CHAPTER 1

WHAT'S NEW IN DREAMWEAVER MX 2004

EVERY YEAR OR TWO, WE SOFTWARE USERS EVERYWHERE GET TO OPEN UP OUR favorite program and discover that things have changed! While we weren't looking, someone sneaked in, rearranged the furniture a bit (not too much, we hope), oiled the squeaky hinges, replaced the old water heater, and generally spiffed things up. We spend the next few weeks metaphorically bumping into things, wondering where the heck our favorite tool went, and discovering all these neat little improvements in how things work.

So what's new in Dreamweaver MX 2004?

THE THINGS YOU'LL NEVER SEE...

You might not see them, but they're here. They're the intangible improvements that just make the program better. Dreamweaver has been retooled for speed and reliability. The program offers full Unicode support, meaning that it can render pages in any language that your computer's operating system can understand. The built-in FTP program is brand-new, faster, and more reliable.

And then there are things you won't see because they're not here anymore. HTML Styles, the Timeline, the Tag Inspector's Tree view (not the Tag Inspector itself, which lives on in the Properties tab of the Selection Inspector), the Answers panel—they're all gone! If you're using Dreamweaver/Windows, Classic Workspace is gone as well. Also gone is support for Windows NT, Windows Me, and Mac OS systems earlier than Jaguar (10.2). Time to upgrade, folks!

...AND SOMETHING YOU WILL!

The first time you launch your brand-new copy of Dreamweaver MX 2004, you'll be face to face with the Start page (see Figure 1.1). More than just a welcome screen, the Start page shows up every time Dreamweaver is running and no documents are open. Its job is to get you started. Choose to open a recently opened document, quickly create a new document, and define a site right from within this one screen. And if you don't like it, you can turn it off in Preferences.

FIGURE 1.1
The Start page, ready
to get you going.

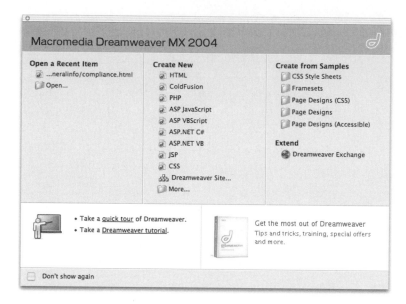

GENERAL INTERFACE IMPROVEMENTS

After the shock of the Start page, the Dreamweaver interface is not that much different from the old MX interface. (Quite a lot of furniture-rearranging went into MX!) But the more you snoop around in there, the more subtle and not-so-subtle differences you'll find.

Insert Bar Categories and Object Groups

Say good-bye to Insert bar tabs. The categories of objects available in the Insert bar are now available from a drop-down menu, and there are fewer categories than before (see Figure 1.2): just Common, Layout, Forms, HTML, Application, and the new and very exciting Favorites. Within each category, you'll find a mixture of objects (indicated by icons) and object groups (indicated by triangle buttons sitting beside object icons). Within the Common category, you have the Hyperlink,

Email Link, and Anchor objects. But then you also have Tables, Images, Media Objects, Template Objects, and more. Tables, Layers, and Layout Tables are all in the Layout category, in addition to some handy items such as Table Rows and Table Columns, and table tags for hand-coding. The most recently used object in each group is the one that displays in the Insert bar. To choose any of the others, click the triangle and choose from the list. While it may be a bit disconcerting at first to hunt around for a particular object only to find it hiding in an object group, you'll quickly learn to love the way your most recently used objects are right there in front of you. After all, if the last layout item you inserted was a table, you'll probably insert more tables before you draw any layers or layout cells.

FIGURE 1.2
The new Insert bar lists its categories in a drop-down menu and contains objects and object groups.

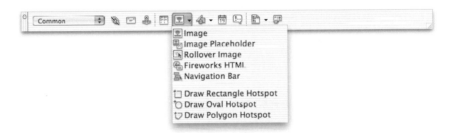

And if you still don't like the way objects are grouped, it's easy to do something about it! Just go to the Favorites category, and you can pick and choose which objects to display there, right there, where you can see them and access them without any hunting or pecking at all (see Figure 1.3).

FIGURE 1.3
The Favorites category in the Insert bar lets you display objects from all categories in one handy place.

Integrated Site Panel (Macintosh)

If you're on the Mac and are opening Dreamweaver MX 2004 for the first time, your first thought may be, "Where the heck did the Site panel go?" It has been integrated into the Files panel group, so it appears in abbreviated mode as one of the cascading panels down the right side of your

monitor, the same way it displays in the Dreamweaver/Windows work-space (see Figure 1.4). Click the Expand button in its upper-right corner, and it undocks and expands to show both halves. Or, of course, you can undock it as you would undock any panel and have your own independent Site window back again.

FIGURE 1.4
The integrated Site panel, new to Dreamweaver/Mac.

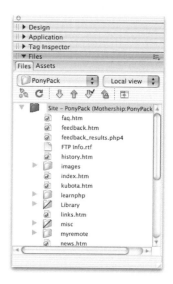

Possibly the best news about this integration is that the Mac Site panel now owns its own set of menu commands, like its Windows counter-part. It's accessible from the panel window's Options menu, and it includes commands such as New File, New Folder, Select Newer Local, and other commands that used to be buried in the Site Files View sub-menu of the main Site menu. How cumbersome was that?

Document-Specific Toolbars (Windows)

For Windows users, a new workspace innovation is toolbars that dock to the Document window instead of to the underside of the Insert bar. Although this may take some getting used to, it's very efficient, putting the toolbar closer to the active area of the document where you're work-ing and enabling you to turn toolbars on and off individually for differ-ent documents. Toolbars can still be undocked by dragging their grabber handles, or they can be docked with the Insert bar, as in MX.

Tag Inspector

The new, redesigned Tag Inspector (Window > Tag Inspector) is a wonderful (and very compact) way of viewing and working with any page element. Like Dreamweaver's very own Swiss army knife, almost everything you'll ever need is in there—even if you didn't know you needed it.

The Attributes tab (see Figure 1.5) is the grown-up version of the Dreamweaver MX Tag Inspector. From this handy and compact little panel, you can set properties for any selected item, from page properties to text properties, to tables and images—you name it. Displayed alphabetically or by category (your choice), each property has its place, along with all the standard browse buttons, color pickers, and dynamic options to help you enter values quickly and accurately.

FIGURE 1.5
The Tag Inspector/ Attributes tab in categorical and alphabetical views.

The Behaviors tab (see Figure 1.6) hosts the redesigned interface for the Behaviors panel, which now includes two options for viewing available event handlers.

The Tag Inspector/CSS tab (see Figure 1.7) is a style rule inspector, a new and useful way to examine and edit the CSS styles applied to objects. View style-formatting elements in categories or alphabetically, and edit them on the spot, without having to go through the CSS Styles panel. If you thought working with CSS was too cumbersome before, get ready for a smooth new stylin' experience!

If all of this seems like *way* too much information for you, then you're a Property Inspector kind of user, and there's nothing wrong with that. Or

you might want to use the Property Inspector for the everyday meat-and-potatoes work you do, and crack open the Selection Inspector for special occasions. Whichever way you work, this new bunch of tools is a welcome addition to the family, putting a wealth of HTML possibilities at your fingertips.

FIGURE 1.6

The Tag Inspector/ Behaviors tab, showing traditional and new display of event handlers.

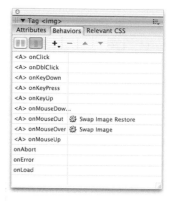

FIGURE 1.7

The Tag Inspector/ CSS tab in alphabetical and categorical views.

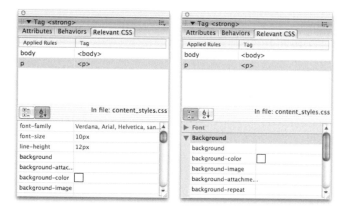

Streamlined Window Menu

It's a little improvement, but it's one that puts a smile on my face. The Window menu now lists all panels and inspectors in one main window, instead of relegating things such as Layers and Frames to the ghetto of the Others submenu. Of course, once I've got my keyboard shortcuts set up and memorized, I probably won't ever visit the Window menu again, but just on general principle, it's nice to see a company of equals there.

DOCUMENT-EDITING IMPROVEMENTS

The intuitive, clean, and powerful Dreamweaver document-editing environment has always been one of the program's strengths, of course. Although the look and feel of the Document window hasn't changed with Dreamweaver MX 2004, various features have been toned up to create a more tightly integrated working experience.

Better Table Editing

For many web designers, tables represent a large part of every day's work activities; yet they're also inherently complex and difficult to handle, even in a graphic environment. Dreamweaver has always had a good set of table-editing tools. Dreamweaver MX 2004 adds two new design aids for building tables.

The Table Widths bar (available from the Document toolbar in the View Options > Visual Aids submenu) displays a horizontal ribbon of width information about any selected table, similar to the information display that accompanies tables in Layout Mode. The bar not only displays dimension information, but it also gives users access to a drop-down menu of selection and editing commands (see Figure 1.8).

FIGURE 1.8
The Table Widths bar, showing table measurements and some handy drop-down menus.

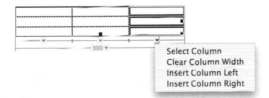

Another viewing aid, Expanded Tables mode (View > Table Mode > Expanded Tables Mode), is a lifesaver for those using borderless tables for page layout. In Expanded Tables mode, Dreamweaver displays all tables with a border, cell padding, and cell spacing so that the table structure is visually obvious, and even tiny cells are easy to see and select (see Figure 1.9). The code behind the table isn't changed, so the table still behaves and displays as normal in the browser; for designing, though, Expanded Tables mode might be an eye-opening experience.

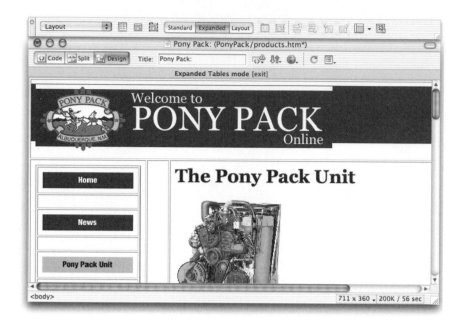

For those of you who like working with Layout mode, it's still there, and a few coding tweaks have improved its reliability. Tables created in Layout mode no longer require a height attribute, although layout cells still do, and the Layout Table Property Inspector now sports a button for deleting row heights. Layout cells are now created with nonbreaking spaces, eliminating the display problems that empty cells once caused in browsers. And it's more difficult to accidentally draw a layout table in midair, creating a table that's accidentally nested inside another table.

Finally, as a very subtle change, deferred table update in Standard mode is a thing of the past. Tables now automatically shrink back to size as soon as large content is deleted, eliminating the need to click outside the table to display the Design view display.

Better Integrated Document Validation

Creating documents that work well in target browsers is crucial to web authoring. So it only makes sense that Dreamweaver's document-validation features should occupy a more prominent place in the interface. And so it is! Dreamweaver can now automatically check documents' browser compatibility on opening, and the Document toolbar sports either a handy OK

icon to tell you all is well or a warning icon to let you know there are problems. Clicking the icon gives you access to settings and controls, including a much-improved interface for choosing browser versions to test against (see Figure 1.10). The main Validate and Check Target Browser commands are still at home in the File menu as well, for those of you who are accustomed to finding them there.

FIGURE 1.10
The Browser Target Check icon and menu in the Document toolbar.

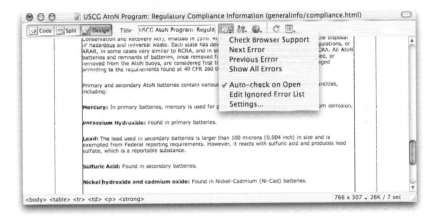

Integrated Graphics Handling

You've inserted an image into your page. Now you realize that it looks awful. You want to resize it, resample it, and fix the color correction and the cropping. Guess what? You can do it all from within Dreamweaver, using the new improved Image Property Inspector (see Figure 1.11). For those of you using Fireworks, the Optimize in Fireworks command (formerly hidden away in the Commands menu) now has its very own button here as well.

FIGURE 1.11
The new Image Property Inspector, with integrated image-editing options.

CSS IMPROVEMENTS

It's more than an improvement. The basic Dreamweaver approach to creating code for your pages has changed to include CSS at all levels. Now, that's a good thing.

CSS Integration

The new CSS style rule inspector (the CSS tab in the Tag Inspector) is only the tip of the iceberg when it comes to changes in Dreamweaver's CSS handling. The CSS Styles panel has been streamlined to include an editing mode only (see Figure 1.12). Why? Because the features for applying styles have all been integrated into the Property Inspector! No longer relegated to special interfaces such as the CSS Styles panel, style sheets are now referenced throughout the interface and are used for basic coding tasks instead of older HTML-based formatting. Where will you see more CSS?

FIGURE 1.12
The new CSS Styles panel, for editing styles only.

The different versions of the Property Inspector now include more CSS information than ever before. The Text Property Inspector no longer lets you switch between "regular" and "CSS" mode; instead, CSS options are front and center (see Figure 1.13). By default, choosing any text formatting from the Property Inspector creates CSS formatting instead of inserting font tags everywhere. And applying classes to tables and other page elements can now be done from their Property Inspectors, although those of you who like right-clicking can still right-click the Tag Selector to apply styles (see Figure 1.13).

FIGURE 1.13
CSS options through-
out the new Property
Inspectors.

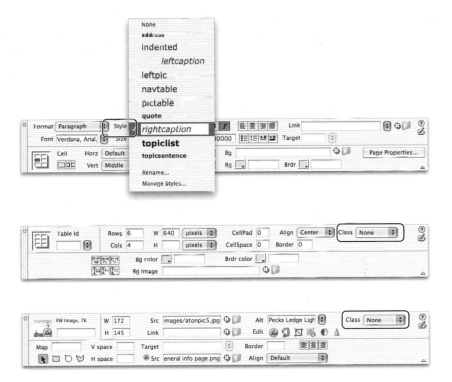

The Page Properties dialog box also has a nifty new tabbed interface and accomplishes tasks such as setting page background color, tweaking link appearance, and such through automatically generated CSS styles (see Figure 1.14).

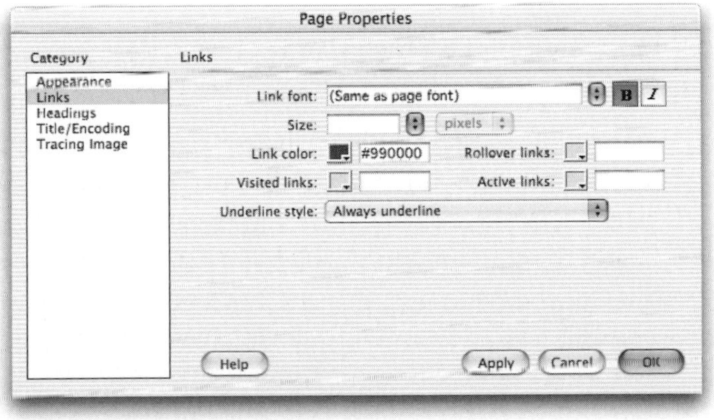

FIGURE 1.14
Setting page proper-
ties the new CSS way.

Of course, you can turn off any of these automatic CSS-writing functions (by going to the Preferences > General dialog box and deselecting Use CSS Instead of HTML Tags). But why would you?

Improved CSS2 Support

Yes, you can still draw layers (the Draw Layer tool is in with the Insert bar's Layout objects). But you can also select any page element, wrap it in a div tag, and apply a custom class or ID, thanks to the new Div object (also in with the Layout objects in the Insert bar). Figure 1.15 shows this nifty procedure happening. The old Netscape-specific layer tag is no longer an option for layer coding. Design view display of CSS-styled elements is improved.

FIGURE 1.15
Wrapping a page element in a div to apply external CSS positioning.

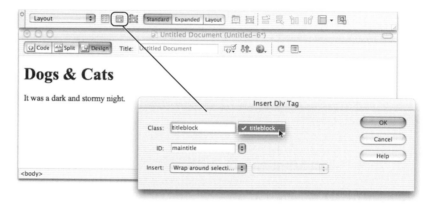

CODE-WRITING IMPROVEMENTS

For all you coders out there, there are goodies for you as well. Right-clicking while in Code view now calls up a contextual menu for easy access to common code-writing tasks, such as creating snippets, converting to lower- or uppercase, and more (see Figure 1.16). For hand-coding those style sheets, you now have CSS code hints at your disposal (see Figure 1.17). The Find and Replace dialog box includes more options—not entirely a coder's tool, but especially important to the geeky. And Dreamweaver offers full XML namespace support as well.

FIGURE 1.16
The new Code view
contextual menu.

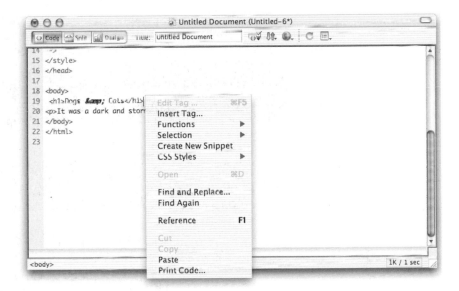

FIGURE 1.17
Hand-coding some
CSS with code hints.

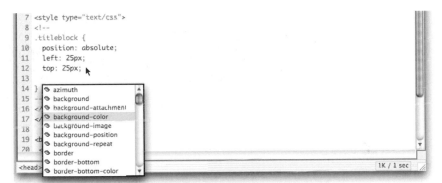

SITE-MANAGEMENT IMPROVEMENTS

In the world of site management, the big news is Contribute. Macromedia's
new program Contribute lets regular folk who aren't web designers easily
update content in prebuilt template pages created in Dreamweaver. Site-
definition options in Dreamweaver MX 2004 include the capability to
manage a Contribute site, coordinating with Contribute users for optimal
site-updating efficiency. Secure FTP (SFTP) connections are now supported
for defining remote sites and testing servers.

Life without a site is also easier, for those times when you just want to get a quick job done without having to define a site (see Figure 1.18). Just choose Computer, Desktop, or one of the nonsite items instead of a defined site, and start working. No longer will Dreamweaver prompt you to move your images to the nearest local root folder or insist on writing absolute file paths because you're not inside that folder. And for uploading, server connections can also be defined independently of site definitions.

FIGURE 1.18
The siteless Site panel and Server Configuration dialog box, for working without a site.

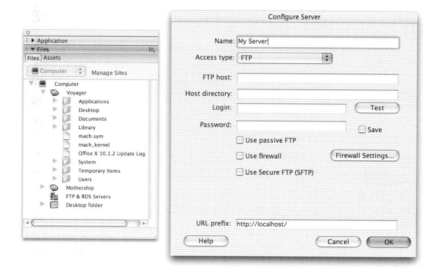

DYNAMIC DATA IMPROVEMENTS

Things continue to improve in the realm of dynamic data, too. Testing server performance is better. ColdFusion support has been beefed up, and, of course, Dreamweaver MX 2004 supports all of the new features in ColdFusion MX. The dynamic objects are much more logically placed and easy to find in the new Insert bar (see Figure 1.19). And if you're accustomed to looking for them in the Server Behaviors panel, they're still accessible there.

FIGURE 1.19
The new Application objects, centrally located and logically organized.

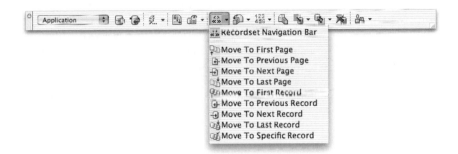

Summary

Now all of you old-time Dreamweaver users know what's new. It's not like it was back in the olden days. If this is your first version of Dreamweaver, then these *are* the olden days. Just imagine how great the program is going to be someday several versions from now, when you're looking back on *these* wild and hairy times. Life—and software—just keeps getting better.

CHAPTER 2

THE DREAMWEAVER WORKSPACE

A BIG PART OF WHAT MAKES DREAMWEAVER MX 2004 SO EFFICIENT AND intuitive to work with, for web design newbies as well as seasoned professionals, is the flexible and streamlined workspace. It's a good idea to take a few minutes to explore the environment, learn where things are, and see how you can set it up to suit your working style and level of expertise.

CHOOSING A WORKSPACE (WINDOWS)

Dreamweaver for Windows uses an integrated workspace, with most windows and panels docked together in one large application window. The first time you launch the program, you're given the choice of two workspaces: Designer and HomeSite/Coder-Style. The Designer workspace is optimized for, well, designers. The HomeSite/Coder-Style workspace is optimized for those who are accustomed to using text editors, especially Macromedia HomeSite. What are the differences?

Comparing Workspaces

The standard Dreamweaver interface, called Designer Style (see Figure 2.1), docks all panels except the Property Inspector, Insert bar, and Results window along the right side of the application window. By default, the Property Inspector is expanded, and the Document window opens in an undocked state showing Design view.

FIGURE 2.1
The integrated workspace with panels on the right (Designer style).

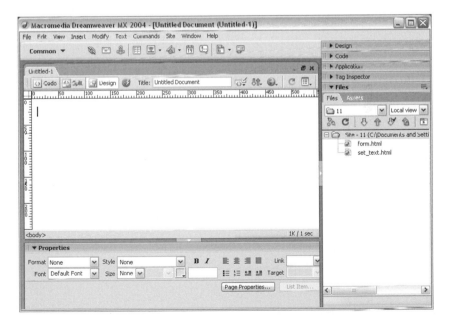

The HomeSite/Coder-Style workspace (see Figure 2.2) docks all panels except the Property Inspector, the Insert bar, and the Results window along the left side of the application window. By default, the Property Inspector is contracted and the Document window opens docked and in Code view.

FIGURE 2.2
The integrated workspace with panels on the left (HomeSite/Coder-Style).

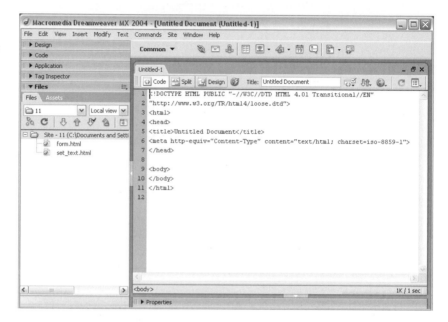

Changing Workspaces

When you've chosen a workspace and gotten to work, you can rethink your choice any time. Just open the Preferences dialog box (Edit > Preferences), go to the General category, and click the Change Workspace button. You can choose between Designer and HomeSite-Coder Style, although you'll have to restart the program for changes to take effect (see Figure 2.3).

FIGURE 2.3
Changing workspaces through the Preferences dialog box.

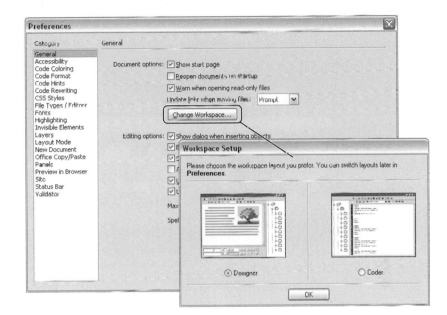

THE START PAGE

New to Dreamweaver MX 2004, you have the option of opening Dreamweaver every day to a friendly, helpful Start page (see Figure 4). In addition to quick links to a Dreamweaver tour and tutorial, you have instant access to do the following:

- Open recent documents or any file (an alternative to choosing File > Open).

- Create new documents of various types (an alternative method of using File > New and using the New Document dialog box, without having to bother with the New Document dialog box). Choosing the More Documents option from this category opens the New Document dialog box.

- Create a new site (an alternative to choosing Site > Manage Sites and clicking the New button).

- Create new documents based on different stationery samples (the same samples available in the New Document dialog box).

- Visit the Dreamweaver Exchange to check out new extensions (an alternative to choosing Help > Dreamweaver Exchange).

FIGURE 2.4

The Start Page, a quick interface for accessing common start-up tasks.

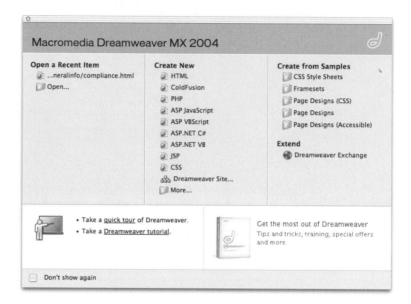

Clicking the Dreamweaver Tour button takes you to the Macromedia website if you're connected to the Internet. Clicking the Dreamweaver Tutorial button opens the Dreamweaver Help system, as if you had chosen Help > Tutorials. So there's nothing in here that you can't also do elsewhere, but it is nice to have all of these handy first-thing-in-the-morning tasks ready and available from one central interface.

If you don't want to be bothered with the Start page, select the Don't Show Again option. To turn the Start page on and off, open the Preferences > General dialog box (Edit > Preferences) and select or deselect the Show Start Page option (see Figure 2.5). If the Start page is enabled, it will display every time you launch the program and whenever there are no open documents.

FIGURE 2.5
Enabling or disabling
the Start page in
Dreamweaver
Preferences.

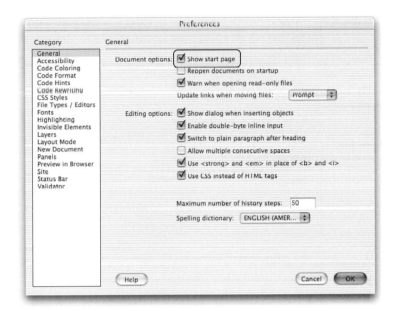

PLAYING WITH PANELS

It's a fact of life that there are lots of panels out there. They're all handy
at one time or another, but boy they sure get in the way when you're not
using them, and it's always hard to find just the one you want when you
want it. Many Dreamweaver tasks involve accessing panels for some reason. Both the Dreamweaver integrated workspace (Windows) and the
semi-integrated workspace (Mac) use a system of docking, grouping,
expanding, and contracting panels to help you streamline your daily
panel use.

Panels and Panel Groups

Any panel can be opened or expanded by choosing it from the Window
menu, which also lists the shortcut keys for opening and closing them.
Most of the Dreamweaver panels live in panel groups, with each panel
available under a tab in the group window. (Well, technically, all of the
panels live in groups, but some panels, such as the CSS Styles panel, live
in groups of one.) The groups are logical, to help you intuitively figure

out which panel goes where. The panel/group title bar includes an options menu for performing panel-related tasks. Figure 2.6 shows a typical panel group with its features highlighted.

FIGURE 2.6
The Code panel group and how it works

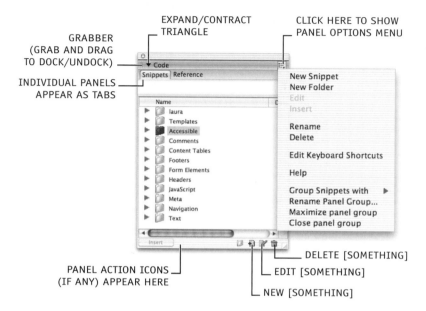

To expand or contract a panel group, click the expand/contract arrow in the panel group's title bar. If necessary, the panel window stretches out to accommodate expanded panels. To expand a panel group and resize it to be as tall as possible, access its options menu and choose Maximize Panel Group.

To adjust the relative height of two panel groups within the window, position the cursor between the two. The cursor turns into a two-headed arrow. Drag up or down to resize.

To close a panel group, access its options menu and choose Close Panel Group. You can open the panel group again by choosing any of its panels from the Window menu.

Showing and Hiding

Sometimes expanding and contracting and resizing isn't enough. You just want things out of the way so you can get a good unencumbered view of your document.

To adjust the amount of space the side panel dock takes up (Windows integrated workspace only), drag the vertical bar that separates it from the rest of the workspace. To toggle the side panel on and off completely, click the triangle in that vertical bar (see Figure 2.7).

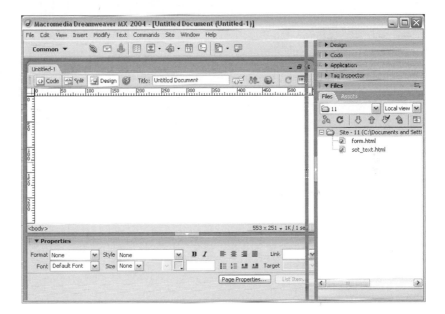

To toggle all panels on and off (Mac and Windows), choose Window > Hide Panels and Window > Show Panels, or just press F4 to toggle back and forth.

Docking and Undocking

Sometimes you just don't want to work with a docked panel. Maybe you find a particular panel (such as the Reference panel) a bit hard to read in its packed-up, docked state. Maybe you have two monitors and want all of your panels spread out across monitor 2 while monitor 1 shows the Document window. Or maybe you're just accustomed to free-standing panels. You're not stuck in the dock!

The grabber edge at the left of the panel's title bar (see Figure 2.6) lets you undock and dock the group. To undock, grab the grabber edge and drag the group out of the panel window. To resize the panel window in its undocked state, drag its lower-right corner (see Figure 2.8).

FIGURE 2.8
An undocked panel
window.

When you undock, you run the risk of losing panel windows. They scoot off the edge of your monitor or tuck themselves away behind things. To get yourself out of this particular pickle, choose Window > Arrange Panels.

To redock, grab the grabber edge and drag the group over other docked panels until a thick black line appears to indicate where you'll be docking. You can even redock the group in an entirely different place from where it started. For Windows users, you can even dock horizontal panels (such as the Results window) in the side dock or move vertically oriented panels (such as the Code group) to the top or bottom of the Document window.

Grouping and Regrouping

Dreamweaver panel groups are supposed to be logical and intuitive, but what if they're not? Or what if you find yourself using only three or four panels, and you get tired of opening and closing three or four panel groups to go back and forth? You can group, ungroup, and even create your own panel groups to create the best panel setup for your working style. And it's all done with the panel window's options menu (refer to Figure 2.6).

Unfortunately, the
Tag Inspector can't
be grouped with any-
thing else.

To move a particular panel into another group, go to the options menu for the original panel window and choose Group Panel With > [whatever group you like!].

To put a panel in a window by itself, go to its options menu and choose Group Panel With > New Group.

To create your own group of favorite panels, just combine the previous steps:

1. Find the first panel that you want in your personalized group, and detach it from its group by going to its options menu and choosing Group Panel With > New Group.

2. In the new panel window you've just created, go to the options menu and choose Rename Panel Group. Call the group anything you like—Favorites, My Panels, you name it.

3. Now, one at a time, find the rest of the panels you want in your group and, for each one, go to its options menu and choose Group Panel With > [whatever you called your panel group]. Note that the Tag Inspector panel cannot be grouped.

You're now free to close or contract all other panel groups and know that you'll always have your favorites at your fingertips (see Figure 2.9).

FIGURE 2.9
Creating a custom panel group.

The Insert Bar and Property Inspector

The Insert bar and Property Inspector are unique panels with their own set of rules. In the Windows integrated workspace, they are docked at the top and bottom of the Document window. They can be undocked, but not grouped with other panels. In the Mac workspace, they are freestanding and can't be docked.

The Insert bar can be viewed in one of two modes: menu mode (the default) or tabbed mode (Dreamweaver MX-style). To switch between modes, choose Show as Tabs from the object category drop-down menu (in menu mode); or choose Show as Menus from the panel options menu (in tabbed mode). Figure 2.10 shows the two styles of viewing the Insert bar.

In the Windows workspace, the Property Inspector can be contracted like any other panel. In Mac and Windows workspaces, the Property Inspector can also be semicontracted to show only its top half by clicking the triangle icon in its lower-right corner (see Figure 2.11).

FIGURE 2.10
Switching between menu and tabbed modes in the Insert bar.

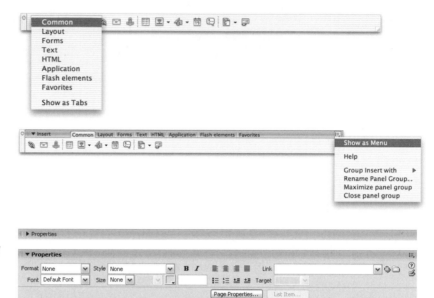

FIGURE 2.11
Changing the Property Inspector from full to abbreviated states (Windows only).

USING THE DOCUMENT WINDOW

Regardless of your working style, the one piece of the interface that you'll probably spend most of your time interacting with is the Document window. It's an intuitive interface with lots of resources, and like most things in Dreamweaver, it can be tweaked and customized to be just exactly what you want.

Docking and Undocking (Windows Only)

In the Windows integrated workspace, you can work with the Document window docked or undocked. A free-standing Document window can fill up as much or as little of the central working space as you like, or it can sit outside the application window altogether if you have a large enough monitor (or two monitors). A docked Document window automatically fills up the central workspace area and sports a tab along its top edge instead of a title bar so you can easily switch among multiple open documents as you work (see Figure 2.12).

To dock and undock the Document window, use the Maximize/Normalize box in its upper-right corner.

FIGURE 2.12
The docked (maximized) and undocked Document window.

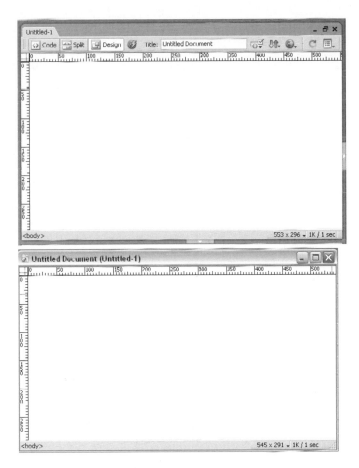

Viewing Documents

To work with documents, you generally have to look at them. The Document window gives you all sorts of choices for how to do that.

Working with Code, Working with Design

The most basic choice you must make when working with a document is whether you want to look at code or a more graphical environment.

Design view (View > Design) enables you to see the page approximately as it will look in the browser (see Figure 2.13). Although this isn't a true WYSIWYG preview, it lets you interact with all page elements in a graphic environment. Nongraphical page elements such as head content, comments, and scripts can be viewed in iconic form by choosing

these options in the View menu and the View > Visual Aids submenu. Other viewing aids for Design view include these:

- **Rulers (View > Rulers)**—Rulers can be set across the top and left edges of the Document window. Use the commands in the View > Rulers submenu to hide and show rulers, change ruler units (although pixels are the most useful), and change the origin point for measuring relative to specific places on the page.

- **Grid (View > Grid)**—A customizable grid can be displayed behind the contents of the document to help align page elements. Use the commands in the View > Grid submenu to hide and show the grid, snap to grid lines, and change the grid's size and appearance.

- **Tracing image (View > Tracing Image)**—A GIF, JPG, or PNG file is displayed behind the contents of the Document window, to be used as a layout guide. Use the commands in the View > Tracing Image submenu to load a tracing image and position it in relation to the page. Use the Page Properties dialog box (Modify > Page Properties) to adjust the tracing image's opacity so it's less obtrusive as you work.

- **Table borders, layer borders, frame borders (View > Visual Aids submenu)**—The edges of tables, layers, or frames are displayed with a thin or dotted line for editing purposes only (see Chapter 8, "Building Tables," for more).

- **Table widths (View > Visual Aids > Table Widths)**—An information strip is displayed across every table in Design view, indicating column and table widths (see Chapter 8 for more).

- **Table mode (View > Table Mode submenu)**—Several different ways of displaying tables are provided for editing purposes only (see Chapter 8 for more).

- **Image maps (View > Visual Aids > Image Maps)**—Image map hotspots are displayed as translucent colored shapes for editing purposes only (see Chapter 5, "Working with Images," for more).

- **Invisible elements (View > Visual Aids > Invisible Elements)**—Any piece of code that wouldn't normally be seen in Design view is made visible as an icon. Use the Preferences/Invisible Elements category to determine what kinds of invisible code are represented by icons.

Code view (View > Code) shows only the raw HTML code for the page (see Figure 2.14). Code view is essentially Dreamweaver's built-in text editor. Some features and functions, such as adding behaviors and drawing layers, are not available in Code view. Non-HTML documents, such as CSS style sheets and script files, can be viewed only in Code view. For a full discussion on working with Code view, see Chapter 27, "Writing Code in Dreamweaver."

Code and Design view (View > Code and Design) splits the Document window horizontally so that you can see Design view and Code view at the same time (see Figure 2.15). Many people find this view to be the most convenient because it enables them to see exactly where they are in the code as they are designing. This view proves convenient when dealing with complex coding tasks such as selecting a particular row or column in an embedded table. By default, Code view is in the upper portion of the window. You can move it to the bottom by choosing View > Design View on Top.

Code view and Design view are more than just different views. They represent different ways of working. Different options appear in panels, or different commands are grayed out, depending on which view is active. In Code and Design view, when both views are visible, one or always has

focus—that is, Dreamweaver considers it the active view. To give a particular portion of the Document window focus, click in that half of the window. You can also choose View > Switch Views, or Ctrl/Cmd-`, to switch between Code view and Design view, or to switch the focus from code to design in Code and Design view.

FIGURE 2.14
The Document window showing a page in Code view.

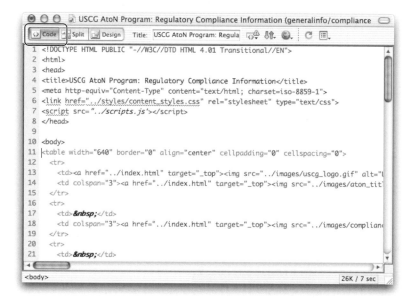

FIGURE 2.15
The Document window showing a page in Code and Design view.

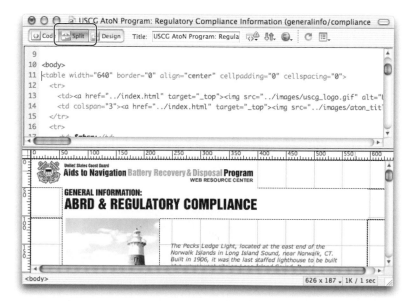

Live Data View

If you use Dreamweaver to create data-driven websites, Design view normally displays your pages with placeholders marking where the server will eventually insert information from a database. For instance, an online catalog page viewed in Dreamweaver will display placeholders for each catalog item's names, prices, and descriptions. Engaging Live Data view makes Dreamweaver replace these placeholders with actual information from a database, giving you a much better preview of what your page will eventually look like online. Live Data view is covered in detail in the section "How Dynamic Sites Work in Dreamweaver" in Chapter 21, "Building Dynamic Sites with Dreamweaver."

Status Bar

Located at the bottom of the Document window, the status bar provides a wealth of information about your page. It also enables you to access your code and panels with a quick click (see Figure 2.16).

FIGURE 2.16
The status bar shown here at the bottom of an undocked Document window.

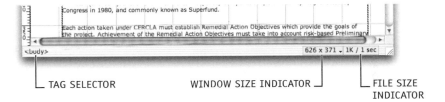

Window Size

The Window Size indicator tells you, in pixels, the current width and height of the "live" area of the Document window. (The *live area* is the part of the window where there's actually content, as opposed to toolbars and status bars and other so-called "chrome" elements.) This can be important information if you're trying to design your pages to fit within common browser window sizes (and who isn't?).

The Window Size indicator reports only the size of the Design view portion of the window. If the Document window is displaying Code view,

the Window Size indicator disappears. If the Document window is displaying Code and Design view, the indicator shows the size of the Design view portion of the window.

If you're working in the integrated workspace (Windows only) and have your Document window docked (maximized), the Window Size indicator shows the size of the visible portion of the window (for example, from the bottom edge of the Insert bar to the bottom of the Document window, and from the left edge of the application window to the vertical divider that begins the panel dock).

The Window Size indicator also includes a pop-up menu that quickly resizes the Document window to any of several default sizes that match the window sizes of browsers at common monitor resolutions. Choose from this pop-up menu to quickly check how your page contents will fit into some common window sizes. You're not limited to the default window sizes Dreamweaver has provided, either. For instance, if you're designing for an intranet and you know that your target audience will all have browser windows set to 600×300, you can add that set of dimensions to the pop-up menu. Just do this:

1. From the Window Size indicator pop-up menu, choose Edit Sizes. This opens the Status Bar category of the Dreamweaver Preferences dialog box (see Figure 2.17).

2. In the Preferences dialog box, edit the list of window sizes as you like.

   • To change any of the existing sizes, just select one of the dimensions shown and enter a new number.

   • To add a new size, click in the area below the existing entries to activate it, and type in a new dimension. Your new entry can have width, height, or both.

3. When you're done, click OK to close the Preferences dialog box. From now on, your new entry appears in the Window Size indicator pop-up menu.

FIGURE 2.17
Adding a default
window size to the
Window Size indicator
pop-up menu.

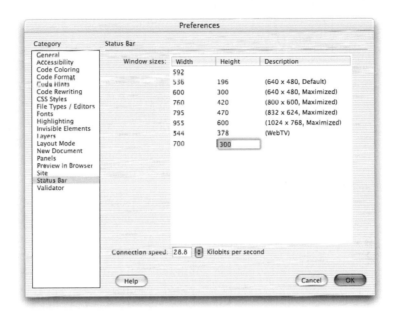

Document Size/Download Time Indicator

The Document Size/Download Time indicator displays two related pieces of information: the file size for the current document and all of its embedded media, and the estimated time that this material will take to download. Unless you have a corner on the market of extremely patient visitors, this is crucial information to have at your fingertips as you're creating your pages. The file size indicator (on the left) calculates the size of your current HTML file itself as well as the sizes of any images, Flash movies, or other files that will need to download before your page can display in a browser, rounded off to the nearest kilobyte (K). The estimated download time calculates how long that much content will take to download over a specific connection speed, rounded to the nearest second. For instance, if your page consists of a 1K HTML document and a 27Kbps image, at a connection speed of 28.8Kbps it will take approximately 1 second to download. The display for this setup would look like this: 28K/1 sec.

The default connection speed for calculating download time is 28.8Kbps, or kilobits per second (the speed of a fairly old modem, or a new modem at peak traffic times). You can change this speed to suit whatever connection speeds you think your target audience will have. For instance, if you're producing an online film festival for high-end users who are all going to have some sort of broadband access, you'll want to set your

connection speed at several hundred kilobits per second. To adjust the connection speed, do this:

What are some standard speeds? Telephone modems can theoretically connect at up to 56K, but federal regulations limit phone-line transfer rates to somewhere between 51K and 53K. ISDN connections can range from 56K to 112K. Cable and DSL connections range from 112K to 1M (one thousand kilobits per second). Don't forget that when determining your visitors' probable connection speed, individual connections can be much slower than the standards.

1. Click the Window Size indicator and choose Edit Sizes from the drop-down menu. This opens the Preferences/Status Bar dialog box.

2. In the Connection Speed text input field, enter whatever value you think represents an average download speed for your target audience.

3. When you're done, click OK to close the dialog box. The status bar now displays its download time based on document size and this new connection speed.

Tag Selector

The Tag Selector (see Figure 2.18) lets you keep one eye on where your code is while you're working in Design view. Based on the fact that HTML pages are built from a series of nested tags, the tag selector indicates at all times where the insertion point or selection is in relation to the tag hierarchy of the page. Because Design view displays only the visible body content of the page, the body tag is always the leftmost element shown here. If the insertion point is inside an h1 tag, the Tag Selector displays this structure:

<body> <h1>

If the insertion point is inside a table cell, inside a table row, inside a table, the Tag Selector displays this:

<body> <table> <tr> <td>

FIGURE 2.18
The Tag Selector in action.

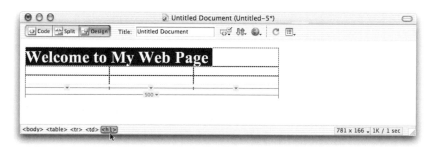

If an entire tag and its contents are selected, the Tag Selector displays that tag in boldface.

Best of all, you can use the Tag Selector to select tags. Click any tag displayed there, and the entire tag and its contents are selected in Design

view. Right-clicking a tag in the Tag Selector opens a contextual menu for performing tag-related tasks such as stripping a tag while leaving its contents intact (Remove Tag), applying a CSS style to the tag (Set Class), and applying ID attributes (Set ID).

Toolbars

Dreamweaver includes various toolbars that can show at the top of the Document window to help you work. All toolbars can be accessed from the View > Toolbars submenu or by right-clicking in a blank part of the Document toolbar.

Standard Toolbar

Following the trend in much software, the Standard toolbar gives you easy access to frequently used commands from the File and Edit menus (see Figure 2.19). The Standard toolbar can be toggled on and off by choosing View > Toolbars > Standard. In Dreamweaver/Windows, the Standard toolbar can be undocked by dragging it into the center of the Document window; after it's undocked, redock it by double-clicking its title bar.

FIGURE 2.19
The Standard toolbar in its docked and undocked states.

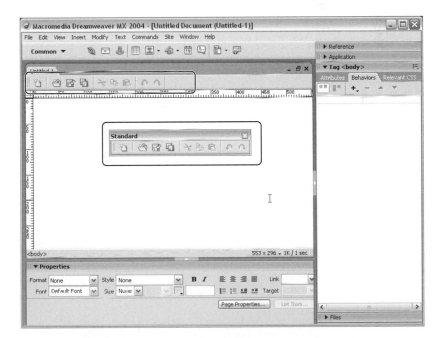

Document Toolbar

The Document toolbar shows an icon view of frequently accessed commands related to working with the Document window (see Figure 2.20). Changing document views, previewing in the browser, validating, and more are all a mouse click away. The Document toolbar can be toggled on and off by choosing View > Toolbars > Document.

FIGURE 2.20
The Document toolbar.

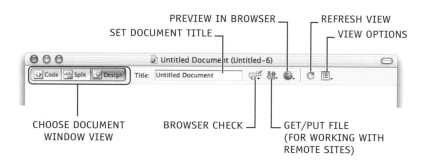

GETTING HELP

If you are having difficulties with your pages or Dreamweaver itself, you can get help in many places. With Dreamweaver Help, the Reference panel, and the Dreamweaver Support Center at the Macromedia website, the answer is most likely within reach. This section explains your Help options.

General Assistance: The Reference Panel

Do you have piles of reference books surrounding you as you work? If so, the Reference panel is ready to be your best friend (see Figure 2.21). This panel contains the complete text from several web reference guides, including O'Reilly's *HTML Reference, CSS Reference, JavaScript Reference,* and *Sitespring Project Site Tag Reference; Wrox ASP 3.0 Reference; JSP Reference; Macromedia CFML Reference;* and the *UsableNet Accessibility Reference.*

FIGURE 2.21
The Reference panel, showing contextual help for HTML.

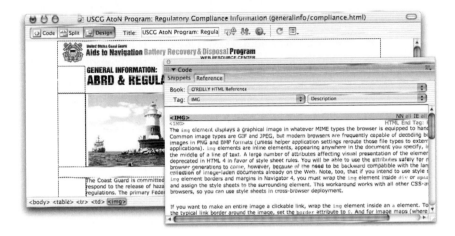

You can use the Reference panel on its own to look up information, or you can use it in tandem with the Document window to get contextual help information. To look up contextual help on whatever tag or script you're currently working on, do this:

1. Click inside the element you want to reference.

2. Choose Window > Reference.

3. The Reference panel opens, showing a description and sample syntax for the selected item.

Dreamweaver Assistance

Dreamweaver has *Dreamweaver Help* that covers the basic use of every element of the program. Dreamweaver Help is a valuable resource for any questions concerning the properties of Dreamweaver.

To access Dreamweaver Help, choose Help > Using Dreamweaver. This launches your operating system's Help application with Dreamweaver Help showing. Figures 2.22 and 2.23 show Dreamweaver Help for Windows and Macintosh.

FIGURE 2.22
Dreamweaver/
Windows Help.

FIGURE 2.23
Dreamweaver/
Mac Help.

Summary

Dreamweaver has an intuitive, highly customizable interface that puts almost every object and function within easy reach. Most options can be reached with one or two clicks. There is almost always more than one way to insert an object or change a property within the Dreamweaver interface. Spend some time getting used to the interface, and try the different ways of performing common tasks. The more familiar you are with the interface and the options available to you, the better you can take full advantage of Dreamweaver functionality.

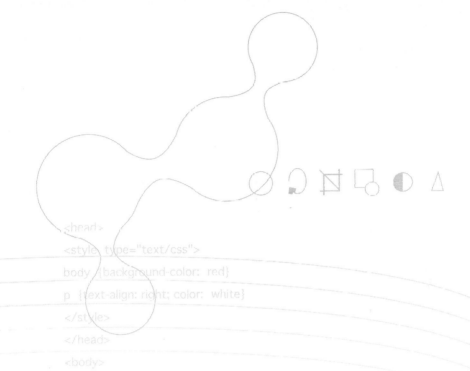

CHAPTER 3

CREATING AND WORKING WITH DOCUMENTS

THIS CHAPTER COVERS THAT MOST BASIC OF TASKS—CREATING A NEW document, setting it up, and turning it into a web page. Unless you're a complete Dreamweaver newbie, you've probably done this before.

THE BASICS OF CREATING DOCUMENTS

Dreamweaver isn't just for HTML anymore, although that still might be the main kind of page that many users will want to work with. With Dreamweaver MX 2004, however, just about any kind of text-based web document can be created, edited, and sometimes even graphically rendered in Design view. This includes not only HTML, but also all the various live data document types, such as ASP, CFM, PHP, and JSP; support document types, such as CSS and JS; and the alphabet soup of document types such as XML, XHTML, and WML.

Because of these choices, creating a new document might still be one of the most basic things you can do in Dreamweaver—but it's no longer the simplest. This section covers the New Document dialog box, which enables you to create documents from scratch, as well as perform various techniques to bring documents and data into Dreamweaver from other sources.

You also can create new documents through the Site panel, but the options differ slightly. See the section "Working with the Site Panel" in Chapter 18, "Site Publishing and Maintenance," for more on this.

New Document Dialog Box

When you choose File > New or press Ctrl/Cmd+N to create a new document, by default the New Document dialog box appears (see Figure 3-1). This dialog box presents you with a wealth of options for creating almost any kind of web document.

Types of Document to Create

Most of the dialog box is taken up by the many options for creating different document types. The leftmost column of choices represents the categories of document types: Basic, Dynamic, Template, and so forth.

Many of these types are beyond the scope of this chapter and are referenced later in this book. Table 3.1 lists the categories along with some of their entries and a brief description of each. To create a standard, plain-vanilla HTML page, use the Basic > HTML option. Select the Basic category from the left column and HTML from the right column.

FIGURE 3.1
The New Document dialog box.

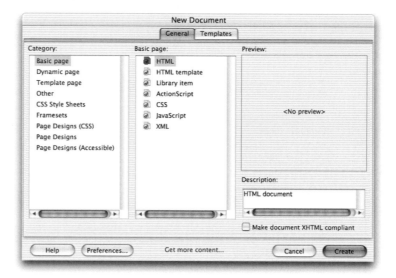

Because you have such an overwhelming number of choices to sift through, the dialog box includes a description area in its lower-right corner to help you. Select any file type from the second column and read a quick description of what it's for before you choose to create that kind of document. For some choices, you also can see a preview in the upper-right corner.

Note that although Dreamweaver can create any of the document kinds listed here, not all of them display in Design view. Only the file types intended for creating viewable web pages will show a usable preview in Design view. Other file types, such as JS, CSS, and TXT, must be viewed and edited in Dreamweaver Code view.

TABLE 3.1 **Document Types Available in the New Document Dialog Box**

Category	Description
Basic Page	These are the most commonly used document types for websites that don't involve server-side scripting and live data. They include HTML and XML for creating viewable web pages, and other file types that will hold supporting information for web pages (for instance, JS for JavaScript and CSS for style sheet information). In addition, with library items and templates, you can create special documents for use with Dreamweaver sites. (See Chapter 21, "Building Dynamic Sites with Dreamweaver," for more on Dreamweaver library items and templates.)
Dynamic Page	These file types create web pages that will use server-side scripting to connect with databases and provide dynamic data websites. The entries in this category represent all the live data technologies Dreamweaver supports: ASP, ASP.NET, ColdFusion, PHP, and JSP. (See Chapter 22, "Creating Dynamic Pages," for more on live data sites.)
Templates Page	The entries in this category enable you to create Dreamweaver templates (predefined documents with special Dreamweaver coding for design team productivity) using a variety of web languages, including good old HTML and various languages related to live data sites.
Other	This catchall category enables you to create just about any kind of text-based document you can imagine, including TXT files.
CSS Style Sheets	Cascading Style Sheets (CSS) enable web authors to store page-formatting information outside the web pages themselves, in external CSS documents that can be referenced by many pages in a website. This category contains a whole selection of predefined CSS documents. (See Chapter 11, "Using Cascading Style Sheets," to learn all about CSS.)
Framesets	Framesets are collections of individual documents that will be displayed together in one browser window. This category contains a selection of predefined framesets—including all documents needed to create a frame-based web page. When you choose from this category, you're creating several new documents at once! (To learn what frames are and how to work with them, see Chapter 10, "Designing Frame-Based Pages.")
Table-Based Layouts and Page Designs (Accessible)	These categories contain predefined "stationery" web pages—Page Designs HTML pages with basic layout setup and placeholder elements (Accessible) ready for you to customize. The accessible designs have been specially created to be accessible to visitors with disabilities. (See the section "Making Your Pages Accessible" at the end of this chapter for more on this.)

Stationery

As Table 3.1 shows, Dreamweaver ships with a variety of predefined page layouts that are yours for the customizing. They're in the Page Designs and Page Designs (Accessible) categories. Dreamweaver also comes with predefined CSS documents, ready to be applied to your documents to quickly add text and layout formatting.

To create a web page based on one of the stationery HTML pages, select an entry from either of the Page Designs categories and click OK. Dreamweaver creates a new document with the placeholder content and formatting in place (such as the one shown in Figure 3.2). Save this document as part of your website and customize its content to create your own new web page quickly.

FIGURE 3.2
A new document based on the Data: Comparative Grid stationery.

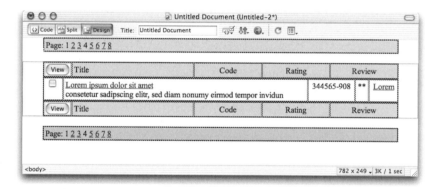

Creating a CSS document based on the choices in this dialog box won't give you a page that can be viewed in a browser—CSS files are meant as supporting files for HTML and other viewable documents. To create a CSS style sheet from one of the stationery choices listed here, select an entry from the CSS category and click OK. Dreamweaver creates a CSS file (it won't display in Design view) that contains a list of styles for formatting HTML pages. Save this document in your website with the .css file extension. To make use of your new CSS document, you must link one or more HTML pages to it. (See Chapter 11 for instructions on doing this.)

It's general use to refer to files that create documents that browsers can display—files that hold web pages, in other words—as HTML files. This is true even though many viewable document types, such as ASP, don't have the .html or .htm filename extensions. Throughout this book, when you read

about creating and working with HTML files, know that this generic term includes documents with .shtm, .shtml, .asp, .cfm, .jsp, .php, and possibly other file extensions. As long as the document uses HTML coding to create a page that the browser can display, it can be generically described as an HTML document.

XHTML Compliance

As long as you're choosing one of the file types that creates a viewable "HTML page," the dialog box offers you the choice of making your new document XHTML-compliant or not. XHTML is the newest flavor of HTML, intended to eventually replace HTML. XHTML is based on XML. It has some very slight syntactical differences from HTML and is stricter in its rules than HTML. The browsers of the future will require XHTML to create *valid* documents. If you tell Dreamweaver to make your new document XHTML-compliant, it will create slightly different syntax as it writes code for you.

If you're creating web pages that just need to work properly in the popular browsers—Netscape Navigator, Internet Explorer, Opera, and a few others—you don't need to worry about XHTML compliance quite yet. All that the standard browsers require is HTML.

New Document Preferences

By default, when you choose File > New, Dreamweaver presents you with the New Document dialog box, with HTML as the default file type and XHTML compliance turned off. To change these and a few other defaults, click the Preferences button at the bottom of the New Document dialog box. This opens the Preferences > New Document dialog box (see Figure 3.3). Note that this is the standard Dreamweaver Preferences dialog box. You can access this same dialog box by choosing Edit > Preferences and choosing the New Document category from the list on the left side of the dialog box.

If you like, you also can change the default file extension that your default file type comes with—for HTML files, you can change from .html to .htm, for instance. This is a little bit more involved, however. From the New Document Preferences dialog box, click the link to the document type XML file (shown in Figure 3.3). This opens Dreamweaver Help at the "Document Type Definition File" section that provides instruction on modifying the

Dreamweaver document type configuration information. (Of course, you can always override the default file extension when you save your files just by typing in your own extension.)

FIGURE 3.3
New Document
Preferences.

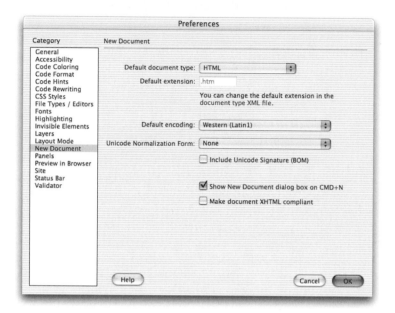

WORKING SMART WITH DOCUMENTS IN DREAMWEAVER

How do you make the most of your documents in Dreamweaver? Make sure they're valid. Make sure they will work properly in all browsers that you think your visitors will be using. Finally, make sure they're accessible.

Checking Page Validity

Validation is an important concept in the web development world. *Validation* is the process of checking the code of an HTML, XML, or XHTML document to make sure it is properly coded (with correct syntax and no nonstandard tags or attributes) before it has to be displayed in a browser. Part of the reason today's browsers are so large and unwieldy is that they are programmed to deal with all sorts of invalid code, even to guess how a page should be presented if the syntax or elements are

incorrect. In an ideal browsing world, each page's code would be checked for validity—validated—before the browser tried to display it; invalid pages would not display at all. The browsers could be lean and mean because they would be able to predict that only correctly coded pages would ever come their way.

If you're just getting started in web design, or if you're a professional on tight deadlines, you can put off worrying about validation for now. None of the major browsers requires it—yet. But eventually, they all will.

Validating Document Markup

Dreamweaver offers a validation service for all HTML documents.

To check the validity of a document, open the document you want to validate and choose File > Check Page > Validate Markup. After a moment or two, the Results window opens, showing the Validation tab, with your document's report card showing (see Figure 3.4).

You can also validate the current document or the current site by opening the Results window (Window > Results), pressing the green Validate button in the upper-left corner, and choosing Validate Document or Validate Entire Site (see Figure 3.4). If you have files selected in the Site panel, the Validate menu will also include the option Validate Selected Files in Site.

FIGURE 3.4
Validating an HTML document in Dreamweaver.

Determining Validation Settings

Validation involves checking your document(s) against a standard; there are all sorts of standards out there, from HTML 2.0 to XHTML strict and beyond. To see what standard Dreamweaver is using to validate your documents, and to change the standards as needed, choose Edit > Preferences > Validator, or, in the Results window, click the Validate button and choose Settings. Both of these commands open the Preferences > Validator dialog box (see Figure 3.5).

FIGURE 3.5
The Preferences dialog box showing the validation settings.

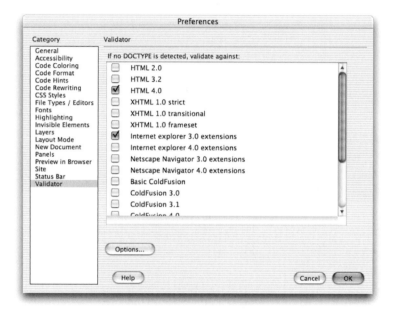

Validating XML

If you're working with any kind of XML (including XHTML), validation is crucial. Browsers (and other interpreters) will generally not process invalid documents. To validate an XML document, choose File > Check Page > Validate as XML. Note that because XHTML documents are really XML, you can also use this command to test their validity.

Checking Against Target Browsers

Okay, your pages all validate, so why don't they function right in your audience's favorite browser? Browsers have quirks and don't always adhere to standards. Most web designers end up memorizing their most

unfavorite browser quirks and work around them. But not all of us can memorize everything. For us, Dreamweaver comes with a database full of information about which browsers support what.

Automatic Checking

Target browser checking is so important that Dreamweaver automatically checks every page you open as soon as you open it, and displays the Browser Target Check icon in the Document toolbar (see Figure 3.6). If your document passes all checks, you'll see an OK icon; if not, you'll see an alert icon. To see a list of problems, click the Browser Target Check icon and choose Show All Errors, or open the Results window (Window > Results) and bring the Target Browser Check tab to the front (see Figure 3.7). All items listed with yellow alert icons are warnings— they aren't supported by one of your target browsers, but that shouldn't cause problems on the page. All items listed with red stop-sign icons are errors; they might cause some unpleasant results in the target browser.

FIGURE 3.6
The Target Browser Check display in the Document toolbar.

FIGURE 3.7
The Results window showing target browser warnings and errors.

If you don't want your pages checked automatically, click the Target Browser Check icon in the toolbar and deselect the Auto-Check on Open option.

Manual Checking

In addition to this automatic checking, you can perform document- or site-wide browser checks any time you like. To check the current document, click the Target Browser Check icon in the Document toolbar and choose Check Browser Support. To check documents or a site, open the Results Window (Window > Results), bring the Target Browser Check tab to the front, and click the green button (see Figure 3.8). Use the drop-down menu in the Results window to display document-wide or site-wide alerts and errors.

FIGURE 3.8
Using the Results window to check browser support.

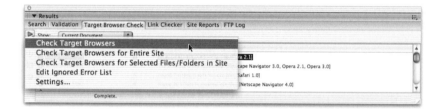

Determining Which Browsers to Check For

Target browser checks are really meaningful only if you choose which browsers are important to you. Do this by clicking the Target Browser Check button in the toolbar and choosing Settings. In the dialog box that appears, select which browsers and versions you want to check against. Then click OK to close the dialog box.

Making Your Pages Accessible

Your pages preview beautifully in the major browsers. They pass the proper validation tests, so you know you're being a good coding citizen. But are they accessible? Accessible web pages are designed to be usable by people with visual, auditory, motor, or other disabilities. This includes people using screen readers and other special software and hardware to browse the Internet. For the World Wide Web to be truly universal, it needs to be accessible.

Accessibility Standards

Various standards exist to specify exactly what makes web pages accessible. The most important of these for you, the web designer, are these:

- **Section 508**—Section 508 of the Federal Rehabilitation Act states that any website for use by government employees or for the purpose of disseminating government information must comply in some very specific ways with the Americans with Disabilities Act. Though Section 508 itself applies only to federal government–related sites, many state governments have adopted it for websites under their jurisdiction; many corporations have also voluntarily adopted its standards.

- **W3C Web Accessibility Initiative (WAI)**—The World Wide Web Consortium (W3C) has created a detailed set of prioritized rules for accessibility. Many of these match the Section 508 rules, but this standard goes beyond Section 508.

How can you learn more about these accessibility standards? Your best friend for accessibility education in Dreamweaver is the Reference panel. Open this panel and, from the Book drop-down menu, choose UsableNet Accessibility Reference. You now have at your disposal all sorts of information on different standards and how to apply them (see Figure 3.9).

FIGURE 3.9
The Reference panel, showing accessibility information from UsableNet.

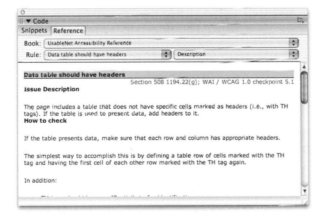

To learn more about applying Section 508 and WAI rules, see the sections throughout this book's chapters on making different page elements accessible.

For more information on Section 508, visit www.access-board.gov/sec508/ guide/1194.22.htm. For more on the W3C WAI, visit www.w3.org/WAI/. For information on accessibility in general, visit www.usablenet.com.

Dreamweaver Accessibility Options

To help you create accessible web pages without compromising your efficiency, Dreamweaver MX 2004 gives you quick access to each of your page element's accessibility attributes. To enable accessibility attributes, choose Edit > Preferences and, in the dialog box, go to the Accessibility category (see Figure 3.10). The list of options represents different page elements that have special accessibility attributes in HTML. For each item you select, every time you click an object to insert that object, its dialog box will include those special attributes. (For more on accessibility options for individual page elements, see the accessibility sections in subsequent chapters throughout this book.)

FIGURE 3.10
The Preferences dialog box showing the Accessibility settings.

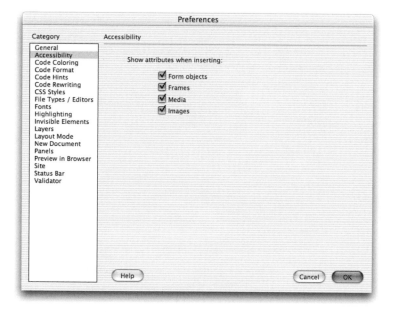

Checking Accessibility

Just as you can check validity and browser support, you can check your pages and sites for accessibility. Dreamweaver offers various tools for this.

To run an accessibility report on your current document or site, do this:

1. Choose Site > Reports.

2. When the Site Reports dialog box opens, choose Accessibility and choose whether to run the report on the current document, on the entire site, or on selected files in the site.

3. Before running the report, click the Report Settings button and choose which standards to check against. Click OK to close this dialog box.

4. Click Run to run the report.

Dreamweaver processes your pages and displays its results in the Results window. Figure 3.11 shows this process happening.

FIGURE 3.11
Running a site-wide accessibility report.

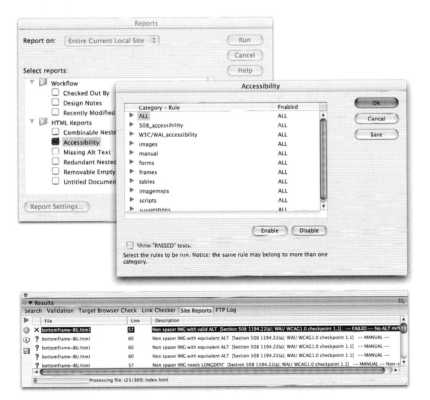

SUMMARY

This chapter covered some of the most basic tasks you can perform in Dreamweaver, those related to creating and working with documents. The next several chapters cover the various aspects of working with documents in more detail—text, images, links, and head content. After that, basic training is over and it's off to the world of web design and beyond.

```
<head>
<style type="text/css">
body {background-color: red}
p {text-align: right; color: white}
</style>
</head>
<body>
```

CHAPTER 4

WORKING WITH TEXT

TEXT IS THE HEART AND SOUL OF THE WORLD WIDE WEB—A FAST-LOADING, flexible, and easily editable component that arguably has the potential to communicate more and better than anything else on the web. This chapter covers the basics of creating well-structured text in Dreamweaver MX 2004, the difference between structural markup and visual formatting, and how to handle text wisely as an important part of every web page you build.

TEXT BASICS

You can't get much more basic than text in a web page. But considering that probably 90% of what you're producing as a web designer is text, it's worth getting a really solid foundation in how HTML text works and how it can go wrong.

Text in the Browser

If you've worked at building web pages for any length of time, you know the drill. HTML is a structural markup language. Its primary job is to describe the logical structure of page elements, such as text, so that the logic of the page is clear to any person or device reading it. For text formatting, HTML uses block-level tags, applied to chunks of text to indicate their role in the page (see Table 4.1); and character-level tags, applied to a word or two within a block, to emphasize or identify those words (see Table 4.2).

TABLE 4.1 **Common Block-Level Structural Markup Tags for Text**

Tag	Description	Browser Styling	Sample
p	Paragraph of body text	Default size and font, usually 12-point Times unless changed in the user's preferences	`<p>Once upon a ⇒time, there was ⇒a frog...</p>`
h1 to h6	Headings, levels 1–6 (h1 is a main heading, h2 is a subhead, and so on)	Bold, larger than default size, with size varying from h1 (largest) to h6 (smallest)	`<h1>Welcome to My ⇒Web Page</h1>` `<h2>All About ⇒Me</h2>`

Tag	Description	Browser Styling	Sample
ul, li	Unordered list (ul) containing list items (li)	Indented, with bullets for each list item	```<ul>` ` <li>Apples</li>` ` <li>Oranges</li>` ` <li>Peaches</li>` `</ul>```
ol, li	Ordered list (ol) containing list items (li)	Indented, with numbers or letters for each list item	```<ol>` ` <li>Preheat oven</li>` ` <li>Make cookie dough</li>` ` <li>Put cookies in oven</li>` `</ol>```
blockquote	Paragraph of quoted text	Indented on both sides	```<p>As Lincoln said:</p>` `<blockquote>Four score and seven years ...</blockquote>` `</p>```
dl, dt, dd	Definition list (dl) consisting of term to be defined (dt) and definition (dd)	Indented definition under term being defined	```<dl>` ` <dt>lemon</dt>` ` <dd>yellow citrus fruit</dd>` ` <dt>lime</dt>` ` <dd>green citrus fruit</dd>` `</dl>```

TABLE 4.2 **Common Character-Level Structural Markup Tags**

Tag	Description	Browser Styling	Sample
em	Emphasize	Italic	```<p>This is <em>very</em> important.</p>```
strong	Strongly emphasize	Bold	```<p>This is <em>extremely</em> important.</p>```

Text in Dreamweaver

In Dreamweaver, you create text by typing it in or by copying and pasting it from other programs. Typing, editing, and selecting functions work just like they do in word-processing programs. The spelling checker (Text > Check Spelling) lets you check the spelling of a selection or an entire document against the main Dreamweaver dictionary as well as your personal dictionary.

You apply HTML structure to text using the Text Property Inspector, Text objects in the Insert bar, and the various commands in the Text menu. Figure 4.1 shows the Property Inspector and Text objects as they relate to each other and to the markup tags in Tables 4.1 and 4.2.

FIGURE 4.1
The Text Property Inspector and Text objects in Dreamweaver.

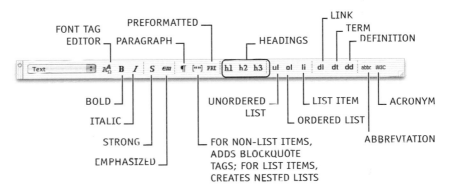

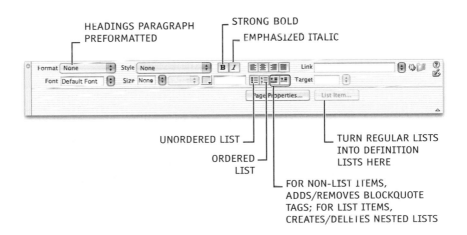

WORKING SMART: BRINGING IN TEXT FROM OTHER PROGRAMS

If the text you need in your page already exists in another program, or if you just prefer typing in another program, you need to get that text into Dreamweaver efficiently. Fortunately, there are several mechanisms for doing this.

The Ins and Outs of Copying and Pasting

Working with Word? The rules are different. See the section "Importing Text from Microsoft Word," later in this chapter, for information on this.

You can easily bring text into Dreamweaver by copying and pasting from other programs. But life will be much easier if you're smart about doing this. After you've copied your text to the Clipboard from another program, you have your choice of three commands for bringing it into Dreamweaver: Edit > Paste, Edit > Paste Text, and Edit > Paste HTML. There are also two matching commands for copying: Edit > Copy and Edit > Copy HTML. What's the difference?

The Paste Command

If you're in Design view, Edit > Paste or Edit > Paste Text turns whatever text is on the Clipboard into text in your Dreamweaver document. All formatting is lost. Paragraph breaks are converted to br tags. No other HTML tags are added. Dreamweaver converts any special characters that it recognizes—things such as apostrophes, quotes, dashes, copyright symbols, and so forth—from the system-specific coding that word processors employ to generic HTML entities. (HTML entities are discussed in depth later in this chapter.)

If you're in Code view, Edit > Paste strips all formatting from the text on the Clipboard and puts that text wherever the insertion point is in your document, with no conversion of special characters. So, for instance, if the text on your Clipboard contains this:

```
<b>Howdy there, fellas.</b>
```

using Edit > Paste from Design view will actually paste the following into your code at the insertion point:

<b>Howdy there, fellas.</b>

The angle brackets will show up in the browser, and the text won't be bold. Using Edit > Paste from Code view with the same Clipboard contents, that code will be put unaltered into your HTML source code, and in a browser it will display like this:

Howdy there, fellas.

The Paste HTML Command

How does the Paste HTML command fit in? If you're in Design view and choose Edit > Paste HTML, it has the same effect as if you had switched to Code view and chosen Edit > Paste. In other words, it pastes your text unaltered into the source code of your document. All formatting, including line and paragraph breaks, is stripped out, and no special characters are converted.

If you're in Code view, the Paste HTML command is not available.

Copying vs. Copying HTML

The same principles work in reverse for when you need to get text or HTML code out of Dreamweaver. If you're in Design view and choose Edit > Copy, you'll put the visible text that you have selected on the Clipboard. If you're in Design view and choose Edit > Copy HTML, or if you're in Code view and choose Edit > Copy, you'll put the actual HTML source code for your selection, including page text, on the Clipboard.

Getting Text (and More) from Word and Excel

For all you Microsoft Office users out there, your web development life just got a lot easier. New to Dreamweaver MX 2004, you can easily and quickly bring even complex content into Dreamweaver from Word and Excel documents while preserving most of their formatting and creating decent HTML code.

Copying and Pasting

Copy anything in a Word or Excel document—text, tables, pictures—and paste it into Dreamweaver Design view using Edit > Paste or Edit > Paste Text. That's all there is to it! The pasted content comes in nicely formatted and structured.

Text Formatting

Copied and pasted paragraphs from Word come in as proper paragraphs, not text separated by line breaks. Word's Normal text style is turned into a CSS class called `MsoNormal`, which is tucked into an internal style sheet for the Dreamweaver document. Paragraphs that have been assigned Word's heading styles (Heading 1, Heading 2, and so on) come in as HTML heading tags (`h1`, `h2`, and so on), with additional inline styles to convey formatting. Text like this, brought in from Word:

Chapter 1

It was a dark and stormy night.

gets turned into the following style declaration in your document's head:

```
<style type="text/css">
<!--
p.MsoNormal {
margin:0in;
margin-bottom:.0001pt;
font-size:12.0pt;
font-family:"Times New Roman";
}
-->
</style>
```

and the following code in the document body (where your insertion point was when you pasted):

```
<h1><span style="font-family:Arial;font-size:16.0pt;">Chapter
➥1</span></h1>
<p class="MsoNormal">It was a dark and stormy night.</p>
```

Tables

Tables pasted from Word and spreadsheets pasted from Excel come into Dreamweaver translated into HTML tables that preserve the formatting of the original through the use of CSS classes, like this:

```
<table class="MacTableGrid">
<tr>
<td width="118" valign="top">
➡<p class="MacNormal">State</p></td>
<td width="118" valign="top">
➡<p class="MacNormal">Capital</p></td>
</tr>
```

Figure 4.2 a shows a portion of an Excel spreadsheet as it appears when pasted into Dreamweaver.

FIGURE 4.2
An Excel document before and after pasting into Dreamweaver.

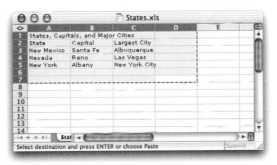

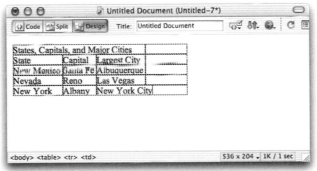

Importing Word and Excel Documents (Windows Only)

The copy-and-paste method works well for bringing in chunks of content. But if you're working in Windows, you can more efficiently turn an entire Word or Excel document into HTML with Dreamweaver's import commands. Do it this way:

1. Create or open a Dreamweaver document to import into.

2. Switch to Design view (the commands don't work from within Code view).

3. Choose File > Import > Word Document or File > Import > Excel Document. Browse to choose the file to import, and click OK to close the dialog box.

There's your nicely formatted HTML content!

Remember, though, that Word documents can sometimes be long (tens or hundreds of pages), and web pages shouldn't be that long. To bring a long Word document into Dreamweaver, break it up into a sequence of documents and import each separately, or select parts of the document at a time and use the copy-and-paste method to put each segment into a separate HTML document. In Dreamweaver, you'll need to add links to the HTML pages you create if you want them function as a unit.

Working with Word HTML

Microsoft Word can also create its own HTML using its Save as Web Page or Save as HTML command. Unfortunately, Word doesn't generate the nicest HTML (see Figure 4.3 for a sample). The code it puts in your document is a mix of HTML and XML code, with an abundance of font tags or CSS styles and countless meta tags. It bloats the file, slows download and browser parsing, and makes further editing really painful. Yuck!

If you have the choice, you'll get better results if you let Dreamweaver do the HTML generating, using the copy-and-paste or import methods discussed earlier in this section. But you might not have control over this part of the development process. How do you make the best of

your Word-generated HTML? By carefully setting your options in Microsoft Word before exporting and by using Dreamweaver features to tidy things up afterward.

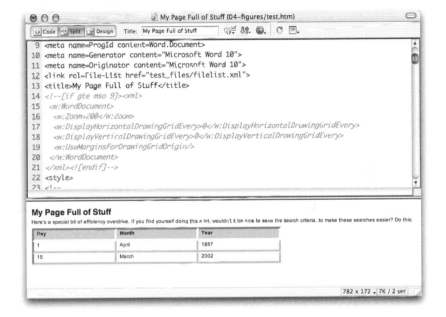

FIGURE 4.3
HTML code generated by Microsoft Word, as viewed in Dreamweaver Code and Design view.

Getting Ready in Word

You can do several things in Microsoft Word to get the cleanest, most web-friendly code possible from it.

First, make sure the code-creation options are set efficiently. Depending on your version of Word, you might find these options in different places. But the settings you should look for and set are as follows:

- Set your target browsers to more than just Internet Explorer. A fairly safe choice is Internet Explorer 4.0 or Netscape Navigator 4.0. Disable all features not supported by these browsers.

- Use CSS for font formatting. (This avoids having numerous font tags throughout the document.)

- Don't allow PNG as a graphics format.

- Set the encoding to Unicode or Western European (ISO). This is especially important because, by default, Word chooses to encode

pages according to the platform you're on. Your special characters end up in a Windows-specific or Mac-specific format that could cause problems for browsers.

- If your document includes graphics, make sure the default resolution is something reasonable, such as 72 or 96.

In Word XP, choose Tools > Options. In the dialog box that appears, bring the General tab to the front and click the Web Options button. In Word X for Mac, choose Word > Preferences > General. In the dialog box that appears, bring the General tab to the front and click the Web Options button.

Next, depending on your version of Word, choose File > Save as Web Page, or File > Save as HTML, or File > Save, and use the Save dialog box to choose one of the web formats. However you get here, you'll have two basic choices: to save the complete contents of the file as a web page or to save a filtered or display-only version of the file. What's the difference? If you save the complete contents, Word includes all sorts of code so that at some time in the future you will be able to reimport the HTML document into Word. That puts a lot of extra junk in there. Unless you really want this ability, choose the filtered or display-only option.

Cleaning Up in Dreamweaver

In Dreamweaver, open the Word-generated HTML as you would any other HTML document. Then choose Commands > Clean Up Word HTML. You are presented with the Clean Up Word HTML dialog box (see Figure 4.4). Table 4.3 lists the clean-up options you have for tidying things up.

FIGURE 4.4
The Clean Up Word HTML dialog box.

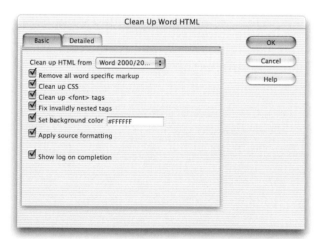

TABLE 4.3 **Clean Up Word HTML, Basic Options**

Option	Description
Remove All Word-Specific Markup	Removes all XML from HTML tags and other formatting specific to Microsoft Word.
Clean Up CSS	Removes tags that refer to CSS, including inline CSS styles (as long as the parent style shares the same style properties). It also removes style attributes beginning with mso and non-CSS-style descriptions. This is beneficial because Microsoft Word HTML relies heavily on CSS styles for formatting, most of them being document-level styles that increase page-loading time in the web browser.
Clean Up <font> Tags	Removes the font HTML tags and converts the default body text to size 2.
Fix Invalidly Nested Tags	Removes invalid font tags. Invalid font tags are those found in spots where the font tag shouldn't be, according to the W3C. Specifically, these are the font tags outside the paragraph and heading (block-level) tags.
Set Background Color	To use a hexadecimal value to set the background color of your document, enter it into the Text field box. Without a set background color, the document will have a gray background. By default, the background color is white, or #FFFFFF.
Apply Source Formatting	Applies the source formatting options that you specified in your sourceformat.txt file. This file is located in your Configuration folder. (See Chapter 28, "Customizing and Extending Dreamweaver," for more about setting your preferences.)
Show Log on Completion	Check this box to see a log listing what changes have been made.

You can use the options in the Detailed tab to specify exactly what changes are included in the conversion.

After you make your selections, click OK. Dreamweaver processes the file, and a cleaned-up version of the page appears in the Document window.

Even after you've cleaned up, you may find unwanted tags or attributes in your code. In particular, an internal style sheet might exist, containing one or more classes called Section1, Section2, and so on. These classes are applied to div tags surrounding the body contents. And throughout the entire page, you might find numerous elements that have been assigned the Normal class, even though that class is not defined internally

or in a linked style sheet. A little fancy finding and replacing can get rid of these items. Do it like this:

1. Open the Find and Replace dialog box (Edit > Find and Replace).

2. Set the search scope to Document.

3. To remove the div tags, set the search type to Specific Tag. In the Search For area, enter **div** as the tag to remove, and press the – button to remove any other search criteria. From the Action drop-down menu, choose Strip Tag. This removes the div tags without deleting any of their contents. Figure 4.5 shows what the Find and Replace dialog box should look like with these settings in place. Click Replace All to complete the search.

FIGURE 4.5
The Find and Replace dialog box, ready to strip all div tags from the current document.

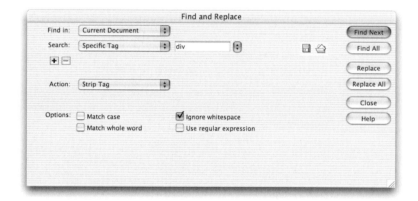

4. To remove the Normal class assignments, set the search type to Source Code. In the Search For field, enter **class="Normal"**. Leave the Replace With field empty. Figure 4.6 shows the dialog box with these settings in place. Click Replace All to complete the search.

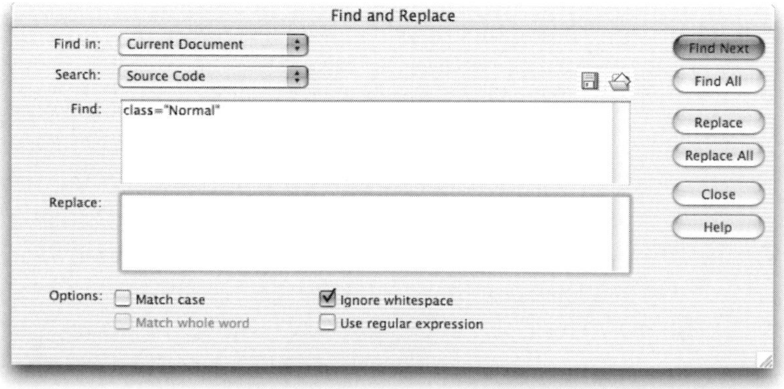

FIGURE 4.6
The Find and Replace dialog box, ready to strip all instances of the Normal class from the current document.

5. When you're done, close the Find and Replace dialog box.

To remove the internal style sheet, you can perform another Specific Tag search, or you can open the CSS Styles panel (Window > CSS Styles), select all internal styles, and click the trash can icon at the bottom of the panel.

 For more information about finding and replacing, see the section "Advanced Find and Replace" in Chapter 27, "Writing Code in Dreamweaver."

Tabular Data

Tabular data is text that's already in a table—data from a spreadsheet, for example, or a table in your word-processing program or from a database. To display that data on a web page, you need it in an HTML table. Although many of these programs can export HTML for you, it's generally not very clean HTML. If your table exists in Microsoft Word or Excel, of course, you can just copy and paste it into Dreamweaver, as described earlier in this chapter. If your table exists in any other program, your best bet for getting it easily and cleanly into Dreamweaver is using the Import Tabular Data command. Here's how it works:

1. In the originating program (a spreadsheet, for example), save or export in a *delimited* format. This means that the program creates a text file in which some character—usually a comma or tab— separates the contents of each cell, and a return indicates the end of a row.

2. In Dreamweaver, open a document and place the insertion point where you want the tabular data to appear. Choose the Tabular Data object from the Layout Insert bar, or choose File > Import > Tabular Data, or Insert > Table Objects > Import Tabular Data. A dialog box appears (see Figure 4.7) in which you select the text file to import, specify what the delimiting character is, and assign any table-formatting characteristics you like. (You can always change these later using the Property Inspector, so it's not crucial to get them exactly as you want them here.) When you click OK, Dreamweaver creates a new table containing the text from the file, split into cells and rows based on the delimiter. Figure 4.8 shows this happening.

FIGURE 4.7
The Import Tabular Data dialog box.

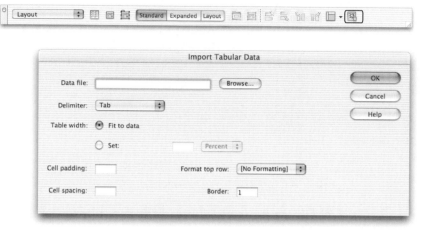

FIGURE 4.8
Importing data from a spreadsheet into Dreamweaver.

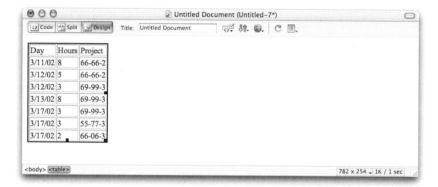

After Dreamweaver builds the table containing your imported data, it behaves like any other table, as if you had constructed and populated it here in Dreamweaver. There's no dynamic link to the text file you imported, so nothing bad will happen if you delete or move that file.

One word of warning, however: The Import Tabular Data command doesn't recognize merged cells. If your original spreadsheet or table contained any of these, the table that Dreamweaver creates will be incorrectly structured (see Figure 4.9). To fix this problem, you'll have to manually add `rowspan` or `colspan` values to the problem cells. To fix the table shown in Figure 4.9, for instance, select the cell in the top row and use the Tag Inspector, Quick Tag Editor, or Code view to assign a `colspan` of 3.

FIGURE 4.9
A spreadsheet document with merged cells creates an incorrectly structured table in Dreamweaver.

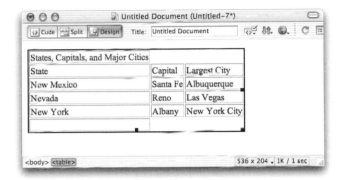

WORKING SMART: CREATING TEXT STRUCTURE

As a web designer, you need to work as efficiently as possible with text. This includes creating and editing it efficiently, and having a good idea what makes well-structured text.

Well-Structured Text: Making Text Accessible

The name of the game for good HTML is separation of form and content. Text in an HTML document is structured with tags that indicate the logical purpose of each piece of text: heading, subheading, paragraph, list, and so on. This is *content*. *Form* is how that text is presented so that its logical structure is apparent. Form can be controlled by the browser, screen reader, or other device; it can also be affected by Cascading Style Sheets, which indicate how certain logical elements should be handled.

Why is this distinction important? For one thing, it's more efficient. Setting every single heading in a website to a certain size, font, and color—referred to as *presentational markup*—is tedious and difficult to

update. Identifying every single heading as a heading and then letting the browser or a style sheet control the formatting of all headings—called *structural markup*—is much more efficient.

Not only is it more efficient, but structural markup is more flexible and, therefore, more accessible. A screen reader, for instance, won't know that some large, bold text on the page is supposed to be a heading—but it does know that text structured with the h1 tag is a heading. The W3C's accessibility guidelines include several recommendations that encourage structural, as opposed to presentational, markup for text:

3.3 Use style sheets to control layout and presentation.

3.5 Use header elements to convey document structure and use them according to specification.

3.6 Mark up lists and list items properly.

3.7 Mark up quotations. Do not use quotation markup (such as blockquote tags, for instance) for formatting effects such as indentation.

For this reason, the font tag and its attributes (size, color, and face) have been deprecated in HTML in favor of using Cascading Style Sheets for formatting; and bold and italic (b and i tags) are discouraged in favor of em (emphasis) and strong tags. Font, bold, and italic all relate to visual presentation only.

Using Dreamweaver to Create Well-Structured Text

Dreamweaver can help you create properly structured text, but only if you work with the program.

Let Dreamweaver Substitute em and strong for b and i

By default, Dreamweaver is set up to do this. Whenever you use the B and I buttons in the Text Property Inspector, the program adds em and strong tags. You can change this setting in the Preferences dialog box (see Figure 4.10). Don't! The default setting is better.

FIGURE 4.10
The Preferences dialog box setting for good coding of bold and italic text.

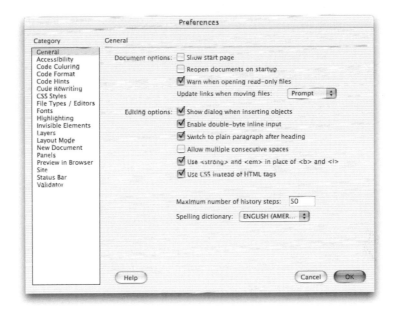

Don't Use Indent and Outdent Improperly

The Indent and Outdent buttons on the Property Inspector look a lot like similar controls in word-processing programs, but they're not! When applied to regular paragraphs of text that aren't list items, they add blockquote tags. When applied to items in an ordered or unordered list, they create subcategories of the list. These are their correct structural uses. If you just want to indent a paragraph of text, but it isn't a block quote, use CSS to create an indented style of paragraph. If you want your list items indented farther than they are by default, use CSS to modify the li tags.

Check out Chapter 11, "Using Cascading Style Sheets," for all the ins and outs of Cascading Style Sheets.

Use All Tags According to Their Structure, Not Their Appearance

This is just an extension of the previous point. Think structurally when applying tags and presentationally when applying style sheets. The top level of headings in a document should be h1, not h2 or h3. If the h1 tag creates text that is too big for your taste, use CSS to modify its presentation instead of just not using it. Definition list formatting is only for definition lists, not to create staggered indent effects. And so forth. At least some of your visitors will thank you. You'll thank yourself when you're maintaining this document later. Your colleagues will thank you when they have to update the document the next time you go on vacation. Like eating your vegetables and buttoning up your overcoat, these are just the right things to do.

Fixing Badly Structured Text

What if you inherit a page that violates these rules? Dreamweaver has a variety of tools to help you fix problems.

Removing *font* Tags

font tags are never a good idea. To remove one font tag, do this:

1. Place the insertion point inside the text that is being formatted with the font tag.

2. In the Tag Selector, find the font tag and right-click it. From the contextual menu, choose Remove Tag (see Figure 4.11). This deletes the font tag without disturbing the text itself.

FIGURE 4.11
Using the Tag Selector to remove an individual font tag.

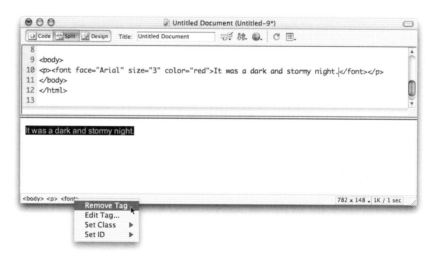

To quickly remove all font tags from one or more documents, perform a Specific Tag search, like this:

1. Choose Edit, Find and Replace.

2. When the Find and Replace dialog box opens, set the search scope to whatever you desire.

3. Set the search type to Specific Tag. In the Search For field, enter **font**. Click the – button to eliminate all other search options.

4. In the Actions drop-down menu, choose Strip Tag. Figure 4.12 shows what the dialog box should look like at this point.

5. Click Replace or Replace All to perform the search.

6. When you're done, click Close to close the dialog box.

FIGURE 4.12
Using a Specific Tag
search to remove all
font tags from a
document.

FIGURE 4.12
Using a Specific Tag
search to remove all
font tags from a
document.

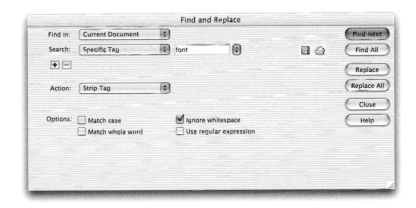

Replacing Bold and Italic with Strong and Emphasis

You can use another Specific Tag search to change b and i tags to strong
and em. Do this:

1. Choose Edit > Find and Replace.

2. When the Find and Replace dialog box opens, set the search scope to
   whatever you desire.

3. Set the search type to Specific Tag. In the Search For field, enter **b**.
   Click the – button to eliminate all other search options.

4. In the Actions drop-down menu, choose Replace Tag. In the text
   field that appears, enter **strong**. Figure 4.13 shows what the dialog
   box should look like at this point.

FIGURE 4.13
Using a Specific Tag
search to replace all
b tags with strong.

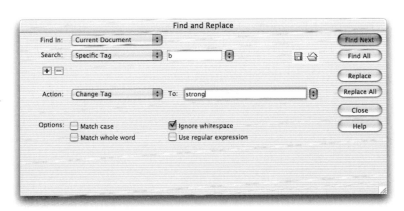

5.   Click Replace or Replace All to perform the search.

6.   Repeat the previous steps, replacing i with em. When you're done, click Close to close the dialog box.

You can use this same technique to get rid of blockquote tags, replacing them with p tags, although it's wisest to choose Replace instead of Replace All so you can examine each occurrence and make sure it's not really a quotation that needs a blockquote tag.

Stripping Out Multiply Indented Lists

A *multiply indented list* consists of one ordered or unordered list inside another, not for the purpose of creating a sublist, but simply to increase the indent. The code looks like this:

```
<ul>
   <ul>
      <li>Apples</li>
      <li>Bananas</li>
   </ul>
</ul>
```

To eliminate these occurrences one at a time, you can select any item in a list, find the double set of ul or ol tags in the Tag Selector, right-click on one of the two tags, and choose Remove Tag from the contextual menu. To quickly find and eliminate them across an entire document or site, you can perform a Specific Tag search for a ul or ol tag inside another ul or ol tag (see Figure 4.14), but you'll have to replace them one at a time and carefully examine each occurrence because the search will also find legitimate nested lists.

FIGURE 4.14
Using a Specific Tag search to find all nested unordered lists.

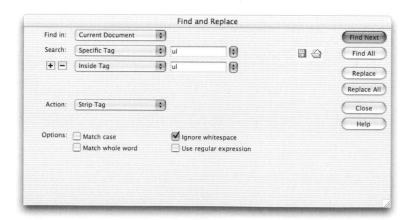

Line Breaks, Nonbreaking Spaces, and Whitespace

Whitespace is a visual concept and, therefore, is related to formatting, not structure. So why discuss it here? Because there's nothing wrong with a little whitespace, as long as it doesn't actually interfere with structure.

Line Breaks: The Good and the Bad

In Dreamweaver, pressing Return or Enter ends the current paragraph and begins a new paragraph. In the source code, this ends one block (paragraph, heading, list item, and so on) and starts a new one. In Design view as well as in the browser, all breaks between blocks are displayed with a double space. This is often called a *hard wrap*.

Sometimes you want a new line but don't want a new block element. You don't want the extra space or you don't want to create a new list item, for instance, In these cases, press Shift+Return or Shift+Enter. This ends the current line and begins a new line. In the source code, a br tag is entered within the current formatting block. In Design view and in browsers, it creates a new line with no extra spacing, bullets, and so on. This is often called a *soft wrap*.

Soft-Wrapping Woes

Line breaks are very easy to abuse, however, and can cause problems if you're not careful. What happens, for instance, if you carefully insert line breaks throughout your text and the browser rewraps the text because of user settings or window size? Figure 4.15 shows what ugly results can happen.

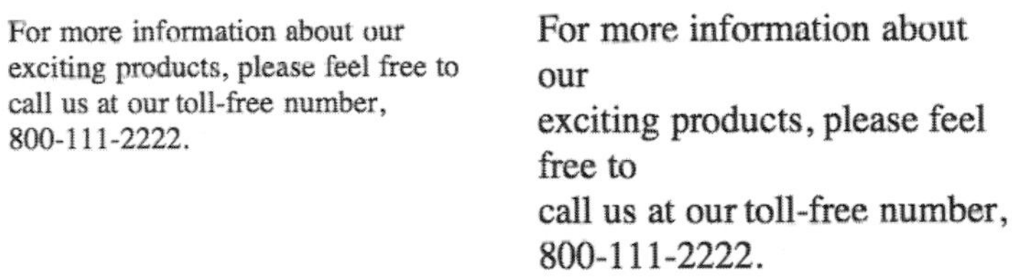

FIGURE 4.15 Soft-wrapping as you hope it might look (left) and as it can look (right) in the browser.

For more information about our exciting products, please feel free to call us at our toll-free number, 800-111-2222.

For more information about
our
exciting products, please feel
free to
call us at our toll-free number,
800-111-2222.

Soft-Wrapping and Structure

Remember also not to use line breaks to create bad structuring. If you want no extra space between a title and its following text, for instance, don't just separate the two with a line break. This obliterates the structural difference between title and text. Instead, use CSS to eliminate the extra space, like this:

1. In the CSS Styles panel, create a new style, either by redefining the tag involved or by creating a custom class.

2. When the CSS Style Definition dialog box comes up, choose the Box category.

3. In the Margin controls, deselect Same for All and set the bottom margin to a negative amount. Figure 4.16 shows this happening.

4. If you defined your style as a custom class, select the text and use the Property Inspector or Tag Inspector to apply it.

FIGURE 4.16
Creating a CSS Style that will eliminate the extra space between two block elements.

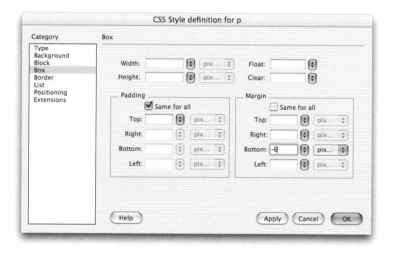

 CSS control of the bottom margin doesn't display correctly in Netscape 4.*x.*

Nonbreaking Spaces

A *nonbreaking space* ( ) is just what it sounds like: a space that is guaranteed not to wrap to the next line, no matter how the automatic text wrap happens. But it's more than that. Browsers ignore extra whitespace in HTML code. But a nonbreaking space creates a space between words or other elements that the browser is not allowed to ignore. The

easiest way to create a nonbreaking space in Dreamweaver is to press Shift+Ctrl+Spacebar (Windows) or Opt+Spacebar (Mac). But you can also create one by choosing the Nonbreaking Space object in the HTML Insert bar or Insert > HTML > Nonbreaking Space.

Dreamweaver also creates nonbreaking spaces for you in a few situations. Any time you create an empty paragraph, for instance, Dreamweaver inserts a nonbreaking space to force the browser to pay attention to the paragraph. (Completely empty paragraphs are considered meaningless whitespace and are ignored by browsers.) The program also inserts nonbreaking spaces into empty table cells, for the same reason that some browsers don't display empty table cells correctly.

Making Whitespace with Empty Paragraphs

Admit it, how many times have you done this? Hit the Return key a few extra times to create a big whitespace between page elements? Guess what? That's cheating! Dreamweaver makes it so easy, inserting those nonbreaking spaces in your empty paragraphs to make sure they display. But it's not really good structure. What's logical about a paragraph full of nothing? A much better way to add space between items is (you guessed it!) CSS.

All About Lists

Everybody loves lists. Whether they're bulleted lists or numbered lists—unordered or ordered, in HTML-speak—they help create read-at-a-glance content for web visitors in a hurry. You can do a lot to make your lists better looking and better structured.

Refining List Appearance with List Types

You don't want round black bullets in your bullet lists? You want "abc" instead of "123" in your numbered lists? This is a simple matter of setting the type attribute for the list or list item. The code looks like this:

```
<ul type="square">
<ol type="a">
```

List types can be set in Dreamweaver in the List Properties dialog box, available from the List Item Property Inspector. To make this happen in Dreamweaver, place the insertion point somewhere within the list and,

in the Text Property Inspector, click the List Item button. This opens the List Properties dialog box (see Figure 4.17).

From here, you can use the List Type drop-down menu to specify what kind of list it is. Even though this is called List Type, it doesn't supply a type attribute for the list; instead, it changes the tag that creates the list:

- **Ordered (ol)**—Creates a numeric, alphabetical, or otherwise ordered list

- **Unordered (ul)**—Creates a bulleted list

- **Directory (dir)**—Creates a multicolumn directory list (this tag is deprecated).

- **Menu (menu)**—Creates a single-column menu list (this tag is deprecated).

Depending on what you choose here, different options become available in the rest of the dialog box.

To determine the list's type attribute, use the Style drop-down menu. Table 4.4 lists the possible types for different list kinds.

TABLE 4.4 **Options Available for List Styling Through the List Properties Dialog Box**

Kind of List	Style	HTML
Unordered	[Default]	No type attribute is added; the browser determines style.
	Bullet	type = "disc"
	Square	type = "square"
Ordered	[Default]	No type attribute is added; the browser determines style.
	Number(1,2,3)	type = "1"
	Roman Small (i,ii,iii)	type = "i"
	Roman Large (I,II,III)	type = "I"
	Alphabet Small (a,b,c)	type = "a"
	Alphabet Large (A,B,C)	type = "A"
Directory List	—	—
Menu List	—	—

For ordered lists, you're also given the opportunity to specify where the list count starts (at 1, 2, 3, and so on). Enter a number in here, even if you've chosen a non-numeric type such as Alphabet. This adds a `start` attribute to the `list` tag, like this:

```
<ol start="5">
```

Finally, in the bottom of the dialog box, you can choose a New Style, which adds a `type` attribute to the particular list item you had selected when you opened this dialog box:

```
<ol type="1">
    <li>
    <li type="a">
    <li>
```

This changes the type of only that one list item.

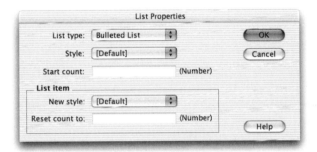

Fancier Bullets with CSS

Bullet types are nice, but what if you want graphic bullets for your unordered lists? CSS can help you! Do it this way:

1. Start by using a web graphics program to create the GIF or JPEG graphic that you want to use as a bullet.

2. Back in Dreamweaver, create a new CSS Style redefining the `ul` (unordered list) tag. Do this by choosing Text > CSS Styles > New CSS Style, or by using the New Style button in the CSS Styles panel.

3. When the CSS Style Definition dialog box appears, go to the List category. In the Bullet Image field, browse to select your bullet. You can leave the Position field blank or choose inside from the drop-down

menu to include the bullet in the indentation for the list items (this makes the indent look larger).

4. Click OK to close the dialog box. From now on, any unordered list governed by the style sheet will use that graphic as its bullet. Figure 4.18 shows the whole procedure in action.

FIGURE 4.18
Creating a CSS style to use an image for list bullets.

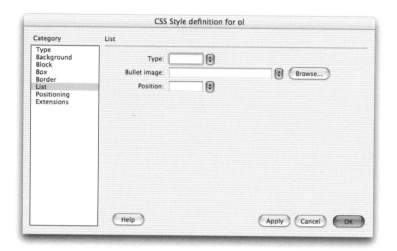

Of course, this isn't the only way CSS can help you format your lists. Font, text size, color, and more can all be set using CSS. To increase or decrease the amount of indentation given to list items, or the vertical space between list items, set the margin properties (available in the Box category of the CSS Style Definition dialog box). See Chapter 11 for more.

Taking Advantage of Special Characters

When working with text, you will no doubt encounter a need for special characters such as accented letters, copyright symbols, or the angle brackets used to enclose HTML elements. To use such characters in an HTML document, they must be represented in the HTML by special codes called HTML entities. They take the form &code, in which code is a word or numeric code indicating the actual character you need to display onscreen. There are hundreds of HTML entities for special characters. Table 4.5 lists some of the most common ones.

TABLE 4.5 ## Commonly Used HTML Entities

Name	Appearance	Keyboard Shortcut (WIN) *	Keyboard Shortcut (MAC)	HTML Entity
Opening Single Quote	'	Alt+0145	Opt+]	‘
Closing Single Quote (Apostrophe)	'	Alt+0146	Shift+Opt+]	’
Opening Double Quote	"	Alt+0147	Opt+[	“
Closing Double Quote	"	Alt+0148	Shift+Opt+[	”
Em Dash	—	Alt+0151	Shift+Opt+-	—
En Dash	–	Alt+0150	Opt+-	–
Copyright Symbol	©	Alt+0169	Opt+G	©
Trademark Symbol	™	Alt+0153	Opt+2	™
Registration Symbol	®	Alt+0174	Opt+R	®

*Windows keyboard shortcuts are ASCII codes and must be entered by pressing and holding the Alt key, typing all four numbers specified, and then releasing the Alt key. The numbers must be typed using the numeric keypad, and Number Lock must be on.

Inserting Special Characters As You Work

Automatic insertion of entities based on keyboard shortcuts might not work if your document doesn't have the default encoding scheme (Latin-1). See Chapter 3, "Creating and Working with Documents," for more on encoding schemes and Dreamweaver.

Some special characters are easier to insert than others. To insert an ampersand, for instance, just press Shift+7 while in Design view, and Dreamweaver will substitute the correct HTML entity (&). If you know the keyboard shortcuts your operating system uses to create other characters, you can also use those in Design view, and Dreamweaver will enter the correct code. On Macintosh, for instance, Shift+Opt+] creates an apostrophe. In Dreamweaver, it creates the ’ HTML entity. Table 4.5 lists Windows and Macintosh keyboard shortcuts for special characters.

The most commonly used HTML entities are easily accessible in Dreamweaver through the Insert > HTML > Special Characters submenu. When you want to insert one of these characters, just put the insertion point where you want it to appear and choose one of the commands here (see Figure 4.19).

FIGURE 4.19
Using the Insert menu to insert special characters.

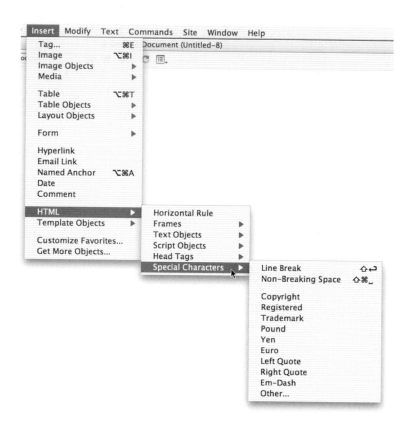

If the special character you need is not listed, choose the Other Character object from the Insert bar (refer to Figure 4.19) or use the Insert > HTML > Special Characters > Other command. This opens a new window from which you can choose a special character (see Figure 4.20). When you click a character icon, it appears in the text field box at the top of the window. You also can type your own special character code into the box.

FIGURE 4.20
The Insert Other Character dialog box.

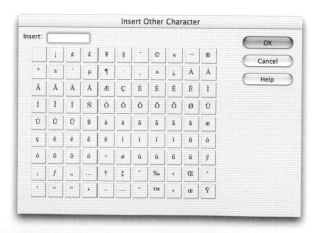

Finding and Replacing to Insert Special Characters

If you've got a whole page full of text in front of you—or, worse, an entire site's worth of pages—that have already been typed without the benefit of HTML entities, the last thing you want to do is hunt through it to replace items one by one. It's time for a little finding and replacing! Do it this way:

1. Open one of the documents you want to edit, and make sure you're in Design view.

2. Find one occurrence of the character you want to change. If you want to insert real (curly) apostrophes instead of straight single quotes, find an example of this. Delete this character and use the Insert bar or Insert menu to insert an HTML entity.

3. Select the special character you just inserted and choose Edit > Copy.

4. Choose Edit > Find and Replace. Choose a search scope (Current Document, Entire Site, and so on) as desired. Set the Search In drop-down menu to Text. In the Search In field, type the character you're going to replace—the straight quote, double-hyphen, and so on. Click inside the Replace With field and Edit > Paste to get the special character in there.

5. Choose Replace or Replace All. The search might take a few seconds, depending on your search scope. When it's done, Dreamweaver will tell you how many replacements it made. Click OK to close that dialog box, and click Close to close the Find and Replace window.

6. Repeat this procedure for any other special characters you want to use.

Here's a special bit of efficiency overdrive. If you find yourself doing this a lot, wouldn't it be nice to save the search criteria to make these searches easier? Do this:

1. Follow the steps just listed, up to the point where you're looking at a Find and Replace dialog box with all of the correct search criteria in place for a particular special character.

2. Instead of searching or closing the window, click the Save button; it looks like a computer disk. Choose to save your criteria in any folder you like that you'll be able to find and remember later. When you're done saving, close the Find and Replace dialog box.

3. The next time you want to search and replace this special character, open the Find and Replace dialog box and click the Load button; it looks like a file folder. Browse to your saved criteria and load them. Then perform the search as usual. Pretty handy!

Do you often use a special character that isn't on the Insert bar? Adding a simple bit of code such as a special character to the Insert bar is not difficult. It's covered in the section "Creating Object Extensions" in Chapter 29, "Creating Your Own Extensions."

Lorem Ipsum and Other Bits of Greek

Have you ever had to build a web page out of text that doesn't exist yet? Your boss or client promised to get you that copy for the home page by Friday, but it just didn't happen—and now you need to design the page. For years, designers have been using fake text, often called *greeking*, just to fill the spaces and indicate what the final design will look like without having any actual text. Weirdly enough, this greeking is usually created from a form of fake Latin (not Greek), always starting with the words *Lorem ipsum*:

> Lorem ipsum dolor sit amet, consetetur sadipscing elitr, sed diam nonumy eirmod tempor invidunt ut labore et dolore magna aliquyam erat, sed diam voluptua.

It doesn't mean anything, but it looks good. It lets you see what the finished design will look like, estimate how many words will fit in a given area, and so forth.

In Dreamweaver, stationery-based designs created from the New Document dialog box's Page Designs category are built with this greeking (see Figure 4.21). So are many of the predefined snippets available in the Snippets panel.

How can you easily put greeking into your documents? Many designers have a special text file that they just open when needed and copy from. But if you want to be a little bit slicker, you can download one of the fake text extensions available on the Dreamweaver Exchange. These include Latin Text, Insert Celestial TechnoBabble, and Insert Corporate Mumbo Jumbo.

To visit the Exchange, choose Help > Dreamweaver Exchange, or launch your browser and go to www.macromedia.com/cfusion/exchange.

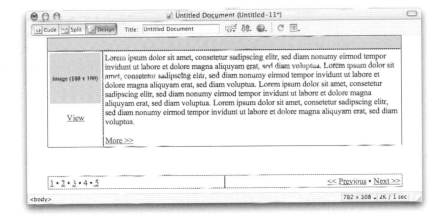

Check Spelling: Build (and Share) Your Own Personal Dictionary

Whenever you check your spelling (Modify > Check Spelling), Dreamweaver consults its own dictionary as well as your personal dictionary. You're also given the chance to add new words to your personal dictionary (see Figure 4.22). But what if you need a lot of your own words added to your dictionary? It's no fun to add them one at a time through the Check Spelling dialog box. And you don't have to!

Dreamweaver keeps its spelling dictionaries in two places. The main dictionaries consist of a series of TLX and CLX files in the main Configuration folder, which is in the Dreamweaver application folder. The user's personal

dictionary doesn't exist until you've added at least one word through the Check Spelling dialog box. So start by opening or creating a document and typing in a word that you know is not in the dictionary (such as your name or any weird made-up word). Then check spelling (Modify > Check Spelling) and, when Dreamweaver tries to correct your made-up word, click the Add to Personal Dictionary button.

Edit Your Personal Dictionary

Dreamweaver creates your personal dictionary as a text file called Personal Dictionary.tlx, which you can find in your personal application support folder. If you're using Windows 98, look here:

```
c:\Program Files\Macromedia\Common\Personal Dictionary.tlx
```

For any other version of Windows, look here:

```
c:\Users and Documents\user name\Application Data\Macromedia\
➥Common\Personal Dictionary.tlx
```

Substitute your username where indicated here. If you're the only user on your computer, you might have to look in the Default User or All Users folder.

Unless you have Windows configured to show invisible files, the Application Data folder will be invisible. To make it visible, choose Tools > Folder Options and bring the View Options tab to the front. Select Show Hidden Files.

If you're on a Mac, look here:

```
/Users/user name/Library/Application Support/Macromedia/Common/
➥Personal Dictionary.tlx
```

Substitute your username where indicated here.

Open this file in a text editor. The contents will look something like this:

For more on how Dreamweaver is configured, see the section "How Dreamweaver is Configured" in Chapter 28.

```
#LID 24941
Gutman i
spuddly i
```

Each spelling entry consists of a paragraph containing the word to be spelled. To add more words, just type them in here, separating each with a hard return. Make sure to also add a return after the last word, or Dreamweaver won't see it.

Share Your Personal Dictionary

When you've gone to all this trouble, you might want to share your dictionary with coworkers. Just put a copy of your Personal Dictionary.tlx file into the other user's personal application support folder, using the same file paths listed here.

Fixing Text Structure Problems in Dreamweaver

In this exercise, you start with a web page that has already been built—but built incorrectly. Your job is to identify the problems and fix them as efficiently as possible, using Dreamweaver to help you. Before you start, download the **chapter_4** folder from the book's website at www.peachpit.com to your hard drive. Define a site called Chapter 4, with this folder as the local root folder.

1. Open the **faq.html** file and examine it in Dreamweaver and in the browser. How does it look? What's bad about the way it's coded?

2. In Dreamweaver, put the cursor somewhere inside the first paragraph and check the Tag Selector. This indented paragraph was created with a blockquote tag. The paragraph isn't a quotation, so it shouldn't be inside a blockquote. In the Tag Selector, right-click the blockquote tag and choose Remove Tag from the contextual menu. Dreamweaver replaces it with a p tag. That's better.

3. Now place the cursor inside any of the questions. What's wrong here? They're formatted using the dt (definition term) tag and then formatted with the font and b tags. Lots of things are wrong here! Because there are several questions in the document, it's more efficient to deal with these items using Find and Replace.

    Choose Edit > Find and Replace. When the dialog box opens, set the Search In drop-down menu to Current Document. Using the instructions earlier in this chapter, perform a Specific Tag search that strips all font tags.

    Next, perform another Specific Tag search that finds all b tags and replaces them with strong tags.

    Finally, perform one more Specific Tag search to find all dt tags and replace them with p tags.

4. That takes care of the questions. How about the answers? To examine one, place the insertion point inside an answer and take a look at the Tag Selector. These items are formatted with the dd (definition data) tag. Perform another Specific Tag search, replacing dd tags with p tags.

5. Now how does your page look? There's a lot of space between questions. Can you tell why? (Hint: Try to put the insertion point inside the empty space between questions.)

   There are extra empty paragraphs between each question. That's not a terrible thing, but it's not good. To get rid of these, follow the instructions earlier in this chapter to perform a Source Code search, finding all instances of <p> </p> and replacing them with nothing.

6. What else is wrong with the text in this document? If you know about definition lists, you might suspect that there's a dl tag lurking somewhere; a definition list always consists of a dl tag surrounding one or more pairs of dt and dd tags. Place the insertion point anywhere in any question or answer, and look at the Tag Selector. You'll see a dl tag in the document hierarchy.

   To get rid of this tag, right-click it in the Tag Selector and choose Remove Tag from the contextual menu. Figure 4.23 shows what the document should look like in the browser by the time you're finished.

FIGURE 4.23

The faq.html exercise file, after removing all presentation markup and eliminating structural problems.

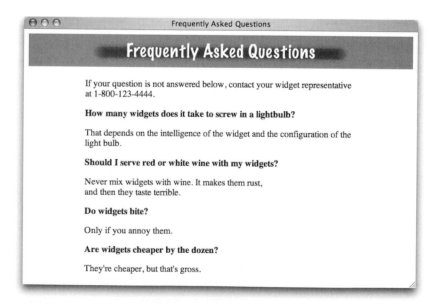

This document now has well-structured text markup. The only problem is, it doesn't look nearly as nice as it did before you started. How do you get it back to its beautiful self without compromising this structure? That's right! Apply CSS. Read all about it in Chapter 11.

SUMMARY

This chapter looked at HTML and text—in particular, at different ways of getting text into Dreamweaver, how to work efficiently with text, and the importance of creating well-structured text. The flip side of this coin is using Cascading Style Sheets to format your well-structured text.

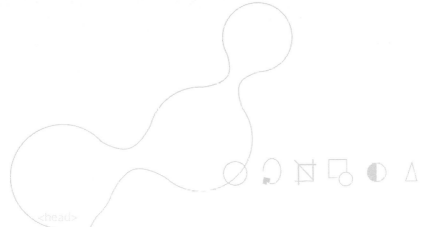

CHAPTER 5

WORKING WITH IMAGES

IMAGES PROVIDE MUCH OF THE ARTISTRY AND VISUAL APPEAL OF THE WEB. Used with care and imagination, images can add sparkle and charm; used without discretion, they can slow download times to a crawl and cause more annoyance than enjoyment. Understanding graphics and being able to manipulate them on web pages is critical to a web designer's success. This chapter takes a quick look at the basics of images, the browser, and Dreamweaver. It then examines the various ways images are used in web pages, including background images and sliced image tables. We also look at a few image niceties, including spacer GIFs, lowsrc images, and image placeholders. We finish up with a look at Dreamweaver/Fireworks integration.

IMAGE BASICS

Images are not complicated to use in the browser, but like everything, they have their rules and quirks; the more you know about those the better. This section covers the basics: how images work in web pages and how they fit into the world of Dreamweaver.

Images in the Browser

Images generally are inserted into web pages using the img tag, like this:

```
<img src="fido.gif" width="100" height="100">
```

The code tells the browser where to look for the image file that should be displayed in this space and how big a space to leave. The src attribute is a relative or absolute link to a GIF, JPEG, or PNG file. It's a required attribute because, without it, there is no image! Strictly speaking, neither width nor height is required, but if they're omitted, the browser has no way of knowing how much space to leave for the image, which slows its display of the web page. So these attributes are almost always present. Table 5.1 lists these and other commonly used attributes for the img tag.

TABLE 5.1 **Commonly Assigned Attributes of the img Tag**

Attribute Name	Description	Required?	Values
name id	Used for identification	N	Text string
src	The file containing the image	Y	URL
width height	Dimensions of the image	N	Number of pixels
alt	Text to display or read if the image can't be viewed	N	Text string
border	Width of the border surrounding the image	N	Number of pixels
vspace hspace	Vertical/horizontal padding on either side of the image	N	Number of pixels

Attribute Name	Description	Required?	Values
lowsrc	Alternate image to display while the main image is loading	N	URL
align	Determines how the image aligns with other elements in the same block	N	Top, left, right, center, and so on
usemap	Associates the image with an image map	N	Name of image map

The image files themselves must be in a format that the browser recognizes and is capable of displaying. Currently, those formats are GIF, JPEG, and PNG (though browser support for PNGs is spotty at best, and most web designers stay away from them). The GIF format is best suited for nonphotographic images with limited colors where crispness is required. GIFs can also contain animation and transparency effects. The JPEG format is best suited for photographs and other images containing many colors or subtle color shifts.

Images in Dreamweaver

Dreamweaver makes it easy to work with images—so easy, in fact, that you may be in danger of losing sight of what's really going on behind the scenes. The following sections go over the basic procedures for working with images in Dreamweaver, pointing out a few potential pitfalls along the way.

Inserting Images

You can get images into Dreamweaver in a variety of ways. You can insert them using the Image object in the Inset bar or the Insert > Image command (see Figure 5.1). If you have a site defined, you can also drag and drop images from the Site or Assets panel into the Document window. Remember that when you insert the image, Dreamweaver doesn't actually embed it in the page like a table or list; it inserts the document- or root-relative path to the image file. Especially if you're using document-relative paths, Dreamweaver works best if you have saved your file before inserting the image so that it can calculate the relative path between the document and image file.

FIGURE 5.1
Inserting an image
using the Image
object.

For more on the Assets panel, see the section "Managing Site Assets" in Chapter 18, "Site Publishing and Maintenance." For more on document-relative, root-relative, and absolute paths, see the section "The Basics of Links" in Chapter 6, "Links and Navigation."

Working with Images

Most image properties can be set in Dreamweaver by using the Image Property Inspector (see Figure 5.2). For setting all other properties, use the Selection Inspector or the Edit Tag command.

FIGURE 5.2
The Image Property
Inspector.

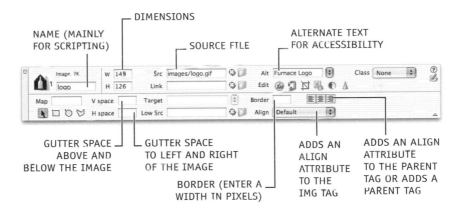

Resizing Images

Images can be resized by changing their width and height values in the Property Inspector or by dragging their selection handles in the Document window. Remember, though, that it's best not to resize images in Dreamweaver or anywhere outside your graphics-editing program. Resizing an image in HTML just tells the browser to display it larger or smaller than it really is. Displaying it larger than It should be enlarges the pixels, distorting the image and making it look pixelated

and fuzzy. Displaying it smaller makes the pixels smaller than can be displayed in the browser, so you're just wasting pixels and bandwidth.

You can always tell if an image has been resized in Dreamweaver by selecting it and checking the Property Inspector. If the width and height fields show their values in bold, those are not the original dimensions of the image. You can restore the image to its proper dimensions by clicking the Reset Size button in the Property Inspector, or by clicking the W and H next to the width and height fields.

However, as with all rules, there are a few exceptions. GIF images made from solid colors or stripes can be stretched without distortion, as long as the stretch occurs along the length of any stripes. This increases image size without increasing file size and is good for bandwidth efficiency.

Aligning Images

Setting image alignment with the Property Inspector can be confusing for the uninformed because the inspector contains two sets of alignment commands: the Align drop-down menu and the left/center/right alignment buttons (see Figure 5.2). What's the difference?

The Align drop-down menu adds an alignment attribute to the img tag itself, like this:

```
<img src="fido.gif" width="100" height="100" align="left">
```

Refer to Table 5.1, and you'll see that this attribute determines how the image aligns with other items in its block. Most commonly, this is text surrounding the image. Setting this attribute is similar in many ways to setting a text wrap or runaround option in page-layout programs.

The left/center/right alignment buttons are for text alignment. If a text element, such as a p tag, surrounds the image, clicking one of these buttons adds an align attribute to that element. If no text element is present, clicking one of these buttons adds a div tag and adds the alignment to that, like this:

```
<div align="left">
  <img src="fido.gif" width="100" height="100">
</div>
```

If the image is inside a table cell, a more efficient way to control its alignment within the cell is to add an alignment attribute to the table cell. This is done a different way, by selecting the table cell (clicking outside the image but inside the cell to create an insertion point will do) and using the Horiz and Vert drop-down menus to set the cell's align and valign properties. The code looks like this:

```
<td align="left" valign="middle">
  <img src="fido.gif" width="100" height="100">
</td>
```

Editing Images

Double-clicking any image in the Document window opens a dialog box where you can change the src file for the image. Selecting the image and, in the Property Inspector, clicking the Edit button launches a web graphics application and opens the image for editing in that application. What graphics program launches? That depends on your which external graphics editor you have defined in Dreamweaver. To check (or change) that setting, do this:

1. Choose Edit > Preferences to open the Preferences dialog box, and go to the File Types/Editors category (see Figure 5.3).

FIGURE 5.3

Setting the preference for the external graphics editor.

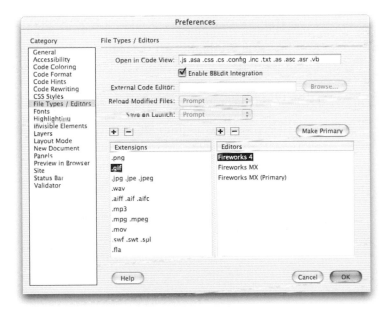

2. In the Extensions list, choose GIF. What appears in the Editors area as the primary editor? If the graphics program that you want to use isn't listed, click the + button at the top of this list to add a program. Select your favorite program and click the Make Primary button.

3. Repeat this procedure for JPEG and (if you'll be using PNGs) PNG.

4. When you're done, click OK to close the dialog box. The next time you click the Edit button in the Image Property Inspector, whatever program you defined as primary for the type of image you have selected will launch.

To enable Dreamweaver/Fireworks integration, Fireworks must be defined as the primary graphics editor for GIFs and JPGs. See the section "Dreamweaver/Fireworks Integration" later in this chapter for more on this.

WORKING SMART WITH IMAGES

As simple as the basic mechanics of images are, there are countless ways to work with them, to have trouble with them, and to be creative with them. And Dreamweaver has a host of image-related features to make your pictorial web work as fun and efficient as possible.

Making Your Images Accessible

Images are inherently inaccessible to people with visual disabilities. Your job as a web author is to make them accessible by providing alternate text descriptions, short and long. Images are included under Section 508, § 1194.22(a):

> A text equivalent for every non-text element shall be provided (e.g., via alt tags, longdesc, or in element content).

The main mechanisms for accomplishing this in HTML are alt and longdesc, both attributes of the img tag.

- **alt**—This contains a short text equivalent for an image. It is used any time the image cannot be seen, which means that even graphical

browsers will display it if the image can't be displayed. (Internet Explorer also displays `alt` text when the mouse hovers over an image, although it isn't what `alt` was intended for.) Every image in your document should include an `alt` attribute. Images that have no significance, such as spacer images, should include an empty `alt` attribute.

If you want an image to display a ToolTip without violating any W3C standards, add the `title` attribute to the image with a short text message. Some browsers display this in ToolTip form; others display it in the status bar.

*   **longdesc**—If your image's meaning can't be summed up in the brief `alt` text, you can optionally assign a `longdesc` attribute. This attribute should contain the URL of a page with a full-text description of the image. (So far, this attribute isn't very well-supported. But your job as web author is to provide the options, not to deal with failures of assistive technology.)

Using these guidelines, various image tags in a document might look like this:

```
<img src="fido.jpg" alt="Fido with his favorite toy">

<img src="spacer.gif" alt="">

<img src="statemap.gif" alt="State Map showing company district
➥divisions" longdesc="statemap_desc.htm">
```

The last of these examples requires that you also create an HTML document called usmap_desc.htm, which contains as much text as necessary to convey the information in the image.

Making Images Accessible in Dreamweaver

Images are prime culprits in inaccessible web pages because, by their very nature, they're not accessible to those with visual disabilities. The solution to this problem is to always provide text equivalents of some kind for all images on your pages.

Before the Fact: Set Accessibility Options

Before you start inserting images, make sure you have accessibility options for Images turned on (Edit > Preferences/Accessibility). When

this is enabled, the next time you insert an Image object you'll be presented with a second dialog box, allowing you to set alt and longdesc (see Figure 5.4). If you don't enter values for either attribute, that attribute won't be added to your document.

FIGURE 5.4

The Image Tag Accessibility Attributes dialog box in action.

After the Fact: Property Inspector, Tag Inspector, Edit Tag Command

After you've inserted your image, you can set alt text at any time by selecting the image and using the Property Inspector. longdesc can be added or edited with the Tag Inspector or the Edit Tag command.

- **Empty alt text for spacer images**—According to the rules, non-significant images, such as those that contain purely decorative elements or spacers, should be given empty alt attributes. This stops screen readers from having to read the image information. To create an empty alt attribute in Dreamweaver, use the Alt drop-down menu in the Property Inspector to choose <empty> (see Figure 5.5).

FIGURE 5.5

Using the Property Inspector to add an empty alt attribute to a spacer image.

- **Searching for missing alt text**—Not sure whether you used alt text for every image in the site? You can search for images without alt attributes in the current document, folder, or site. Choose Site > Reports, and select the Missing Alt Text report (see Figure 5.6). Here's a warning, though: This report identifies any empty alt attributes (as described in the previous paragraph) as missing, which, of course, they're not.

FIGURE 5.6
Running a site report
to look for missing
alt text.

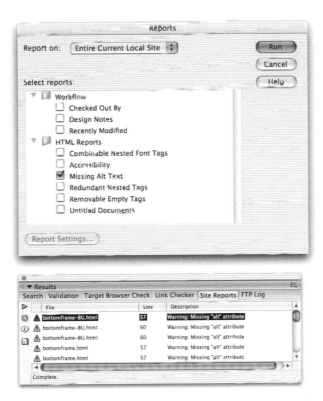

Integrated Image Editing

New to Dreamweaver MX 2004, certain basic image-editing activities, such as cropping, resampling, and handling image enhancement, can now be performed on images from within Dreamweaver. Of course, Dreamweaver isn't primarily an image editor, so leave the sophisticated image-editing tasks to Fireworks, Photoshop, or whatever your graphics editor of choice is. But for quick adjustments on-the-fly, they're a great innovation. The image-integration features are part of the Image Property Inspector (see Figure 5.7), ready for action whenever you select an image that has been placed in a Dreamweaver document. They're also available in the Modify > Image submenu. They can be used on any image that's placed in a Dreamweaver document, but they're most commonly useful for photographic images, in which subtle color differences are important and cropping is often required.

It might take some getting used to, but remember that any change you make using these tools affects the image file itself, unlike other changes the Property Inspector lets you make. The width and height fields, for instance, just alter the dimensions the image displays at in the page, not the image file's actual dimensions.

FIGURE 5.7
The Image Property Inspector, highlighting the image-editing tools.

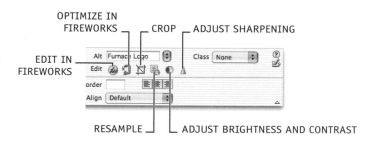

 In addition to adding image-integration features, the new Image Property Inspector includes an Optimize Image in Fireworks button. For more information on this and other Fireworks integration features, see the section "Dreamweaver/Fireworks Integration" later in this chapter.

Cropping Images

Cropping means cutting away part of the image so that some of it is lost. The resulting image is still rectangular (cropping isn't like masking or other sophisticated transparency effects). But parts of it have been chopped away.

To crop an image in Dreamweaver, select it and either click the Crop button in the Property Inspector or choose Modify > Image > Crop. Dreamweaver warns you that this will change the original image. Click OK to close the alert window. The image now displays with a cropping rectangle in front of it (see Figure 5.8).

The area inside the rectangle will be the area that remains after you've cropped the image. Drag the selection handles on the edges of the area and reposition them to determine where the image should crop. The parts of the image that fall outside this rectangle will display with a gray film over them, indicating that they'll be deleted if you crop the image.

When you've adjusted the cropping rectangle to your liking, either press Enter or double-click inside the image to confirm the change and crop the image.

FIGURE 5.8
Cropping an image in
the Dreamweaver
Document window.

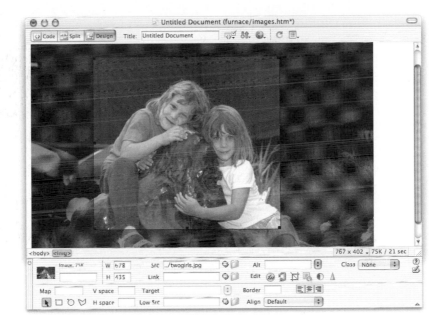

How do you cancel once you've started cropping? Click in the Document
window outside the image to deselect it. This closes the cropping window without changing the image.

Adjusting Brightness and Contrast

Brightness determines the overall lightness level of an image. If you
increase the brightness of an image, all colors in the image get uniformly
lighter. If you decrease brightness, they get uniformly darker. Contrast
determines how light the light areas of the image get, how dark the dark
areas get, and how many midtones the image contains. A high-contrast
image has very light and very dark tones, but very few midtones. A low-
contrast image has lots of midtones, but the light areas aren't much
lighter than the midtones, and the dark areas aren't much darker.

To adjust the brightness or contrast of an image, select it and click the
Brightness/Contrast button in the Property Inspector, or choose Modify >
Image > Brightness/Contrast. A dialog box opens (see Figure 5.9) with
slider controls for brightness and contrast. Move the sliders up and
down to change the image, or enter numbers in the input fields. When
you're done, click OK to close the dialog box and change the image.

FIGURE 5.9
Adjusting brightness
and contrast of
an image in
Dreamweaver.

Adjusting Sharpness

Sharpening an image makes its details look sharper, more in focus. It might even give the illusion that it's adding detail to the image. What sharpening does is look for areas in the picture where dark pixels meet light pixels. Assuming that these meeting points represent details in the image, such as the edge of a face against a background or a nose against a cheek, the contrast between light and dark along the edge is exaggerated. This makes the edge stand out more. Because the very nature of the digitizing process can make images look slightly soft and fuzzy, sharpening is an important tool for digital editing.

To adjust sharpening for an image in Dreamweaver, select it and click the Sharpen button in the Property Inspector, or choose Modify > Image > Sharpen. The Sharpen dialog box appears, with a sharpness slider (see Figure 5.10). Move the slider from left to right to increase sharpness. When you're done, click OK to change the image.

It's important to realize that although adjusting brightness and contrast or increasing sharpness can make the details of an image stand out more than they did before, none of these commands can create details where there were none before. Furthermore, every time you adjust the image, you're distorting it and losing data. It's a bad idea to adjust the same image more than once or twice.

FIGURE 5.10
Sharpening an image
in Dreamweaver.

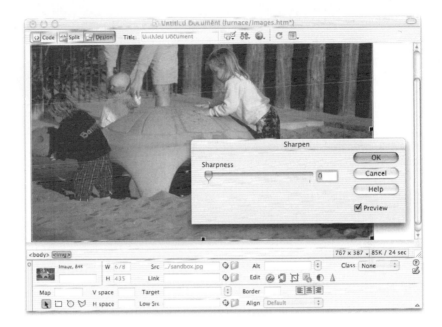

Resampling Images

Each pixel-based image has a certain number of pixels in it. When you resize an image in Dreamweaver by selecting it and changing its width and height properties in the Property Inspector, you're not actually changing the number of pixels or anything else about the image file itself. You're just telling the browser to display the existing pixels of the image bigger or smaller. That's why images resized to be larger using this method look fuzzy and pixelated.

Actually changing the number of pixels in an image is called *resampling*. The computer either subdivides pixels, thus adding to the total number, or combines pixels, reducing the total. Resampling always introduces at least some distortion into the image because the computer doesn't always guess right about what color to make the subdivided or combined pixels. But an image that has been resampled to make it bigger generally looks better than an image that has just had its existing pixels enlarged.

Resampling in Dreamweaver isn't relevant unless you've already resized the image by changing its width and height properties (either

through the Property Inspector or Tag Inspector, or by dragging its edges in the Document window). After you've done that, the Resample button in the Property Inspector becomes enabled. Select the image and click this button to subdivide or combine pixels so that the image's actual dimensions match the altered width and height properties in the HTML.

Images As Backgrounds

Ever since browsers started supporting images, web page creators have been using—and misusing!—images as background elements. Image backgrounds are commonly assigned to pages, tables, and layers. A background image can be tiled horizontally and vertically to fill an assigned space. Text and other graphic elements can be placed in front of the background image without using CSS layering techniques. Background images can be as straightforward as a repeating wallpaper pattern behind the page (as in Figure 5.11) or can be more sneakily applied as nonrepeating watermarks, side banners, and so on (as in Figure 5.12).

FIGURE 5.11
A wallpaper-style background image applied to a page.

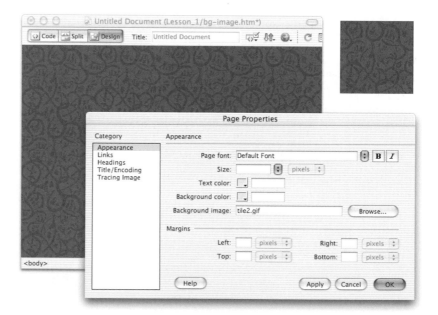

FIGURE 5.12
Background images
used as side banner
and watermark
images.

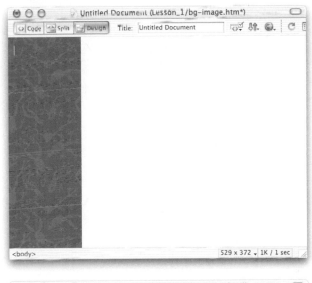

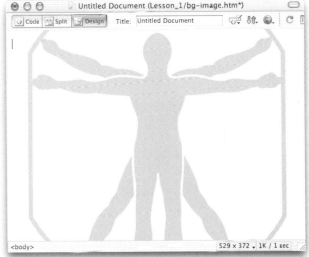

Tiled Image Backgrounds the Old-Fashioned Way

Long before CSS came on the scene, images were being used as background elements, courtesy of the background attribute. Assigning a background attribute to the body tag gives a repeating image background for the entire page. Assigning a background attribute to a table, table row, or table cell, tiles a repeating image behind just those elements.

```
<body background="flowers.jpg">
<table background="polkadots.gif">
```

In Dreamweaver, apply a background image to a page (i.e., to the body tag) by choosing Edit > Preferences, going to the General category, and deselecting the Use CSS instead of HTML Tags option. Then choose Modify > Page Properties and change the background color in the Appearance category of the dialog box. Assign backgrounds to tables and other page elements by using the Bg image field in the Property Inspector (see Figure 5.13).

FIGURE 5.13
Assigning (non-CSS) background images to page elements in Dreamweaver.

This method of assigning background images is still valid HTML and might be all you need, but it has its limitations compared to CSS:

If your target audience might be using Netscape 4, be aware that when a background image is applied to a table without using CSS, it will be tiled incorrectly.

- There is no way of controlling image tiling. The browser automatically tiles the image as often as needed, horizontally and vertically, to fill available space. Although this isn't necessarily a bad thing, it might not always fit the bill.

- There is no way of controlling image positioning. The tiling starts in the upper-left corner and repeats from there.

Image Backgrounds with CSS

Now in the days of CSS, the theory of background images hasn't changed, but we have a more efficient and powerful means of applying them. Redefined page elements and custom classes can all contain various background-image properties, like this:

```
background-image: url(myimage.gif);
background-attachment: scroll;
background-repeat: repeat-x;
background-position: 0px 2px;
```

Table 5.2 lists these style properties and what they mean.

TABLE 5.2   ## CSS Style Properties for Background Images

Property Name	Values	Description
background-image	URL(URL string)	The image to use in the background
background-repeat	repeat-x, repeat-y, no-repeat	How to tile the image (x is horizontal, y is vertical)
background-position	Two coordinates	Where to position the background in relation to its parent element (the page, table or table cell the background is attached to)
background-attachment	scroll, fixed	Whether the background should scroll or remain fixed when the page scrolls in the browser window

To assign a background image to any page element (including the body tag itself), use CSS by defining a style that includes background properties. Like this:

1. Open the CSS Styles panel (Window > CSS Styles) and click the New Style button at the bottom of the panel, or right-click in the CSS tab of the Tag Inspector and choose New Rule.

2. When the New CSS Style dialog box opens, choose whether to create your style in the current document or in a separate style sheet document, and whether to redefine an existing HTML tag or create a custom class. If you're assigning a page background, redefine the body tag. If you're assigning a background to a table, table row, or table cell, ask yourself whether every single table, row, or cell is going to have this same background (probably not). If not, create a custom class for your background image.

3. Click OK to close this dialog box and open the CSS Style Definition dialog box. In that dialog box, go to the Background category and assign your various image properties (see Figure 5.14). When you're done, click OK to close this dialog box.

4. If you redefined an HTML tag (such as body), you're done. If you created your background in a custom class, you'll need to apply it to the table or other page element that needs a background. Do this by selecting that element so its tag appears in the Tag Selector, right-clicking the tag in the Tag Selector, and choosing from the Class submenu that appears.

To assign a background image to the page itself (i.e., to the body tag), you can either use the preceding steps to redefine the body tag; or you can choose Edit > Preferences and, in the Preferences dialog box, go to the General category and make sure the Use CSS instead of HTML tags option is selected. Then choose Modify > Page Properties and use the Background Image field in the Appearance category to assign an image (see Figure 5.15). Dreamweaver will automatically create a CSS style that redefines the body tag for you.

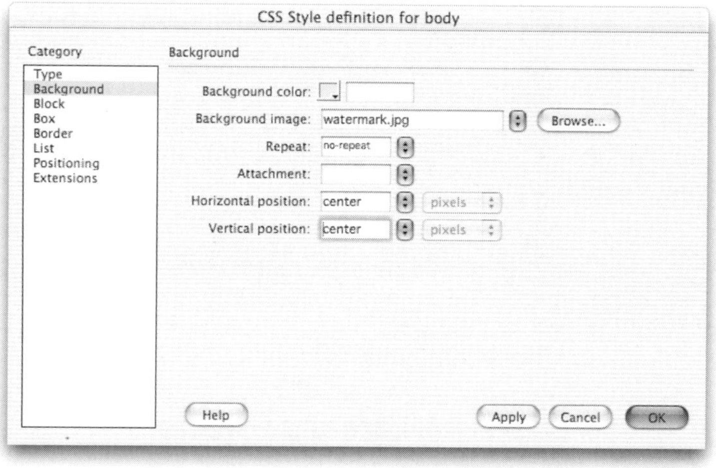

FIGURE 5.14
Creating a CSS Style that adds a background image to a page or page element

FIGURE 5.15
Using the Page
Properties dialog box
to create a CSS-based
page background.

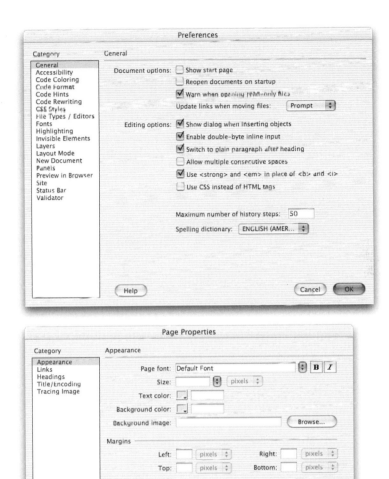

 See Chapter 11, "Using Cascading Style Sheets," for a full discussion of CSS.

Creative Background Effects

Budding web designers always want to know how to create those cool
integrated text-and-graphics effects they see in so many websites. Often
the answer involves creative background effects.

Use Vertical Tiling to Create Sidebar Graphics

How many left-side navigation sidebars have you seen in your life?

They've been around forever (see Figure 5.16). With CSS, creating them and making them efficient is simple. Do this:

FIGURE 5.16
A typical web page with sidebar graphic for navigation controls.

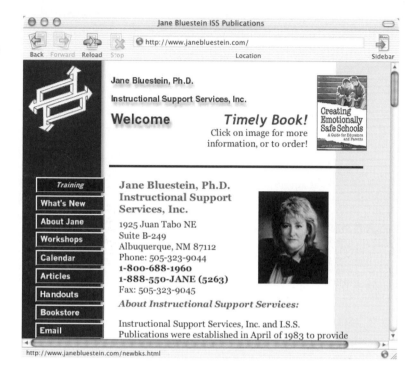

1. In your graphics program, design the sidebar graphic the way you want.

2. Presumably, you want the sidebar to extend from top to bottom of every page, but only on one side. The idea is to tile the image vertically but not horizontally. Still in your graphics program, ask yourself how short the image can be to create the result you want when tiled vertically. The most efficient sidebar graphics are only a pixel or two high and are as wide as the sidebar (see Figure 5.17).

FIGURE 5.17
A sidebar graphic before and after cropping in Fireworks.

When you've determined the ideal dimensions, crop the image to that size (or create an image slice that size) and export it.

3. In Dreamweaver, create a CSS style following the instructions in the previous section, setting the Repeat option to repeat-y.

If you need to design your page backgrounds without CSS for some reason, you can still stop the image from tiling horizontally by making it wider than the browser window. Before CSS came along, it wasn't at all uncommon to see background images that were 1 pixel high and a few thousand pixels wide.

Put Colored Tables in Front of Wallpaper

As long as there have been background images on web pages, there have been a few designers who put text in front of wallpaper-type patterns. It's almost never readable unless the pattern is so subtle that it's hardly visible.

A creative solution to this problem is to put the text in a solid-colored object (such as a table cell or layer) that sits in front of the page background (see Figure 5.18).

FIGURE 5.18
The Crayola website gets to be colorful and readable by putting solid-colored table cells in front of a patterned page background.

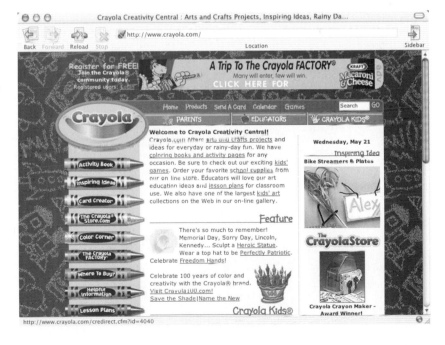

Mix and Match to Create Efficient, Flexible Image Effects

The next time you're getting ready to drop an image in a navigation bar, title banner, or sidebar, ask yourself whether mixing and matching background and foreground images, or background colors and images, can help you.

Figure 5.19, for instance, shows a title banner that stretches and shrinks with the browser window. How was that built? With a 100% width table containing a foreground image aligned left and a 1-pixel wide background image tiled horizontally across the table.

FIGURE 5.19
A flexible title banner created from a mixture of background and foreground graphics.

Figure 5.20 shows a nonrectangular-looking layout box, created from a table that mixes background cells, colors, and foreground images. No magic HTML skills are involved here—just some sneaky application of basic tables and images. Not only are these designs graphically inventive, but because they rely on reused images and background colors, they're efficient for downloading as well.

FIGURE 5.20
A mixture of images and colored table cells creates a striking layout shape.

Images and Page Structure

No image is an island unto itself. In web design, images are key players in building web pages. Because web pages today are largely structured with tables, images work within tables to create page structure. They can work invisibly as spacers stabilizing table structure, or visibly as part of table-based layouts and sliced image tables. This section looks at both of those uses.

Single-Pixel GIFs

A *single-pixel GIF* is just what it sounds like: a GIF image consisting of only a single pixel, usually made transparent. These little units are popular with web designers because they easily solve some common layout problems and contribute to some interesting design possibilities. They're often referred to as *spacer GIFs* or *shims*.

Creating Single-Pixel GIFs

A single-pixel GIF can easily be created in any web graphics program. Just open a new document with the canvas size set to 1×1 and canvas (or background) color set to transparent. Then save or export as a GIF with transparency enabled. Figure 5.21 shows this happening.

FIGURE 5.21
Creating a transparent single-pixel GIF image in Fireworks.

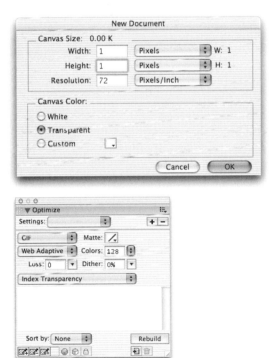

Single-Pixel GIFs in HTML

The most common use for single-pixel GIFs in HTML design is to prop open table cells and stabilize table structure. Insert one of these transparent images into an otherwise empty table cell, and assign the image

whatever width and height you want the table cell to have. A very solid table can be constructed by adding an extra row or extra column that consists of nothing but differently sized transparent GIFs. Designers call these *control rows* and *control columns*.

When Fireworks generates sliced image tables for you, or when Dreamweaver creates a table in Layout mode or uses the Convert Layers to Table command, the programs add control rows and columns filled with transparent GIFs. The programs even create the single-pixel GIF images for you! Fireworks calls its transparent GIFs spacer.gif. Dreamweaver calls its transparent GIFs either spacer.gif or transparent.gif. If you've used any of these table-generating features, you probably already have at least one transparent single-pixel GIF in your site folder. Feel free to use it.

Using Single-Pixel GIFs in Dreamweaver

Nontransparent single-pixel GIFs have also been used on web pages as colored rules and square bullets. Because each GIF can be only one color, resizing won't distort it. Increasingly, however, CSS is being used to generate this kind of effect.

You insert a single-pixel GIF the same way you would insert any image. The only problem is, these images are tiny, so they can be difficult to see in Design view. Insert the single-pixel GIF this way:

1. Insert the image as normal. It will automatically be selected when it appears in the document.

2. Don't deselect it or you'll have a hard time finding it again. Immediately use the Property Inspector to assign width and height. Also assign an empty `alt` label (by choosing `<empty>` from the Alt field drop-down menu).

    If you lose a single-pixel GIF, select the items around it and go to Code view. Somewhere in the selected code, you'll find the `<img>` tag. Change the width and height there.

3. Even after it has been resized, the transparent image is impossible to see (it's transparent!). But if you know approximately where it is, you can click around in the general area until you find it.

Sliced Image Tables

What's a sliced image table? It's what you get when you create a layout (such as a navigation bar or title banner) in a web graphics program, divide it up with slice objects, and export the HTML and images. What's wrong with sliced image tables? Nothing, really. They're usually tightly

structured and well-behaved in browsers, and our lives are a lot easier for having them around. But the page structure they create is not as simple or as flexible as it might be. The complex tables they build can take longer to display in the browser than simpler tables, and they sometimes generate more images than they need to.

What can you do to streamline your image-heavy layouts? Whether you decide to construct your own tables or to clean up tables exported from graphics programs, here are some things to watch out for.

One Cell, Multiple Images

When a graphics program generates a sliced image table, every image gets its own table cell. That's not always necessary. Figure 5.22 shows a horizontal navigation bar created from a row of images. Taken on their own, these images don't need to be in a table at all, and if they are in a table, they can occupy one big cell. Just be sure to set the cell to nowrap (enable the No Wrap option in the Table Cell Property Inspector) so the images all stay in one line.

FIGURE 5.22
A row of buttons created in separate table cells (top) and in one big table cell (bottom).

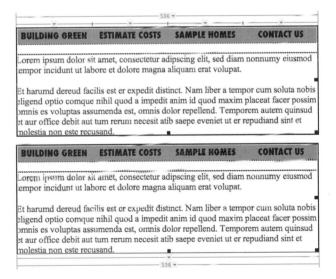

Vertical sets of images aren't quite as straightforward to handle without a multirow table, but it can be done. Separate the images with a line break (press Shift+Enter to insert a br tag), or place them in one table cell or layer that has a width assigned that matches the image width.

Image Padding vs. Spacers

Sliced image tables insert spacer images wherever items need to be separated, but that's not always necessary. Side-by-side (or top-to-bottom) images can also be separated by padding them with vspace and hspace (non-CSS) or padding (CSS), or by adding cellpadding to the table cells they're in. Figure 5.23 shows a row of three buttons separated simply by assigning hspace to the middle image; hspace assigns space on both sides of an image, so only the middle image needs it to separate all three images.

FIGURE 5.23
A row of buttons created in one table cell, separated by hspace.

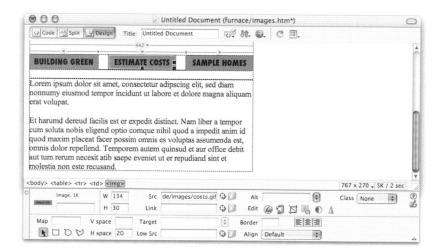

Reuse, Resize, Replace

Sliced image tables also tend to generate a separate image for each cell in the table, even though it would sometimes be more efficient to reuse one image more than once. Images are also generated at full size, even though sometimes a smaller image could be resized to create the same effect. Examine your sliced images and determine whether this is happening. If it is, replace multiple images with instances of one. Replace larger images with smaller ones. Pay special attention to the spacers that get tucked in all the nooks and crannies. For efficiency, all invisible spacers should be created from one single-pixel GIF. (See the section "Single-Pixel GIFs," earlier in this chapter, for more on this use of graphics.)

Figure 5.24 shows a navigation bar with rollover effects that could easily be created by reusing one single triangle graphic.

FIGURE 5.24
A sliced image table that could be streamlined with resized graphics.

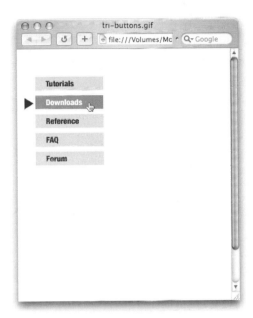

Streamlining Table Generation in Fireworks

If you use Fireworks to create your sliced image tables, follow these guidelines to help the program generate efficient HTML and images:

- Carefully align all slice objects to create as few rows and columns as possible.

- Draw slice objects wherever graphics need to be generated, leaving empty areas only where a page or table background should show through.

- Choose File > HTML Setup and use the Table tab in the HTML Setup dialog box to fill empty cells with a spacer image.

- When exporting, deselect the option Include Areas Without Slices. (Table cells generated from areas without slices will be filled with a resized single-pixel spacer GIF.)

Incorporate Background Elements
Web graphics programs generally don't generate background images or rely on background colors as part of their output. But you can be smarter

than that! Analyze your table structure and see how many images you can replace with background elements. Figure 5.25 shows a typical image table that could use cell colors for its backgrounds.

FIGURE 5.25
A sliced image table that could use cell background colors instead of foreground images to create its effect.

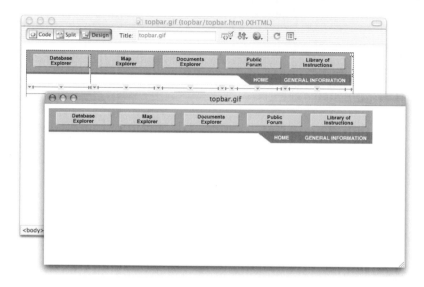

Respect the Table Structure

If you're making your own tables to hold images, it's up to you to make the table solid and stable. But before you start altering a Fireworks- or Photoshop-generated table, make sure you understand its original structure so you don't break it. Sliced image tables are stable because of how they're structured. Fireworks tables, for instance, have the following structural characteristics:

For more on table stabilization, see the section "Making Tables Behave" in Chapter 8, "Building Tables."

- Individual cells have no measurements, but the overall table has a pixel-based width.

- A "control row" and "control column" of single-pixel GIFs have been placed at the top and right edges of the table to keep its internal elements from shifting. These items are there for good reason; if you disturb them, the table might not display properly in the browser.

Figure 5.26 shows the diagrammed structure of a typical Fireworks-generated table.

FIGURE 5.26
A Fireworks-generated table, expanded to show its structure.

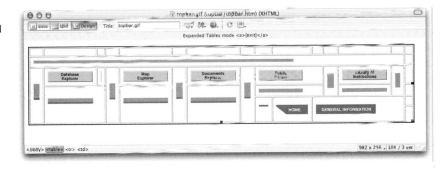

Positioning Images with CSS-P

As long as your target audience doesn't include Netscape 4.*x* or any older browsers, you can create some wonderful layout effects with CSS-positioned images that seem to float above the rest of the page. Figures 5.27 and 5.28 show some examples of this in action. To create a CSS-positioned image in Dreamweaver, do this:

FIGURE 5.27
A CSS-positioned image hugging the right edge of a title banner layout.

POSITION: ABS
RIGHT: 0
TOP: 0

FIGURE 5.28
A CSS-positioned image at the left edge of a banner, overlapping various elements beneath it.

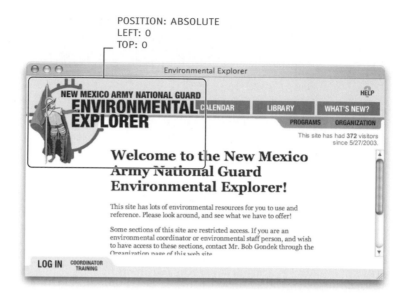

POSITION: ABSOLUTE
LEFT: 0
TOP: 0

1. Create the image as normal.

2. Insert the image in a document by placing the insertion point at the beginning of the body content and then using the Insert bar or Insert > Image command. Make sure the image isn't inside any other tags, such as tables, paragraphs, or headings.

3. Open the CSS Styles panel (Window > CSS Styles) and click the New Style icon (or right-click in the CSS tab of the Tag Inspector and choose New Rule). When the dialog box opens, choose to create a custom class called .image or .logo or some other descriptive name like that. Click OK to close the dialog box.

4. In the CSS Style Definition dialog box, go to the Positioning category. Choose Absolute Positioning, and assign any numeric value to either Left or Right, and either Top or Bottom. (The values don't matter because you can change them later.) Click OK to close this dialog box.

5. In the Document window, select the image. In the Tag Selector, right-click the img tag and choose your custom class from the Set Class submenu.

6. Your image is now positioned through CSS. You can adjust its position on the page by clicking its edge so that the Layer Property Inspector appears, and dragging or nudging it on the page. Your image will also float above all other non–CSS-positioned elements on the page.

One word of warning about floating images like this: If the image is a GIF with transparency effects, you might have to think carefully about how to antialias (or alias) the edges so that it blends in smoothly with whatever it's floating over.

Lowsrc: Your Low-Bandwidth Friend

Lowsrc is one of the unsung heroes of the HTML world. So many wonderful things on web pages work best only for high-bandwidth users, but lowsrc is at its best for low bandwidth. What is *lowsrc*? It's an alternate image you can specify that will appear in the browser window as a placeholder until a larger, slower-to-download image is ready to appear. Let's say you have a really terrific photo of Niagara Falls or astronauts landing on Mars, and you really need it on your web page, but it's a whopping 30K or more. Create an alternate version of the image, with the same dimensions, but very simple, that weighs in at 1K, and specify it as a lowsrc for the main image. The user with a slow connection will see the lowsrc image on the page until the main image downloads and is ready to display.

To create and insert a lowsrc image, follow these steps:

1. In your web graphics program, open the large image. It's probably a full-color GIF or JPEG in glorious technicolor.

2. Change the export/optimization settings to create a two-color GIF (black-and-white is popular, but any two colors will do), tinkering until you get the file size down as low as possible, and export or save to create the GIF. (There's not much point in a lowsrc image that doesn't download almost instantly.)

3. In Dreamweaver, insert the main image in your page wherever you like.

4. With the image selected, look in the Property Inspector for the Low Src field. Browse or point and shoot to select the lowsrc version of the image.

That's it! You won't be able to preview your lowsrc version locally because the main image will appear too quickly. But on a slow connection, the effect looks almost like animation, taking advantage of the slow appearance of the main image.

Blocking Out Layouts with Image Placeholders

How many times have you had to design a page around text and graphics that don't yet exist? Have you ever been right in the swing of building a page when you realized you needed a graphic you hadn't created yet, so you had to stop and put something together before continuing? Graphic designers in the print world use greeked text and FPO (for placement only) image placeholders. In Dreamweaver, you can use one of the fake text generators to create some greeking for you in a hurry. And you can use the Image Placeholder object to create the code for a picture of any size, until the real thing comes along. Figure 5.29 shows what it looks like.

FIGURE 5.29
An image placeholder (along with some greeked text) in Dreamweaver Design view and in the browser.

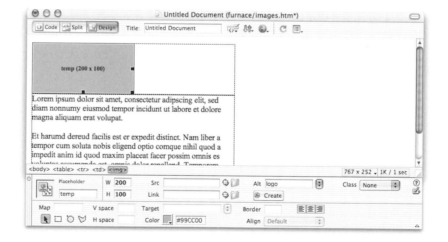

For more on greeking, see the section *"Lorem Ipsum* and Other Bits of Greek" in Chapter 4, "Working with Text."

Inserting Image Placeholders

To create and insert an image placeholder in Dreamweaver, do this (as shown in Figure 5.30):

1. With your document open, place the insertion point wherever you want the temporary image inserted.

2. In the Common Insert bar, choose the Image Placeholder object from the Images objects, or choose Insert > Image Objects > Image Placeholder from the menu.

3. The Image Placeholder dialog box appears. Assign a width and height to determine how much space the image will occupy, a color for the placeholder (gray is a good choice if you don't want the placeholder to distract you from your main color scheme), alt text for accessibility and to display in the browser, and a name that will appear in the placeholder in Design view to remind you what's supposed to go there. (The name has to be valid for scripting purposes, so don't use any spaces or special characters.) When you've set these options, click OK to close the dialog box and insert the placeholder.

FIGURE 5.30
Inserting an image placeholder.

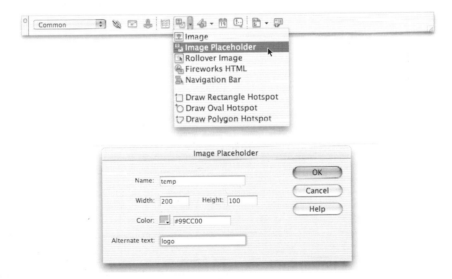

If you examine the code for your placeholder, you'll see that it's a regular img tag, with an empty src attribute and an inline CSS style attribute setting the background color. There's nothing nonstandard about this coding, so the browser has no trouble interpreting it. Because there's no source and the image can't actually be displayed, the browser uses the background color and alt text in its place.

Working with Image Placeholders

Use the image placeholder not just to block out where the final image will go, but also to help you determine its ideal dimensions. Resize it using the Property Inspector or resize handles. The current dimensions are displayed in the placeholder itself, as well as in the Property Inspector. When you're ready to generate your final image, use these dimensions as your guide. After the image has been created, return to Dreamweaver, select the placeholder, and use the Property Inspector to assign an src. After the src file has been set, the placeholder turns into a regular Dreamweaver image object.

If you're using Fireworks, creating the final image from the placeholder is even easier than that. When you're ready to create the image, select the placeholder and, in the Property Inspector, click the Create button. This launches Fireworks and opens a new document with the canvas size set to your placeholder's dimensions. Create the final image and click the Done button in the Fireworks window; Fireworks walks you through saving and exporting before returning you to Dreamweaver.

Dreamweaver/Fireworks Integration

If you use Dreamweaver for your web editing and Fireworks for graphics building, you can take advantage of some powerful features integrating the two programs.

For Dreamweaver/Fireworks integration to work, you must have assigned Fireworks to be your primary graphics editor in Dreamweaver Preferences. See the section "Editing Images," earlier in this chapter, for more details on doing this.

How Integration Works

How does integration across the Macromedia product line work? More important, how can you not get in its way as it's working? The various programs of Studio MX 2004 talk to each other by leaving each other HTML comments and Design Notes.

HTML comments show up in any Fireworks-generated HTML, telling Dreamweaver any important details about how the HTML was generated, what source file created it, and so forth:

```
<!-- Fireworks MX Dreamweaver MX target.  Created Wed May
➡21 11:48:11 GMT-0600 2003-->
```

```
<!-- fwtable fwsrc="mydog.png" fwbase="mydog.jpg" fwstyle=
➡"Dreamweaver" fwdocid = "742308039" fwnested="0" -->
```

When you select a Fireworks-generated table in Dreamweaver, if it sees these comments, it shows the special Fireworks Table Property Inspector and enables launch-and-edit.

Design Notes are tiny XML files with the .mno filename extension, stored in folders named _notes. You've probably seen them on your hard drive and maybe wondered what they were. Whenever you export an image from Fireworks into a folder that is part of a Dreamweaver local site, Fireworks creates a Design Note named after the exported file, with the .mno extension added. So, mydog.jpg creates a Design Note file called mydog.jpg.mno. It puts this MNO file in a folder called _notes, located in the same folder where the image has been exported. If there isn't a _notes folder, it makes one. Inside the MNO file is this little bit of XML:

```
<?xml version="1.0" encoding="iso-8859-1" ?>
<info>
    <infoitem key="fw_source" value="/images/mydog.png" />
    <infoitem key="fw_slice_info" value="0 c8 64 0 0 71 64
    ➡0" />
</info>
```

Back in Dreamweaver, when you insert that image and then select it, the program looks for the MNO file. If it finds one, it knows that this is a Fireworks-generated image and you get the special Fireworks Image

Property Inspector. It also knows the location of the PNG file that generated this image, which makes launch-and-edit possible. If the image was created from a slice in Fireworks, the MNO file also includes a line of code indicating which slice generated it.

How can you goof up this system? By deleting the HTML comments, _notes folders, or MNO files! Deleting the comments disables integration features for Fireworks-generated HTML items, such as sliced image tables. Deleting the _notes folder or MNO file disables integration features, such as launch-and-edit, for individual images.

Insert Fireworks HTML

The Fireworks HTML object provides an easy method of getting a sliced image table, along with any JavaScript it uses for rollovers and such, into an existing Dreamweaver document. Why is this important? Most people don't generally use Fireworks to generate entire web pages. Instead, they build only the navigation bar or only the title banner in Fireworks and create the rest of the page in Dreamweaver. Fireworks HTML is much too restrictive to work well for general-purpose, text-heavy page layouts. The Fireworks HTML object fits nicely into this workflow. Use it like this:

1. In Dreamweaver, build the layout for your page, including whatever layout tables and CSS layers are required for formatting. Leave space for the sliced image table.

2. In Fireworks, create a file just the size of the navigation bar, title banner, or other page element you want to build here. Create your graphics, draw slice objects, assign links and behaviors, and do whatever else you need to.

3. Before you export, choose File > HTML Setup. In the HTML Setup dialog box, make sure the HTML Style is set to Dreamweaver HTML. This causes Fireworks to add the comments Dreamweaver needs for integration to work properly.

4. When you export, be sure to select HTML and Images in the Export dialog box.

5. In Dreamweaver, open the document where the Fireworks elements should be inserted, and place the insertion point where the items should appear.

6. From the Insert bar, choose Fireworks HTML (see Figure 5.31). When the dialog box opens, browse to select the HTML file that Fireworks generated (don't worry about finding the images—Dreamweaver will find them). Unless you plan to reinsert this Fireworks HTML in another Dreamweaver document, select the option Delete File After Insertion. When you're done, click OK to close the dialog box and perform the insertion.

FIGURE 5.31
Inserting Fireworks
HTML into a
Dreamweaver
document.

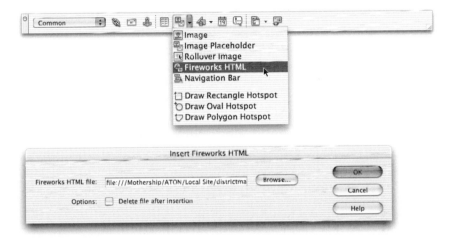

In your Dreamweaver document, you now have the Fireworks table and any related JavaScript code, along with HTML comments identifying them. From now on, when you select the table, Dreamweaver will display the special Fireworks Table Property Inspector. In addition to the regular table properties, this inspector lists information needed for launch-and-edit.

Launch-and-Edit

Launch-and-edit is the generic term Macromedia uses to describe a key feature in its cross-program integration: the capability to select an item generated in one program (such as Fireworks or Flash) from within another program (such as Dreamweaver) and automatically launch the parent program, open any required source file, make desired edits, and

return to the launching program. For Dreamweaver/Fireworks integration, this means selecting a Fireworks-generated image or table, clicking the Edit button in the Property Inspector, and having Fireworks automatically launch and open the source PNG file, ready for editing. The basic process is simple:

1. In Dreamweaver, select the image or table and click the Edit button in the Property Inspector. Or, right-click the image and, from the contextual menu, choose Edit with Fireworks.

2. When Fireworks comes to the forefront, its document window will have a special launch-and-edit bar at the top (see Figure 5.32). Make whatever edits you like and, when you're done, click the Done button.

FIGURE 5.32

The Fireworks Document window in launch-and-edit mode.

3. Fireworks now saves the PNG file, re-exports as needed, generating new images or HTML, and closes the file.

4. Dreamweaver comes back to the forefront and reloads any changed images or HTML.

This sounds great! But what can go wrong? After you've imported Fireworks HTML into Dreamweaver, you have to be careful about what you do with it there if you ever want to use launch-and-edit to update it. Changing links, alt text, and other nonstructural information in the HTML generally isn't a problem. But if you make any structural changes to the table (such as the table simplifications discussed earlier in this chapter) and then try launch-and-edit, you'll be warned that Fireworks will overwrite those changes when it updates your HTML. Don't let that

happen! The same thing will happen even if you select an individual image within the sliced image table and try to use launch-and-edit: Even though you might want to update only that one image, Fireworks will regenerate the entire table.

On-the-Fly Optimizing

One of the coolest integration tools is the capability to reoptimize images on the fly from within Dreamweaver. Let's say you've imported that animated dancing baloney for the "what's new" page, and when you get it into Dreamweaver you realize that you should have optimized it as a JPEG, or the GIF transparency isn't working, or the animation timing is off. Select the image and choose Commands > Optimize Image in Fireworks, or right-click the image and choose Optimize Image in Fireworks, or click the Optimize in Fireworks button in the Property Inspector. Fireworks launches and takes you directly to a special version of the Export Preview dialog box called Optimize Image. There you can update your optimization settings and click Update; Fireworks re-exports the image with the new settings and returns you to Dreamweaver. Figure 5.33 shows this happening.

FIGURE 5.33
The Optimize Image in Fireworks command at work.

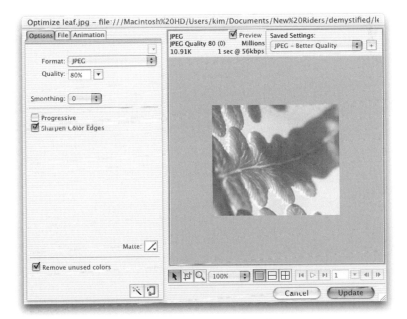

On-the-fly optimizing is especially handy when it comes to resizing files. You might be working on a page with several images in place and realize that one of the images needs to be bigger or smaller—but you're not supposed to resize images in Dreamweaver, so what do you do? Resize the image, leave it selected, and choose Commands > Optimize Image in Fireworks (or right-click the image and choose the command from the contextual menu). When the Optimize Image dialog box opens, the file will be set to optimize at its new size. After you've clicked Update and returned to Dreamweaver, take a look at the width and height indicators in the Property Inspector. You'll see that they're no longer in bold, meaning that the image has now been properly resized.

Visit the Exchange: Fireworks Integration Extensions

If the built-in integration features between Dreamweaver and Fireworks aren't enough for you, the Dreamweaver Exchange has several extensions that do even more. These include two free extensions authored by Macromedia: InstaGraphics Extensions for Dreamweaver MX and Web Photo Album 2.1 for Dreamweaver MX.

InstaGraphics Extensions for Dreamweaver MX 2004

According to Macromedia, this extension enables you to instantly create Fireworks Web graphics directly from Dreamweaver without expert design skills and without even knowing Fireworks. It includes three items: the Convert Text to Image command, the Convert Bullets to Images command, and the Fireworks Button object.

- **Convert Text to Image command**—As its name suggests, this command creates an image of any Dreamweaver text, with the font and style of your choice (see Figure 5.34). You can tell it to change all selected text or all text in the document within certain tags (such as all h1 text). You can find this command in the Commands menu.

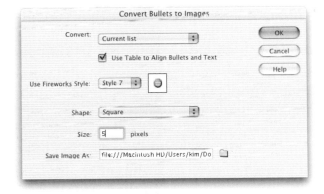

- **Convert Bullets to Images command**—Convert any or all unordered lists in your document into lists built from graphic bullets and tables for good formatting (see Figure 5.35). You choose the size and style of bullet, and Fireworks even makes sure it blends with your document's background color. (Note that when you're done with the command, your list isn't technically a list anymore because it's not within ul tags.) You can find this command in the Commands menu.

- **Fireworks Button object**—This object works much like the Flash Button object that's been in Dreamweaver for a few versions now. It lets you choose a button style, assign your own text and link information, and create a button with rollover code already applied (see Figure 5.36). It's like a shortcut for you creating the button and its

rollover state, adding the Swap Image behavior, exporting the whole shebang from Fireworks, and bringing the HTML into Dreamweaver. It's quite a timesaver as long as you like the button styles that it gives you to choose from. You can find this object in the Insert bar's Media tab.

FIGURE 5.36
The Fireworks Button object, part of the InstaGraphics suite of extensions.

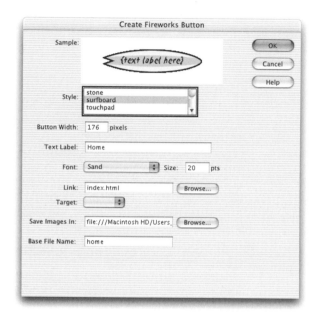

Web Photo Album 2.1 for Dreamweaver MX (Macromedia)

This popular extension lets you create your own HTML photo album from existing photos on your computer. You choose the graphic style and other details, and you choose which photos to include. It generates thumbnails, HTML pages for display, the whole works. The interface takes the form of a wizard walking you through easy steps, so it's very intuitive (see Figure 5.37). You can find this command under the Commands menu.

You can use the Web Photo Album 2.1 command if you don't have Fireworks on your system, but you won't be able to generate thumbnails.

Create Web Photo Album
Photo album title: Product Descriptions
Subheading info: Our line of products are pictured helc
Other info:
Source images folder: file:///Macintosh HD/Users/kim/Doc
Destination folder: file:///Macintosh HD/Users/kim/Doc
Browse...
Browse...
OK
Cancel
Help
Thumbnail size: 100 x 100
Show filenames
Columns: 5
Thumbnail format: JPEG - better quality
Photo format: JPEG - better quality
Scale: 100 %
Create navigation page for each photo

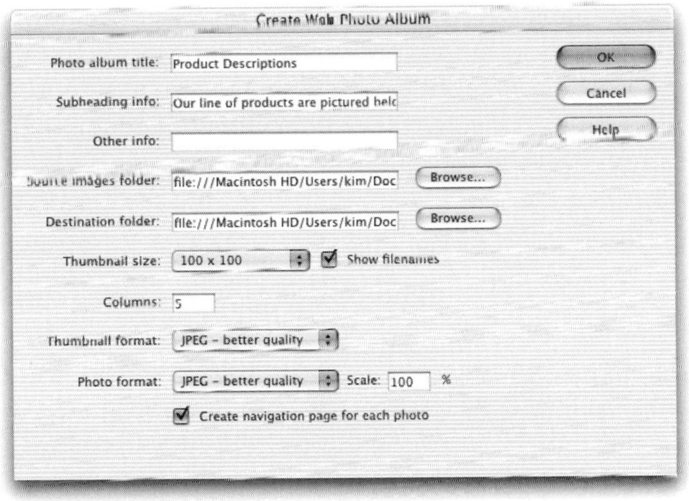

FIGURE 5.37 The wizard interface for the Web Photo Album 2.1 command.

EXERCISE 5.1

Putting Images Together into a Complex Title Banner

In this exercise, you bring together various graphics to create a well-structured, efficient title banner that mixes sliced images and background images. Before you start, download the **chapter_05** folder from the book's website at `www.peachpit.com` to your hard drive. Define a site called Chapter 5, with this folder as the local root folder.

1. Figure 5.38 shows the title banner you need to create. It should contain rollover buttons and should be flexible, stretching all the way across the browser window as it resizes.

BEAR Essentials
BEARS
COATS & HATS
BEAR REPAIR
PALS

FIGURE 5.38 Layout for a title banner and navigation bar, to be created in Dreamweaver and a web graphics program.

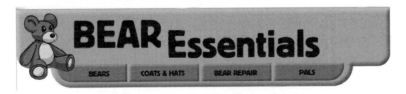

The first issue you need to deal with is how this layout is best created. What kind of sliced (or nonsliced) images will it need? How should it be constructed? For the exercise, the following strategy will be used:

The nonflexible title and navigation bar in the center can be created in Fireworks (or other graphics program). The stretchy bar will be created by a mixture of background and foreground images, placed in a flexible table.

As a bonus for you Fireworks users, the chapter_5 folder also contains the source PNGs that these graphics were built from. top_left.gif, top_right.gif, and top_shim.gif were all exported from beartop.png. The sliced image table was exported from beartop-nav.png.

2. In the chapter_5 folder, open **main.html**. This file is where you'll construct the finished layout. It currently contains a flexible table set to 100% wide, with placeholder text indicating what will go in each cell. Figure 5.39 shows this file.

FIGURE 5.39
The file where the title/navigation banner will be built.

3. Before starting work, choose Edit > Preferences. Go to the Accessibility category and enable accessibility options for images.

4. Start by defining the background image. Open the CSS Styles panel (Window > CSS Styles) and go to Edit Styles mode; you'll see that the body tag has been redefined for this document (setting page margins to 0). Select that style in the CSS Styles panel and click the Edit Style button at the bottom of the panel to open the CSS Style Definition dialog box.

    In this dialog box, go to the Background category. For Background image, click the Browse button and choose top_shim.gif (in the chapter_5/images folder) as the source. To see how the tiling options work, move the dialog box so you can see your Document window and click the Apply button. Try choosing different options in the Repeat drop-down menu and clicking Apply to see how these options work. Finish up by setting the Repeat option to repeat-x,

which will repeat the image across the top of the page. Click OK to close the dialog box.

5. Now you'll add two foreground images to make the top banner look rounded at its ends. In the leftmost cell of the table, delete the word *left* and, in its place, insert the top_left.gif image. When the accessibility options dialog box comes up, leave the alt field blank—this is a purely decorative image and shouldn't have any text in its alt label. After the image has been inserted, use the Property Inspector to set its alt text to <empty>.

6. Repeat the previous step for the rightmost cell of the table, deleting the word *right* and inserting the top_right.gif image. Again, assign an empty alt label.

7. The rounded banner effect is almost ready to preview. In the middle cell of the table, delete the word *navbar* and, using the Property Inspector, set the width of the table cell to 100%. This forces the left and right images to the outer edges of the window so that they look like a natural end to the background banner. Figure 5.40 shows what your page should look like at this point.

FIGURE 5.40
A background/ foreground image combination creating a flexible bar across the top of the browser window.

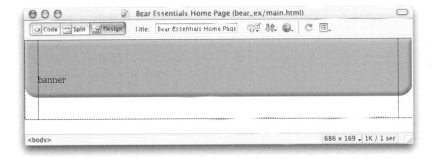

8. Now for the sliced image table that forms the central portion of the title/navigation banner. Place the insertion point in the center table cell and, from the Insert bar, choose Fireworks HTML. When the dialog box opens, choose to insert the banner.htm file. For purposes of the exercise, it doesn't matter whether you delete the file after insertion. Click OK to close the dialog box. Figure 5.41 shows the results.

FIGURE 5.41

A sliced image table sitting on top of a flexible background graphic.

FIGURE 5.41
A sliced image table sitting on top of a flexible background graphic.

Don't worry if you don't have Fireworks on your system. The Fireworks HTML will still work.

9. The sliced image table looks almost perfect in its place, but it needs a few refinements. First, align it in the center of its table cell by clicking in the cell area outside the banner (so your insertion point is in the center cell of the main table); in the Property Inspector, set the Horiz drop-down menu to Center.

Next, the sliced image table has a white background color applied to it. Select the table and, in the Property Inspector, find and delete the #ffffff background color.

The table is also 1 pixel too low compared to the graphics around it. That's because of the control row across the top of the table. Although it can sometimes be dangerous to delete the control row, in this case it won't destabilize the table. Remove it by selecting the BEAR Essentials title image, which is in the second row of the table. Press the up arrow key once to move the insertion point to the cell that contains the title image. Then press the up arrow key once more to move the insertion point into a cell in the 1-pixel-high control row at the top of the table. Choose Modify > Table > Delete Row. Your sliced image table scoots up slightly and snuggles right into place.

At this point, check your page in a browser. The banner resizes with the browser window, but because of the interaction of background and foreground images, it still looks like a graphic unit.

10. For the finishing touch, you need to add the bear in the upper-left corner. It will be inserted as a CSS-positioned image that sits in front of the banner and hugs the upper-left corner of the browser window. Start by selecting the main table and pressing the left arrow key to

move the insertion point to the very beginning of the body content. Then insert the bear_orange.gif image. When the accessibility options dialog box appears, enter an alt label of **teddy bear**. The new arrival pushes your existing tables out of alignment in Design view (see Figure 5.42). Don't panic!

FIGURE 5.42

Inserting the bear image temporarily messes up the layout.

11. At the bottom of the CSS Styles panel, click the New Style button. When the New CSS Style dialog box opens, choose to make a new custom class for the current document only. Call the class `.bearlogo`. Click OK to close this dialog box and open the CSS Styles Definition dialog box.

    In this next dialog box, go to the Positioning category. Set the Type drop-down menu to Absolute, and enter **0** in the Left and in the Top input fields. Any page element to which this style is attached will now be positioned at the upper-left corner of the window. When you've done this, click OK to close the dialog box and create the style.

12. In the Document window, select the bear image. In the Tag Selector, find the img tag. Right-click on it and choose Set Class > bearlogo from the contextual menu. Your bear jumps into place, and the table adjusts itself.

    If the layout still looks odd in Design view, that's probably because of the limitations of the Design view display. Preview the page in a browser to see the actual effect. The title/nav banner stretches and centers itself, and the bear sits atop everything else, even overlapping the navigation bar if the window gets small enough. The result should match the original sample picture you saw back in Figure 5.32.

SUMMARY

This chapter looked at some of the ins and outs of designing web pages with images. In addition to the basics, image accessibility issues were covered, along with working smart with background images, sliced image tables, and single-pixel GIFs. We also looked at Dreamweaver/Fireworks integration and the new integrated image-editing features built into Dreamweaver MX 2004.

CHAPTER 6

LINKS AND NAVIGATION

IF YOU HAVE EVER SURFED THE WEB, YOU KNOW HOW CONVENIENT IT IS TO simply click some underlined text and be magically transported to a new place on the Internet that gives you the information you desire. These hyperlinks are both simple to create and extremely powerful. You will need to know how to create this navigation technique to build a useful website.

THE BASICS OF LINKS

To use links effectively, you first need to know how they work in the browser and how Dreamweaver MX 2004 handles them. The following sections look at the anchor (a) tag, what it can do, and how Dreamweaver can help you insert and manage your links.

How Links Work in the Browser

Hyperlinks are created by surrounding a page element with the anchor, or a, tag. The href attribute, which stands for hypertext reference, specifies the link's destination, like this:

```
Read the <a href="http://www.nytimes.com">New York Times</a> on
➥the web.
```

or

```
<a href="http://www.nytimes.com"><img src="nytimes_pic.gif"></a>
```

In the browser, linked text is marked in some way so that it is clearly distinguishable from ordinary text, usually underlined and bright blue; after being visited, the same link usually is rendered in purple. By default, linked images are displayed with a border in the same colors, although most web designers override that default. When over a link, the cursor usually changes into a hand with a pointing finger to indicate that this item is clickable (see Figure 6.1).

FIGURE 6.1
By default, link text is usually displayed by browsers underlined and colored blue.

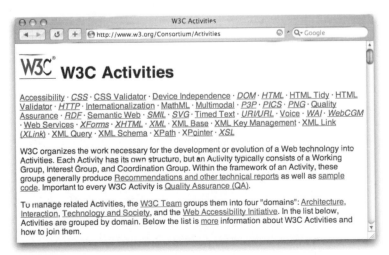

Absolute vs. Relative Paths

URL stands for universal resource locator. A *URL*, or web address, is essentially a pointer to a given document or object located on the Internet, given as a path describing how to get to the document. URL paths can be absolute, document-relative, or root-relative.

An *absolute URL* is an Internet address that contains all the information your computer could ever want to know about the location being requested. This information includes how the information is to be retrieved, including its protocol, domain, directory, and filename:

```
http://www.mfa.org/exhibitions/upcoming.htm
```

Why is the protocol so important? All sorts of different web addresses can be accessed using absolute URLs, including web pages, email addresses, FTP sites, and more. The protocol indicates what kind of resource is being requested. Table 6.1 lists the most commonly used protocols and their meanings.

TABLE 6.1 ## Protocols for Creating Absolute URL Paths

Protocol	Description	Example
`http://`	Hyptertext Transfer Protocol, used to request web pages	`http://www.macromedia.com`
`ftp://`	File Transfer Protocol, used to access files stored on FTP servers	`ftp://ftp.mydownloads.com/`⬦`myfiles.zip`
`mailto:`	Mail Protocol, used to send email messages	`mailto:laura@rocketlaura.com`

A *relative path* is a shortened form of address in which various parts of the address—the protocol, site address, and directory—might be inferred from other information available.

A *document-relative path* gives only the information needed to go from the current document to the desired page. To link between two pages in the same directory (as shown in Figure 6.2), only the filename is necessary, like this (linking from mypage.html):myotherpage.html.

To link to a second page that's deeper within the folder structure than the calling page, use the folder name and filename, like this (linking from mypage.html):myfolder/mythirdpage.html. To link to a second page

that's higher in the folder hierarchy, use ../ to indicate each level to climb up, followed by the filename: (linking from mypage.html):../index.html.

FIGURE 6.2
An example directory structure that might be used with document-relative linking.

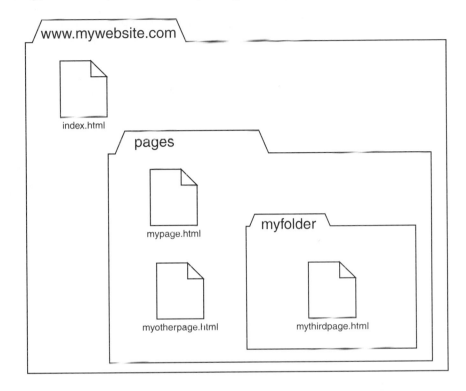

To move up and down the hierarchy, use as many folder names or ../ indicators as needed, one for each level:

`pages/myfolder/mythirdpage.html`

`../../index.html`

A *root-relative path* establishes the relationship between a file and the root of the site. The root of the site is what you would consider the general name of the site, such as `www.macromedia.com` or `www.mfa.org`:

`/index.html`

`/pages/mypage.html`

`/pages/myfolder/mythirdpage.html`

Root-relative links always have a slash in front of the pathname, as you can see.

Why would you want to use root-relative paths? It saves time later if you need to do some reorganization of documents on your site. If you have your company newsletter online and you move the monthly articles to a directory called Archive when the new issue goes online, root-relative links will save you the time it would take to change links within last month's page to reflect the new path structure.

If you want to preview your pages locally inside a browser and without a web server, you must use document-relative paths. Web browsers can't understand what local root folder you are using, so the only paths that can be followed are relative to the document currently being viewed.

Also be warned that not all web servers are configured to handle root-relative paths correctly. Check with your server administrator before employing this kind of link in your site.

Targets

By default, when you click a link, the new document opens in the current browser window, replacing what was in it previously. However, HTML enables you to specify that a link should open in a new browser window or on a frame-based site in a particular frame. This is written using an optional attribute of the anchor tag, <a>, called target. If you want the new document to open in a separate window, the target attribute needs to be set to _blank:

```
<a href="http://www.macromedia.com" target="_blank">Click
➥here!</a>
```

Other values for the target attribute are discussed in Chapter 10, "Designing Frame-Based Pages."

Links in Dreamweaver

Creating links is a common task when creating a website, as you can imagine. Luckily, Dreamweaver makes this task quick and easy. Now that you understand the basic principles of URL paths, you are ready to use Dreamweaver's Property Inspector to add links to your site.

Whenever an image or text element is selected in Design view, the Property Inspector includes a set of link fields and controls for specifying link information (see Figure 6.3).

FIGURE 6.3
The Text (top) and
Image Property
Inspectors, both
showing their link
controls.

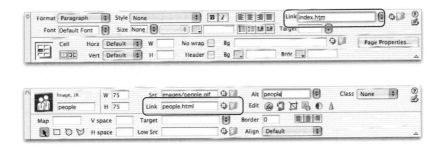

Assigning Absolute Links

All absolute links must be typed into the Link field of the Property Inspector. Be sure to type the complete link, including the protocol.

If you're working within a defined Dreamweaver site, you can also use the Assets panel to help manage your absolute URLs. Open the Assets panel (Window > Assets) and bring the URLs category to the front (see Figure 6.4).

FIGURE 6.4
Using URL assets to
manage absolute
URLs.

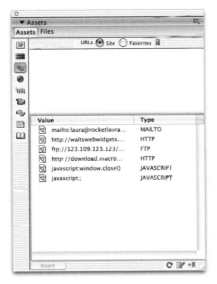

Assigning Relative Links

To assign a relative link, select the element and then either type the relative URL in the Link input field of the Properties Inspector or use the Browse or Point-to-File icons. Using either of these methods causes

Dreamweaver to construct a document-relative or root-relative path to the specified location.

If you do not save your file before inserting an image or creating a link, Dreamweaver does not understand where this HTML document is located. Therefore, you will get a message reminding you to save the file. Until you save the file, Dreamweaver creates a link specific to your workstation. This link will not necessarily work after you upload your document, so get into the habit of saving your new documents into the proper directory as soon as you create them.

To browse for a link, click the Browse button (the folder icon) next to the Link field and, from the dialog box that appears, browse to the desired file. Choose whether to create a document-relative or root-relative link (see Figure 6.5).

FIGURE 6.5
Browsing for document- or root-relative links.

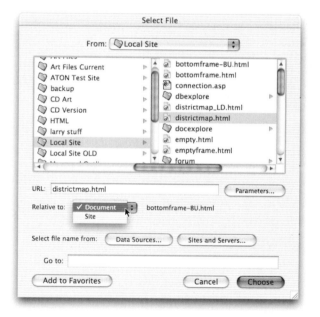

To use Point-to-File, you need to have the Site panel or other Dreamweaver documents open in addition to the current document. Click on the Point-to-File icon (it looks like a rifle sight), and drag from there until the cursor is on top of the document you want to link to, either its file icon in the Site panel or its Document window (see Figure 6.6).

FIGURE 6.6
Creating a relative
link using Point
to-File.

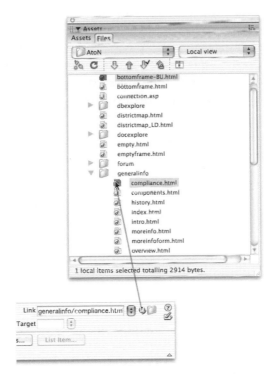

Document-Relative vs. Root-Relative Links in Dreamweaver

Every time you browse to create a relative link, Dreamweaver gives you
the option of creating that link as document-relative or root-relative.
Note that this setting is sticky—if you change it, it stays that way until
you change it again. This is not retroactive (it does not change links that
are already set relative using another method).

When you create a relative link using Point-to-File, you aren't given the
option of choosing what kind of relative link to create. Instead, whatever default you established the last time you browsed to a relative
URL will be used. To change the default, assign at least one link using
Browse, choosing the desired kind of link in the Select File dialog box.
Also, root-relative links can't be previewed locally in your browser.
Within Dreamweaver, if you preview a page containing root-relative
links, Dreamweaver temporarily converts those URLs into document-
relative paths. When you click a link in the previewed page, it will
work, but any paths on subsequent pages will not work locally because
they are site-root–relative. For this reason, you will be able to preview
only one page at a time.

Email Links

An *email link* is just another kind of absolute URL path. Dreamweaver gives you a few different ways to create email links. The simplest is to use the Property Inspector. Select the text or image you want to use for the link, and in the Link field of the Property Inspector, enter the address, complete with its `mailto:` protocol:

`mailto:youraddress@domainname.com`

Figure 6.7 shows this happening. Note that there is no space after the colon.

FIGURE 6.7

Using the Property Inspector's Link field to enter an email address.

If you prefer not having to remember and type the `mailto:` protocol every time you enter an email link, Dreamweaver also provides an Email Link object. To use it, follow these steps:

1. To create an email link from an image, click the image to select it. To create an email link from text, either enter the text and select it or position the cursor where you want the text to go.

2. Choose the Email Link object from the Insert bar (Common category), or choose Insert > Email Link from the Dreamweaver main menu (see Figure 6.8).

3. When the Insert Email Link dialog box appears, enter the email address you want to link to (without the `mailto:` protocol) and click OK.

FIGURE 6.8

The Email Link object and its dialog box.

After you've inserted an email link this way, if you look at the Property Inspector, you'll see that the Link field shows the absolute URL, exactly as if you had typed it yourself.

To avoid confusing yourself, it's safest to pick one method for inserting email links and stick to it—either typing the full URL into the Link field or using the Email Link object. If you mix and match, you might find yourself adding the mailto: protocol when you shouldn't, or forgetting to add it when you should.

NAVIGATION METHODS AND TOOLS

Using links involves a lot more than just pointing images and text to other web pages. Named anchors, image maps, and jump menus all provide alternative means of linking. Rollovers and navigation bars make simple graphic links into interactive page elements. And Dreamweaver lets you build them all.

Named Anchors

Isn't it nice when you visit a website where the designers have taken the time to make links that allow you to navigate within a long page so that you don't have to scroll up and down to find what you're looking for? You may have seen this on a FAQ page, where you can click a frequently asked question and read only the answer to that particular question. When you make a link to a specific place in a document—rather than just linking to the document itself—you are creating what's called a *named anchor link*.

How Named Anchors Work

In HTML, a named anchor is an a tag with no href, but with a name attribute:

```
<a name="outerspace"></a>
```

The named anchor itself is invisible. But other text or image links can link to it by including its name in their href attributes:

```
<a href="#outerspace">

<a href="destinations.html#outerspace">

<a href="http://www.rocketlaura.com/destinations.html#
➥outerspace">
```

The first of these examples links to a named anchor in the current document (# means "in this document"). The second two link to a named anchor in another document, referenced with a relative or absolute URL. If the outerspace anchor is located halfway down the page in the destinations.html file, all links will open that page and cause the browser window to scroll halfway down.

Creating Named Anchors

To create a named anchor in Dreamweaver, follow these steps:

1. In the Document window, in Design view, place the insertion point where you want the named anchor.

2. From the Insert bar (Common category), select the Named Anchor object or choose Insert > Named Anchor (see Figure 6.9).

3. In the dialog box that appears, type a one-word name for the anchor and click OK.

FIGURE 6.9
Inserting a named anchor.

If you have invisible elements set to show, the anchor marker appears in Design view at the insertion point (see Figure 6.10). If you don't see the anchor marker, choose View > Visual Aids > Invisible Elements (or the Visual Aids submenu in the Document toolbar's View Options menu). The little gold anchor icon might look as if it has moved the page contents around it out of position. This is an illusion of Dreamweaver

Design view. In the browser, the icon will be invisible and won't take up any space.

When naming your anchors, be careful not to use any spaces or special characters in the name. Also remember that these names are case-sensitive. Finally, make sure you are not putting the anchor itself inside a layer because this will fail in Netscape 4.

FIGURE 6.10
A named anchor as it appears in Design view if invisible elements are showing.

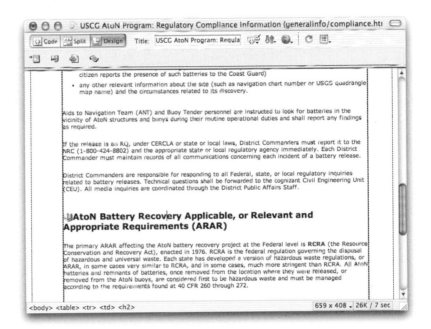

Linking to Named Anchors

Dreamweaver gives you several options for linking to named anchors.

Using the Property Inspector: Select the text or image from which you want to create the link. If the anchor is within the current document, just type the pound sign (#) followed by the anchor name into the Link field (see Figure 6.11). If the anchor is in a different file, enter the file path (by typing or browsing for it) and then type # followed by the anchor name.

FIGURE 6.11
Using the Property
Inspector to link to a
named anchor.

FIGURE 6.11
Using the Property
Inspector to link to a
named anchor.

Using Point-to-File: The Point-to-File icon also can be used for linking
to named anchors. Select the text or image to be made into a link, click
the Point-to-File icon, and drag it to the anchor marker on the page
(see Figure 6.12). You can use Point-to-File to link to an anchor in
another document, as long as both documents are open. Just point to
the other document (which activates it) and then to the anchor within it.

FIGURE 6.12
Using Point-to-File to
link to an anchor.

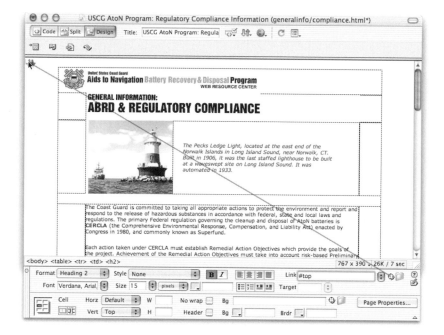

Image Maps

An *image map* is a graphic image that has various "hotpots" that function
as links. Coordinates that form rectangles, circles, or polygons within the
image determine the hotspots. Figure 6.13 shows a typical example of
an image map at work.

FIGURE 6.13

The Dulles
International Airport
site uses a map of
the terminal for
navigation.

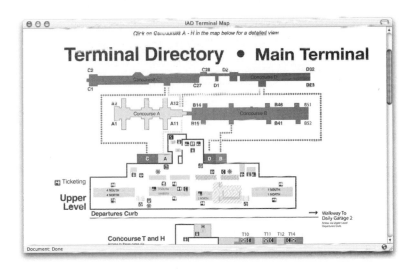

How Image Maps Work

Two types of image maps exist: *server-side image maps* and *client-side image maps*. With server-side image maps, the coordinate information is stored on the server, which can slow the loading of the linked pages considerably. Client-side image maps contain all the mapping information in the same HTML file in which the image resides. Client-side image maps are preferable for several reasons:

- Links are resolved more quickly because there is no need for the information to be accessed from a remote server.

- The user can be shown the destination URL when mousing over a hotspot.

- Image maps can be tested locally.

The code for a client-side image map consists of two parts: the img tag, with a usemap attribute linking it to the map, and a map tag that contains the coordinates. It looks like this:

```
<img src="images/library.gif" width="534" height="120"
 border="0" usemap="#libmap">
<map name="libmap">
  <area shape="rect" coords="41,23,196,85" href="page1.html">
  <area shape="rect" coords="205,25,350,87" href="page2.html">
</map>
```

The map tag can be anywhere within the document's body section; it doesn't have to sit anywhere near the img tag.

Creating an Image Map

Dreamweaver has tools for creating, configuring, and editing image maps and their hotspots, without having to worry about the code behind them. The Dreamweaver hotspot tools create client-side image maps.

To create an image map in Dreamweaver, follow these steps (see Figure 6.14):

1. In the Document window, select the image you want to make into an image map.

2. In the Map area of the Image Property Inspector, type a unique, one-word name for the image map.

3. Define the image map hotspots by using one or more of the Hotspot tools. Notice there are multiple tools to create all kinds of hotspots.

FIGURE 6.14

The Image Property Inspector showing the Map tools.

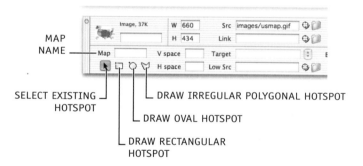

MAP NAME

SELECT EXISTING HOTSPOT

DRAW IRREGULAR POLYGONAL HOTSPOT

DRAW OVAL HOTSPOT

DRAW RECTANGULAR HOTSPOT

To draw rectangular or circular hotspots, select the relevant hotspot drawing tool and drag the pointer over the image in the Document window to create a rectangular or circular hotspot.

Polygonal hotspots can be fun to create, but don't get carried away. Compared to a square or circle, it takes a lot of code to describe the geometry of a fiddly polygon. That can slow your page display.

Creating polygonal hotspots is a bit trickier. To use the polygon tool, select the tool and, in the Document window, click once over the image for each corner point of the desired polygon-shape hotspot. Finish by returning to the Property Inspector and clicking the Arrow tool (in the Map section) to close the shape. It's crucial to officially finish drawing the polygon hotspot by clicking the arrow tool. If you don't do this, every mouse click that you make inside the image will continue adding corners to your polygon. If this happens to you, click the Arrow tool to leave polygon-drawing mode, select the tangled-up hotspot you've created, and delete it.

New to Dreamweaver MX 2004, you can also choose one of the hotspot objects from the Images group in the Common Insert bar.

Working with Hotspots

After you create a hotspot in Dreamweaver, you can select it and set its properties using the Hotspot Property Inspector (see Figure 6.15). The inspector's Link, Target, and Alt fields function exactly the same as those you fill in when you create a simple image hyperlink and can be completed in the same way.

FIGURE 6.15
The Hotspot Property Inspector.

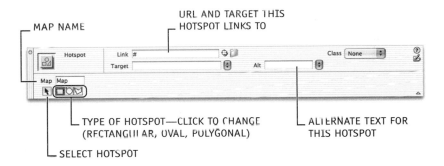

To edit the hotspot after you've created it, use the Arrow button (found in the Hotspot Property Inspector). Click in the hotspot's central area to select it. Drag to move it. To reshape it, click and drag any of the selection points that appear around the selected hotspot's edge (see Figure 6.16).

FIGURE 6.16
Using the Arrow tool to reshape a hotspot.

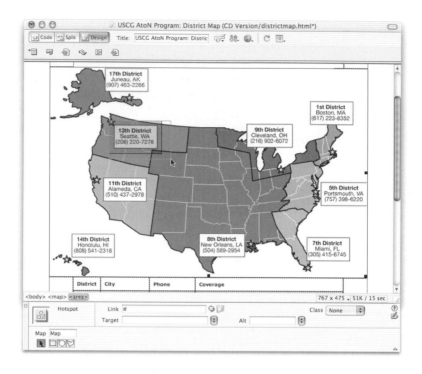

EXERCISE 6.1

Creating an Image Map in Dreamweaver

In this exercise, you create a simple image map using Dreamweaver. Before you begin, download the **chapter_06** folder from the companion website at www.peachpit.com to your hard drive and define a Dreamweaver site named Chapter 6 with the folder **chapter_06** as its root directory.

1. Open the file **image_map.html**. Click once on the green navigation bar image to select it. In the Property Inspector, on the bottom left, click the blue square icon near the word *Map*.

2. Now hover the cursor over the navbar image; you'll notice that the cursor has turned into a crosshair. Click and drag to form a rectangle around the word *Home*. The rectangle should show as a shaded turquoise-blue region; if it does not, go to View > Visual Aids and be sure that Image Maps is checked. If you make a mistake, just be sure that the blue hotspot is selected and press the Delete button on your keyboard.

3. When you've drawn a hotspot you're satisfied with, leave it selected and use the Property Inspector to link it to the file **home.html**. For alternate text, enter **Go to Home Page** in the Alt field (see Figure 6.17), and press Enter or Tab (or click anywhere in the Document window) to activate the Property Inspector change.

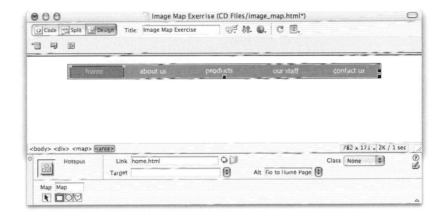

An image map needs a name attribute. You can assign it one of your own choosing using the Property Inspector; if you don't, Dreamweaver will name it Map. This is perfectly adequate, but you might find a more descriptive name helpful, especially if you have more than one image map on a page.

4. Create hotspots linking the other words on the navbar image to the corresponding pages in the **chapter_06** folder; each link on the navbar has an HTML document with the corresponding name (such as **about_us.html**). Save and preview in a browser.

Jump Menus

A *jump menu* is a `form select` item that displays as a drop-down list of options. Clicking an option is the equivalent of clicking any other kind of link. A jump menu can provide links to local or remote documents, email links, or links to any other type of file that can be linked to within HTML (see Figure 6.18).

FIGURE 6.18
A jump menu in action.

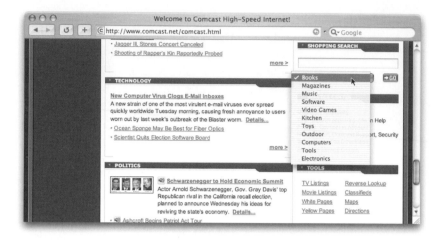

For more about form objects, see Chapter 9, "Working with Forms."

A jump menu often includes a menu selection prompt, such as Country or Choose One, which displays at the top of the list. Clicking a list option activates the link.

Jump menus are best used in specific applications. Generally, when saving space is important, when the user does not need to see all the menu options at once, or when there are a great deal of menu items, a jump menu is appropriate.

Creating a Jump Menu in Dreamweaver

Dreamweaver makes creating jump menus simple. Just follow these steps (see Figure 6.19):

1. Open your document in Design view and position the cursor where you want the jump menu to appear.

2. In the Insert bar, go to the Forms category and choose the Jump Menu object, or choose Insert > Form > Jump Menu.

3. When the Insert Jump Menu dialog box opens, specify what entries will appear in the jump menu and what location to send the browser to when visitors choose this option. Type the text labels desired into the Text field; click the plus (+) button to add them to the menu. Use

the Browse button to choose URLs, or type them manually. You also can use this dialog box to set your jump menu's options, such as whether to include a Go button. (See the following sections for more on this.)

FIGURE 6.19
Inserting a
jump menu.

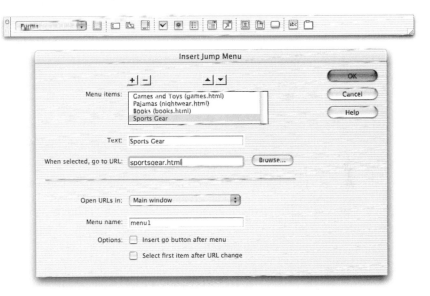

Jump Menu Code

The code for a jump menu consists of a `<form>` and enclosed `<select>` tag and JavaScript—in the guise of the jump menu or Jump Menu Go behavior—to make it go. After you've inserted the jump menu, if you have invisible elements set to show in your document, you'll see the red rectangle of the form surrounding your jump menu. If you select the jump menu, you'll see the appropriate behavior in the Behaviors panel (see Figure 6.20).

Even if the jump menu is not being used in an actual interactive form, some browsers require that any form item be enclosed in `<form>` tags. Therefore, Dreamweaver inserts them automatically.

FIGURE 6.20
A jump menu as it appears in Design and Code view.

```
17 <body>
18 <form name="form1">
19 <select name="menu1" onChange="MM_jumpMenu('parent',this,0)">
20 <option value="games.html" selected>Games and Toys</option>
21 <option value="nightwear.html">Pajamas</option>
22 <option value="books.html">Books</option>
23 <option value="sportsgear.html">Sports Gear</option>
24 </select>
25 </form>
26 </body>
```

To Go or Not to Go

When you create your jump menu, you have the option of building it as a pop-up menu only or as a pop-up menu with an associated Go button. A Go button is a form button labeled Go, which activates the jump menu when it's clicked.

To avoid having to use a Go menu to activate your first menu entry, don't make the first entry a destination. Give it a text label of Choose One or Destination, and leave the value (URL) field blank.

Jump menus don't need Go buttons because normally the menu activates as soon as a visitor chooses a destination from the menu. But what happens when the visitor's desired destination is already appearing in the menu? For instance, the destination might be the default menu choice (the first item in the list of specified destinations), or the visitor might have arrived at the page using the browser's Back button. For such occasions, the Go button provides a means of activating the menu without changing the selected destination.

To include a Go button when defining your jump menu, select the Insert Go Button After Menu option in the Insert Jump Menu dialog box.

Using Jump Menus with Frames and Multiple Windows

Jump menus can be used to load new pages into new windows or into different windows of a frameset. To specify this, use the Open in Main

Window option for each URL when defining the jump menu's destinations (see Figure 6.19).

If the jump menu opens its destination URL in a separate window, you're presented with another decision: After the destination has been loaded, do you want the jump menu to continue displaying the entry for the loaded destination, or do you want it to revert to displaying its default (first) entry? Probably, if you're opening the destination in a new browser window (assigning a target of _blank), you want the menu to revert; if you're opening the destination in a separate frame within the same browser window, you don't (see Figure 6.21). Whether the jump menu reverts is determined by the Select First Item After URL Change option in the Insert Jump Menu dialog box.

FIGURE 6.21
A jump menu in a frameset opening a new URL in a different frame (the jump menu is not reverting to its initial selection).

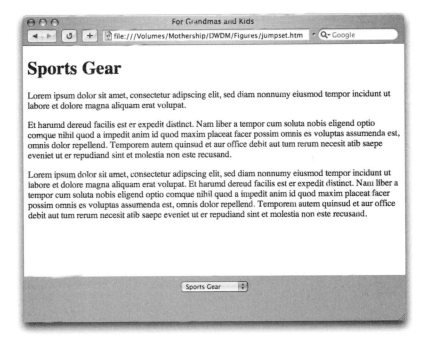

Editing a Jump Menu

After a jump menu has been created, you can edit the menu itself and its "jumping" functionality using the Property Inspector and the Behaviors panel. You also can edit, add, or remove Go buttons.

The Jump Menu Property Inspector

Select the jump menu to view the Jump Menu Property Inspector (see Figure 6.22). This is actually nothing more than the List/Menu Property Inspector with jump menu entries in place. In addition to changing the jump menu from a pop-up menu to a list, if you want (so that several entries appear at once), you can edit the destinations from here by clicking the List Values button.

FIGURE 6.22

The List/Menu Property Inspector for a jump menu.

The Jump Menu Behavior

Select a jump menu and, in the Behaviors panel, you'll see that the jump menu behavior has been added to the form element using the onChange event trigger. (This means that the behavior will execute any time the menu selection is changed.) Double-click that behavior, and the Jump Menu behavior dialog box opens. This dialog box is almost identical to the Insert Jump Menu dialog box—it's missing only the Menu Name and Insert Go Button options, which can be defined only when the jump menu is created.

Playing with Go Buttons

If you created your jump menu with a Go button, the button has the Jump Menu Go behavior applied, to be triggered by onClick. This behavior is really nothing more than an alternate means of calling the Jump Menu function. Double-click to edit the behavior, and you'll see that the only option it allows for is which jump menu clicking the button should trigger.

If you decide that you don't want a Go button after all, you can safely select and delete your Go button at any time.

After having created your jump menu, if you decide that you really do want a Go button, you can add one by doing this:

1. Insert a form button within the form that contains your jump menu. (Put the insertion point directly after the jump menu and choose Insert > Form Objects > Button.)

2. Using the Property Inspector, set the button's label to Go.

3. Select the button and, from the Behaviors panel, assign the Jump Menu Go behavior to it.

TIP

Go buttons don't have to be form buttons. Any page element that can have a link applied to it—including text links and images—can be used to trigger the Jump Menu Go behavior.

Most visitors prefer jump menus that jump to their destinations as soon as they choose from the menu. However, if you want your menu to activate *only* if visitors first make a selection and then click the Go button, do this:

1. Create the jump menu with a Go button, or use the previous instructions to add a Go button later.

2. Go to Code and Design view. In the Design portion of the Document window, select the jump menu.

3. In the Code portion of the window, find and examine the code for the menu (the `select` item). Delete the event handler and function call, as shown here (code to be deleted is shown in bold):

    ```
    <select name="menu1" onChange="MM_jumpMenu('parent',this,0)">
    ```

Note that, after you've done this, Dreamweaver will not recognize the `select` item as a jump menu anymore, so you won't be able to use the Behaviors panel to edit its behaviors.

Rollovers

With all the new and creative site designs, how does a visitor understand when something is a hyperlink? Typically, a navigation link will change in some way when the cursor is over it. For example, a text link might change color or size or change from normal to bold. By making some sort of visual change in the link, the link is saying "I'm clickable!" This type of feature is known as a *rollover* and is usually applied to images.

A rollover actually consists of two images: the *primary image*, or *up* image, which displays when the page first loads; and the *secondary image*, or *over* image, which the browser substitutes for the primary image when the cursor moves across the primary image. The two images must be the same size. If they are not, the secondary image will take on the dimensions of the primary image.

Creating a Rollover in Dreamweaver

Image rollovers can be created easily in Dreamweaver, thanks to the Rollover Image object. If you want to create a rollover, you insert an image that automatically turns into another image when the cursor is placed on it.

To insert a rollover image, just follow these steps (see Figure 6.23):

1. With your document open in Design view, place the insertion point where the image should be inserted. In the Insert bar (Common category), from the Images objects, choose the Rollover Image object.

2. The Insert Rollover Image dialog box opens. Type a name in the Name field. Images that will be used in a rollover must be named; if you don't name your image, Dreamweaver will assign it a default name.

3. Use the Browse button to browse for the Original (Up) image and Rollover (Over) image, or type the filename and path for each into the field.

4. Check the Preload Images box if you want this option. (See the next section for more on preloading.)

5. Provide alternate text in the Alternate Text field. (This becomes the primary image's alt attribute.)

6. Use the Browse button to browse to and select the URL to send the visitor to when the rollover image is clicked, or enter **javascript:;** for a null link if the link shouldn't go anywhere.

7. Click OK to insert the rollover image.

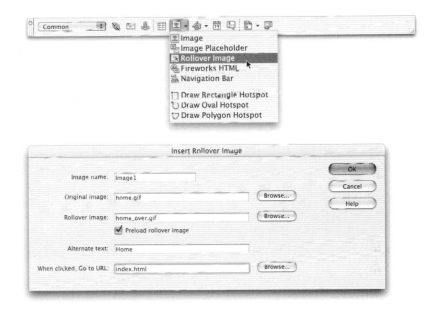

Preloading and Rollovers

Normally, the browser downloads page resources—including images— the first time they appear on a page. This means that your Up image is downloaded, but because your Down image is not displayed—and possibly will never be displayed—it is not downloaded. When someone places the cursor on your up image, the over image is fetched. This can take time, ruining the entire rollover effect. Your user might move the mouse off the up image before the over image ever gets a chance to display! If you preload the over image, that second image is ready and waiting to be displayed. It's possible that it will never be called upon. That doesn't matter. If it is called upon, it will display immediately. When you choose the Preload Images option in the Rollover Image dialog box, Dreamweaver writes JavaScript telling the browser to download the primary and secondary images when the page first loads, thus eliminating that delay. Therefore, it's a good idea to make sure this option is selected when using the Rollover Image object.

Editing Rollover Images

Using the Rollover Image object is actually a shortcut for the more complex Dreamweaver procedure of inserting an image, assigning it a link, and adding a Swap Image and Swap Image Restore behavior to it. After

you have inserted a rollover image, it becomes simply an image with a link and a behavior applied (see Figure 6.24). To edit the image and its link, select it and use the Property Inspector. To edit the rollover code, select the image and, in the Behaviors panel, double-click the Swap Image behavior. This gives you access to the Swap Image dialog box, from which you can change the secondary image and preloading options (among other things).

FIGURE 6.24
A rollover image revealing itself to be a linked image with several behaviors applied.

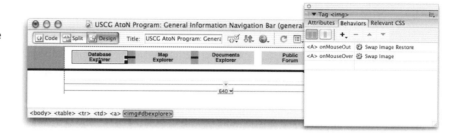

To learn more about Swap Image and how behaviors work, see Chapter 13, "Interactivity with Behaviors."

Navigation Bars

The term *navigation bar* can refer to any set of links arranged horizontally or vertically on a web page. Generally, these are a prominent feature of a website and remain consistent from page to page, providing an easy way for the user to move between pages and files. A navigation bar (or navbar) can be made of text links, linked images, or an image map. A more elaborate type of navigation bar is often made with sets of images that change based on the actions of the user, using JavaScript. Dreamweaver provides the Navigation Bar object to make creating this kind of navbar simple.

Each button or element in a Dreamweaver navigation bar can have up to four states. Two states determine the standard rollover functionality (see Figure 6.25):

- **Up**—The image shown when the user hasn't yet interacted with the element.

- **Over**—The image shown when the pointer hovers over the up image. The element's appearance changes to signal that it is interactive.

FIGURE 6.25
The Up and Over states of an image in a navigation bar.

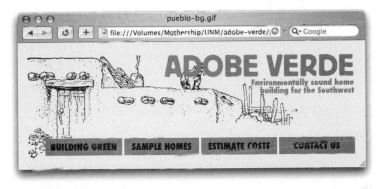

Two other states determine how the image will appear when the page it links to is currently being displayed—for instance, what should the Home button look like on the home page? They are (see Figure 6.26):

- **Down**—When the navbar doesn't actually navigate among multiple pages (usually this occurs when it's in a frameset), this is the image that appears after the user clicks the element. When an element is clicked and a new page loads, the navigation bar, still displayed, shows the clicked element with a changed appearance to signify that it has been selected.

- **Over While Down**—When the pointer is rolled over the down image, this image appears.

FIGURE 6.26
The Down and Over
While Down states
of an image in a
navigation bar.

It isn't necessary to include all four states in every navbar. Often just the Up, Over, and Down states are used.

Creating a Navigation Bar

To create a navigation bar, you first need to oil up your web graphics program and create the graphics you'll need for whatever button states you plan to use. Then come back to Dreamweaver, open a document, place the insertion point where the navigation bar should appear, and do this (see Figure 6.27):

1. In the Common Insert bar, from the Images objects, choose the Navigation Bar object or choose Insert > Image Objects > Navigation Bar from the menu.

2. The Navigation Bar dialog box appears. Each element corresponds to a button in the navbar, and each button has up to four states. One by one, name your elements and use the plus (+) button to add them to the navbar. Use the Browse buttons to assign images for the different states.

FIGURE 6.27
Inserting a naviga-
tion bar.

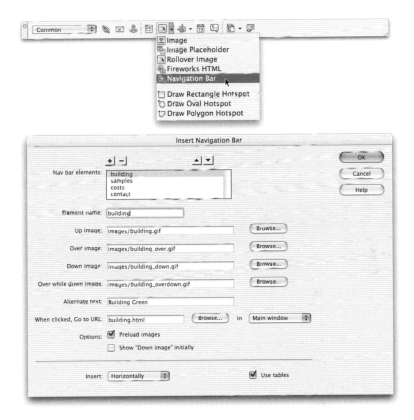

3. Supply alternate text in the field by that name, and use the Browse button to specify the URL to which the user should be sent when the button is clicked in the When Clicked, Go to URL field. Choose the window or frame in which you want the URL to open in the field just to the right of the URL field.

4. Choose Preload Images if you want. (See the discussion on preloading images in the "Rollovers" section of this chapter.) Choose Show Down Image Initially if you want that particular element to be in its Down state when the page loads. This is appropriate, for instance, on a home page, where you would want the Home button to indicate that you are already on the Home page.

5. At the bottom of the dialog box are two more options. Choose to insert your navigation bar horizontally or vertically, and choose whether you want HTML tables to be used.

6. Click OK to insert the navigation bar.

Editing a Navigation Bar

After a navigation bar has been inserted, it consists of several images, each of which has several Set Nav Bar Image behaviors applied to it. If you chose to have your navigation bar structured as a table, it will also include a `table` tag (see Figure 6.28).

FIGURE 6.28
A navigation bar inserted and ready for editing.

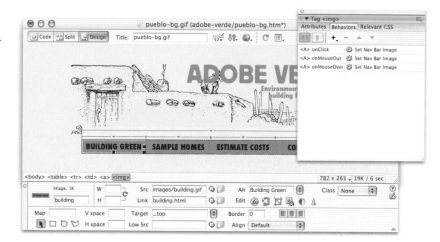

You're free to rearrange the images in the navigation bar, adjust the properties of the table that contains them, change the URLs the images link to, and even delete some images, without disturbing the navigation bar.

To edit the entire navigation bar at once, choose Modify > Navigation Bar. This opens the Modify Navigation Bar dialog box, which is very similar to the dialog box you used to create the navigation bar.

To edit the various rollovers that make up the navigation bar, select any image in the group and, in the Behaviors panel, double-click any of the three Set Nav Bar Image behaviors. The dialog box that appears contains two tabs: The Basic tab lets you adjust the rollover settings for the currently selected image. The Advanced tab lets you set some very fancy image changes for the other images in the navigation bar, based on what's happening to the selected image (see Figure 6.29).

In the Insert Navigation Bar dialog box, you can select an element and use the up-pointing and down-pointing triangle icons near the top of the box to change the order of the elements in the navbar.

FIGURE 6.29

The Basic and Advanced tabs of the Set Nav Bar Image behavior dialog box.

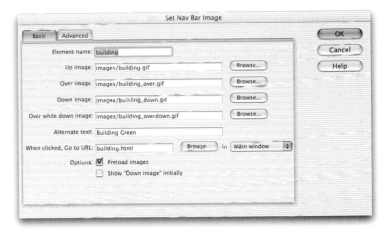

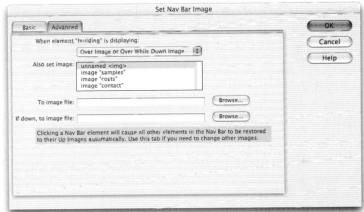

Creating a Navigation Bar with Dreamweaver

Dreamweaver makes building a navbar easy, but you still have to create the images needed. You'll need an image for each element (or button) in each state. In this exercise, you make a navigation bar using all 4 states for each of 4 buttons; the 16 images needed are already in your **chapter_06/images** folder. In Exercise 6.3, you'll place the same navbar on other pages so that you can see the Down and Over While Down states in action.

1. If you haven't yet, download the **chapter_06** folder from the companion website to your hard drive, and define a Dreamweaver site named Chapter 6 with the folder **chapter_06** as its root directory.

2. Open a new blank document and name it **seasons.html**.

3. From the Dreamweaver main menu, choose Insert > Interactive Images > Navigation Bar. This opens the Insert Navigation Bar dialog box. You'll insert four buttons: Winter, Spring, Summer, and Fall. Each has four states.

4. For the first item in the navigation bar, start with the Element Name field and type in **Winter**.

   For Up Image, click Browse and, from the **images** folder, choose **winter_up.gif**. For Over Image, click Browse and choose **winter_over.gif**. For Down Image, click Browse and choose **winter_down.gif**. For Over While Down Image, choose **winter_overdown.gif**. For When Clicked, Go to URL.

5. Then click the plus (+) button at the top of the dialog box to add another button.

6. Repeat step 5 to create the Spring button. Continue adding items and filling in fields to create the Summer and Fall buttons.

7. Select Preload Images and choose Insert Horizontally. Then click OK to insert the navbar into the document.

8. Save and preview in the browser (see Figure 6.30). You can see how the Over state works; however, because the pages you have linked to don't exist yet, you'll get a "Page Not Found" message when you click the links. Just use your browser's Back button to return to the Seasons page. In Part II, "Designing with Dreamweaver," you'll create the linked pages so that you can see the Down and Over While Down states in action.

FIGURE 6.30
Previewing the navigation bar in seasons.html.

Using a Navbar Across Multiple Pages

In this exercise, you'll place the navbar you created in Exercise 6.2 on three other pages.

1. Open **seasons.html**.

2. Choose File > Save As, and save the file with a new name, **winter.html**. Change the page title to **Winter**. Choose Modify > Navigation Bar to open the Modify Navigation Bar dialog box.

3. In Navbar Elements, select winter. At the bottom of the box, select Show "Down Image" Initially and click OK. Save.

4. Open **seasons.html** again and repeat steps 2 and 3, naming the new page **spring.html** and changing its title. In the Modify Navigation Bar dialog box, select Spring and select Show "Down Image" Initially.

5. Open **seasons.html** again and repeat steps 2 and 3 again, creating **summer.html**.

6. Open **seasons.html** again and repeat steps 2 and 3 again, creating **fall.html**.

7. Preview **seasons.html** in the browser.

Each page should show the Over state when the pointer rolls over the image, and the page for each particular season should display the appropriate button in a darkened state. When you're on the Spring page and you roll over the darkened Spring button, you'll see the Over While Down state (see Figure 6.31).

FIGURE 6.31
The spring.html page as it appears in a browser demonstrating the Down (top) and Over While Down (bottom) states of the navigation bar.

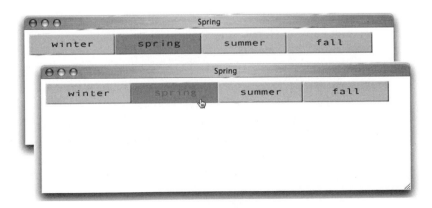

WORKING SMART WITH LINKS

Links are at the heart of web interactivity, and there's a lot you can do to make them more powerful, more fun, and more interactive—and even more accessible!

Making Your Links Accessible

There's nothing inherently inaccessible about links. But your job as a web author involves making them easier to deal with. In a graphical interface, the user can glance quickly down each page hunting for exactly the links needed. But a screen reader reads the entire page from top to bottom, and links can easily get lost in the shuffle. The user who wants to jump right into the page content doesn't want to listen to a dozen links in the top navigation bar. The user who wants to head straight for the links at the bottom of the page doesn't need to listen to the entire page being read before getting there. Section 508, § 1194.22(o), states:

> A method shall be provided that permits users to skip repetitive navigation links.

There's no magic HTML tag or attribute for taking care of this, nor does Dreamweaver have a magic bullet for you. But that doesn't mean it's difficult! The solution is as easy as adding an extra link at the top of any set of repetitive links. Do it this way:

1. At the end of your set of links, immediately before the main page content starts, insert a named anchor. Call it something sensible like main. (For details on creating anchors, see the section "Named Anchors" earlier in this chapter.)

2. At the beginning of the set of links, insert text or an image and link it to that anchor. The text might say Skip Navigation or Skip to Main Content.

If you don't mind that the skip-navigation link is visible, your job is done. But you can also hide it. To create a truly invisible link, use a single-pixel transparent spacer GIF as your image. Give it some alt text, such as Skip to Main Content or Skip Navigation, and link it to the anchor. Screen readers will read the alt text, but graphical browsers will completely pass over the image.

The code for an invisible skip-navigation setup looks something like this:

```
<a href="#main">
  <img src="spacer.gif" width="1" height="1" alt=Skip to main
  ➥content>
</a>
[navigation bar or other set of links goes here]
<a name=main></a>
[main page content goes here]
```

Figure 6.32 shows how it looks as it's being created in Dreamweaver.

FIGURE 6.32
Using a transparent
spacer image as a
skip-navigation link.

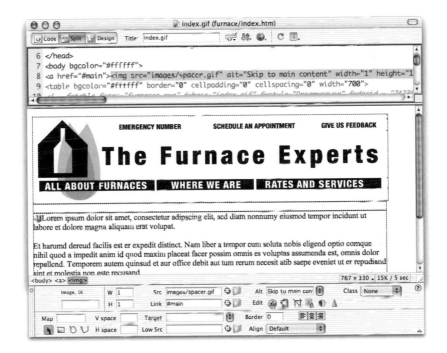

Special Requirements for Image Maps

Of course, image maps are made from images, so all image-accessibility guidelines—most important, the use of alt labels—apply. In addition, Section 508, § 1194.22(e), states:

> Redundant text links shall be provided for each active region of a server-side image map.

Client-side image maps don't require redundant text links because each hotspot in the map has its own alt attribute.

On a less-official note, be aware that image maps are more accessible if their hotspots are large and easy to click on. They should be more or less uniform in size, if not in shape, and large enough that they can be easily found by the cursor. A hotspot should always correspond to a portion of the graphic that clearly communicates the URL destination; if words aren't used, universally understandable icons (such as a mailbox for an email link) should be employed.

Dressing Up Your Links with CSS

By default, links are highlighted in the browser with bright blue. Linked text gets a blue underline; linked images get a blue border. Visited links get a purple underline or border. Although some web pundits argue that we shouldn't mess with these settings (or visitors might get confused and not recognize them as links), most web designers do something to customize link appearance.

Linked Images

When is the last time you saw an image on a web page with a big blue border surrounding it? Not for a while, probably. Borders around linked images can be turned off by specifically setting the image's border attribute to 0. Every time you add a link to an image in Dreamweaver, this happens automatically (see Figure 6.33).

FIGURE 6.33
Creating borderless linked images in Dreamweaver's Code and Design view.

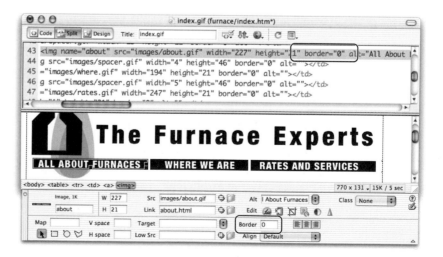

Linked Text

The appearance of linked text—text color, whether there's an underline, and so forth—can be controlled by using CSS to redefine the a tag. You can approach this task in one of two ways in Dreamweaver: through the Page Properties window or through the CSS Styles panel.

Using the CSS Styles Panel to Control Link Appearance

This is the slow way to do it, but it gives you more of an idea what's happening under the hood and also gives you more options. For instance, you can save your link formatting styles in an external style sheet for sharing across a site using this method.

To change the basic appearance and behavior of all linked text, open the CSS Styles panel and create a new style. In the New Style dialog box, choose to redefine the a tag for the current document only or in a separate style sheet (see Figure 6.34). When the CSS Style Definition dialog box opens, make any choices you want. All linked text will be styled as you choose here. The most commonly set options are all in the Type category:

- To customize link color, choose from the Color field.

- To remove the underline, set the Decoration to None.

- To make your links appear in Bold, choose Bold (or any of the bold settings).

Other, more sophisticated text link effects can be created using the a: pseudoclasses. To do this in Dreamweaver, open the CSS Styles panel and create a new style. In the New Style dialog box, choose CSS Selector and choose one of the following from the drop-down menu that appears (see Figure 6.35):

- a:link controls how regular links will look (similar to redefining the a tag).

- a:hover controls how links will look when the user rolls over them.

- a:visited controls how visited links look (those that the user has been to recently).

- a:active controls how links look when the user has clicked on them.

FIGURE 6.34
Redefining the anchor tag to control link appearance.

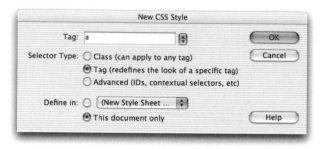

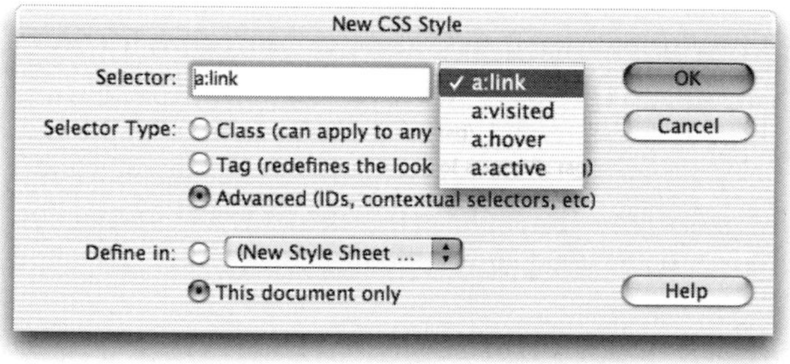

FIGURE 6.35
Creating CSS pseudo-classes to determine how rolled-over, visited, and active links will appear.

When you choose to create one of these styles, the CSS Style Definition dialog box opens, and you can assign any formatting you want to your hovered-over, visited, or active links. One of the most popular effects currently is to hide the underlines on linked text but have it reappear when

the user rolls over the text. Do this by defining the a:hover class and, in the Type category of the Definition dialog box, setting Decoration to Underline.

Using Page Properties to Control Link Appearance

If you don't want to go through the time of setting up multiple styles in the CSS Styles panel, you can quickly set up link appearance in the Page Properties window. Just choose Modify > Page Properties and go to the Links category (see Figure 6.36). The most commonly set options for regular, rolled-over, visited, and active links all appear here.

FIGURE 6.36
Using the Page Properties dialog box to set link appearance.

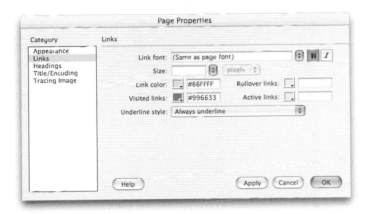

When you make your choices using this method, Dreamweaver adds all necessary CSS styles (a, a:hover, and so on) to an internal style sheet within the current document.

For more on internal and external style sheets, including how to export styles into external CSS documents, see Chapter 11, "Using Cascading Style Sheets."

Assigning Link Colors Without CSS

There is a pre-CSS way to control normal, active, and visited link colors on a page by adding attributes to the body tag:

```
<body link="#FFFF00" alink="#FF0000" vlink="#00FF00">
```

There's no real reason to use this method, unless you're targeting very old browsers (version 3 and below). But you can tell Dreamweaver to

create your link colors this way, if you prefer. In the Preferences/ General dialog box (choose Edit > Preferences and go to the General category), deselect the option Use CSS Instead of HTML Tags. The next time you choose Modify > Page Properties, the Links category won't appear. Instead, go to the Appearance property and set link colors there. You won't be able to change any other link characteristics, such as removing underlines or creating hover effects, because those require CSS.

Setting URL Parameters

Links can also be to pass information from page to page for scripting purposes. This is done in the form of URL parameters. Information passed as a parameter is coded as a name/value pair appended to the end of the URL, separated from it by a question mark (?). Multiple parameters are separated from each other by an ampersand (&). If any of the passed values includes a space, it must be encoded as a plus sign (+) or an ASCII value (%20). A URL with passed parameters looks like this:

`mypage.html?username=fred+jones&password=logmein`

The page at the end of this link (mypage.html, in this case) can then use JavaScript or any kind of server-side processing to make use of the parameters. (This is the same kind of URL that occurs when you submit a form using the GET method.)

Adding URL Parameters to Links in Dreamweaver

To add URL parameters to your links in Dreamweaver, you can always manually type the parameter into the Link field in the Property Inspector, if you remember the syntax and don't mind doing some typing. But it's easier to let Dreamweaver help you. Click the Browse button to browse for a link. When the Select File dialog box opens, choose the file to link to and click the Parameters button to open the Parameters dialog box (see Figure 6.37). In this window, enter each name and value that you need to be passed. Click OK twice to close both dialog boxes, and you'll see your fully constructed URL in the Property Inspector's Link field.

FIGURE 6.37
Creating a link with
passed parameters
in the Select File
dialog box.

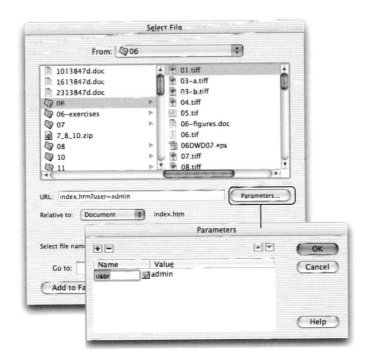

Using JavaScript to Process URL Parameters

Why would you want to do this? Presumably, you're using some kind of
scripting on the linked page, or there's not much point in it. Data-driven
pages that use server-side technology, such as ColdFusion or PHP, use
URL parameters extensively. But you can also process passed information
with JavaScript. Unfortunately, Dreamweaver doesn't come with any prebuilt behaviors for doing this, but if you don't mind a small amount of
code-writing, you can create some very useful effects.

For instance, what if visitors might link to the current page from several
other places in your site, and you want to customize the information
that you present based on who they are? Insert the following script code
into your document wherever you want the customized content to
appear:

```
<script language="JavaScript">
var params = location.search;
//collect the passed parameter as a variable called x
var x = params.substring(x.indexOf("=")+1,x.length);
```

```
//if the parameter has a certain value, enter some content
if (x =="parents") document.write('<h1>Hello, Parents!</h1>');
//if the parameter has another value, enter different content
else if (x =="students") document.write('<h1>Hello, Students!
➥</h1>');
//otherwise, enter some default content
else document.write('<h1>Hello!</h1>');
</script>
```

The JavaScript comments (shown in bold here) describe what the script is doing. It's creating a different heading to display on the page, depending on the value of the passed parameter.

You can modify this script to collect any single URL parameter and display optional page content. Just copy the following framework code into your Dreamweaver document wherever you want the customized content to appear:

```
<script language="JavaScript">
var params = location.search;
var x = params.substring(x.indexOf("=")+1,x.length);
if (x=="value1") document.write('content here');
else if (x=="value2") document.write('content here');
else document.write('default content here');
</script>
```

Customize the code to your needs like this:

- For the code shown in bold, enter your own information (parameter values, custom content).

- You'll always want to test for at least one value, so always include the line that begins with `if`.

- For any additional values that you want to have custom content for, include an `else if` line. Duplicate this line as many times as you want, to add more options.

- What happens if there is no passed parameter? If you want default content, use the `else` statement. If you don't want to display any content, you don't need to include the `else` statement.

You can make life even easier on yourself by turning each of these lines into a snippet so you don't have to type it by hand every time:

1. Open the Snippets panel (Window > Snippets).

2. Right-click the JavaScript Snippets folder, and choose New Snippet from the contextual menu. For the snippet name, enter something such as **Parameter-if**. For type, choose Block. Type the **fif-statement** from the code listed earlier into the text area, like this:

    ```
    if (x=="value1") document.write('content here');
    ```

    Click OK to close the dialog box.

3. Repeat this process to create a Parameter If-Else snippet and a Parameter Else snippet.

4. Finally, create one more snippet. Call it **Parameter-Wrapper**. For type, choose Wrap. In the Insert Before text area, enter this:

    ```
    <script language="JavaScript">
    var params = location.search;
    var x = params.substring(x.indexOf("=")+1,x.length);
    ```

    In the Insert After text area, enter this:

    ```
    </script>
    ```

To use your new snippets, create a document, go to Code view, and do this:

1. Place the insertion point where the parameter-testing script should go.

2. From the Snippets panel, select the Parameter-If snippet and click the Insert button. When the generic code is pasted into your document, change value1 and content here to whatever you need.

3. For each additional else-if or else line that you want to add, create a new blank line in your code and insert the appropriate snippet. Then customize the value and content portions of the code.

4. Finally, select all of the lines of code that you just created, and insert the Parameter-Wrapper snippet. This wraps your if statements in the script needed to process parameters.

Passed parameters are used extensively when constructing data-driven pages. For more on using passed parameters, see Chapters 22, "Creating Dynamic Pages," and 23, "Further Dynamic Techniques." For the full story on snippets, see Chapter 27, "Writing Code in Dreamweaver."

Spiffing Up Email Links with Parameters

URL parameters can also be used with email addresses to specify extra things, such as subject and cc. This means that when the user clicks the link and the email program launches, it opens a new message window with all of this information already in place. Table 6.2 lists some email-related URL parameters and what they do.

TABLE 6.2

URL Parameters for Use in Email Links

Parameter	Values	Description
cc	Email address	Adds a cc (carbon copy) recipient to the email message
bcc	Email address	Adds a bcc (blind carbon copy) recipient to the message
subject	Text string	Adds a subject line to the message
body	Text string	Adds text to the body of the message

An email address with URL parameters in place looks like this:

```
mailto:johndoe@xyz.com?subject=Info%20Request&Cc=sallysmith
➥@xyz.com&Bcc=bigbrother@xyz.com
```

Figure 6.38 shows how an email message window looks when activated by this link.

FIGURE 6.38
An email message window as it appears when the email link that called it includes parameters.

Unfortunately, you can't use Dreamweaver's handy Parameters window to add parameters to an email address because the Parameters window is called from the Select File dialog box, accessed when you browse to choose a file to browse to. An email address can't be browsed to because it's an absolute URL.

But you can add parameters by manually entering them in the Property Inspector's Link field (which is very tiny) or, of course, directly into Code view. Just remember to include all the proper punctuation: ? to start, & between parameters, and %20 where you want spaces inserted.

Using Links for JavaScript

Web designers use anchor tags for more than just linking from page to page. Rolling over or clicking on a link in a web page can trigger JavaScript events, which means the a tag can have behaviors attached to it.

Null Links and Behaviors

If you want a piece of text to trigger a Dreamweaver behavior, it needs to first be made into linked text. Images can trigger behaviors without being linked images, but by having the link turns the browser's cursor into a hand, without which the user might not know to click on the image. You want the user to click on the link, but you don't want the link to actually go anywhere—it just needs to trigger the behavior. You need to create a null link. That's an a tag with an href value that does nothing.

To create a null link, select your text or image and type **javascript:;** into the Property Inspector's Link field (see Figure 6.39). The code ends up looking like this:

```
<a href="javascript:;">Click here!</a>
```

This tells the browser not to do anything when the link is pressed.

FIGURE 6.39
Creating a null link
in the Property
Inspector.

It's also possible to create a null link by entering the pound sign (#) in the Link field (that's easier to type!). This link points to the current page, so it essentially does nothing in the browser. But if your link is toward the bottom of a long scrolling web page, clicking it might cause the browser to jump to the top of the page. For that reason, it's not used much anymore. The `javascript:;` link is safer.

Entering JavaScript into the HREF

If you like creating your own JavaScript code, and just have a short little chunk of code to type, you can also enter it into the `href` attribute directly, preceded by the keyword `javascript`:

```
<a href="javascript:alert('You clicked me!');">Click here!</a>
```

If you're fond of this kind of coding, you probably know all about this already. But did you know that you can enter this information in the Link field of the Property Inspector? The only problem is, the input field is awfully tiny, so it can be hard to see what you're doing (see Figure 6.40).

FIGURE 6.40
Using the Property Inspector to create a JavaScript link.

SUMMARY

Hyperlinks are an essential and defining feature of the World Wide Web, and a skillfully designed navigational system is one of the highest-priority considerations in the creation of a website. In this chapter, you learned about linking URLs, about how links appear in the browser, and what these appearances say to the user. You looked at email links and named anchors, and you tried out several widely used types of navigation controls: image maps, jump menus, linked rollover images, and multistate navigation bars. You also got to take your links beyond the basics, using URL parameters, CSS formatting, and JavaScript in links. Now you're all set to go places on the web!

```
<head>
<style type="text/css">
body {background-color: red}
p {text-align: right; color: white}
</style>
</head>
<body>
```

CHAPTER 7

UTILIZING HEAD CONTENT

IN YOUR FRENZIED RUSH TO CREATE THE BEST, MOST BEAUTIFUL, KNOCK-their-socks-off web page, don't overlook the unglamorous but entirely practical world that lives inside your document head. This chapter discusses what goes into the head. You'll also see how Dreamweaver handles head elements such as search keywords, page refreshes, and document encoding. And you'll see how you can use these and other tools to maximize your working efficiency and web presence.

THE BASICS OF HEAD CONTENT

Head content might not be glamorous, but it's also not difficult to understand and is extremely useful. This section looks at how head content is coded in HTML and interpreted by browsers, search engines, and so on. It also covers the interface for working with head content in Dreamweaver.

How Head Content Works in the Browser

A standard HTML page contains a head tag and a body tag. The body contains all the page content that will actually display in the browser window. The head contains a variety of information that won't display (at least, not directly), although it can be accessed to determine how the page will be handled. Some head content is accessed by the browser; some is accessed by other programs, such as server software, search engines, and validation software; and some might not be accessed at all, except by humans who might view or edit the code. The W3C specifies several elements that a well-formed head section could use. Unfortunately, the browsers have not yet fully implemented them all, so you can't take full advantage of the head.

Table 7.1 lists the standard head elements, along with a brief description of each.

TABLE 7.1 **Standard HTML *<head>* Elements**

Tag	Purpose	Browser Support	Example(s)
title	Contains the page title, to be displayed in the browser window title bar and user bookmark menu	Yes	`<title>Webley's Web` `➥Widgets</title>`

Tag	Purpose	Browser Support	Example(s)
link	Specifies a relationship between the current document and another document	For use only with style sheets	`<link rel="stylesheet"` ➥`href= "widgetstyles.css"` ➥`type="text/css">`

base	Specifies a URL and/or target, to which all document links will be relative	Yes	`<base href="http://`
			➥`www.webwidgets.com/">`
			`<base target="_top">`

meta	Acts as a generic tag for adding miscellaneous information to the document (for example, keywords and character encoding)	Yes	`<meta name="generator"`
			➥`content="Dreamweaver">`
			`<meta http-equiv=`
			➥`"Content-Type"`
			➥`content="text/html;`
			➥`charset=iso-8859-1">`

script	Encloses JavaScript or other script statements for the browser to execute, or links to an external script file	Yes	`<script language=`
			➥`"JavaScript">`
			`function helloWorld() {`
			`window.alert("Hello,`
			➥`world!");`
			`}`
			`</script>`

style	Encloses CSS style sheet information to affect the display of the current document	Yes	`<style type="text/css">`
			`a {`
			`font-weight: bold;`
			`text-decoration: none`
			`}`
			`</style>`

How Head Content Works in Dreamweaver

Dreamweaver provides two main interfaces for dealing with head content: the menu of Head objects in the HTML category of the Insert bar, for adding content to the head; and the Head Content view option, along with Property Inspectors for each kind of content, for examining and editing head content.

Viewing and Editing Head Content

Head content shows up in Design view as a bar across the top of the Document window, showing an icon for each element present in the document head (see Figure 7.1). Choose View Options > Head Content to toggle the head content display on and off. (The View Options menu can be accessed from the Document toolbar or from the View menu.) Note that Head Content won't show up as a view option unless you're in Design view or Code and Design view.

FIGURE 7.1
Displaying head content as icons in Design view.

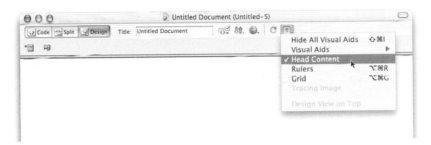

To examine or edit a head element, click its icon in the display bar and use the Property Inspector to view and change the element's attributes.

You can also rearrange head elements by dragging their icons around in the head content bar. The order of elements in the head usually doesn't matter, though, because each element serves a different function and is called on when needed, regardless of position.

Adding Head Content

Dreamweaver inserts some head elements (title, script, and style, for instance) automatically as you create and edit pages. Other commonly used head elements have corresponding objects in the HTML category of the Insert bar (see Figure 7.2). If you want to add an element that isn't in the Insert bar, you must enter it in Code view, either by typing it yourself or using the Tag Chooser.

You can also increase your <head> content options by searching the Macromedia Exchange for Dreamweaver for an extension that does what you want.

FIGURE 7.2
Head elements in the
Insert bar.

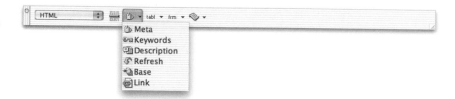

You can insert head elements from either Design or Code views, but with a few important differences. If you're working in Design view, placement of the insertion point isn't crucial when working with head content. No matter what element in the <body> you might have selected when you insert, Dreamweaver knows to put head content in the head. If you have one of the icons in the head element display selected when you insert, Dreamweaver places the new element immediately after the selected element. If no head elements are selected when you insert, Dreamweaver inserts the new head element at the end of all other head content.

If you're working in Code view when you insert a Head object, the code for the object is inserted wherever the insertion point is—even if that means inserting it outside the <head> section entirely, or even inserting it within another HTML tag. (Obviously, unless you know your way around HTML tag syntax, it's safer to use Design view for adding your Head objects.)

If you like working in Code and Design view, remember that either the Design or the Code portion of the Document window must always have focus. If you insert Head objects while the Code portion has focus, your insertion point must be in a proper location within the <head> tags for the object to be correctly inserted.

WORKING SMART WITH *META* TAGS

Meta means "about." The purpose of the meta tag is to store information about the current document for possible processing by browsers, servers, search engines, or even lowly humans viewing the source code. For each different kind of information you want to store, you use a different meta tag. HTML documents can have as many meta tags as needed, all stored in the head.

How *meta* Tags Store Information

Information is generally stored in the meta tag as a name/value pair, using the name and content attributes:

```
<meta name="generator" content="Dreamweaver">
```

Over time, certain name/value pairs—such as keywords, description, and refresh—have become standard in HTML use and are collected and processed by browsers and search engines. However, web authors also are free to create any desired name/value pairs to store other document-related information. Many popular HTML editing programs, for instance, use a generator meta tag when generating code, to sneak some free advertising into user documents. Some web authors let potential code-borrowers know whom they're borrowing from with an author tag, as follows:

```
<meta name="author" content="Julius Marx">
```

The various meta tags are useful enough that Dreamweaver supplies several objects representing different kinds of meta information. The following paragraphs examine these.

The Character-Encoding *meta* Tag

This kind of meta tag isn't in the Insert bar. Dreamweaver inserts it automatically into every HTML document it generates. The code looks like this:

```
<meta http-equiv="Content-Type" content="text/html;
charset=iso-8859-1">
```

(See the following section for more on http-equiv, which is used here in place of name.)

This standard meta tag tells the browser what character set to use in representing the text portions of the page. ISO-8859-1 refers to Latin-1 encoding, used for most western European languages. Examples of other encodings include ISO-8859-5 (Cyrillic) and SHIFT_JIS (Japanese). Unless you know what you're doing, don't mess with this tag.

meta Tags and the Generic Meta Object

Ultimately, every meta tag consists of a name and some content, so the Dreamweaver generic Meta object is the perfect bare-bones tool for inserting custom meta information. Figure 7.3 shows the generic meta tag being inserted.

FIGURE 7.3
Inserting meta content with the generic Meta object.

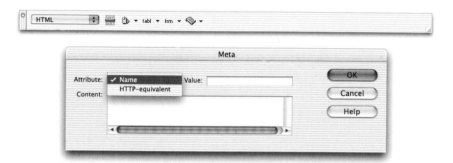

To insert a meta tag, follow these steps:

1. In the Insert bar, go to the HTML category and, from the Head objects, choose the Meta object.

2. In the dialog box that appears, use the pop-up menu to choose either the name or http-equiv attributes to include. (The http-equiv attribute maps the attribute and its respective name to the HTTP response header for processing. Unless you know specifically what you want and are sure that http-equiv is appropriate, use the name attribute.)

3. In the dialog box's Value text field, enter the value you want the name (or http-equiv) attribute to have.

4. In the dialog box's Contents text area, enter the value you want the content attribute to have.

Figure 7.3 shows how the dialog box insertion areas translate into the finished meta tag code. Why not use this generic object to insert all meta content? The meta tags that use standard keywords, those that a browser

or other agent will be processing, also require standardized syntax for their content. Dreamweaver's specialized Meta objects take care of those syntax requirements for you. Dreamweaver does not include all the meta tags that you might want to use. Table 7.2 lists some of those meta tags not included with Dreamweaver.

TABLE 7.2 **Some Useful *meta* Tags Not Included in the Dreamweaver Insert Bar**

Syntax	Description/Purpose
`<meta http-equiv="expires" content="15 Apr 2001 23:59:59 GMT">`	Specifies a date after which the browser cache for the current page will expire. This guarantees that visitors' browsers won't show an out-of-date version of the page. The date and time should be formatted as shown. The time information is optional.
`<meta http-equiv= "Set-Cookie" content=cookie_name =cookie_value; expires=1 Jan 2002 23:59:59 GMT">`	Sets a cookie with whatever name and value are specified in place of cookie_name and cookie_value (for example, favorite_color=green). The expiration information is optional; if it's not present, the cookie expires when the browser is shut down.
`<meta http-equiv="pragma" content="no-_cache">`	Prevents the browser from caching the page. Note that Internet Explorer versions 4 and later ignore this tag.
`<meta http-equiv= "Content-Script-Type" content= "text/language_name">`	Specifies the language to be used in all `<script>` tags within the document. The content string might read text/javascript or text/vbscript, for instance.

Meta Keywords and Descriptions

Undoubtedly the most commonly used and most generally practical of the meta tags are those that help search engines locate and retrieve information about documents. The most common of these are keywords and description. They're used like this:

```
<meta name="keywords" content="Marx Brothers, humor,
➥vaudeville, movies, Groucho, Harpo, Chico, Zeppo, Gummo">
➥<meta name="description" content="An unofficial look at
➥America's kings of slapstick and wisecracking. With links
➥and freebies.">
```

The `meta keywords` tag contains a comma-separated list of words that web visitors might type into a search field; these should lead them to the current document. The `meta description` tag contains a few sentences that can be used in a search results page to represent the current document. A Dreamweaver object represents each of these (see Figure 7.2). To insert either into your head section, choose the object from the Insert bar or menu and enter the appropriate information in the dialog box. Figures 7.4 and 7.5 show these tags being inserted (in Design and Code views).

FIGURE 7.4
The meta keywords tag being inserted and later inspected using the Keywords object.

FIGURE 7.5
The meta description tag being inserted and later inspected using the Description object.

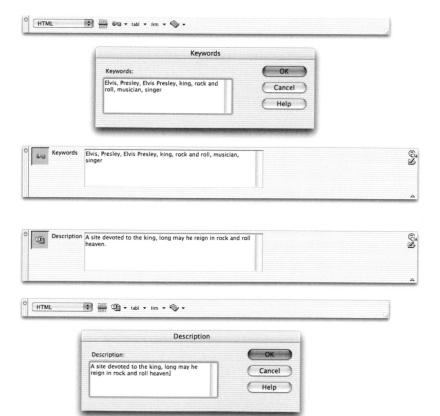

Maximizing Searchability

Using keywords and descriptions, and using them well are two different things. The more you know about how search engines work and how to take full advantage of their offerings, the better your standings in the search results will be.

There is much more to this subject than will fit in this chapter. Luckily, the Web is full of wonderful resources. A great place to start is World of Design (www.global-serve.net/ ~iwb/ search_engine/ killer.html). This site includes articles, tutorials, and a host of useful links related to meta tags and search engines in general.

Search engines work by sending out automated programs, called *robots* (or *web crawlers*, *spiders*, or *bots*) to index web pages. *Indexing* consists of retrieving documents and recursively retrieving all documents referenced (that is, linked) from those documents. Robots determine which pages to start indexing by various means, including when a web page author or webmaster registers the page with the search engine. When a visitor accesses the search engine and enters one or more search words, the engine returns results based on its analysis of the documents it has retrieved. Results are based on matched keywords; matched words in the description, the page title, visible document content, links, and alt text are commonly searched as well.

Here's the code for how a sample head section is set up for maximum searchability:

```
<head>
<title>The Web Widgets Construction Materials Home Page</title>
<meta name="keywords" content="web, widgets, construction
➥materials, building tools, web tools, snarflators,
➥crambangers, diffusion devices, child, children, diffuse,
➥diffusion, ....."> 
<meta name="description" content="The Web Widgets Construction
➥Materials Company, home to a vast selection of snarflators,
➥crambangers and other web tools. Visit us for daily specials
➥and our unique how-to section.">
<!--The Web Widgets Construction Materials Company, home to a
➥vast selection of snarflators, crambangers and other web
➥tools. Visit us for daily specials and our unique how-to
➥section.-->
</head>
```

What elements make this code so searchable?

- **Page title**—The information in the title tag is descriptive and readable (it can be searched, and it might show up on some search results pages) and uses several words present in the keywords list.

- **Keywords**—Keywords are case-sensitive and are in the plural where appropriate. (If the keyword is singular and the user searches using a plural, no match will be found.) No words are repeated except where necessary. (Unnecessary repetitions either are ignored or are considered "spamming" and might get the entire site banned from the search engine.) The keywords list is approximately 900 characters long, which is the maximum length accepted by some search engines (some engines accept as many as 1,024).

- **Description**—The description uses words from the keywords list. It is slightly less than 200 characters long, which is the maximum acceptable length for most search engines (some accept fewer). Note that if your description or keywords are too long, they won't be considered in the search; it doesn't necessarily mean that the robot will reject the page.

- **Comment**—A comment is inserted, repeating the contents of the description. This is to address those few robots (most notably Excite and Magellan) that do not search meta tags.

Limiting Searchability

Wait a minute: Why would you want to stop robots from indexing your documents? Quite simply, you might have a number of reasons. Certain areas of a website might contain private or secure data. If your site uses frames, you might not want framed pages to be indexed outside their framesets. Certain areas, such as ASP and CGI folders, might contain scripts that will run when accessed, with undesirable results. On a large site, the increased traffic of robots indexing every single page might be a drain on the web server.

You can limit robot traffic in two ways, one of which Dreamweaver can help with.

- **The robots.txt file**—This file, which resides on the server, can specify certain folders within a site that robots should not index. Using robots.txt, you can isolate these site areas from all robots or from specific robots. The contents of the file might look something like this:

```
USER-AGENT: *
DISALLOW: /asp/
DISALLOW: /cgi-bin/
DISALLOW: /private_folder/
```

The disadvantage of using robots.txt is that each web server must have only one such file, located in a folder at the root level of the server. Customizing it is, therefore, the province of the server administrator, not the individual web authors.

- **The `meta robots` tag**—Less reliable than robots.txt, but more easily accessible, is adding a `meta` tag to your document with a name of "`robots`" and one or more of the following values, in a comma-separated list, for content: `all`, `none`, `index`, `noindex`, `follow`, and `nofollow`. To explicitly allow access to all links within a page, use the following code:

```
<meta name="robots" content="all, follow, index">
```

To deny access to a page and its links, use this:

```
<meta name="robots" content="none,noindex,nofollow">
```

To allow access to the current document but not its links, use this:

```
<meta name="robots" content="index,nofollow">
```

Because Dreamweaver does not offer a specific Meta Robots object, use the generic Meta object to insert this tag. From the Head tab of the Insert bar, click the Meta object. Figure 7.6 shows a `meta robots` tag being added to a document, with typical settings in the dialog box.

FIGURE 7.6
Using the generic
Meta object to insert
a `meta robots` tag
into a document.

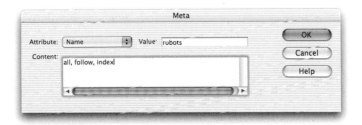

EXERCISE 7.1

Making a Document Searchable

In this exercise, you set up the Walt's Web Widgets home page to take maximum advantage of search engines. The files for this exercise (and the following exercises) are on the book's website at www.peachpit.com in the **chapter_07** folder. If you haven't done so already, download those files to your hard drive so that you can work and save changes. Figure 7.7 shows Walt's home page.

FIGURE 7.7

Walt's Web Widgets home page (main.html) as it appears in a browser.

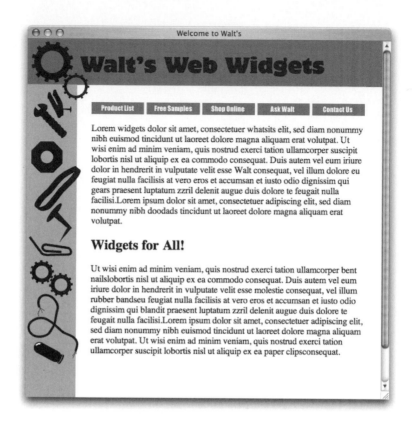

Walt's Web Widgets sells widgets—also known as doodads, gewgaws, thingamajigs, and whatsits. His stock consists of, among other things, bent nails, rusty screws, anonymous keys, rubber bands—you name it, Walt's has it. When people need just the perfect little piece of junk for a very particular job, Walt wants them to find him. Keep that in mind as you're filling out the keywords and description for this page.

1. From the **chapter_07** folder, open **main.html**. You will be setting up searchability for Walt's home page. In the Document window, show the head content (View > Head Content, or use the View Options icon in the toolbar). In the Insert bar, choose the HTML category and find the drop-down menu of Head objects.

2. Start with keywords. Remember, you want to end up with 900 characters, if possible, to take full advantage of your allotted space in the search engine's index. From the Insert bar, click the Keywords icon to insert a meta keywords tag. In the dialog box, enter as many words

related to widgets—and Walt's stock in general— as you can think of, separated by commas (spaces are optional). Use the following to help you get started:

```
widgets, doodads, thingies, thingy, thingummies,
➡thingummy,thingamajigs, thingimajigs, whatsits, geegaws,
➡gewgaws, odds and ends, junk, stuff, paper clips, bent
➡screws, rusty nails, wire pieces, rubber bands, string,
➡washers, nuts, bolts, screws, pushpins, tacks, thumbtacks
```

Remember to use the plural rather than the singular, and not to repeat words unnecessarily. Note that in the sample words shown here, some plurals and singulars appear (thingies, thingy). That's because the plural and singular are spelled differently; in this case, users searching for the singular won't find it from the plural. Also note that alternative spellings (geegaws, gewgaws) are included. If you can think of a common way that people tend to misspell (or mistype) words, those variants also are good items to add to the list. That 900-character limit is higher than you might think!

How fun is it to keep counting characters as you go? Not much. Unfortunately, Dreamweaver, unlike some text editors, has no tool for automatically counting words or characters. If you have a text editor that can count characters, you could use it as an external code editor. Or, you could create the keyword list in a word processor that can count. Alternatively, if your JavaScripting skills are up to it, you might decide that this is a dandy opportunity to create a custom Dreamweaver exten-sion—a keyword counter! See Chapter 29, "Creating Your Own Extensions," for more on writing extensions.

3. Check the page title. Hmm, "Welcome to Walt's" might look nice in the Bookmarks list, but it doesn't contain any real information, and—more important for the search engines—it contains no key-words. Change the page title to something more suitable: "Walt's Web Widgets: Widgets, Doodads, and Thingies."

4. Add the meta description tag. From the Insert bar or menu, choose the Description object. In the dialog box, enter a 100–200 character description of Walt's—maybe something like this:

Visit Walt's Web Widgets for the world's largest supply of
➥doodads, thingummies, and whatsits, all at unbelievable
➥prices. We can find hard-to-get items.

5. Repeat the description in a comment. No, you don't have to type it
    in again! Just do this:

    • From the head content display bar in the Document window,
      select the Description icon.

    • In the Description Property Inspector, select the text you entered
      and copy it.

    • Go to Code view and place the insertion point just before the
      closing `</head>` tag.

    • In the Insert bar, go to the Common category and choose the
      Comment object, which inserts the opening and closing com-
      ment tags. (Or, you can just type `<!-- -->`.)

    • Put the insertion point between the two double dashes, and
      paste.

    The new comment appears in your head section, immediately fol-
    lowing the description. You'll see the little comment icon in the
    head content display bar.

6. Finally, give the robots some instructions letting them know that
    they can search Walt's entire site. (Walt has no secrets!) In the Insert
    bar, click the generic Meta object. Set the dialog box entries to match
    those shown in Figure 7.6.

Walt's Web Widgets is now ready to go public!

meta refresh

Another standardized and popular kind of meta tag is the meta refresh
tag. This tag, when present, is processed by the browser, causing the
page to either reload itself or load a new page after a set amount of time
has elapsed. To reload the current page after 10 seconds, the syntax
looks like this:

```
<meta http-equiv="refresh" content="10">
```

To load a new page after 5 seconds, the syntax looks like this:

```
<meta http-equiv="refresh" content="5;URL=pagetwo.html">
```

refresh tags that reload the current page are often used with pages that contain dynamic data, such as breaking news, stock quotes, or the time and temperature. They're also used with web cam pages—every few seconds, the page reloads and a new web cam picture is automatically loaded into place. refresh tags that load new pages are often used with redirection pages: "Our site has moved!" They're also used with splash screens that show a brief welcome message or graphic for several seconds and then whisk viewers away to the true home page.

The Meta Refresh Object

In Dreamweaver, you insert refresh tags using the Refresh object, as shown in Figure 7.8. Choose the object from the Insert bar or menu, and enter the number of seconds that should elapse before the refresh and whether to load a new page or reload the current page.

FIGURE 7.8
A meta refresh tag being inserted and later inspected, using the Refresh object.

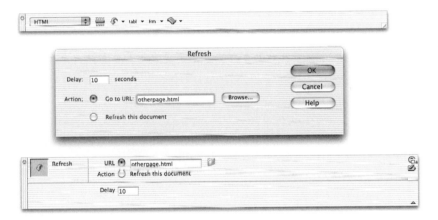

Tips for Refreshing

Although using the tag is nice and straightforward, as with all things there are issues to consider:

- Unfortunately, refresh tags are not used only by the good guys. They also are used for much more sleazy purposes by disreputable sites (porn sites, for instance), allowing visitors to bookmark seemingly innocuous pages, such as "Aunt Bee's Quilting Zone," that are actually automatic links to "Hot Babes R Us" or "How to Construct a

Nuclear Bomb." For this reason, some search engines will not index pages that contain refresh tags.

- Deciding how long to pause before refreshing (especially if the refresh will load a new page) requires some thought. How long is too long? If there is content on the current page (an animation, text to read), how long is long enough?

- If the refresh will be going to a new page, you might consider including a clickable link to that new page so impatient users don't have to wait the required number of seconds.

EXERCISE 7.2

Create a Refreshing Splash Page

To get some experience with the refresh tag, you can use the Web Widgets files from the preceding exercise. In the **chapter_07** folder, along with **main.html**, is **splash.html**, shown in Figure 7.9. Open that file now. It contains an animated logo and welcome message, and Walt wants his customers to see it for a few seconds before going on to visit the rest of the site.

FIGURE 7.9
The Walt's Web Widgets splash page (splash.html), as it appears in the browser.

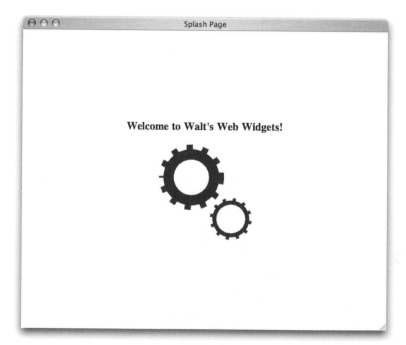

No matter what size the browser window is, the page content of **splash.html** will be vertically and horizontally centered onscreen. The effect is created by placing the content in a table with a width and height of 100% and cell alignment of center (horizontal) and middle (vertical). The height attribute for tables isn't official HTML, but currently all browsers support it, and it's an easy way to create a swell effect.

1. To begin, add the refresh tag. In the Insert bar, go to the HTML category and, from the Head objects, choose Refresh. When the dialog box appears, choose **main.html** as the file to load. How long should you have visitors wait? Start by entering **10** seconds in the Delay field.

2. Before proceeding any further, try it out in a browser. Choose File > Preview in Browser and then sit and wait until the refresh occurs. (If it doesn't occur, go back to Dreamweaver and double-check your steps!) Is 10 seconds too long? Try 5 seconds—or find your own best delay time.

3. What about the viewers who don't want to wait at all? For them, you will add a regular link to **main.html**. You can add the link to the animated logo itself, or you can add a line of text, **click to enter**, beneath the logo. Alternatively, you can do both, just to cover all your bases. After you've done that, try it out to make sure it works before proceeding.

4. Finally, change the scenario. What if the splash page has something on it that people might want to read? Perhaps it's a joke, an introductory sentence or two, or an interesting news tidbit. Add some lines of text to the page so that it looks like the page shown in Figure 7.10.

5. Now preview the page in a browser and imagine you're a first-time visitor. Maybe you want a few more seconds to read the text. Or maybe you think the delay time you've chosen still works fine. Just remember, the more there is to absorb on the page, the longer you might want to delay.

Why do websites have splash pages? First, there's a psychological reason. You're "framing the picture," mentally putting visitors in the mood for the website to come. Obviously, this goal is more appropriate for some websites (entertainment sites, online brochures) than others (informational sites). Second, there's a technical reason. While the viewer is seeing the splash page, you can be performing a browser check, starting the download of large graphics or media files that will be needed later, checking cookies, and so forth.

FIGURE 7.10
The final Web Widgets splash page, with its added content, ready to entertain and divert visitors.

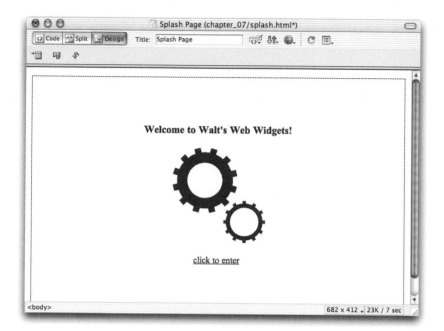

WORKING WITH OTHER HEAD CONTENT

You'll probably spend more time using the various Dreamweaver Meta objects than using either of the other Head objects, but both link and base have their uses as well.

Base Tags and the Base Object

In HTML, the purpose of the base tag is to provide an absolute URL or a link target that the browser will automatically use to resolve all links within the document. It sounds more complicated than it is.

Base Tags and Absolute URLs

When a browser encounters relative URLs in an HTML document, it constructs absolute addresses from them by accessing a "base" URL, usually that of the current document itself. If your web page address is http://www.yourcompany.com/index.html and the page contains a link to images/spacer.gif, the browser combines those two addresses to construct an absolute URL for the image: http://www.yourcompany.com/images/spacer.gif.

If your document head uses the base tag to specify an alternate URL, like this:

```
<base href="http://www.webwidgets.com/store/">
```

all relative links in the document now are calculated relative to that address. So,

```
<a href="pricelist.html">Home</a>
```

resolves to this:

```
http://www.webwidgets.com/store/pricelist.html
```

Likewise,

```
<img src="../images/spacer.gif">
```

resolves to this:

```
http://www.webwidgets.com/images/spacer.gif
```

These addresses will be used even if the actual URL of your document is entirely different, like this:

```
http://www.homepagesRus.com/index.htm
```

When would you want to use the base tag to override your document's own URL for relative addressing? You would want to on two occasions:

- When creating mirror sites, where sets of pages on different web servers refer to a common resource pool of images or pages, base makes it possible to just port the pages to the mirror server. Using base, the relative links can be made to point to resources that are on the original server.

- When inserting HTML into email messages, all links must be either absolute or relative to a specified base. This is because email messages have no URL for the email browser to use in constructing absolute paths. (Note that some email software, most notably Hotmail, cannot correctly construct URLs using base. It's safer, therefore, to just use absolute URLs throughout and not specify a base.)

Base Tags and Link Targets

Targets in links determine in which browser window a linked document will appear. Valid targets include the assigned name of any open window or frame in a frameset, or any of the generic targets—such as _blank for

a new window, or _top for the main window in a frameset. The normal link syntax looks like this:

```
<a href="widgets.html" target="_blank">
```

However, if the document head includes a base tag that points to a target, like this one, all links in the document are opened in that target window exactly as if the target were specified in each individual link:

```
<base target="_blank">
```

A link coded as this behaves as thought it were coded using the full targeting syntax:

```
<a href="widgets.html">
```

Why would you want to use the base tag to specify targets document-wide instead of specifying them individually for each link? It results in more efficient HTML, especially if your page contains many links (a resources or bibliography page, for instance). It makes life easier because you don't have to remember to specify every single target; it also makes editing simpler, if you change your mind about where links should be targeted. Instead of changing dozens of individual links, you need change only the base tag.

If you specify a target using the base tag, does that mean every single link in your document absolutely must use that target? No—you can override the base target for specific links by specifying a different target for the link itself. So, if the `<head>` section specifies `<base target="content">`, but a link on the page specifies `<a href="mypage.html" target="nav">`, that particular link will open in the window named nav.

If you're a smart Dreamweaver user, of course, you could use a tag-specific Find and Replace to quickly change all those targets instead of using the base tag. Tag-specific searches are discussed in Chapter 27, "Writing Code in Dreamweaver."

Using the Base Tag in Dreamweaver

To insert a base tag into a Dreamweaver document, use the Base object in the Insert bar or menu, as shown in Figure 7.11. This object enables you to enter a URL and a target name. As with any head content, as long as you're in Design view when you insert it, it doesn't matter where the insertion point is when the object is chosen; the base tag automatically is inserted into the head.

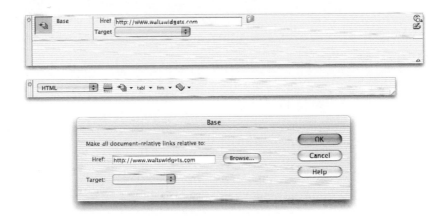

Remember the following few tips when working with the base tag in the Dreamweaver environment:

- **Use only one base tag per document.** Dreamweaver won't stop you from inserting multiple base tags in your document, but it's not legal HTML. Don't do it.

- **Remove empty href attributes.** If you specify a base target and no base URL, Dreamweaver writes the code for the base tag like this (problem code is highlighted):

```
<base href=" " target="_blank">
```

Although this is technically legal, it can cause the browser to misinterpret all the links on your page. (A link to spacer.gif is resolved to http://spacer.gif, which is a meaningless address.) Avoid the problem by going to Code view and manually deleting the empty href attribute.

- **Type in the absolute URL.** Although Dreamweaver allows you to browse to choose the base URL, doing this creates a relative address. For standard use, the base tag requires an absolute address.

- **Don't forget the final slash (/).** The browser ignores any part of the URL that falls after the final slash. The following base URLs are considered equivalent:

```
http://www.webwidgets.com/
http://www.webwidgets.com/index.html
http://www.webwidgets.com/images
```

If you find yourself repeatedly using the base tag for targeting and manually removing code, you might want to download Massimo Foti's Base Target object from the Macromedia Exchange for Dreamweaver.

- **Preview pages with base URLs.** After you have specified an absolute base URL, you won't be able to properly preview the page (in Dreamweaver or your browser) until you've uploaded all relevant files to the server. If you really want to preview the page while you're working locally, you need to substitute the address of your local site folder. This is a URL beginning with the `file://` protocol. To access that information, open one of your site's documents in Dreamweaver and use Preview in Browser (F12) to view the page in any browser. Look at the URL in the browser's address field—the path ends in the name of the temporary file, but it should begin with the absolute URL of your local site folder, like this (the local folder address is shown in bold):

  ```
  file:///Power%20Girl/Web%20Widgets/Local%20Site/
  ➥TMP2onxb308wp.htm
  ```

  Copy the relevant part of the address from the browser and paste it into your base tag. (Be sure to include the final slash!)

  ```
  <base href=" file:///Power%20Girl/Web%20Widgets/
  ➥Local%20Site/">
  ```

  After you've done this, you can preview locally, but not by using Dreamweaver's Preview in Browser feature. You'll need to open the page manually from the browser. And, of course, don't forget to restore the proper base URL before uploading the page.

- **Don't use the Site panel to move files.** When you have a base URL in place, you're in charge of the relative links. If you rearrange your site's file structure using the Site panel's File view, Dreamweaver tries to update all relative links—don't let it! It will corrupt the links and nothing will work. To be safest, do your file rearranging outside of Dreamweaver, using your operating system's file management (Windows Explorer or Macintosh Finder).

EXERCISE 7.3

Add a Base Target to a Page's Links

Back to Walt's Web Widgets for this exercise. Walt has decided that he wants all the subject pages on his site to open in a new browser window so the visitor never leaves the home page. You can accomplish this quickly by adding a `<base>` tag specifying a target of `_blank`.

1. From the **chapter_07 folder**, open **main.html**. Make sure that head content is showing, and that the Insert bar is showing the Head category. It doesn't matter what in the Document window you have selected.

2. In the Insert bar, click the Base object. When the dialog box appears, leave the URL field empty. From the pop-up target menu, choose _blank. Click OK to exit the dialog box.

3. Set the Document window to show Code and Design view. In the Head content display bar, click the Base object icon to select your newly inserted base tag. This action also should select the code for the base tag, in Code view.

4. In Code view, delete the href attribute from the base tag so the tag reads as follows:

```
<base target="_blank">
```

That's it! Preview the page in a browser and click any of the page's links. Each should open in a new window.

Link Tags and the Link Object

With the link tag, it's theoretically possible to specify all sorts of complex relationships between web documents. This includes specifying certain documents as next and previous in a series, linking alternative-language versions of pages, linking page glossaries, and much more. Unfortunately, none of the major browsers supports this functionality yet, although Lynx (a text-based browser) and iCab (a Macintosh browser) do, to some extent. For current use, the only reliable implementation of the link tag is to link external style sheet documents (see Chapter 11, "Using Cascading Style Sheets," for more on this).

SUMMARY

Did you ever think so much could be going on behind the scenes of a web document? The various head elements might not be visible in the browser, but they are capable of doing a lot. By taking advantage of them, you can make coding links easier (base), make your page available to search engines (meta), and perform all sorts of other nuts-and-bolts tasks.

PART II:
DESIGNING WITH DREAMWEAVER

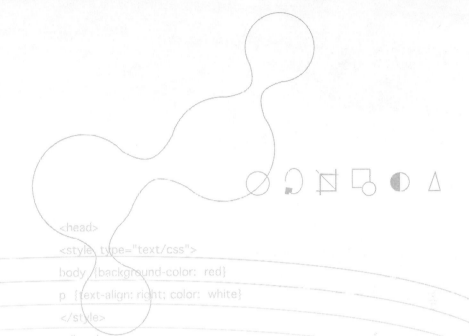

CHAPTER 8

BUILDING TABLES

AH, TABLES. FOR MOST WEB DESIGNERS TODAY, TABLES ARE THE MEAT AND potatoes of what we do every day. They can also be the bane of our existence. We use them for data display and for page layout. They're not inherently difficult to understand, but table code can quickly get cumbersome and difficult to keep track of. And browsers so often don't treat them right. This chapter goes over some table basics, looks at how Dreamweaver MX 2004 works with tables, and then covers different ways to maximize table-making power in the Dreamweaver environment.

TABLE BASICS

Tables themselves aren't difficult to understand, but they're constructed from many bits and pieces, and working with them in Dreamweaver and in the browser is a complex process.

Tables in the Browser

In HTML, tables are created with the table tag. Each table consists of a number of rows, specified by tr (table row) tags. Each row consists of cells, specified by td (table data) or th (table header) tags. Nowhere is the number of columns specified; that's determined by the number of cells in the rows. The basic code framework for a two-row, two-column table looks like this:

```
<table>
  <tr>
    <th>[header cell contents here]</th>
    <th>[header cell contents here]</th>
  </tr>
  <tr>
    <td>[cell contents here]</td>
    <td>[cell contents here]</td>
  </tr>
</table>
```

This table includes one row of header cells and one of regular data cells. Note that none of the tags involved requires any attributes. Various optional attributes determine how the table will look and behave, including dimensions, border, treatment of cell contents, and so on. Table 8.1 lists the most commonly used attributes and what they're for. Many more attributes are possible, some included in the HTML specification and others for use by particular browsers. (Check the Dreamweaver Reference panel for a more comprehensive list.)

TABLE 8.1   **Commonly Assigned Attributes Used with Tables**

Attribute Name	Description	ApplyTo	Values
name id	Used for identification.	table, tr, td, th	Text string
width (height)	Table or cell dimensions. (Only width is part of the HTML specification, although height may be recognized by browsers.)	table, td, th	Number (pixels) or percent value
border	Whether the element has a border surrounding it.	table, td, th	Number
cellpadding	Gutter space within each cell, between cell edge and contents.	table	Number (pixels)
cellspacing	Space between each cell.	table	Number (pixels)
bgcolor	Background color of the element.	table, tr, td, th	Color, identified by number or name
background	Background image for the element.	table, tr, td, th	URL of an image file
align	Horizontal alignment of cell contents	table, tr, td, th	left, center, right
valign	Vertical alignment of cell contents.	tr, td, th	top, middle, bottom, baseline
colspan, rowspan	How many columns or rows the cell spans—the HTML mechanism for merging cells.	tr, th, td	Number (of columns or rows)

Tables in HTML were originally developed for use in displaying tabular data (see Figure 8.1), but web designers adopted them for use in page layout (see Figure 8.2). With the advent of CSS positioning, tables should be reverting to their original use. However, inconsistent browser support of CSS means that, so far, tables are still the safest best for page layout.

FIGURE 8.1

A table used for displaying tabular data in a web page.

Collections

Collection	Description
Contents	Contains all the items appended to the application through a script command
StaticObjects	Contains all the objects appended to the application with the HTML <object> tag

Methods

Method	Description
Contents.Remove	Deletes an item from the Contents collection
Contents.RemoveAll()	Deletes all items from the Contents collection
Lock	Prevents other users from modifying the variables in the Application object
Unlock	Enables other users to modify the variables in the Application object (after it has been locked using the Lock method)

Events

Event	Description
Application_OnEnd	Occurs when all user sessions are over, and the application ends
Application_OnStart	Occurs before the first new session is created (when the Application object is first referenced)

FIGURE 8.2

A borderless table used for setting the layout of a web page.

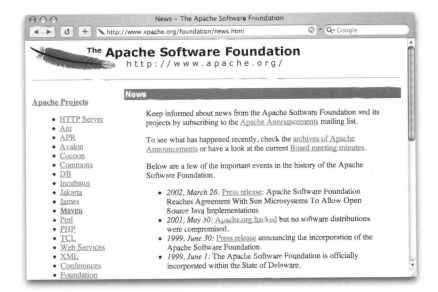

Tables in Dreamweaver

Because tables are so important, Dreamweaver has a variety of tools and commands for working with them. Some are safer to use than others, and some are more intuitive than others. No matter what your working strategy is, you'll undoubtedly find something in here that you like.

Table Interface Choices

Of course, your first decision, as with anything in Dreamweaver, is whether you want to work with tables in Design view or Code view. But even within the Design view environment, you have choices. What should the table-making interface be like? What visual aids do you need?

Choosing a Table Mode

To choose a table mode, go to the View menu and choose from the options in the Table Mode submenu; or, in the Layout Insert bar, choose one of the three Table Mode buttons (as shown in Figures 8.3–8.5). In either case, you have three choices:

- **Standard mode (View > Table Mode > Standard Mode)**—This default table mode displays tables in Design view approximately how they will look in the browser (see Figure 8.3). It's the mode most experienced Dreamweaver users prefer, but it can be awkward if your table includes a complex structure or tiny cells.

FIGURE 8.3
A page layout table viewed in Standard mode.

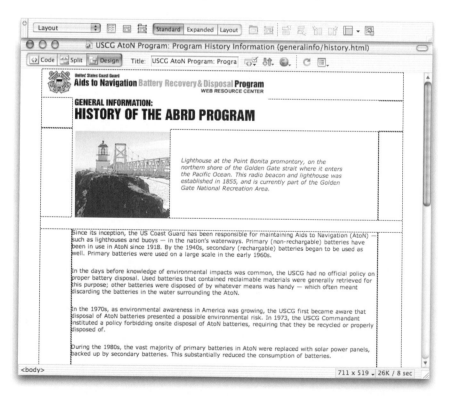

- **Expanded Tables Mode (View > Table Mode > Expanded Tables Mode)**—This mode, which is new to Dreamweaver MX 2004, displays tables in Design view with artificially added spacing between and within the cells, and with a visible border even if the table has no border (see Figure 8.4). This mode sacrifices some of the WYSIWYG qualities of Standard mode to make table structure easier to see and table elements easier to select and work with. Working in Expanded Tables mode is the same as working in Standard mode, but with some additional viewing assistance as you go.

FIGURE 8.4

The same page layout table viewed in Expanded Tables mode.

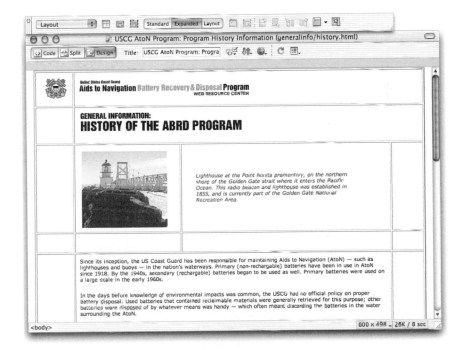

- **Layout Mode (View > Table Mode > Layout Mode)**—Layout mode is more than a means of viewing tables (see Figure 8.5); it's a whole alternative way of working with tables. Although it's very intuitive and attractive to web design beginners, it has its own set of dangers and can lead to badly structured pages. Layout mode is covered in depth later in this chapter (see the section "Working in Layout Mode").

FIGURE 8.5
The same page layout table viewed in Layout mode.

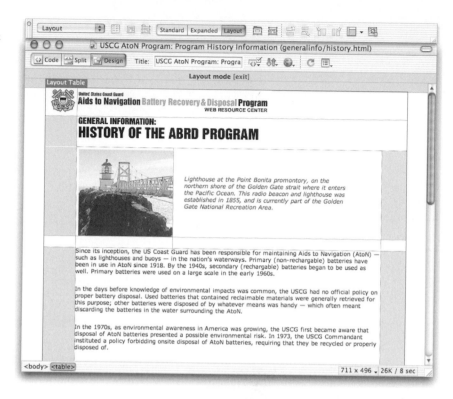

Table-Viewing Aids

Whether you're working in Standard or Expanded Tables mode, you have a few extra bits of visual aids that you can call on in the Design view interface:

- **Table Widths (View > Visual Aids > Table Widths)**—New to Dreamweaver MX 2004, the Table Widths visual aid shows a horizontal bar across the bottom or top of any selected table (see Figure 8.6). The bar indicates any table or cell dimensions. Clicking its triangle icons also gives you access to some extra help in selecting elements and setting table properties. The Table Widths visual aid works in either Standard or Expanded Tables modes.

FIGURE 8.6
A selected table showing the Table Widths visual aid.

- **Table Borders (View > Visual Aids > Table Borders)** If you're working in Standard mode, this visual aid shows the edges of borderless tables as dotted lines, so the table structure is visible in Design view, even if it won't be in the browser (see Figure 8.7). Because Expanded mode includes always-visible borders, this aid isn't needed in that mode.

FIGURE 8.7

A borderless table in Design view, with and without the Table Borders visual aid.

Inserting Tables

For more on table accessibility attributes, see the section "Making Your Tables Accessible," later in this chapter.

To insert a table (unless you're working in Layout mode), use the Table object in the Layout Insert bar, or choose Insert > Table. Both of these methods open the Insert Table dialog box (see Figure 8.8). In the dialog box, specify the basic structure of your table and click OK to insert the table. Note that, other than specifying rows and columns, you don't have to specify values for any table characteristics while inserting. Also, all table structure and attributes can be edited later through the Property Inspector, so nothing is set in stone here.

FIGURE 8.8
Inserting a table.

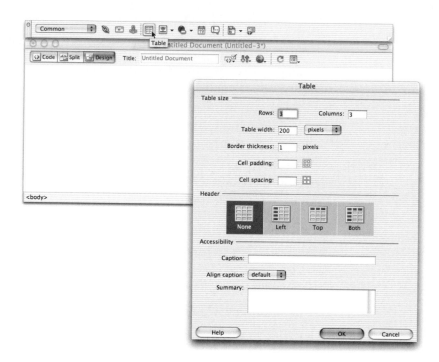

The Table object always remembers the values you used the last time you inserted a table, so you probably won't have to deal with every item every time you create another table.

Have you ever looked at the code for a brand-new table and seen that each cell contains ? What's that doing in there?

This is the HTML entity for a nonbreaking space. Some browsers don't properly display empty table cells, so Dreamweaver doesn't let you create them. Every time it sees an empty cell, it tucks a nonbreaking space in there. As soon as you put content in the cell, Dreamweaver removes the space. Delete the content, and the space is back! That's a nice bit of housekeeping taken care of for you.

Selecting Tables

Working with tables means selecting tables, rows, columns, and cells—and that's not always easy. The more you're familiar with the different selecting options and techniques, the more efficiently you'll work with tables. The two main techniques for selecting are by clicking and dragging various items inside the Document window, and by using the Tag Selector. You can also use keyboard shortcuts to navigate around the table and select items within it. For the most part, use the method you like best; sometimes one method works better in a given situation than another, though, so it's a good idea to be familiar with all of them.

Selecting from Within the Document Window

Some people are just born clickers-and-draggers. Clicking something in the Document window is the most intuitive way to select things for most people. With tables, though, there are so many possibilities!

- **Selecting individual cells**—First, if all you want to do is set cell properties in the Property Inspector, you don't have to actually select the cell. Just click inside the cell to put the insertion point there, and the cell's properties show up in the lower half of the Property Inspector. To actually select a cell, Ctrl/Cmd-click inside the cell. To select more than one cell at a time, Ctrl/Cmd-click in as many cells as you like. To select multiple contiguous cells, you can also place the cursor inside one cell and drag across as many cells as you like; or click in the first cell, hold down the Shift key, and click in another cell.

- **Selecting rows**—Select a row by selecting all of the cells within it.

- **Selecting columns**—You can select a column by selecting all of the cells within it. If the Table Width bar is showing, you can also click the triangle in the width indicator for that column and choose Select Column (see Figure 8.9).

- **Selecting the table**—Select the table itself by clicking its edge. This takes a surprising amount of hand-eye coordination. You also run the risk of accidentally dragging the edge of the table—and, therefore, resizing it—while clicking. A handy, and safer, shortcut, is to right-click inside any table cell and choose Table > Select Table from the contextual menu. If the Table Width bar is showing, you can also click the triangle icon of the table width indicator and choose Select Table.

FIGURE 8.9
Using the Table Widths indicator to select a table column.

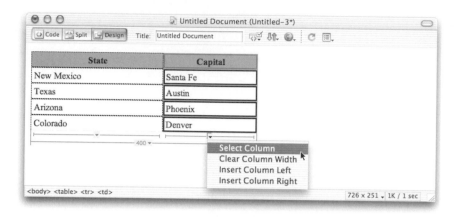

Selecting with the Tag Selector

The Tag Selector can be your best friend when you're working with tables. First, you can use it as an indicator of where you are in your table's structure. Click inside any cell, or select any cell or row, and the Tag Selector displays the structure of the table around you (see Figure 8.10). Plus, of course, the Tag Selector is great for selecting tags. Just click inside any cell to place the insertion point there; then click on the td tag in the Tag Selector to select the cell, the tr tag to select the row that encloses that cell, or the table tag to select the entire table. The Tag Selector is your author's favorite method of selecting tables.

The Tag Selector is less useful for selecting multiple elements or for selecting table columns (because columns have no tag associated with them).

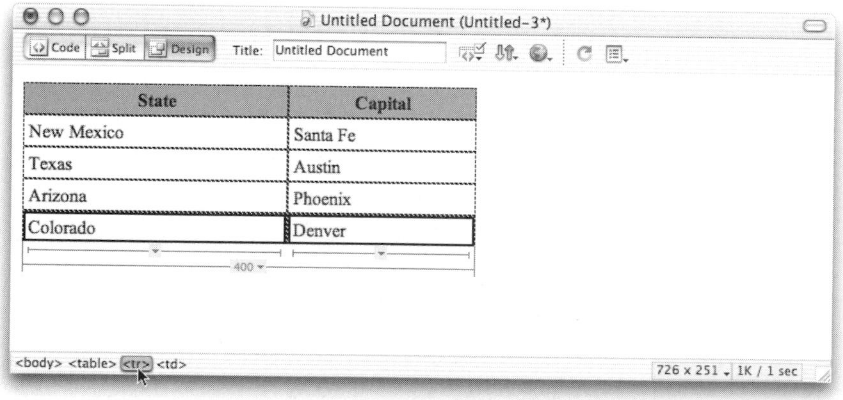

FIGURE 8.10
Using the Tag Selector to select a table element.

Keyboard Navigation and Selection

Dreamweaver has made working with HTML tables very similar to working with tables in word-processing programs or spreadsheets, so your favorite keyboard-access methods from those other programs will work here, too.

To move from cell to cell, press Tab (move forward) or Shift+Tab (move backward). Or, use the arrow keys to move through the contents of your cells and to move from cell to cell.

To select a cell from the keyboard, make sure the insertion point is inside that cell and press Ctrl/Cmd+[(that's the opening square bracket key). This is the keyboard shortcut for Edit > Select Parent Tag. When you have the first cell selected, you can select adjacent cells by pressing the arrow keys. Or, you can press Ctrl/Cmd+[again to select the row containing that cell, and Ctrl/Cmd+[again to select the entire table.

Setting Table Properties

Like just about everything in Design view, tables and cells have associated Property Inspectors to help you work with them. Select a table, and the Table Property Inspector appears (see Figure 8.11). Place the cursor inside any cell, and the lower half of the Property Inspector shows table cell properties (see Figure 8.12). Although table rows have no associated inspector, when all cells in a row are selected, the Property Inspector shows row properties in the cell property area.

FIGURE 8.11
The Table Property Inspector.

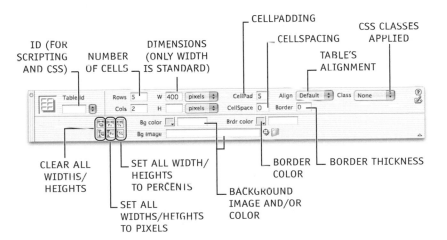

FIGURE 8.12

The Property Inspector showing table cell (or row) properties.

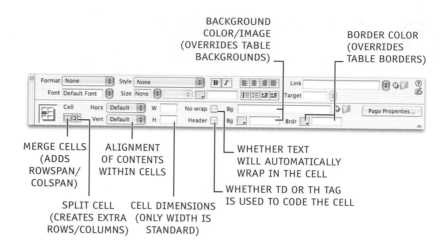

BACKGROUND
COLOR/IMAGE
(OVERRIDES TABLE
BACKGROUNDS)

BORDER COLOR
(OVERRIDES
TABLE BORDERS)

MERGE CELLS
(ADDS
ROWSPAN/
COLSPAN)

ALIGNMENT
OF CONTENTS
WITHIN CELLS

WHETHER TEXT
WILL AUTOMATICALLY
WRAP IN THE CELL

WHETHER TD OR TH TAG
IS USED TO CODE THE CELL

SPLIT CELL
(CREATES EXTRA
ROWS/COLUMNS)

CELL DIMENSIONS
(ONLY WIDTH IS
STANDARD)

Most of the properties shown in these two Inspectors match up to those shown in Table 8.1. Others can be looked up in the Reference panel (Window > Reference). Read over these few tips and "gotchas" about the Property Inspectors and their settings, though:

- Empty fields in the cellpadding and cellspacing fields mean that these properties won't be set, which means that the browser determines cellpadding and cellspacing. Most browsers add 2 pixels for each. To create a table with no cell padding or spacing, set both of these properties to 0.

- Aside from the table border property itself, most border-related properties (border color, individual cell borders, and so on) are non-standard HTML and won't work in all browsers. Use these with caution, preview carefully, and check the Reference panel as needed for more information.

- Although the width property is standard HTML, the height property is not. Assigning a height to tables or cells can also cause browser display problems. Avoid setting height unless you have to; if you do need to assign heights, be sure to preview carefully in all target browsers.

- Many properties dealing with a table's visual display, such as border, bgcolor, and alignment, can be more efficiently set using CSS. (See the discussion on CSS and your tables later in this chapter.)

- When you use the Background property to set a background image for your table, the chosen image tiles to fill the entire background. Netscape 4 doesn't display this tiling correctly.

If you're looking for some quick formatting of a data table, check out the Format Table command in Dreamweaver's Commands menu. It hasn't been updated in awhile and it uses some cumbersome coding, but it contains dozens of quick-and-easy formatting templates for data display in a table. While you're at it, check out the Sort Table command, also in the Commands menu. Very handy!

Changing Table Size and Structure

How big do you want your table to be? How many rows and columns should it have? What about merging cells across columns or rows? All of these common tasks can be performed using the Table Property Inspector, the Document window, and the Modify > Table menu.

Setting (and Removing) Dimensions

You can set table and cell dimensions by typing numbers in the Property Inspector or by clicking and dragging table and cell edges in the Document window. Although the click-and-drag method is certainly more immediately gratifying and intuitive, it's very dangerous because it's so easy to lose track of which dimensions Dreamweaver is adding where. It's also frustrating because tables don't always resize the way you think they will when you're happily dragging edges around.

- **Setting pixel- and percent-based dimensions**—In the Table Property Inspector, use the drop-down menu to choose a pixel- or percent-based dimension. A *percent-based* table width causes the table to resize based on the width of the browser window it's in, or (for tables that are nested inside other elements) the width of the page element containing the table. In the Property Inspector for cells, there's no drop down menu, but you can still create cells with percent-based dimensions. Just type a % after the width or height number in the input field. Percent-based cell widths take up that percentage of the table's width. (So, if you're assigning percent-based widths to all columns in a table, make sure that your percents add up to 100%.)

- **Converting between pixels and percents**—The Table Property Inspector also gives you a set of buttons for converting pixel-based dimensions to percent-based dimensions, and vice versa, for the entire table (and all of its cells).

- **Removing dimensions**—For removing dimensions, the Table Property Inspector gives you the Clear Column Widths and Clear

Row Heights buttons—very handy if you end up with too many dimensions or the wrong dimensions in a table and want to start over. If you have the Table Widths bar showing, you can also click the triangle under any column and choose Clear Column Width.

Adding and Removing Rows and Columns

When you inserted the table, you specified how many rows and columns it should have. But plans change. Nothing is set in stone.

- **Using the keyboard**—To add a row to the bottom of a table, place the insertion point in the last cell in the table (at the bottom right) and press Tab. There's a new row! This makes adding rows as you type contents quick and easy. (The added row has the same attributes as the row above it.)

- **Using the Property Inspector**—To add or delete a row or column at the end of a table, you can select the table and change the number of rows or columns. If you replace a larger number with a smaller number, Dreamweaver deletes the bottom row or rightmost column (and its contents). If you make the number larger, Dreamweaver adds a row at the bottom or a column at the right.

- **Using the Document window**—To delete a row or column, select it and press Delete. Any contents are deleted as well, of course.

- **Using the Table Widths bar**—To insert a column, click the triangle under the column to the left or right of where you want to insert, and choose Insert Column Left or Insert Column Right.

- **Using the menus**—The Modify > Table submenu (also available in the contextual menu if you right-click within a table) has a whole range of handy commands, including commands for adding and removing rows and columns.

  - **Insert Row/Insert Column**—Inserts a row or column directly before (above or to the left of) the row or column containing the insertion point

  - **Insert Rows or Columns**—A much more flexible command that presents you with a dialog box for inserting as many rows or columns as you like, before or after the insertion point

  - **Delete Row/Delete Column**—Removes the row or column containing the insertion point

- **Using the Insert bar**—New to Dreamweaver MX 2004, the Layout Insert bar includes objects for inserting rows and columns into tables (see Figure 8.13).

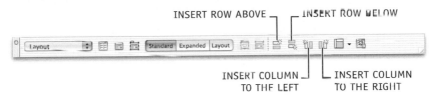

Merging and Splitting Cells

You can also change a table's structure by merging and splitting cells. To merge two or more cells, select them and either choose Modify > Table > Merge Cells or click the Merge Cells button in the Property Inspector (see Figure 8.12). To split a cell into two or more cells, place the insertion point inside the cell and either choose Modify > Table > Split Cells or click the Split Cells button in the Property Inspector. A dialog box appears, asking how you want the cell split (see Figure 8.14). Choose your options and click OK to close the dialog box and split the cell.

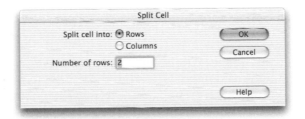

What happens when you merge cells? Dreamweaver applies the rowspan or colspan attribute to one of the selected cells, and removes the other cells. Content from all selected cells is moved into the remaining cell. If it makes more sense to simplify the table's structure another way, however—for instance, if you've just merged cells across every row in a two-column table, creating, in essence, a one-column table—Dreamweaver rewrites the table structure that way. It's possible to create some very sophisticated table structures with merged cells, if you let Dreamweaver take care of rowspan and colspan, nothing will go wrong with the code.

What happens when you split cells? When you split a cell into columns, Dreamweaver increases the number of columns in the table and adds a colspan attribute to all other cells in the current column. That's a pretty

major structural change. The same thing happens when you split a cell into rows: The total number of rows in the table is increased, and row-span is added to other cells as needed.

Although there's nothing inherently wrong with merging or splitting cells, don't use *these* commands as a crutch to shore up badly structured tables. It's much better planning to figure out ahead of time how many rows and columns a table needs, and where cells need to be merged, than to start without planning ahead and merge and split until you've lost track of how the table is built.

WORKING SMART WITH TABLES

When you've got the hang of working with tables, it's time to make them work for you. You want them to look nice, keep their shape, and use efficient formatting. You want them to be accessible. And you can do all of that in Dreamweaver!

Controlling Table Dimensions

Absolutely the hardest thing about designing with HTML tables is making sure they keep their dimensions in the various browsers. They stretch. They shrink. They come apart at the seams. What can you do to avoid these dimensional disasters?

Don't Use Dimensions Unless You Have To

Remember, tables don't need to have dimensions at all. Tables without dimensions tend to shrink around their contents, sizing themselves automatically. Sometimes this is all that you need. And sometimes you need only a few strategically placed dimensions.

Try it! Select a data or layout table that has been causing you fits, and click the Clear Column Widths and Clear Row Heights buttons in the Property Inspector to remove all dimensions (see Figure 8.11). How does it look? If the table contains short bits of text that are wrapping when they shouldn't, try selecting each cell where that's a problem and turning on the No Wrap option in the Property Inspector. Your dimensional problems may be over.

If your table needs dimensions, start by setting only a few. Maybe setting a width for the overall table will be enough, and the cell widths will take care of themselves. If your table columns are still funky, assign cell widths. You don't need to give every single cell a width—just one in each column.

When you've got dimensions in place, make sure they don't contradict each other. One of the primary causes of table misbehavior in browsers is conflicting dimensions. If you set each column of your table to have a width, either remove the table's overall width or make sure the numbers add up. (The table's overall width must include the widths of all columns as well as cellspacing, cellpadding, and non-CSS borders.) If your columns are percent-based, the total percent must add up to 100%. If the table width is percent-based, don't assign pixel widths to all columns. And so on. The more you work with dimensions, the more important it is to do the math. Dreamweaver won't create mathematical impossibilities in the code it writes for you, but the program won't stop you from doing it yourself.

Finally, even though Dreamweaver gives you opportunities to set heights for your tables and cells, remember that this attribute is not part of the HTML specification and, more to the point for your designs, doesn't always play nicely in browser displays. Assign widths as you like, but let your content determine height. If you really do need to assign a height, make sure you test it thoroughly in all target browsers.

Use Control Rows and Columns When Necessary

Have you ever wondered why sliced image tables generated by programs such as Fireworks generally don't fall apart in the browser? They're coded with control rows and columns. An old designer's trick for creating stable tables takes advantage of this fact by building tables around invisible "spacer" graphics that prop open the table to exactly the right size. A *control row* is an extra row added to the top or bottom of a table, built with no merged cells and containing an invisible single-pixel GIF in each cell set to the width desired for that column. A *control column* is an extra column added to the left or right of a table, built with no merged cells and containing a single-pixel GIF in each cell set to the height desired for that row.

You don't necessarily need both. If your table's height is stable and only the width needs help, you need only a control row. If you want to stabilize width and height, add the column as well.

Figure 8.15 shows a control row and column in action. Adding one or both of these items to your tables, and managing them, can be a chore—but they're worth their weight in gold for table stability.

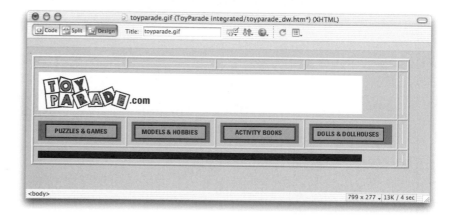

 To create a control row, you first need the spacer graphic to put in its cells. You can easily build one in Fireworks or any other web graphics program by creating a new image with a 1 × 1 pixel canvas and saving or exporting it as a transparent GIF. Every time you export a sliced image table from Fireworks, it generates a spacer image (spacer.gif). Dreamweaver generates a spacer image when you build a flexible table in Layout mode (spacer.gif) or when you convert Layers to Tables (transparent.gif).

USING FLEXIBLE WIDTHS SENSIBLY

Believe it or not, flexible tables are often harder to create than fixed-width tables. This is because although you want the overall table to have a flexible width, you probably don't want all columns to resize. Generally, flexible tables are built with one flexible column and one or more fixed-width columns. Getting this column to flex while that one doesn't takes a few extra steps.

Flexible tables that mix fixed and flexible columns almost always do better with a control row to help them. For each fixed-width column in the control row, insert a spacer graphic as described in the previous section, sized to the desired column width. For the flexible-width column, insert a spacer graphic sized to whatever minimum width you want for this column; then assign the cell itself a width of 100%. That means the cell

should take up 100% of the space available to it, which is the entire width of the table, minus the fixed widths being propped open by the spacer graphics in your other columns. Figure 8.16 shows the control row set up for a flexible table.

FIGURE 8.16
A flexible-width table using a control row for stabilization.

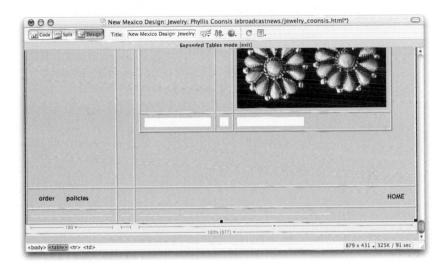

If you want to make sure the right columns are flexing in your flexible-width table, try temporarily assigning each cell a different background color. When you preview in the browser, you'll see clearly what's flexing and what isn't.

Making Your Tables Accessible

According to some accessibility pundits, tables are inaccessible tools of the devil and should never be used. But really, there's nothing wrong with using tables for displaying data or organizing page layout, as long as you follow the rules for making them accessible. It's not even that hard!

Accessibility for Data Tables

Section 508 has very little to say about tables, and what it does say applies only to data tables. Section 508, § 1194.22(g) and 1194.22(h), state:

> Row and column headers shall be identified for data tables.

and

Markup shall be used to associate data cells and header cells for data tables that have two or more logical levels of row or column headers.

The first of these rules is applicable to any simply structured data table and can be accomplished using the th (table header) tag with the id attribute and the td (table data) tag with the headers attribute:

State	Capital City
New Mexico	Santa Fe

```
<table>
   <tr>
      <th id="State">State</th>
      <th id="Capital City">Capital City</th>
   </tr>
   <tr>
      <td headers="State">New Mexico</td>
      <td headers="Capital City">Santa Fe</td>
   </tr>
</table>
```

The second rule applies to more complex data tables, where more than one axis of information is presented. It can be taken care of by using the scope attribute to specify whether the header cell controls a row or column:

	Store 1	Store 2
Chocolate Bars	355	20
Popsicles	25	500

```
<table>
   <tr>
      <th> </th>
      <th id="Store #1" scope="row">Store #1</th>
      <th id="Store #2" scope="row">Store #2></th>
   </tr>
   <tr>
      <th id="Chocolate Bars" scope="col">Chocolate Bars</th>
      <td headers="Store #1 Chocolate Bars">355</td>
      <td headers="Store #2 Chocolate Bars">20</td>
   </tr>
```

```
<tr>
    <th id="Popsicles" scope="col">Popsicles</th>
    <td headers="Store #1 Popsicles">25</td>
    <td headers="Store #2 Popsicles">500</td>
</tr>
</table>
```

Caption and Summary

Section 508 says nothing about using captions or summaries for tables, although the W3C's Web Accessibility Initiative (WAI) suggests a priority 3 guideline to provide summaries for tables. However, many accessibility experts suggest using these to enhance your table's accessibility. A table's caption is a short sentence summarizing the contents of the table, which will appear in all browsers and can be visually styled using CSS. It looks like this in the code:

```
<table>
<caption>States and their capital cities</caption>
    [etc]
</table>
```

A summary is similar in functionality, but will not appear in a graphical browser. It looks like this in the code:

```
<table summary="States and their capital cities">
    [etc]
</table>
```

Because a caption and summary perform the same task, you don't need both.

Accessibility for Layout Tables

Section 508 says nothing about layout tables. Although the W3C generally frowns on using tables for layout purposes (believing you should be using CSS instead), it offers the following guidelines for ensuring that they're accessible:

Do not use tables for layout unless the table makes sense when linearized. Otherwise, if the table does not make sense, provide an alternative equivalent (which may be a linearized version). [priority 1]

If a table is used for layout, do not use any structural markup for the purpose of visual formatting. [priority 2]

Keeping in mind that screen readers read tables in a linear fashion, from left to right and top to bottom, make sure that whatever content is in your layout table makes sense when read that way. If it doesn't, either restructure the table or provide a link to another page that contains the same material presented in a linear fashion (that is, without a table). Furthermore, don't use any of the markup usually associated with data tables—table headers, captions, summaries, and so on—for layout tables. Structurally (as well as graphically), layout tables should be invisible.

Making Tables Accessible in Dreamweaver

The Dreamweaver Table object makes it easy to create accessible data and layout tables. Just think carefully about how you fill out the options in the Insert Table dialog box, and the job is pretty much done. After you've created a table, it's harder to add, edit, or remove the accessibility attributes because most of them don't appear in the Property Inspector.

Header Cells and the *scope* Attribute

When you insert a table that will be used to present tabular data, be sure to choose one of the Headers options in the Insert Table dialog box to place your header cells in the first row, first column, or both. The table will be created with th tags for these cells, with the scope attribute already applied to each (see Figure 8.17). Pretty nice!

If you're creating a layout table, be sure to choose the None option for Headers, and no th tags will be added to the table.

After you've created the table, if you change your mind about what should and shouldn't be a header, select each cell in question and use the Header option in the Property Inspector to turn cells into headers or data cells. If you do this, however, be sure to keep track of the scope attribute! If you change existing header cells into data cells (by deselecting the Header option), the scope attribute remains in place, which it shouldn't because data cells don't have a scope. Because scope doesn't appear in the Property Inspector, you need to edit the code directly or use the Selection Inspector or the Tag Editor dialog box (Edit > Tag) to remove it. If you turn data cells into header cells (by selecting the Header option), no scope attribute is added. According to Section 508, you don't need the scope unless you have more than one level of header; but if you do have a complex table that requires scoping, you'll have to add the correct scope attribute by editing the code or using the Selection

Inspector. Dreamweaver also won't stop you from doing something illegal, such as having too many header cells or having headers in illogical positions.

FIGURE 8.17
Creating header cells with the Table object.

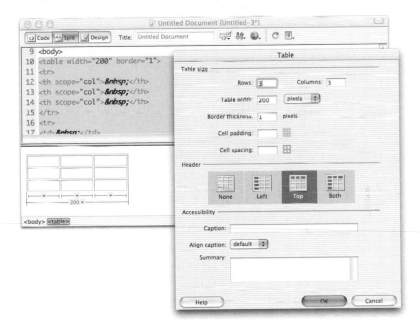

Captions and Summaries

To add a caption or summary to a table while you're inserting it, just fill in the appropriate fields in the Insert Table dialog box. The caption displays in Design view (as well as in the browser window), so it's easy to see, select, and edit its text after it's in place. To edit the caption properties (such as alignment), use the Selection Inspector. The summary won't display, so you'll need to use the Selection Inspector or Tag Editor to work with it—or even to remind yourself that it's there.

What if your table already exists and you want to add one of these items? The summary is coded as an attribute to the table tag, so you can select the table and use the Selection Inspector to add it.

It's a trickier proposition to add a caption to an already existing table. Because the caption is coded in its own tag and not as a table tag attribute, you can't use the Edit Tag command or Selection Inspector to create it. But you can do it in Code view:

1. In Design view, select the table. (This is just to help you find the code for the table after you switch views.)

2. Switch to Code view or Code and Design view, and find the opening table tag. Put the insertion point immediately after the tag.

3. In the HTML Insert bar, from the Table object group, choose the Table Caption object (see Figure 8.18). This inserts an empty caption tag in the code.

4. Between the opening and closing caption tags, enter the text you want for your caption.

FIGURE 8.18
Inserting a caption with the Table Caption object.

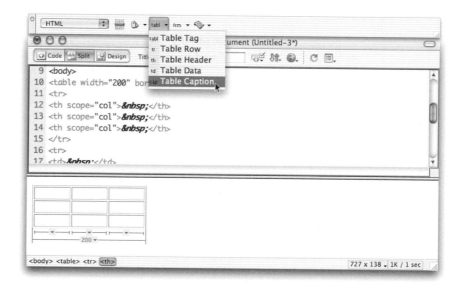

 For more in-depth information on table accessibility, see one of the books written specifically on web accessibility, such as Joe Clark's excellent *Building Accessible Websites* (New Riders, 2001).

CSS and Your Tables

Cascading Style Sheets make it possible to do some wonderful things to table display, all without cluttering up your table code with extra attributes. As always with CSS, be sure to preview in your target browsers to make sure your CSS formatting is supported. Some older browsers (such as Netscape 4) don't interpret all aspects of CSS table formatting properly.

Applying CSS to Tables

You can apply CSS to tables by redefining the table, tr, th, or td tags in your style sheet; or, you can define custom classes or IDs and apply those to any of the table tags.

To apply a custom class or ID to a table, select the table and use the Class drop-down menu in the Table Property Inspector. Or, right-click on the table tag in the Tag Selector and choose Set Class or Set ID from the contextual menu (see Figure 8.19).

FIGURE 8.19
Using the Tag Selector to apply a custom class to a table.

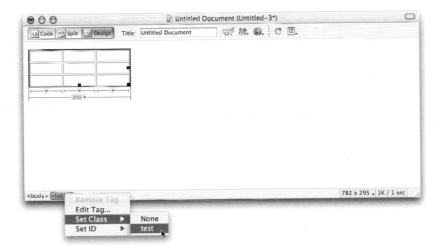

To apply a custom class or ID to a table cell, select the cell and use the Class drop-down menu in the top portion of the Property Inspector, or right-click the td, th, or tr tags in the Tag Selector and choose Set Class or Set ID from the menu.

CSS Properties and Table Formatting

Applying CSS to your tables can replace traditional HTML formatting for borders, backgrounds, widths, alignment, and even cell padding in tables. No matter which of the following properties you choose to style with CSS, remember to remove those properties from your table's HTML so you don't have any formatting conflicts.

Border Effects

To create a border as part of your table's style, create a new style and, in the CSS Style Definition dialog box, go to the Border category (see Figure 8.20). Here you can choose to assign a border to all four sides of a table element or only certain sides. You can specify solid, dashed, dotted, and other border styles (although not all are equally well supported in browsers, so be sure to check your results). Your border can be a pixel-based or other width. And it can be any color. You can also mix and match so that maybe the top border is black and fat, while the bottom border is gray and thin.

You can apply a border effect to any table element, but the tr tag doesn't always display borders properly, so you might want to apply it to tables and cells only.

FIGURE 8.20

Applying a border to a table style.

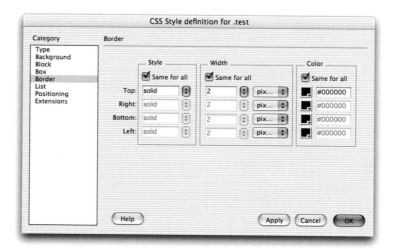

Background Colors and Images

Tables, rows, and cells can also have background colors and images applied to them using CSS styles. Create a new style and, in the CSS Style Definition dialog box, choose the Background category (see Figure 8.21). If you choose a background image, you can also control whether it tiles and how it positions itself within the element by using the Repeat, Horizontal Position, and Vertical Position options.

Width and Cell Padding

Table and cell width, and table cell padding can be controlled by CSS box properties. To access these properties in the CSS Style Definition dialog box, choose the Box category. Set the width field to any pixel, percent, or other type of value you desire. To adjust cell padding, set the Padding options. Warning, though: Not all browsers treat the CSS padding property well, so either preview carefully in your target browsers or don't use CSS to control cell padding. Cell spacing is also better coded without CSS.

Aligning Cell Contents

You can center cell contents horizontally and vertically by using the CSS block properties. To access these properties in the CSS Style Definition dialog box, choose the Block category. Use the Text Align field (for horizontal alignment) and the Vertical Alignment field (for vertical alignment).

EXERCISE 8.1

Creating a CSS-Styled Data Table

In this exercise, you'll build a data table and create CSS styles for table formatting. Along the way, you'll make sure it's accessible. Before you start, download the **chapter_8** folder from the book's website at www.peachpit.com to your hard drive. Define a site called Chapter 8, using the **chapter_8** folder as the local root folder.

1. Create a new file. Save it in your site folder as **holidays.html**. Figure 8.22 shows what you're going to create in this file.

FIGURE 8.22

The holidays.html table as it will look when completed.

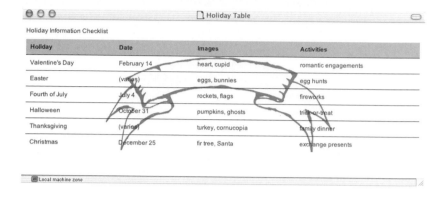

2. Working in either Standard or Expanded Tables modes, insert a table with the following settings:

   rows: 2

   columns: 4

   width: 500

   cellpadding: 10

   cellspacing: 0

   border: 0

   For headings, choose to create a row of header cells across the top of the table (a look at Figure 8.22 will tell you why). For the caption, enter **Holiday Checklist**. Leave the summary blank. Clock OK to close the dialog box and insert the table.

3. Enter the following headings into the header cells across the top of the table: Holiday, Date, Images, Activities. In the next row, enter your favorite holiday and its information. Keep adding rows and holiday entries until you have four or five entries. (Remember, you can press Tab while in the last cell of the table to quickly add a new row.)

4. Now that you have data in the table, select it and remove the width. The data will hold it open.

5. Open the CSS Styles panel and click the New Style button to create a new style. Create a new custom class called .holiday for this document only (see Figure 8.23). Click OK to open the CSS Styles Definition dialog box.

FIGURE 8.23
Creating the holidays custom class.

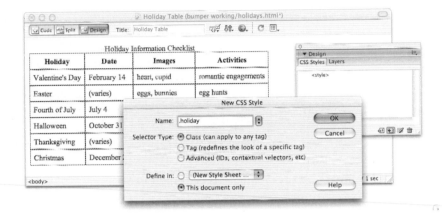

6. This custom class will be applied to the entire table. It's going to hold only two items: text-formatting options and a width indicator. In the Type category of the CSS Style Definition dialog box, set whatever type formatting you like—font, size, color, and so on. When the style is applied, this will govern all type within your table. Go to the Box category and set the Text Align option to Left. This will left-align all text within the table.

    To set the table width, go to the Box category. In the width field, type **100%**.

    Click OK to close the dialog box and create the custom class.

7. In the Document window, place the insertion point inside the table you created. In the Tag Selector, find the table tag and right-click on it. From the contextual menu, choose Set Class > Holiday (see Figure 8.24). You just used the Tag Selector to help you select a table and apply a CSS class. Very nice! The text in your table changes its formatting, and the table width stretches across the page.

FIGURE 8.24
Using the Tag Selector to select a table and apply a CSS class to it.

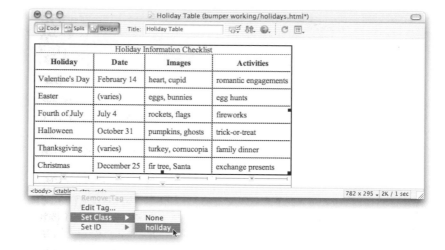

8. You want to apply a certain set of style formatting to all header cells in the table, but not necessarily to all header cells in all tables throughout the document. So, you'll define a contextual selector that applies only to header cells that occur within elements governed by the holiday class.

   In the CSS Styles panel, click the New Style button. Create a new CSS Selector with the name `.holiday th` (see Figure 8.25). In the CSS Style Definition dialog box, go to the Background category and assign a background color. Click the Apply button to see the new style take effect. Adjust the background color, if you like. Then click OK to close the dialog box and create the style.

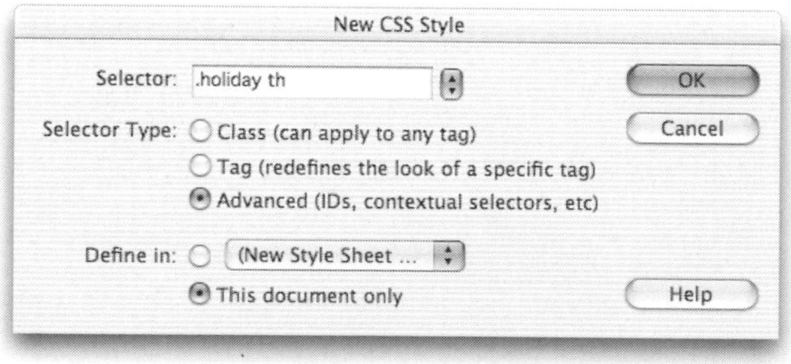

FIGURE 8.25
Creating a contextual selector to format all headers within a holidays-styled element.

9. Now you'll do the same thing to format all data cells within the holiday table. In the CSS Styles panel, click the New Style button.

Create a new CSS Selector with the name .holiday td. In the CSS Style Definition dialog box, go to the Border category. Set a solid, black, 1-pixel border across the top only (see Figure 8.26). Click OK to close the dialog box and create the style.

FIGURE 8.26

Creating a top border for each table cell in the holidays table.

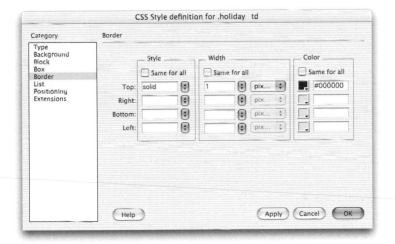

10. To control the appearance of the caption, you'll redefine the caption tag. (This will affect all captions, regardless of whether they're part of a holiday table.) In the CSS Styles panel, click the New Style button and redefine caption. In the CSS Style Definition dialog box, to increase the space between the caption and the table, go to the Box category and set a bottom padding of 10 (see Figure 8.27). When you're done, click OK to close the dialog box.

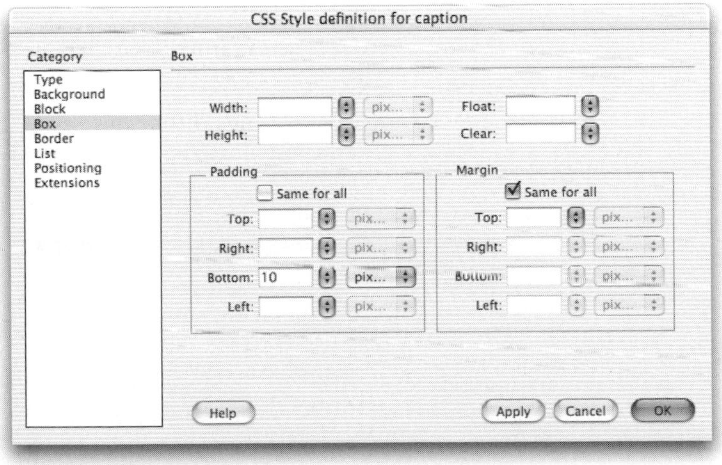

FIGURE 8.27

Using padding to separate a table caption from its table.

11. Finally, experiment with a table background. In the CSS Styles panel, select the holiday style and click the Edit Style button. When the dialog box opens, go to the Background category and click the Browse button to choose a background image. From the **category_08** folder, choose the **brown_ribbon.gif** file. Move the dialog box so you can see the table, and click the Apply button. Experiment with different settings to see how they look. To re-create the example shown in Figure 8.22, set the Repeat to No-Repeat and the Vertical and Horizontal positions to Center and Bottom, respectively. When you're done, click OK to close the dialog box.

12. Take your CSS-styled table for a test drive in as many different browsers as you can. How does it fare?

USING TABLES FOR PAGE LAYOUT

Eventually, we'll all be using CSS for all of our page formatting and layout needs, and tables will be relegated back to their original, more limited function as tabular data displayers. Unfortunately, that day isn't quite here yet. So, you use tables to arrange page content, and they work just great—as long as you follow the rules, respect the quirks of browser display, and develop a good working strategy.

What's Your Working Strategy?

Here's the million dollar question: Exactly how *do* you go about translating all of your table knowledge into a page layout? Or translating that beautiful layout idea you have in your head into HTML tables? Well, every designer approaches things differently. But here's my favorite working strategy for bringing order to chaos, and one that has worked well for my web design students:

1. Sketch out your layout on paper or in your favorite computer graphics program.

   Remember, the computer is not a designer. And HTML is not a friendly environment for creative brainstorming. Always know where you're going before you start building an HTML page. If you're comfortable with pencil and paper, start drawing your layout idea there.

(It doesn't have to be a work of art!) If you're really at home in a graphics program, such as Fireworks or Freehand or whatever you like, do it there. This has the added advantage of giving you a head-start creating any graphic elements you'll need for your page.

2. Figure out how a grid-like table structure will fit over that layout. (Draw the table structure.)

   Remember to keep the table structure as simple as possible without compromising your design, and use multiple stacked or nested tables if you need to. Plan to use extra cells rather than cell padding or cell spacing to create gutters between page elements. (Gutter cells are more adjustable than HTML padding and more reliable in the browser than CSS padding.) You should also start planning at this point where to incorporate background elements such as background graphics and cell colors.

3. Decide whether you want your layout to be fixed or flexible. If it's flexible, which columns should flex? If not, how do you want to align it in larger browser windows?

   Not all layouts respond well to flexing across a browser window. Of those that don't, layouts with sharp, clean, well-defined left and right edges work very well in fixed form centered in the browser window.

4. In Dreamweaver, build the table(s).

   Don't worry about dimensions right now. You'll probably want to set some kind of table width when you start, but it's only temporary, to make the table easier to work with. Just make sure the tables have the right number of rows and columns, and merged cells where needed. While you're at it, also set the table's cell spacing, cell padding, and borders to 0, and set your cell's vertical alignment to top.

5. Insert your page content.

   This means creating your graphics, assigning background elements, and putting in text (or fake text), links, and so on. If your page uses

a sliced image table (navbar, banner, and so on) created in a graphics program, insert that now as well.

6. Use whatever strategies are needed to stabilize the dimensions (as outlined earlier in this chapter).

    If the fates are smiling on you, the table might be stable and perfect now. If so, you're done! If not, start by assigning an overall table width (fixed or flexible). Then add a control row or column. By the time you've done all of these things, the layout should be nice and secure.

EXERCISE 8.2

Translate a Layout into a Table-Formatted Page

In this exercise, you're going to create the layout shown in Figure 8.28 using HTML tables. If you haven't done so already, download the **chapter_08** folder from the book's website to your hard drive, and define a site called Chapter 8 with this as the root folder. All files for this exercise are in the **chapter_08/fixed** folder.

FIGURE 8.28

The desired layout for the Wildlife Friends web page.

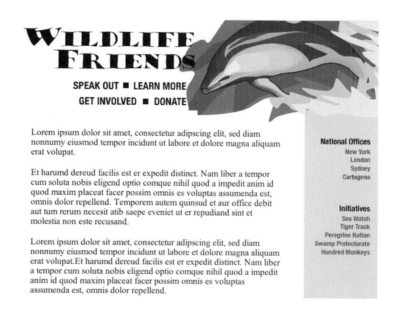

1. The first step has already been done for you. The layout has been sketched out so you know where you're going. Now you need to determine how this layout will break down into one or more tables. The title banner across the top can be created from a sliced image table, and so can the navigation bar down the right side. Your job is to determine what the overall page structure will be, leaving holes for those two nested tables. Figure 8.29 shows the sample layout with a table grid drawn over it, indicating the table that needs to be built. This will be a fixed-width layout, so none of the columns needs to flex.

FIGURE 8.29
The proposed table structure for the layout.

2. Now you need to build that table. In Dreamweaver, create a new file. Save it in the **chapter_08/fixed** folder as **index.htm**. With that file open, create a table with 4 rows, 2 columns; no cell padding, cell spacing, or border; and 640 pixels wide (which is how wide the desired layout is). Because it's intended for layout and not data display, don't create any headers, caption, or summary. Figure 8.30 shows this happening.

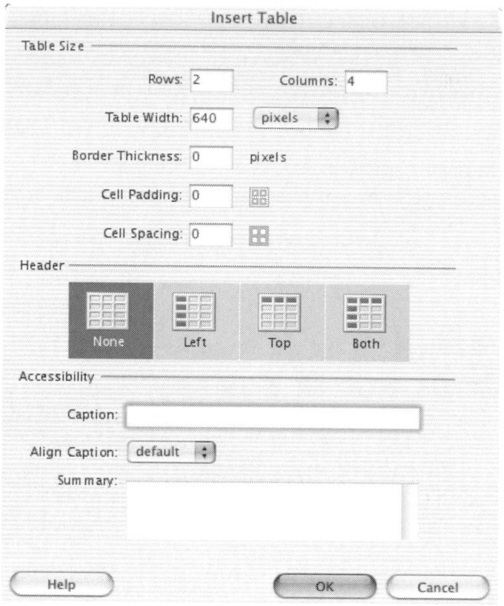

FIGURE 8.30
Creating the table for the Wildlife Friends layout.

To make your table match the grid structure, merge all cells in the top row. While you're at it, type a quick reminder in each cell so you know what they're for (and so the text props them open and makes them easier to see without having to go into Expanded Tables mode). Figure 8.31 shows this happening.

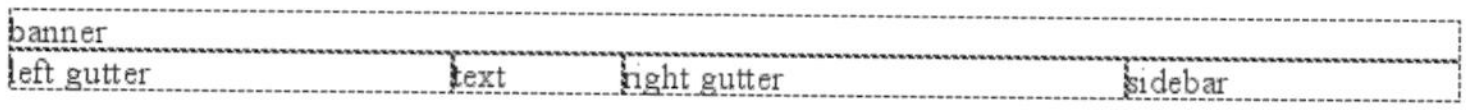

FIGURE 8.31
The table with its structure set up for the layout and notes in place.

While you're getting the table ready, select each cell in the second row and use the Property Inspector to assign it a vertical alignment of top. When those cells have real content, you'll want it to float to the top.

3. Now start putting the content in the page. The title banner is a Fireworks sliced table. To insert it, delete the text from the top cell of your table, leave the insertion point in that cell, and choose the

Fireworks HTML object from the Insert bar (it's in the Common category, Image objects). When the dialog box opens, browse to the wildlife-top.htm file in your **chapter_08/fixed** folder. Click OK to insert the table and close the dialog box. Your layout now looks like that shown in Figure 8.32.

FIGURE 8.32
The Wildlife Friends layout with the title banner in place.

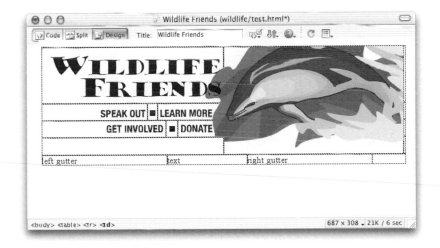

For more on sliced image tables, from Fireworks and other graphics programs, see Chapter 5, "Working with Images."

4. Another sliced image table goes in the sidebar. Delete the text in the rightmost cell and leave the insertion point in place. Choose the Insert Fireworks HTML object again, and this time insert the **wildlife-side.htm** file, also in the **chapter_08/fixed** folder. Your layout now looks like Figure 8.33. Nothing's in quite the right place yet, but you're not panicking because you're not finished!

5. You now need some text to put in the center of the page. If you have one of the filler-text extensions installed, use it to fill in several paragraphs of greeking. If not, open the **filler-text.htm** file in your **chapter_08** folder, copy the text from that file, and paste it into the appropriate table cell in your layout. The layout probably looks really odd now, but it's about to get better.

6. A control row is the most guaranteed way to stabilize this puppy. Select the table and, in the Table Property Inspector, change the number of rows from 2 to 3. This adds a new row at the end of the table. Control rows shouldn't have merged cells (cells with rowspan attributes) in them. Make sure yours has four unmerged cells.

When you've got the control row in place, delete the gutter text from the two cells in the previous row; you won't be needing them anymore.

FIGURE 8.33
The layout with title banner and sidebar in place.

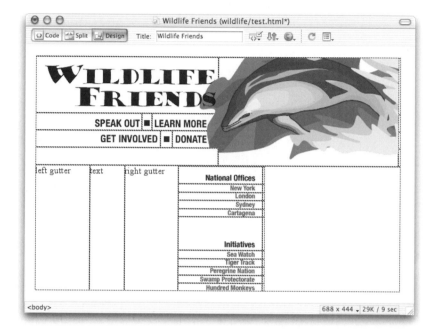

7. Here's where the math comes in. The entire layout is 640 pixels wide. Selecting the sidebar nested table tells you that this column needs to be 150 pixels wide. If you make each of the text gutters 30 pixels wide, how wide should the text column be? Add those three numbers and subtract the total from 640; you come up with 430. So, the control row structure should look like this:

    30 + 430 + 30 + 150

    To make this happen, place the cursor in the leftmost cell of the control row and insert the spacer.gif image from your **chapter_08/fixed/ images** folder. As soon as the image is in place, and without deselecting it, set its width to 30. Also use the drop-down Alt menu in the Image Property Inspector to set its alt text to <empty>. (That's for accessibility.)

    Repeat this procedure for the other cells in this row, using the widths you just figured out.

8. As soon as you insert the last spacer image, if you deselect the table the control row seems to disappear. Why is that? Dreamweaver puts nonbreaking spaces in empty table cells, remember, and this gives them a certain automatic height. But when you put a 1-pixel-high spacer image in a cell, Dreamweaver removes the nonbreaking space. When all cells in the control row have spacer images in place, the row becomes 1 pixel high—and pretty hard to see!

If you want to see that your control row is still in place, you can turn on Expanded Tables mode (View > Table Mode > Expanded Tables Mode), which separates all cells and shows the control row.

Your layout is now complete! Because it's a fixed-width layout, though, it hugs the left edge of the browser window. To center it in the browser window, select the layout table (the big table, not the little nested ones) and, in the Table Property Inspector's Align drop-down menu, choose Center. The table now floats to the middle of any large browser window.

EXERCISE 8.3

Build a Flexible-Width Layout Using Table Structure

In this exercise, you'll build a slightly different version of the Wildlife Friends page. The desired layout is exactly like that shown in Figure 8.27, but this time, the center column of the layout table should stretch. Because this exercise builds on skills covered in the previous exercise, make sure you don't try this one until you've finished that one.

The table structure required for the flexible-width layout is diagrammed in Figure 8.34. Note that the banner graphic has been modified slightly so that the title and links on the left no longer touch the dolphin on the right. That's because these two elements need to hug opposite edges of the browser window as the page flexes, so they must be completely separate items. The top banner also has a light blue background, so it will still look like a banner if the left and right elements drift far apart in a large browser window.

Note also that, to accommodate this grid, two separate, stacked tables make for a much simpler solution than one large, complex table.

FIGURE 8.34
Table grid for the Wildlife Friends page, with an arrow indicating the part of the layout that should stretch.

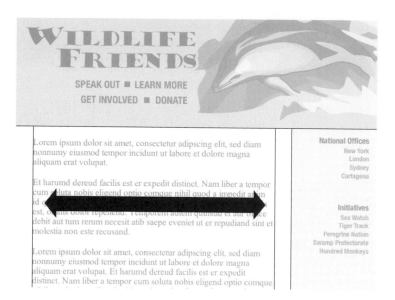

1. In Dreamweaver, create a new file. Save it in the **chapter_08/flex** folder as **index.html**.

2. Build the first of the page's two tables. This table should have one row and two columns, and a width of 100%. As with all layout tables, set `cellpadding`, `cellspacing`, and `border` to 0. Figure 8.35 shows how the table should look when it's built, with temporary text indicating which page elements will go in each cell.

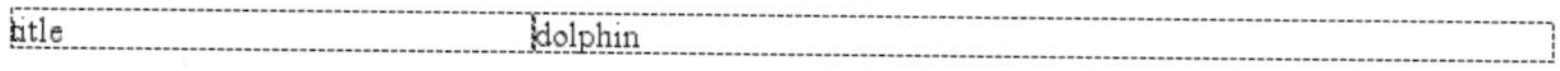

FIGURE 8.35
The first table for the flexible Wildlife Friends layout.

title	dolphin

3. To build the second table, select the table you already have and press the right arrow key to place the insertion point immediately after this table. Then insert another table. This one requires one row and four columns. The second table automatically stacks under the first one. Figure 8.36 shows what the tables should look like, with placeholder text.

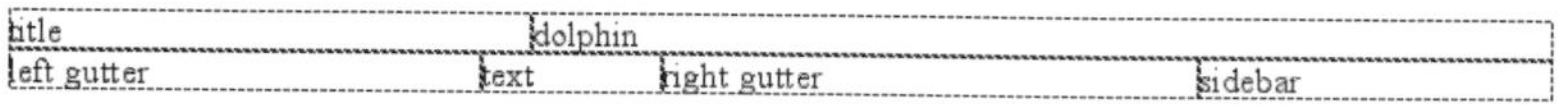

FIGURE 8.36
Adding the second table for the layout.

title	dolphin		
left gutter	text	right gutter	sidebar

(If one table has two columns and the other has four, why not just create one two-row table and merge cells in the top row? Look at the grid in Figure 8.34, and you'll see that the columns won't line up, so one table won't work.)

4. Now to fill in the banner elements in the top table. Start by setting the horizontal alignment of the left cell to Left, and the horizontal alignment of the right cell to Right. Remember, it's usually easier to set cell alignment before the cell has its contents in place.

   Delete any placeholder text from the left cell (title) and, with the insertion point still inside this cell, use the Insert Fireworks HTML object to insert the **wildlife-top.htm** file from your **chapter_08/flex folder**.

   Now delete placeholder text from the right cell (dolphin), and insert the image dolphin.gif (from the **chapter_08/flex/images** folder) into this cell. Figure 8.37 shows what the page should look like at this point.

FIGURE 8.37
The flexible layout with its top elements in place.

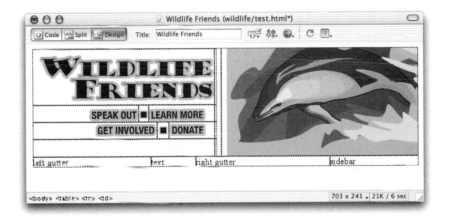

5. Now you need to create the blue background across the entire banner. Select the top table. In the Table Property Inspector, find the Bg Color button. Click the button to open the color picker, and use the color picker's Options menu to turn off the Snap to Web Safe option. Then move the cursor over the blue background color of the dolphin and click to sample that color. Figure 8.38 shows all of this happening.

   With this color in place, preview your page in a browser and see how the layout behaves as it's resized.

FIGURE 8.38
Setting the color of
the top table to
match the dolphin
graphic.

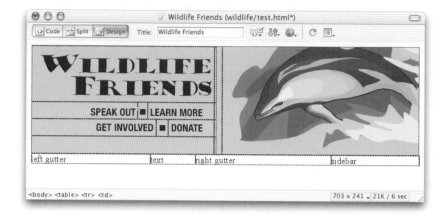

6. Now for the bottom table. The central cell needs some filler text. Either use a filler text–generating extension or open the **filler-text.htm** file, in the **chapter_08** folder, select the text inside, copy it, and paste it into the text cell of your layout's bottom cell. Set the vertical alignment for the cell to top.

   The cell on the right needs the sidebar element. Delete any placeholder text in that cell, and use the Insert Fireworks HTML object to insert the **wildlife-side.htm** file in your **chapter_08/flex** folder. Also set the background color of this cell to #E4ECEE (a light bluish-gray). At this point, your layout should look like Figure 8.39.

FIGURE 8.39
The flexible-width
Wildlife Friends lay-
out, with all page
elements in place.

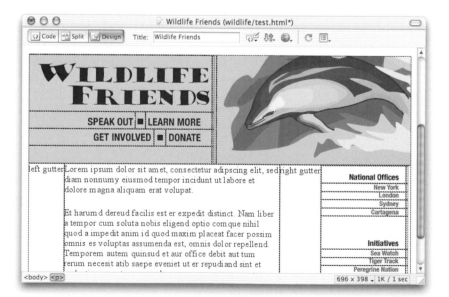

7. Now add a control row to the bottom of the second table. Following the same instructions as in the previous exercise, insert spacer images into each cell, with the following widths:

30 + 1 + 30 + 150

Now select the control cell in the text column, and set its width to 100%. If you're having trouble selecting (or even seeing) the control row cells, switch to Expanded Tables mode while you work.

You should also remove any placeholder text in the two gutter cells at this point. Preview your layout in a browser—it should look like Figure 8.40. Congratulations!

FIGURE 8.40
The flexible-width layout, finished so far.

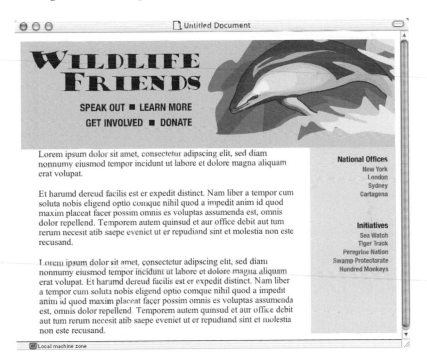

EXERCISE 8.4 — Adding CSS Formatting to the Wildlife Flex-Width Layout

In this final exercise, you'll tweak the flexible-width layout built in the previous exercise by replacing some of its formatting with CSS. This layout might not work in older browsers, but it gives you a good idea how layout tables and CSS can complement each other. The finished page will look like Figure 8.41.

FIGURE 8.41

The finished CSS-enhanced flex-width layout for Wildlife Friends.

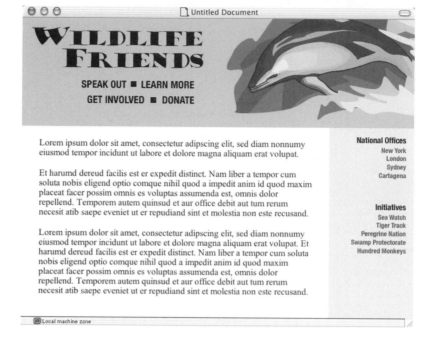

1. To start, the layout will look nicer if it really hugs the browser window edges. In the CSS Styles panel, click the New Style button to create a new style. In the dialog box that appears, choose to redefine the body for the current document only. When the CSS Style Definition dialog box opens, go to the Box category and set the margin for all sides to 0. Figure 8.42 shows this happening.

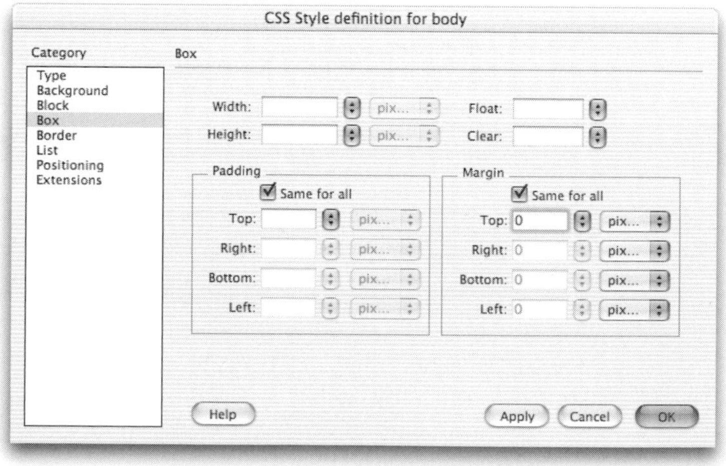

FIGURE 8.42

Using CSS to remove page margins for the current document.

After you've done that, click OK to close the dialog box. Your flexible table now flexes all the way to the edges of the window.

2. Next, you're going to refine the banner so the elements will overlap, if necessary. You'll do it by defining the dolphin as a background image in the banner table.

The top banner table needs to be only one column wide for the new layout, so select the table and, in the Table Property Inspector, change the number of columns from 2 to 1. That deletes the dolphin, but because the table width is 100%, it doesn't stop the banner from stretching across the entire page.

Also remove the background color from the table; you'll be using CSS for that.

3. Now you need to create a style to handle the banner display. Create a new style, a custom class called .banner. In the Style Definition dialog box, go to the Background category. Set the background color to #98CEED (the same blue that's in the dolphin picture). For the background image, choose the dolphin.gif image. Set the repeat value to no-repeat, and the horizontal alignment to right (see Figure 8.43).

FIGURE 8.43
Using CSS to create the top banner's color and add the dolphin picture.

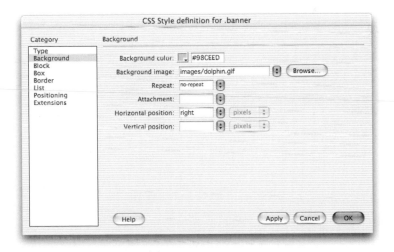

When you're done, click OK to close the dialog box, and use the Property Inspector or Tag Selector to apply the banner class to your

top table. Your layout shouldn't look much different than it did before you re-created it. But preview it in a browser and see what happens when the window resizes (see Figure 8.44). That's a bit fancier than it was before, although it won't display properly in Netscape 4 or older browsers.

FIGURE 8.44
The CSS-formatted banner, flexing in the browser window.

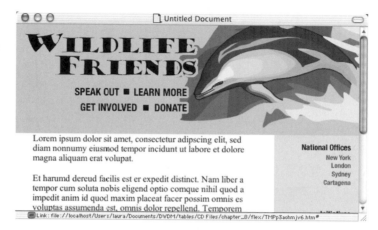

4. The other improvement you'll make is to ensure that the light gray sidebar color goes all the way to the bottom of the window, regardless of how long the page content and the content table are. You do this by defining the gray bar as part of the page background instead of the table background.

First, remove the gray background color from the sidebar table cell. Next, in the CSS Styles panel select the body style and click the Edit Style button. When the dialog box opens, go to the Background category. Set the page's background color to white. For the background image, browse to the **gray_bg.gif** image in the **chapter_08/flex/images** folder. This image is a 150 × 1 solid gray. Choose to repeat vertically only (repeat-y), and set the horizontal alignment to right (see Figure 8.45). This creates a 150-pixel-wide solid gray bar from top to bottom of the page, along the right edge. When you're done, click OK to close the dialog box.

Now preview the page in a browser (see Figure 8.46). See how the sidebar doesn't just end in the middle of nowhere?

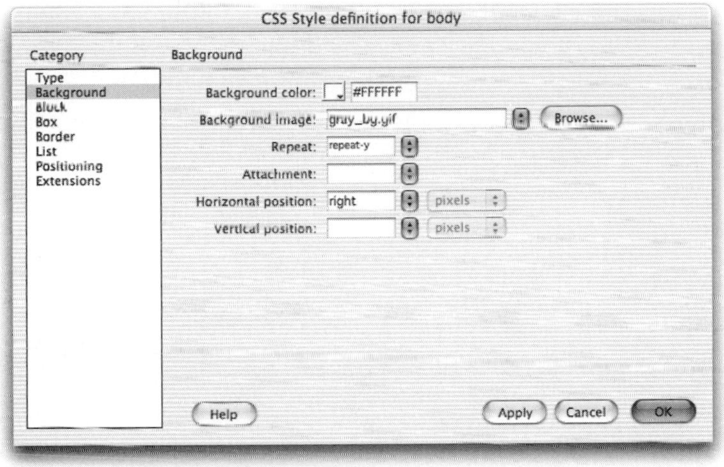

FIGURE 8.45
Creating a gray sidebar from a page background image, using CSS.

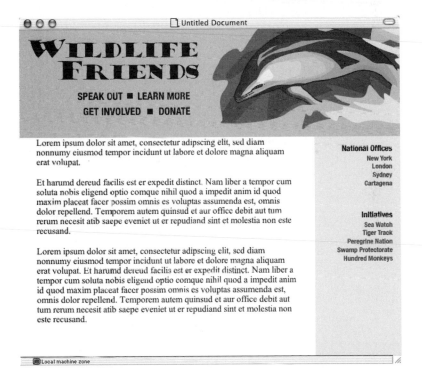

FIGURE 8.46
The Wildlife Friends layout with fully extended sidebar.

5. One more refinement is in order. The text in the main cell snuggles up a little bit close to the top banner. You could fix this problem in a non-CSS manner (safe for just about all browsers) by splitting the text

cell into two rows, putting a spacer image in the top cell and the text in the bottom cell. Figure 8.47 shows this happening.

FIGURE 8.47
Adding a horizontal gutter between banner and text by adjusting the bottom table structure.

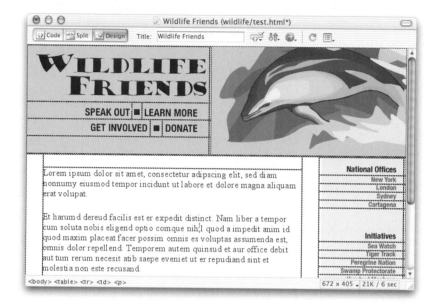

But as long as you're using CSS, why not simply add some padding to the top of the table cell? Create a new custom class called `.text-cell`. In the Style Definition dialog box, go to the Box category and set the top padding to 20 (see Figure 8.48). When you're done, click OK to close the dialog box and create the style.

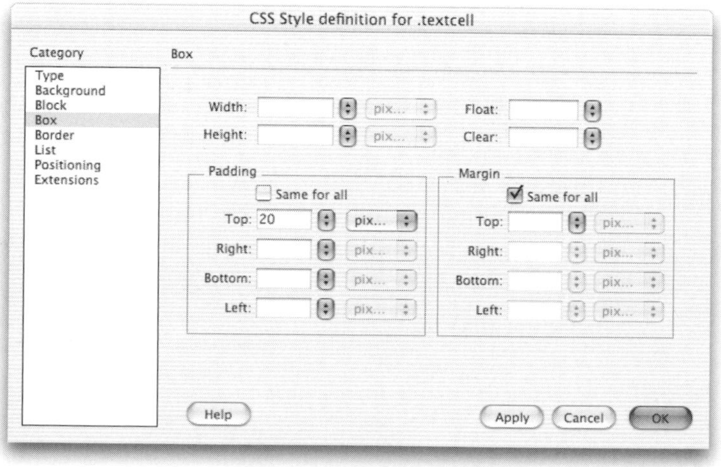

FIGURE 8.48
Using CSS to add cell padding to the top of a table cell.

Finally, select the cell containing your page's text and use the Property Inspector or Tag Selector to assign the textcell class to this cell. The text bumps down from the top of the cell, all without having to add a gutter cell! Your Wildlife Friends layout is complete.

Layout Tables and Layout Mode

Layout mode is an alternate way of viewing and working with layout tables, in which the tables and cells appear more like rectangular boxes full of content than like HTML tables—something like the text boxes and picture boxes that print designers are familiar with from Quark-XPress and InDesign. To create the layout, draw some boxes, Layout Table boxes and Layout Cell boxes. To adjust the layout after it's been created, adjust the size and shape of your boxes. Meanwhile, behind the scenes, Dreamweaver is creating and adjusting the HTML table code for you.

Is Layout mode a good thing or a bad thing? It depends on your point of view. Many designers find it nicely intuitive to click and drag to create their tables. Others don't like Layout mode because it can be used as a crutch to avoid learning proper table-structuring techniques. But if you really prefer the Layout mode interface, you can still take charge of your table structure—if you know what you're doing and always keep an eye on the code.

Getting Around in Layout Mode

To activate Layout view, choose View > Table Mode > Layout Mode, or click the Layout Mode button in the Layout Insert bar (see Figure 8.49). If this is the first time you've been to Layout mode, you'll get an alert window telling you about Layout mode. You can safely close it—it's informational only. When Layout mode is engaged, a yellow highlight at the top of the Document window indicates that you're in Layout mode. In the Insert bar, within the Layout objects, the Layout Table and Draw Layout Cell objects become available for use, while the table tag becomes disabled.

FIGURE 8.49
Layout mode and how
to get there.

DRAW LAYOUT TABLE ⎯⎯ ⎯ DRAW LAYOUT CELL

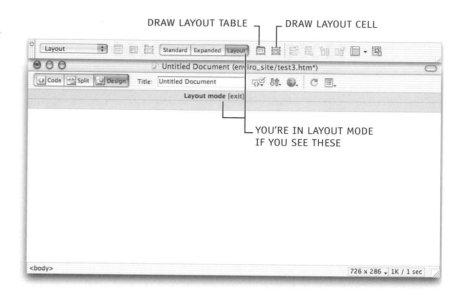

L YOU'RE IN LAYOUT MODE
IF YOU SEE THESE

Drawing Layout Tables

To draw a layout table, choose the Layout Table object and follow the instructions that appear in the Document window's status bar, clicking and dragging to draw a rectangle where you want your table to be. This rectangle will become a table tag in your code, sized to match the rectangle you've drawn.

On your page, the new table appears outlined in green (see Figure 8.50). At its top is the Column Header area, which displays the column's width in pixels. In this case, the table consists of only one column, so this width will also be the table's width. (See the following for more on setting up flexible, percent-based layout tables.)

FIGURE 8.50
Drawing a table
with the Layout
Table object in
Layout mode.

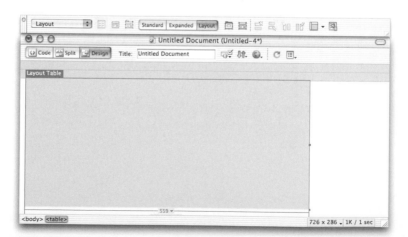

Layout tables can be placed in empty page areas, nested within existing tables, or drawn around existing cells and tables. Like all HTML tables, they cannot overlap each other.

Drawing Layout Cells

To draw a layout cell, choose the Draw Layout Cell object from the Insert bar (see Figure 8.49) and, again, follow the instructions that appear in the status bar, clicking and dragging inside the layout table to create the cell. The cell displays in the Dreamweaver Document window with a blue outline (see Figure 8.51). Because cells must exist within a row and column grid, the layout table containing your cell might show additional subdivisions—these are other cells in the HTML table that are being created as you work. The layout table's column header now shows the widths for all columns.

FIGURE 8.51
A layout cell inside a layout table.

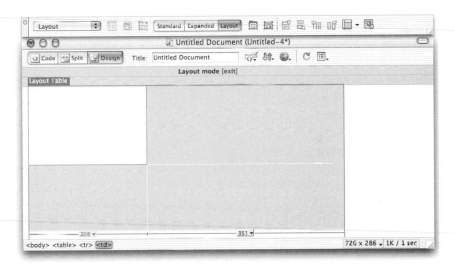

Layout cells can exist only within a layout table. If you draw a layout cell without drawing a layout table first, Dreamweaver creates the layout table for you.

Cells must stay within a row-and-column grid but can span several rows or several columns. They cannot overlap, however. Dreamweaver helps you stay within this structure by snapping new cells to existing cells, or to the side of the page, if you draw them within 8 pixels.

Manipulating Table Structure in Layout Mode

A major attraction of Layout view is that, after you've created your page layout in this way, you can adjust it much more intuitively than you can when working with HTML tables in Standard view. In addition to using special Property Inspectors for layout tables and cells, you can interactively resize and reposition your layout directly in the Document window.

To resize a layout table or cell interactively in the Document window, select it and use the selection handles to drag the edges. Note that resizing a nested layout table resizes the table itself and the cell of the parent table that contains it. To move a layout cell or nested layout table, click and drag or use the arrow keys to move it 1 pixel at a time. Hold down Shift while using the arrow keys to move 10 pixels at a time. Remember, cells can't be moved or resized beyond the borders of their parent tables, and no overlapping is allowed.

Using the Layout Mode Property Inspectors

Layout tables and cells each have their own Property Inspector, enabling you to set all the standard table and cell properties, just like in Standard mode (see Figures 8.52 and 8.53). Some properties, such as width and height, cell padding and spacing, and background color, are the same as those you would find in the Property Inspector for a standard table. But there are some obvious differences. For instance, `cellpadding` and `cellspacing` for the table are set to 0, assuming that you'll be using gutter cells for your layout. Each cell has a default vertical alignment of `top`, again assuming that you want any table content to float to the top of its cell. Width can be specified as a fixed pixel width or `autostretch`, which means 100%. Tables and cells can be assigned background colors but no background images. Other input fields that aren't useful in Layout mode are also gone.

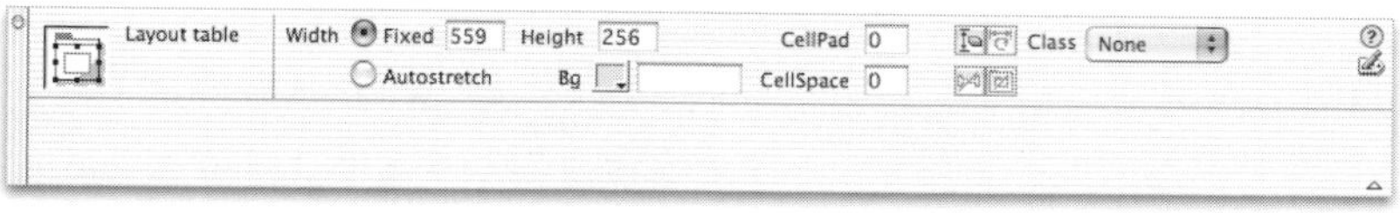

FIGURE 8.52
The Layout Table
Property Inspector.

Autostretch Tables and How They Work

When you first create a layout table, it has a fixed width. You turn it into an autostretch table by assigning either the table itself or one of its columns to have an autostretch width instead of a fixed width. When you do this, Dreamweaver assigns the table and one of its columns a width of 100%. All other columns in the table retain their fixed widths. An autostretch layout table must have only one column, designated as autostretch.

The first time you create an autostretch column or table for a particular site, Dreamweaver asks whether you want to use a spacer image to stabilize table structure (see Figure 8.54). As discussed earlier in this chapter, spacer images are a good idea, so the default is Yes. Note that Dreamweaver even offers to create the spacer image for you—or, if you already have a spacer image, select that one. Whatever choices you make here set a preference for this site. You can change that preference at any time in the Preferences/Layout view dialog box (see Figure 8.55).

FIGURE 8.54
Setting a spacer
image for an
autostretch table.

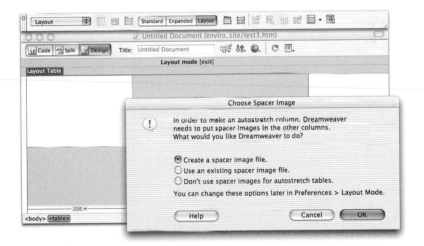

FIGURE 8.55

Setting spacer image preferences for a Dreamweaver site.

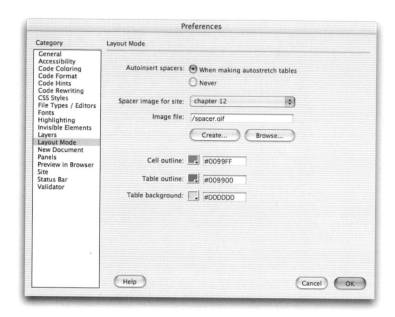

The Coding Behind Layout Mode

What's happening behind the scenes when you build a table in Layout mode? Dreamweaver is writing table code for you, of course. For a fixed-width table, no control row or column is generated, but the table and the first row of cells each has an assigned (pixel-based) width. The first column of cells also has a height. To remove that height, select the table, go to the Property Inspector, and click the Clear Row Heights button. It's a pretty normal-looking table!

For flexible-width (autostretch) tables, the coding is similar to that suggested earlier in this chapter in the "Controlling Table Dimensions" section. If you told Dreamweaver to use a spacer image, a control row is added to the bottom of the table with spacer images in all of its cells. The top cell of the autostretch column has also been assigned a width of 100%.

Working Smart with Layout Mode

So, you love the click-and-drag atmosphere of table generation that Layout mode offers, but you don't want to be a bad HTML citizen, creating sloppy page layouts. What can you do?

- Keep the principles of good table design in mind. Even though you're clicking and dragging, create simple table structures with no unnecessary rows or columns.

- When you've got some content in your cells, clear row heights to get rid of those unsupported height attributes.

- Keep an eye on the code you're creating, the same as you would in Standard mode. Go back to Standard mode as often as you like, to see how your table holds up under scrutiny.

- If you're creating a fixed-width table, remember that Dreamweaver hasn't created a control row for you. Create one for yourself if your table needs stabilizing.

SUMMARY

Tables are one of the mainstays of a web designer's life, useful for data display and page layout. In this chapter, you learned how tables work in HTML and what you can do with them. We also covered the wide range of tools and commands Dreamweaver puts at your disposal for working with tables. In addition, we explored techniques and strategies for creating functional, stable tables for page layout, and how to approach translating page layouts into table terms. The following chapters in this part of the book look at other aspects of page design with Dreamweaver, including forms, frames, and CSS.

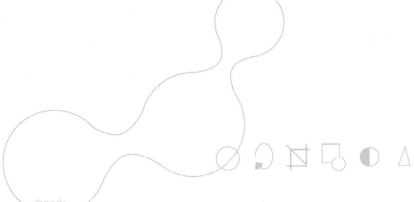

```
<head>
<style type="text/css">
body {background-color: red}
p {text-align: right; color: white}
</style>
</head>
<body>
```

CHAPTER 9

WORKING WITH FORMS

A FORM ALLOWS YOU, THE DEVELOPER, TO ASK STRUCTURED QUESTIONS OF the visitor, enabling you to elicit desired information. With a form, you can just ask for the visitor's name and email address; you also can have visitors take a survey, sign a guest book, provide feedback on your site, or even make a purchase. Forms are standard tools for the web designer. This chapter covers how forms work in the web environment, the basics of creating forms in Dreamweaver MX 2004, how to make your forms attractive and accessible, and different ways that JavaScript and Dreamweaver behaviors can make your forms more interactive.

FORM BASICS

The HTML code that you create in Dreamweaver (or any other web-authoring program) is only part of what is required for a form to do its job. Forms require a *script* (a set of instructions, generally a text file, which is executed within an application) for the information input to the form to be processed.

Form-Processing Scripts

The most common way to process form data is a common gateway interface (CGI) script. CGI scripts are typically written in Perl or another programming language, possibly C++, Java, VBScript, or JavaScript.

Forms also can be processed by server-side technologies such as ASP, ASP.NET, ColdFusion, PHP, or JSP, which function essentially in the same way as CGI scripts. In conjunction with these technologies, forms are commonly used to collect information to be added to databases.

Before creating interactive forms, check with the administrator of the server where you plan to host the website and find out what type of scripting technology is supported. Perl CGI scripts are very commonly supported, and some host companies will even provide these scripts already set up for use on their servers.

The specifics of setting up scripts are beyond the scope of this book, but at the end of the chapter, you'll find some web resources that will point you in the right direction.

The HTML Behind Forms

The HTML code for form creation is not very complex. A form tag surrounds various kinds of input, select, and textarea tags—collectively called *form controls* or *form elements*—interspersed with text labels, tables, and whatever other page elements are required to create the form layout. The code for a very simple form might look like this:

```
<form name="myForm">
  Username:<input type="text" name="username"><br>
  E-Mail:<input type="text" name="email"><br>
  <hr>
  <input type="submit" value="Submit">
</form>
```

The `form` tag itself officially defines an area of the page as a form and specifies what action should take place when the form is submitted. A form's action is the address of a file. When the user clicks the Submit button, the information entered into the form's various fields is sent to this address. In some situations, a form might not require the `<form>…</form>` tag pair; this might be the case with a client side–only form, which doesn't involve sending information to a server. Some browsers, however (particularly Netscape 4), will not display form elements outside of a `<form>` block, so it's best to include it.

Table 11.1 shows commonly assigned attributes of the `form` tag and what they mean.

TABLE 11.1 Commonly Assigned Attributes of the *form* Tag

Attribute	Function of Attribute
name	Assigns an identifier to the entire form element. This value is particularly useful when using scripts that reference the form or its controls.
action	Specifies the URL to be accessed when the form is being submitted. The URL might be to a CGI program or to an HTML page that contains server-side scripts.
method	Forms might be submitted by two possible HTTP methods: GET and POST. This attribute specifies whether the form data is sent to the server appended to the ACTION attribute URL (GET) or as a transaction message body (POST).
target	Allows a window or frame destination other than the current one to be specified as the location to load the HTML page that has been designated to be returned by the server after the form data is processed.
enctype	Sets a MIME type for the data being submitted to the server. For typical form submissions sent by the POST method, the default MIME type is the correct one.

Within a form, input, textarea, and select elements create text fields, check boxes, radio buttons, submit buttons, and other form elements. Other HTML elements, such as tables, images, and text, can also be used to provide instructions, labeling, and layout for the form. Table 11.2 lists the most commonly used form elements, along with a quick peek at the code that creates them.

TABLE 11.2 ## Form Elements and Their attributes

Form Element	Tag	Example
Text field	input	`<input type="text" name="myText" size="10"` ➥`maxlength="50">`
Password field	input	`<input type="password" name="myPassword" size="10"` ➥`maxlength="50">`
Check Box	input	`<input type="checkbox" name="myCheck" checked>`
Radio group	input	`<input type="radio" name="myRadio" value="1">True` `<input type="radio" name="myRadio" value="0">False`

Button	input	`<input type="button" value="Click Me!">`
		`<input type="submit" value="Submit Form">`
		`<input type="reset" value="Reset Form">`

List/menu	select	`<select name="mySelect">`
		  `<option value="1">True</option>`
		  `<option value="0">False</option>`
		`</select>`

Text area	textarea	`<textarea name="myTextarea" cols="10" rows="5">`
		  `text input goes here`
		`</textarea>`

Image field	input	`<input type="image" name="myImage"` ➥`src="myButton.gif">`
File	input	`<input type="file" name="myFile">`
Hidden field	input	`<input type="hidden" name="myField">`

Figure 9.1 shows a form that uses a variety of input and other elements, as it appears in the browser.

FIGURE 9.1
Form elements in the browser.

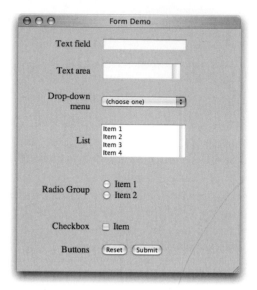

How Forms Work in Dreamweaver

Dreamweaver makes building HTML forms very easy. All common form tags can be added using the Forms category of the Insert bar (see Figure 9.2). The same objects also are available by choosing items from the Insert > Form submenu.

FIGURE 9.2
The Forms Insert bar.

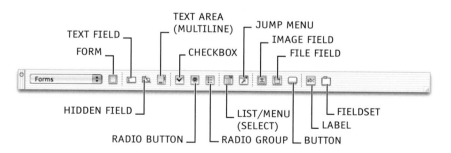

To build a form in Dreamweaver, start by inserting a form object. If you have invisible elements showing, the form will appear as a red box; it's important to keep track of that box so that you make sure to put your form objects inside it. (To turn on invisible elements, choose View > Visual Aids > Invisible Elements.) When the form is selected, the Form Property Inspector appears (see Figure 9.3).

FIGURE 9.3
The Form Property
Inspector.

TIP

Forms can be hard to
select because you
have to click exactly
on the red box out-
line. Use the Tag
Selector instead.
Place the insertion
point anywhere
inside the form, and
in the Tag Selector,
find the form tag
and click on it. That
selects your form.

If you try to insert a form element without having first inserted a form,
Dreamweaver will offer to insert the form automatically. Although this is
handy, Dreamweaver might not create the form exactly where you want
it. It surrounds the current form element and its label with a form tag,
but no other page elements. For instance, if you have created a table to
hold your form elements, Dreamweaver places the form inside the table,
not surrounding it.

With the form in place, use form objects to add form elements inside
the red box. You can also insert any nonform elements, such as images,
text, a table to control the layout, and so on. Each form element has its
own Property Inspector, as shown in Figures 9.4 through 9.8. Pay special attention to the names you give your form fields because the script
that processes the form may require certain naming conventions to be
followed.

FIGURE 9.4
Property Inspectors
for the Dreamweaver
text field elements.

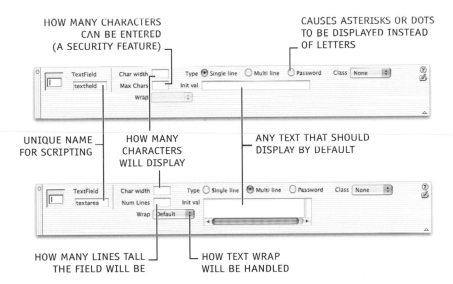

FIGURE 9.5
Property Inspector for the List/Menu form element.

UNIQUE NAME FOR SCRIPTING

DROP-DOWN MENU OR MULTI-ITEM LIST

FOR LISTS, HOW MANY LINES HIGH

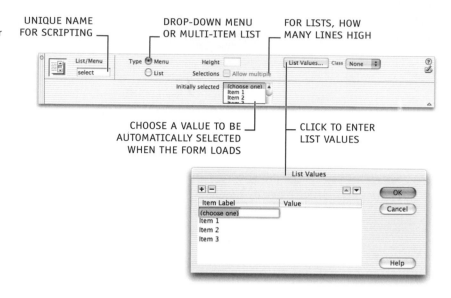

CHOOSE A VALUE TO BE AUTOMATICALLY SELECTED WHEN THE FORM LOADS

CLICK TO ENTER LIST VALUES

FIGURE 9.6
Property Inspector for the Checkbox form element.

UNIQUE NAME FOR SCRIPTING

VALUE THE FORM WILL RETURN TO SCRIPTS IF THIS ITEM IS CHECKED

DEFAULT STATE

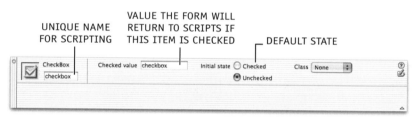

FIGURE 9.7
Property Inspector for the Radio button form element.

VALUE THE FORM WILL RETURN TO SCRIPTS IF THIS ITEM IS SELECTED

DEFAULT STATE

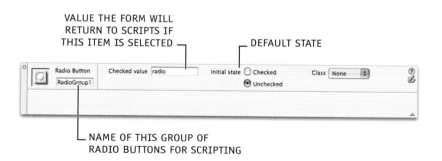

NAME OF THIS GROUP OF RADIO BUTTONS FOR SCRIPTING

FIGURE 9.8
Property Inspector
for the Button form
element.

TEXT THAT WILL APPEAR
IN THE BUTTON

ACTION TO TAKE
WHEN THE BUTTON
IS PRESSED

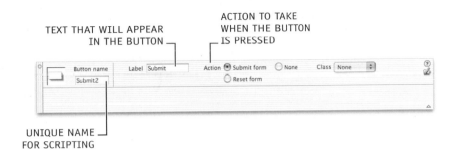

UNIQUE NAME
FOR SCRIPTING

When naming forms and form elements, keep a few things in mind. First, don't use spaces or special characters. Second, it is a good idea to use names that clearly identify the form or element's role. Third, develop your own *naming conventions*, and be consistent. Either don't use capitals at all or use them in a consistent way; either don't abbreviate English words at all or abbreviate in a consistent way; either use underscores between words or run the words together. This helps you to remember the names you create and avoid typos. Finally, be aware that scripting languages have certain *reserved words* that have special meaning and can cause problems. The word *date* is a common example. You might want to research which reserved words exist in the scripting language you're using, especially if you run into problems that seem to have no other explanation.

WORKING SMART WITH FORMS

Forms aren't glamorous, but there are plenty of ways to make them look and function at their best. Dreamweaver can help you make your forms accessible to all visitors, to look their best, thanks to CSS formatting, and to be more interactive with the addition of Dreamweaver behaviors.

Making Your Forms Accessible

Because the whole purpose of forms is to be accessed and interacted with, form accessibility is a big issue. If a user can't use the mouse, how can he select a form field to type information into? If he can't see your page layout, how can he tell which form field is for the username and which is for the email address? Consequently, various rules, guidelines, and options apply to making acceptably accessible forms.

According to Section 508, §1194.22(n):

> When electronic forms are designed to be completed online, the form shall allow people using assistive technology to access the information, field elements, and functionality required for completion and submission of the form, including all directions and cues.

That sounds like a lot! Luckily, browsers and operating systems take care of some of this for you, such as making it easy to activate form fields for the mobility-impaired. And the HTML specifications provide several mechanisms (some more well supported than others) for helping:

- **Labeling**—Even a user who can't see your form's layout should be able to tell without a doubt what each text field, check box, or other element is for. To accomplish this, every form element should include a label tag containing a text label that explains what information this element collects (username, password, phone number, favorite color, and so on).

- **Tab indexing**—A user who can't use a mouse should be able to use the Tab key to activate all form elements in order. The browser should allow this automatically (at least, on Windows or Mac OS X), but you can help users by adding a tabindex attribute to at least the first form element and optionally to all form elements. tabindex takes a number as its value, indicating the order in which elements can be tabbed through. So, the first element in the form should have a tabindex of 1, the second element should a tabindex of 2, and so forth.

- **Access keys**—Ideally, a user who can't use a mouse should be able to enter a key command that will activate a particular form field. For instance, type **F** to activate the First Name field. This bit of accessibility is not well-supported in browsers, however, and can conflict with OS-level shortcut keys, so it is not often used.

Using these guidelines, the basic code for an accessible form might look like this:

```
<form name="theForm">
  <label for="username">User Name:</label>
  <input type="text" name="username" id="username" tabindex="1"
➥accesskey="n">
```

```
<label for="pword">Password:</label>
  <input type="password" name="pword" id="pword" tabindex="2"
  ➥accesskey="p">
  <input type="submit" name="submit" id="submit" label="Submit"
  ➥tabindex="3">
</form>
```

In this example, each item has a tabindex. Each item except the Submit button has a label and accesskey attribute. (The Submit button needs no accesskey: It is always accessed by pressing Return and needs no text label because it contains its own internal label attribute.) The form would also be acceptably accessible without the accesskey attributes.

Labels can be coded implicitly—wrapped around the form element being labeled:

```
<label>User Name
    <input type="text" name="username" ... >
</label>
```

Or, they can be coded explicitly—placed next to the form element:

```
<label for="username">User Name</label>
    <input type="text name="username" ... >
```

According to the U.S. Access Board (www.access-board.gov), explicit labels are more reliable. They also allow for more design freedom.

Before the Fact: Set Accessibility Options

Before you create your form, make sure you have accessibility options for Forms turned on (Edit > Preferences/Accessibility). When this is enabled, the next time you use the Insert bar or menu to create a form element, you'll be presented with a dialog box letting you assign label, tabindex, and accesskey attributes (see Figure 9.9). Note that the same dialog box appears regardless of whether you're inserting a Submit button, a textarea, or another form element. It's up to you to know, for instance, that a Submit button can do without explicit labeling. The form object itself doesn't call up an accessibility dialog box because no special treatment is necessary for form tags.

The accessibility dialog box gives you choices for how your labels are coded and how they appear. To create explicit labels (coded separately from the form element rather than wrapped around it), choose Attach Label Tag Using for Attribute. To create implicit labels, choose Wrap with Label Tag. Whichever option you choose, use the Position choices to specify where the label should appear in relation to the form element (before or after). As mentioned earlier, explicit labels are more flexible and reliable. Implicit labels are easier to manage, however, because there is no for attribute to keep track of and no chance that the label and its related form element will become separated.

FIGURE 9.9
The InputTag Accessibility Attributes dialog box in action.

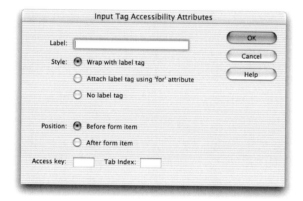

Remember that the text in the label tag will display in the browser window as regular text. So, when laying out your form, don't enter the text separately if you're going to use the accessibility dialog box to generate a label.

Working with *tabindex* and *accesskey*

To add or edit either the tabindex or accesskey attributes for an already existing form element, use the Edit Tag command (Style Sheet/Accessibility category) or Tag Inspector (see Figure 9.10). Neither of these attributes appears in the Property Inspector, but they are available in the Tag Inspector's CSS/Accessibility category.

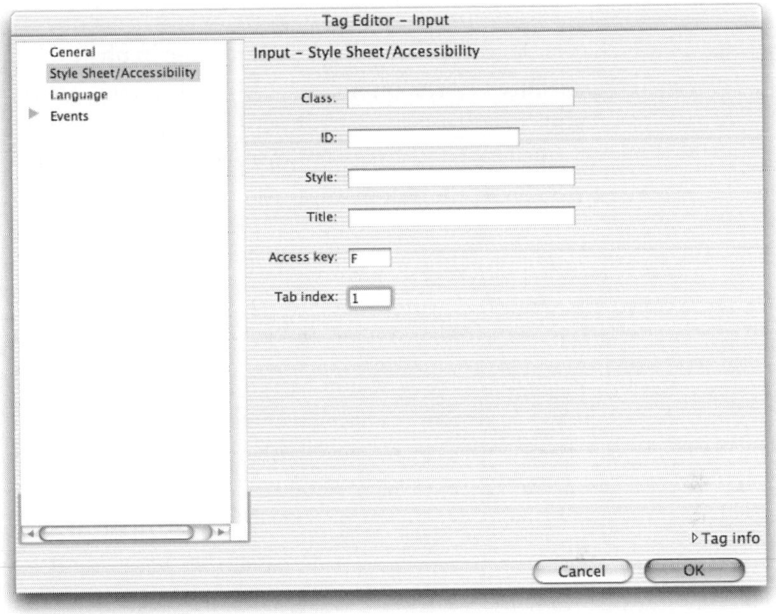

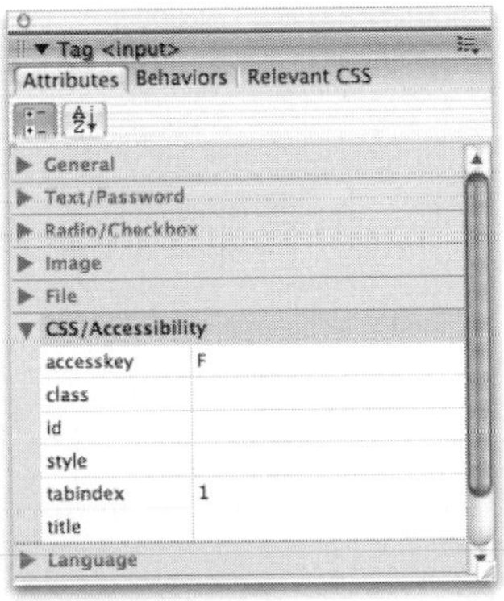

FIGURE 9.10
Setting tabindex
and accesskey in
the Edit Tag dialog
box and Tag
Inspector.

Forget About *accesskey*

The smart money says, don't bother with accesskey unless you have a really good reason to do so. It's not well-supported, and it can actually cause conflicts with the user's operating system.

Apply *tabindex* Only as Needed

The tabindex attribute can be applied to other page elements besides form elements (the object and a tags, for instance), to allow users to skip directly to important page content. If the form is an important part of your page, however, you probably want users to be able to tab directly

there, so don't clutter the page with other `tabindex` attributes. Not every form element needs to have a `tabindex` because after the user has activated the first field, built-in browser/OS tabbing features will take the user to additional fields. However, if you want to control tabbing order (especially if you want to override browser/OS defaults), you can apply the attribute to all elements.

Use Nonconsecutive *tabindex* Values

Note that `tabindex` values don't have to be consecutive. If your first field has a `tabindex` of 10 and the second has a `tabindex` of 300, the tabbing order will still go from a smaller to a larger number. You can use this to your advantage! If you think there's any chance you might be coming back later to add more form fields to the beginning or middle of your form, don't assign consecutive `tabindex` values to every field in the form. For instance, what if you have 20 fields and want to add a new field or two between the address (`tabindex=3`) and phone number (`tabindex=4`)? You'll have to renumber almost every field in the form. Either don't assign `tabindex` to all form fields, or give the address field a number such as 10 and the phone number a higher number, such as 15 or 20.

Working with Labels

Labels are different from `tabindex` and `accesskey` because they're coded as separate tags rather than attributes of the `form` element tag. They also create visible elements on the page.

If you've created form elements without labels, using regular text to identify them, you can easily convert that text into a label. Just select it and, in the Insert bar (Forms category), choose the Label object (see Figure 9.11). This wraps a `label` tag around your selected text. Because labels display in Code view, it also activates Code view so you can see the code being added. Note that the tag is entered without a `for` attribute, so it's not connected with any form field. You'll have to enter the `for` attribute in Code view or in the Tag Inspector.

Labels display in Design view as regular text, with no visual indicator that they're labels. If the insertion point is inside a label, though, the Tag Selector will display the label tag in its hierarchy. The Property Inspector doesn't recognize labels, so use the Tag Inspector to edit label properties such as the all-important `for` attribute.

FIGURE 9.11
Using the Label
object to turn
existing text into
a form label.

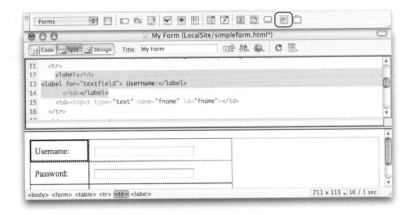

EXERCISE 9.1

Create an Accessible Form

In this exercise, you'll create a form that uses various types of form elements. Figure 9.12 shows the finished page you're aiming for. Before you
start, download the **chapter_09** folder from the book's website at
`www.peachpit.com` to your hard drive and define a site called Chapter 9,
using that as the root folder.

1. In the **chapter_09** folder, open **evalform.html**. This page contains
    a main layout table holding a navigation bar across the top and a
    nested table to contain the form. Open the CSS Styles panel, and
    you'll see that several styles have already been defined in an external
    style sheet attached to this document. If you switch to Code view
    and examine the head of the document, you'll see that the style
    sheet has been attached using the `import` directive. These style sheets
    won't be recognized by Netscape 4, so you don't need to worry that
    your CSS formatting will render the form inoperative.

2. This will be an accessible form, so start by turning on Dreamweaver's
    accessibility features. Open the Preferences dialog box (Edit >
    Preferences), and in the Accessibility category, enable accessibility
    options for form elements.

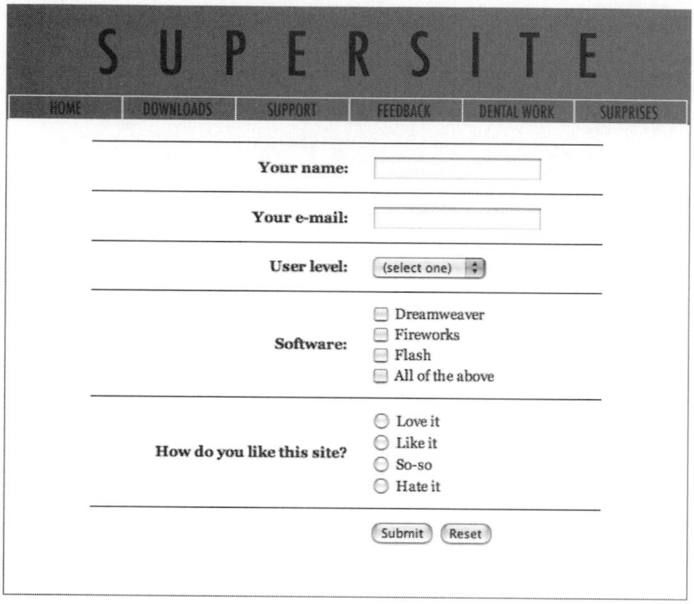

FIGURE 9.12
The finished Supersite Evaluation form.

3. The `form` tag needs to surround the table. Select the nested table (it shows up in the Tag Selector as table.formtable) and choose Edit > Cut. Then, with the insertion point still where the table used to be, insert a Form object from the Insert bar. Make sure invisible elements are showing (View > Visual Aids > Invisible Elements) so you can see its red outline. With the form still selected, in the Property Inspector, change its name to evalForm. Leave the other form properties alone for now.

Place the insertion point inside the form and choose Edit > Paste to put the layout table back in place. (Normally, when you're working, it's best to create the form object first, but it's nice to know how to add a form after the fact, for those times when you forget!)

5. The first row needs a text field and a label. Place the insertion point in the first cell and insert a text field. When the Input Accessibility dialog box appears, set the label to Your Name:, and choose to attach the `label` tag using the `for` attribute. For Position, choose Before Form Item. Leave `tabindex` and `accesskey` empty for now. Figure 9.13 shows what the dialog box should look like.

FIGURE 9.13

The Accessibility Options dialog box for the first text field in the Supersite form.

This inserts the label and text field both in the first cell, which you don't want. Deselect both items and then drag the form field into the second table cell.

You also need to give the text field a good name. Select it and, in the Property Inspector, set its name to fullname. When you've done that, select the text label and use the Tag Inspector to make sure the for attribute also says fullname (see Figure 9.14). (If it doesn't match, it's worse than useless!)

FIGURE 9.14

Make sure the text field's label matches the text field's name.

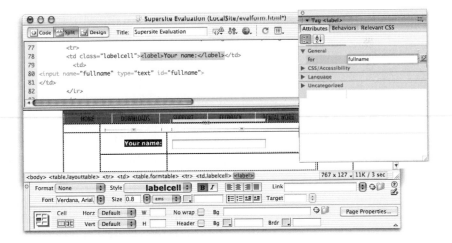

6. Repeat this procedure to create the second row of the table, which should contain a text field named email, with the label Your Email:.

7. For the next row, insert a List/Menu object. When the accessibility dialog box appears, choose User Level: for the label. Use the same

technique to move the form field to a separate cell. Name the select element **userlevel**, and make sure the label is updated as well.

In the Property Inspector, click the List Values button to open the list values dialog box. Set the list values to the following:

- (Select One)
- Novice   novice
- Intermediate   intermediate
- Advanced   advanced
- Power User   power

When you're done, click OK to close the dialog box and, in the Property Inspector, set Select One to be the default selected option. Figure 9.15 shows this happening.

FIGURE 9.15

Setting the list values for the userlevel drop-down menu.

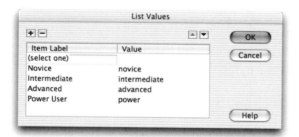

8. The next table row contains a set of check boxes. The text in the left cell is not a label for any one element, so just type **Software:** into the table cell.

   In the right cell of this row, insert a check box. Label it **Dream-weaver** and name it **dw**. For the checked value, enter DW and leave the initial state as unchecked. You need to add a line break after this element. Do it this way: Place the insertion point within the Dreamweaver label, use the Tag Selector to select the label tag that surrounds it, and press the right arrow key to move the insertion point after the label. Then press Shift+Return to create a soft return (br tag). Insert another check box, labeled **Fireworks** and named **fw**, with check value FW and initial state unchecked. Repeat this procedure to create two more check boxes: one labeled **Flash** and named **fla**, with a checked value of FLA, and one labeled **All of the Above**

and named **all**, with a checked value of ALL. Every check box should have an initial state of unchecked.

9. In the next row, there's a radio group. In the left cell, type in **How Do You Like This Site?** In the right cell, insert a radio group. This inserts as many radio buttons as you like. When the dialog box opens, name the group eval and create the following radio buttons:

- Love It   4

- Like It   3

- So-So   2

- Hate It   1

Set the list to be separated by line breaks. Figure 9.16 shows what the dialog box should look like when you're done. Click OK to close the dialog box.

FIGURE 9.16
Creating the eval
radio button
group for the
Supersite form.

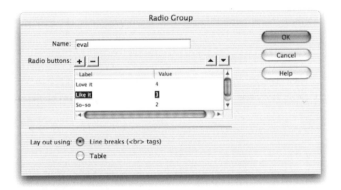

Select the Love It radio button and, using the Property Inspector, set it to be selected by default. (If users are too busy to fill out this part of the form, assume that they loved the site!) Check out the code for these buttons, and you'll see that they've been added with implicit labeling; the input tag is nested within the label. Explicit labeling is recommended, but implicit labeling has the advantage that you don't have to keep track of the for attribute.

10. In the last row, insert two buttons in the right cell. For each, set the labeling to no label tag; you don't want your buttons to have

text labels sitting next to them because they have their own labels on them.

When both buttons are inserted, select the left one. You'll see that it's automatically a Submit button, but you can make it a Reset button. Choose Reset from the Action options in the Property Inspector. This automatically changes the button's label as well as its type. Its name becomes submit2. Change it to Reset.

Formatting Forms

With forms more than any other type of page content, you're at the mercy of the browser for what things will look like. Text fields, drop-down menus, check boxes—each browser and platform determines how these will appear. At the same time, it's crucial that your forms look tidy and inviting so that users will want to fill them out and will find them intuitive. The two main weapons in your form-formatting arsenal are tables and CSS. You also have the choice of substituting images for Submit and Reset buttons.

Form Layout with Tables

Tables help keep page elements aligned and organized. Organization is especially important when it comes to forms. Many designers organize forms in tables with one row per line of form elements, and optionally a separate column for labels, as is shown in Figure 9.17. Cell padding (applied via the Property Inspector or specified in a CSS style) or gutter cells can be used to separate the form elements from each other.

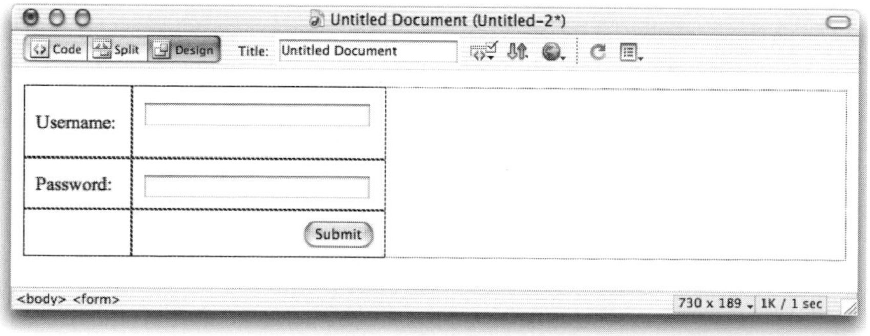

FIGURE 9.17
Using a table to control form layout.

For more on tables and layout, and their related accessibility issues, see the sections "Using Tables for Page Layout" and "Making Your Tables Accessible" in Chapter 8, "Building Tables."

Remember as you're doing this, however, that the form still needs to linearize well, or it won't be accessible. Screen readers read tables from left to right and top to bottom, so keep labels and form elements next to each other in the same row rather than putting the label on one row and its associated form element on the row below.

If you're using Dreamweaver's accessibility options to create your form labels and you want to put the form in a table in which labels and form elements are spread across different cells (as shown in Figure 9.1), be sure to use the Attach Label Using for Attribute option. This inserts the label and form element as separate tags. Dreamweaver inserts them both into the same table cell, but you can select either and drag it to another cell when it's in place.

Form Formatting with CSS

One of the frustrating aspects of designing HTML forms has always been how little control you have over their appearance. With CSS, things are looking up. By redefining form and form element tags and applying custom classes, you can add borders and backgrounds, determine sizes, and more. As usual with CSS, results aren't equally well supported across all browsers and for all form elements, so some experimentation and previewing is in order. But you can still do some nice things with your forms' appearance for most visitors (see Figure 9.18).

With its limited support of CSS, Netscape 4 offers a particular challenge when it comes to form design. Not all styles display properly. But much more important, in some cases text fields can become nonfunctional, no longer accepting input. Obviously, this is unacceptable. A workaround is to create a style sheet that Netscape 4 won't see, using the import directive. See the section "Using Linked and Imported Style Sheets to Create a Netscape 4–Friendly Site," in Chapter 11, "Using Cascading Style Sheets," for full details.

FIGURE 9.18

A form customized with CSS, as it appears in Internet Explorer 5, Netscape 6, Opera 5, and Safari 1.

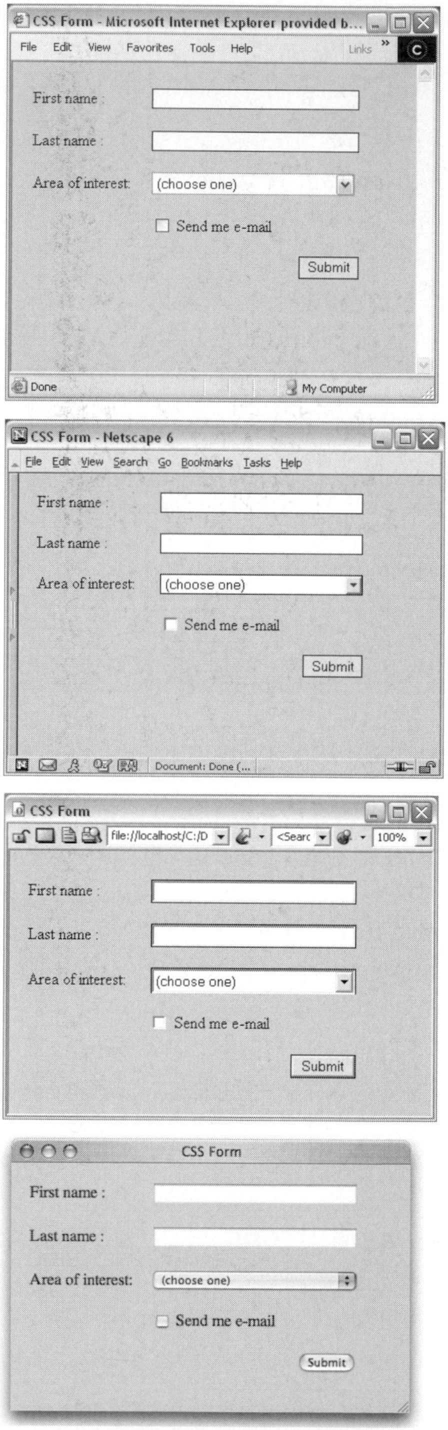

- **Text boxes**—Text fields and text areas can benefit from having borders and backgrounds applied, type properties specified for their input, and width controlled (use absolute sizes only).

- **Buttons**—You can use borders and backgrounds to control the appearance of buttons such as Submit and Reset. Width and height can also be used to control size (use absolute sizes only), although be careful that text display isn't chopped off.

- **List/menus**—Use borders, backgrounds, and type properties to control drop-down menus and lists in forms. You can also assign width (absolute sizes only), but be careful not to truncate text display.

- **Radio buttons/check boxes**—Not much can be done with these elements. Backgrounds and borders can be applied, but the effect isn't very nice.

- **Labels**—If you're using the label tag for all text labeling of form elements (and you should be, for accessibility!), you can use any CSS formatting that you would apply to any text elements on a page.

When designing style sheets for your form elements, it's better to apply custom classes and contextual selectors than to redefine tags. Different form elements use different tags, so it's easier to apply one class to input, select, and textarea tags than to redefine all three. The input tag, in particular, is used for so many different kinds of form elements (text fields, radio buttons, check boxes, buttons) that redefining this tag to suit each kind of element at once is difficult. Borders and backgrounds, for instance, work on text fields and buttons but don't apply nicely to radio buttons and check boxes.

Just because it's possible doesn't mean that it's always a good thing to do it. Don't forget that the primary purpose of forms is to be useful and easy to fill out. Colored backgrounds and other odd effects can interfere with that.

Using Images as Buttons

If you don't like the way the browser displays your Submit and Reset buttons, and if CSS doesn't give you enough options, you can always use image buttons instead (see Figure 9.19). To do this in Dreamweaver, use

the Image Field object. When you choose this object, Dreamweaver presents you with a standard Select File dialog box to choose a GIF or JPEG image. But the image is inserted into your form as an input tag, with code like this:

```
<input type="image" name="imageField" border="0" src=
➥"myCloseButton.gif">
```

FIGURE 9.19
A form with images substituted for the Submit button.

If you have accessibility options for form elements turned on, the standard Input Accessibility Options dialog box appears. As with regular buttons, you don't have to supply a label because the button will be its own label. But be sure to supply alt text for your image button, as you would with any image. When the image button is selected, the Image Field Property Inspector appears (see Figure 9.20).

FIGURE 9.20
The Image Field Property Inspector.

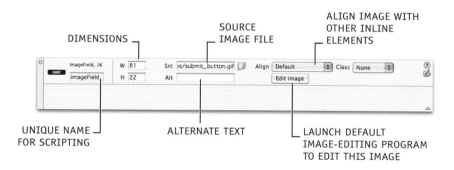

EXERCISE 9.2

Dress Up a Form with CSS Formatting

In this exercise, you'll format the form created in the previous exercise using CSS styles to control form elements' appearance.

1.   Open **evalform.html** from the **chapter_9** folder. It already has CSS styles governing text formatting. You'll be adding styles to govern form elements.

2. In the CSS Styles panel, click the New Style button. When the New Style dialog box opens, choose to create a custom class called .fieldborder, to be defined in the formstyles.css external document. Click OK to open the CSS Style Definition dialog box.

   Go to the Border category. Leave Same for All Options selected and choose to create a solid 1-pixel black border. Click OK to close the dialog box.

3. Select the first text field and, using the Property Inspector's Class drop-down menu, assign the fieldborder class. Repeat this procedure for the second text field, the list/menu, and the Reset and Submit buttons.

4. Preview the results in as many browsers as you can to see how the formatting is supported.

The Ins and Outs of Form Processing

Forms collect information and pass it along for processing. That's the mysterious "back end" of web development that front-end designers usually know nothing about. But it's important, even for front-end folks, to get a sense of how everything fits together and to build better and more efficient forms.

Understanding the *action* Attribute

It all starts with that age-old question: What happens to forms when they're submitted? When a user presses the Submit button, the browser looks in the form tag for an action attribute. The action attribute holds the address of a receiving file that can presumably do something to process the form's input, like this:

```
<form name="theForm" action="http://www.mysite.com/cgi-bin/
➥myscript.cgi" method="GET">
```

The browser sends that information to that receiving file's address using one of two methods:

- With the GET method, the browser adds the information to the end of the receiving file's address as URL parameters, like this:

  ```
  http://www.mysite.com/cgi-bin/myscript.cgi?fname=Fred&lname=
  ➥Smith&favcolor=blue
  ```

- With the POST method, the browser sends the information as a separate packet of information

The POST method is more secure and can transmit larger amounts of data. GET is often used by search engines and for other nonsecure purposes.

Even though the form is usually submitted to a script file, it doesn't have to be. It can be submitted to any file. A form tag like this

```
<form name="myForm" action="thankyou.html" method="get">
```

will send the information to a "thank you" page, and because that's a regular HTML page, it will display in the browser window. The "thank you" page might contain JavaScript for processing the information, or it might just ignore the information and display as any normal web page would.

A form tag like this

```
<form name="myForm" action="mailto:laura@rocketlaura.com">
```

will send the form's information to an email address, which will cause the user's email program to send the named recipient a message containing all of the form data.

The mailto solution is very easy to implement but is very limited. If a user is on a machine that doesn't have a default email client installed (at the library or a cybercafe, for instance), the form will not send, but it will also not alert the user that there's a problem. Internet Explorer displays a security warning when the user submits the form, alerting the user that the submission method is open to being read by third parties. This is enough to scare quite a few users into hitting the Cancel button. In other browsers, the email-composition window will open, but nothing will be filled in.

Client-Side Form Processing with the Set Text of Text Field and Change Property Behaviors

Forms can also partake of purely client-side scripting (for example, JavaScript carried out by the browser). Interacting with form elements—choosing items from a drop-down menu, selecting a check box, and so on—can trigger JavaScript behaviors. And form elements can be dynamically updated by a JavaScript without having to reload the entire page.

Together, these two facts make it possible to create forms that adapt their information display as the user is interacting with them.

In Dreamweaver, the Set Text of Text Field and Change Property behaviors give you access to some of this client-side processing. Set Text of Text Field lets you dynamically change the text in any of your form's text fields. With Change Property, you not only can change text in a text field or area, but you also can change the selected item in a drop-down menu or change the selected state of radio buttons and check boxes.

To use the Set Text of Text Field behavior, start by creating a form with at least one text field that you want to change. Next, select the page element that you want to trigger the change. This can be another form element, linked text, an image, or any other element that can have behaviors attached to it. From the Behaviors panel Actions list, choose Set Text > Set Text of Text Field. When the dialog box appears (see Figure 9.21), enter any text that you want to appear there.

FIGURE 9.21
The Set Text of Text
Field dialog box.

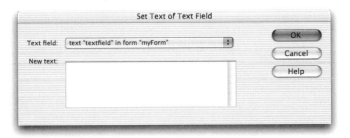

The text that you enter doesn't have to be plain old text. Any valid JavaScript function call, property, global variable, or other expression can also be embedded in the text. A JavaScript expression must be placed inside braces ({}). So, an expression like this:

```
The URL for this page is {window.location}
```

would display text like this:

```
The URL for this page is http://www.mysite.com/mypage.html
```

To use the Change Property behavior, Start by creating a form with either a text field, a text area, a list/menu, a radio group, or a check box that you want to dynamically change. Next, select the page element that you

want to trigger the change. From the Behaviors panel Actions list, choose Change Property.

When the dialog box appears (see Figure 9.22), it has a variety of options to choose from because this is a generic behavior that can be used on more than just form elements. From the Type of Object menu, choose the type of form element you want to change. From the Named Object list, choose the particular element that you want to change. The Property list then gives you a choice of all changeable properties for this element, as supported by different browsers. Luckily, all but the oldest browsers support changing basic properties of form elements. For different form elements, here are your options:

- For check boxes and radio buttons, the checked property determines whether the item is selected. To change this, enter **true** or **false** in the Value field at the bottom of the dialog box.

- For text fields, password fields, and text areas, the value property determines what text appears. To change this, enter the text that you want to appear in the Value field at the bottom of the dialog box. Unlike the Set Text of Text Field behavior, JavaScript expressions entered in the value field aren't evaluated.

- For select elements (for example, list/menus), the selectedIndex property determines which item in the list is selected. It works like this: Each item in the list has its own index number, starting from 0 for the first item. Determine the index number of the item that you want to have selected, and enter it in the Value field at the bottom of the dialog box.

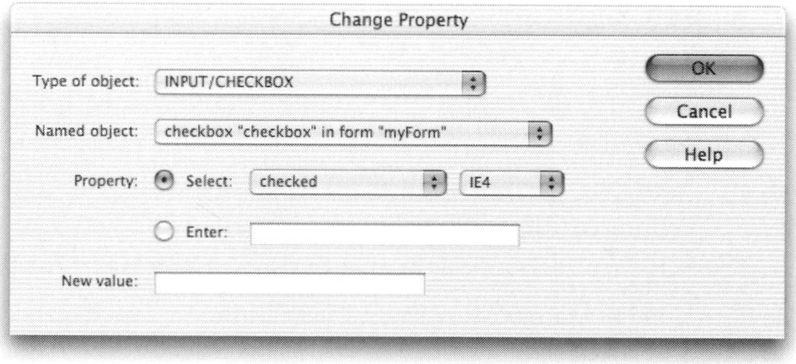

FIGURE 9.22

The dialog box for the Change Property behavior, with form element property changes showing.

EXERCISE 9.3

Using the Set Text of Text Field Behavior

In this quick exercise, you'll get a chance to see some more client-side form processing. You'll also see how form elements can be used to trigger behaviors. If you haven't done so already, download the **chapter_9** folder from the book's website to your hard drive and define a site called Chapter 9, using that as the local folder.

1. In the **chapter_9** folder, open **mathpage.html** and examine it. You'll see that it contains a form with several text fields and a Submit button (see Figure 9.23). Select each form field; you'll see that their names are num1, num2, and finalnum. Select the form; you'll see that its name is myForm. These are all important bits of information for processing the script.

   Can you guess what the game is? The user should be able to type two numbers in the top two fields, click the button, and get a result.

FIGURE 9.23
The mathpage.html form, ready to do some calculating.

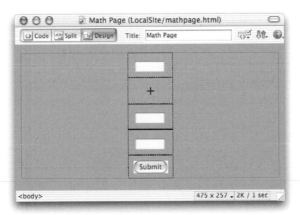

2. This form requires some processing of information, but it doesn't need to talk to a web server. It doesn't need to call an actions page, either. So, it doesn't need a Submit button. Select the Submit button and, in the Property Inspector, change its Action from Submit to None. You've just canceled the Submit button's built-in functionality. Now change its value to Calculate.

3. When the user clicks the Calculate button, the finalnum text field should display the result of adding the previous two fields. The Calculate button needs to trigger the Set Text of Text Field behavior.

   Select the Calculate button. In the Behaviors panel, click the + and choose Set Text > Set Text of Text Field from the Actions list. When the dialog box opens, enter the following:

   `{myForm.num1.value + myForm.num2.value}`

   The brackets indicate that you're entering a JavaScript expression. The expression tells the browser to add the values of the num1 and num2 fields, within myForm. Click OK to close the dialog box.

4. In the Behaviors panel, double-check the behavior's event handler. It should be onClick. If it's anything else, change it.

4. Try it out in a browser. Enter two numbers in the top fields and click the Calculate button. There's some client-side form processing in action and dynamic updating of form elements.

EXERCISE 9.4

Using Change Property to Dynamically Update a Form

In this exercise, you'll tweak the Supersite form you built earlier in this chapter. When the user changes one form element, you'll use that to trigger changes in other form elements.

1. Start by opening the **evalform.html** file that you worked on earlier. The check boxes include an All of the Above option. Presumably, if the user checks this option, the three check boxes above it should also be checked.

   Select the All check box (the one labeled All of the Above). In the Behaviors panel, click the + button and choose Change Property from the Actions list. When the dialog box appears, choose Input/Check Box for the Type of object, and the dw check box for the Name of Object. The property to change should default to checked. In the drop-down menu of target browsers, choose IE4. In the New Value field at the bottom of the dialog box, enter **true** (see Figure 9.24). Click OK to close the dialog box.

FIGURE 9.24
Using the Change
Property behavior to
change the checked
property of one check
box, triggered by
another check box.

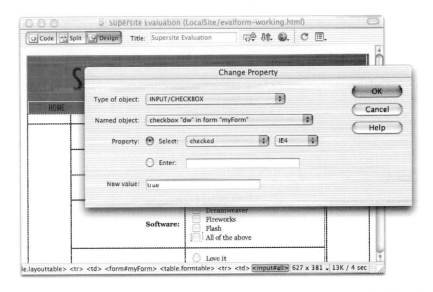

2. When the behavior is inserted, note the event handler specified in the Behaviors panel. It should be `onClick`.

3. Try it out in the browser. Clicking the All of the Above check box not only checks it, but it also checks the Dreamweaver check box.

4. Repeat the procedure two more times, adding two more instances of the Change Property behavior to the All check box to change the Fireworks and Flash check boxes.

5. Now, if you use all of that software, you must be a power user. So how about also changing the userlevel List/Menu? Again, select the All check box and add a new Change Property behavior. This time, choose Select for the object type, userlevel for the object name, and `selectedIndex` for the property. Leave the browser drop-down menu at IE4. The Power User option is the fifth item in the list, which gives it an index number of 4 (counting starts from 0, remember). So, enter 4 in the New Value field (see Figure 9.25). Click OK to close the dialog box.

6. Try this out in a browser. Checking the All of the Above button turns on all other check boxes and sets the User Level drop-down menu to Power User. That's how form elements can dynamically update themselves based on user input.

FIGURE 9.25
Using the Change
Property to change
the selected item in
a drop-down menu.

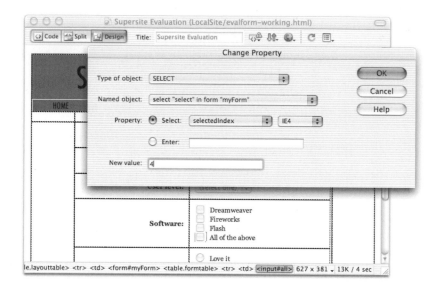

Form Validation with the Validate Form Behavior

There's no point in submitting a form if vital information is missing or incorrectly entered. In fact, depending on the script that will be processing the form and how much error-checking it has built in, missing information might cause errors on the server. The most efficient course of action is to make sure all required form entries are present and valid before submitting the form. This is generally done using a JavaScript that executes when the user clicks the Submit button. The process is called *form validation*.

Dreamweaver's Validate Form behavior lets you specify that certain fields must be filled in and/or must include a certain kind of content (such as a number or email address) before the form is considered valid. To use the behavior, do this:

1. First, completely design your form and make sure all form fields have been named.

2. You can attach the behavior to the form itself or to the Submit button. To attach the behavior to the form, put the insertion point inside the form and use the Tag Selector to select the form tag. To attach the behavior to the Submit button, select the Submit button.

3. In the Behaviors panel, click + and choose the Validate Form behavior from the Actions list. In the dialog box that appears (see Figure 9.26), all text fields in your form are listed by name. For each field, select the field and choose whether it's required and whether it requires a specific kind of information. When you're done, click OK to close the dialog box.

4. If you chose to attach the behavior to the form, make sure the Behaviors panel shows that the behavior is added to the onSubmit event handler. If you attached it to the Submit button, make sure the behavior is added to the onClick event handler.

FIGURE 9.26
The Validate Form behavior dialog box.

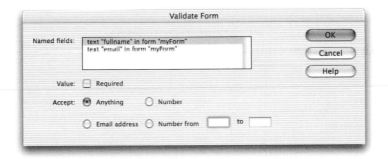

Regardless of where you attached the behavior, it will execute when the Submit button is clicked, before the form is submitted. If there's a problem, it will stop the form from being submitted and display an error message (see Figure 9.27).

FIGURE 9.27
An invalid form (missing required information) causes the Validate Form behavior to display an alert message like this one.

You can test the Validate Form behavior offline by previewing it in the browser because it gets executed by the browser. Only if the form is valid will the browser try to submit it.

The behavior validates only text fields, not drop-down lists or any other form element.

Unless you're very comfortable with JavaScript, you probably don't want to go messing around with how the Validate Form behavior behaves. But as long as you're a careful typist, you can customize the text of the alert message that appears when a form is invalid. Go to Code view, find the `MM_validateForm()` function, and within that find the line of code that looks like this:

```
} if (errors) alert('The following error(s) occurred:
➥\n'+errors);
```

You can enter your own brief statement in place of the text marked in bold here. If your message contains any apostrophes or single or double quotes, however, you'll need to escape them by typing a backward slash (\) in front of them:

```
} if (errors) alert('Your form can\'t be submitted because:
➥\n'+errors);
```

Your customized message should stay in place even if you edit the behavior.

EXERCISE 9.5

Attaching the Validate Form Behavior to the Submit Button

In this exercise, you attach the Validate Form behavior to the form's Submit button to check the text fields in your form before submitting it to the server. This exercise builds on Exercises 11.1 and 11.2, which should be completed before you proceed with this exercise.

If you haven't done so yet, download the **chapter_09** folder from the book's website to your hard drive. Define a site called Chapter 9, with this folder as the local root folder.

1.   Open your **evalform.html** document from Exercise 11.1. Select the Submit button at the bottom of the form.

2.   In the Behaviors panel, click the plus (+) button and, from the Actions list, choose Validate Form. This opens the Validate Form dialog box.

3.   Select the text field you named fullname. Select Required so that the field has to contain some data. From the Accept options, select Anything.

4. Then select the text field you named email. Again, select Required. This time, however, from the Accept options, select Email Address. This requires that this field at least contain an at sign (@) to be accepted.

5. Click OK to insert the behavior.

6. Save the document and preview it in a browser. You can test the form, to some extent, without having it actually connected to a script; when you press Submit, the browser will return an error message because you haven't specified a place to submit the data. Before you receive that error message, however, you can observe the Validate Form behavior in action. Try submitting the form without filling in a name; you should get an error message in the form of a small gray browser pop-up box. Then try it with a name filled in, but with an invalid email address containing no at sign (@); you should get another error message.

SUMMARY

Forms are an important part of the web developer's toolkit, crucial to exchanging information with site visitors. In this chapter, we covered how forms work to capture data on the web and process it, as well as the basics of the HTML code used to build forms, and how to use Dreamweaver to quickly add forms and form elements to an HTML document. We looked at making forms accessible, how to dress them up with CSS, and how JavaScript behaviors can enhance their functionality.

Of course, this is only the front end of form development. The back end—connecting the form to the application needed to process it—is obviously crucial. You're encouraged to see this book's chapters on using server-side languages (Chapters 21–26) and to look into using the many available Perl CGI scripts and the wealth of information on CGI on the web.

```
<head>
<style type="text/css">
body {background-color: red}
p {text-align: right; color: white}
</style>
</head>
<body>
```

CHAPTER 10

DESIGNING FRAME-BASED PAGES

FRAMES PROVIDE THE WEB DEVELOPER WITH A PAGE-DESIGN TOOL VERY different from any other. With frames, rectangular areas of a page can be specified as distinct "windows" into which content can be loaded and reloaded, independent of the rest of the page.

Many developers love frames for the design freedom they allow and the solid browser support behind them. Using frames, it's possible to create easy-to-maintain, complex, interactive interfaces that could otherwise be built only from less reliable and more difficult scripting methods. Many developers hate frames, citing usability issues such as the inability to bookmark specific pages in a frameset and the difficulty some users have printing framed pages, as well as the extra challenges frame-based websites present during authoring.

This chapter goes over the basics of working with frames in the browser and in Dreamweaver MX 2004, and then looks at specific frame-related topics, such as making your frames accessible, making them searchable, and working smart to deal with other frame-usability issues. We also take a look at iframes.

FRAME BASICS

When you view a frame-based page in the browser, what you're really seeing is several HTML documents at once, loaded into the individual *frames* of a *frameset*. Figure 10.1 shows a frame-based page as it appears in the browser, along with a peek at its actual frameset structure.

FIGURE 10.1

A basic frame page.

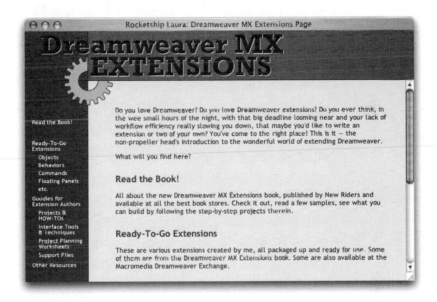

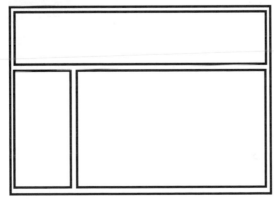

Frames in the Browser

The frameset page contains no body tag. Instead, it consists of a frameset tag with several frame tags nested inside it, indicating how the page should be divided and what document should appear in each frame. The basic code structure looks like this:

```
<frameset cols="80,*">
    <frame src="navbar.html" name="navFrame">
    <frame src="intro.html" name="mainFrame">
</frameset>
```

Any HTML page can appear in the frames of the frameset. No special coding is required for these pages.

Framesets can also contain other frameset tags, to create more complex layouts:

```
<frameset cols="80,*">
    <frame src="navbar.html" name="navFrame">
    <frameset rows="134,*">
        <frame src="banner.html" name="titleFrame">
        <frame src="intro.html" name="mainFrame">
    </frameset>
</frameset>
```

The frameset and frame tags are part of the HTML 4 specification and have been supported by browsers starting with IE3 and NN4. Tables 10.1 and 10.2 list commonly assigned attributes for each tag.

TABLE 10.1 ## Commonly Assigned Attributes of the *frameset* Tag

Attribute Name	Description	Required?	Values
name id	Used for identification	No	Text string.
cols rows	Defines the number of columns or rows in the frameset	Yes	Comma-separated list, with one entry for each column or row. Each list element can be a pixel or percent value, or * for a relative value.

continues

TABLE 10.1   ## Commonly Assigned Attributes of the *frameset* Tag *continued*

Attribute Name	Description	Required?	Values
framespacing	Specifies the amount of space between frames (similar to cell spacing in a table)	No	Number of pixels.
frameborder	Specifies whether to display a border between frames	No	yes/no.
border	Specifies the width of the border between frames	No	Number of pixels.

TABLE 10.2   ## Commonly Assigned Attributes of the *frame* Tag

Attribute Name	Description	Required?	Values
name id	Used for identification	No	Text string
src	Specifies the page to display in this frame	Yes	URL
frameborder	Specifies whether to display a border around this frame	No	yes/no
bordercolor	Specifies the color of the border	No	Color
marginwidth marginheight	Specifies the gutter space between the frame edge and its content (similar to cell padding in a table cell)	No	Number of pixels
noresize	Specifies whether the user will be allowed to resize the frame (frames are resizable only if the borders are visible)	No	—
scrolling	Specifies whether scrollbars will appear around the frame	No	yes/no/auto

Linking within framesets requires the use of the target attribute as part of the link:

`<a href="mypage.html" target="mainFrame">`

Table 10.3 lists the various targets that can be specified in links.

TABLE 10.3 **Possible Target Values for Use with Frameset Navigation**

Target Value	Description	Example
The name of any frame in the current frameset	Opens the specified document in the named frame.	`<a href="mypage.html"` ↪`target="mainFrame">`
_top	Replaces all framesets, opening the document at the top level of the browser window.	`<a href="mypage.html"` ↪`target="_top">`
_parent	Used within nested framesets, replaces the frameset that contains the link. This can be the top frameset or a nested frameset.	`<a href="mypage.html"` ↪`target="_parent">`
_self	Opens the document in the same frame that contains the link (same as using no target).	`<a href="mypage.html"` ↪`target="_self">`
_blank	Opens the document in a new browser window outside of the parent frameset.	`<a href="mypage.html"` ↪`target="_blank">`

Frames in Dreamweaver

The coding for frames is not difficult, but like so much in HTML, frames can be cumbersome to deal with if you're just working with code. The Dreamweaver visual environment lets you easily create entire multi-document framesets and view and manage your framesets and framed pages with relative ease.

Creating Frames

In Dreamweaver, frame-based pages can be created manually or by using one of the prebuilt framesets that ship with the program. To create a frame-based page manually, follow these steps:

1. Create or open a document that has no framesets in it.

2. Choose Modify > Frameset > Split Frame Left, Split Frame Right, Split Frame Up, or Split Frame Down.

When you have a frameset created, you can further divide it by choosing the splitting commands again or by Alt/Opt-dragging from a frame edge.

To build a page using one of the prebuilt framesets in Dreamweaver, do one of the following:

- Choose File > New and, in the New Document dialog box, on the General tab, choose from the Framesets category.

- Create or open a document and choose one of the Frame objects in the HTML Insert bar; or, choose Insert > HTML > Frames > [any frameset].

Frames that Dreamweaver builds for you have many coding niceties already built in, such as setting scrolling and resize properties. Frames that you build yourself do not, so you have to be more careful to assign their properties wisely.

Working with Frames

The hardest aspect of working with frames is that you're always working on multiple pages at once (the frameset and the framed pages). Dreamweaver offers a variety of tools to make this easier for you, including the Property Inspector, the Frames panel (available under Window > Frames), and the Tag Selector (at the bottom of the Document window).

- **Frames panel (see Figure 10.2)**—This panel always gives you a visual representation of the frames in your current frameset. Clicking anywhere in the Frames panel activates the frameset document. Clicking in a particular frame in the panel selects that `frame` tag. Clicking the black border around the frames selects the `frameset` tag.

FIGURE 10.2
The Frames panel, diagramming a nested frameset.

- **Tag Selector (see Figure 10.3)**—This handy item always tells you which portion of which open document you have selected. If the Tag Selector lists the frameset, frame, or noframes tags, you are working on the frameset document. If it lists only the body tag and its contents, you're working on one of the framed pages.

FIGURE 10.3
The Tag Selector, with a frame element in a frameset selected.

- **Property Inspector (see Figures 10.4 and 10.5)**—As always in Dreamweaver, use the Property Inspector to assign properties for whatever element is selected. For the most part, the inspector is self-explanatory. The method for setting frameset row and col properties, however, deserves a note. When a frameset tag is selected, the proxy icon on the right indicates how many rows or columns the frameset has been divided into. To set the size of that row or column, click it in the proxy and set the Value and Units fields.

FIGURE 10.4
The Frameset Property Inspector.

FIGURE 10.5
The Frame Property Inspector.

How Frameset Resizing Works

What happens when the browser window resizes? All framesets must fill the entire browser window. If you build your frameset the manual way (instead of using the prebuilt framesets), you are responsible for making sure that this happens.

If you want all rows or columns in your frameset to resize proportionally when the browser window resizes, set Units for all rows or columns in the frameset to Percent. You must also make sure that the numbers in the Value fields add up to 100% for the frameset.

If you want one row or column to stretch and others to remain fixed, set Units for the fixed rows or columns to Pixels and choose a number for the value. For flexible rows or columns, set Units to Relative and don't assign a value. At least one row or column must have a Relative value, or the frameset won't resize properly!

After you've made these unit/value assignments in the Property Inspector, you can safely resize frames by dragging their borders in the Document window.

Linking to Frames

Any time you want a linked page to appear within a specific frame or browser window, the link should be targeted. In Dreamweaver, use the Property Inspector to assign targets.

WORKING SMART WITH FRAMES

So much for the basics. Now for the fun stuff. What can you do to really take advantage of frames, and how can Dreamweaver help you? The following sections discuss some common strategies for dealing with frame usability and accessibility issues, as well as some handy uses for frames that you might not have thought of.

Making Your Frames Accessible

Usability experts might argue about the dangers and advantages of frames, but frames offer no more accessibility issues than any other navigation or layout method.

According to Section 508, § 1194.22(i):

> Frames shall be titled with text that facilitates identification and navigation.

What does this mean in practical terms? Screen readers and other text-based browsers present a frame-based web page by listing the titles or names of the frames available, and allowing users to navigate between the frames. So it's crucial to supply meaningful information here. How do you do this?

For each frame tag in the frameset document, do the following:

- Use the `name` attribute to identify the frame's purpose.

- Use the `title` attribute to identify the frame's purpose (this can be the same as the `name` attribute or a slightly longer, more descriptive version of it).

Within each HTML document that will appear in a frame, do this:

- Use the `title` tag to describe the contents of this page.

- Where appropriate, start the body content with a descriptive heading.

Using these guidelines, the basic code for an accessible frameset document might look like this:

```
<frameset cols="80,*">
    <frame src="navbar.htm" name="navigationBar" title=
    ➥"Navigation Bar">
    <frame src="main.htm" name="mainContent"  name="Main
    ➥Content">
</frameset>
```

The relevant code for one of the framed documents (main.htm, for instance), might look like this:

```
<html>
<head>
    <title>Walt's Widget World: Overview of
    ➥Widgetizers</title>
</head>
<body>
    <h1>Overview of Widgetizers</h1>
    [etc]
</body>
</html>
```

Making Frames Accessible in Dreamweaver

Dreamweaver's accessibility tools make it easy to build accessible framesets every time. But you do have to remember to use them!

Before the Fact: Set Accessibility Options

Before you create your frameset, make sure you have accessibility options for Frames turned on (Edit > Preferences/Accessibility). When this is enabled, the next time you choose a Frame object from the Insert bar or use the New Document dialog box to create a frameset, or choose one of the Insert > HTML > Framesets commands to insert a prebuilt frameset, you'll be presented with a dialog box letting you assign a title attribute for each frame in the frameset (see Figure 10.6). Note that this dialog box assigns the title attribute for the frame tag. This is not the same as assigning a page title for documents within the frameset. Note also that you can't alter the frame names within this dialog box—you can change only the titles.

FIGURE 10.6
The Frame Tag Accessibility Attributes dialog box in action.

If you create your frames manually (using one of the Modify > Frameset > Split commands), this dialog box won't appear.

After the Fact: Tweak Existing Framesets

After you've created your frameset—whether you've used Dreamweaver frame objects or defined your frameset manually—use the Property Inspector, the Selection Inspector, or the Edit Tag command to change properties as needed.

- **Use the name attribute wisely.** Names such as `leftFrame` or `bottomFrame` might be fine and dandy for use in link targets, as in this code:

  ```
  <a href="main.htm" target="topFrame">
  ```

  But names like this don't do anything to describe the frame's purpose in the layout, so they aren't very accessible. Instead, use names such as `navigationBar`, `titleBanner`, or `mainContent`. When you let Dreamweaver create frames for you, the default frame names aren't very descriptive. After all, Dreamweaver doesn't know which frame you'll be using as the navigation bar or title banner. So, after Dreamweaver has built your frameset, take a few moments to rename the frames. You can use the Property Inspector, the Selection Inspector, or the Edit Tag command for this.

- **Supply titles**—If you didn't have accessibility options for frames enabled before you started, or if you created your frameset manually, your frames still need titles. To do this, use the Tag Selector to select a frame tag and find the `title` attribute in the Attributes tab of the Tag Inspector (CSS/Accessibility category). You can also switch to Code view and right-click a frame tag, and choose Edit Tag to open the Edit Tag dialog box (Style Sheet/Accessibility category). Figure 10.7 shows these two methods of assigning frame titles.

- **Set page titles and headings (where appropriate)**—Do this in the individual documents that will appear in the frameset. All pages should have their `title` tag set, using Modify > Page Properties or the Page Title field in the Document toolbar. Including a heading in the text is more of a suggested guideline than a required rule, and it really applies only to content page. (When is the last time you saw a frameset in which the navigation frame started with a big h1-level heading that said Navigation?)

FIGURE 10.7
Setting a frame title
in the Edit Tag dialog
box and Tag
Inspector.

Making Your Frames Searchable

One of the oldest arguments against using frames is that search engines
can't properly search them. Frameset documents have no body tag, and
search engines don't read frame tags. So, any text or links contained in
your framed pages will never be found. If you want anybody to find your
website, that's a bit of a deal-breaker! But it isn't entirely accurate. You
can easily make your framesets searchable by utilizing the noframes tag,
which provides body content for any device that can't read frame tags.
The code looks like this:

```
<frameset cols="80,*">
   <frame src="navbar.html" name="navFrame">
   <frame src="intro.html" name="mainFrame">
</frameset>
<noframes>
   <body>
```

```
[searchable body content goes here]
    </body>
</noframes>
```

When frames first came on the scene and not all browsers supported them, web authors often put messages in the `noframes` content along the lines of "Your browser doesn't support frames, so you can't see our website." These days, smart designers use `noframes` to target search engines.

Working with *noframes* Content in Dreamweaver

Dreamweaver automatically adds a `noframes` tag to every frameset it builds—you just need to take advantage of it. Access `noframes` content this way:

1. Open a frameset document and make sure you're in Design view.

2. Choose Modify > Frameset > Edit NoFrames Content.

The Document window changes to display the body section within the `noframes` tag, and you're ready to use any Dreamweaver tools to construct alternate page content for the frame-less (see Figure 10.8). The Tag Selector displays the `noframes` tag.

FIGURE 10.8
Editing noframes content in Design view.

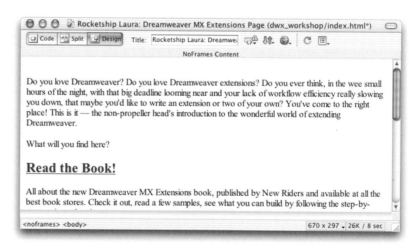

When you're done working on your `noframes` content, choose Modify > Frameset > Edit NoFrames Content again to toggle back into regular frame-viewing mode.

You can also switch to noframes content if you're working in Code view by putting the insertion point within the noframes tag and then switching back to Design view.

What to Include in *noframes* Content

Search engines look through keywords and descriptions, page titles, and body content, and they follow links from the main page to all other pages in your site. Keywords, descriptions, and page titles are stored in the head section of the HTML document, so they work the same in frameset documents as they do in any document. But you want to put body content and links in your noframes area for the search engines to find. Text content is the most important because search engines don't look at images, but they do pay attention to image filenames and alt text.

To quickly get all relevant content from your framed pages into the noframes area, you can do this:

For more on keywords, descriptions, and how to target search engines, see the section "Optimizing for Search Engines" in Chapter 7, "Utilizing Head Content."

1. In regular (frames) view, click inside one of your framed pages and choose Edit > Copy.

2. Choose Modify > Frameset > Edit NoFrames Content to switch to noframes view.

3. Edit > Paste.

4. Switch back to regular view and repeat this procedure for all frames in your frameset. Remember, as long as you have included navigation links in your noframes content, the search engine will be able to navigate through the rest of your site from here.

Navigating Within Frames

As long as you're careful to target your links properly, setting up basic navigation within framesets is easy. But you can employ several strategies to dress up your framesets beyond the basics—and Dreamweaver, as always, can help you.

Changing Multiple Frames at Once

The user clicks a link in the navigation frame and a new page appears in the content frame. But what if you want that one user click to load a new

page in the content frame and the banner frame? Sometimes you just need to change two frames at once, and the regular old anchor tag just isn't up to it. You need a little JavaScript to help out. The Dreamweaver Go To URL behavior lets you do it quickly and easily. Do it this way:

1. Open a frameset document with at least three frames (one to hold the navigation and two to be changed). Look at the Frames panel to remind yourself what the three frames are named. You'll need this information shortly.

2. Select the graphic or text that will become the link.

3. In the Property Inspector's Link field, enter **javascript:;** to create a null link (a link that goes nowhere).

4. With the link still selected, open the Behaviors panel (Window > Behaviors) and click the + to assign the Go to URL behavior.

5. When the Go to URL dialog box appears, all frames in your document will be listed. Select the first frame that you want to change (this is why it's important that you know what your frame names are) and click the Browse button to select the new page that should appear in that frame. Note that an asterisk now appears next to that frame name in the dialog box, indicating that you've set a new URL to appear there.

6. Do the same for the second frame that you want to change. Select it in the list and click Browse to set the link. If you want to change more than just two frames, keep selecting frame names and setting links.

7. When you're done, click OK to close the dialog box. That's it!

After you've inserted this behavior, if you examine your document in Code view, you'll see that Dreamweaver has inserted an MM_goToURL() function, which resets the page in each specified frame by changing that frame's location.

Navigating to Specific Pages Within Framesets

One of the usability issues with frame-based websites is that visitors can't bookmark specific pages within a frameset; they can bookmark only the frameset itself. This can be very frustrating, especially in large, information-rich sites where visitors want to head straight for certain

content pages. Once again, it's JavaScript and the `location` object to the rescue, although for this you have no handy Dreamweaver behavior to fall back on.

How It Works

When you're linking to a specific page in a frameset, you essentially want the link to say, "Load index.html (the frameset page) and then also put catalog.html (the desired content page) in the content frame." You can do this by adding a URL parameter to the link, like this:

```
<a href="index.html?page=content.html">
```

The URL parameter is everything that appears after the ? in the path. Of course, the browser doesn't know what `page=content.html` means. So, you then have to add some JavaScript to the framework page telling the browser that whatever page is named in the URL parameter should appear in the content frame.

Setting up the frameset document to parse URL parameters is the hardest part of the procedure. It involves creating the JavaScript that loads different content pages as needed. This JavaScript must be added as a function in the head section and a function call attached to the body tag. In Dreamweaver, do it this way:

1. Open the frameset document.

2. Examine the Frames panel to see what your frames are named. In particular, note the name of the frame that all content pages will be loaded into.

3. Select the frameset (make sure it's showing as bold in the Tag Selector at the bottom of the Document window).

4. Choose View > Head Content so that the gray head content area appears at the top of the Design view portion of the Document window. Click inside this area to activate it so Dreamweaver knows that you want to insert your first batch of code here.

5. In the HTML Insert bar, choose the Script object. When the Script dialog box opens, make sure the language is set to JavaScript and enter the following code in the Content field (see Figure 10.9):

```
<!--
function loadPage(){
var myParameters=window.location.search;
if (myParameters==""){
   return;
}
var contentPage=myParameters.substring(myParameters.indexOf
➡("=")+1,myParameters.length);
mainFrame.location.replace(contentPage);
}
//-->
```

FIGURE 10.9

Inserting a function that will use a URL parameter to determine frame content.

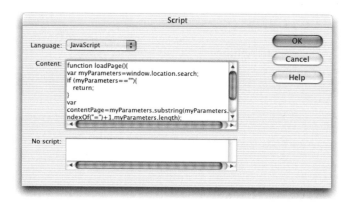

For more on the Script object, see the section "Writing JavaScript in Dreamweaver" in Chapter 27, "Writing Code in Dreamweaver."

This code collects any URL parameters in a variable called myParameters. It then figures out what filename appears after the equals sign in the parameter, and it sets the location of a frame called mainFrame to that filename. In your code, you'll want to substitute the name of your content frame for mainFrame before proceeding.

When you've checked your code and made sure that the correct frame name is in place, click OK to close the dialog box. A new script icon appears in the head content area of the document window.

6. This function must execute when the frameset is loaded, which means that the `frameset` tag needs to call it `onLoad`. With frameset selected, choose Modify > Edit Tag. When the Edit Tag dialog box opens, go to the Events > onLoad category. Select the `onLoad` event and enter the following in the content area (see Figure 10.10):

   ```
   loadPage()
   ```

FIGURE 10.10
Inserting the function call that will execute the `loadPage()` function.

7. When you're done, click OK to close the Edit Tag dialog box.

When this code is in place, all you need to do is access it from any page that links to the frameset. Let's say that your main frameset page is called index.html, and you want it to load with a page called catalog.html in the content frame. The URL that appears in the browser's address field needs to say something like this:

```
http://mydomain.com/index.html?page=catalog.html
```

You can try this out by previewing your frameset page in the browser and manually typing in the question mark and URL parameter. (If the specified page doesn't automatically load, double-check the JavaScript code that you entered in your script against the code listed here.)

To link to the frameset from another page in your site, do this:

1. In Dreamweaver, open the page that will link to your frameset. Select the text or graphic that should link to the desired page.

2. In the Property Inspector, click the Browse button that appears next to the Link field. Browse to your frameset document.

3. Before closing the Select File dialog box, click the Parameters button. Another dialog box opens. Enter the page for the parameter name, and enter the name of the content page as its value (see Figure 10.11).

FIGURE 10.11
Using the Parameters dialog box to assign a URL parameter for frame navigation.

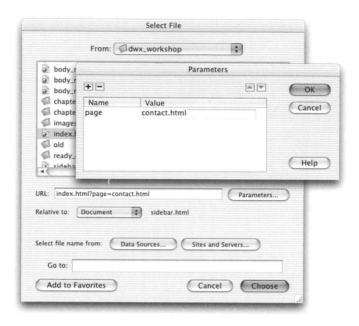

4. Click OK to close the Parameters dialog box, and choose to close the main dialog box. In the Property Inspector, the Link field should now contain the URL and its parameters, separated by a question mark.

Note that you don't have to browse to create your URL and parameters if you don't want to. If you're comfortable typing things in by hand and understand the rules of URL parameters, you can just type into the Link field. (The rules are these: No spaces around the question mark or equals sign, and no quotation marks around the value.)

Also note that all of the previous samples assume that all files are in the same folder, although this isn't always the case. The URL parameter must contain an absolute URL or a URL relative to the frameset document. Dreamweaver doesn't help you figure that out. If your catalog page is in a subfolder called departments, for instance, the finished link will look like this:

```
index.html?page=departments/catalog.html
```

Make It a Snippet!

If you use frames with any regularity, you might want to save the loadPage() function as a snippet for future insertion. Remember,

though, that the function call must also be inserted every time this function is used, and the snippet will insert only the main function. You'll have to add the function call manually. You can do this in the Behaviors panel like this:

1. In the Tag Selector, select the **body** tag.

2. In the Behaviors panel, click the two-column display icon so all events display.

3. Find the onLoad event. In the column next to it, type **loadPage()**. Figure 10.12 shows this happening.

FIGURE 10.12
Using the Behaviors panel to add the event handler for the loadPage() function.

What About the Exchange?

As of this writing, no third-party extension is available on the Macromedia Exchange for direct frame navigation. New extensions are being posted all the time, however, so keep checking!

Allowing Visitors to Bookmark Pages

When you have the loadPage() script set up in your frameset document, it's easy to make sure that all pages are individually bookmarkable. Every time a user bookmarks a page, the browser bookmarks whatever is appearing in its address field. You just need to make sure that all internal navigation in your site uses URL parameters so that the address field always contains the framework page and its page parameter.

Keeping Pages in Frames

One of the big worries for authors of frame-based websites is this: What happens if users accidentally stumble on one of your framed pages, naked and without its parent frameset? This can easily happen if, for

instance, a search engine finds one of your content pages and sends the user there. If your page contains no indication of what website it belongs in and (even more important) has no way of navigating back to the parent website, this user will never find you! Your content page will be an orphan in cyberspace. There are various strategies for heading off this disaster at the pass, ranging from automatic scripted solutions to simple navigation additions. The frame-wranglers out there refer to this as *frame jamming* or *frame stuffing*.

Quick and Easy: Navigation Footer

You can eliminate the orphan frame problem simply and quickly by always including navigation and identification somewhere in every framed page. An unobtrusive little footer like that shown in Figure 10.13, for instance, will ensure that any visitor to this page will know where the page belongs and how to get there. No scripting or other fanciness is required.

FIGURE 10.13
Additional navigation and identification in the footer of a framed page guarantees that this page will never be a dead end for visitors.

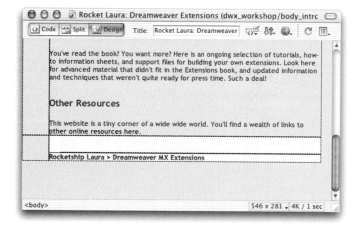

Quick Navigation Footers with Snippets

You can design your navigation any way you like, but if you just want to get it done fast, you might check out the snippets that ship with Dreamweaver. In the Snippets panel (Window > Snippets), check out the Navigation/Horizontal folder. The sample footer shown in Figure 10.13 was built in less than five minutes from the Pipe as Separator snippet, with a little modification.

See Chapter 27, "Writing Code in Dreamweaver," for more on snippets, and Chapter 21, "Building Dynamic Sites with Dreamweaver," for more on library items.

Make Your Footer into a Library Item

Presumably, you're using framesets because you like their efficiency. After you've created your navigation footer, turn it into a Dreamweaver library item so you can easily drag and drop it into many pages and update it efficiently from the library.

Add Some Scripting: Conditional Footer Information

With just a little bit of extra effort, you can streamline your framed pages by making the navigation/identification described in the previous section conditional so that it appears only if the page is being viewed without its parent frameset. The coding is slightly tricky, but it may be worth the effort for you—and, as usual, Dreamweaver can provide help along the way.

Here are the basic steps:

1. Open a page that will normally appear in a frameset, and create the navigation/identification content that should appear if the page isn't in its frameset.

2. Now for the tricky part. Select the content you just created and switch to Code view. The code must appear without any line breaks, and all single quotes or apostrophes must be "escaped" by typing a backward slash (\) in front of them. You need to edit the selected portion of your code to meet these requirements. You can do this manually or by using Edit > Find and Replace. This code won't work:

```
<table>
<tr>
<td>Joe's Website</td>
</tr>
</table>
```

But this code will:

```
<table><tr><td>Joe\'s Website</td></tr></table>
```

3. Now select your cleaned-up code and choose Edit > Cut.

4. Leave the insertion point where it is, and in the Insert bar, choose the Script object.

5. When the Script Insertion dialog box appears, make sure JavaScript is the language chosen in the drop-down menu. Type the following (no typos) into the Content field (see Figure 10.14):

```
<!--
if (self == top) document.write(' ');
//-->
```

FIGURE 10.14
Creating a Script object to display conditional footer information.

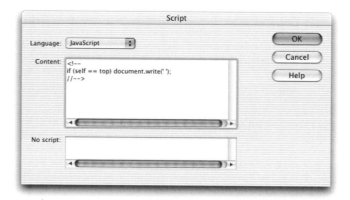

6. Place the cursor between the two single quotes and choose Edit > Paste. This should put your cleaned-up code in the content window.

7. Now place the cursor in the No Script content field and choose Edit > Paste again. (Why do this? For accessibility, any JavaScript that causes page content to display—such as this script—should have a no-script alternative. If the user's browser isn't capable of interpreting the JavaScript, it will display the navigation by default.)

8. Click OK to close the dialog box. In Code view, this portion of your page should now look something like this:

```
<script language="JavaScript">
<!--
if (self == top) document.write('<table><tr><td>Joe\'s
➥Website</td></tr></table>');
//-->
</script>
<noscript>
    <table><tr><td>Joe\'s Website</td></tr></table>
</noscript>
```

Pay attention to the color coding in the code! If all is well, all of the code that you pasted inside the JavaScript (not the code in the noscript tag) should appear in one color and style. If it doesn't, you missed a hard return or single quote in there somewhere.

9. When you return to Design view, the conditional content will appear only as a gold script icon. To edit this script in the future, select its icon and, in the Property Inspector, click the Edit button. The noscript content will appear as normal in Design view.

This bit of scripting probably wasn't much fun, but you can save yourself some work in the future by making it a snippet.

To create a snippet that contains all the code you just inserted, do this:

1. In Design view, select the script icon that represents your conditional content, and copy it (choose Edit > Copy).

2. Open the Snippets panel (Window > Snippets) and right-click the JavaScript snippet folder. Choose New Snippet from the contextual menu.

3. When the Snippet dialog box appears, the code that you just copied should already be in the Content field. Give your snippet a name and description. Set its type to Block (see Figure 10.15). When you're done, click OK to close the dialog box.

FIGURE 10.15
Turning the conditional navigation into a snippet.

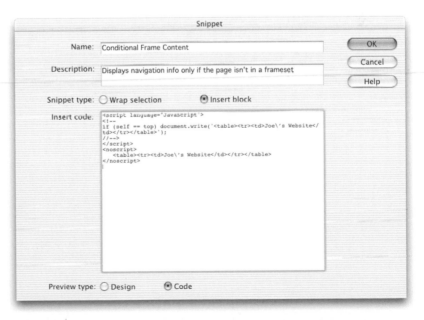

4. The next time you want to insert this content into a page, just drag and drop this snippet from the Snippets panel to the appropriate place in your document.

You can also create a snippet that contains only the JavaScript shell so that you can add different conditional content in the future. Do it this way:

1. Open the Snippets panel (Window > Snippets) and right-click the JavaScript snippet folder. Choose New Snippet from the contextual menu.

2. When the Snippet dialog box opens, give your snippet a name and description. Set its type to Wrap (see Figure 10.16).

FIGURE 10.16
Creating a more flexible conditional content snippet.

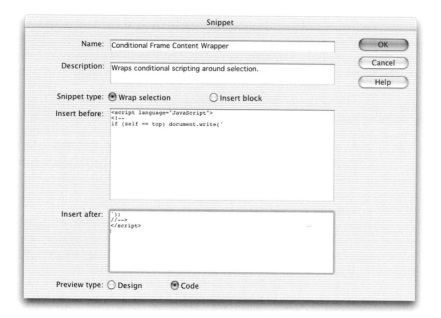

3. In the Insert Before content field, type the following:

```
<script language="JavaScript">
<!--
if (self == top) document.write('
```

Make sure there are no empty returns following this text.

4. In the Insert After content field, type the following:

```
');
//-->
</script>
```

5. When you're done, click OK to close the dialog box.

The next time you want to insert any conditional navigation into a frameset, do this:

1. In Design view, create the navigation or other element that should appear only if the page is not in a frameset.

2. Switch to Code view. Remove all line breaks and insert a backslash (\) in front of all apostrophes and single quotes.

3. Select all of the cleaned-up code.

4. Open the Snippets panel, select your conditional content snippet, and click the Insert button at the bottom of the panel. This wraps the JavaScript coding around your content.

Visit the Exchange

If you want a little help with your conditional navigation, you might try the Write If Frameset object, available on the Macromedia Exchange. This object works much like the wrapped snippet described in the previous section. It has the limitation that any code you insert must be free of returns and double quotes. It also requires the frameset tag to have an id attribute.

Frame-Jamming Scripts

You also have the option of automating the entire process so that whenever a page loads without its parent frameset, it automatically reloads itself inside the frameset. It's done by means of an automatically executing JavaScript. Unfortunately, Dreamweaver won't automatically write this script for you. But you have several other options for getting the frame-jamming code inserted, including building on the loadPage() script defined in the previous section and using any of the jamming scripts available on the Exchange.

Do-It-Yourself Jamming with *loadPage()*

Do-it-yourself frame jamming requires that your frameset document be equipped with the loadPage() function and function call described in the previous section. If you don't have that code in place, take a few minutes to go through that section now.

When your frameset document is set up, each content page that you want automatically jammed back into the frameset needs to have some scripting added to its head section. Do it this way:

1. Open the content page that you want to jam.

2. Choose View > Head Content so that the head content area is showing, and click in that area to activate it.

3. In the Insert bar, choose the Script object. When the Script dialog box appears, make sure that the language drop-down menu is set to JavaScript, and enter the following code in the Content field:

```
<!--
if (top == self) location.replace("frameset.html?page=
➥content.html");
//-->
```

    Substitute the name of your frameset document and your content page, where indicated in bold. Can you see how this script changes the location object to a new URL? And how the URL includes parameters which will be used by the loadPage() command in the main frameset?

4. When you're finished, click OK to close the dialog box. The script appears as a script icon in the head content area.

 You can save this piece of code as a snippet to save yourself the trouble of retyping it in the future. But you'll always have to tweak it to specify the page names you need.

Visit the Exchange: Frame-Jamming Extensions

Not interested in doing all of this coding yourself? The Macromedia Exchange lists several extensions that insert frame-jamming code similar to the code presented here. These include Find Parent Frameset (Subhash Robin), Frame Jammer (Hal Pawluk), and Frame Stuffer (Hal Pawluk).

Getting Out of Frames

Navigating into a frameset is only half of the frames navigation story. Sometimes you also need to get your pages out of frames. This can be done automatically, through frame-busting JavaScripts, or manually through targeted links.

Frame Busting

Frame busting generally deals with problems in other people's frame-sets rather than your own. Have you ever seen one of your web pages tucked inside somebody else's frameset? That happens when the frame-set author, either on purpose or by accident, links to your page without proper targeting (see Figure 10.17). Because putting someone else's web page in your frameset can suggest that the other site is somehow a subsidiary of yours, lawsuits have been fought over this bit of sloppy Internet etiquette.

FIGURE 10.17
The Macromedia web-site, absorbed into someone else's frameset.

A simple bit of JavaScript added to your web page can guarantee that it never appears inside a frameset. Unfortunately, Dreamweaver won't auto-matically write this script for you. But you have several other options for getting the frame-busting code inserted.

Do-It-Yourself Frame Buster

The code for busting frames isn't complicated, so if you don't mind a modicum of typing, you can easily build a script and reuse it. Do it this way:

1. Open an HTML document where you want the frame-busting code inserted.

2. Choose View > Head Content so that the gray strip of head content icons appears at the top of the Document window. Click inside the head content bar to activate it.

3. In the HTML Insert bar, from the Script object group, choose the Script object.

4. When the Script Insertion dialog box appears, make sure JavaScript is the language chosen in the drop-down menu, and type the following into the Content field (see Figure 10.18):

```
<!--
if (self != top) top.location.replace(self.location);
//-->
```

FIGURE 10.18

Creating a script object containing frame-busting code.

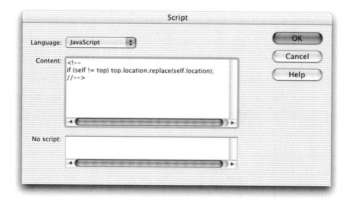

5. Click OK to close the dialog box. The script appears as an icon in the head content area of the Document window. Your page is now busted!

6. To edit this script in the future, select its icon in the head content area and, in the Property Inspector, click the Edit button.

When you've done all this, you can save yourself the trouble of doing it again by saving the code as a snippet.

Visit the Exchange: Frame-Busting Extensions

If you'd rather take advantage of other people's busting code than write your own, the Dreamweaver Exchange lists several third-party extensions to insert frame-busting scripts. These include the Frame Buster (Rabi Sunder Raj) and Break Out Of Frames (Thierry Koblentz) objects, and the Bust Frames (Triptych) behavior.

Print-Friendly Pages

Another usability issue that plagues frame-based websites is the difficulty users have printing individual frames. Nothing is more frustrating to a user trying to print your content than to end up wasting printer ink and paper, accidentally printing a colorful, graphics-heavy navigation frame. The easiest fix to this problem is to provide a link to a print-friendly version of each content page. What's a print-friendly version? The content frame by itself, with no other banners or sidebars.

To create a print-friendly link, just do this (see Figure 10.19):

1. Create an unobtrusive text or graphic link that says something like "Click here for a print-friendly version of this page."

2. Using the Property Inspector, assign a link to the page itself, targeted to a blank window.

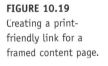

FIGURE 10.19
Creating a print-friendly link for a framed content page.

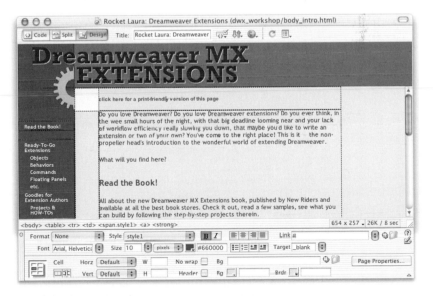

Creative Graphic Effects with Frames

Part of the fun of frame-based sites is being able to create unusual layout and graphic effects. The following sections cover a few of these, along with special instructions for using Dreamweaver to build them.

Letterbox Framesets

A *letterbox frameset* is an arrangement of frames that centers the page in the browser window, surrounded by background or border elements. Figures 10.20 and 10.21 show some different letterbox effects. In the first, the Macnab Design site floats in the center of a gray background, creating the same effect that multimedia CD-ROM presentations often have. In the second, more complex incarnation of letterboxing, the Web Monster home page sits in the middle of the browser window, surrounded by a striped border and black background. If the browser window gets small enough that not all of the main page shows, the striped border still hugs the edges so that the layout looks complete. As these examples show, the central portion of the letterbox can be fixed and surrounded by flexible borders, or the central portion can be flexible and surrounded by fixed borders.

FIGURE 10.20
The Macnab Design site uses a letterbox frameset to center its layout vertically and horizontally in the browser window.

FIGURE 10.21

The Web Monster site uses a complex letterbox frameset to surround its main layout with a border and background.

Do-It-Yourself Letterbox Frameset

Dreamweaver has no letterbox Frame objects, so you construct them manually using the various Modify > Frameset >Split commands. Do it this way:

1. Create a new document. In the New Document dialog box, choose Framesets/Fixed Top, Fixed Bottom.

2. Place the cursor inside the middle frame and choose Modify > Frameset > Split Frame Left to create a vertical frame division nested inside the horizontal division.

3. Alt/Opt-drag left or right from that vertical split to create a second vertical split. (At this point, check the Frames panel to make sure you've got one frameset split twice instead of a frameset nested inside another. If you've accidentally created the latter, choose Edit > Undo and perform the second split again.)

4. Position the horizontal and vertical divisions approximately where you want them, remembering that your layout will sit entirely in the center frame.

5. Open the Frames panel and select the outermost of the two nested framesets. In the Property Inspector, set the borders to None and the border width to 0. To create a fixed center frame, use the Property Inspector's proxy to set the top and bottom frames to Relative height

and set the middle frame to a set number of pixels (your choice). To create a flexible center frame, use the proxy to set the middle frame to Relative height and set the top and bottom frames to a certain number of pixels.

6. Now repeat this process with the innermost frameset. Set the borders to None and the border width to 0. To create a fixed center frame, use the proxy to set the left and right frames to Relative and the center frame to a set number of pixels. To create a flexible center frame, use the proxy to set the middle frame to Relative and the left and right frames to a set number of pixels.

7. The outer frames won't have content, so they don't need scrolling. Select each of the outer frames (top, bottom, left, right) and set the Scroll drop-down to None. It's your choice whether you use scrolling for the center frame. (Neither site in Figure 10.20 or 21 used scrollbars in the center frame.)

8. Finally, because the outer frames will all be the same, you can use the same HTML file to fill each frame. Place the insertion point inside one of the outer frames, and save that file with a generic name such as bg.html. Set its background color to black, gray, or whatever color you want your background to be. Then use the Frames panel to set the Src for each remaining outer frame to the same file.

Visit the Exchange: Letterbox Frameset Extensions

If you like letterbox framesets enough that you might want to use them repeatedly, you might want to visit the Macromedia Exchange and download Project Seven's Letterbox Frameset extension. This command, which appears under the Modify > Frameset submenu, creates a fixed-center letterbox layout.

Splitting Background Graphics Across Frames

Some of the most graphically creative framesets on the web disguise their frame-ness through clever use of background color and images. Figures 10.22 and 10.23 show different uses of this technique. In the first example, one large abstract background graphic stretches across frames invisibly until the content area is scrolled. In the second, a photographic background appears across both frames, at full intensity on the home page and faded back in the other content pages.

FIGURE 10.22
A page from Lynda Weinman's site uses a very nonrectangular background graphic across a left-side navigation frame and right-side content frame.

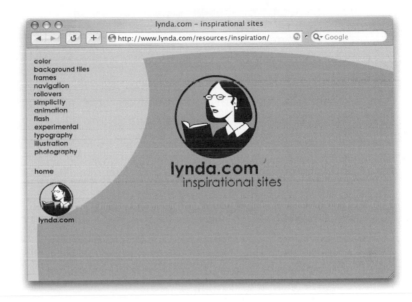

FIGURE 10.23
The website for the movie *Titanic* places a photograph across the top navigation frame and bottom content frame.

Spreading graphics across frames doesn't work well in Netscape 4 because there is no way to make the graphic reliably align across frames.

The technique for doing this isn't hard, but it requires a little bit of thinking outside the box because most web graphics programs don't provide easy tools for making it happen. Using Fireworks and Dreamweaver, you can do it this way:

1. In Dreamweaver, create a frameset. Pay attention to the frame dimensions.

2. In Fireworks, create a new document with a large enough canvas size to cover both frames.

3. Create a background graphic that covers the entire canvas area.

4. Draw slice objects with the same sizes and positions as your frames. If necessary, adjust the background graphic to suit the slice sizes.

5. Optimize and export from Fireworks, choosing Export Images Only and Export Slices.

6. Back in Dreamweaver, assign each exported image to be the background image for a frame. Use CSS to assign background images if you want to control their tiling.

EXERCISE 10.1

Maximizing the Usability and Accessibility of a Frame-Based Site

In this exercise, you'll assemble a frameset from individual files and use the techniques covered in this chapter to make sure it's accessible, searchable, and easily navigable. Before you start, download the **chapter_10** folder from the book's website at www.peachpit.com to your hard drive. Define a site called Chapter 10, with this folder as the local root folder.

1. Start by examining the files that will go into this frameset. The bearnav.html file contains the navigation bar that will sit at the top of each page. The bearbottom.html file contains an information bar that will sit at the bottom. The intro.html, coats.html, repair.html, and pals.html files contain content that will sit in the middle. The files are built using graphics that smoothly blend between frames, softening the rectangular frame shapes. Figure 10.24 shows how the assembled pieces will look.

FIGURE 10.24
The Bear Essentials main frameset as it will look when assembled.

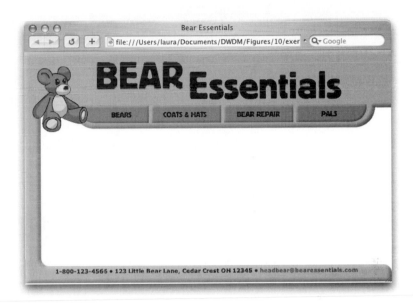

2. You want your frameset to be accessible, so before creating it, take a moment to choose Edit > Preferences. Go to the Accessibility category and enable the option for Frames. (You can enable the other options as well, if you want.)

3. The initial content page is **intro.html**. Open this file. In the HTML Insert bar, find the Frame object that creates Top and Bottom Frames, and click it. This creates a frameset around the content page. (See how the center content area of the object's icon is blue? That means the current document will end up in that frame.)

   While you're inserting, Dreamweaver asks you what titles to give your three frames. Title them like this:

Frame Name	Title
bottomFrame	Contact Frame
mainFrame	Content Frame
topFrame	Navigation Frame

4. After the frameset has been created, open the Frames panel (Window > Frames) and click anywhere in it to activate the frameset document. The Tag Selector should now begin with `<frameset>`. Choose File > Save Frameset. Save the file in your **chapter_10** folder as **index.html**.

5. In the Frames panel, click in the topFrame area. This selects the `frame` tag that controls this frame in the frameset document. The Tag Selector should now say `<frameset><frame>`. In the Property Inspector, find the Src field and use the Browse button or point-and-shoot icon to link to **bearnav.html**. The top navigation bar should now appear in your Document window.

6. In the Frames panel, click the bottomFrame area. Use the Property Inspector to change this frame's `src` to **bearbottom.html**. Figure 10.25 shows how the page should look so far. The measurements are a little bit off!

FIGURE 10.25
The Bear Essentials frameset, with all elements in place—but the dimensions are slightly off.

7. You need to make the top and bottom frames large enough to show their contents, and no larger. In the Document window, examine the bottom bar picture. If you select one of the corner graphics, you'll see that they're each 42 pixels high. If you similarly examine the graphics in the top frame (you'll have to drag the frame divider down a bit to see the whole thing), you'll see that the title banner is exactly 150 pixels high. The bottom and top frames should therefore be exactly 42 and 150 high, respectively.

In the Frames panel, click the border around the frame diagram. This selects the `frameset` tag, where all frame dimensions are specified. In the Property Inspector's frameset proxy, select the top frame and set the row to 150 pixels. Then select the bottom frame in the proxy and set the row to 42 pixels. Finally, select the middle row and

make sure the measurements are set to Relative. Figure 10.26 shows what the page should look like with proper frame dimensions.

FIGURE 10.26
The Bear Essentials
frameset, with dimen-
sions properly set.

Preview the frameset in a browser. It should look like Figure 10.24. Resizing the browser window should expand the middle frame without distorting the framing graphics.

8. The frameset is basically functional. Your next task is to make it accessible. The default frame names that Dreamweaver supplied are not very descriptive, so replace topFrame with **navFrame**, and bottomFrame with **contactFrame**. Replace mainFrame with **contentFrame**. (These names are very similar to the titles you entered earlier.)

Each frame must also have a descriptive page title. Currently, the content pages all have proper titles, but all other pages are Untitled Documents.) Assign page titles like this:

Frame/File	Page Title
navFrame/bearnav.html	Bear Essentials: Navigation Bar
contactFrame/bearbottom.html	Bear Essentials: Contact Information

These page titles serve accessibility and searchability needs, in that each mentions not only the page description but also the site name.

9. The frameset page should have keywords and a description in its head, but that's outside the scope of this exercise. See Chapter 8, "Building Tables," for more on assigning these.

10. Assign links, using targeting, as follows (Figure 10.27 shows this happening):

Button	Link	Target
Bears	intro.html	contentFrame
Coats & Hats	coats.html	contentFrame
Repair	repair.html	contentFrame
Pals	pals.html	contentFrame

11. When you're done, check the results in the browser. You should be able to navigate to all four content pages without disturbing the frameset.

12. Now you need to add some noframes content to the frameset document to help search engines find the page. Start in the navigation frame. Select the table that contains the navigation bar and choose Edit > Copy. Then choose Modify > Frameset > Edit NoFrames Content, click inside the Document window, and choose Edit > Paste.

Choose Modify > Frameset > Edit NoFrames Content to return to normal frame viewing and select all the content in the main frame. Return to noframes editing and paste this content after the navigation bar.

Finally, do this one more time to get the contact information from the contact frame into the noframes area.

Note that the links in the navigation bar are still correct because the bearnav.html file and the index.html file are both in the same folder. If they were in different folders, the links here would have to be adjusted. Also note that it's not the most efficient practice to copy the entire navigation bar to the noframes area, graphics and all, although it is the quickest. To be more efficient, delete the navigation bar and manually enter a text version of the title and links.

Figure 10.28 shows how an efficient, graphics-free version of the noframes content might look in Design view.

FIGURE 10.28
The graphics-free noframes content for Bear Essentials.

13. Now you need to make sure that the framed pages properly link back to their parent pages. Close the frameset document and open intro.html (it's easier to work with the document when it's not being viewed through the frameset). In the table cell immediately below the page's text, insert a text-only navigation bar. You can use one of the Navigation snippets to build it, or you can create your own from scratch. When you're done, it should look like Figure 10.29.

FIGURE 10.29

The text-only navigation bar at the bottom of intro.html.

Where exactly should the links go? That depends on whether you want to link immediately back to the frameset or whether you want to let the visitor navigate among the content pages without returning to the frameset. For this page, link as follows:

Text	Link	Target
Home	index.html	_top
Bears	intro.html	(none)
Coats & Hats	coats.html	(none)
Repair	repair.html	(none)
Pals	pals.html	(none)

To test your frameless navigation, copy this navigation bar and paste it into **coats.html**, **repair.html**, and **pals.html**. Then try viewing any of these pages in the browser. You can navigate around quite happily without the frameset, or you can click the Home link and get the frameset back.

14. As an optional step, try making the navigation appear only if the page doesn't appear in its frameset. To do this, open **intro.html** (or any of the framed page files) and follow the steps in the section "Add Some Scripting: Conditional Footer Information," earlier in this chapter.

15. How about allowing visitors to link directly to individual framed pages? To do this, you must add the `loadPage()` command to the frameset. Open **index.html** and follow the instructions in the "Do-It-Yourself Jamming with `loadPage()`" section, earlier in this chapter.

When you've got the code in place, preview **index.html** in the browser. The intro page should display in the middle frame. Then manually revise the URL in the browser's address field to include `?page=repair.html` and click the browser's Reload button. The frameset should load with the repair page in place.

16. How can you make use of this parameter passing? It's most useful when linking to the frameset from outside it. But you can also use it to help visitors bookmark framed pages. To do this, open **repair.html** and, in the right table cell, type the following:

Click here before bookmarking this page.

(To make the text look nice, choose Paragraph formatting and assign the note CSS style.) Select the text and link it to `index.html?page=repair.html`. Figure 10.30 shows this happening.

FIGURE 10.30
Adding a book-marking option to a framed Bear Essentials page.

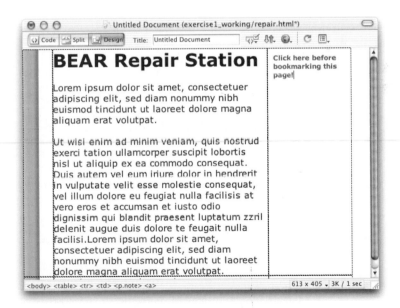

Try this out in the browser. If you click the link, the page reloads with a revised URL in the browser's address field. If the visitor then bookmarks the page, the bookmark will call up this particular page.

17. Now, how about linking to a printer-friendly version of the page? Underneath the note you just entered, add a new paragraph:

`Click here for a printer-friendly version of this page.`

Select the text and link it to **repair.html**, with a target of _top.

THE WORLD OF IFRAMES

Frames are not supported by Netscape 4.

Like a regular frame, an *iframe* (or inline frame) defines a rectangular area inside a browser window that displays a portion of another document. Unlike standard frames, however, iframes exist within ordinary HTML documents, inside the body tag, just like any other page element (image, table, and so on). Figure 10.31 shows a sample of an iframe at work. Iframes are useful for many of the same reasons standard frames are: They allow partial page contents to change without reloading the entire page, they allow certain page content to scroll while other content remains stationary, and so on. They also have the same accessibility requirements as frames. They're part of the HTML 4 specification and are currently supported by all major browsers.

FIGURE 10.31
An iframe allowing portions of one document to show inside a rectangular window in another.

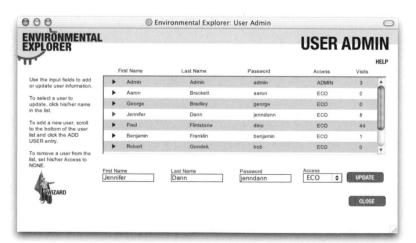

Iframes in Dreamweaver

Dreamweaver only partially supports iframes. Iframes cannot be inserted within Design view, they don't display in Design view, and their properties don't appear in the Property Inspector.

Creating Iframes

The two mechanisms for inserting iframes are the Tag Chooser and the Floating Frame object. To insert an iframe into a page using the Tag Chooser, do this:

1. Create the document that will hold your main layout, determining where in the page layout you want the iframe to appear. This should be a rectangular area, which can be placed inside a table cell or CSS layer, or anywhere other HTML block elements (such as images and paragraphs) can be placed.

2. Create another document to be viewed inside the rectangular area of the iframe. The entire layout of this document does not need to fit inside the iframe area, but if the layout is larger than the iframe area, it will have to scroll.

3. In the main document, place the insertion point where the iframe should appear. At this point, you have your choice of inserting the iframe with the Tag Chooser or the Floating Frame (Code view only) object.

4. Choose Insert > Tag to access the Tag Chooser. From the HTML Tags/Page Elements/General category, choose iframe and click Insert.

5. The Edit Tag dialog box opens. In the General category, assign any properties desired, using Table 10.4 for reference.

6. When you're done assigning properties, click OK to close the Edit Tag dialog box and then Close to close the Tag Chooser. Your iframe won't display in Dreamweaver Design view, but a look at Code view will show you that it's there.

To insert an iframe using the Floating Frame object, prepare your files as specified in steps 1–2, and then do the following:

1. Switch to Code view. Within Code view, place the insertion point where you want the iframe to appear.

2. In the HTML Insert bar, choose Floating Frame from the Frames object group. (This object is available only from within Code view.)

This inserts the iframe tag with no properties, so it won't be functional unless you assign properties separately.

TABLE 10.4 ## Main Attributes of the *iframe* Tag

Attribute	Values	Required	Description
src	Absolute or relative URL	Yes	The file that should appear in the iframe area
width height	Number, in pixels	Yes	The width and height of the iframe rectangular area
scrolling	true, false	No	Whether scrollbars will appear in the iframe
marginwidth marginheight	Number, in pixels	No	The gutter between the edges of iframe area and its content
border	true/false	No	Whether a visible border surrounds the iframe
align	left, right, top, middle, bottom	No	How the iframe aligns with surrounding content

Working with Iframe Properties

After the iframe is created, you can use the Tag Inspector or the Edit Tag dialog box to examine and set its properties. Iframes can't be seen in Design view, but can they be selected using the Tag Selector.

You can select an iframe from within Design view. Just click in the Document window where the iframe should be, and it will appear in the Tag Selector. Of course, if you can't see the iframe, you might have trouble clicking exactly where it is—or even remembering exactly what it is. And unlike many other invisible elements (form tags, for instance), iframes themselves don't display any little gold invisible element icon in Design view. But you can insert a comment between the opening and closing tags of your iframe to help you find it because comments do show gold icons. Do it this way:

1. Go to the Preferences/Invisible Elements dialog box and turn on the icon for Comments. This tells Dreamweaver to display comments as a gold icon when invisible elements are showing.

2. Switch to Code view and place the insertion point between the opening and closing iframe tags.

3. From the Common Insert bar, choose the Comment object. This inserts the framework code for a comment. Type a few words inside the framework, such as "iframe goes here."

From now on, whenever invisible elements are showing, you can select the gold comment icon, and the Tag Selector will display the iframe tag. Click the tag indicator in the Tag Selector to select it, and you can set its properties.

To set iframe properties, choose Modify > Edit Tag to open the Tag Editor, or use the Attributes tab of the Tag Inspector. Iframe properties are detailed in Table 10.4.

Visit the Exchange: Iframe Extensions

Iframes are useful little items and are fairly popular. Several extensions are available on the Macromedia Exchange to help insert and edit them.

SUMMARY

This chapter looked at how to build frame-based web pages in Dreamweaver and how to maximize their accessibility, searchability, and navigability. We examined how frames work in the browser, what built-in tools Dreamweaver has to help create framesets, and how to stretch those tools and extend the program where needed, to make the most of frame-based design.

CHAPTER 11

USING CASCADING STYLE SHEETS

CASCADING STYLE SHEETS (CSS) OFFERS A WAY TO EXTEND THE FORMATTING capabilities of your web page beyond the limitations of HTML. CSS enables you to define and change the look of your website quickly and easily. This chapter discusses CSS: what it is, why it is, and how to use it.

CSS Basics

As great as CSS is, it's a big, new scary world if you've never been here before. This look at the basics covers how CSS came to be, what it does and how it works, and what tools Dreamweaver MX 2004 has on tap to help you create it.

A Little History Lesson

The original concept for HTML was that of a language used to mark up text to describe the different structural elements of a document. HTML tags identified which portion of a document was a heading, which portions were paragraphs, which portion was part of a list, and which words needed to be emphasized. The browsers were designed to interpret these structural elements in such a way that the text onscreen made sense to the reader. Not every browser displayed text the same; one might show text marked emphasize in italics, and another might show that text in bold, but either way, the text was emphasized. The goal was readable documents that would display with structural definition across a variety of platforms (see Figure 11.1).

FIGURE 11.1
Basic structural markup tags as they display in a browser window.

Presentational Markup and Its Problems

With the advent of graphical browsers and the rapid expansion of the Web came the demand from HTML authors for new tags that would specify presentational effects rather than just structure. Designers were no longer satisfied to specify that a word needed to be emphasized somehow; they wanted to be able to specify exactly how the word would be emphasized (by bolding, for instance). In response to this pressure, physical elements such as b and i began to enter the language. Soon a structural language was evolving into a presentational one, and the font tag for styling text came into wide usage.

Website designers were happy to have some control over presentation, but as they stopped using structural formatting, it was no longer possible to deduce the structure of the information from the source. This has a number of negative repercussions, including the following:

- The code produced doesn't convey anything about the meaning of the text being presented. Structurally, these pages are just strings of letters. A speech-synthesis browser, for example, will read text marked with <h1> tags as a main heading; it will read text marked to be rendered in large type and bold just like any other text.

- Unstructured markup is much more difficult to maintain. Text marked up logically according to the meaning of the content results in clean code that makes sense.

- Unstructured pages are very difficult to index. If page headings and section headings are clearly marked, search engines can use them to enable the user to perform targeted searches for relevant information.

This Is a Job for CSS

The W3C quickly recognized that the nature of HTML was being changed by the increasing use of presentational markup and that a solution was needed. As a direct response, work began on Cascading Style Sheets; in 1996, CSS was made a full W3C Recommendation.

CSS is designed to allow the web designer a lot of control over how pages display, while retaining the basic essence of HTML as a structural language. It allows for much more complex and varied presentation of text than HTML ever could, permitting styling such as the creation of

borders, the amount of space around elements, variations on capitalization, decoration (such as underlining), letter spacing, and many other possibilities.

Almost as exciting is the lightening of the web developer's workload brought about by the use of linked style sheets, in which a single change to a style declaration can affect specifically targeted text site-wide.

CSS is clearly the direction of things to come for web designers and should be part of the toolkit of any serious web designer.

With the proliferation of new and alternative web-browsing devices such as cellular phones, handhelds, personal digital assistants, and web TV, logical document structuring might well become critical. In conjunction with CSS, this approach allows for very different presentations as determined by the device being used to view the page—exactly as in the original concept for HTML.

The Nuts and Bolts of CSS

A *Cascading Style Sheet* at its most basic is a set of instructions that defines how an HTML document is going to display. The great thing about CSS is that it can be defined in an external file, or sheet. This external sheet first is read by the browser and then applies the rules to the specified content on the page. In this way, the style and formatting of the page are separate from the content. This is an important concept in designing web pages. It also gives you a powerful and detailed way to update your entire website.

You can create a style sheet that defines your text as Arial, 12 pixel, red, bold, and left-justified with a blue background. Attach your sheet to all the pages on your site, and all your text will appear that way. If you have a change of heart, you can change that one style sheet and make the text Times, 28 pixel, green, italic, and right-justified. Save that new sheet, and the entire website is automatically updated.

CSS also enables you to do things that HTML just can't do. You can set a layer on your page to be scrollable. This way, you can have a window in the middle of your page with scrollable content. You can define different colors for every facet of a table border. You can set custom graphics for bullets, and you can remove the underline from hyperlinks.

Although browser support is getting better with every release, some browsers do not display all CSS elements, nor do they display some elements in the same way. It is always a good idea to test your page in multiple browsers. One important idea of CSS is that if the style is not supported in the browser, the information will still be there—it will just not show the offending styles.

IE 5 and above and Netscape 6 and above do a fine job of displaying most CSS elements. Netscape 4 has some limitations.

CSS gives you unprecedented control over your page. The W3C is now recommending the use of CSS for page formatting. You would do well to explore the possibilities of CSS in your web design.

A Note About Semantics

A *style*, or *style rule*, is generally defined as a set of parameters for a tag or a class.

A *sheet* is the file that contains the styles. A sheet can contain many styles.

Anatomy of a Style

At the heart of CSS is the style. Understanding how styles work and what flavors they come in is crucial to using them wisely.

CSS Selectors

The easiest of the styles to understand is the CSS selector. A *selector* is any HTML element or tag. To affect the appearance of the tag, you apply a set of rules that defines how the tag should display in the browser.

The basic format of a selector style is this:

```
selector {property:value}
```

The selector is the tag being changed. The property is the name of the property being set. The value is the value of the property being set.

A basic CSS example is this:

```
p {color: green}
```

This sets any text within the <p></p> tags to green for any page that uses this style.

You also can group several settings into one style:

```
p
{
color: green;
text-align: right
}
```

This sets the green text to the right of the page.

If you want to assign multiple tags the same style, you can list them in the selector:

```
p,div,H2
{
color: green;
text-align: right
}
```

Notice that a comma separates each tag, a full colon separates the property from the value, and semicolons separate properties.

Contextual Selectors

Contextual selectors are another way of applying styles to specific tags. This is a bit more specialized because a selector works by being applied only when a certain condition or set of tags is present.

For instance, you can create a CSS selector that you want to be applied only to anchor tags that are within lists. So, you would set up a selector that looks for a tag combination of li a (list item, anchor) and then applies the style. All linked elements not in lists are not affected by this style.

```
li a
{
color: red;
font-weight: bold;
text-decoration: none;
}
```

Classes

You can have more than one set of styles for a tag. The most flexible method of defining more than one set of styles is to specify classes. A *class* is a set of style rules that can be applied to any element, unlike a

redefined HTML tag, which is *automatically* applied to all specified elements, like this:

```
.red {color: red}
h2.green {color: green}
```

When you want to specify a particular class in a tag, it would look like this:

```
<h2 class="green">This is Green text</h2>
```

This tells the tag to use the green class. Because this is applied directly to this tag, it influences this tag only. `<h3 class="green">This is not green text</h3>` is not affected because the `.green` class is directly associated with the `<h2>` tag.

You can use the `red` class with any tag, and it would apply because it is not assigned to a specific tag. So, the following would actually display properly:

```
<h2 class="red">This is Red Text</h2>
<h3 class="red">This is Red Text</h3>
```

Pseudoclasses

The most common usage of *pseudoclasses* is to display links in different states: Link, Visited, Hover, and Active. These are preset definitions for link styles that differentiate Links, Active (links that are being clicked on), Hover (when mousing over a link), and Visited (links that have already been visited). You can use selectors to define a style for each of these states. The order of their use in the CSS file is important: It must be Link, Visited, Hover, Active, or their functionality will not work as desired. An example is this:

```
a:link{text-decoration:underline}
a:visited{text-decoration:overline}
a:hover{text-decoration:none}
a:active{text-decoration:none;cursor:wait}
```

Pseudoclasses work with IE 4+ and Netscape 4+, but the a:hover effect won't show up in Netscape 4.

Styles and Style Sheets, and Where They're Kept

Styles can exist in a document as individual styles placed inline with the document or they can be grouped in collections called *style sheets*. A style sheet can be internal or external, depending on where it is stored relative

to the document that it's formatting. The following sections discuss the relative advantages and disadvantages of inline styles, internal style sheets, and external style sheets.

Inline Styles

Inline styles are those defined directly within the tag on the page. The CSS is written right into the tag as an attribute, like this:

```
<input type="text" style="width:150px; border:1px solid
➥#000000;">
```

Although an inline style takes precedence over all other styles, it affects only the particular tag it's attached to. No other instances of the input tag, for instance, are affected by the width and border options set here. This is the least efficient way of using CSS in a web page.

Internal Style Sheets

Internal style sheets are defined within the actual HTML page in the head region using the style block. This way, the styles are available to the whole page without being dependent on another file.

A typical internal style looks like this:

```
<head>
<style type="text/css">
body {background-color: red}
p {text-align: right; color: white}
</style>
</head>
<body>

<p>This paragraph is white.</p>
<p>So is this paragraph.</p>
```

As you can see, if you want to move all paragraphs in the document to the left and change their color, just edit the CSS in the head; the changes will be made automatically to all paragraphs in the document.

External Style Sheets

External style sheets enable you to take full advantage of the capabilities of CSS. External style sheets contain all the styles and definitions in an external file with a .css extension. This is arguably the best way to store

your styles. Using this method, the style information is completely independent of the HTML code. You can change the look and feel of your entire site just by editing this external file. The site automatically updates depending on the information in that sheet after it is uploaded to the server. After you learn all the options that CSS presents to you, you can take full advantage of this functionality.

A typical external style sheet is *linked* to the page by code like this:

```
<link href="styles.css" rel="stylesheet" type="text/css">
```

Or, it is *imported* into it like this:

```
<style type="text/css">
<!--
@import url("styles.css");
-->
</style>
```

HTML tags, including comment tags, should *never* be included in external CSS files because they can cause your CSS to not be interpreted correctly in the browser. (CSS comments are allowed, just not HTML comment tags. To create a comment line in CSS, start it with two forward slashes [//].)

The actual style sheet file just has a list of selectors and classes listed, as follows:

```
p
{
color: green;
text-align: right
}

.red {color: red}
h2.green {color: green}
```

After you link the external style sheet to all pages in your site, you just change the settings in the file and save and upload—and everything updates. This is the tremendous advantage of using CSS!

Cascading and Inheritance

One of the advantages of CSS styles is that they all work together, if needed, and can overwrite each other as needed. Cascading and inheritance work together to make this cooperation happen.

Cascading refers to the use of multiple styles and sheets and the order in which they are read. The order in which the styles appear within the code determines which particular trait will display. If the external style

sheet says that h2 text should be blue, but there is an inline style on a particular h2 tag that says the text should be yellow, the yellow will win because it is closer to the actual text code.

Inheritance means that in styles that cascade, the closer style will overwrite only those parameters that both styles share. In the preceding example, if the external style says that the h2 tag should be right-justified, the inline style will not overwrite that because it does not have a parameter that controls justification. Therefore, the h2 tag will be yellow because of the inline style, but it will inherit the right-justification from the external style.

CSS in Dreamweaver

Dreamweaver has a full set of tools for helping you design, create, manage, and preview a CSS-based website. In fact, starting with Dreamweaver MX 2004, CSS is everywhere in the code the program writes and the interface you work with.

The CSS Styles panel (Window > CSS Styles) is the central location for manipulating and controlling styles and style sheets. From this panel, you can create, edit, and examine styles, and manage external linked or imported style sheet documents (see Figure 11.2).

FIGURE 11.2
The CSS Styles panel, showing internal and external style sheets and style definitions for the current document.

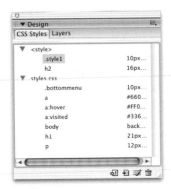

Dreamweaver MX upgraders, are you missing the Apply Styles mode? It's gone! Apply styles from the Tag Inspector or the Property Inspector.

Creating a New Style

To create a new style in the CSS Styles panel, click the New CSS Style button. You can also create a new style by right-clicking in the Tag Inspector's Relevant CSS tab and choosing New Rule, by choosing New from the Style drop-down menu in the Property Inspector, by choosing Text > CSS Styles > New from the main menu, or by right-clicking in an empty portion of the Document window and choosing CSS > New.

Whichever method you choose, the New CSS Style dialog box appears (see Figure 11.3). From here, you can determine what kind of style you want to create and where you want to put it.

Choose the type of style you want to create from the Selector Type options. Your choices are these:

- **Class (can apply to any tag)**—If you choose this option, use the Selector field to enter a name for your class. Class names should start with a period, but if you forget to type the period, Dreamweaver will insert it for you.

- **Tag (redefines the look of a specific tag)**—If you choose this option, use the Selector field to specify a tag to redefine, either by typing it into a field or by choosing it from the drop-down menu.

- **Advanced (contextual selectors and so on)**—Use this category for anything that doesn't fit in the other two, such as pseudoclasses, contextual selectors, and IDs.

  To create a pseudo-class, choose this option and use the Selector field drop-down menu to choose a pseudoclass—or, you can type the pseudoclass name manually.

  To create a contextual selector, choose this option and type the names of your contextual selectors into the Selector field. For a contextual selector that combines li and a, for instance, type li a in the field. For a selector that combines the custom class .footer and a:link, type .footer a:link in the field (don't forget the period in front of the class name, or the selector won't work).

  To create an ID, choose this option and type ID#*name* in the Selector field, substituting the name of your ID for *name*. (IDs are discussed in the next chapter.)

In the bottom portion of the dialog box, you can choose to save the style in an internal style sheet, which will be added to your document's head, or an external style sheet, which will be saved in a CSS document and attached to the current HTML document. If you want to put the style in an external document but you don't have one, choose the New Style Sheet Document option, and Dreamweaver will help you create one now.

FIGURE 11.3
The New CSS Style
dialog box.

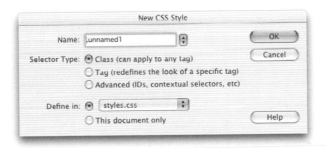

After you've decided what kind of style to create, click OK to close the New CSS Style dialog box. This automatically opens the Style Definition dialog box, ready for you to specify what formatting the new style should include by defining style parameters.

Defining Style Parameters

The interface for specifying CSS style formatting is the Style Definitions dialog box. This dialog box appears as soon as you create a new style and every time you want to edit existing styles. Its eight different windows cover different aspects of CSS control.

As you're working, note that Dreamweaver MX 2004 now renders most CSS elements in the Design window. However, it is still a good idea to preview the page in multiple browsers to make sure that your pages will actually render correctly.

Type

The Type category lists options for formatting text (see Figure 11.4). Some options are self-explanatory; some are not so much. Most of these settings will display well across browsers and in Dreamweaver Design view.

FIGURE 11.4
The CSS Style Definition dialog box, showing the Type category.

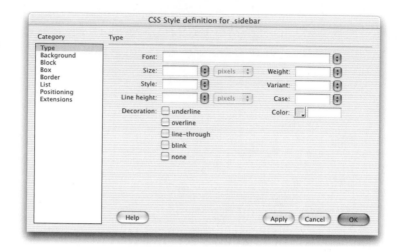

- **Font**—Select the font group to be used in the style. You can edit this list by clicking the down arrow and choosing Edit Font List. For more information on font usage, see the sidebar "Specifying Fonts in CSS."

- **Size**—Specify a font size. Notice that you can choose a number value or absolute size values. Absolute size values set the medium value to the default settings of the user's browser or defined styles rules and then scale from there.

- **Style**—Set the font to normal, italic, or oblique. The difference between italic and oblique is this: *Italic* is a distinct version of the font. Most fonts have an italic version. *Oblique* is simply the original version of the font that has been angled by the computer. In reality, there is usually no difference between the two in the browser, but there can be variances between fonts and sizes. If this distinction is critical, test both settings in the browsers.

- **Line Height**—This determines the height of a single line of text. If you are more used to working with print projects, this is comparable to line spacing or leading. Normal line height is calculated based on type size; lines will be approximately 20% larger than the type size. Absolute line height can be assigned based on any of the measurement systems covered in the following sidebar.

- **Weight**—This determines the boldness of the font. The number values (100–900) are absolute settings, whereas Bolder and Lighter

are relative to the default weight. Note that boldness is not always rendered the same way across browsers; always preview in several different browsers if you choose any setting here other than Normal or Bold.

- **Variant**—This setting determines whether lowercase letters will be substituted with small capital letters.

- **Case**—Determine the capitalization of the text: all uppercase, all lowercase, or with every word capitalized.

- **Color**—This determines the color of the font.

- **Decoration**—This sets options for lines on the text. Use the None option for removing the underline from hyperlinks.

Background

The *Background category* (see Figure 11.5) controls how the background is rendered. Note that with CSS, you can control the background of every block element. This means that every paragraph, layer, table, or other discrete element can have its own background style. To apply a background to the whole page, you must apply background formatting to the body tag.

FIGURE 11.5
The CSS Style Definition dialog box, showing the Background category.

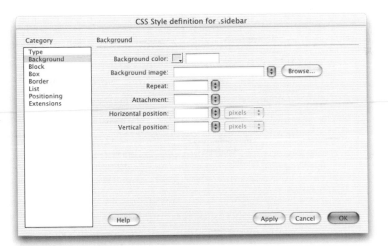

- **Background Color**—This sets the background color of the element.

- **Background Image**—This sets a tiling or nontiling background image behind the element. The remaining settings in this category all determine how a background image will display.

  - **Repeat**—This setting controls tiling for a background image. You can choose to repeat, not repeat, repeat horizontally only (repeat-x) or vertically only (repeat-y).

  - **Attachment**—This option determines whether a background image will scroll with the page or remain static, allowing the page to scroll over it.

  - **Horizontal Position and Vertical Position**—These settings determine the placement of the background image. Choose Left, Right, or Center/Middle to align the image relative to its parent element. Enter a numeric distance to offset the image from the parent's upper-left corner.

In the Dreamweaver window, the image set here might show up in the upper-left corner of the Design window. Preview in the browser for a correct look at the page. Also, there are browser limitations with some background images settings, especially with Netscape 4. As always, test in multiple browsers for compatibility.

Block

Block elements are discrete pieces of HTML. For instance, a paragraph is a block-level element. For CSS reasoning, it is considered a block of code; when applying a custom class to a paragraph, it affects only the code between the opening and closing paragraph tags. This way, each paragraph is treated as a separate element. Most block elements have an opening and closing tag. This is distinct from *inline elements*, which can be placed anywhere within a block element. An image, which doesn't have a closing tag, is a good example of an inline element.

The Block category (see Figure 11.6) of the CSS Style Definition dialog box contains options for specifying how block elements are presented on the page.

FIGURE 11.6
The Block CSS Style Definition dialog box, showing the Block category.

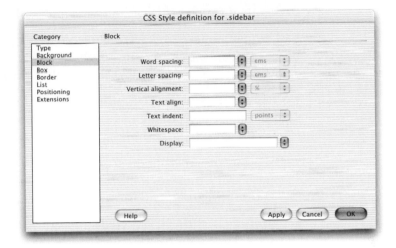

- **Word Spacing**—Use this setting to define the amount of space between each word.

- **Letter Spacing**—Use this setting to define the space between each letter in a word.

- **Vertical Alignment**—This setting determines the vertical aspect of word spacing. You can use it to specify subscripts and superscripts.

- **Text Align**—This setting determines the horizontal alignment of a text block: Left, Right Center, or Justify. Check in the browser when using Justify because browser support is inconsistent (and pretty darn ugly even when it does work).

- **Text Indent**—This setting determines the indentation of the first line of a block of text. (To indent an entire block of text, use Margin or Padding in the Box category.)

- **Whitespace**—This setting determines the whitespace, or empty space, within the block element. Normal collapses multiple spaces into one space. Pre leaves multiple spaces. Nowrap does not permit line wrapping without a break tag.

- **Display**—Controls fundamental aspects of the block element, including whether the element displays and how the tag behaves. Test these settings carefully because there is limited browser support for the Display option.

Box

Every block-level element in a page, such as a paragraph, is considered to live in its own rectangular box shape, which can be arranged using the box CSS settings. Some of these settings are used in conjunction with the positioning controls to create CSS positioning (discussed fully in Chapter 12, "CSS Positioning, Dreamweaver Layers, and Page Layout"). Note that some of these settings will show up only in the browser. Preview frequently to check your page.

Use the Box category (see Figure 11.7) of the CSS Style Definition dialog box to control element placement and spacing on the page.

FIGURE 11.7
The CSS Style Definition dialog box, showing the Box category.

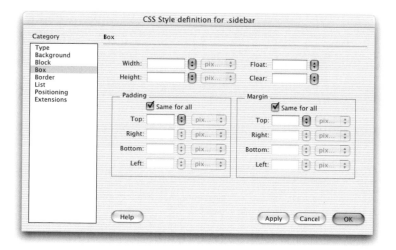

- **Width and Height**—These determine the width and height of the element.

- **Float**—Float is used to separate an element from the rest of the page. Other elements will flow and wrap around this element as if it were something like an image. Only with an image will this setting show up in Design view.

- **Clear**—Clear is used to define an area that does not allow elements to overlap. A layer that appears on a side set to Clear will be moved below the clear area. This keeps block-level elements from occupying the same horizontal space.

- **Padding**—Padding determines the space between the contents of the block element and its border (or its margin, if a border is not set).

It's similar to the cellpadding attribute for tables. You can set the padding on all four sides of an element independently by deselecting the Same for All check box.

- **Margin**—Margin determines the amount of space between the element's border and other page elements around it. It's similar to cellspacing for tables, or vspace and hspace for images and media elements. You can set the margin on all four sides of an element independently by deselecting the Same for All check box.

Border

Border options are used to set a border around the specified element. It is this border from which the box padding and margin are referenced. It's similar to a table border, but with more possibilities.

Use the Border category (see Figure 11.8) of the CSS Style Definition dialog box to set the border of a page element.

FIGURE 11.8
The CSS Style Definition dialog box, showing the Border category.

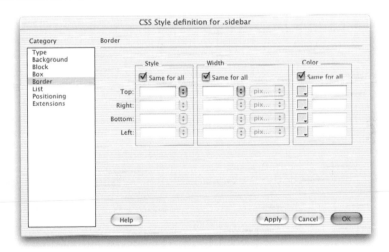

- **Style**—Choose from Dotted, Dashed, Solid, Double, Groove, Ridge, Inset, and Outset. Browser support for these differs.

- **Width**—Set the width for the border, as a number of pixels or non-numeric Thick or Thin.

- **Color**—Choose a color for the border.

Note that, as with padding and margin settings, the border can be applied to all four sides of an element independently. Use this independence to create effects such as paragraph rules.

List

The List category (see Figure 11.9) provides options for dressing up your numbered or bulleted lists.

FIGURE 11.9
The CSS Style Definition dialog box, showing the List category.

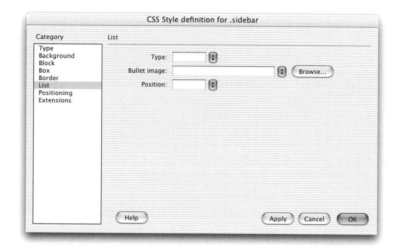

- **Type**—For bulleted (unordered) lists, choose the type of bullet to display: Disc, Circle, or Square. For ordered lists, choose what kind of alphabetical or numeric numbering to use: Decimal, Lowercase Roman Numerals, Uppercase Roman Numerals, or Upper- and Lowercase Letters.

- **Bullet Image**—For bulleted lists, specify an image to use as the bullet. Press the Browse button to link the image.

- **Position**—This setting determines how the list item wraps and indents. Choose Outside to wrap the list item to an indent, or Inside to wrap the item to the margin.

Positioning

The options in the Positioning category (see Figure 11.10) determine where the page elements will appear on your page—called *CSS Positioning*, or *CSS-P*. Although CSS positioning can be applied to most block-level elements, it is generally used with div tags. See Chapter 12 for a full discussion on CSS positioning.

FIGURE 11.10
The CSS Style
Definition dialog
box, showing the
Positioning category.

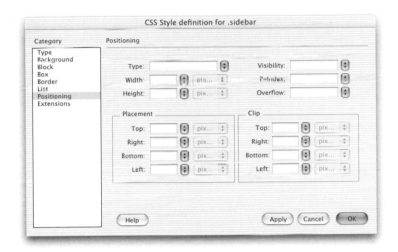

- **Type**—This determines what kind of positioning controls the element. Absolute positioning places the block element relative to the upper-left corner of the page. Relative positioning determines placement relative to the spot in the document where the positioning style appears in the document. Static positioning places the block element in the same location in which it appears in the document.

- **Visibility**—This controls the initial visibility of the element. Inherit gives the element the same visibility setting as the parent tag. Visible makes the element visible. Hidden makes the element invisible. These options are used with JavaScript to hide and show page elements dynamically. See Chapter 14, "Controlling Layers with JavaScript," for a full discussion on visibility and scripting.

- **Width and Height**—These are the same as the width and height settings in the Block category. They define the dimensions of the block element.

- **Z-Index**—The z-index setting determines the stacking order of elements on a page. It takes a numeric value. Elements with lower numbers will appear below higher-numbered elements. Stacking order is relevant only for CSS-positioned elements that overlap. See Chapter 12 for more on using z-index.

- **Overflow**—This is used when the content of an element is larger than its specified width and height, and determines what happens to that extra material. Visible allows all the content of the layer to

be shown simultaneously, no matter what the size setting is. Hidden strictly enforces the layer's size and cuts off any content that overflows this layer size. Scrollbars adds scrollbars to the layer whether it needs them or not. Watch for browser support on this if you are displaying important content. Auto creates scrollbars only when needed.

- **Placement**—Use these settings to specify where a CSS-positioned element will display. For absolutely positioned elements, all values are relative to the corners of the browser window. See Chapter 12 for a full discussion of this.

- **Clip**—This setting is used to specify the part of the layer that is visible. Use it when you want to hide a part of the layer without Overflow controls. It can be used in combination with JavaScript to create interesting effects.

Extensions

Options in the Extensions category (see Figure 11.11) are used for special considerations and customization. They haven't been as widely adopted by browsers as most of the other settings here, so tread carefully—and preview often—when using them.

FIGURE 11.11
The CSS Style Definition dialog box, showing the Extensions category.

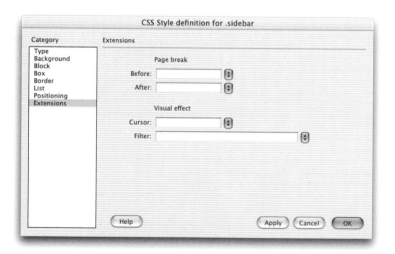

- **Page Break**—Use this for setting page breaks when setting up a page for printing. Use this setting for determining whether the page break comes before or after this element.

- **Visual Effect**—Use this to change the look of the cursor when it is over the element with this setting. Most browsers do not support this setting.

- **Filter**—This setting lets you apply special effects to images on the page. As of this writing, they work only in IE 4+.

Working with Styles

Style management happens in the CSS Styles panel, the Tag Inspector, the Property Inspector, the Tag Selector, and elsewhere.

Applying (and Unapplying) Styles

The beauty of redefined HTML tags is that they don't need to be applied. When a tag is redefined in your style sheet, every occurrence of it automatically takes on whatever formatting you specified. Contextual selectors and pseudoclasses work the same way.

Custom classes, on the other hand, need to be applied to an existing tag. Dreamweaver gives you various ways to do this:

- **Using the Property Inspector (see Figure 11.12)**—The Text and Table Property Inspectors include a drop-down menu of classes available for the current document. Just select the object/text that you want the class applied to, and then select the style from the drop-down menu to apply it. To unapply the class, choose None from the menu.

FIGURE 11.12

Applying custom classes in the Text Property Inspector and the Table Property Inspector.

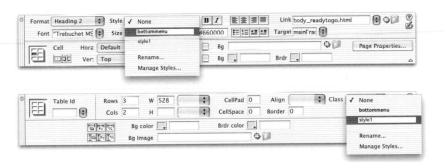

- **Using the Tag Inspector (see Figure 11.13):** In the Attributes section of the Tag Inspector, from the CSS/Accessibility category, type in the name of the class to apply.

FIGURE 11.13
Applying a CSS class with the Tag Inspector

- **Using the Tag Selector (see Figure 11.14)**—Right-click any tag in the Tag Selector and, from the contextual menu that pops up, choose Set Class to see a list of available classes. Choose one to apply it. To unapply a class, choose None.

FIGURE 11.14
Applying a custom CSS class with the Tag Selector.

- **Using the CSS Styles menus (see Figure 11.15)**—The CSS Styles menu includes a list of currently available classes. Access it under the Text menu or by right-clicking on a page element and using the contextual menu. To unapply a class, choose None.

After a tag has a class applied to it, the Property Inspector's drop-down Class menu shows that class, and the Tag Selector displays the tag with the class name after it.

FIGURE 11.15
Applying a custom
class with the CSS
Styles menu.

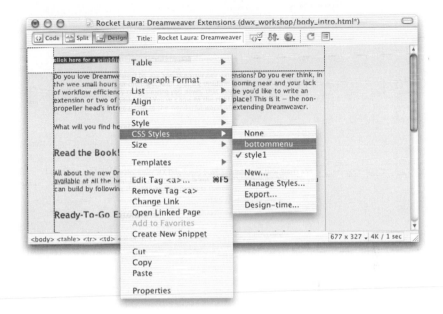

Managing Styles with the CSS Styles Panel (and Elsewhere)

The CSS Styles panel displays what styles you have defined, what their properties are, and where they're located (internally or externally).

- To edit any style, select it in the panel and click the panel's Edit Style button. This opens the CSS Style Definition dialog box, where you can change any properties you want.

- To rename any class, select it in the panel and choose Rename from the panel's Options menu.

- To delete a style, select it in the panel and click the panel's Remove Style button (the trash can). For custom classes, though, it doesn't delete the places where the style has been applied in your document.

You can also manage your styles from various other points in the Dreamweaver interface. From the main menu, choose Text > CSS Styles and use the Edit or Rename commands. You can also get to this sub-menu by right-clicking in the Document window and choosing CSS Styles from the contextual menu. Another interface for managing styles can be accessed by choosing Text > CSS Styles > Edit from the main menu. This command opens a <style> window, which displays all styles defined internally in the current document and all attached style sheets.

Select a style and click Edit to edit it, or select a style sheet and click Edit to open a second window showing this sheet's styles. Those of you who started using Dreamweaver before MX will recognize this as the old style-editing interface. It's very cumbersome compared to the CSS Styles panel, however, so unless you're familiar with it and love it, you're better off not using it.

Inspecting Styles

Once you've got styles happening in your document, you want to keep tabs on what classes have been applied, where CSS formatting is happening, and so on. The Property Inspector, the Tag Selector, and especially the brand-new glorious Tag Inspector can help you there.

Inspecting Styles with the Property Inspector

If your selection calls up the Text or Table Property Inspectors, any applied classes will show up in the Class drop-down menu (with formatting applied, where possible). For text selections, the Property Inspector also displays some of the basic text formatting that any redefined tag or custom class has applied to this item (see Figure 11.16). Be careful here, though! Changing any of these settings doesn't update your current style. Instead, it creates a new style and applies it to the text element in addition to whatever styles may already be there.

FIGURE 11.16
Inspecting styled text with the Property Inspector.

Applied Classes and the Tag Selector

When a class has been applied to a tag, it appears in the Tag Selector along with that tag (see Figure 11.17). Pay attention to this! It's a great way to keep tabs on where your classes are being used. The Tag Selector won't tell you if a tag has been redefined, however, or if there's a contextual selector at work.

FIGURE 11.17
The Tag Selector, showing several applied classes.

The Tag Inspector/CSS Rule Inspector

The Attributes tab of the Tag Inspector indicates, in its CSS/Accessibility category, whether a class has been applied to a selection. But that's just the start of the fun. The Relevant CSS tab of the Tag Inspector—also called the CSS Rule Inspector—is a wonderful compact interface for examining and editing styles that have been applied to your page elements (see Figure 11.18).

- **Examining applied style rules**—The top portion of the window indicates what CSS style rules are currently affecting the item you have selected in your document. That style rule might be a custom class, a redefined tag, or a combination of both. For custom classes, it also indicates what tag the class has been applied to.

- **Examining style properties**—Select a rule in the top portion of the window, and the bottom portion displays an exhaustive list of CSS formatting options, including any values that have been set in this rule. You can choose to display the list in categories (the same categories used by the CSS Style Definition dialog box) or alphabetically.

- **Editing styles**—Best of all, any changes you make to the style properties listed here will change the style you have selected. So, if you have one paragraph in your document selected and it's controlled by a redefined p tag, you can change the p rule formatting options here to reformat all paragraphs document-wide. If the redefined p tag is housed in an external style sheet, you've just reformatted paragraphs throughout your entire site, and all without having to go to the CSS Styles panel and opening the CSS Style Definition dialog box.

FIGURE 11.18
Using the CSS Rule Inspector to examine a styled text paragraph.

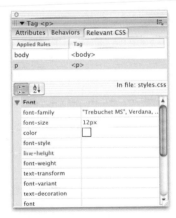

Formatting a Page with an Internal CSS Style Sheet

In this exercise, you'll spiff up the formatting of the Zoo Visit home page with CSS, stored in an internal style sheet. Before beginning, download the **chapter_11** folder from the book's website at www.peachpit.com to your hard drive. Create a site called Chapter 11 with this as the local root folder.

1. From the **chapter_11** folder, open **index.html** and examine it (see Figure 11.19). As far as table-based layout goes, not much else is happening. The text is created entirely from structural markup, leaving the browser to interpret all h1, h2, p, and a tags.

FIGURE 11.19

The Zoo Visit page before any CSS formatting has been applied.

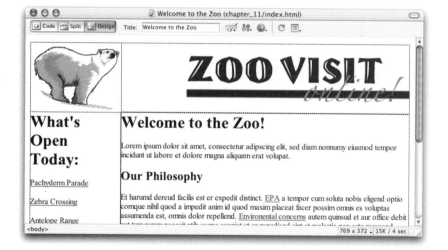

2. To start, a few page properties need tweaking. That means redefining the body tag. In the CSS Styles panel, click the New Style button. When the New Style dialog box opens, choose to redefine the body tag for This Document Only (see Figure 11.20). Click OK to close this dialog box.

    The CSS Style Definition dialog box opens automatically. You want to set the page margins to **0**, and you want to set the page background. Page margins are in the Box category, so go there now. Set the margins to **0** for all sides.

FIGURE 11.20
Redefining the body
tag for the current
document only.

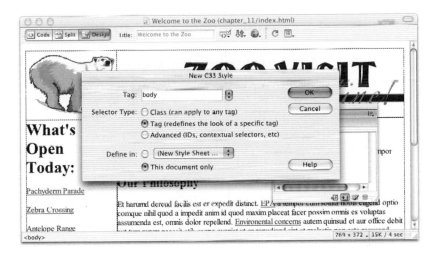

Now go to the Background category. Set the background color to **white** (just in case some browser doesn't default to a white background). For the background image, browse to the **blue_bar.gif** file (in images folder) and set the Repeat to **repeat-y** (vertical only). Click OK to close the dialog box. The page looks better already! Redefining the body is often where a CSS makeover starts.

3. Now for some basic text formatting: redefining the p tag. Create a new style, redefining the p tag for the current document only. When the Style Definition dialog box opens, go to the Type category and choose the Georgia font list. Set the size to .9 em. (See the section "Specifying Dimensions in CSS" for more on ems.) Click the Apply button to see your changes take effect. Then click OK to close the dialog box.

4. You want the h1 and h2 tags to be redefined as well, to use the same font list but with larger em sizes. Create those styles now. Experiment with the sizes until you get results you like. Choosing basic text formatting is often another early step in CSS formatting.

5. Now for a custom class or two. You don't want to alter the page margins, but the text in the main cell shouldn't run all the way to the right margin. This cell (and only this cell) needs some padding. In the CSS Styles panel, create a new style that makes a custom class called `.maincontent` (don't forget to start with a dot). In the Style Definition dialog box, go to the Box category and set the padding for the right side only to **30** pixels (see Figure 11.21).

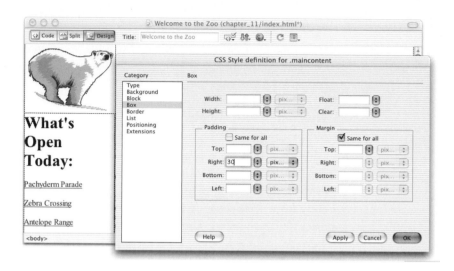

Click the Apply button; it has no effect in the document. That's because this is a custom class and needs to be applied. Click OK to close the dialog box.

In the Document window, put the insertion point in the main text area somewhere and use the Tag Selector to select the td tag that contains it. In the Property Inspector's Class drop-down menu, choose maincontent. You now have a right margin. The Tag Selector lists this cell as td.maincontent.

6. But wait! The maincontent style needs some bottom padding as well so that it doesn't smash into the footer. In the CSS Styles panel, select the maincontent style and click the Edit Style button. When the Style Definition dialog box opens, go to the Box category and add a bottom padding of **20** pixels. Click the Apply button to test your style. The change takes effect because this class has already been applied. Click OK to close the dialog box.

7. You're on your own now. To format the footer cell, create a custom class called .footer that adds **20** pixels of padding on all sides, and apply it to the bottom-right cell of your table.

8. One final item: The contents of the footer cell need to be right-aligned, which means editing the footer class. Select the table cell containing your footer. In the Selection Inspector, go to the CSS tab and open the Block category. Find the Align setting, and set it to Right. That's a quick way to edit a style sheet!

Working with Style Sheets

Style management is also about managing style sheets, both internal and external. All of this management can be done through the CSS Styles panel as well.

Attaching Style Sheets

Although you can use the CSS Styles panel to create style sheets, you also can attach existing style sheets. If you are adding more pages to a website that has a series of premade styles, you can easily attach those style sheets to your new pages and apply them as you want. They will act no differently from styles created in Dreamweaver. Redefined HTML tags will automatically update, and the list of custom classes should appear in the CSS Styles panel.

To attach an existing style sheet using the CSS Styles panel, simply click on the Attach Style Sheet button in the lower left of the panel. You can also choose Attach Style Sheet from the Class drop-down menu in the Property Inspector. Or, you can choose Text > CSS Styles > Attach Style Sheet from the main menu, or right-click in the Document window and choose CSS Styles > Attach Style Sheet.

Whichever method you choose, you are prompted to browse to the .css file and to choose whether to link or to import. The difference between these two is slim: Link uses an href to link to the sheet, while Import uses a style or URL link to find the file. Netscape 4 supports only the Link method. Other newer browsers can support either.

Click OK to complete the linking. The redefined HTML tags and selectors are applied automatically, and the list of the custom classes will be available throughout the interface.

If you imported your style sheet, it will display in the CSS Styles panel within the `<style>` tag indicator. That's because the `import` directive appears within a `style` tag. If you linked the style sheet, it will simply appear in the CSS Styles panel as itself (see Figure 11.22).

FIGURE 11.22
The CSS Styles panel, showing a linked and imported style sheet.

Working with External Style Sheets

When you have an external style sheet attached to a document, you can work with its styles the same way you would work with internal styles: through the CSS Styles panel and other interface elements discussed here. But every time you change a style in an attached sheet, Dreamweaver is actually changing the CSS document, not your open HTML document. This can be a little bit disconcerting until you get used to it. For instance, you might save your HTML, change a style definition, and then try to undo that change, only to find out that you can't because the change wasn't made to the current document.

Some web authors find this frustrating, so Dreamweaver gives you the option of automatically opening an external style sheet behind the current document whenever you work on one of its styles. That way, when you change a style, the change is made in the open style sheet and the style sheet isn't saved. If you want to undo the change, you can, or if you want to undo several changes, you can activate the CSS document and choose File > Revert.

The disadvantage of Dreamweaver opening the CSS document and not automatically saving it after every change is that you need to remember to save it periodically, even though it's not the main document you're working on. (You're working on your HTML document.) Every time you want to preview in a browser, for instance, you have to remember to activate the CSS document and save it, or any style changes you've made recently won't appear in your preview. If Dreamweaver should (heaven forbid!) crash while you're working, or if the power goes out and your computer shuts down unexpectedly, and you haven't remember to save both your HTML and your CSS file recently, you've just lost a lot of editing changes.

By default, Dreamweaver doesn't open the CSS document automatically. To change this preference, choose Edit > Preferences/CSS Styles and select the Open _CSS Files When Modified option (see Figure 11.23).

 The Preferences/CSS Styles dialog box also gives you various options for writing shorthand CSS code. By default, they're deselected. Unless you already write your own CSS code by hand and like to use shorthand, you can leave these preferences as is.

FIGURE 11.23
The Preferences dialog box for CSS Styles, including the option to automatically open external CSS documents when they're edited.

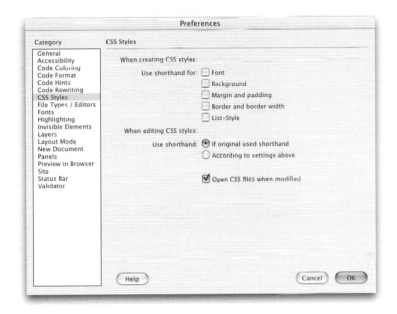

Removing Style Sheets

To remove an external style sheet, select it in the CSS Styles panel and click the Delete CSS Style (trash can) button. Note that this doesn't actually delete external CSS documents! It deletes only the link or import statement in your current document that connects the two.

An internal style sheet can't be deleted. Instead, select the individual styles within it and delete those.

Exporting Style Sheets

Exporting means moving styles from an internal to an external style sheet. Exporting becomes important if you create a style internally when you meant to create it externally, or create it internally and then later change your mind.

To export an internal style sheet from the CSS Styles panel, choose Export Style Sheet from the panel's Options menu. You can also choose Text > CSS Styles > Export from the main menu, or right-click in the Document window and choose CSS Styles > Export.

Whichever method you choose, Dreamweaver prompts you to create a new CSS document. When you've done this, click OK to close the dialog box. The new style sheet is created. Unfortunately, if you were hoping to

remove the internal style sheet and link your current document to the external style sheet, that doesn't happen. Your current document remains unchanged. To complete the operation, you'll have to delete all internal styles and use the Attach Style Sheet button to link or import the newly created CSS document.

If you want to copy just one or two styles to an external document, not your entire style sheet, select them in Code view and cut and paste them into a CSS document. The CSS Styles panel can help you with this, too. Select one of the styles in the panel and, from the Options menu, choose Go to Code. (You can also right-click the style and get the same Options menu.) Or, just double-click the style name to accomplish the same thing.

Creating a Style Sheet from Scratch

Maybe you don't want to create your external style sheet as you go. Maybe you know already what your styles will be, and you just want to build the style sheet without having a document open. You can do it! Just choose File > New and, in the New Document dialog box, choose Basic Pages/CSS as your document type.

This file will open in Code view because there's nothing to display in Design view. But that doesn't mean you can't use design tools to work on it. Using the CSS Styles panel or any other Dreamweaver method you prefer, create as many new styles as you want. Make sure the New Style dialog box is set to create the style This Document Only so that the code gets written in the document you have open. When you're done, save and close. Now you can link or import this style sheet into as many HTML documents as you want.

| EXERCISE 11.2 | **Moving Internal Styling to an External Style Sheet** |

This exercise builds on the previous exercise, moving the internal styles that you created there to an external style sheet. You won't be able to do this exercise until you've done that one.

1. Start by opening **index.html** in your **chapter_11** folder. Examine the CSS Styles panel, and you'll see the various internal styles you defined earlier. You want to make those styles external so you can apply them to other pages. (For some of you, this is a typical design

scenario, starting internally and then deciding external would be better. It's also good practice working with style sheets.)

2. In the CSS Styles panel, open the Options menu and choose Export Style Sheet. When the dialog box opens, choose to call your style **main.css** and save it in the **chapter_11** folder.

3. Now you need to get rid of the internal style sheet to make room for the new external styles. In the CSS Styles panel, select each style and click the Delete button to get rid of them all. Back to square one!

4. Now click the Attach Style Sheet button in the CSS Styles panel. When the dialog box opens, choose to Link to the main.css document (see Figure 11.24), and click OK to close the dialog box. Styles are back!

FIGURE 11.24
Attaching the main.css style sheet to the Visit Zoo page.

5. To finish, the footer needs some spiffing up. How about a border to separate the footer from the content area? Select the footer cell and, in the Property Inspector, find the Class drop-down menu. From this menu, choose Edit.

When the Style Definition dialog box opens, go to the Border category. Deselect Same for All for all options, and create a top border that's solid, 2 pixels thick, and the same orange color that's in the zoo title graphic (see Figure 11.25).

Click OK to close the dialog box. There's a lovely horizontal line separating the footer from the rest of the page.

FIGURE 11.25
Creating a horizontal
rule effect with a
top-only border style.

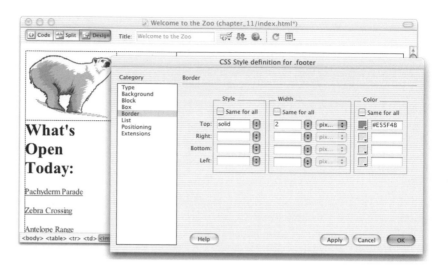

WORKING SMART WITH CSS

CSS is wonderful not only because it's new and efficient, but because it's powerful. To make the most of Cascading Style Sheets, you have to be smart about using them.

Specifying Fonts in HTML (and CSS)

A lot of text-formatting chores got a lot better when CSS came along. Without CSS, you don't have as many text sizes to choose from, you can't indent or set margins, and so on. But the world of font choices is still the same as it always was. The CSS Style Definition dialog box, just like the non-CSS tools you used in previous Dreamweaver versions, gives you a drop-down menu of (not very exciting) font groups to choose from instead of the glamorous list of cool typefaces you desire. Why?

HTML, Fonts, and Browsers

Fonts do not embed themselves in web pages, and there's no mechanism for linking a font to a web page the way you link graphics and other media. (There are lots of technical and legal reasons for that.) This means that the end user will be able to display your beautiful web page using only the fonts that he has installed on his computer. If your

page calls for a font that a particular user doesn't have installed, your text will display in his browser's default font—usually Times New Roman.

The first strategy for dealing with this problem is to specify only fonts that your visitors are likely to have on hand. Of course, all computer setups are different, but almost all Windows systems have Times New Roman, Arial, Georgia, Verdana, and Courier New. Almost all Mac systems have times, Arial, Helvetica, Georgia, Verdana, and Courier.

The second strategy is to specify more than one font, leaving the user's browser to go through the list of supplied choices for one that it recognizes as being on the system. This is often called using fallback fonts, font groups, or font lists. Because the browser stops at the first font that it recognizes, the strategy is to start with fonts that maybe not everybody has and work down toward the more common fonts, ending with a generic font category such as serif or sans serif. This system expands the possibilities greatly, even if you stick to the fonts that visitors on different systems are likely to have. Table 11.1 lists some fairly common font choices that can be useful in font lists.

TABLE 11.1 ## Reasonably Common Serif and Sans Serif Fonts on Mac and Windows, According to Category

Mac	Windows	Category
Times	Times New Roman	Serif
Georgia	Georgia	Serif
Book Antiqua	Book Antiqua	Serif
Palatino	Palatino Linotype	Serif
New York	—	Serif
Arial	Arial	Sans serif
Helvetica	—	Sans serif
Verdana	Verdana	Sans serif
Trebuchet MS	Trebuchet	Sans serif
Comic Sans MS	Comic Sans	Sans serif
—	Tahoma	Sans serif

Verdana (sans serif) and Georgia (serif) are both good choices for body text on websites. A type designer named Matthew Carter, who was hired by Microsoft to create two very readable screen-based families, developed them especially for screen reading.

Font Lists in Dreamweaver

Dreamweaver offers you the following font-face combinations:

- Arial, Helvetica, sans serif

- Times New Roman, Times, serif

- Courier New, Courier, mono

- Georgia, Times New Roman, Times, serif

- Verdana, Arial, Helvetica, sans serif

If none of these strikes your fancy, you can edit these or add your own lists in the Edit Font List dialog box (see Figure 11.26). You can access this window from any drop-down menu of fonts in Dreamweaver by choosing Edit Font List at the bottom of the menu. You can also choose Text > Fonts > Edit Font List.

FIGURE 11.26
The Edit Font List dialog box.

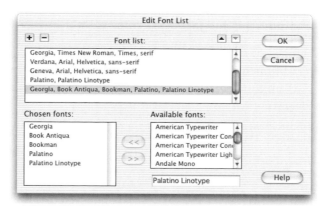

To create a new font list, select the Add Fonts in List Below entry in the font list area, or click the + button at the top of this area. From the two fields in the bottom half of the dialog box, the Chosen Fonts area on the left shows the fonts in your font list. The Available Fonts area on the right lists the fonts installed on your computer. The text field underneath this area lets you specify any font not on your system. The idea is,

you select or type in a font on the right, press the << arrow, and copy the font to the list on the left. To remove a font from the list, click the >> arrow.

Add as many fonts as you want to your new combination, starting from the most desirable and ending with the most generic. Always finish a font combination with a generic font family; these can be found at the very end of the Available Fonts list.

When you're finished, click OK to close the Edit Font List dialog box.

You can add fonts and can remove fonts, but you can't rearrange fonts in this dialog box. If you get your fonts in the wrong order, you'll have to remove them and add them again to get back to where you want to be.

Specifying Dimensions in CSS

When it comes to specifying the sizes of things, CSS presents you with an embarrassment of riches. Embarrassing because who the heck knows what all of those choices mean? There are many different ways to define sizes, but they generally fall into two groups: absolute and relative. *Absolute sizes* are unchangeable, no matter where they are used:

- Points (pt) and picas (pc) come from the print world. A point is 1/72 of an inch. A pica is 12 picas, or 1/6 of an inch.

- Millimeters (mm) and centimeters (cm) are standard metric lengths. A millimeter is 1/100 of a centimeter. (For the nonmetric, 2.54cm equal 1 inch.)

- Inches (in) are standard lengths in the regular world, although they're rarely used in the web world. An inch equals .394 of a centimeter.

- Pixels (px) are the standard way of defining sizes on computers. Most elements on the web page are defined in pixels. A pixel is one small block of monitor space, the physical building blocks of your screen. A pixel is *defined* as a fraction of an inch on the screen. The difficulty of using pixels is that Macs and PCs have chosen different fractions for determining size. And to confuse the issue even more, the CSS spec pegs the "reference pixel" at about 90 pixels per inch, which, sadly, neither operating system uses. But pixels remain the most-used measuring entity around.

Relative sizes are bigger or smaller than some defined length:

- **Percentage (%)**—A universal concept, a percentage value is *X*% bigger than a standard value. The question for development is, bigger compared to what? Percent-based sizes always use the default setting of the parent tag as the baseline size. For instance, if the default size of a font is 10 units, setting the font to 120% makes the font show at 12 units. Setting the percent value to 20% shows it at 2 units. Another example is tables. Set a table to be 80% wide, and it will show as 80% of the window because the body tag is the parent element. Set a table cell to 80%, and it will take up 80% of the table because the table tag is the parent element.

- **Em**—An em is an obscure but useful value. It is defined as equal to the point size for a given font element. If a font is set as 12 pixels, then 1 em equals 12 pixels. This way, you can set a custom class to be 2 em of a certain setting—say, the previous font. If you apply this class to a piece of text, it will be 2 em big, or 24 pixels.

- **Ex**—This is a relative setting that is based on the height of a lowercase *x* in the chosen font. Although this can be of great help when using a certain font, keep in mind that different fonts have different relative *x* sizes. One font's *x* can be half the size of a capital letter, and another font's x can be 60–70%. This will make ex render differently between fonts.

CSS and Accessibility

There's nothing inherently inaccessible about CSS; it's just a formatting language. In fact, CSS is so handy that disabled web surfers often use their own style sheets to enhance functionality. For instance, a low-vision person might use a style sheet that specifies very large text, or a color-blind person might use a style sheet that changes all colors to black on white. The job of the web designer, in relation to these people, is to stay out of their way. How do you do this?

According to Section 508, § 1194.22(d):

> Documents shall be organized so they are readable without requiring an associated style sheet.

No matter what kind of styles you have applied to your document, it should be readable and functional without them. (It doesn't have to be pretty—just functional.) Also, because user-specified style sheets are external, you don't want to override those styles with styles you've defined internally—use external style sheets, not internal style sheets or inline styles.

Section 508 doesn't go any further than this, but the W3C's Web Accessibility Initiative guidelines add a recommendation that addresses formatting issues in general:

> Use relative rather than absolute units in markup language attribute values and style sheet property values [priority 2].

In other words, set your font sizes—and other sizes—to percentages or other relative settings rather than points or pixels.

Dreamweaver doesn't offer any magic gadgets to help you design your CSS for accessibility because you don't need them. Just use common sense when creating styles and style sheets. You can, however, use Dreamweaver's Design Time Style Sheets feature to help preview how your pages will fare in an alternate environment. Do it this way:

1. Create a new CSS style sheet document (choose File > New, and choose Basic Pages/CSS as the document type). With this document open, use the CSS Styles panel to redefine the basic HTML tags for text display in large-print style (200% size, black, Georgia, for instance). Redefine the body tag to have a white background color. Or, choose whatever visibility changes one of your target users might have in a custom style sheet. Save this file with a descriptive name such as **access.css**.

2. Now open one of your HTML documents that has been formatted with a beautiful, elegant external style sheet.

3. In the CSS Styles panel, go to the Options menu and choose Design Time Style Sheets. When the dialog box appears (see Figure 11.27), find the Show Only at Design Time section and click the + button. Browse to select your access.css style sheet.

   Now find the Hide at Design Time section and click the + button. Browse to select the style sheet that's currently attached to this page.

FIGURE 11.27
The Design Time style
sheets interface.

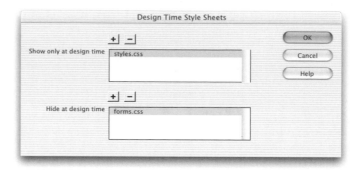

4. When you're done, click OK to close the dialog box. Dreamweaver now displays your document with the alternate style sheet. Wow! Is it readable? Is there some local formatting in there, getting in the way of big, black, bold text (or whatever your accessibility style sheet specified)? If the page is functional like this, you've done an accessible job applying CSS.

5. To put things back to normal, go back to the CSS Styles panel Options menu, choose Design Time Style Sheets again, and, for both sections in the dialog box, select the style sheet listed. Then click the – button.

Getting Specific with Contextual Selectors

Contextual CSS selectors—styles that take effect only under certain conditions—drastically expand the power of what you can do with CSS formatting. As was outlined earlier in the chapter, they're easy to create in Dreamweaver. Taking advantage of them is just a matter of getting your mind used to thinking in contextual terms.

Creating Multiple Link Styles for a Page

Imagine this scenario: Your pages all have a navigation sidebar, with CSS-formatted text links instead of images. They also have a footer with some redundant text links. And the main content area of each page may or may not include inline links in the text. Do all of these links have to look the same? No! By defining some contextual selectors, you can create different link styles for each different need. Do it this way:

1. For the text links in the main content area, either redefine the a tag (and its pseudoclass brethren) or leave it to display using browser defaults. Visitors are used to seeing underlined blue links in text, so don't mess with a good thing.

2. For the sidebar, create a custom class called .sidebar, and apply it to the table cell or div element that contains the sidebar elements. You can use the sidebar style to apply whatever formatting you like—background color, text formatting, anything.

Why is it .sidebar a and not a .sidebar? Because the link is going to be inside the table cell or div that has the sidebar class applied to it. The a .sidebar class would control a sidebar-styled element located inside a link. The parent tag comes first; then comes the enclosed, or child, tag.

3. Now create a contextual selector. In Dreamweaver's New CSS Style dialog box, choose the Advanced option and, in the input field, enter **.sidebar a:link** as the name of your style. This will affect only links within elements that have the sidebar class applied to them—in other words, only the links in your page's sidebar area. These links will be mimicking a traditional navigation bar, so remove underlines, make them bold, change fonts, and do whatever you like.

4. To give your sidebar links rollover effects, create another new contextual selector. Call this one **.sidebar a:hover**, and assign whatever color changes or other hover changes you like.

5. Repeat this procedure for the footer links: Create a custom class called .footer and apply it to the table cell or div that contains the bottom navigation elements. Then define contextual selectors such as .footer a to control the appearance of these links.

Quick Styling of Table Cells

Here's another scenario: You have layout tables throughout your site, but you also have a few dozen very large data tables scattered across the site that you want to display a certain way. And you want to control it all as efficiently as possible. You can use custom classes to format the tables, but the disadvantage of classes is that they must be applied. And the formatting you have in mind must be applied to individual table cells, not just tables. Do you have to create a custom class for data table cells and then go through your entire site, applying custom classes to a dozen or more table cells in each document? No! You apply a custom class to your data tables and use a contextual selector to apply the cell formatting. Do it this way:

1. Create a custom class called .datatable. Give it whatever formatting characteristics you like for your data tables—maybe a nice background color or text formatting for table contents. Apply this class to all data tables.

2. Now create a contextual selector. In Dreamweaver's New CSS Style dialog box, choose the Advanced option and, in the input field, enter **.datatable td** as the name of your style. Assign centered alignment, assign borders, and assign any formatting that must be applied on a cell-by-cell basis. When you finish, your data table cells are formatted immediately because the custom class has already been applied.

When you start thinking in contextual terms, you'll increase your CSS efficiency and be able to tackle bigger projects without blanching.

EXERCISE 11.3

Use Contextual Styles to Format Links and Other Page Content

In this exercise, you'll continue to build the Zoo Visit site, using contextual styles to create several different link styles.

1. The links in the main content area need to be color-coordinated to match the page background bar, but otherwise they should be left alone. The links in the sidebar need different formatting. Those in the footer still need different formatting.

   Start with the main text links in the content area. To define those, you'll just redefine the anchor tag. Create a new style that redefines the a tag; make sure the style gets saved in the main.css style sheet, not in the current document. In the Type category of the Style Definition dialog box, select the color chip and sample your page's blue sidebar to create the text link color. When you click OK to close the dialog box, all links on your page turn that shade of blue. The links in the sidebar disappear entirely.

2. Now it's time to set up the sidebar. Create a custom class called .sidebar, to be stored in the main.css style sheet. You don't want the sidebar content to smash up against the edges of its table cell, so it's time for more padding. Assign a left and right padding of 10 and 20 pixels. Click OK to close the dialog box.

Try applying the class through the Tag Selector this time. Place the insertion point in the sidebar cell. In the Tag Selector, find the td tag that contains the selection, and right-click. From the menu that appears, choose Set Class > sidebar.

3. Now that there's a custom class, you can create some contextual selectors for what's inside it. Create a new style and, in the New Style dialog box, choose Advanced. For your selector's name, enter **.sidebar a:link** (don't forget to type the dot at the beginning). Click OK to close the dialog box. Figure 11.28 shows this happening.

FIGURE 11.28
Creating the .sidebar a contextual style.

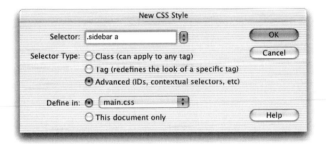

TIP

What if it doesn't work? Open main.css and double-check the name of the contextual style. Is the dot missing? Is anything else wrong? If there's the smallest typo, it won't work.

When the Style Definition dialog box appears, you get to choose how the links inside the sidebar will appear. Set the color to white, the font to the Arial list, the weight to bold, and the size to 90%. (This means 90% of what the size would be without this style.) Click OK to close the dialog box and create the style. The links in the sidebar are styled!

4. The sidebar links would also benefit from rollover effects. That requires another contextual style. Create a new style, of the Advanced type, with the name .sidebar a:hover. In the Style Definition dialog box, change the text color to black and set the decoration to Underline. Click OK to close the dialog box.

5. There are several more opportunities for contextual styles on this page. Do you know what they are? The heading in the sidebar uses an h1 tag because it's the main heading in the sidebar, but it should look different from the real main heading. How can a contextual style help you there? The links in the footer also need their own styling. To contrast with the main content of the page, they should be in Arial and should colored orange to match the divider bar that

you added to the footer previously. What contextual style will fix this formatting problem? (Answers: `.sidebar h1` and `.footer a`.)

Your challenge: Can you make these styles happen?

Working with Multiple Style Sheets at Once

Thanks to the properties of inheritance and cascading, you can have an external and internal style sheet, or multiple external sheets, controlling the same document at the same time. Remember that the *cascading* in CSS means that styles can be additive and that the code closest to the actual element trumps higher-level style rules. Understanding the benefits and drawbacks of combining sheets will enable you to take full advantage of CSS.

Using Internal and External Style Sheets Together

Why would you want to use an internal and an external style sheet? You might have a whole set of site-wide styles that govern the entire look and feel of your pages. But you've got this one page, with content that's unlike any of your other pages and with formatting requirements of its very own. You still want it to have the company look and feel, but you need a few extra tweaks for this page alone.

It's easy to mix and match internal and external when you use the CSS Styles panel to build your styles. Every time you create a new style, use the Define In settings to choose where the style code goes.

Just remember that, according to the rules of cascading and inheritance, the internal style sheet always wins any style wars. You want to define as many styles as you like externally and then selectively override just the styles that should be different for the internal style sheet. If the external style sheet defines the p tag to be Arial 12-pixel left-aligned text with line spacing of 15 and a color of black, and your current page needs blue text, redefine the p tag internally—but include only the specific property that needs changing, color. That way, if the company font changes from Arial to Georgia, you won't have to fix this page.

Using Multiple External Style Sheets

This is where life really gets interesting. If you're a good planner, you can create modular design effects for maximum CSS efficiency even on a large site. Imagine: You've got a site-wide style sheet that defines page margins, basic fonts and sizes, and nothing else. That applies to all pages in the site. Then each department has its own style sheet that defines a custom color scheme to apply to the page background and text. And across all departments, you've got some common types of pages, such as input forms, that have their own style requirements. Figure 11.29 shows how you might attach these style sheets to create a lovely, well-organized style cascade.

FIGURE 11.29
Diagramming a site's use of multiple external style sheets.

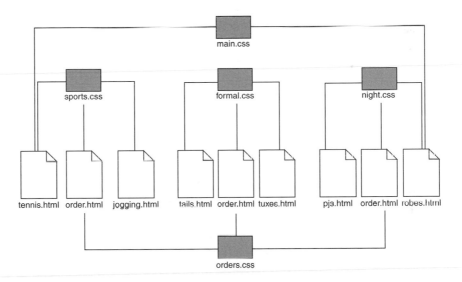

Order Matters!

You can link, or attach, as many style sheets as you want to an HTML document. According to the rules of cascading, the one at the bottom of the list has precedence (because it's closest to the page content in your document). Because the one at the top of the list is farthest away, it will be overridden by all others. So, the farther down the list a style sheet is, the higher its priority is.

How It All Works in Dreamweaver

You can get yourself into trouble attaching multiple external style sheets if you're not careful.

First, by default, Dreamweaver adds newly attached style sheets to the bottom of the style list. This is true whether they're linked or imported or a mixture. If you can, attach them in order, from lowest priority to highest priority. Their order in the CSS Styles panel display is the same as their order in your document.

What can you do if your style sheets are in the wrong order? You can't use the CSS Styles panel itself to rearrange them, unfortunately. You can switch to Code view, find the code for both styles, and cut and paste to rearrange them.

Second, it is possible (and even legal) to import a style sheet into another style sheet. If you have an external style sheet selected in the CSS Styles panel when you attach another one, Dreamweaver will import the new style sheet into the one you had selected instead of attaching it to your current HTML document. If this happens, the newly attached style sheet will appear indented in the style list, and you'll need to open the other style sheet in Dreamweaver, find the code that imported the second sheet, and delete it.

EXERCISE 11.4

Using Multiple Cascading Style Sheets

It's time for the coup de grace in the Zoo Visit site. By the end of this exercise, you'll see some of what's possible using external Cascading Style Sheets.

1. To start, the main.css style sheet needs to be applied to more than one page. Open **zebra.html**. In the CSS Styles panel, click the Attach Style button and choose to Link the main.css style sheet to this file. Some, but not all, of your formatting appears. What's missing?

   You need to apply the maincontent, sidebar, and footer classes, that's what! Using the Property Inspector, the Selection Inspector, or any of the other methods mentioned earlier in this chapter, apply all three of these classes to the appropriate table cells.

   Repeat this procedure to attach the main.css style sheet to **zebra_form.html**. If you're feeling really frisky, you can attach all of the pages: the monkey section, the elephant section, and so on. But the only one you'll be using in the exercise is the zebra.

2. Now for the subsidiary style sheet. Take a look at one of the two zebra pages you just edited. Both of the pages in the zebra section need their own special treatment; they need a purple background graphic (instead of blue) and a purple color for links to match. Everything else about them should match the main page. You need a zebra style sheet, to override a few of the properties in the main style sheet.

Open **zebra.html,** go to the CSS Styles panel, and create a new style. Choose to store this style in a new style sheet document, not main.css. Because you need this style to change the page's background graphic, set it to redefine the body tag. Click OK to close this dialog box. When Dreamweaver asks what to call your new CSS document, call it **zebra.css** and save it in the **chapter_11** folder.

When the Style Definition dialog box opens, go to the Background category and set the background image to **purple_bar.gif** in the images folder. Set the Repeat option to repeat-y and click OK to close the dialog box. The zebra's sidebar color changes, but all other styles from the main page are still in place.

The zebra.css style sheet also needs to redefine the a tag so that its color matches the purple sidebar. Create a new style to be stored in zebra.css that redefines the a tag. In the Type category of the Style Definition dialog box, set the color to match the purple sidebar (see Figure 11.30).

FIGURE 11.30
The zebra section of the Zoo Visit website, with its own color scheme on top of the main style sheet's formatting.

3. Now apply the zebra style sheet to the other of your two zebra pages. Open **zebra_form.html**. Attach the zebra.css style sheet to this file, and there's your new color scheme!

4. So now the zebra_form.html page is being formatted by two separate style sheets. But wait, there's more! All of the order form pages throughout the site need some form styling, which can be found in the forms.css style sheet. Attach this style sheet to the **zebra_form.html** document to see a CSS triple-play (see Figure 11.31).

FIGURE 11.31
The zebra's order form page, using three external style sheets to make its magic.

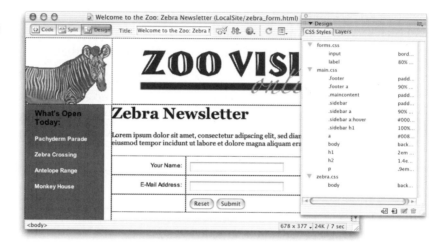

If you're really curious, finish up the site! The elephant page needs brown_bar.gif as its sidebar; the monkey page needs green_bar.gif.

Using Linked and Imported Style Sheets to Create a Netscape 4–Friendly Site

As mentioned earlier, Netscape 4 doesn't support the import directive for attaching external style sheets to web pages. You can use this to your advantage, to create one set of styles for newer browsers and another set for Netscape 4. Do it like this:

1. As you build your web page, create an external style sheet to hold all CSS formatting, and attach it to the page. Call the style sheet something like **styles.css**.

2. When you're finished, preview the page in Netscape 4 and see what doesn't work there. Determine how you could simplify the styles to make it work acceptably.

3. In Dreamweaver, duplicate styles.css as ns4_styles.css or some similar name. Open it in Dreamweaver and use the CSS Styles panel to edit the problematic styles so they're Netscape-friendly. Save and close.

4. Open your web page again. In the CSS Styles panel, select and remove the styles.css attached style sheet. (You're removing it so you can reattach it in the proper order.)

    Attach the Netscape-friendly style sheet, being sure to specify the Link method as you do. Then reattach the main style sheet, using the Import method.

What's going to happen here? Reading from top to bottom, any newer browser will see the linked style sheet, but will then also see the imported style sheet. Because the imported style sheet appears second, it will take precedence for displaying content. Netscape 4 will see the linked style sheet and will link it. It will then completely ignore the imported style sheet and display its content according to the simpler set of rules.

Summary

CSS is an important aspect of web design, and it will become only more important in the future. This chapter acquainted you with CSS and the basics of its structure, use, and possibilities. This chapter discussed the theory of separating content from style, cascading and inheritance, and ways to link to styles. Experiment with CSS, using the styles provided or creating styles of your own. Try using all the different parameters available to you, and then check them in both browsers to get an idea of how they react.

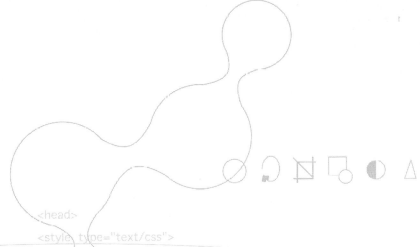

CHAPTER 12

CSS Positioning, Dreamweaver Layers, and Page Layout

CASCADING STYLE SHEETS CAN DO A LOT MORE THAN SPECIFY FONTS AND ADD table backgrounds. CSS positioning properties can also be used to control the layout of a web page by controlling the position of page elements. In addition to the CSS tools covered in the previous chapter, the Dreamweaver MX 2004 Layer object, Layers panel, and Layer Property Inspector provide a friendly and powerful graphic interface for working with CSS positioning. This chapter covers how CSS-P works and how to use Dreamweaver's Layer interface to make CSS-P work for you.

What is a *layer*? If you search an HTML reference, you'll find that there is an old Netscape 4–specific tag called layer, but this is not what is meant by the term in Dreamweaver or by most web developers who use it today. Rather, *layer* is an intuitively understandable term for one or more page elements that, through application of CSS properties, are positioned and layered above other page contents. Throughout this chapter and this book, that's the way in which the term is used.

LAYER BASICS

To work well with CSS layers in Dreamweaver, you must first understand where they're coming from and what they're doing. With that groundwork, you can make the most of them without painting yourself into any nasty corners.

CSS-P and Layers in the Browser

The original CSS1 specification covered various text and other formatting options for page content in HTML. But the W3C wasn't finished there. CSS-P introduced the capability to govern how elements are positioned on the page (*P* is for positioning). An expanded version of CSS-P then became part of the CSS2 standard. In addition to positioning, CSS-P allows page elements to be assigned a width, visibility, and even depth (z-index), allowing elements to be layered on the page. (Hence, the term *layer*.)

How CSS Positioning Works

Table 12.1 lists some of the style attributes possible with CSS-P and CSS2, and what they can do. Of these, positioning has been the most exciting to web designers. Through positioning controls, any page element can be turned into a free-standing entity, and—theoretically, at least—web designers need no longer be slaves to the tyranny of tables for simple things such as putting page contents where they want them.

TABLE 12.1 **CSS-P and CSS2 Styles**

Style Property	Values	Description
position	static, absolute, relative, or fixed	Positions the element on the page (see the text for details).
left, right, top, bottom	Measurement in pixels, percent, and so on	Specifies the element's distance from the edge of its parent element.
width, height	Measurement in pixels, percent, and so on	Specifies the element's dimensions.
z-Index	Number	Specifies the element's place in the stacking order. Higher numbers are in front of lower numbers.
Visibility	true/false	Specifies whether the element is visible (used mainly for scripting purposes).
Clip	clip: rect(top right bottom left)	Specifies whether the entire element will display or whether only a rectangle within the element's width and height will display.
Overflow	visible, hidden, scroll, auto	Determines what happens to content that won't fit within the width and height of the element.

Positioning Types

Positioning comes in three flavors: *absolute, relative,* and *static.* These types work like this:

- **Static positioning** makes the element a static part of the document's normal flow. This is where the element would sit on the page if no positioning were specified. The element appears on the page as part of the normal flow of elements. The code for static positioning of an element might look like this:

  `<h1 style="position:static;">Howdy!</h1>`

- **Absolute positioning** places the page element an absolute distance from the edges of the browser window or the item's parent element. This distance can be specified in pixels, percent, or other units of

measurement supported by CSS. The code for absolute positioning of an element might look like this:

```
<h1 style="position:absolute; left:0px; top:0px; ">
➥Howdy!</h1>
```

Assuming that this element isn't inside a table, div element, or other page element, it's a direct child of the body tag and hugs the upper-left corner of the browser window, regardless of what other page elements might proceed it in the HTML flow.

- **Relative positioning** places the page element relative to other page content. This is similar to static positioning, in that the element's default position is after or below elements that precede it in the HTML and before or above elements that follow it in the HTML. But a relatively positioned element can be offset from its default position by assigning left, top, right, or bottom values. The code for relative positioning of an element might look like this:

```
<h1 style="position:relative; left:50px; top:10px; ">
➥Howdy!</h1>
```

Assuming that this element occurs below a table on the page, the code here will move its left edge to be 50 pixels to the right of where it would otherwise sit below the table, and move its top edge 10 pixels down from where it would otherwise sit.

- **Fixed positioning** is similar to absolute positioning, except that when the page scrolls in the browser window, fixed elements do not scroll with it. The code for fixed positioning of an element might look like this:

```
<h1 style="position:fixed; left:0px; top:0px; ">Howdy!</h1>
```

Assuming that this element is not nested in any other elements (except the body itself), it will hug the upper-left corner of the browser window and will stay there even if the user scrolls down the page to view other content. (Unfortunately, fixed positioning is not as well-supported as the other positioning types, even in modern browsers.)

Positioning and Nesting

Positioning gets more complex when elements are nested inside other elements. In most browsers, and in the CSS-2 specification, how an element's positioning is interpreted depends on whether the element's

parent also has positioning specified—and specified as nonstatic. If the parent has no position attribute set or has the position set to static, a child with absolute position will be positioned relative to the closest ancestor with absolute or relative positioning. If no such ancestor exists (including the document body), the child will be positioned relative to the window.

Applying Positioning to Page Elements

A page element can be positioned with an inline style definition, like this:

```
<h1 style="position:absolute; left:150px; top:80px">Howdy!</h1>
```

Or, it can be positioned by assigning it a custom class that includes positioning, like this:

```
.logotest { position: absolute; left:150px; top:80px; }
<h1 class="logotest">Howdy!</h1>
```

And because a particular style definition that includes positioning may be used only once in a document, the CSS style information can also be attached to a page element's unique ID attribute, like this:

```
#logotest { position: absolute; left: 150px; top: 80px; };
<h1 id="logotest">Howdy!</h1>
```

If the style definition shown here is placed in an external style sheet document and is attached to a number of HTML pages, each page can have one element with the logotest ID, which will have its placement controlled by the style.

As with all CSS, the inline method is the least efficient because the information can never be reapplied to any other page elements in this or any other document.

Using *div* and *span* as Page Elements for Positioning

Theoretically, any page element can be absolutely positioned using CSS-P. Block elements (such as tables, headings, and paragraphs) are most commonly used for this, although inline elements (such as images) can also be used. But what if you want to position a group of elements, such as a heading and a following paragraph? You would enclose the entire group in a tag that doesn't have any of its own characteristics to interfere with page display, and apply a custom class or inline style to that tag. The two

tags used for this are div (block element) and span (inline). Coding for positioning a group of elements might look like this:

```
<div style="position:absolute; left:150px; top:80px;
width:200px">
    <h1>Howdy!</h1>
    <p>Welcome to my brand-new website!</p>
</div>
```

or this:

```
<span style="position:absolute; left:150px; top:80px;
width:200px">
    <h1>Howdy!</h1>
    <p>Welcome to my brand-new website!</p>
</span>
```

div and span elements can be nested inside each other. Other HTML elements nested inside div and span elements can also have positioning applied, like this:

```
<div style="position:absolute; left:150px; top:80px;">
    <h1 style="position:absolute; left:50px; top:50px;">
    Howdy!</h1>
</div>
```

How Layers Work in Dreamweaver

Dreamweaver layers provide an interface for dealing with CSS-P in Design view. Like any tool, they can be used or abused. Remember to always keep track of what's happening in the code while you're working with layers.

Drawing and Inserting Layers

The simplest and most intuitive way to get into building layers is to insert Layer objects with the Draw Layer object, found in the Layout Insert bar (see Figure 12.1). To use this tool, choose it from the Insert bar, position the cursor in the Document window, and drag to draw. When you're done, Dreamweaver displays a layer fitting your dimensions.

FIGURE 12.1
The Draw Layer object.

You can also choose Insert > Layout Objects > Layer, which inserts a layer with default dimensions and positioning into the document.

If you check Code view after your layer is created, you'll see that Dreamweaver built it as an empty div tag with an inline style where absolute positioning, dimensions, and stacking index are specified:

```
<div id="Layer1" style="position:absolute; width:200px;
➥height:115px; z-index:1; left: 113px; top: 117px;"></div>
```

Absolutely positioned elements don't require all of these attributes, but they're all supplied by default.

Working with Layer Properties

Select your layer, and the Layer Property Inspector appears (see Figure 12.2). You can use this to change or remove any properties, or to change the tag used for the layer from div to span. To change the defaults for inserting layers, you can also choose Edit > Preferences/Layers (see Figure 12.3). Or, you can change your layer's size and position interactively by moving or resizing it in the Document window.

FIGURE 12.2
The Layer Property Inspector.

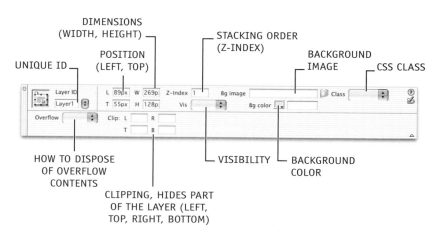

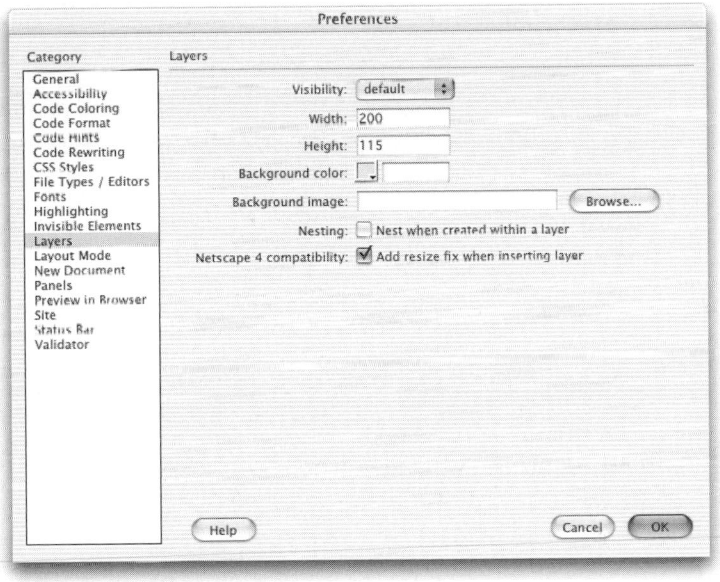

FIGURE 12.3
Setting layer
preferences.

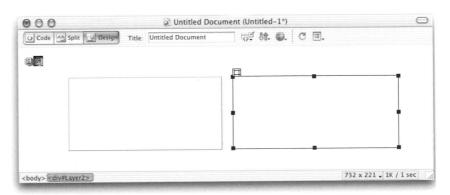

Invisible Elements: Layer Markers

Because layers created with the Layer object use absolute positioning,
their placement in the Design view layout isn't necessarily anywhere near
where their code has been inserted. The code for the layer might be
immediately after the opening body tag, while the layer itself sits at the
bottom of the page. To help you keep track of the code, Dreamweaver
gives you the option of seeing code icons where the code itself sits. To
enable these, go to Preferences (Edit > Preferences) and, in the Invisible
Elements category, make sure the Anchor Points for Layers option is
selected. Then from the View Options menu, choose Visual Aids and
select Invisible Elements. Figure 12.4 shows these visual aids at work.

FIGURE 12.4
Showing invisible
anchor points for
layers.

Managing Layers with the Layers Panel

The Layers panel (see Figure 12.5) helps you manage your layers. It tells at a glance how many layers your document contains, what their names are, what their stacking order is (which is in front, which is behind), and whether they're visible. (Invisible layers are not too useful for creating page layout, but are a staple of DHTML scripting.) You can also use the Layers panel to select layers that might otherwise be tricky to select, either because they're invisible or because they're stacked behind some other layers.

To access the Layers panel, choose Window > Layers. After the Layers panel has been opened, it appears as part of the Advanced Layout panel group, docked with your other panels.

FIGURE 12.5
The Layers panel, a vital layer-management tool.

The layers you've placed on the current page are shown in the panel as a list of names that reflects their stacking order (or z-index). The stacking order can be manipulated by dragging layers up and down in the list.

The left column with the eye icon at the top enables you to change the visibility of layers. See Chapter 14, "Controlling Layers with JavaScript," for more on playing with layer visibility.

You can allow or disallow overlapping layers by checking or unchecking the Prevent Overlaps box. As discussed earlier, overlapping layers are at more risk of misbehaving in browsers than layers that don't overlap. You might also want to disable overlapping if you think you might later want to turn your layers into a table for a more browser-compatible layout. (You can do this with the Modify > Convert > Layers to Table command, although it creates unwieldy table structure.)

Designing with Layers in Design View

If you're a visual sort of person who feels quite at home creating and manipulating design elements in programs such as QuarkXPress or Photoshop, you'll love how intuitive it is to create page designs using layers in Design view.

Selecting Layers

A layer has three possible selection states, each represented in Design view by a different graphic state (see Figure 12.6):

- When the layer is selected, it displays a little white box in its upper-left corner, as well as eight solid black squares around its perimeter. The white box is the selection handle. The black squares are resizing handles.

- When the insertion point is inside the layer, the layer appears as a box with a selection handle but no resize handles. The layer appears this way just after it has been inserted because Dreamweaver assumes that you want to start putting content in the newly created layer right away.

- When the layer is not selected, it appears as a plain beveled box, with no selection or resize handles.

FIGURE 12.6
The three different appearances of a layer in the Document window.

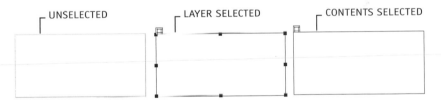

To select a single layer, do one of the following:

- Click one of the layer's borders. (This is straightforward and obvious, but it requires a bit of hand-eye coordination to click precisely on the layer border.)

- Click inside the layer so the selection handle shows in the upper-left corner, and click the handle. (This is a slower two-step process, but it requires less-accurate clicking.)

- Click inside the layer and use the tag selector at the bottom of the Document window to select the div or span tag that is the layer.

- If invisible elements are showing, click the layer's layer marker.

- In the Layers panel, click the layer's name.

To select multiple layers from within the Document window, click on the borders or selection handle of the first layer you want to select and then Shift-click anywhere within each additional layer. If invisible elements are showing, you also can Shift-click on each layer marker, in turn. To select multiple layers using the Layers panel, Shift-click the names of the layers you want to select. (Discontiguous selections are allowed.) No matter which selection method you use, the last layer that you select will show its resizing handles in black; other selected layers will show resizing handles in white.

Naming Layers

Each layer in a document must have a unique ID. When you create a layer, Dreamweaver gives it an ID based on the naming scheme Layer1, Layer2, Layer3, and so on. Layer IDs are used for CSS reference and also for any scripts that reference the layers. Layer names must be one word only, with no special characters.

Although you don't *need* to change your layers' default names, it is a good idea to give your layers names that are more descriptive than Layer1 or Layer2 so that you can easily identify them as you work. Even better, name them according to a naming scheme in which each layer's name tells you something about its position or function. For example, you might name a layer containing a navigation bar LayerNav, and a layer holding the page footer LayerFooter.

You can use the Layers panel or Property Inspector to change a layer's name. Double-click the layer in the Layers panel and type the new name into the text field area, or change the name in the Layer ID field of the Property Inspector.

Inserting Content into Layers

Inserting content into a layer is simple: Just click inside the layer and insert in the usual way. Content can be inserted using the Dreamweaver Insert bar or Insert menu, dragged from the Assets panel or from elsewhere on the page, or pasted from the Clipboard.

Drag-Resizing Layers

To size a layer in the Document window, first select it so that its resize handles show. Then just click and drag any of its resizing handles. Use the corner handles to resize horizontally and vertically at the same time, or use the noncorner handles to resize in one direction only.

Moving Layers Around

Be careful not to grab the layer in its middle and drag. You won't be able to move the layer this way, and you might accidentally drag its contents (an image, for instance) out of the layer entirely.

To change a layer's position from within the Document window, just grab it either by the selection handle or over the border, and click and drag. The cursor turns into a four-headed arrow when it moves over the selection handle, or a grabber hand when it moves over the border, to indicate that clicking and dragging is possible.

To nudge a layer a pixel at a time, select it and use the arrow keys to move it. To nudge a layer 10 pixels at a time, hold down Shift while using the arrow keys to move it.

Aligning Layers

Graphic designers migrating from the print world will be happy to know that Dreamweaver has a lovely feature for aligning layers. To align one or more layers with a border of another layer, do this:

1. Determine which layer you want the other layer(s) to align to (which layer will remain stationary, in other words, as the others shift to align with it).

2. All layers will be aligned to the last layer selected. So, using any of the selection techniques outlined earlier, select the layers you want to align, selecting the aligned-to layer last. (Its resize handles will show in black, indicating that it will remain stationary.)

3. Go to Modify > Align and, from the submenu, choose one of the alignment options (Left, Right, Top, or Bottom).

Figure 12.7 shows several layers being aligned to one stationary layer.

FIGURE 12.7
Using Modify > Align to align two layers to a third.

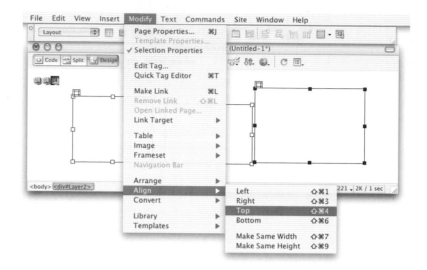

Matching Layer Sizes

Following the procedure for aligning layers, you also can modify layers so that their dimensions match. To do this, just select your layers, go to Modify > Align, and choose Make Same Height or Make Same Width. As with aligning, the last layer selected determines the final height or width of all selected layers.

Nesting Layers

A *nested layer* is a layer created inside another layer. The code looks like this:

```
<div id="Layer1" style="position:absolute; width:200px;
➥height:115px; z-index:1; left: 200px; top: 200px;">
  <div id="Layer2" style="position:absolute; width:100px;
  ➥height:100px; z-index:1; left: 50px; top: 50px;">
    [Layer2 content goes here]
  </div>
  [Layer1 content goes here]
</div>
```

Nesting is often used to group layers. A nested layer moves along with its parent layer and can be set to inherit visibility from its parent.

To create a nested layer, use any of the following procedures:

- Place the insertion point inside an existing layer and choose Insert > Layer.

- Drag the Draw Layer button from the Insert bar and drop it into an existing layer.

- Click the Draw Layer button in the Insert bar, hold down Alt/Opt, and draw a layer inside an existing layer.

- In the Layers panel, select a layer and then Ctrl/Cmd-drag the layer's name onto the layer that you want to be its parent.

- If invisible elements are showing, drag the child layer's layer maker inside the parent layer.

After one layer is nested inside another, the child layer (the nestee) might jump to a new location in the Document window. This is because the layer's position is now being calculated relative to the parent layer's position. This also means that from now on, if you move the parent layer, its child moves with it—but if you move the child, the parent won't move.

Figure 12.8 shows how nested layers appear in the various areas of the Dreamweaver interface. In the Document window, if invisible elements are showing, the gold anchor points indicate nesting status. In the Layers panel, a nested layer is shown with its name indented under its parent layer. Click the plus/minus (+/−) button to the left of the parent layer name to show or hide its children.

FIGURE 12.8
One layer nested inside another as they appear in Design view, the Tag Selector, and the Layers panel.

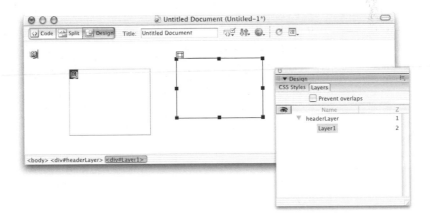

Not all browsers respect the relative positioning of parent and child. If accurate and predictable positioning of page content is important to you, test your pages thoroughly in a variety of browsers, or don't use nested layers.

EXERCISE 12.1

Creating a Basic Layer Page

In this exercise, you'll build a simple page layout using layers. For the Student Ministries home page, you want to place some images on a page so that some of them overlap one another and some are transparent, allowing the images beneath to show through. You've chosen layers to achieve this result. Figure 12.9 shows the final effect you're looking for.

FIGURE 12.9
The desired layout for the Student Ministries home page.

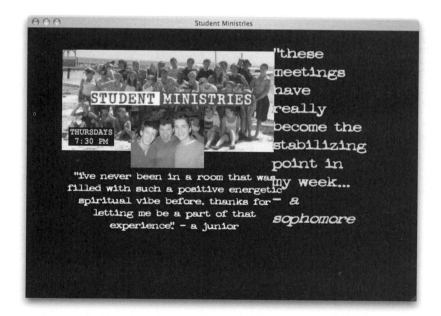

Before you start, download the files from the **chapter_12** folder on the book's website at www.peachpit.com to your hard drive. Define a site called Chapter 12, with this folder as the local root folder. All the files for this exercise are in the **chapter_12/ministries** folder.

1. Select File > New to create a new HTML document. Save it in the **chapter_12/ministries** folder as **student_ministries.html**. To get your workspace ready for layer work, open the Layers panel

(Window > Layers). To achieve the desired layout, you'll need to create overlapping layers; if Prevent Overlaps is selected in the Layers panel, deselect it.

2. Create your first layer by drawing it. In the Insert bar, click the Draw Layer button. The cursor changes to a crosshair, ready for drawing. In the Document window, drag to draw a layer roughly the size and shape shown in Figure 12.10. (You'll adjust the size later.)

FIGURE 12.10
Drawing the first layer.

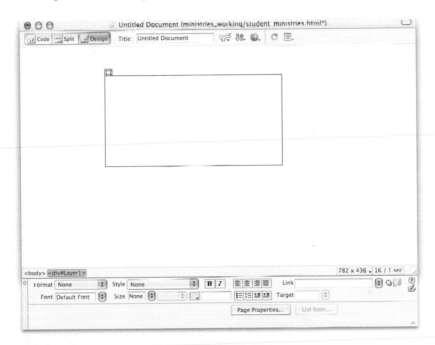

3. Now put some content—an image—inside the layer. Click inside the layer to give focus to its content area. Go to the Insert bar and click the Image button. When the Select File dialog box opens, browse to the file **images/student_ministries.jpg** (in the **chapter_12/ ministries** folder) and insert it.

4. To create the second layer, click the Draw Layer button again and draw a layer roughly the size and shape shown in Figure 12.11. For this layer's content, insert the **images/three_guys.jpg** image.

   Note that you need to place the layers and their graphics only approximately at this point. Later, you'll position them exactly the way you want them.

FIGURE 12.11

The second layer drawn in the Document window.

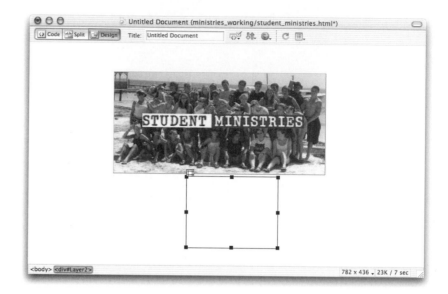

5. Add two more layers, inserting **images/quote1.gif** into the first and **images/quote2.gif** into the second. These images will look a little funny at this point because they're designed to sit in front of a black background. You're working on a white background for now because layers are hard to see and select against a black background. You'll switch the background color later. Your document should now look somewhat like Figure 12.12.

6. Now add a nested layer. You want to place another graphic so that it displays along with the Student Ministries graphic, regardless of how you rearrange the layers. To do this, you'll nest a layer within the layer containing that graphic. Click the Draw Layer button on the Common tab of the Insert bar to choose the Draw Layer object. Starting from within the layer that holds the Student Ministries graphic, Alt/Opt-drag to draw a new, smaller layer. When you've done this, put the cursor inside the new layer and insert the **images/thursday.gif** graphic into it.

7. You're getting quite a collection of layers here. Before proceeding any further, take a moment to name them. In the Layers panel, select the layer that Dreamweaver has named Layer1. Double-click its name and give it a more useful name: **studentministries**. (Layer names must consist of only letters and numbers.) Rename Layer2 **threeguys**.

FIGURE 12.12
The student_ministries.html file with four layers drawn and content inserted.

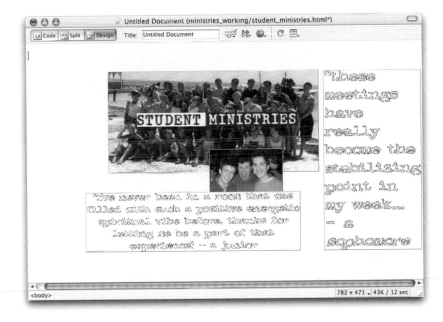

Can you see a naming convention developing here? Each layer is being named after the image it contains, minus the filename extension. Continuing this convention, rename the other three layers. When you're done, your Layers panel should look like the one shown in Figure 12.13.

FIGURE 12.13
The newly named layers of student_ministries.html as shown in the Layers panel.

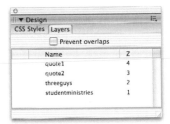

8. To change the page background, choose Modify > Page Properties. In the Appearance category, find the Background color setting and use the color picker to assign a color of black (#000000). Figure 12.14 shows this happening.

    Click OK to close the dialog box. Your page now shows a black background. Try selecting your layers. It is a little trickier. If you feel comfortable working with the black background, leave it. If not, just choose Edit > Undo to undo the change and return to the white background.

FIGURE 12.14
Changing the page background color.

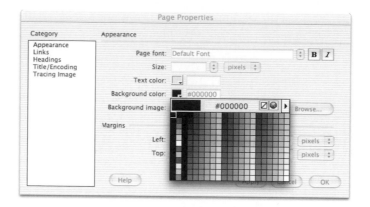

9. You've added images to each layer, but the size of the layer doesn't reflect the size of the image, and it is best if they are set to exactly the same dimensions. First, select the **studentministries.gif** image and examine the Image Property Inspector. You'll see that the image has a width of 417 and a height of 198.

   The studentministries layer should have these same dimensions. Select this layer either by clicking its name in the Layers panel or by clicking one of the layer's edges in the Document window. You can tell that the layer is selected when the Layer Property Inspector appears (not the Image Property Inspector or Text Property Inspector). If you're working with a white background, you can also see the eight solid black squares around the perimeter of the latter.

   Set the W value of the studentministries layer to 417px and the H value to 198px. (Remember to add the px after the number, with no space in between.)

10. Repeat this process for the remaining layers. Select each image, remember or jot down its dimensions, and then select the image's containing layer and assign the W and H values to those dimensions. (Remember to add the px.)

11. Next, arrange the layers on the page by dragging them, and arrange their stacking order as necessary using the Layers panel. If you want, you can imitate the design shown in Figure 12.9, or you can be creative and come up with your own. Remember that the whole point of using layers here is to enable you to overlap your images somewhat, so be sure to experiment with some overlapping. You'll probably want to leave your background color black from this point on, to

In the Layer Property Inspector, be careful not to confuse the L and T (Left and Top) fields with the W and H (Width and Height) fields.

see the design the way it is intended, and you'll want to save and preview in a browser frequently.

12. Save your page and preview in a browser. Note that some older browsers might have problems displaying this page.

WORKING SMART WITH LAYERS

Those are the basics of Dreamweaver layers. What's beyond the basics? Exploring the relationship between layers and CSS-P, and really taking advantage of what Cascading Style Sheets can do for your page layout.

Layers As Styled Objects

Although the Layer object is definitely the most obvious way to go about making layers in Dreamweaver, the story doesn't end there! Any page element whose style includes an absolute or relative positioning property gets treated as a layer in Design view. This is great news because you might not like the way the Layer object codes things, but you still want to take advantage of the niceties of the layer interface in Design view.

Creating Layers Through CSS

To create a CSS-positioned element that will function as a layer without using the Layer object, you need to define a style that includes absolute or relative positioning information. If the style is a custom class or ID, you also need to apply it to a page element. Do it this way:

1. Define a new style, using the CSS Styles panel or other method.

2. When the New Style dialog box opens, create a custom class by choosing Class and entering a name in the Selector field. Or, create an ID selector by choosing Advanced and entering a pound sign followed by a name in the Selector field (see Figure 12.15). You can choose to create the style internally or externally. Click OK when you're ready to proceed.

Class or ID? If you're sure that the element will only ever appear one time on a page, define it as an ID. Classes are more for items that might be reused within a document.

3. When the CSS Style Definition dialog box opens, go to the Positioning category. From the Type drop-down menu, choose Absolute or Relative. Then enter values in the Left, Top, Right, or Bottom fields (see Figure 12.16). Be careful not to assign self-contradictory values! Don't assign a Left value and a Right value, or a Top value and a Bottom value.

4. Before leaving the CSS Style Definition dialog box, you can assign whatever other style characteristics you like, or if you're interested only in positioning, consider the style defined with only these elements in place. When you're done, click OK to close the dialog box.

FIGURE 12.15
Defining a style based on an ID selector.

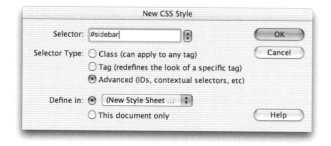

FIGURE 12.16
Creating a CSS style that includes absolute positioning.

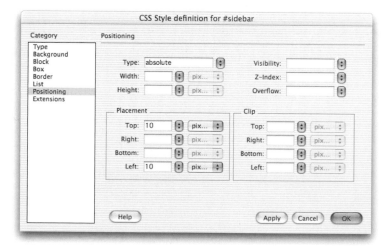

You can also right click the tag in the Tag Selector and choose from the Set Class or Set ID submenu. But this will not assign the style to the tag itself; rather, it will insert a span tag with the appropriate class or ID.

Applying the Positioning Style to an Existing Page Element

You can now apply this class or ID. Select a page element that you want to position (h1, img, or another). If your style is a class, use any of the methods outlined in the preceding chapter to apply it. If your style is an ID, you can apply it in the Attributes tab of the Tag Selector (ID is in the CSS/Accessibility category of attributes) by typing in its name (without the pound sign.

As soon as you do this, the positioning moves your element, and your element appears in Design view surrounded by a layer box (see Figure 12.17). As long as this layer box is selected, the Property Inspector shows your element as a layer. If you click inside the layer box, the original element's Property Inspector appears.

If you defined your style as a class, you should also assign an ID to your new "layer" page element. You can do this with the ID field in the Layer Property Inspector.

FIGURE 12.17
Assigning a style containing positioning information to an image.

Creating a *div* Element to Hold the Style

Or, you may want to apply your new style to a div tag, which can contain multiple elements. Dreamweaver provides the Div object for just such occasions. Just do this (as demonstrated in Figure 12.18):

1. If you already have page content that you want to wrap the div tag around, select it. Otherwise, put the insertion point where you want the div tag and its contents inserted.

2. Choose the Div object from the Layout Insert bar, or choose Insert > Layout Objects > Div from the main menu. The Insert Div Tag dialog box appears.

3. If you defined your style as a class, choose it from the Class drop-down menu in the dialog box. Enter a unique one-word ID in the ID field.

4. If you defined your style as an ID, choose it from the ID drop-down menu in the dialog box. (Note that only unused IDs appear in this menu. Unlike classes, an ID can be used only once in a document.)

5. The Insert option enables you to specify exactly where the div should appear. If you have content selected, it will default to wrap around this content. If nothing is selected, it defaults to the position of the insertion point. But you can also choose to insert the tag immediately before or after certain other tags, such as the body.

When you've chosen your settings, click OK to close the dialog box and insert the div tag. You now have a layer created from a div tag—but unlike a Dreamweaver-created layer, this one derives its positioning, dimensions, and other layer properties from your custom class or ID.

FIGURE 12.18
Inserting a div object with positioning determined by a custom class.

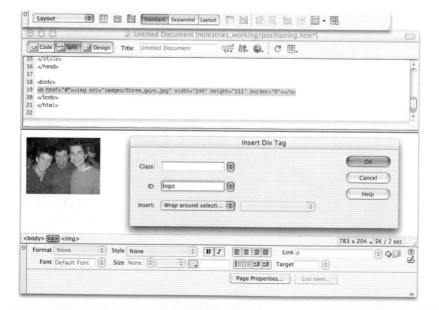

Working with CSS-Styled Layers

Working with layers created this way is basically the same as working with Layer object layers, with one important distinction. Every time you change the properties of your new layer by using the Property or Tag Inspectors, by using the Layers panel, or by adjusting the layer in the Document window, the style is updated. This happens even if the style is housed in an external style sheet.

What are the advantages to creating your layers this way rather than using Dreamweaver's Layer object to create them? First, it takes advantage of CSS's separation of form and content. Because the style information is in its own class or ID, your page code isn't cluttered with positioning information in the content area. If the style is defined in an external style sheet, it can be applied to multiple pages across your site for site-wide formatting that includes positioning. The positioning information can also be unapplied by simply removing the style assignment, so pages can be quickly updated.

In addition, the CSS Styles panel enables you to create positioning effects that are not possible with Layer object layers, such as assigning a position based on right or bottom instead of left and top. This means that you can create page elements that hug the right or bottom edge of the browser window instead of the left top. Here's a warning, however: The Property Inspector displays only left and top positions, so if you define your layer with CSS using right/bottom positioning, you won't be able to see or change its properties from there. If you move the layer in Design view, Dreamweaver will add left/top positioning rather than adjusting the original right/bottom coordinates. This creates a mathematical anomaly that will cause problems in the browser.

EXERCISE 12.2

Designing a Set of Web Pages Using CSS Positioning in an External Style Sheet

This exercise lets you see how powerful CSS-P can be. You'll create a set of IDs in an external style sheet, attach them to elements within several documents within a site, and use the Dreamweaver layers interface to quickly format the entire site by formatting one page. Along the way, you'll also get a good look at how forms separate content to make a more flexible website.

If you haven't done so already, download the files from the **chapter_12** folder on the book's website to your hard drive. Define a site called Chapter 12, with this folder as the local root folder. The files for this exercise are all in the **chapter_12/enviro_site** folder. To make working with the exercise's external style sheet easier, choose Edit > Preferences, go to the CSS Styles category, and deselect the **Open CSS files when modified** option.

1. Begin by opening any one of the six HTML documents that comprise the Enviro "minisite." Examine the page in Design view and Code view to see that it's built from unformatted images and text. The page isn't very pretty yet (see Figure 12.19) because there is no layout—this is just content without formatting. A look at the CSS Styles panel will show you that an external style sheet is attached, but it contains only a body tag redefinition. All the pages in this folder are built exactly the same way, with comparable content.

FIGURE 12.19

One of the documents in the Enviro site (chapter_12/enviro_site) showing unstructured content ready for styling.

2. Your first task is to create all the CSS building blocks (such as the IDs) that this content requires. Don't close the document you've been examining. Open the CSS Styles panel (Window > CSS Styles or expand the Design panel group).

   Click the New Style button to open the New CSS Style dialog box. Choose the Advanced option, and enter **#banner** in the Selector field. Save the style in the attached siteStyles.css document (see Figure 12.20). Click OK to close the dialog box.

FIGURE 12.20
Creating the first ID
for the Enviro site.

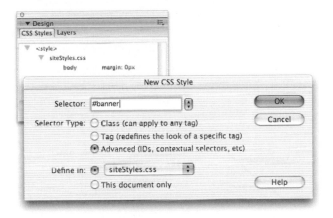

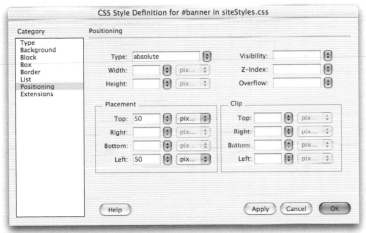

3. The CSS Style Definition dialog box opens. For now, you need to set only one property. Go to the Positioning category and set the Position drop-down menu to Absolute (see Figure 12.20). Set the left and top values to 50 pixels. When you've done that, click OK to close this last dialog box.

4. In addition to the #banner ID you just created, you need an ID for each positionable page element. In the CSS Styles panel, right-click the #banner ID and choose Duplicate. Name the duplicate **#maintitle** and click OK to close the dialog box.

    Repeat this duplication procedure to create the following additional styles:

For more on working with external style sheets, see the section "External Style Sheets" in Chapter 11, "Using Cascading Style Sheets."

#bodycopy

#handsbutton

#dropsbutton

#scalebutton

#stampbutton

#peoplebutton

#phonebutton

For now, don't worry about assigning any unique properties to these styles. Figure 12.21 shows what your CSS Styles panel should look like when you're finished.

FIGURE 12.21
All the ID styles needed for the Enviro site documents.

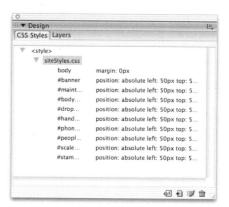

5. Here's where the fun starts! By applying the IDs with their absolute positioning to your various page elements, you'll be creating Dreamweaver layers. Start with the banner (the banner graphic at the top of the page). Your strategy for this element is to apply the banner ID to the image itself. Select the image. Open the Tag Inspector and bring the Attributes tab to the front. If you're viewing your attributes by category, expand the CSS/Accessibility category and find ID. Otherwise, scroll through the list to of attributes and find ID. Type banner into the input field next to this attribute (no pound sign!). Figure 12.22 shows this happening.

FIGURE 12.22

Applying the banner
ID to the banner
image.

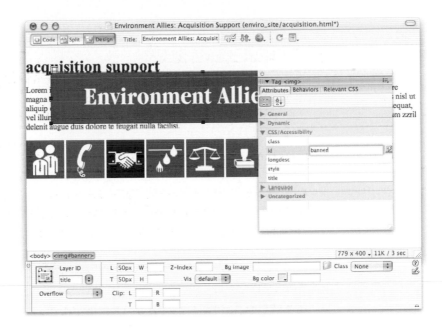

6. Next, you'll apply the #maintitle ID to the page's main heading by applying it directly to the h1 tag. Repeat the process in Step 5, using the Tag Inspector to assign an ID of **maintitle** to the h1 tag.

    Look at the interesting happenings! In Code view, the h1 tag now has an ID. In Design view, the heading looks like it's in a layer (complete with resize handles and the layer tab at the upper left). If you click the borders or the tab of this layer, the Property Inspector shows properties for a layer. If you click within the text of the heading, the Property Inspector shows text controls. The Tag Selector shows the heading and ID.

7. Now you need to assign the #bodycopy ID to the document's main text. Although you could apply the ID directly to the p tag, what if you eventually want more than one paragraph of text in your pages? You can't have more than one bodycopy ID in the document, so it's best to wrap the paragraph in a div tag.

    Start by selecting the paragraph. It's important to select the entire paragraph, including its surrounding tags. To make sure you're doing

this properly, place the insertion point somewhere inside the paragraph and then find and click the p tag in the Tag Selector. This selects the text and opening and closing tags.

Now select the graphic and, from the Layout Insert bar, choose the Div object. In the dialog box that appears, set the following:

- Leave the Class input field empty.

- From the ID drop-down menu, choose bodycopy.

- Leave the Insert drop-down menu at Wrap Around Selection.

Click OK to close the dialog box and insert your new div tag. Figure 12.23 shows this happening.

FIGURE 12.23
Using the Div object to wrap a div tag around the body text and assign the body-copy ID.

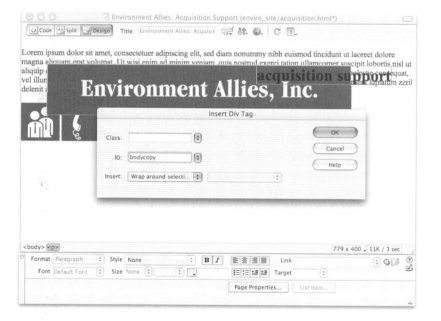

8. Finally, each navigation image in the document must have the appropriate "button" class applied to it. Again, although you could apply the classes directly to the images, this isn't a good idea because each image is actually an img tag wrapped in an a tag. It's best to create a div for each one. For each image, select the image and use the

Tag Selector to select the a tag surrounding it; then insert a Div object. It should be fairly clear which style goes with which button—the dropbutton style goes with the button called dropbutton, which has a picture of water drops on it, and so forth.

Figure 12.24 shows the page layout as it appears with everything turned into layers (but no organizing or formatting yet).

FIGURE 12.24
The acquisitions.html page, with all page elements assigned custom classes and being treated as layers.

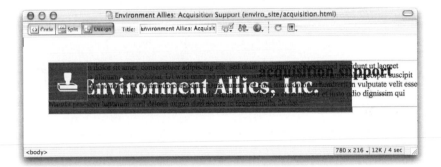

9. Your next step is to add formatting information to your IDs. You do this by using the Dreamweaver layers interface and the CSS Styles panel. Start by using all the various layer tools introduced earlier in this chapter to position your page elements where you want them. Drag layers to move or resize them, use the Property Inspector to change their position or size numerically, and use the arrow keys to nudge them or the Modify > Align commands to align them.

You can also take this opportunity to add text formatting to the title and bodycopy IDs, if you want. For each of these, select the ID in the CSS Styles panel and click the Edit Style button at the bottom of the panel to change the style.

When you're done formatting, check your document in Code view. You'll see that no formatting code has been added! Other than the added ID assignments and the added div tag around the banner, the document code looks just the same as it did at the beginning of the exercise.

10. The true power of CSS is that classes stored in external style sheets can control many documents simultaneously. To get an idea how that works, you have six HTML files to play with in the **chapter_12/ enviro_site** folder. As soon as you apply the custom classes to any of these documents, they immediately adopt the formatting of the page you just made.

    Open one of the remaining HTML documents and do this:

    Repeat steps 5–8 to apply the IDs to your page elements. As you work, the layout and formatting that you created in the first file magically take over your page. (The new formatting might hide some page elements under others, making them inaccessible. If this happens, choose Edit > Undo for the last style assignment you did and apply the styles in a different order so that all elements remain accessible.)

    How industrious do you feel? To see how this technology works, it's important to get at least two pages formatted. If you want more practice, format more than two. But leave at least one page unformatted because you'll need it for the next exercise.

11. From now on, no matter which of your formatted documents you're working on, any change in position, size, text formatting, or other layer properties will change the style sheet itself and the layout of all documents. Try it and see how efficiently you can restructure your entire set of pages. How many different possible layouts can you create?

    In particular, try out effects like these:

    - Although it can't be done from the Layer Property Inspector, layers can also be measured based on their distance from the right or bottom edge of the browser window. Edit your various button classes by removing the L and T values and replacing them with R and B values (see Figure 12.25). R (right) measures the distance between the right edge of the layer and the right edge of the browser window; B (bottom) measures the distance between the layer's bottom and the browser window's bottom. You can set either or both of these to hug either or both edges.

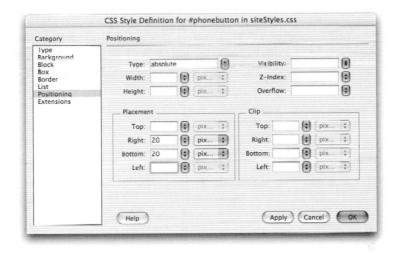

- Try setting the text layer to a percent-based value less than 100%. Note that you can use percent-based settings even if the element doesn't start at L or T set to 0. A text layer with its left edge at 200px and its width set to 75% will stretch and squash while still leaving margins on either side of itself (one fixed and one slightly flexible margin). You can also remove the text layer's width property entirely, which allows text to flow all the way to the right edge of the page.

- This last option won't work if you have the banner ID applied directly to the img tag. But if you remove the banner ID from the img tag and instead wrap the image in a div tag and apply the ID to that, you can set the banner layer's width to 100%, and L and T to 0. Then set its background color to match the blue of the banner image. For all your pages, the banner now bleeds off the top and sides of the page, no matter how big the browser window. You can also center the title graphic inside the layer by opening the .banner style, choosing the Block category, and setting the Text Align drop-down menu to center.

Using variations of these settings, you can create flexible layouts in which different page elements hug different edges of the browser window. Just because you're not using tables doesn't mean you can't have liquid layouts! Figure 12.26 shows an alternate layout that uses several of these methods.

FIGURE 12.26
A flexible alternate layout for the chapter_12/enviro_site pages.

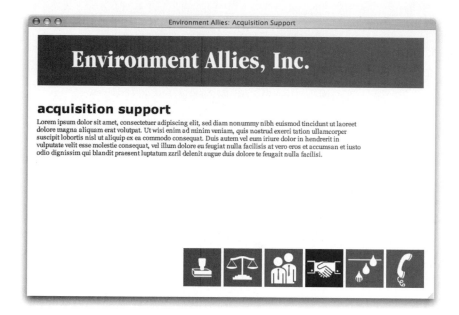

Browser Support for Your Layers

Unfortunately, CSS-P is still somewhat on the bleeding edge as far as browsers are concerned. No browser earlier than version 4 can interpret CSS-P. Any of the newer browsers that promise standards compliance should render your pages correctly. But there's still a lot of room for interpretation in dealing with the CSS standards, so you should always tread lightly when using layers in your pages.

Gracefully Degrading

In web development, a page that functions acceptably in older or non-standard browsers, even though its fancier features may not be supported, is said to gracefully degrade. Maybe your layer-based formatting won't look its best, but the page is still readable and its links and other features are functional. How do you make sure your layer-based page gracefully degrades? Make sure the content is presented in a logical, readable order even without any positioning cues. This is also how to make a layer-based page accessible.

How can you check to see whether your page will display acceptably without its layer-based formatting? Probably the easiest solution is to disable style sheets in your browser. If your layer formatting is built into

an external style sheet, you can also use Dreamweaver's Design Time Style Sheets option to temporarily hide the style sheet. Both of these methods are covered in the section "Making Your Styles Accessible," in Chapter 11. Figure 12.27 shows a gracefully degrading layer-based page with and without its associated style sheet.

EXERCISE 12.3

Making Sure a Layer-Based Site Gracefully Degrades

In this exercise, you'll work more on the Enviro site you created in the previous exercise. You'll check to see how your page linearizes without layer-based formatting, and you'll make any necessary adjustments.

1. Start by opening one of your formatted pages from the Enviro site. To see how it will look and behave without its style sheet, open the CSS Styles panel and, from the panel Options menu, choose Design Time Style Sheets. In the Hide at Design Time category, press the + button and choose siteStyles.css. Click OK to close the dialog box. Figure 12.28 shows this happening.

FIGURE 12.28

Using Design Time Style Sheets to hide the siteStyles.css external style sheet.

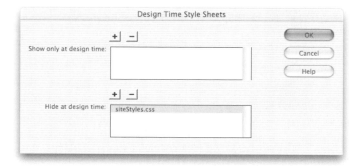

2. What does your page look like now? Probably something like the one shown in Figure 12.29. It's not bad—it's definitely readable. For accessibility, make sure the page elements are in a logical order: banner, title, body copy, buttons. If they're not in this order, switch to Code view and rearrange the tags so they are.

3. The navigation buttons also display oddly, with one button per line. Why is this happening? Because you put each button in its own div tag, and the div tag is a block-level element. Block-level elements are like paragraphs—they must exist on their own, not inline with other elements. The simplest way around this is to replace each of these div tags with a span tag. Earlier in the chapter, you saw that either div or span can be used for CSS-P. But the span element is an inline element and won't force each image to be on its own line.

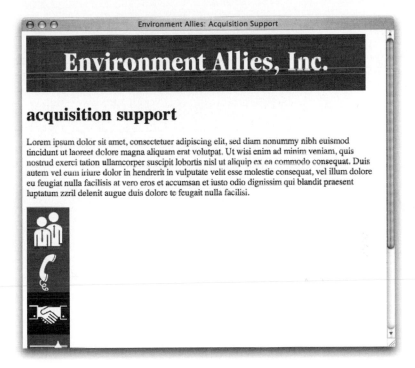

Unfortunately, Dreamweaver doesn't offer a handy Span object. How can you fix this problem? A fairly simple solution is to use Find and Replace to selectively replace div tags with span tags. Do it this way (see Figure 12.30):

- Choose Edit > Find and Replace.

- In the dialog box, choose Current Document as your scope and Specific Tag as the search type. Search for all div tags containing img tags.

- For the Action, choose Change Tag to span.

- Click the Replace All button.

  After Dreamweaver has finished its search, select one of your navigation buttons. It's now contained in a span tag. The unformatted layout of your page looks much more compact now.

4. Finally, when you're done testing, go to the CSS Styles panel and, from the Options menu, choose Design Time Style Sheets. In the Hide at Design Time area, select the siteStyles.css document and press the – button so that your style sheet is no longer hidden. Click

OK to close the dialog box. Your styles are restored, and your page is back to its formatted self!

FIGURE 12.30
Finding div tags containing images and replacing them with span tags.

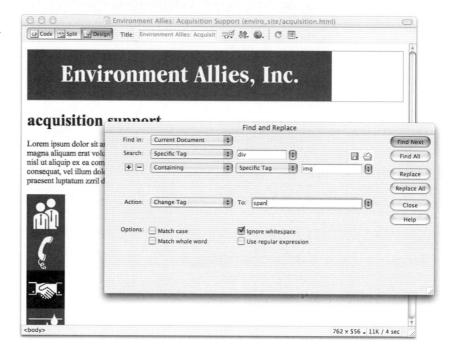

The Netscape 4 Problem

Netscape 3 and earlier don't support layers. Netscape 6 and later are more standards-compliant and render them properly. But Netscape 4 remains a constant challenge for web designers in its quirky treatment of CSS standards. Netscape had a proprietary tag of its own, layer, for implementing layer effects, and it didn't support the official CSS specification very well. If Netscape 4 users are part of your target audience, what can you do?

The Netscape 4 Resize Problem and Fix

One infamous quirk in Netscape 4 happens when a visitor to your page resizes the browser window while viewing your CSS-P layout. The browser resizes and moves layers, pretty much destroying what you've built. The solution is to add a JavaScript to the page that triggers when the window is resized, forcing the page to refresh and eliminating the problem. Dreamweaver automatically adds this JavaScript for you if you tell it to.

To set up Dreamweaver so it automatically inserts this JavaScript, go to Layer Preferences (see Figure 12.3) and choose the Netscape 4 Compatibility option. A JavaScript function is added to your document's head, and a function call is added to the body tag with the onResize event handler.

To add or remove this JavaScript after you've created a document, open the document and choose Commands > Add/Remove Netscape Resize Fix.

Creating a Netscape-Only Version

For more on the Check Browser behavior, see the section "Targeting Multiple Audiences: The Check Browser Behavior," in Chapter 13, "Interactivity with Behaviors."

If Netscape 4 compatibility is very important to you (if a high percentage of your audience uses this browser) and you don't think the gracefully degrading solution discussed earlier will do what you need, you might consider creating an alternate version of the page that uses the Netscape layer tag instead of div, span, or any other CSS-formatted element. Do it this way:

1. Save a version of your page (with a handy title such as **index_netscape.htm**).

2. In this page, remove all CSS-formatted tags and replace them with content wrapped in layer tags. The syntax for the layer tag looks like this:

```
<layer left="300" top="300" width="200" height="200"
➥bgcolor="orange" z-index="3">
   [content goes here]
</layer>
```

Because Dreamweaver has no object for this, you'll have to code it by hand. Code hints will help you with the syntax as you type.

3. In the original CSS-formatted page, add a Check Browser behavior to be triggered by onLoad. If the browser is Netscape 4, redirect the user to your alternate page. For other browsers, stay on the current page. Be sure not to send any users of other browsers—including Netscape 6+ users—to this page because none of these browsers recognizes the layer tag.

If you want to investigate CSS positioning further, try these free, highly recommended online tutorials:

MaKo's CSS Positioning Tutorial: www.mako4css.com/Tutorial.htm

Denis Wilford's Flexible Page Tutorial: http://deniswilford.com/graphic/tut1/tut1a.html

BrainJar's CSS Positioning Tutorial: www.brainjar.com/css/positioning/default.asp

SUMMARY

CSS-P is the future of page layout. And the Dreamweaver interface for creating and working with layers provides an intuitive and visual environment for creating and working with this kind of page design. Whether you use Dreamweaver-generated layers right "out of the box" or create your own styles with positioning attributes, you can use Design view to arrange them and the Property Inspector to set their attributes. The next chapter covers another use for layers—probably their most popular use so far in the web community: controlling them with JavaScript to create DHTML interactivity.

PART III:

INTERACTIVITY, DHTML, AND MULTIMEDIA

CHAPTER 13

INTERACTIVITY WITH BEHAVIORS

BEHAVIORS ARE USER-FRIENDLY PIECES OF JAVASCRIPT PREBUILT BY Dreamweaver MX 2004 that enable you to create advanced inter-actions within a page without actually having to script them yourself. With the many popular Dreamweaver behaviors, you can create dynamic, advanced interactive page elements such as rollover images and pop-up menus that greatly enhance your site. You can even create redirection scripts that will load alter-nate pages depending on the user's browser.

This chapter covers an introduction to JavaScript fundamentals, how Dreamweaver writes JavaScript, and how to attach and work with behaviors in Dreamweaver.

Basics of Behaviors

The basic mechanics of using Dreamweaver behaviors are simple—
although, as usual, the more you know about what's happening behind
the scenes when you apply that Swap Image or other behavior, the better
off you'll be.

How Behaviors Work: JavaScript and HTML

HTML was originally designed for scientists and researchers to put their
documents in an electronic format that could be shared and viewed over
a wide range of computers. Therefore, it is primarily designed to display
static text with a simple, basic structure. The current state of the web has
stretched HTML way beyond the purpose for which it was designed. The
rising needs of early web developers created a demand to extend the
basic functionality and interactivity of the Web. JavaScript was developed
and incorporated into HTML to satisfy this demand.

What Is JavaScript?

JavaScript is a scripting language loosely based on the Java programming
language. A *scripting language*, by definition, is not self-executable. This
means that it is a set of instructions that are read and executed by another
program—in this case, the browser. This is in contrast to Java, which is
a compiled language. This means that the code is compiled or packaged
into a self-contained program that can be run by itself.

Because it is a scripting language, you do not need a special program
with which to write the script. Scripting languages can and are written
as text files. The browser reads the script and executes the functions it
finds there.

Working with Events and Actions

A Dreamweaver behavior, like most JavaScript interactions, consists of
an *event* and an *action*. When the user clicks something, that's an event.

That event (clicking) triggers an action such as a new window opening, a sound playing, or a picture changing.

The browser is on the alert, constantly watching for events. When the browser detects an event, it looks to see if there's an *event handler* that contains a series of instructions for handling that event. Those instructions are the action (a window popping open, a sound playing, and so forth.)

An action is made up of one or more scripting statements that are *do* statements, imperatives that command—do this, do that, then do the other thing! When an action might get performed more than once on a page, it's more efficient to combine all of those imperative statements into a single unit called a *function*. A function is a recipe for action. When there are functions involved, the event handler doesn't have to say, "Do this; do that; do the other thing." The event handler can simply say, "Go find this function and perform the actions it specifies."

Working with Behaviors in Dreamweaver

The central headquarters for working with behaviors is the Behaviors panel (Window > Behaviors). In previous versions of Dreamweaver, it was its own panel, but new to Dreamweaver MX 2004, it's an integrated part of the Tag Inspector (see Figure 13.1)—because, of course, the panel displays only behaviors that are attached to the current selection.

FIGURE 13.1
The Behaviors panel, now an integrated part of the Tag Inspector.

ONLY EVENTS THAT HAVE BEHAVIORS ARE SHOWN

ALL EVENTS ARE SHOWN

Choosing Where to Attach a Behavior

To attach a behavior to any page element, you must first select an element that can have behaviors attached to it. This includes links (text or image), images, form elements, and the body of the page itself.

Images and Links

Images and links—the img and a tags, to be specific—respond to being clicked on or rolled over, so attach a behavior to this kind of object when you want the user to be able to trigger it with a mouse-click or by a movement of the mouse. Image rollovers and status bar changes are popular behaviors for these objects.

Null links, or links that don't go anywhere, are often used to trigger behaviors. A null link has a pound sign (#) or the keyword javascript:; as its href value. To create a null link in Dreamweaver, enter one of these values in the Link field of the Property Inspector. The javascript:; link involves more typing, but is preferable because the # link can cause minor browser problems. For more information on null links, see the section on "Using Links for JavaScript" in Chapter 6, "Links and Navigation."

Form Elements

Form elements, such as input, select, and submit tags, can respond to being clicked on or to having data entered into them. Attach a behavior to this kind of object when you want it to be triggered by the user entering text in a text field, choosing from a drop-down menu, pressing a Submit button, and so on. The Form Validation behavior can be attached to a Submit button so that it executes when the form is submitted.

To select the body tag, either click in an empty area of the Document window to deselect everything else, or go to the Tag Selector and click the body tag indicator there.

The Page Body

The page itself, represented by the body tag, can respond to being loaded or unloaded, to the window being resized, and to other page-related or window-related events. Attach a behavior to the body when you want it to execute automatically as the page loads or unloads. Preloading images, checking for plug ins, and checking browser versions are generally actions that occur when the page loads.

Attaching the Behavior

When you have the desired element selected, go to the Behaviors panel. Double-check the panel's title bar, which should be displaying the tag that you want your behavior attached to (body, a, img, and so on). Click the + button to access the Actions list. This list displays all behavior actions installed on your computer. Those that are inappropriate for your current selection and document are grayed-out. You can't choose the Validate Form behavior, for instance, if there's no form in the current document.

Choose an action from the list, and that behavior's dialog box opens. All behaviors display dialog boxes. Fill in any required options and click OK to close the dialog box; the behavior is applied.

After the behavior has been applied, it shows up in the list of behaviors whenever this page element is selected.

Choosing Event Handlers

When you apply a behavior, Dreamweaver assigns a default event to trigger the action—usually onMouseOver for images, onLoad for pages, and so forth. You can change this triggering event by clicking it in the Behaviors panel to access a list of possible events.

Be aware, though, that not all browsers support all events. Older browsers, for instance, respond only to onMouseOver events for images and text. To tell Dreamweaver what events to display, you need to tell it what browser you're targeting. Do this by clicking the + button to access the Actions list and choosing Show Events For (see Figure 13.2). Pick a browser setting from the submenu here.

In general, the number of events available goes up as the browser version goes up. The safest choice that still gives you a variety of events is 4.0 and Later Browsers.

 To make sure you're using events that are supported by the browsers your audience will be using, be sure to pay attention to any warnings Dreamweaver's Browser Check errors list, accessible from the Document toolbar. For more on browser checking, see the section "Checking Against Target Browsers" in Chapter 3, "Creating and Working with Documents."

FIGURE 13.2
Choosing a target
browser group to use
when determining
behavior events.

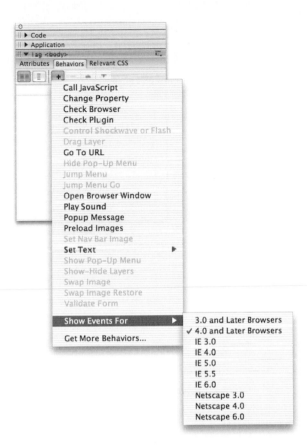

Inspecting and Editing Behaviors

Whenever you select an item in the Document window, any behaviors
that have been applied to it appear in the Behaviors panel. One item
can have multiple behaviors applied to it, even triggered by the same
event handler. Event handlers appear in the panel in alphabetical order,
although they won't execute that way. (Even though onMouseOut is
alphabetically before onMouseOver, the mouseout event can't logically
happen before the mouseover event.)

If more than one behavior is triggered by the same event, the actions
portion of the panel indicates the order in which the actions will occur.
Use the up and down arrows at the top of the panel to rearrange them.

To delete a behavior, select it and press the – button at the top of the panel.

To change any of the behavior's settings, double-click the name of the
behavior or the little gear icon next to it. This opens the dialog box associated with that behavior, ready for inspection or editing.

WORKING SMART WITH BEHAVIORS

The fun of using Dreamweaver behaviors is what you can do with specific behaviors to snazz up your page or make it that much more functional. The hard part is getting used to the quirks each behavior brings with it and knowing how to use each one well.

The Ins and Outs of Selecting Linked Images

If you want a behavior to be triggered by rolling over or clicking an image, you have a choice: Make the image a null link and attach the behavior to the a tag, or attach the behavior directly to the img tag. The first gets coded like this:

```
<a href="#" onMouseOver="[behavior code]">
  <img src="dog.jpg">
</a>
```

The second gets coded like this:

```
<img src="dog.jpg" onMouseOver="[behavior code]">
```

There are two advantages to creating a link and using that to trigger the behavior. First, if the image is a link, the cursor will change when the user rolls over it, which means that the user is more likely to recognize this as something he can interact with and click on. Second, Netscape 4 doesn't support attaching behaviors to the img tag, so the behavior might not work unless you attach it to a surrounding link.

Because Netscape 4 doesn't support adding actions to images, if you have your Behaviors panel set to display events for 4.0 and Later Browsers, or 3.0 and Later Browsers, Dreamweaver won't let you assign an action directly to an image. If you select an image and choose a behavior, the program looks for a link surrounding the image. If there isn't one, it adds a null link. Then it attaches the behavior to that link.

To make the whole process more user-friendly, however, Dreamweaver still treats the behavior as if it were associated with the image. If you select the image, the Behaviors panel will display the behavior, but with an <A> indicator in the event handler area (see Figure 13.3). (Previous versions of Dreamweaver displayed the event handler in parentheses.)

This means that the actual code for the behavior has been put in the **a** tag. You can inspect and edit the behavior, even though, strictly speaking, the tag that you have selected (img) has no behaviors attached to it.

FIGURE 13.3
The Behaviors panel showing behaviors for a link surrounding the selected image.

But what if you want your behavior attached to the image itself and not the link? Select the image, find the behaviors with the <A> event handlers, and use the drop-down menu to assign a non-<A> event handler (see Figure 13.4). This moves the code from the link to the image. Note that to show event handlers for the image itself, you need to show events for one of the later browser versions—I.E. 4+ or Netscape 6.

FIGURE 13.4
Reassigning the event handler to attach a behavior to an image instead of its link.

Targeting Multiple Audiences: The Check Browser Behavior

With the Check Browser behavior (see Figure 13.5), you can set up your site to show different content depending on the browser the user is using. Although this might increase the number of pages in your site, you can be assured that they will be viewed as you designed them without browser-incompatibility concerns.

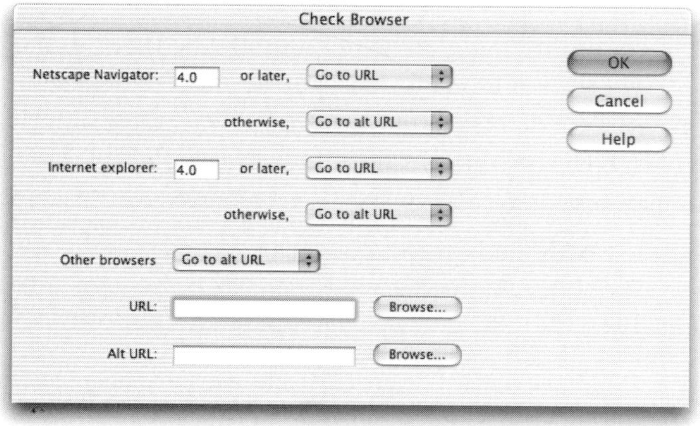

FIGURE 13.5

The dialog box for the Check Browser behavior.

This might be required only if you have a lot of DHTML, with animated layers and other elements that might be prone to cross-browser issues. This behavior uses JavaScript to determine the browser name and version and then automatically links to the determined path.

To use this behavior, you are deciding a few things. The behavior decides among IE, Netscape, and others. For testing this behavior, you need at least three browsers installed. Also, you need to make pages that let you know that it is working. For instance, you need to make a page that says "This is Netscape" or "This is IE" and "This is the other page."

There are also a couple of ways to set this up. Because the behavior is going to happen as the page is loading, you can set up an empty page that contains only the behavior. It will then direct you to the correct page. Or, for browsers that don't support JavaScript or those that have disabled it, put the behavior on the initial page. This page should have content for those users. Others will be directed accordingly.

You have three choices for redirection:

- Stay on This Page

- URL

- Alt URL

Using these combinations, you can set up your redirection. You also have browser versions to consider. By default, they are set to 4.0. So, the behavior is asking, "What browser is it?" but also "What version?" Those with version 3 browsers can be sent somewhere else.

For this example, you will set up the behavior so that the other browser will stay on the same page and so that IE and Netscape users will be redirected. Again, you will need at least three different browsers installed to really see this. For this requirement, you can have a combination such as Netscape 3 and 6, and IE 4 or above.

1. With the initial or JavaScript-free page open, click on the plus (+) button of the Behaviors panel. Choose Check Browser.

2. For URL, browse to the page you have created for Netscape 4 and above users. For Alt URL, choose the page you created for IE 4 and above users. All others are going to stay on this page.

   For Netscape 4.0 or later, choose Go to URL. For Otherwise, choose Stay on This Page.

   For Internet Explorer 4.0 and later, choose Go to Alt URL. For Otherwise, choose Stay on This Page.

   For Other browsers, choose Stay on This Page.

3. Save and preview in the various browsers to confirm that everything is working as planned.

You can use the browser version number to further refine the behavior. You can have extended functionality in pages designed for IE 5.0 and higher. If someone comes in with IE 4.0, you can send that user to less-complicated pages. This might be useful if you are using other behaviors that use 5.0 events. You can redesign these behaviors to work with 4.0 events for these viewers.

Keep in mind that this behavior is not foolproof. As with every stage of development, be sure to test all your functionality as you go.

Tiny Bits of Hand-Coding: The Call JavaScript Behavior

Call JavaScript is a behavior that inserts JavaScript code that you write yourself. Instead of inserting some prewritten JavaScript action, however, the behavior adds whatever JavaScript statement(s) you specifically tell it to add. To use this behavior, open a document; select the element that you want to trigger the behavior; and, from the Behavior panel's Actions list, choose Call JavaScript. In the dialog box that appears, type in whatever JavaScript statement or statements you want to execute (see Figure 13.6). Separate multiple statements with semicolons.

FIGURE 13.6
The Call JavaScript behavior in action, being used to insert a simple one-line chunk of JavaScript code.

This is a handy behavior for quickly adding bits of JavaScript code to a document, without having to worry about coding event handlers, functions, and function calls, and even without having to leave Design view. Of course, you can't really use the behavior unless you know enough JavaScript syntax to know what code you want to add, so it's not for everybody. But if you want to dip your toes in the JavaScript waters just a bit without having to master event handlers and such, Call JavaScript might be just what you need. Table 13.1 shows some handy one- and two-line code statements that can be entered into the Call JavaScript dialog box.

Note for hand-coders: Because Dreamweaver behaviors must always insert their JavaScript as a noncustomizable function and a function call with parameters, Call JavaScript can lead to more cumbersome coding than if you just dipped into Code view and added the code there. For more on Dreamweaver's JavaScript tools, including Call JavaScript, see the section "Writing JavaScript in Dreamweaver" in Chapter 27, "Writing Code in Dreamweaver."

TABLE 13.1 **Some Simple JavaScript Statements to Use with the Call JavaScript Behavior**

JavaScript Code	What It Does	Special Instructions
`history.back()` `history.forward()`	Sends the browser back or forward as if the user had clicked the browser's Back or Forward buttons.	—
`window.close()`	Closes the current browser window. This is useful when multiple browser windows are open.	—
`window.resizeTo` `(width,height)`	Resizes the current browser window to the specified dimensions. This is handy when the page first loads. Select the body tag and attach it using the onLoad event.	Substitute numbers for *width* and *height*.
`document.formname.` `textfieldname.focus()`	Puts the insertion point in a specified text field, in a specified form. This is useful when a page contains a form because the user can immediately start typing in the first text field as soon as the page loads. Select the body tag and attach it using the onLoad event.	Substitute the name of your form and the name of the text field you want to put the insertion point in.

Opening New Browser Windows: Beyond the Simple Pop-Up

The Open Browser Window behavior (see Figure 13.7) opens a new browser window. You can specify what page appears in that window, and you get to determine exactly what the window looks like: how big it is, whether it's resizable, and even what bits of window "chrome" (button bar, status bar, scrollbars, and so on) it displays. This behavior is great when you want a message to pop up, but you want it to look nicer than the generic browser alert window called up by the Show Pop-Up Message behavior; or when you want to open a page in a new window, but you need more control than simple _blank targeting can offer.

FIGURE 13.7
The Open Browser
Window dialog box.

 You don't need to use JavaScript just to display a web page in a new browser window. You can accomplish that with a standard hyperlink by setting its target attribute to _blank. With this targeting method, however, you can't control the size or appearance of the browser window. For that, you need the behavior.

To use the Open Browser Window behavior, start by creating or getting the URL for the page that you want to appear in the new window. Then open the page that you want to trigger the behavior from; select a page element; and, from the Behaviors panel's Actions list, choose Open Browser window.

In the dialog box that appears, enter the specifics for the new window.

If you want to make sure your visitors don't mistake this new window for the main browser window behind it, and if you want to save screen space, don't turn on all the chrome elements. In fact, most designers leave most of them off (see Figure 13.8). But it's a good idea to leave the resize control and scrollbars on, in case your users need them.

It's also a good idea to give the new window a name (a simple, one-word name will do). Why? If your main page has several links to new windows, or if the user clicks on your one link to the new window several times, you probably don't want this to open multiple new windows. It can get awfully crowded in there! But if the new window has a name, the browser knows not to open more than one of it. If you call your window **mini**, for instance, and the user opens it, loses it behind something else, and then tries to open it again, the browser will see that mini already exists and will bring it to the front instead of spawning another window.

 It's not the most common situation in the world, but if you want to include a link in the main window that changes the page in the new window, you can use the new window's name as the link's target, like this:
`<a href="otherpage.html" target="mini">`.

FIGURE 13.8
A little browser
window, with and
without chrome.

WITH CHROME

WITHOUT CHROME

Window Size Issues

When deciding what size to make your window, be aware that not all browsers or platforms size their windows the same. (Table 13.2 shows some sample size variances.) You don't want content failing to display properly because the window isn't big enough.

TABLE 13.2 **A 400 × 400 Browser Window As It Displays in Different Platform/Browser Combinations**

Platform	Browser	Viewable Window Area
Windows	IE	400 × 400 (no chrome) 385 × 420 (all chrome)
Windows	Netscape/Mozilla	400 × 400 (no chrome) 400 × 400 (all chrome)
Mac	Safari	400 × 400 (no chrome) 400 × 350 (all chrome)
Mac	IE	415 × 415 (no chrome) 415 × 415 (all chrome)
Mac	Netscape/Mozilla	400 × 400 (no chrome) 400 × 400 (all chrome)

Window Placement

By default, the new browser window that opens appears tucked up into the upper-left corner of the user's screen. Unfortunately, the behavior doesn't include an option for changing that. But you can fix that if you don't mind just a small amount of hand-coding.

When the behavior is in place in your document, go to Code view and look in the head section for this function:

```
function MM_openBrWindow(theURL,winName,features) { //v2.0
  window.open(theURL,winName,features);
}
```

Determine, in pixels, how far away from the upper-left corner you want the window to appear. You need to supply it as x,y coordinates (x = horizontal, y = vertical). Then add the following to code to the function:

```
function MM_openBrWindow(theURL,winName,features) { //v2.0
 newWin = window.open(theURL,winName,features);
 newWin.moveTo(x,y);
}
```

For x and y, substitute the horizontal and vertical coordinates you determined earlier.

Or, if you're up to a slightly longer bit of typing, you can get the window to center itself on the user's computer screen, no matter what size it is. Instead of the previously added code, change the function like this:

```
function MM_openBrWindow(theURL,winName,features) { //v2.0
 newWin = window.open(theURL,winName,features);
 newWin.opener.name="main";
 newWin.moveTo((screen.width/2)-200,(screen.height/2)-200);
}
```

This one's trickier because you have to watch out for all those parentheses in the fourth line. But that's all there is to it! Note, however, that the code written here centers a 200 × 200 browser window. Change the occurrences of 200 in the fourth line to the width and height you have specified for your new window.

Be aware, though, that after you've made these tweaks, this isn't a plain out-of-the-box Dreamweaver behavior anymore. If you edit it through the Behaviors panel, your custom code can be overwritten.

Closing the New Window

All of your computer-savvy users will know how to close the new little window you've opened by clicking its Close box. But it's a nice idea, for those who don't know, to give them an easy-to-see little Close button in the window itself (see Figure 13.9). It's just a matter of opening the page that will display in the little window, adding a text or graphic link to its layout, and attaching a bit of JavaScript to it that tells the browser to close the window. Dreamweaver has no behavior for this, but it's so easy that there's not much need for one. Just select your Close text or graphic and, in the Property Inspector's Link field, type this:

```
javascript:window.close()
```

FIGURE 13.9
A little browser window with a Close button.

Figure 13.10 shows how the whole procedure looks in Dreamweaver.

FIGURE 13.10
Creating the Close button for display in a little browser window.

This short bit of JavaScript code could also be added using the Call Java-Script behavior. The resulting code that gets added to your page is more compact if you add the code through the Link field, however.

Creating a Controller Window

One possible use for a small new browser window is to contain links to exciting places in the main website (see Figure 13.11). Some designers refer to this as a *controller window*. It works this way: The links in the small window are regular hyperlinks that are targeted to the main window, so clicking them opens the linked page in that window. The trick is, the main window needs to have a name to use as the target value.

FIGURE 13.11
A controller window with links that should load in the main browser window.

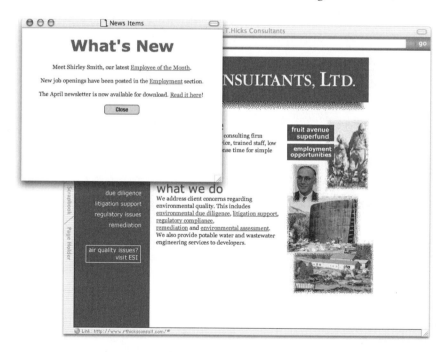

Controller windows can also be used to open a third browser window and control the pages that appear in that window. In these cases, the main window sits behind the two new windows.

Naming the main window is usually done by the same script that opens the new window—the Open Browser Window behavior, in other words. By default, the behavior doesn't do this, but, guess what? A little code tweaking can easily meet this challenge.

When the behavior is in place in your document, go to Code view and look in the head section for this function:

```
function MM_openBrWindow(theURL,winName,features) { //v2.0
  window.open(theURL,winName,features);
}
```

Now change it to look like this:

```
function MM_openBrWindow(theURL,winName,features) { //v2.0
 newWin = window.open(theURL,winName,features);
 newWin.opener.name="main";
}
```

You can substitute any one-word name you like for main. Just remember what you enter here because you'll need it for targeting your links later.

EXERCISE 13.1 ## Creating a Pop-Up Controller Window

In this exercise, you'll create a miniwindow that pops up from the Kenswear home page, directing visitors to highlighted pages within the site. If you haven't done so yet, download the **chapter_13** folder from the book's website at www.peachpit.com and create a site with this as the root folder. The files for this exercise are in the **ken** folder.

1. In the **ken** folder, open **index.htm**. This is Ken's home page, which links to his three main departments (Sportswear, Formalwear, and Businesswear). There's also a What's New? button pointing visitors directly to whatever pages Ken wants to highlight this month.

    Also open **whatsnew.htm**. This is the file that will appear in the pop-up window.

2. In the index.htm file, select the What's New? button. This button needs to trigger behaviors without actually linking anywhere, so in the Property Inspector's Link field, type **javascript:;**.

3. With the button still selected, open the Behaviors panel, click the + button, and choose Open Browser Window. When the dialog box appears, enter **whatsnew.htm** in the URL field (or you can browse to this file). Set the size to 300 × 300 and leave all chrome elements turned off. Name the window **whatsnew** (see Figure 13.12). Click OK to close the dialog box.

FIGURE 13.12
Configuring the Open
Browser Window
behavior for the
Kenswear site.

Preview the page in a browser. Clicking the What's New? button opens a little window with the whatsnew.htm page displayed in it.

4. The whatsnew.htm page has a Close button in it so that users know for sure how to get rid of the window. Open that file (if it's not already open) and select the Close button. In the Property Inspector's Link field, type **javascript:window.close()**.

   To see this effect in the browser, go back to index.htm and preview it in the browser. Click What's New? to open the little window, and click Close to close it.

5. Next, refine the behavior so that it moves the window away from the upper-left corner of the screen and sets the scene for linking back to the main window. In index.htm, switch to Code view and examine the document head. There are a lot of functions in there! Find the `MM_openBrWindow` function and change it to look like this (new code is in bold):

```
function MM_openBrWindow(theURL,winName,features) { //v2.0
  newWin = window.open(theURL,winName,features);
  newWin.moveTo(200,200);
  newWin.opener.name = "main";
}
```

When you're done, preview it in the browser to make sure the behavior still works and that it moves the window away from the upper-left corner.

6. Now it's time to take advantage of that code by putting links into the pop-up window. In **whatsnew.htm,** select the link to the tuxedo page. In the Property Inspector, browse to **formalwear/tuxedo.htm** for the Link and enter **main** into the Target field (see Figure 13.13).

FIGURE 13.13
Targeting a link from the pop-up window to its parent.

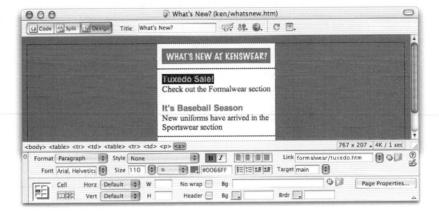

Try it! Save the What's New file and then go back to the home page and preview it in the browser. You should be able to open the little window and then click the tuxedo link to change the main window.

Note that, when you click the link in the little window, the main window regains focus and comes to the front. The little window hasn't closed—it's just behind the main window. If you want the controller window to remain visible, go back to the What's New file, use the Tag Selector to select the body tag, and in the Behaviors panel, click the + button and add the Call JavaScript behavior. When the dialog box opens, enter the following in the code field (see Figure 13.14):

```
window.focus()
```

Click OK to close the dialog box. In the Behaviors panel, change the event from onLoad to onBlur. What does this do? Every time the whatsnew window loses focus (gets sent to the back), it brings itself back to the front. Now when you try the site, clicking the tuxedo

link in the What's New page changes the page in the main window, but doesn't hide the little window.

FIGURE 13.14
Using the Call JavaScript behavior to ensure that the What's New window stays in front of other browser windows.

FIGURE 13.14
Using the Call JavaScript behavior to ensure that the What's New window stays in front of other browser windows.

7. It's time to see how naming the little window works. Open **business-wear/index.htm** and select the What's New? button there. Repeat what you did in steps 2 and 3 to add a null link to the button, and use it to open a new browser window. Use the same settings as before for the new browser window, and make sure you name the window **whatsnew**, just like you did before.

When you've done this, try the site in a browser. Start on the home page, and click the What's New? button to open the little window. Leaving the little window open, go back to the home page and click the Businesswear link. This takes you to the page where you just added the second Open Browser Window behavior. Click the What's New? button on this page. Instead of opening a new window, the original little window just comes to the front!

Advanced Image Swapping: Disjoint Rollovers

Swap Image (see Figure 13.15) is undoubtedly the most popular of the Dreamweaver behaviors because it's nice and stable and it creates rollovers. Everybody loves rollovers! In the world of web design, they've become an expected way of making buttons announce to the world that they're buttons and can be clicked on. But Swap Image can also be used to create more complex effects, such as disjoint rollovers.

FIGURE 13.15
Dialog box for the
Swap Image behavior.

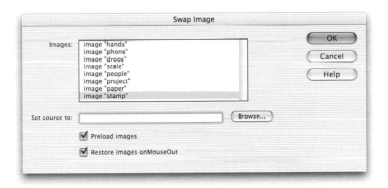

Swap Image and Disjoint Rollovers

The Swap Image behavior changes the value of the src property of an img tag so that another image is displayed in the original image's place. No rule says that the image being swapped has to be the image that the behavior is attached to. When the behavior is triggered, it can swap any image in the current document. When an image swaps because the user clicked on or rolled over something other than the image itself, it's referred to as a *disjoint*, or *complex*, rollover.

Only a few rules are involved in working in Swap Image:

- The behavior can swap only one image for another; it can't make an image appear where there was none before. But one image can be an invisible image, such as a spacer GIF.

- The original image and the swapped image will display with the same width and height, so it's best if they're the same size to start.

- The images must be named—that is, the Image Property Inspector must show a one-word name in the Name field in its upper-left corner. If you don't supply a name, Dreamweaver assigns a default (Image1, Image2, and so on). But for complex situations such as disjoint rollovers, this is very hard to work with, so it's best to name the image before beginning. And don't change the names when the behavior is in place!

The Swap Image behavior is easier to understand if you remember that the img tag itself is just a placeholder in the document, where the browser is reserving space and expecting to display an image. The src attribute determines which image will fit into the space. The width and height attributes determine how much space to reserve. The Swap Image behavior swaps only the src, not the width or height. That's why the swapped image must display at the same size as the original. On another note, that's also how Dreamweaver's Placeholder Image object works, by creating an img tag with no src.

Creating a Disjoint Rollover

To build a disjoint rollover, make sure you have a named image in your document and another image file somewhere in your site ready to swap for it. Then do this:

1. Select the page element that should trigger the swapping. This can be another image, a piece of linked text, or whatever you like.

2. In the Behaviors panel, click the + to access the Actions list, and choose Swap Image.

3. When the Swap Image dialog box appears, take a look at the list of images in the upper portion of the window. That's a list of all images in your document, identified by name. If you currently have an image selected in the document, it will be selected here.

   In the list of images, select the name of the image that you want to swap. (See why it's important to name things?)

4. In the lower half of the dialog box, browse to select the image you're swapping with. Notice that the image list now shows an asterisk next to the name you had selected. This image will be swapped.

When you're done choosing images to swap, make sure the Preload Images and Restore on MouseOut options are set the way you want them, and click OK.

Performing Multiple Image Swaps

Not only can you swap any image with the Swap Image behavior, but you can also swap more than one image at a time with the same behavior. For

instance, you might have a navigation bar button selected. You can assign one Swap Image behavior that will create a standard rollover and swap some other image on the page at the same time.

To perform multiple image swaps at once, go through the steps outlined in the previous section, but before closing the dialog box, repeat steps 3 and 4 to swap another image. Do this as many times as you want. Each image that will be swapped shows up in the dialog box's image list with an asterisk by its name, so you can spot them easily as you're scrolling through the list.

Swap Image and the Different Event Handlers

You're also not limited to swapping images on rollover. Maybe you want the image to change when it's clicked on instead of when it's rolled over, or in addition to the rollover swap. You can swap images for onMouseOver, onMouseDown, onMouseUp, onClick, or onMouseOut to create some interesting interactive image effects! (Remember to check that your target browsers support the events you use, though.)

EXERCISE 13.2

Creating a Clickable Slide Show with Swap Image

In this exercise, you'll use some fancy image-swapping to create a clickable slide show for an art gallery. If you haven't done so already, download the **chapter_13** folder from the book's website to your hard drive and define a site with this as the root folder. The files for this exercise are in the **chapter_13/gallery** folder.

1. Start by opening **index.html** and examining it. It contains a table-based layout consisting of a title picture and four numbered buttons, separated by a transparent spacer graphic (see Figure 13.16).

   Pay particular attention to the images. Select each, and you'll see that they all have names that are descriptive of the purpose they'll have in the slide show: pic, pictitle, one, two, three, and four. The name of the spacer graphic (pictitle) tells that it's doing more than taking up space here! It's going to be swapped for other images as the slide show progresses.

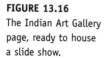

FIGURE 13.16
The Indian Art Gallery page, ready to house a slide show.

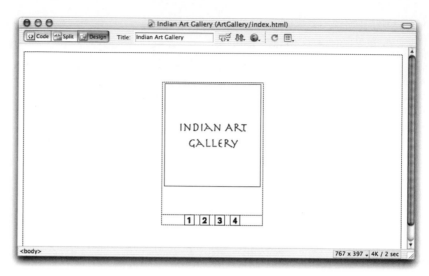

2. Clicking the first button needs to make a picture appear in place of the introductory slide (the image named pic) and needs to make that picture's title appear in place of the spacer graphic (the image named pictitle).

Select the One button. In the Behaviors panel, click the + and choose the Swap Image behavior from the Actions list. Do you recognize your named images in the image list? This list is a lot less daunting when your images have descriptive names.

You want to swap the pic image, so select pic from the image list. Click the Browse button and choose **sunchief.jpg** from the **gallery/images** folder.

You also want to swap the pictitle image, so select pictitle and then browse to the **sunchief_title.gif** image from the **gallery/images** folder. Do you see how asterisks are appearing by the names of images you've swapped?

Finally, you do want to preload images, but you don't want to restore on mouseOut because these aren't going to be rollovers. Deselect that option. Figure 13.17 shows what your settings should look like at this point. Click OK to close the dialog box.

FIGURE 13.17

The Swap Image dialog box showing settings for swapping the pic and pictitle images, without restoring them upon onMouseOut.

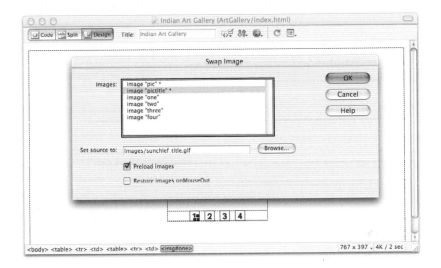

3. Examine the Behaviors panel, and you'll see that the behavior has been added with a default event of <A>onMouseOver (the <A> means a null link was created, which is fine). Select this event and, from the drop-down menu, choose <A>onMouseUp or <A>onClick. If neither of those events shows up in your list, click the + button and, from the bottom of the Actions list, choose Show Events For > 4.0 and Later Browsers.

4. Preview in the browser to see what happens when you click the One button. Both images change!

5. You're on your own for this one. Repeat the previous steps so that the Two button shows the lizard, Three shows the buffalo, and Four shows the fish. The image filenames make it clear which one is which. When you're done, you should be able to preview in the browser and click on any numbered button to view a picture and its title.

   (Are you wondering why the pictures and their associated titles are in separate images? For optimization, the pictures need to be JPGs and the titles need to be GIFs.)

6. Now for some extra fancy stuff. You want each button to be visibly selected while its picture is showing. To do this, you're going to swap more images; this time, each button will swap for a selected version of itself when it's clicked on.

Select the One button and go to the Behaviors panel. Because you want to swap the button graphic upon onMouseUp or onClick, and you already have a Swap Image behavior for that event, you don't need to add another one. Instead, double-click on the behavior's name in the panel to open it for editing.

When the dialog box opens, pic and pictitle both have asterisks by their names, to indicate that they're already being swapped. Make sure the image named One is selected (it should be, by default) and browse to **one_selected.gif** in the gallery/images folder. Click OK to close the dialog box.

7. Repeat this procedure to swap the other three buttons with their selected versions (again, the filenames should be self-explanatory).

Now preview in the browser again. Clicking the One button should change it to black, as well as display the sunchief picture and title. Clicking the Two button changes it to black—but the one button is still black! Eventually, all of your buttons will turn black because you haven't restored any of them.

8. You might think of using the Swap Image Restore behavior for this, but that's a very specialized behavior that works only in straightforward rollover situations. Instead, you need to do some more swapping.

Select the One button and, in the Behaviors panel, open its Swap Image behavior up for editing. In the image list, select Two. When the One button is clicked, Two should revert to its nonselected state, so swap this image for **two.gif** (in the gallery/images folder). Select Three and swap it for **three.gif**; then select Four and swap it for **four.gif**. You don't know which of these may be selected when the user clicks the One button, so you'll swap them all.

Repeat this procedure for the other three buttons. By the time you're done with each Swap Image dialog box, all of the images in the image list should have asterisks. By the time you're done with the whole project, you should be pretty comfortable swapping images! Figure 13.18 shows the finished slide show in action.

FIGURE 13.18
The Indian Art Gallery
slide show in its
final form.

FIGURE 13.18
The Indian Art Gallery
slide show in its
final form.

Cascading Menus the Easy Way: The Show Pop-Up Menu Behavior

The Show Pop-Up Menu behavior (see Figure 13.19) lets you create a submenu of links that will appear when the user clicks on a link on your page. This behavior is modeled after the behavior of the same name in Fireworks MX 2004, although, unlike its Fireworks cousin, it creates only text-based menus, where Fireworks can also generate image-based menus. If you open a document in Dreamweaver that contains a Fireworks-generated pop-up menu, Dreamweaver recognizes the code as a pop-up menu.

FIGURE 13.19
Dialog box for the
Show Pop-Up Menu
behavior.

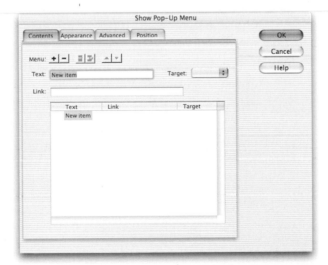

To use this behavior, you need to attach it to an image or a hyperlink. Insert an image on your page. Select the image and then open your Behaviors panel. Select Show Pop-Up Menu. Then follow these steps:

1. On the opening screen, enter the name of the menu item. This is the text that will appear on the button. Then assign the text a link by browsing to another page or entering in a URL. You can set the target here if you are using Frames.

2. Click the plus (+) button to add this menu item. Click the Indent Item button if you want to create a submenu off the next-higher menu item. Items will continue to be indented until you click the Outdent Item button. Use the up and down arrow buttons to arrange the order in which the menu items will appear.

3. When you have completed adding your menu items, go to the Appearance tab. Here you determine the look of your menus.

4. Select whether this will be a vertical or horizontal menu. The Preview area gives you an approximate look of the menu. Choose the font name, size, and style of the menu text. Choose a justification setting. Choose the text and cell colors for the Up and Over states.

5. When set there, go to the Advanced tab. Here you can specify specific settings of your menu. Because there are really tables, you can set cell width and height, padding and spacing, and delay time. You can also specify borders and specific colors of the borders. (These settings might be browser-dependent.)

6. Now go to the Position tab. This tab lets you specify the position of the pop-up menus relative to the image to which they are attached. If you want, you can specify any pixel number for the X and Y values.

7. Click OK, and your pop-up menu is built. It will not show up in the Design window, so choose Preview in Browser to see it in action.

EXERCISE 13.3

Building a Pop-Up Menu

In this exercise, you will create a pop-up menu using Dreamweaver's built-in behavior. This is a very popular way to quickly build an advanced navigation system.

If you haven't done so yet, download the **chapter_13** folder from the book's website to your hard drive. Define a site called Chapter 13, with this folder as the local root folder.

1. Open a new HTML document and save it as **pop_up.htm**.

2. Insert the **navigation.gif** image (from the **chapter_13** folder on the website) onto the page. Make sure that it is selected on the page.

3. In the Behaviors panel, click the plus (+) button and select Show Pop-Up Menu. The wizard shown in Figure 13.19 displays.

4. In the contents panel, type **Macromedia** in the Text field. In the Link field, type **http://www.macromedia.com**.

5. Click the plus (+) button. Type **Dreamweaver**. In the Link Field, type **http://www.macromedia.com/dreamweaver**.

6. Click the plus (+) button again and type **Fireworks**. In the Link field, type **http://www.macromedia.com/fireworks**.

7. Click the Indent Item button. This indents Page 3 relative to Dreamweaver and creates another level of pop-up menu.

8. Click the Appearance tab. This panel is where you determine the look of the menu.

9. You can choose between Vertical Menu and Horizontal Menu. Look at both options, but choose Vertical Menu. Leave the rest of the default options.

10. Go to the Advanced tab. Leave the defaults here, but notice that these options are equivalent to table settings. Dreamweaver is actually creating tables to make these menus.

11. Go to the Position tab. This menu enables you to set the position of the menu relative to the image to which this behavior is attached. This is a nice improvement from the Fireworks 4 implementation of this feature!

12. Click the leftmost button. This makes the menu appear from the lower-right corner of the image.

The Hide Menu on the onMouseOut Event option should be checked. This makes the menu disappear when you move off it, and it adds a Hide Pop Up Menu behavior to your Behaviors list. This behavior is used only in conjunction with a pop-up menu and should be added only with this check box.

13. Click OK to create the menu. It will not be functional in the Design window.

14. Preview in the browser and test your menu.

Efficiency Enhancer: Externalizing Your Behavior Code

Experienced scripters know that any code that will be used repeatedly should be accessed from a single, shared resource for greatest efficiency. This makes the code easier to read and edit, and it also trims download time and browser overhead—especially if the code is extensive. When dealing with JavaScript in HTML documents, this often means moving the functions to a linked JS file that can be shared between HTML documents.

Any time you use a Dreamweaver behavior repeatedly across a site, you have an opportunity to streamline your code by moving the function code to a shared file. Dreamweaver even helps you. You must cut and paste the function code to a new JS file, and create a link between the two documents. You can then easily share that JS file between documents, and Dreamweaver will recognize its presence.

To move one or more function calls to a shared JS file, follow these steps:

1. Open an HTML file that contains one or more applied behaviors that you know you'll be reusing in other documents.

2. In Code view, scroll to the <head> section of the document and find the <script> tag containing your behaviors' functions.

3. Select everything between the opening and closing <script> tags (but not the tags themselves), and select Edit > Cut (see Figure 13.20).

FIGURE 13.20

Removing a behavior's function from the document `<head>`.

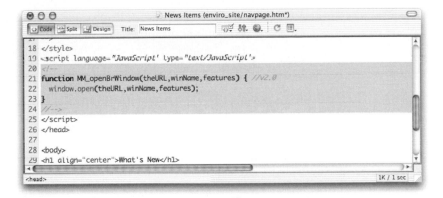

4. Go to File > New to access the new document dialog box. Here, choose the Basic category of files, and choose to create a new JavaScript file.

5. When the new file opens, place the insertion point on a new line after the opening comments and choose Edit > Paste (see Figure 13.21).

FIGURE 13.21

Adding the behavior function to a new shared JS file.

6. Save the file, with the .js extension, into your site. (After you've created this shared file, you can simply add other behavior functions to it later; you don't have to create a new JS file every time. Each site you work on can have its own shared JS file.)

7. Close the JS file, and return to your HTML document.

Your behaviors are now broken until you link your HTML document with the new shared JS file. To link the shared file, do this:

1. Go to View > Head Content so that the Document window shows the little gray strip of icons that represent your document head.

2. Find and select the script icon. (This should select the now-empty `<script>` tag from which you removed the functions.)

3. In the Property Inspector, find the Src field. Click its Browse button, and browse to the shared JS file. (See Figure 13.22).

FIGURE 13.22

Changing a `script` tag to contain a link to a shared JS file.

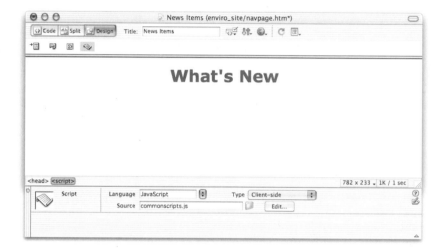

4. After you've done this, save your document and select Preview in Browser. If you did everything correctly, the behavior should still work.

The major benefit of creating JS files is that you can reuse them in other HTML documents. To reuse a shared behavior, follow these steps:

1. Open another document in which you want to use the same behavior. Don't apply the behavior yet!

2. Go to View > Head Content.

3. Open the Assets panel, and choose to view scripts. Your shared JS file will appear there.

4. Drag the shared file from the Assets panel to the head content bar in your Document window. If you examine your code after having done this, you'll see that a link to the shared file has been added (see Figure 13.23).

FIGURE 13.23

Using the Assets panel to link a new HTML document to the shared JS file.

5. Now you can apply any behavior that uses the functions in the shared JS file. Dreamweaver will know not to add the functions to your document because they're already present in the shared file.

If you love the idea of sharing functions but want some help with it, try Paul Boon's "Create and Hot Swap JS Files from Script Tags" extension, available from the Macromedia Exchange.

Thinking Outside the Box: Hijacking Function Calls

When you understand how functions and function calls work in Dreamweaver behaviors, you can extend your use of behaviors by "borrowing" their function calls to put in unusual places, essentially enabling you to attach behaviors to elements not normally allowed by the Dreamweaver interface. For instance, you can call behaviors from within media elements, such as Flash or QuickTime movies. You can even call behaviors from within other behaviors.

It works like this:

1. Start by creating a temporary text link (something you'll delete when you're done). Somewhere in the document, type a word or two of text, and link it to # (a null link).

2. With the new text link selected, open the Behaviors panel and apply the behavior whose function call you want to borrow. (Maybe you want to call the Pop-Up Message behavior from within a Flash button, for instance. You would start by applying that behavior to your temporary text link.) Configure the behavior as desired. Test it in a browser to make sure it does what you need it to do.

3. In Code view, find the code for your text link (see Figure 13.24). It will include the function call from the behavior, like this (function call is shown in bold):

   ```
   <a href="#" onMouseOver="MM_popupMsg('Hello, world!')">click
   me</a>
   ```

FIGURE 13.24
Creating a function call by applying a behavior to a temporary text link.

Select and copy the function call code—all the code between the double quotes, starting after onMouseOver= (just like the bold code shown here). Don't include the quotes themselves, though!

4. You are now free to attach this function call to any other behavior or page element. To add the function call to Flash Button or Text, for instance, double-click the Flash object to open its editing window. In the Link field, type **javascript:** and then paste your function call (see Figure 13.25). For the Pop-Up Message behavior, the call should be javascript: MM_popupMsg('Hello, world!').

FIGURE 13.25
Adding the borrowed
function call to a
Flash object.

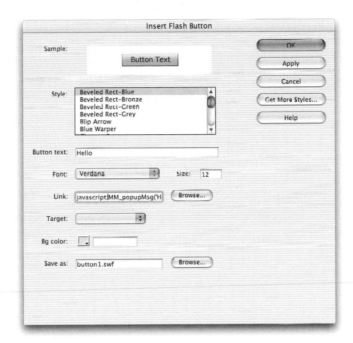

5. Delete the temporary text link. Be careful here, however! If you just select the link in Design view and delete it, Dreamweaver removes the function as well as the function call. Instead, go to Code view and delete the item there. (After you've deleted the link, look through the document head to make sure the main function is still present.)

See Chapter 14, "Controlling Layers with JavaScript," for examples of using this technique to call behaviors from other behaviors. See Chapter 16, "Building Web Pages with Flash," for examples of using the technique with media elements.

SUMMARY

Behaviors go a long way toward giving your web page advanced functionality and that professional flair. They enable you to go well beyond the limitations of basic HTML.

Other behaviors are available, and these are discussed throughout the book in chapters relevant to their specific functionality. You also can download and install any other functions in Dreamweaver that will go beyond the set included here. You can find these at the Macromedia Exchange for Dreamweaver, discussed in Chapter 28, "Customizing and Extending Dreamweaver."

In the next chapter, you will learn about even more behaviors and how they relate to using layers in your page design.

CHAPTER 14

CONTROLLING LAYERS WITH JAVASCRIPT

SO FAR IN THIS BOOK, YOU HAVE LEARNED WHAT CSS IS AND HOW IT CAN be used as a sophisticated page layout tool. The next two chapters cover the dynamic aspect of DHTML—how to use JavaScript to control CSS page content. The current chapter examines the various Dreamweaver MX 2004 behaviors for controlling layers, including determining visibility, changing layer content, and setting other properties; the next chapter focuses on performing these activities over time—or in other words, animating your layer control.

DYNAMIC HTML BASICS: LAYERS AND SCRIPTING IN THE BROWSER

DHTML is a series of overlapping technologies for creating *dynamic web pages*—pages capable of responding in complex ways to user interactions—without using server-side processing, plug-ins, or other helper applications. CSS and JavaScript are the key players in DHTML, along with various proprietary technologies such as Netscape's JSS (JavaScript style sheets) and Microsoft's ActiveX filters.

For more about CSS and layers, see Chapter 12, "CSS Positioning, Dreamweaver Layers, and Page Layout."

About the DOM

The heart of live data page control is the DOM. The *DOM*, or Document Object Model, is a hierarchical description of the structure of objects in an HTML page. In scripting terms, an *object* is an element that can be accessed and altered by scripting commands. The browser window is an object, for instance; with scripting, you can determine what size it is and what location (URL) it's currently displaying, and you can even tell it to change its location to a new URL. The document currently being displayed in the window is an object—so is a form sitting in the document and each input field inside the form. A JavaScript statement such as this one enables you to climb up the document "tree" to talk to a text field inside a form, inside the document that is currently inside the browser window, and then to change that text field's value:

```
window.document.theForm.textField1.value="Hello world"
```

By accessing that value, you have just navigated the DOM.

Like everything else about computers, the DOM develops and has versions. Basic form access, such as that shown here, is part of the Level 0 DOM. Dynamic HTML, which accesses other page elements, requires the more developed Level 1 DOM. Only browsers 4.0 and above can understand the Level 1 DOM; therefore, only those browsers can handle DHTML.

DOM Incompatibility

The DOM is important to you because all DOMs are not the same. The W3C has set out a standard for how the DOM should function in HTML pages. But browsers follow the standard to different degrees. The Mozilla/Netscape 6 DOM is closest to the standard. The Internet Explorer DOM has some differences. The older Netscape 4 DOM varies quite a bit from the standard. This means that, even if you consider only the two major browsers, you have three different DOMs to deal with.

In general, DHTML authors have a choice of the following:

- Pick one browser to design for, and ignore the rest.

- Try to be as inclusive as possible by using only features that work everywhere.

- Try to be reasonably inclusive, but also use new features by putting two or more sets of code in each page, each directed at a different browser.

Dreamweaver's DHTML Authoring Strategy

One of the reasons Dreamweaver is popular as a DHTML authoring tool is that it shields designers from most of these compatibility problems. All of its layer-related behaviors are written with the proper JavaScript to work as well as possible in both major browsers. DHTML features that are purely browser- or platform-specific (such as the IE/Windows filters and page transitions) are either not included or not emphasized in the interface.

You can never be completely shielded, however. Certain items will display differently across browsers—and across platforms in different browsers. Certain behaviors will behave differently in different browsers—or they won't behave at all, despite Dreamweaver's robust coding. This chapter focuses on how to use Dreamweaver tools for dynamically controlling layers. Be aware as you go through it that not everything you do will work equally well in all browser/platform situations.

CONTROLLING LAYER VISIBILITY

Visibility control as scripted by Dreamweaver is supported by Netscape Navigator 4 and 6 and Mozilla, IE 4–6, and Opera 5–7 across platforms.

One of the simplest and most reliable layer properties that you can control with scripting is visibility. By dynamically hiding and showing layers, you can create pages that store much more information than is visible at any given time. The designer's buzzword for this is *nested content*. Nested content can include contextual information popping up where needed, drop down navigation menus, and different sets of body content that display as users click navigation controls. The possibilities are limited only by the designer's imagination and ingenuity.

You control layer visibility in Dreamweaver with the Show-Hide Layers behavior. As Figure 14.1 shows, it's simple and straightforward to use.

FIGURE 14.1
The interface for Show-Hide Layers behavior.

The Basics of Showing and Hiding Layers

As with any behavior, start by creating the layer to show or hide, and select the object that will trigger the visibility change. Showing and hiding can be triggered by rollovers, mouse clicks, form data changes, or even pages loading. Then follow these steps:

1. In the Behaviors panel, choose the Show-Hide Layers behavior.

2. In the dialog box that appears, select a layer from the list.

3. Choose the visibility state that you want it to have.

4. Repeat steps 2 and 3 for any other layers you want to change with this instance of the behavior.

Note that you can change the visibility of as many layers as you like in this one dialog box with just one instance of the Show-Hide behavior. If you have three alternate content layers, for instance, one instance of Show-Hide will show one content layer and hide the other two. (That's the scenario being illustrated in Figure 14.1.) Here are a few other tips.

Setting Visibility vs. Changing Visibility

It's important not to confuse the use of JavaScript to change a layer's visibility with the use of CSS to assign the layer's initial visibility. You assign the latter through the Property Inspector or Layers panel (see Figure 14.2). If you want your layer to be invisible from the moment the page starts loading, set its visibility to be hidden here. Only if you want your layer's visibility to change based on user interaction or browser activity do you need to use the Show-Hide Layers behavior.

What's the difference between setting the property initially and using the behavior to set it upon onLoad? Behaviors that execute upon onLoad will execute only after the page has finished loading. For instance, you can create a loading screen by making a layer containing the word Loading and setting it to start out visible but become hidden upon onLoad.

FIGURE 14.2
Setting layer visibility in the Property Inspector or Layers panel.

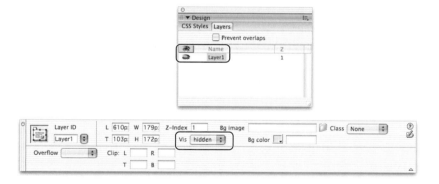

Showing, Hiding, and Default

When you choose the Show-Hide behavior, you have three visibility choices. Show and Hide are self-explanatory. Default sets the visibility state to inherit. If one layer is nested inside another, the child (nested) layer inherits the visibility setting of the parent (nesting) layer.

Choosing Not to Show or Hide a Particular Layer

What if you're in the Show-Hide dialog box, and you've selected a particular layer and set it to show or hide, and then you realize that you had the wrong layer chosen? You don't have to cancel the whole operation. Just choose the same option for the same layer again to toggle it off. If you've set the layer Fred to Show by mistake, for instance, just leave Fred selected and click the Show button again.

Working with Invisible Layers

When you start working with this behavior, you are likely to run into the following situation. You've created a layer that will start out invisible until the user clicks a button or mouses over something that makes it show. How do you continue working with the layer in Design view now that it's invisible? One solution is to leave it visible until you've finished editing the page. The very last thing you'll do before saving, closing, and uploading the file is use the Property Inspector or Layers panel to set the layer's visibility to Hidden.

For any of you who have less-than-perfect memories, however, this is a dangerous idea because it's easy to forget that last step when you're facing down a deadline and have a million things to do. Instead, use the Layers panel to select your hidden layer. Clicking a layer's name in the panel will select it, and as soon as it's selected, it will become visible and will stay visible as long as you're editing its contents. As soon as you deselect it, however, it will disappear again. Making the layer temporarily visible in this way doesn't change the HTML code (that is, the code still defines the layer as being invisible), so there's no danger of it getting uploaded and displayed on the web improperly (see Figure 14.3).

FIGURE 14.3
Selecting an invisible layer in the Layers panel to make it temporarily visible in Design view.

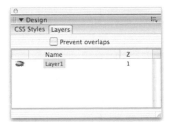

EXERCISE 14.1

Creating a Drop-Down or Cascading Menu

In this exercise, you'll create one of the most popular hidden-layer effects: a graphic menu bar with menus that appear when the mouse rolls over topics on the menu bar. This sort of menu is called a *drop-down menu* when the menu bar is placed horizontally across the top of a page (the menu bars in standard applications), and a *cascading menu* or fly-out menu when the menu bar is vertical and the menus appear to the side. All files for the exercise are located on the book's website at `www.peachpit.com` in the **chapter_14/menus** folder.

If you haven't done so already, download the **chapter_14** folder to your hard drive and define a site with that folder as the local root folder.

1. Start by opening **dropdown.html** and examining its contents and structure. This file contains four layers—one for the menu bar and three for the menus that will appear from it. The three menu layers are nested within the main menu bar layer, so the whole menu system can be repositioned by moving only the main layer. Preview the file in a browser, and you'll see that the first of the menus already contains rollovers for each entry (see Figure 14.4).

FIGURE 14.4
The dropdown.html file, before any Show-Hide Layer behaviors have been applied.

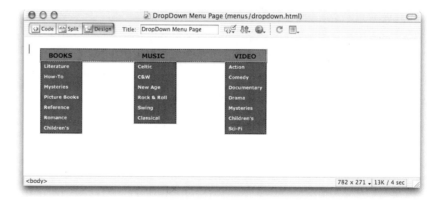

2. When working in depth with layers, an important habit to get into is giving them names you'll recognize when you see them in a dialog box or inspector. Before proceeding with the scripting in this exercise, take a moment to rename the layers. Name them main, books, music, and video.

3. The three books, music, and video layers should initially be invisible. Using the eyeball column in the Layers panel, make the books, music, and video layers invisible by clicking until the closed eye icon shows (see Figure 14.5).

FIGURE 14.5
The Layers panel for dropdown.html, with layers renamed and "eyeballs" closed, signifying that the layers are hidden.

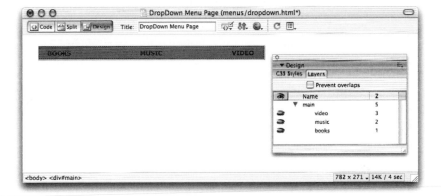

4. You want each menu to appear when the user mouses over the appropriate title in the menu bar. This means attaching the Show-Hide behavior to the three main graphics in the menu bar. Start with the BOOKS image.

- Select the image.

- Open the Behaviors panel and choose Show-Hide Layers from the actions list.

- In the dialog box that appears, from the list of layers, find books and set it to Show (see Figure 14.6).

- When you're done, click OK to close the dialog box.

FIGURE 14.6
The Show-Hide Layers dialog box showing the books layer.

After you've applied the behavior, check the Behaviors panel to make sure the `<A>onMouseOver` event trigger is chosen. (Remember to use the event trigger that appears with `<A>` to ensure maximum cross-browser compatibility. For more on this, see Chapter 13, "Getting Interactive with Behaviors.")

Preview in the browser to make sure the behavior is working. Then repeat the procedure for each of the other two menu topics.

5. After you've applied all three behaviors, the menus should appear on cue—but they never disappear. The mechanics of making that happen aren't difficult—it's just a matter of applying another Show-Hide behavior. But what event should trigger the behavior? That's a matter of strategy.

One strategy is to make each menu button (BOOKS, MUSIC, VIDEO) trigger its own menu to show and the other menus to hide. To accomplish that, select one of the menu title graphics—BOOKS, for instance—and, in the Behaviors panel, double-click its Show-Hide behavior to edit it. For the BOOKS graphic, the books layer should already be set to Show. Select the music layer and set it to Hide; then set the video layer to Hide also. Using this one behavior, you've now created a script that shows one menu and hides the other two (see Figure 14.7).

FIGURE 14.7
The Show-Hide Layers dialog box for the BOOKS menu title, set to show the books layer and hide the other two menu layers.

Repeat this process for each of the three title graphics. Rolling over any menu title should show that title's menu and hide the other two menus.

When you're finished, check out the result in the browser. Assuming that your users will check out each of your menus and then choose a destination from one of them, your menu system should work perfectly. There's one niggling interface flaw remaining, however. What if your visitors check out all the different menus and then decide not to choose a destination from any one of them? After the menus have started showing, there's no way to get all three of them to hide. Again, this is a matter of strategy. What event can be used to trigger all menus hiding?

A sneaky solution is to put another layer behind all of the menu layers, fill that layer with an invisible image, and set that image to trigger all menus hiding when it is rolled over. Figure 14.8 shows this happening.

FIGURE 14.8

Adding a large layer behind the menus, to be used in triggering all menus to hide.

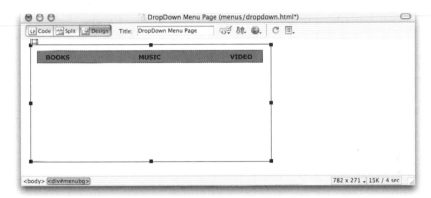

7. Start by drawing a new layer. Make it large enough to cover the entire area of your menu bar and menus. While you're at it, jot down its width and height from the Property Inspector. (Don't nest the background layer in with the main layer, or the effect won't work.) Because it will sit behind the other layers, as a kind of invisible background for them, name it **menubg**.

   Arrange the new menubg layer behind all the other layers by going to the Layers panel and dragging it to the bottom of the list of layers.

With the cursor inside this new layer, use the Image object from the Insert bar to insert **trpix.gif**. This transparent, single-pixel GIF image is located in the **chapter_14/menus/images** folder with the rest of the image files for this exercise. Set the width and height of the image to match the dimensions of your layer.

8. With this large transparent image selected, go to the Behaviors panel and add another Show-Hide Layers behavior. Set this behavior to hide all three menu layers. Set the triggering event to onMouseOver or <A>onMouseOver.

When you're finished, preview the page in a browser. When a menu is showing, moving the mouse away from the menu should hide all menus.

What's happening here? When the mouse rolls over the transparent image, all menus will hide. But when the mouse is over another image, in another layer, which is in front of the transparent image, its event handler is disabled. So, effectively, you've created a trigger that will hide all menus only when the mouse is in the vicinity of the menu system but not actually over any menus or the menu bar.

Should you use onMouseOver or <A>onMouseOver as the trigger for the transparent image? As was discussed in Chapter 13, any time an <img> tag is selected, you have a choice of event triggers with or without <A>. Choosing a trigger with <A> will add the behavior's function call to an <a> tag surrounding the image (and will even create the <a> tag, if necessary). Choosing a trigger without this marker will add the function to the <img> tag itself. Because Netscape 4.x does not support event handlers for <img> tags, it's safer to use the <A> triggers. But adding an <a> tag also causes the cursor to change to a pointing finger. This is the user's cue that a link is present. In the case of your menu system, users will be confused if, any time the mouse gets anywhere near the hidden menus, the cursor changes to indicate a link. That's bad interface design.

For this exercise, try out the menu system both ways—with onMouseOver and <A>onMouseOver. See what the difference means to you. Figure 14.9 shows what the user will see if you choose the safer <A>onMouseOver event handler.

 To access the both onMouseOver events, set the event handlers pop-up menu to show events for IE 4.0.

FIGURE 14.9
The pointing finger cursor appearing over empty space if an <a> tag is added to the transparent image behind the menus.

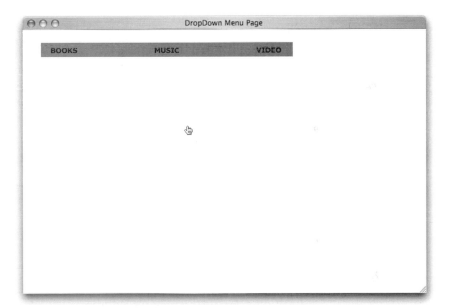

9. Optional challenge: Can you see how the menu system you've just created could function as a vertical menu bar with cascading menus, without any change in scripting? The only changes required are layout changes—altering the table structure of the main layer, the relative positions of the various menu layers, and the dimensions of the invisible image and layer in the background. See if you can create a sideways cascading menu from this file. If you get stuck, check out **cascading_finished.html**, in the **chapter_14/menus** folder, for a completed example. Figure 14.10 shows a cascading menu system in action.

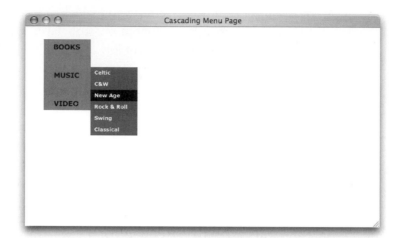

Working Smart with the Show-Hide Behavior

The actual mechanics of applying this behavior are not complicated. However, working with invisible page elements brings up a host of questions that you'll undoubtedly stumble across when you least expect them. Here are a few points to consider.

Downloading and Invisible Layers

Any content within an invisible layer is still considered part of your page. It will download when the page downloads. This has all sorts of ramifications. If your page contains many layers that are initially invisible, and if those layers have substantial content in them, your page will take a while to download even though it looks like a simple, fairly empty page. If a user clicks a button that makes a layer visible, and that layer's contents haven't finished downloading yet, the user will experience a delay. After the page has finished downloading, however, layers that become visible will display immediately. In essence, you've preloaded the contents of those layers.

Triggering JavaScript Actions Within Invisible Layers

Because layers can contain just about anything, your layers might include buttons or text links that have their own behaviors attached to them. Be aware that triggers won't work if a layer is invisible. If you

have a rollover set to open a new window when the mouse moves over it, and that rollover is hidden in an invisible layer, no visitor is going to accidentally trigger the new window opening by moving the mouse over that hidden item.

Media Objects in Invisible Layers

Embedded video, audio, Flash movies, and other media objects can be placed in layers (see Chapter 15, "Plug-Ins, ActiveX, and Java," for more on this), but this limits the functionality of the layers. Depending on the browser, the platform, and the media plug-in involved, the layer might not become properly invisible, or it might not be possible to change layer visibility with scripting. If you want to use media objects in conjunction with DHTML effects like these, test your pages carefully in all target browsers.

CONTROLLING LAYER CONTENTS

An alternative approach to putting nested content on pages is to change the contents of a single layer instead of hiding and showing multiple layers. In Dreamweaver, you do this with the Set Text of Layer behavior.

As coded by Dreamweaver, the Set Text of Layer behavior works in IE 4+, Netscape 4, and Netscape 6/Mozilla. It does not work in Opera 5 and 6, but it does work in Opera 7.

The Basics of Setting Layer Text

The Set Layer Text behavior is tucked away in the Set Text submenu of the Behaviors panel's Actions pop-up menu. Choosing it brings up a dialog box in which you can choose any of your document's layers and enter any text you want to appear in that layer (see Figure 14.11). Whatever you enter here will replace the existing layer contents, regardless of the contents. You can even change the contents of the layer containing the object the behavior is attached to. If you leave the dialog box's input area empty, the contents of the specified layer will be deleted.

FIGURE 14.11
The Set Text of Layer
behavior in the
Behaviors panel
Action list, and the
dialog box it calls up.

Working Smart with Set Text of Layer

What can you do to really take advantage of this behavior?

Setting More Than Text

Despite its name, Set Text of Layer is not limited to text effects. You can use it to put almost any content into a layer, by entering HTML code rather than straight text into the input field of the dialog box. Code such as this will display in a formatted text message in the specified layer:

```
<h1>Welcome!</h1>
<p>Are you ready for the <b>big</b> moment?</p>
```

Tables and images, links, and forms can all be written into layers using this behavior. A more accurate description for the behavior might be "Set HTML Content of Layer."

Here are a few tips to consider when using Set Text of Layer.

Watch Those Quotes

Whatever text or HTML you enter in the dialog box will be inserted into the behavior's function call, like this:

```
onClick="MM_setTextOfLayer('Layer1','','Hello World')"
```

If you have set your Code Rewriting Preferences to URL-encode special characters and attribute values, any HTML source code that you enter will be inserted into your page code looking like this:

```
onClick="MM_setTextOfLayer('help','','%3Cimg src=%22duck.gif%22
width=%2250%22 height=%2250%22%3E')"
```

For a full discussion of functions and function calls in Dreamweaver behaviors, see the section "Working with Behaviors in Dreamweaver" in Chapter 13. For more on the Code Rewriting preferences, see the section "Using Dreamweaver as a Text Editor" in Chapter 27, "Writing Code in Dreamweaver."

Although this code will work perfectly fine in a browser, it isn't too readable if you later want to hand-edit your HTML. You can avoid this mess by going to Edit > Preferences > Code Rewriting (Mac OS X: Dreamweaver > Preferences > Code Rewriting) and disabling both Special Characters options—the Encode Special Characters in URLs and Encode <, >, &, and " in Attribute Values Using & options. With these options deselected, Dreamweaver will escape all quotes with \ and leave all other characters alone. If you do this, however, you must include only single quotes in your HTML code. This code, for instance, will break the behavior:

```
<img src="duck.gif" width="50" height="50">
```

But this code will work fine:

```
<img src='duck.gif' width='50' height='50'>
```

It will be inserted into your page code as the following function call:

```
onClick="MM_setTextOfLayer('violin','','<img src=\'duck.gif\'
width-\'50\' hcight=\'50\'>')"
```

Avoid Hand-Coding

If you want to insert HTML formatting using Set Text of Layer, but you don't want to type all that code yourself, work smart with Dreamweaver.

Create the desired display in Design view, either in the same file you're working on or in a temporary file. Then go to Code view and copy the code from there. Open the Set Text of Layer dialog box, click in the input area, and paste. Remember, though, that Dreamweaver always encloses tag attributes in double quotes. So, if you have disabled the Special Characters options as described earlier, you'll have to replace all double quotes with single quotes, either by hand or by using the Find and Replace command, before the behavior will work.

Don't Include Media Objects

Some browsers won't display embedded media properly when the <embed> code appears as part of this command. Media objects and layers often don't mix well.

EXERCISE 14.2

Setting Layer Text to Display Context-Sensitive Information

This exercise builds an interactive illustration that puts different data in an information layer depending on what part of the illustration the mouse rolls over. All the files for the exercise can be found in the **chapter_14/ violin** folder on the book's website.

1. Open and examine **violin_write.html**. This file, pictured in Figure 14.12, presents the user with a picture of a violin. Image map hotspots will be used to trigger a behavior that puts different information in the help layer as the user's mouse rolls over those parts of the illustration. If you browse this file, you'll see that some of the hotspots already trigger basic text-only information to appear. You'll be adding the same behavior to the remaining hotspots and then dressing up the way the contextual information displays. (To see the final presentation in action, browse to **violin_write_finished.html**.)

2. Select the hotspot at the top of the violin picture. Open the Behaviors panel and choose Set Text of Layer from the Actions list. In the dialog box, choose the help layer from the pop-up menu, and type the word **Scroll** in the input field. When you have finished, make sure the event triggering the action is onMouseOver. Figure 14.13 shows the dialog box with information entered.

FIGURE 14.12
The violin_write.html
presentation as it
should appear in
the browser when
complete.

FIGURE 14.13
The Set Text of Layer
dialog box, set to
enter a simple text
message in the help
layer.

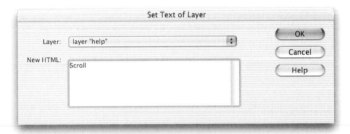

You also need to blank out the help layer when the mouse rolls off the violin scroll. With the same hotspot selected, add another instance of the Set Text of Layer behavior. Choose the help layer from the pop-up menu again, but this time leave the input field blank (enter no text). When you're done, change the trigger event to onMouseOut.

Repeat the procedure for the hotspot directly below this one, configuring it to show the word Neck upon onMouseOver. Make sure you

preview in the browser to make sure you've coded the effect properly before proceeding to the next step.

3. Now make the Scroll and Neck messages a bit fancier. Select the top hotspot and double-click its onMouseOver behavior to edit the text that will appear. Replace the original message with this code:

```
<h1>Scroll</h1>
<p>Scrolls are curly and brown, and have wooden pegs
➡sticking _out of both sides.</p>
```

Close the dialog box and choose Preview in Browser. Rolling over the violin scroll should now display information like that shown in Figure 14.14.

FIGURE 14.14

The Set Text of Layer behavior used to display HTML-formatted text.

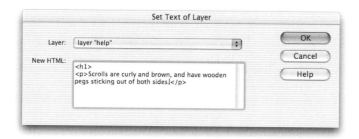

4. After you've verified that your behavior is working, check your code to see how the HTML was inserted into the function call. (You can do this quickly by going to Code and Design view and selecting the hotspot in the Design View portion of the Document window.) Depending on how your URL encoding preferences are set, you might see a mess like this:

```
<area onMouseOver="MM_setTextOfLayer('violin','',
➡'%3Ch1%3EScroll%3C/h1%3E%0D%3Cp%3E Scrolls are curly and
➡brown, and have wooden pegs sticking out of both
➡sides.%3C/p%3E')" shape="rect" coords="65,3,145,89"
➡href="#">
```

To clean up this code, go to Edit > Preferences, and choose the Code Rewriting category. Deselect both Special Characters options. When this is done, return to the Behaviors panel and double-click the scroll hotspot's Set Text of Layer behavior to open its dialog box. You

don't need to change anything in the dialog box; just click OK. Check your code again, and you should see a more readable function call than before:

```
<area onMouseOver="MM_setTextOfLayer('violin','','
➥<h1>Scroll</h1><p> Scrolls are curly and brown, and have
➥wooden pegs sticking out of both sides.</p>')"
➥shape="rect" coords="65,3,145,89" href="#">
```

5. For the Neck hotspot, use Dreamweaver to help write the formatted code. Create a new Dreamweaver file, and save it in the **chapter_14/violin** folder as **temp.html**.

   In **temp.html**, type the following text:

   ```
   Neck
   Violin necks are long and skinny, and since they're made of
   ➥wood they're not much good for swallowing.
   ```

   Now use the Property Inspector to format the first line as <h1> and the rest as <p>.

   Go to Code view, select all the HTML code for the formatted text, and copy it. (If you copy directly from Design view, you'll get only the text, not the formatting code.)

   Back in **violin_write.html**, select the Neck hotspot and open its Set Text of Layer behavior for editing. Delete the contents of the input field and paste in the HTML code from the temporary file. Preview in the browser again; rolling over the Scroll and Neck hotspots should display similarly formatted text in the help layer. If you changed your Code Rewriting preferences in the previous step, your page's source code should contain a nice, readable (nonencoded) chunk of HTML in the Neck hotspot's function call.

6. To make things even fancier, replace the <h1> title with a GIF image, again using the **temp.html** file as a handy code-creating workshop.

   Open **temp.html** (or bring it to the front) and go to Code and Design view. In the Design portion of the Document window, delete the heading; in its place, insert the image **scroll.gif**. Figure 14.15 shows how the revised scroll message should appear in the temp file.

FIGURE 14.15
Creating a fancier chunk of display information in temp.html.

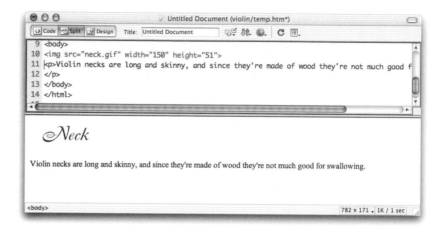

If you have disabled URL encoding in your preferences, you'll need to replace all double quotes with single quotes. To do this, go to Edit > Find and Replace. Set your search parameters to Current Document and Source Code. Search for double quotes (") and replace with single quotes ('). Because this is only a temp file, go ahead and click the Replace All button to perform the search quickly.

When this is complete, activate the Code view portion of the Document window, and select and copy all the code for the image and text. Then go back to **violin_write.html**, open the Scroll hotspot's behavior for editing, and replace its contents with the new code.

7. Preview your violin page in the browser. If you entered your code correctly, you should see a result like that shown in Figure 14.12. If your browser preview doesn't work properly, double-check the code for your page. The scroll hotspot's event handler should contain escaped single quotes.

Let Dreamweaver's color coding work for you. If your pasted code contains incorrect quote marks, the improperly terminated string literals will turn black. If the quote marks are correct, the entire function call (everything after onMouseOver=) will be blue.

8. If you want to complete the violin-browsing experience and get some practice with this behavior, repeat the previous steps to dress up the rest of the violin hotspots. All the required GIF images are in the **chapter_14/violin** folder.

Using CSS Layer Styles to Format Text

A lovely, efficient way to put nicely formatted text into a layer without having to enter and re-enter the HTML formatting for each new set of text is to assign a custom CSS class to the layer itself. It works this way (see Figure 14.16):

1. Create the layer you're going to be targeting with the behavior.

2. Using the CSS Styles panel (or the CSS tab of the Tag Inspector), create a new custom class. Include any text formatting, positioning, or layer formatting you want in this style.

3. In Design view, select the layer and apply the style to it.

After this is done, whenever you Set Text of Layer, you need to enter only the text itself. All formatting will be supplied.

FIGURE 14.16
Setting up and applying a CSS class to control the formatting of a layer that will have its content set dynamically.

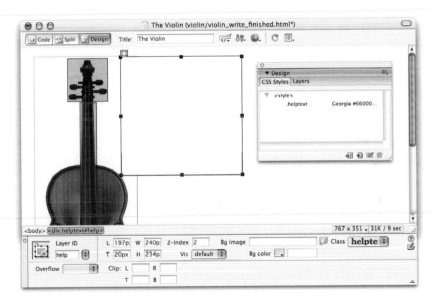

Set Text of Layer or Show-Hide Layers?

Repeatedly setting the text of a single layer can create a similar effect to starting with a stack of hidden layers and showing them one at a time. Why choose one method over another?

- **Loading and preloading.** If all of the document's content is present when the page initially loads (as it is when using Show-Hide Layers), it will all display immediately when called on. Depending on your project, you might decide that this is a good thing or a bad thing. If

you know ahead of time that users are probably going to access all the content, you'll want to download it as soon as possible—so use Show-Hide Layers. If you think users will probably want to access only one or two layers' worth of contents, you might not want to make them wait for the other layers' content to download—so use Set Text of Layer.

- **Simple text changes.** If your content all consists of similarly formatted text, it will probably be more efficient to create and edit content using Set Text of Layer. You can use a CSS style applied to the layer to control formatting, and you need enter only unformatted text in the behavior's dialog box.

- **Different content, identical layers.** If your content will all appear in the same position on the page, it's easier to format, resize, and position one layer than several. Use Set Text of Layer.

- **Browser compatibility.** Setting layer text as it is scripted in the Dreamweaver behavior is supported by all current versions of Netscape and IE, but not by versions of Opera earlier than Opera 7. If this extra browser support is important to you, stick with Show-Hide Layers.

DRAGGING AND DROPPING LAYERS

It's easy in Dreamweaver Design view to move layers around on the page, but after the page is created and published on the web, everything is cemented in place. Or is it? With the Drag Layer behavior, you tell layers to track the coordinates of the user's mouse. You can use this scripting to create repositionable navigation menus and pop-up windows, drag-and-drop games, shopping carts, and even slider controls.

 Note that the Drag Layer behavior as implemented in Dreamweaver will not work in Netscape 6 or in Opera before version 7.

The Basics of Dragging and Dropping

Applying the Drag Layer behavior is not as straightforward as applying the other layer behaviors because it must be triggered when the page loads, not when the user presses the mouse down on a layer. What

you're doing is declaring a given layer to be "draggable"—after that, it's up to the user to drag it around or not. To set up a draggable layer, follow these steps:

1. Open or create a document that has at least one layer in it.

2. Deselect all page content or use the tag selector to select the <body> tag.

3. Open the Behaviors panel and choose the Drag Layer behavior from the Actions list. In the dialog box that appears, use the pop-up menu to select the layer that you want to be draggable. Configure any other settings as desired, or leave the default settings in place.

4. Make sure the event triggering the action is onLoad.

That's it! For the life of this document, the layer is draggable. Figure 14.17 shows the Drag Layer behavior dialog box.

FIGURE 14.17
The Drag Layer behavior dialog box in Basic and Advanced modes.

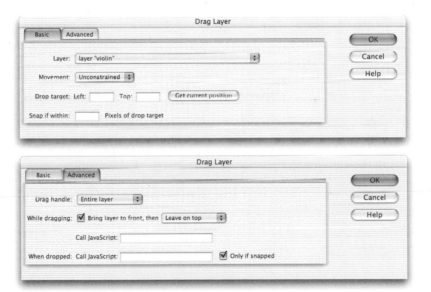

Draggability Options

You can customize a layer's draggability in various ways. You can control which portion of it is draggable, where and how far it can be dragged, what happens to its z-index (position in the stacking order) as it is dragging, and what should happen when the user drops it. Some

of these options can be tricky to use, but they are responsible for the power of the behavior.

Constraining the Drag Area

If you apply no constraints, the user is free to drag the layer anywhere within the browser window. Depending on why you've made the layer draggable in the first place, you might want to limit users to dragging only within a certain area. If you're creating a game, for instance, you might want the draggable game pieces to stay within the defined game boundaries.

Assigning a constraint area is easy: Just select the Constraint option from the Movement menu in the Basic tab of the Drag Layer dialog box.

The tricky part is determining what constraint values to specify in the four text fields. These fields all ask the same question: Starting from its current position, how many pixels up/down/left/right should the layer be allowed to move? Depending on what kind of constraint you're trying to create, figuring out these values can be simple or can require some tinkering and thought.

If you love solving engineering problems and are good at diagramming and math, you probably don't need any help with this. For everybody else, here's a simple strategy:

1.   Grab a pencil and paper, and in Dreamweaver open the History panel.

2.   Select the layer you want to constrain, and write down its starting L (left) and T (top) positions.

3.   Drag the layer to the topmost, leftmost position you want it to go. Note the new T (top) position, and subtract it from the starting T value. That's your "up" value. Note the new L (left) position, and subtract it from the starting L value. That's your "left" value.

4.   Drag the layer to the bottommost, rightmost position you want it to go. Note the new T position, and subtract the original T value from it. That's your "down" value. Note the new L position, and subtract the original L value. That's your "right" value.

If you're not sure which value to subtract from which, just remember that all constraint numbers must be positive integers, or 0. (A value of 0

means the layer isn't allowed to move in that direction.) Subtract the smaller value from the larger one. Figure 14.18 shows a form you might find handy for your note taking.

original (L): [   ]   original (T): [   ]

− leftmost (L): [   ]   − topmost (T): [   ]

_____

UP value: [   ]   **LEFT value:** [   ]

rightmost (L): [   ]   bottommost (T): [   ]

− original (L): [   ]   − original (T): [   ]

_____

DOWN value: [   ]   **RIGHT value:** [   ]

Assigning a Drop Target (and Snapping to It)

A *drop target* is the location where you want the user to drop the layer. If you're creating a game, such as a matching game, this would be the location of the correct answer. If you're creating a shopping cart interface, this would be the cart graphic that tells you the user wants to buy an item. This option is specified in the Basic tab of the Drag Layer dialog box.

You specify the drop target as Left and Top coordinates, which represent where the upper-left corner of the layer should be when it's dropped. Because it's almost impossible for a user to drop a layer on exactly those coordinates (not 1 pixel right or left, up or down), you enable snapping and assign a "snap-to" distance, also measured in pixels. If the user drops the layer within that many pixels of the target, the layer snaps into place and is officially on target.

How do you figure out what values to use for the drop target? The dialog box gives you a helpful Get Current Position button—click the button,

and the current coordinates of the draggable layer are entered. This is useful, however, only if the layer is currently sitting at its target location. Therefore, one way to approach the problem is to close the dialog box, move the layer to its desired destination, return to the dialog box, and click the button. Then close the dialog box again and move the layer back to its starting position.

Another way to handle this situation is to move the layer to the drop target destination, write down the coordinates, and then choose Edit > Undo or use the History panel to put the layer back where it started. Then go to the dialog box and type in the values you wrote down. (The second method has the advantage of putting your layer back in exactly the same position where it started.)

Specifying a Drag Handle

Do you want the user to be able to click anywhere on the layer to start dragging it, or can he drag only from a particular location (such as a handle)? If your layer contains a puzzle piece or shopping item, for instance, you probably want the entire layer to be draggable. If it's an interface item, however, like a miniwindow or pop-up message, you'll probably want users to drag it only by its title bar (just like a real computer window).

Choose the Area Within Layer option from the Drag Handle menu in the Advanced tab of the Drag Layer dialog box. Text fields will appear, asking you to specify the drag handle's left edge, top edge, width, and height. The left and top measurements are relative to the left and top of the draggable layer. To use a temporary layer to determine the appropriate values for a drag handle, follow these steps (demonstrated in Figure 14.19):

1. Draw a temporary layer to use as a proxy for the drag handle. Resize and position this layer to where you want the handle to be.

2. Jot down the new layer's W, H, L, and T values from the Property Inspector.

3. Select the draggable layer, and jot down its L and T values. The temporary layer's W and H values will become the drag handle's W and H.

4. Subtract the draggable layer's L and T values from the temporary layer's L and T values, to get the drag handle's L and T values.

5. When you're done, delete the temporary layer.

FIGURE 14.19
Using a temporary layer to determine measurements for a drag handle.

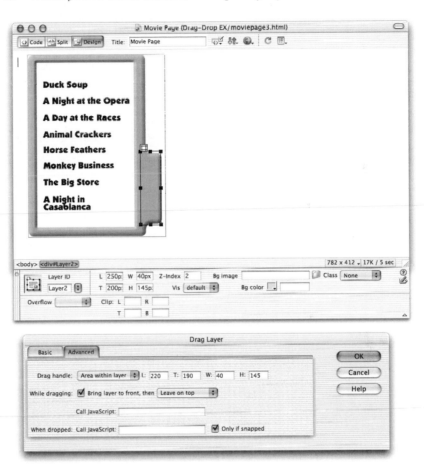

If you repeatedly find yourself scratching your head over pixel coordinates and measurements, try using an onscreen pixel ruler utility. You can find plenty of them available at shareware sites such as www.download.com.

Changing the Z-Index

The *z-index* determines which layers are on top of which other layers. While a layer is being dragged, it should probably be on top—dragging a layer that goes behind other layers is a weird experience. When the layer is dropped, you might want it to stay on top, or you might want it to

return to its normal position in the stacking order. Use the Advanced tab of the dialog box to specify how the z-index is treated.

EXERCISE 14.3

Creating a Draggable Shopping Cart Interface

In this exercise, you use the Drag Layer behavior to create a graphic shopping experience in which visitors can drag shopping bags into a cart. All the files for this exercise can be found on the book's website in the **chapter_14/shoppingcart** folder.

1. Start by opening **shopping.html** and examining its contents (see Figure 14.20). All the page elements are in place, and the layers have been given descriptive names. None of the scripting has been added.

FIGURE 14.20
The shopping.html file, ready for adding behaviors.

2. You want all three shopping bag layers to be draggable, so you need three instances of the Drag Layer behavior, each triggered when the page loads. Deselect all page content or use the tag selector to select <body>. Then open the Behaviors panel and create a Drag Layer behavior for each shopping bag. Preview in the browser to make sure the bags are indeed draggable.

3. For your first refinement, limit the draggable area for the shopping bags. You don't want users dragging and dropping bags on top of

the title bar or shopping instructions, so define an official "shopping area" from the bottom of the title bar to the bottom of the shopping cart, and from the left edge of the price fields to the right edge of the shopping cart.

Before plunging back into the dialog boxes, you need to calculate the Up, Down, Left, and Right constraint values for each bag. Using the method outlined earlier (or any other method you like better), determine the values for each bag. Then configure each Drag Layer behavior instance with the correct numbers. Figure 14.21 shows the editing dialog box for the redbag layer, with appropriate values entered.

FIGURE 14.21

The Drag Layer dialog box for the redbag layer, showing its correct constraint values.

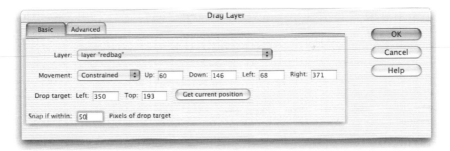

4. Now set drop targets for all three bags.

   Move all three bags to where you think their final destination should be in the cart (see Figure 14.22). For all three, jot down their L and T values. Then use Edit > Undo or the History panel to put the bags back to their original positions, and enter each bag's values in the appropriate Drag Layer dialog box. For each bag, enter a snap-to distance of 100 pixels.

5. You want each bag to come to the front as you're dragging it. When the bags are dropped, however, you need to reset the z-index so that they end up sitting inside the cart rather than on top of it. Open each Drag Layer behavior and bring the Advanced tab to the front. Make sure that Bring to Front is selected, and choose Restore z-index from the pop-up menu.

6. Try it! In browsers that support the Drag Layer behavior, you should be able to drop items in the shopping cart or leave them lying around the window—but not outside your official shopping rectangle.

FIGURE 14.22
The desired location of all three shopping bags after they're dropped in the cart.

Triggering Actions with Drag and Drop

Being able to drag items around onscreen might be fun, but it can really be useful when you use it to trigger other actions. If the layer is a slider, if it's a game, or if it's a shopping cart, you might need to know three things:

- That an object is currently being dragged
- That an object has been dropped
- That an object has been dropped on target

Calling JavaScripts from the Drag Layer Behavior

Another handy one-liner to use with Drag Layer is location= 'anypage.html', which will cause the browser to go to the specified relative or absolute address as soon as an item is dropped on a target.

In Dreamweaver, you use the Call JavaScript options in the Drag Layer dialog box's Advanced tab to trigger other actions based on the user's dragging and dropping. As you can see from the dialog box, the behavior can be configured to trigger a script as soon as the user starts dragging, when the user drops the layer, or only when the user drops the layer on target. Any JavaScript statement(s) entered into the appropriate input field will execute when the specified condition is met. In the dialog box shown in Figure 14.23, for instance, dropping the layer on target will pop open an alert window with a short message.

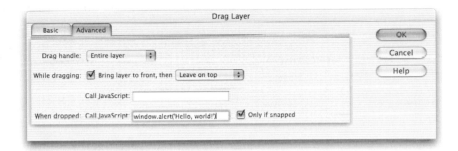

Using Drag Layer to Trigger Another Behavior

If you want the Drag Layer behavior to trigger scripts longer than a line or two, you don't want to enter the entire script in those tiny little input fields. It's better to create a JavaScript function in the document <head> and enter the function call here. On the other hand, wouldn't it be nice if you could just trigger another Dreamweaver behavior from here, instead of having to manually code scripts? The previous chapter presented a sneaky technique for using behaviors in unusual places by inserting a behavior into a document and then "borrowing" the function call portion of the behavior. In working with the Drag Layer behavior, this means placing the function call from another behavior into one of the Call JavaScript fields, in the Drag Layer dialog box. Figure 14.24 shows this happening.

FIGURE 14.24
Borrowing the function call from the Pop-up Message behavior to use in the Drag Layer dialog box—the Pop-up Message behavior will be executed when the dragged layer is dropped.

EXERCISE 14.4

Responding to Items Dropped in a Shopping Cart

In this exercise, you'll add more functionality to the draggable shopping cart developed in the preceding exercise. If the user drops a shopping bag in the cart, you'll trigger another script that responds in various ways.

1. If you completed the preceding exercise and are happy with your results, open the **shopping.html** page you created. If you would rather start fresh, open **shopping_finished.html** from the **chapter_14/ shoppingcart** folder on the book's website. Whichever file you open, save it as **buying.html**.

2. In the Behaviors panel, open any of the Drag Layer behavior instances to open its editing window, and bring the Advanced tab to the front. In the When Dropped: Call JavaScript text field, type the following code:

```
window.alert('You bought me!')
```

This nice, simple statement makes a pop-up message appear. So that the message appears only if the bag is in the cart, select the Only If Snapped option.

Try the new, improved shopping cart in your browser. Dragging the bag to the cart should call up a pop-up window like the one shown in Figure 14.25.

FIGURE 14.25
Dragging a shopping bag to the cart, and the resulting alert window.

3. Now get your shopping cart to do something fancier by inserting a function call for a Dreamweaver behavior. You'll make your document's three price layers invisible to start, and then have each one become visible as its matching bag is dropped in the cart.

To set up the effect, make each of the price layers (redprice, green-price, blueprice) invisible by closing its eye in the Layers panel.

4. Following the steps outlined earlier, you'll start by adding a fake text link. Create a new, small layer somewhere on your page. Type the words **buy me!**, or some other simple word or phrase, into the layer, and use the Link field in the Property Inspector to link the text to #. Figure 14.26 shows this happening.

FIGURE 14.26

Creating a simple text link as a temporary holder for a function call.

5. With the text link selected, use the Behaviors panel to add a Show-Hide Layers behavior. In the behavior dialog box, configure it to show the redprice layer.

    Before proceeding, test this behavior in the browser to make sure it's working properly.

6. Now copy the function call. Select the text link and go to Code view or Code and Design view. The code for the text—including its `<a>` tag, event handler, and function call—should be selected and, therefore, easy to locate. Deselect the code and select only the function call. Your code and selection should look like this (selected code is shown here in bold):

```
<div id="Layer1" style="position:absolute; left:263px;
➥top:116px; width:138px; height:61px; z-index:7"><a href="#"
➥onClick="MM_showHideLayers('redprice','','show')">buy me!
➥</a></div>
```

Copy the selected code and go back to Design view.

7. Now paste the function call into the Drag Layer behavior. In the Behaviors panel, find the Drag Layer instance that controls the red shopping bag, and open its dialog box. In the Advanced tab, if there's any code written in the When Dropped field, delete it. Then paste the function call into that input field. Your dialog box should now look like the one shown in Figure 14.27.

FIGURE 14.27

The Drag Layer dialog box showing the pasted function call from the Show-Hide Layers behavior.

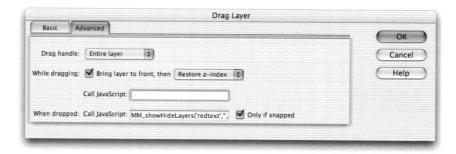

Try the result in your browser. If it doesn't work, check the pasted function call and make sure you pasted exactly the code shown in Figure 14.29 (that is, everything after the `onClick` event handler and between the double quotes).

When in Code view, to quickly determine what JavaScript functions are present in a document, go to the toolbar and click the {} icon to get a pop-up list of functions.

8. Finally, delete the layer containing the text link because you don't need it anymore. Select the layer in Design view, and then go to Code view. Make sure you have everything (including the `<div>` tags) selected, and delete. Then scroll up to the top of the page to make sure the `MM_showHideLayers()` function is still present. After you've done this, check the page in a browser again to make sure the behavior still works.

9. You still need to add the same behavior to the other two shopping bags. Although you could go through the entire process again (yuck) for each bag, with a tiny bit of hand-coding, you can accomplish your task quickly and easily.

Aren't you glad you gave your layers easy-to-remember names such as redprice, greenprice, and blueprice? This is a good example of the importance of good naming conventions as you work.

The function call for Show-Hide Layers should still be on the Clipboard from your preceding copy-paste action. In the Behaviors panel, open another of the Drag Layer instances. In the dialog box, note which shopping bag this instance is controlling (green or blue). Then bring the Advanced tab forward, click in the When Dropped text field, and paste again. Examine the pasted code. Find the reference to redprice, and change the color name to match the color of this bag. Repeat this process for the third Drag Layer behavior instance. All three of your shopping bags should now be scripted.

10. One more revision: What if, after putting an item in the shopping cart, the user decides not to buy that item? When a bag is dragged out of the cart, you want the relevant price layer to hide. You can accomplish this task as well, within the limits of the Drag Layer behavior, by using the While Dragging: Call JavaScript setting in the behavior's dialog box. With just a little more hand-coding, you can even reuse the function calls you've already added.

In the Behaviors panel, open one of the Drag Layer instances and bring the Advanced tab forward. In the second input field (the one you just filled in), drag to select the entire function call entry and copy. Paste that code into the first input field. In the first field, find the reference to show and change it to hide. Everything else remains the same. Your first code entry will read as follows:

```
MM_showHideLayers('greenprice','','hide')
```

The second entry will look like this:

```
MM_showHideLayers('greenprice','','show')
```

Repeat this process for the other two Drag Layer instances, and try the finished page in the browser. As soon as you start dragging a shopping bag, the price disappears; if you drop it in the cart, the price reappears. (If you get stuck, **buying_finished.html** contains the completed exercise.)

CONTROLLING OTHER LAYER PROPERTIES

You've changed visibility, you've changed the contents, and you've dragged layers around. However, those are only a few of the layer properties you can control. Depending on which browser(s) you're scripting for, you can change background color, position, width and height, style, and clipping—you name it. The Dreamweaver general, all-purpose behavior for controlling everything not covered by other behaviors is Change Property.

Using the Change Property Behavior

This behavior isn't just for changing layer properties. It's more of a catchall behavior for changing any property of any scriptable page element. Depending on the browser you're targeting and the DOM it supports (see the discussion on DOMs at the beginning of this chapter), you can change properties for form elements, various kinds of layers, and even images. Figure 14.28 shows the Change Property dialog box with its various parts identified.(See Chapter 9, "Working with Forms," for a discussion of using this behavior with form elements.)

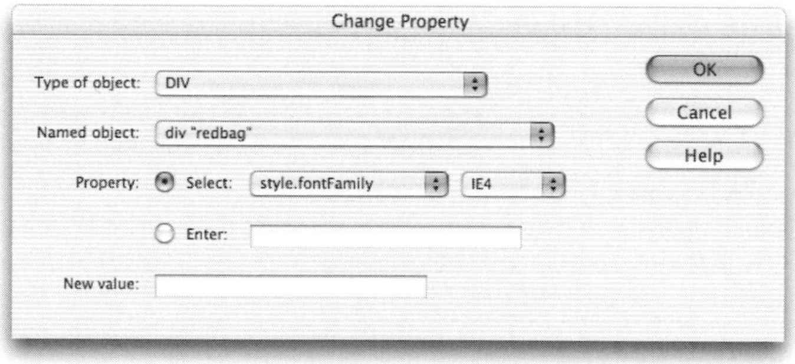

FIGURE 14.28

The Change Property dialog box.

To use Change Property to alter layer properties, follow these steps:

1. Set up your document with whatever layer (or form or image) elements you want to use and change.

2. Select whichever object will trigger the behavior, and choose Change Property from the Behaviors panel Actions list.

3. From the first pop-up menu, choose the tag of the object you want to change (<div>, <layer>, and so on). Unless you have changed the default, a layer in Dreamweaver will be created with the <div> tag.

4. The second pop-up menu will now be populated with all named instances of the chosen tag that appear in your document. From this menu, choose the specific instance you want to control. (Unlike Show-Hide Layers, you can control only one object with each occurrence of this behavior.)

5. Choose a target browser from the pop-up list on the third line of the dialog box. What you choose here will determine what choices will appear in the Property pop-up list to its left.

6. Choose a property to change. If the Property list is empty, the object you have chosen is not scriptable in the DOM of the browser you have targeted. If you want to change a property that isn't on the list but that you know is scriptable, enter it by hand in the text field below.

7. Enter a new value for the property. It's up to you to choose a value acceptable for that property. The Change Property dialog box shown in Figure 14.29 is set to change the font-family of all text within the <div> layer named caption. If the value field for this dialog box didn't contain a valid font name, the property change would have no effect.

Change Property and Browser Compatibility

Because it's a generic behavior with a very basic purpose, Change Property does not necessarily create cross-browser scripts. After you choose a target browser in the dialog box, the script will be entered using the syntax required for that browser. If all you're doing with the behavior is scripting form fields, your script will probably work across browsers because only basic DOM access is required for this kind of page element. If you're scripting layers, your behavior will definitely be browser-specific.

Controlling Netscape Layers

As discussed in Chapter 13, "Interactivity with Behaviors," Netscape 4.*x* functions best if its proprietary <layer> tag is used to create layers, even though layers created with other tags will work there. If you target Netscape 4 in the Change Property behavior and specify that you want to change <div> layers, no scriptable properties will show up in the dialog box. If you choose the <layer> tag to change, however, you'll still be allowed to choose named instances of <div> layers, and the property list will supply a list of Netscape-formatted properties to change. Figure 14.29 shows this strange occurrence in action. This configuration will work fine in Netscape 4 or Netscape 6.

FIGURE 14.29
The Change Property dialog box set up to change the z-index property of a div layer.

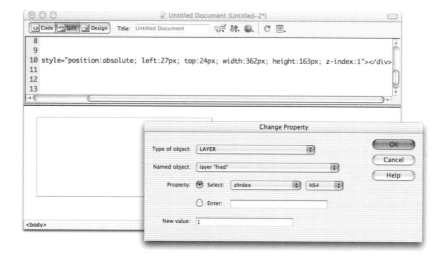

Doubling Up for Multiple Browsers

For some properties, it is possible to target IE and Netscape Navigator just by attaching two instances of Change Property to the same event handler. Figure 14.30 shows two separate configurations of the behavior, each set to change the vertical position of the specified layer on the page. Both behaviors are being applied to one text link, to be activated by onClick. This strategy won't work with all properties. If you attempt to change the layer's background color in this way, for instance, IE interprets the Netscape syntax as a command to change the page's background color.

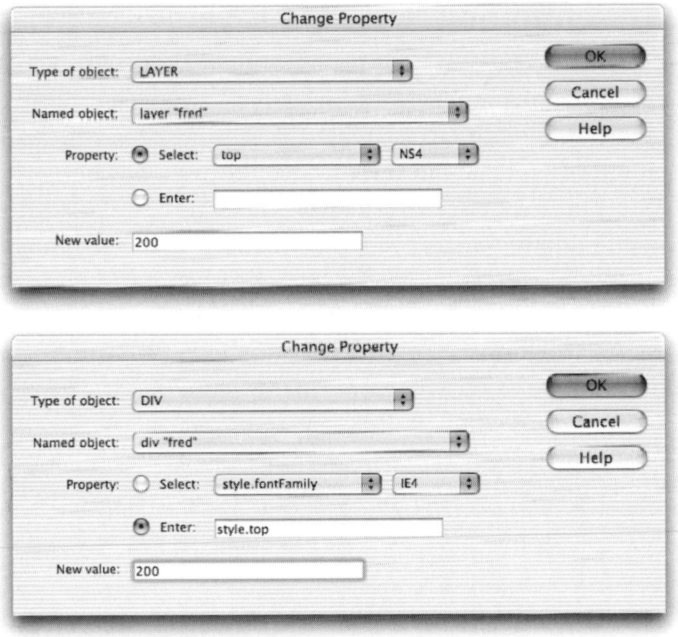

FIGURE 14.30

Two instances of the Change Property behavior, each set up to change the l (top) property of a layer called fred

SUMMARY

Dynamic HTML—the capability to use JavaScript to control page elements such as layers—is an exciting technology with much promise, although browser incompatibility issues turn it into a minefield for designers. In this chapter, you have seen the primary Dreamweaver tools for helping you navigate this minefield safely. You also have seen how you can sometimes push the envelope to make the Show-Hide Layers, Set Text of Layer, Drag Layer, and Change Property behaviors work for you.

CHAPTER 15

PLUG-INS, ACTIVEX, AND JAVA

CHAPTER 14, "CONTROLLING LAYERS WITH JAVASCRIPT," SHOWED HOW DHTML can be used to add complex interactivity and visual effects to web pages—subject only to the limitations of the browser itself. In this and the next chapter, you'll see how you can add different kinds of media and interactivity by extending the browser's capabilities. This chapter discusses how specific plug-ins, ActiveX controls, and Java can enable you to go beyond the browser, and how Dreamweaver MX 2004 helps you work with all of those so-called "rich media" technologies. Because of the extensive integration of Dreamweaver with Flash, Chapter 16, "Building Web Pages with Flash," covers that topic.

EXTENDING THE BROWSER WITH PLUG-INS AND ACTIVEX

The most common way to extend browser functionality and create media-rich pages is through plug-in content. Creating web pages that rely on this kind of browser extension can be a frustrating experience—even in Dreamweaver!—unless you understand the limitations of the technology underneath it and how to use that technology intelligently.

How Plug-In Media Works in the Browser

Browsers are essentially HTML decoders. Their job is to translate the markup instructions in an HTML file into a visible, functional screenful of information. By adding JavaScript to your HTML, you can add a certain amount of interactivity to web pages. By themselves, however, browsers cannot handle the rich variety of media you might want your pages to contain. They cannot display video, they cannot manipulate and present sound, and they cannot present PDF content. Because of browser differences, it's also difficult to reliably create complex interactive content that will work across browsers and across platforms solely through JavaScript and HTML.

Luckily, browsers are extensible: They call on external entities to do what they alone cannot do. In fact, they do this frequently as you surf the Web, whether you're aware of it or not.

MIME Types, Plug-Ins, and Helper Applications

Every time a browser encounters a file, it must determine what kind of file it is and what should be done with it. Browsers do this by examining the file's *MIME type*. The MIME (Multipurpose Internet Mail Extension) type is part of the information the web server usually sends along with the file when a web page is downloaded to a user's computer. The MIME type includes a description of the file's category and helps the browser determine what should be done with it.

As a backup, in case the web server does not send the MIME information with the downloaded file, the browser also examines the suffix, or file-name extension, of all downloaded files.

If the MIME type or filename extension indicates that the file is something the browser can't deal with, it calls on outside help. This help is either a helper application or a plug-in.

A *helper application* is a program that can deal with the file type in question. A helper application can be any program on your computer. Any time the browser comes across a file with an extension of .doc or a MIME type of application/doc, for instance, it will probably attempt to find and launch Microsoft Word or an equivalent word processor that has been defined as the helper application for that kind of file. Any of these programs also can be launched independently of the browser.

A *plug-in*, like a helper application, has functionality that the browser doesn't, but it is not a standalone application. Plug-ins cannot launch and run on their own. Instead, they add functionality to the browser. Plug-ins must reside in the Plugins folder, inside the browser's own application folder. The Flash, QuickTime, and Shockwave plug-ins, as well as the Flash and Shockwave ActiveX controls, are examples of this kind of help. When the browser comes across a file with an extension of .swf or a MIME type of application/x-shockwave-flash, it will probably look for and attempt to launch the Flash Player plug-in.

Netscape Plug-Ins vs. ActiveX Objects

Years ago, to enable web authors to put media content on HTML pages, Netscape developed the capability to add plug-ins to itself; to support plug-in–based media content, Netscape created its own nonstandard HTML tag, <embed>. Although the <embed> tag was never made part of the W3 Consortium's official HTML specification, it was a big hit with users. Internet Explorer adopted the <embed> tag and the plug-in system, and for several years it was the standard method used to insert media into web pages. The code looks like this:

```
<embed src="myMovie.mov" width="32" height="32"
➥pluginspage="http://www.apple.com/quicktime"></embed>
```

Meanwhile, Microsoft was developing its own set of technologies to allow applications of all kinds to share information and work together. Object Linking and Embedding (OLE) and the Component Object Model (COM) eventually developed into ActiveX technology. For web use, Microsoft built into its browser the capability to understand miniprograms called *ActiveX controls*, which could control and share information with ActiveX objects placed on a web page using the <object> tag. ActiveX controls can be written to work with various applications, including Internet Explorer. Microsoft's scripting language, VBScript, can be used to communicate between the ActiveX control and the browser, much as JavaScript (which was developed by Netscape) communicates between plug-ins and the browser. The code looks like this:

```
<object classid="clsid:D27CDB6E-AE6D-11cf-96B8-444553540000"
➥codebase="http://download.macromedia.com/pub/shockwave/cabs/
➥flash/swflash.cab#version=6,0,0,0" width="100%" height="100%"
➥id="framework" align="">
<param name=movie value="framework.swf"> <param name=quality
➥value=high> <param name=bgcolor value=#000000> </object>
```

It's confusing but important to remember that, although IE/Windows no longer supports Netscape-style plug-ins, it does support the embed tag. When the browser sees an embed tag, it first looks for an ActiveX control to handle the content. If there is no ActiveX control, older versions of the browser will look for a plug-in; the newest versions will not.

As a result, there are two ways to insert media content into browsers: as plug-in objects using embed, or as ActiveX objects using object. Two sets of browser technology are available for interpreting that content: Netscape-style plug-ins and ActiveX controls. Only IE supports ActiveX, and because ActiveX is so tied in with Microsoft's other technologies, it works only on the Windows platform. Until recently, both Netscape and IE supported Netscape-style plug-ins, but starting with versions 5.52-SP2, IE/Win no longer supports plug-ins—it supports only ActiveX controls (although it does still support the embed tag for ActiveX content). Although older versions of IE/Win and all versions of IE/Mac theoretically support plug-ins, they don't offer very good support. In Netscape, you can communicate with plug-in content using JavaScript; Internet Explorer does not allow JavaScript access to plug-in objects or ActiveX objects; VBScript can be used to communicate with ActiveX objects, but not with plug-in objects. And because Internet Explorer/Macintosh does not support ActiveX, this severely limits what you can do to control cross-browser, cross-platform media content.

As a web author, you tread daily through this minefield. Dreamweaver helps by offering support for both technologies and by taking care of as many details as it can to make your pages accessible to all.

According to the World Wide Web Consortium's official HTML specification, the object tag is to be used for placing all media elements that the browser can't normally display (including Java applets) on web pages. In practice, however, browser support for this tag is not widespread beyond Internet Explorer's ActiveX technology.

How Plug-In Media Works in Dreamweaver

In Dreamweaver, to insert media content using the embed tag, use the Plugin object. To insert media content using the object tag, use the ActiveX object. Both are located in the Common category of the Insert bar, in with the Media objects. Both are generic objects that can be used with a variety of plug-in and MIME types. Figures 15.1 and 15.2 show both objects and their Property Inspectors. Note that the Property Inspector for ActiveX objects includes an Embed option. When this option is selected, Dreamweaver will insert an object tag and an embed tag for best cross-browser compatibility.

FIGURE 15.1
The Plugin object and Property Inspector.

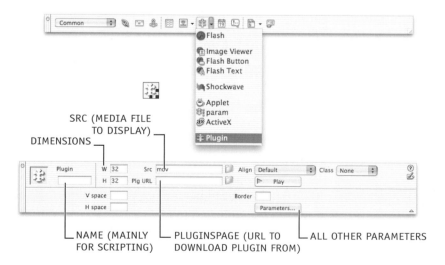

FIGURE 15.2
The ActiveX object
and Property
Inspector.

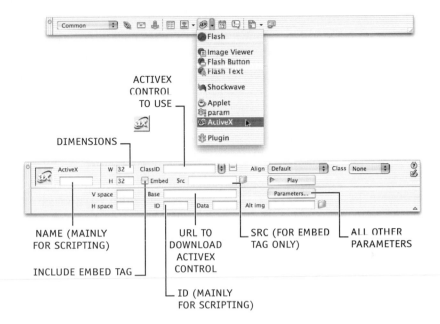

In addition to many standard properties such as width, height, and so forth, the Plugin Property Inspector includes one item that you might not have seen before: Plg URL, which inserts a plug-in's URL.

The ActiveX Property Inspector looks a little more strange and includes several items that might not be familiar to you:

- **classid (Class ID)**—This is the name of the ActiveX control to be used to handle the content. The Shockwave, Flash, and RealMedia controls appear on the pop-up list; names of any other controls must be typed in. After a control name has been manually entered, it appears in the pop-up list until removed (by clicking the minus [–] button next to the pop-up list).

- **codebase (Base)**—Similar to the `pluginspage` attribute for the Plugin object, this optional attribute contains the URL of a site where the required ActiveX control can be downloaded. If a value is entered in this parameter and the user's browser does not have the appropriate control to handle the source file, the control is automatically downloaded, if possible.

- **data**—This attribute should contain the URL of the source file for the content. It's not required by many ActiveX controls (including Flash, Shockwave, and RealPlayer). Some controls, such as Real-Player, require a src parameter instead. (See more on coding for RealPlayer later in this chapter.)

In addition to the previous options, which are added as parameters to the <object> tag, the following will create tags nested within the main <object> tag, both to be used as alternate content:

- **Alt image**—Specifying an image file here adds an <img> tag within the <object> tag. If the required ActiveX control is not available in a particular browser, the image specified here will display in the browser instead.

- **Embed**—If enabled, this adds an <embed> tag inside the <object> tag, to support Netscape on all platforms and Internet Explorer on non-Windows platforms. The src parameter listed in the Property Inspector is used with this tag (not with the <object> tag).

Accessing Plug-In–Specific Parameters

Both the Plugin and ActiveX Property Inspectors must work for any type of embedded media content, for a variety of plug-ins and ActiveX controls. Consequently, they offer only generic properties. Most plug-ins and controls also accept—and sometimes require—their own specific properties that don't appear in the inspector. Dreamweaver has a mechanism for handling this: the Parameters button, located in both the Plugin and ActiveX Property Inspectors. Pressing this button accesses a special Parameters dialog box (see Figure 15.3) into which any attribute's name and value can be entered. It's up to you to know, for each plug-in or ActiveX control, what parameter names and values to use here.

FIGURE 15.3
The Parameters dialog box for adding attributes not available in the Plugin or ActiveX object Property Inspectors.

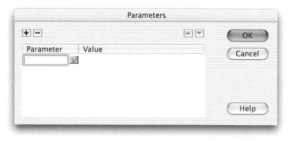

Playing Embedded Content

Dreamweaver doesn't automatically display embedded media content in the Document window; instead, it shows a generic placeholder Click the Play button in the Property Inspector to see and hear the media. As long as you have the relevant plug-in installed in any browser on your system, Dreamweaver will be able to preview the media. (For details on this, see the sidebar "How Dreamweaver Plays Media Content.")

How Dreamweaver Plays Media Content

Dreamweaver uses Netscape plug-ins to play embedded media. Every time you click the Play button to preview a media element, Dreamweaver looks for the required plug-in, first in its own Configuration/Plugins folder and then in the Plugins folders of all installed browsers. If it finds the plug-in, the media will play. If not, the media won't play.

Dreamweaver/Windows users take note, however! Dreamweaver uses plug-ins—not ActiveX controls—to preview media content. If the only browser installed on your system is Internet Explorer, or if your other browser(s) have no plug-ins installed, you will not be able to preview embedded media from within Dreamweaver unless you install Netscape or Opera (or any other browser that uses plug-ins) and configure that browser with the required plug-ins. You can also obtain a copy of the required plug-in—from another computer or from the company that created the plug-in—and copy its class file (such as ShockwavePlugin.class) to your Dreamweaver/Configuration/Plugins folder.

This isn't an issue for Dreamweaver/Mac users because all Macintosh browsers use Netscape plug-ins.

If the particular content you are working with has no related plug-in—only an ActiveX Control—you won't be able to preview it in Dreamweaver no matter what you do. Windows users must preview in the browser; Mac users can't preview at all.

Playing ActiveX Content

Click the Play button in the Plugin or ActiveX Property Inspectors (refer to Figures 15.1 and 15.2) to see and hear the media. As long as you have

the relevant plug-in (not ActiveX control) installed in any browser on your system, Dreamweaver will be able to preview the media. (For more on this, see the previous sidebar "How Dreamweaver Plays Media Content.")

Almost any media element can be accessed without using either `<embed>` or `<object>`, by linking directly to it. To create a link to a media file, just set up a text or image link on a page; then, in the Property Inspector's Link field, browse to the media file. This is a fairly crude way to get media on your website, however, because it gives no control over parameters or scripting.

Working with Specific Plug-Ins

To use plug-in media content effectively on your web pages, you need to familiarize yourself with the various plug-ins and ActiveX controls, and how each works—in the browser and in Dreamweaver.

Shockwave

To learn more about Shockwave, visit www.macromedia.com/shockzone.

Shockwave is a plug-in and related file format that allows content developed with Macromedia Director to be viewed in the browser. Director has long been industry-standard software for developing interactive CD-ROMs. Shockwave is cross-browser and cross-platform, available as a Netscape plug-in and an ActiveX control. According to Macromedia, 167 million users worldwide have the Shockwave plug-in installed. Shockwave movies have the .dcr filename extension.

QuickTime

QuickTime is a cross-platform, system-level extension and browser plug-in that provides synchronized media and interactivity similar to that found in Shockwave and Flash. QuickTime has long been available as a plug-in; recently, in response to Microsoft's decision not to support plug-ins for IE/Windows, Apple has released QuickTime as an ActiveX control as well. According to a recent Apple announcement, 100 million copies of the QuickTime player and browser plug-in have been distributed and installed worldwide. QuickTime movie files use the .mov filename extension.

To learn more about QuickTime, visit www.apple.com/quicktime. For more on the new QuickTime ActiveX control, visit www.apple.com/quicktime/download/qtcheck and www.apple.com/quicktime/products/tutorials/activex.html.

Inserting a QuickTime Object

In Dreamweaver, you can insert QuickTime content using the Plugin or ActiveX objects. For best compatibility with the newest versions of Internet Explorer, it's best to use ActiveX, although be sure to check the Embed option in the Property Inspector so Dreamweaver also generates an embed tag for other browsers. Whichever method you use, the Property Inspector is generic, with no QuickTime-specific options. As with Shockwave, width and height are always set to a default value of 32 × 32 pixels. If the dimensions are set smaller than the original movie size, the movie is cropped; if the dimensions are set larger than the original size, empty space is added around the edges of the movie.

Passing Parameters to QuickTime

QuickTime movies accept a wide variety of parameters. As with other media types, use the Parameters dialog box, accessible by clicking the Property Inspector's Parameters button, to assign these attributes. Table 15.1 shows a list of some parameters commonly used with QuickTime movies.

TABLE 15.1 **Some Useful Parameters That Can Be Used with QuickTime Content**

Parameter	Value	Description
autostart	true or false	Specifies whether the movie starts playing as soon as it loads.
loop	true or false	Specifies whether the movie repeats indefinitely or plays only once.
controller	true, false, qtvr	Specifies whether a controller bar appears at the bottom of the movie, and what kind of controller bar it is. Use the qtvr controller for QuickTime virtual reality movies. (If the controller is visible, set the height parameter to the movie's height plus 16 pixels. Otherwise, the controller will be cropped.)

Parameter	Value	Description
scale	Aspect, ToFit, or a number	Specifies whether the movie appears at its original size, or enlarged or reduced. ToFit scales the movie to match the width and height parameters; Aspect does the same, but without distorting its aspect ratio. A scale value of larger than 1 enlarges the movie; smaller than 1 reduces the size.
volume	0 to 100	Determines the volume of any audio in the movie.
kioskmode	true or false	If true, doesn't allow the user to save a copy of the movie.
starttime	Time, using format 00:00:00:00	Determines at what point in the movie it should start playing.
endtime	(Same as starttime)	Determines at what point in the movie it should stop playing.
href	Absolute or relative URL	If this parameter is present, clicking the URL anywhere on the movie launches the specified URL.
qtnext*n*	Absolute or relative URL	Specifies a movie to play after the current URL movie is finished. The name of the parameter must end in an integer (represented by *n* in the column to the left), like this: qtnext1, qtnext2, and so forth. Multiple qtnext parameters can be used to play a series of movies.
target	myself or the name of a window or frame	If you're loading a new QT movie with the href or qtnextn, use myself to load it into the same place as the original.

EXERCISE 15.1

Adding a QuickTime Movie to a Document, and Setting its Parameters

In this exercise, you'll insert a QuickTime movie into a page using <object>, and experiment to see how you can customize it with parameters. All files for this exercise can be found in the **chapter_15/quicktime** folder on the book's website at www.peachpit.com.

1. Open **quicktime_parameters.html**.

2. Insert a generic ActiveX object. In the Property Inspector, set the basic `<object>` parameters as follows:

   classid (Class ID) = clsid:02BF25D5-8C17-4B23-BC80-D34888ABDDC6B

   width = 340

   height = 256

   codebase (Base) = http://www.apple.com/qtactivex/qtplugin.cab

   (The true height of the movie is 240 pixels, but you're adding 16 pixels for the controller bar that will appear at the bottom of the movie onscreen.)

3. Still in the Property Inspector, select the `<embed>` option, and set its src to bird.mov. (This is the first time you've specified which movie you intend to play.)

4. Click the Parameters button to access the Parameters dialog box. Experiment with the different parameters listed in Table 15.1 to see how they work. In particular, try setting the following:

   - controller = false—Preview the movie, and you'll see that, without the controller bar, there's no way to start or stop the movie. (You'll also have an extra 16 pixels in the movie's height setting.)

   - loop = true

   - autoplay = false—You'll certainly need the controller back on for this one. Otherwise, there's no way to start the movie playing!

   - scale = ToFit—After you've set this parameter, change the movie's width and height so it's really short and squatty. You'll see that the movie resizes to fill the space, even if it means distorting the picture.

   - scale = Aspect and bgcolor = #FF0000—Leave the movie short and squatty, and preview again. The movie won't be distorted anymore, and you'll see the red background color filling in part of your page.

   - href = http://www.newriders.com—When this parameter has been set, clicking the movie in the browser should connect you to the New Riders home page.

The first time you place a QuickTime movie in a document using the ActiveX object, you'll have to type in the classid yourself because it doesn't appear in the ClassID pop-up menu. You have to do it only once, though. After that, Dreamweaver remembers what you typed, and you can simply choose it from the pop-up menu.

- `href` = flowers.mov and `target` = myself—As long as the **flowers.mov** file from the book's website is in the same folder as **bird.mov**, clicking the movie should replace the first movie with the new movie. (Also see what happens if you remove the `target` attribute.)

- `pluginspage` = http://www.apple.com/quicktime/download—As discussed earlier, this is an important parameter for users relying on plug-ins and not ActiveX controls. Within the ActiveX Property Inspector, it must be set using the Parameters dialog box.

Figure 15.4 shows the Parameters dialog box with some of these values in place. For each attribute set, preview in a browser to see the effect on the movie presentation.

FIGURE 15.4
The generic Parameters dialog box showing various optional QT parameters, as used in quicktime_sampler.html.

5. After you've set several parameters, examine your code. You'll see that Dreamweaver has added each of the parameters to both the `<object>` and `<embed>` tags, using the syntax appropriate to each.

Dreamweaver has even added the `pluginspage` attribute to both tags, although it is meaningful only for the `<embed>` tag. If you like your code mean and lean, you can delete the `<object>` `pluginspage` parameter tag—but it isn't hurting anything by being there, and if you delete it, Dreamweaver won't recognize this parameter or show it in the Parameters dialog box.

Windows Media

Windows Media is a comprehensive platform for delivering audiovisual media, including streaming delivery and the capability to combine different media types in complex presentations. It is shipped as part of the Windows operating system, giving it a very wide user base. The player exists as an ActiveX control, with a powerful set of parameters and

scripting controls available to it—but only for those browsing with IE/ Windows. The player is available as a (much less powerful) plug-in for Netscape and Macintosh users. Filename extensions for Windows Media Player include .wma and .wmv.

For playback in the browser, Windows Media Player utilizes metafiles containing pointers to media files. The metafile, not the media file itself, gets embedded into the web page. Windows Media metafiles are written in an XML-derived markup language and have the .wvx (video) or .wax (audio) filename extensions. The file must contain an absolute or relative pathname to the media file. The syntax looks like this:

To learn more about Windows Media, visit www.microsoft.com /windows/ windowsmedia.

```
<ASX version="3.0">
  <entry>
   <ref
href="http://www.mydomain.com/mediafiles/myAudio.wma"/>
  </entry>
</ASX>
```

Inserting Windows Media Objects

Because the Windows Media Player is an ActiveX control, you insert Windows Media content with the Dreamweaver ActiveX object. The steps are as follows:

1. Create the media content.

2. Create the metafile using the preceding syntax.

3. With the Dreamweaver ActiveX object, embed the metafile in the document. Because the classid for Windows Media is not in the Dreamweaver pop-up list, in the Property Inspector, you have to enter the following ClassID manually:

   6BF52A52-394A-11d3-B153-00C04F79FAA6

You should have to do this only the first time you embed Windows Media content—after that, the information will be part of the pop-up list.

Passing Parameters to Windows Media Objects

Table 15.2 lists some of the commonly used parameters accepted by the Windows Media ActiveX control. With these parameters, you can determine how your media object will look and behave on the web page. Most must be added using the Dreamweaver generic Parameters dialog box.

TABLE 15.2 **Some Useful Parameters Accepted by Windows Media Player 7 (This List Is Not Exhaustive)**

Parameter Name	Value	Description
url	Absolute or relative URL	For proper streaming, specify the pathname of the metafile, not the media itself. (Dreamweaver note: If you check the Include Embed option in the Property Inspector and specify an src for that tag, this parameter is entered automatically for you. If not, you must enter it manually using the generic Parameters dialog box.)
width	Number of pixels	The horizontal space that the media and its controller will be allotted on the page.
height	Number of pixels	The vertical space that the media and its controller will be allotted on the page. (The controller itself is 40 pixels high; the information bar above that is 20 pixels high. Values are calculated from bottom to top, so assign a height of 40 to present only a controller bar.)
uimode	Full, mini, or none	How the controller bar appears. (To create invisible media, choose none and set the width and height to 0.)
autoStart	true or false	Whether the media begins playing automatically as soon as the page loads.
playCount	Number of loops	How many times the media will play.
currentPosition	Number of seconds	Where in the media's timeline it begins to play, measured in seconds from the beginning.
currentMarker	Marker number	Where in the media's timeline it begins to play, based on markers inserted into the media. (Use the Windows Media ASF Indexer utility to embed markers.)
volume	0 to 100	How loud audio content will play.
balance	-100 to 100	Whether audio content will play from the left speaker (-100), the right speaker (100), or some combination of both. A value of 0 plays from both speakers equally.
mute	true or false	Whether audio content will play or be muted.

EXERCISE 15.2

Inserting Windows Media Objects

In this exercise, you'll insert two Windows Media files into an HTML page—one containing audio and video, and one containing only audio. All exercise files are in the **chapter_15/windowsmedia** folder.

1. As you did with RealMedia, you start by locating the media and creating metafiles that point to it. The audio file is called **jazz.wma**. The video file is **aspirations.wmv**.

2. You can create the metafiles in a text editor or in Dreamweaver Code view. For the audio file, create a text file and save it as **jazz.wax**. Enter the following code:

```
<ASX version="3.0">
  <entry>
    <ref href="jazz.wma"/>
  </entry>
</ASX>
```

For the video file, create another text file and save it as **aspirations.wvx**. Enter the following code:

```
<ASX version="3.0">
  <entry>
    <ref href="aspirations.wmv"/>
  </entry>
</ASX>
```

If you want to use Dreamweaver's Code view to work with these metafiles, you should change the program preferences to recognize the new filename extensions. Choose Edit > Preferences, go to the File Types/Editors tab, and in the input field for files to open in Code view, add two new extensions: .wax and .wvx.

Note that for the preceding code to work properly, the metafiles and the media files must be stored in the same folder. If you have them stored differently, you'll have to adjust the relative URL accordingly.

3. Now you can insert the metafiles into your document. From your exercise files, open **windowsmedia_sampler.html**.

4. Using the ActiveX object, insert a new media element onto the page. In the Property Inspector, set the width and height to 320 × 240. Set the `classid` as follows:

6BF52A52-394A-11d3-B153-00C04F79FAA6

Make sure the Include Embed option is selected, and set the `src` to **jazz.wax**. When this is done, you can try out your file in the browser. The audio track should play and the Windows Media controller should appear (see Figure 15.5).

FIGURE 15.5
The windowsmedia_sampler.html exercise file with the audio file in place, as it appears in the browser.

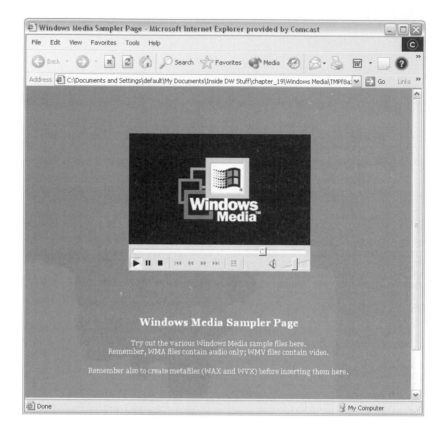

5. Now you add the video. Back in Dreamweaver, with the same exercise file open, add a paragraph break after the first media object and insert another ActiveX object. Set the width and height to 320 × 240. Turn on Include Embed and set the src to **aspirations.wvx**.

6. If you try your file in the browser now, you're in for an overwhelming experience because both files start to play at once. Using the Property Inspector's Parameters button and generic Parameters dialog box, assign each media element an autoStart parameter set to false.

7. Now you adjust how the controls look. This is done with the uimode parameter and the width and height.

    •   **For the video file**—The video doesn't quite fit in the 320 × 240 box you created for it. Set the height to 300 pixels—that adds 40 pixels for the controller and 20 pixels for the information

bar. Now when you play the file in a browser, the movie should fit nicely into its box.

- **For the audio file**—You want your sound to show on the page only as a simple controller, taking up a minimum of space. To start, add a uimode parameter set to mini. This simplifies the control, but doesn't remove the swirling picture above it. To get rid of this, change the height to 40—because the height is calculated from the bottom of the box, this value truncates the display at the top edge of the controller. Figure 15.6 shows this.

FIGURE 15.6

The windowsmedia_sampler.html file, as it appears in the browser when all parameters have been set.

8. Now make the sound loop. To set looping, decide how many times you want the sound to play and set the playCount parameter to that number. (You'll notice that there is no looping parameter.) You might have to change the autoStart=false parameter to autostart=true before the looping will work.

9. Experiment with the other parameters as you like, to see what each can do. As you're experimenting, don't forget to browse in Netscape as well as Internet Explorer (to see how your media fares). If you have access to different computers and platforms, try the files on those systems as well.

Inserting a Shockwave Object

In Dreamweaver, inserting Shockwave content is done with the Shockwave object (shown in Figure 15.7), located in the Media category of the Insert bar. The object inserts Shockwave content using the `<object>` tag, with an included `<embed>` tag.

FIGURE 15.7
The Shockwave object and its associated Property Inspector.

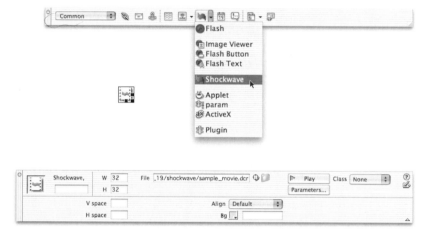

If you have a site defined, you can also use the Assets panel to organize, preview, and insert your Shockwave movies. Just click the Shockwave icon in the panel to view your movies.

The Property Inspector for Shockwave content is fairly sparse because several basic parameters—such as `pluginspage` and `codebase`—are set automatically by Dreamweaver. Note that `width` and `height` are not set automatically; Dreamweaver sets these to a default of 32 × 32 pixels, regardless of the movie's dimensions. You must find the correct movie dimensions in Director itself or by using trial and error in the browser. If the `width` and `height` parameters in the Property Inspector are set smaller than the original movie size, the movie is cropped; if the dimensions are set larger than the original size, empty space is added around the edges of the movie.

Passing Parameters to a Shockwave Object

It's possible to pass all sorts of information to a Shockwave movie in the form of parameters entered in the <object> and <embed> tags, as long as the movie knows what to do with the information it's receiving. These parameters include basics such as autostart and loop, as well as a whole series of parameters that Director authors can tie into the movie's Lingo scripting. Inside Director, these parameters are accessed through the externalParamValue( ), externalParamNumber( ), and externalParamName( ) functions. The parameter defined in Dreamweaver must have exactly the same name as the parameter called in the Lingo code.

To access and assign other parameters for the Shockwave movie, click the generic Parameters button to open the Parameters dialog box. From here, click the plus (+) button to get a list of potential parameters that can be set. (Figure 15.8 shows this happening.)

FIGURE 15.8
The Parameters dialog box for assigning Shockwave-specific parameters.

Adding Sound to Web Pages

If you decide to use targeted media for your sounds, you might consider targeting the Flash plug-in. This means creating an SWF file that contains only an audio element, or an audio element with Flash buttons and other controller elements. (Of course, you have to know enough about Flash authoring to build such an interface.) For more on using Flash and Dreamweaver, see the next chapter.

Adding sound to a web page can be one of the most challenging and confusing media-related tasks. It's not that hard to get browsers to make sounds—just about any computer with a sound card in it will have some sort of sound-capable plug-in for the browser. What's hard is deciding how best to get predictable, desirable results out of your sounds.

Targeted vs. Untargeted Media Placement

You can choose from a number of sound file formats when adding sound to a web page, each with its own strengths and weaknesses. A number of plug-in/ActiveX technologies are also available to handle sounds. Some formats, such as RM files for RealAudio, are proprietary—only one plug-in can handle them. Others, such as AIF and WAV, are supported by a variety of plug-ins. The first choice you'll have to make when determining how to add sound to a page is whether to target a specific plug-in and risk losing audience members by using a proprietary format, or to avoid targeting but give up predictability by using a more generic format.

Table 15.3 shows the main sound file formats currently in use on the Web, along with their supporting plug-ins. Each different plug-in presents the user with a different control panel for handling sounds; each accepts different parameters.

TABLE 15.3 **Specifications of the Major Sound File Formats Available for Web Use**

Filename Extension	Description
.wav	The native format for Windows audio files. Understood widely and offers fairly good compression-to-sound quality.
.aif	The native format for Macintosh audio files. Understood widely and offers fairly good compression-to-sound quality.
.mp3	The latest and greatest file format, not supported by many older plug-ins but quickly becoming a standard. Offers very good compression-to-sound quality.

continues

TABLE 15.3 **Specifications of the Major Sound File Formats Available for Web Use** *continued*

Filename Extension	Description
.au	The native format for UNIX audio files. Understood widely (and the only format available for use in Java), but offers poor compression-to-sound quality.
.mid, .midi	File format for synthesized (that is, computer-generated instead of digitally recorded) sounds. Understood widely, and offers extremely small file sizes. Files contain instructions for playing sounds, which are then implemented by software-based musical instruments within the computer itself.

Working with Untargeted Media

For maximum audience coverage, most web authors don't target specific plug-ins when adding sound to a page. What are the ramifications of this?

ActiveX or Plug-In?

When you place media with the ActiveX object, you must specify a classid (and thus a target ActiveX control). If you want your sound to be untargeted—to play in whatever plug-in or helper application is available on each user's browser—you need to use the Plugin object. (Remember, the Plugin object inserts content using the <embed> tag, and IE/Windows still recognizes this tag, as long as the user has an ActiveX control of some kind to play the sound.)

Dealing with Controllers

The *controller* is the visual representation of an embedded sound clip in a web page. It lets the visitor know that a music clip or other sound is present, and lets the user control its playing. When you design a page with embedded sound, therefore, you need to leave room for this element in the page layout. But how can you do this wisely, when you don't know which plug-in will be handling the sound, and so don't know what size the controller will be? Any page that includes an untargeted sound must be capable of accommodating any of them. Follow these two rules:

- **Think big**—As a general rule, it's better to allow too much space rather than not enough. Small controls, such as the QuickTime controller, can easily float in a large space, but large controls, such as the WinAmp control panel, don't fare too well when squeezed into a small space. Good default width and height settings are 144 × 60. These are the dimensions for the Netscape LiveAudio plug-in and are large enough to accommodate other controls fairly comfortably.

- **Use background color**—Most plug-ins will accept some sort of parameter specifying a background color. This is the color that will appear surrounding the controller (if it's placed in a too-large space). Use this parameter to ensure that any extra space matches the background color of the surrounding page or page elements so that it doesn't look so obviously like a small fish in a large pond.

Overloading the Parameters

Different plug-ins accept different parameters. Therefore, you need to be smart about assigning your parameters. You need to know which parameters are more widely supported than others. You also can double up on, or "overload," the parameters—setting multiple parameters to handle the same sound attribute, to make sure you're covering all of your bases. Table 15.4 lists various useful sound-related parameters, along with strategies for their use in multiple plug-in situations.

TABLE 15.4 ## Some Standard Parameters for Controlling Audio Files

Parameter Name	Value	Description
src	URL	Name of the sound file to play.
width	Number of pixels	The horizontal space the media controller will be allotted on the page. (Controllers will be resized, if possible, to fit the specified width.)
height	Number of pixels	The vertical space the media controller will be allotted on the page. (Controllers will be resized, if possible, to fit the specified width.)
bgcolor	Color	If the width and height values assigned are larger than the controller's dimensions, this color will fill up the rest of the allotted space.

continues

TABLE 15.4   **Some Standard Parameters for Controlling Audio Files** *continued*

Parameter Name	Value	Description
hidden	true or false	Whether the controller should be visible on the page. (Warning: Some browsers won't play a hidden sound.)
autostart, autoplay	true or false	Whether the audio will begin playing automatically as soon as the page loads. Some plug-ins require autostart; some require autoplay. Use both to be safe.
loop	true or false	Whether the audio will play once or loop indefinitely. (Some, but not all, plug-ins will accept a numeric value here.)
volume	0 to 100	How loud the audio will play. Not all plug-ins recognize this value.

EXERCISE 15.3   **Creating a Sound Sampler Page**

In this exercise, you add several sound files in various formats to a web page, to get some practice working with nontargeted sounds. To get maximum benefit from the exercise, after you have finished creating the sampler file, try viewing it from as many different computers and browsers as you can. All files for the exercise can be found in the **chapter_15/audio** folder.

1. To begin the exercise, open **sound_sampler.html**. This file contains a page layout ready to hold different sounds and their controllers.

2. With the file open, use the Dreamweaver generic Plugin object to insert a sound clip into each of the slots in the layout. (Figure 15.9 shows the page layout with audio objects in place—the controllers shown are QuickTime, RealMedia, and Windows Media Player.) Use the sound files in the folder provided with the exercise files. Try one each of the various different file formats, to see how browsers handle

the file types. Use the small slots in the layout to note which file types are being placed so that you can better analyze the results later.

FIGURE 15.9
The
sound_sampler.html
page layout, with
audio objects and
descriptive text
in place.

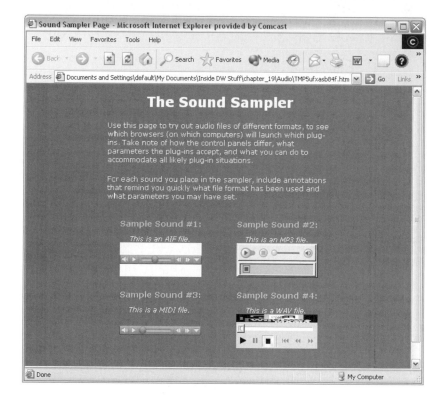

3. For each sound clip placed, set whatever parameters you like. (Use Table 15.4 as a guide.) In Figure 15.9, note that one of the two samples showing the QuickTime controller has been assigned a bgcolor matching the page background; doesn't that look nicer than that ugly white box in the other sample?

4. After you have constructed your sampler file, try it out in the browser. Better yet, try it out in multiple browsers. If you have access to different computers and different operating systems, try it out there as well. Pay attention to all the different results you get. Try to tweak the parameters to get the best results you can, in all the different plug-in/browser/platform situations. When you're done, you can save the file as a reference for future sound use.

Scripting Plug-In Media

Sometimes it's not enough to put media on your pages. Sometimes you want your media to be controllable. You want it to interact with other page elements; you want to replace the standard controller bars and other visual elements with your own tasteful buttons and bows. In other words, you want to script it. Can you script media elements? Yes—and no. Most plug-ins accept a variety of commands. Dreamweaver even has a few built-in behaviors to help you implement those commands. However, they might not always work the way you want them to.

How Media Scripting Works—and Why It Doesn't Always Work

To understand how scripting of media elements works—and doesn't work—in browsers, you need to revisit the browser wars. As you learned in Chapter 13, "Interactivity with Behaviors," JavaScript is the main language used for client-side scripting in the browser. But JavaScript, like the <embed> tag, was originally created by Netscape for use with that browser. In Netscape, it's possible to use JavaScript to pass commands to any plug-in media element that has been inserted using the <embed> tag.

Microsoft not only has its own browser and its own plug-in technology (ActiveX), but it also has its own scripting languages, VBScript and JScript. Media placed on a page using the <object> tag and controlled by an ActiveX control can receive commands using these languages—but not JavaScript.

To further complicate matters, Internet Explorer does not allow any scripting control of standard plug-in content placed using <embed>. What does this mean?

- **Internet Explorer**—It's impossible to send any scripting commands to media that have no ActiveX control.

- **Internet Explorer/Mac**—It's impossible to send scripting commands to any plug-in media because ActiveX and its related technologies don't function outside the Windows operating system.

- **Netscape**—It's impossible to take advantage of the powerful scripting possibilities offered by many ActiveX controls.

The good news is, you're not going crazy when you notice that your media scripting works only in some of the browsers some of the time.

The bad news is, there's not much to be done about it. If your web pages are aimed at a target audience using one browser or one platform, your media-controlling horizons are broader than if you're trying to target the general populace in all its diversity.

Controlling Specific Plug-Ins

Each plug-in or ActiveX control offers its own set of scripting commands that it can accept (to control its media). Sometimes, as with JavaScripting for QuickTime or JScript controls for Windows Media, these commands are extensive and powerful. For more information on this, check the websites listed earlier for each technology.

Controlling Audio: The Play Sound Behavior

The Dreamweaver Play Sound behavior is an excellent example of the perils and pitfalls of scripted media control. It seems simple—create a button or text link, apply the behavior, choose a sound file to play, and whenever the user clicks the button, the sound should play. The only problem is, because of the problems outlined earlier, it works in some browsers, and in others, it doesn't.

If you really want reliable, controllable media, the simplest answer is to avoid browser scripting entirely. Flash, Shockwave, and QuickTime movies all offer internal scripting.

Plug-In Detection

So you've decided to use content that requires one or more plug-ins or ActiveX controls on your website. What do you want to do about potential site visitors who won't have the proper browser setup?

Scripted Detection with the Check Plug-In Behavior

The standard method for invisible plug-in detection is to use a JavaScript that executes when the page loads. That's what the Dreamweaver Check Plugin behavior does.

This behavior can be used in two ways:

- The behavior can be put in the page that contains the media content. If the plug-in is found, the browser stays on the page; if not, the browser is sent to an alternative page.

• The behavior can be put on an empty dummy page. In this case, if the plug-in is found, the browser is sent to the page containing the media; if not, the browser is sent to the alternative page.

The second scenario is more efficient for downloading because it doesn't make visitors without the plug-in wait for a complex page full of media to start loading before they're sent to another page. The first scenario is easier to set up and maintain because there's one fewer HTML file to keep track of.

To use the Check Plugin behavior, follow these steps:

1. Start by creating all the files you'll need. You'll need at least the file containing the media and a page of alternative content. You also might want to create a blank dummy page that will eventually contain only the behavior and nothing else.

2. Open the file you want to insert the behavior into. This might be the media page or the dummy page.

3. In the tag selector, click the <body> tag. The behavior needs to be called from this tag.

4. In the Behaviors Inspector, choose Check Plugin from the Actions list. The dialog box that comes up will look like the one shown in Figure 15.10.

FIGURE 15.10
The Check Plug-in behavior dialog box, with sample entries in place.

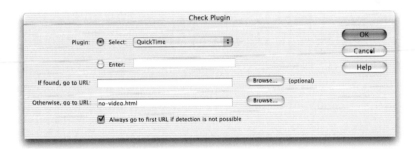

5. From the drop-down menu in the dialog box, choose the appropriate plug-in for which you want to test. The most commonly used plug-ins are available; if a plug-in isn't listed, you must type its name yourself.

6. In the other fields of the dialog box, enter the names of the files you created earlier. If you're adding the behavior to the page containing

the media, leave out the optional If Found destination file. If you're adding the behavior to a dummy page, enter the media page as the If Found destination. Enter the name of the alternative content page as the If Not Found destination.

7. Important: Make sure the option Go to First Page If Detection Is Impossible is selected. Internet Explorer/Mac does not allow JavaScript plug-in detection. If this option is *not* selected, users with that browser will always be sent to the alternative content, even if they have the plug-in (obviously, a very distressing experience).

Limitations of Scripted Detection

If it involves scripting, something can go wrong with it. As noted earlier, some browsers don't allow scripted detection. Also, if you're using the Check Plugin behavior for your scripting, it's important to keep in mind that this script checks only for the presence of a plug-in, not the version. What if your QuickTime content requires QuickTime 5 but the user has only QuickTime 3? The Check Plugin behavior will direct your users to the QuickTime version of your web page, but those users won't be able to access the content. They are high and dry.

You can avoid the problems of scripted detection by using nonscripted visible redirection. In other words, just tell users up front that plug-in media will be used, and give them the chance to choose alternate content or download the plug-in. When users aren't sure whether they have the plug-in, it's a good idea to put some sample plug-in content on the page for them to see, such as, "If you can see the above animation/video/hear the music, you have the plug-in."

EXTENDING THE BROWSER WITH JAVA

If you're tired of playing the plug-in game, there's another totally different way to extend the browser's capabilities: Java.

How Java Works in the Browser

Java is a platform-independent, object-oriented programming language created by Sun Microsystems. (Despite the similarity in names, Java is

not related to JavaScript.) Java can create fully functional, freestanding applications. It also can create miniapplications, called *applets,* that run inside a web browser. Because Java is a complete programming language, similar to C or C++, Java applets can be as powerful and diverse as you like. Java applets are commonly used for everything from online games to animation and special effects to visitor counters, clocks, calculators, and navigation tools.

The Nature of Java

To understand what makes Java so well-suited to web use, you need to know how it differs from other programming languages.

Computers don't directly "understand" C++ or Java or any other so-called high-level programming language. Instead, computers understand a numeric language called *machine code.* After a program is written in a high-level language, it must be compiled, or translated, into machine language. Machine language is platform-specific; this is why your copy of Dreamweaver will run only on a PC or only on a Mac. Programs must be compiled for a certain type of computer, and then they will run only on that type of computer.

To learn more about Java, visit Sun's website at http://java.sun.com. To learn more about implementations of the Java virtual machine, visit Microsoft at www.microsoft.com/java and Apple at www.apple.com/java.

Java is different. Java is compiled to run on a pretend computer called a *virtual machine.* The virtual machine is actually itself a program that is compiled to run on a specific platform. On Windows computers, the virtual machine is Microsoft VM; on Macs, it's Mac OS Run-Time for Java (MRJ). When a Java application or applet is run on a virtual machine, the virtual machine translates the code into platform-specific machine code. Thus, the Java applet itself is platform-independent.

Java Issues

The good news is, Java applets are not only platform-independent, but they're browser-independent as well. As soon as a browser encounters an applet on a web page, it launches the virtual machine and steps out of the way. You don't have any plug-ins to worry about. The only things needed to run a Java applet are a virtual machine (which most computers already have installed) and a Java-enabled browser (which almost all browsers are).

The bad news is, nothing is perfect. Some virtual machines are slower and buggier than others; it takes time to launch the virtual machine,

which can seem like excessive download time to a frustrated user; and, because the virtual machine is running through the browser, complex applets that require lots of processing power can (and do!) crash browsers.

Java also can create security problems. Some so-called hostile applets are actually designed to behave like viruses; others can cause damage to a system accidentally. It's the job of the virtual machine to protect the computer system from these dangers, but virtual machines themselves can never be completely hackproof. Consequently, many institutions that deal in sensitive information will set their firewalls not to accept any Java, and individuals might choose to disable Java in their browser preferences.

Java and Media

Java applets can contain images and sounds, which will then display in the browser without the need for additional plug-ins or system components. All images must be GIFs or JPEGs. All sounds must be AU files. Java cannot handle video; however, it can create animations or "fake video" from a series of still images. Java animations are not as smooth and do not run as quickly as those created in Flash, Shockwave, or QuickTime.

Working with Applets

Working with applets is not like working with Shockwave or Quick-Time movies, or any other kind of web media, because applets are not structured like those elements. Your first encounter with an applet will probably involve the words "What are all these bits and pieces, and where's the applet?"

Class Files

A basic compiled Java applet is a file with the filename extension .class—not .java, which is used for uncompiled source code.

However, an applet often consists of more than just one file. A complex applet might have several class files, of which only one is the applet itself. The others are supporting players that the applet will call on as it works. With some applets, naming conventions make it clear which is the main file—if the program is called Tabulator and there's a class file called tabulator.class, for instance. With other applets, however, it can

be a challenge knowing which class file to actually embed in the web page. (The best applets usually have documentation that spells this out for you.)

Media Files

If an applet uses any media files—images, sounds, movies, and so on—these also will be in separate files, sometimes in separate folders. You must keep the internal folder structure of the applet the way the applet author intended, or the applet won't be capable of finding its media files.

Obtaining Java Applets

Most Java applets are written by Java programmers. There isn't one standard authoring environment for creating them. This is why every applet is so different from every other applet.

If you want to use Java on your website, you can program it yourself, hire someone else to program it, or use one of the many prewritten applets available on the web and elsewhere. Sun's own applet resource page (http://java.sun.com/applets), which has links to other major resource sites as well as a selection of applets to download, is a good place to start looking. Some applets are free, some are shareware, and some are commercial. Some are also better documented than others and allow more customization. Some work better than others do.

Working with Applets in Dreamweaver

Dreamweaver provides several features for working with Java applets, including the Applet object and the Applet Property Inspector. You can use these tools to insert an applet into an existing page or to examine and alter the sample HTML code that usually comes with commercially available Java applets.

Inserting an Applet

In Dreamweaver, use the Applet object, found with the Media objects in the Common category of the Insert bar, to place Java applets on a page. The actual process is simple. Click the Applet object. In the dialog box that follows, browse to the appropriate class file and click OK. There!

You have an applet. If you look at your code, you'll see that the applet has been inserted using the `applet` tag.

Figure 15.11 shows the Applet object as well as the Property Inspector for a Java applet. Because every applet is different, this is another generic inspector, with a Parameters button for adding applet-specific parameters. Aside from the standard parameters, the only two settings available are Code and Base. Code adds a `class` parameter and should be set to the name of the class file. Base adds the `base` parameter and should be set to the URL of the folder, if any, that contains the Java applet files. (It's customary to store an applet in its own folder so that all the files that comprise it can easily be kept together.) As with plug-in media, additional parameters used by specific applets are added with the generic Parameters button.

FIGURE 15.11
The Applet object and the Property Inspector for a Java applet.

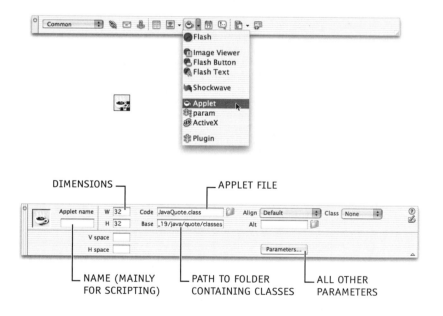

EXERCISE 15.4

Inserting a Java Applet

In this exercise, you insert an applet that puts a continually changing series of quotes on the web page. (This applet is one of several freebies offered at the Sun Java site, http://java.sun.com/openstudio/guide.html. To see it in action on a web page, look on the book's website in **chapter_15/java** for **quote_finished.html**. Figure 15.12 shows a static screenshot from this file.)

FIGURE 15.12
Sun's Java Quotes
applet as it appears
in a web page.

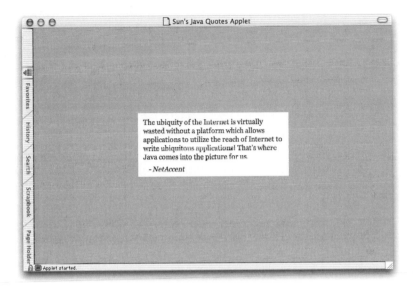

According to the documentation, the applet takes several parameters; Table 15.5 lists them. Some of these parameters might be optional, and others might be required; the documentation doesn't specify. You'll use them all.

TABLE 15.5

Parameters for the Sun Quotes Java Applet, Along with Descriptions and Suggested Values

Name	Value
bgcolor	The background color of the applet in RGB hexadecimal.
bheight	The border height, in pixels.
bwidth	The border width, in pixels.
delay	The delay between frames, in milliseconds.
fontname	The name of the font to be used for the applet.
fontsize	The size of the font, in points.
link	A URL to load if the applet is clicked.
random	true or false, determining whether the quotes should appear randomly or in a set order.
number	The number of quotes.

Name	Value
quote*N*	This parameter must appear once for each quote to be included (*N* is an integer), based on the number of quotes specified. The first quote is quote0, the second quote is quote1, and so on. For each occurrence of the parameter, the value must be a vertical bar (|)–delimited string in which the first item is the quote, the second item is the author, the third item is the RGB hexadecimal text color, the fourth item is the RGB hexadecimal background color, and the last item is the length of time in seconds to display the quote.
space	The distance in pixels between the quote and the author name.

1. To start, find and examine the **Quote** folder, which contains this applet. You'll see several class files. Can you tell by their names which one is the applet?

2. In **chapter_15/java**, open **java_quotes.html**.

   Using the Insert Applet object, insert the applet. The main class file that you should insert (you might have figured this out already) is **JavaQuote.class**. The codebase option should say quote/classes/.

Java is case-sensitive! Make sure all references to files, folders, parameters, and values are in their correct case, or your Java applets won't work.

3. Next, set the width and height for the applet to occupy in your layout. For this applet, there is no required size—the dimensions just determine how much space the quotes will be allotted on the page. If you want your page to match the examples shown here, set your width and height to 300 × 125.

4. Referring to the parameters list in Table 15.5, and using the generic Parameters dialog box, set the parameters for the applet. Experiment until you get results you like.

   (You might find it difficult to see what you're doing when you try to enter the quote parameter because most quotes are fairly long and the dialog box won't show them in their entirety. If you like, you can type each quote first in a text editor, such as Notepad or Simple Text, and then paste it into the parameter's value field. You also can work directly in Dreamweaver Code view, of course, if you feel comfortable there.)

   When you're done, your Parameters dialog box will look something like the one shown in Figure 15.13.

FIGURE 15.13
The Parameters dialog
box, showing entered
parameters and val-
ues for the Sun Quote
Java applet. (Only
the first few parame-
ters are visible.)

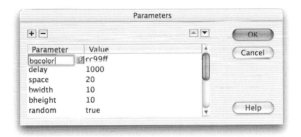

5. Try it in a browser. If everything got entered correctly, your virtual
    machine should load and show you an ever-changing set of quotes.

You might come across a Java applet that has been packaged into one or
more archive files. These files will have filename extensions of .jar, .zip, and
.cab. With an applet like this, it's easiest to just follow the programmer's
instructions that came with the applet and not use Dreamweaver to generate
the code.

SUMMARY

In this chapter, you got a taste of the major technologies available for
adding media content to the web, along with the mechanisms in
Dreamweaver and in the browser that make them work. The next chapter
looks at a particular media technology: Flash.

CHAPTER 16

BUILDING WEB PAGES WITH FLASH

IN TODAY'S WORLD OF PLUG-IN MEDIA, FLASH RULES. YOU CAN INTEGRATE Flash into HTML pages in so many ways, and Dreamweaver offers so many tools for helping you do it, that this chapter focuses solely on working with this one kind of plug-in media content. The discussion covers the specifics of working with the Flash plug-in, as well as special Dreamweaver features for coordinating Flash and HTML content.

HOW FLASH WORKS IN THE BROWSER

Flash content is plug-in–based media, following all the rules and restrictions of QuickTime, Shockwave, and the other media covered in the preceding chapter. The file format for online Flash movies is SWF (pronounced "swiff"). Most Flash media is created in the Macromedia Flash authoring program—although, since Macromedia opened up the format to other developers, more content is being developed in other programs as well. Viewing SWF movies requires the Flash Player, which is available as a plug-in and an ActiveX control. Macromedia estimates that 98% of the web-browsing public has some version of the Flash Player installed. Internet Explorer 6 for Windows comes with the ActiveX control preinstalled.

Like the plug-in media covered in the previous chapter, a Flash movie is embedded in an HTML page, using the object tag and the embed tag, to accommodate all browsers. The code looks like this:

```
<object classid="clsid:D27CDB6E-AE6D-11cf-96B8-444553540000"
➥codebase="http://download.macromedia.com/pub/shockwave/cabs/
➥flash/swflash.cab#version=5,0,0,0" width="365" height="250"
➥title="myflashmovie" >
  <param name="movie" value="myflashmovie.swf">
  <param name="quality" value="high">
  <embed src="myflashmovie.swf" quality="high"
➥pluginspage="http://www.macromedia.com/shockwave/download/
➥index.cgi?P1_Prod_Version=ShockwaveFlash" type=
➥"application/x-shockwave-flash" width="365" height="250"">
  </embed>
</object>
```

The classid and pluginspage attributes shown here allow browsers to link directly to the pages on the Macromedia website where the ActiveX control or plug-in can be downloaded and installed.

How Flash Works in Dreamweaver

Dreamweaver makes the process of putting Flash movies into web pages easy—although the more you know about how Flash operates, the more you'll be able to take advantage of it.

To insert a SWF movie into an HTML document in Dreamweaver, use the Flash object, found under the Media menu on the Common Insert bar (see Figure 16.1), or use the Insert > Media > Flash command.

FIGURE 16.1
The Flash object as it appears in the Insert bar.

Don't confuse the regular Flash object with the Flash Text or Flash Button objects. Use the Flash object to insert Flash movies that already exist; use the others to create new, simple Flash movies for navigation or titling purposes.

If you're working within a defined Dreamweaver site, you can also add Flash movies to your documents from the Assets panel (see "Assets Management" in Chapter 18, "Site Publishing and Maintenance," for more on this). The Assets panel also gives you a chance to play each Flash movie to preview it before inserting it in a document (see Figure 16.2).

Like other media elements, the Flash movie appears in your document as a gray box. When it's selected, resize handles let you resize it dynamically in the Document window, and the Flash Property Inspector appears (see Figure 16.3). Pressing the Play button in the Property Inspector plays the movie. The inspector contains all the basic properties that all media have

in HTML, such as width and height, as well as a number of parameters specific to the Flash plug-in. For any parameters not covered here, the Parameters button opens a window for entering name/value pairs.

FIGURE 16.2
Viewing a Flash movie in the Assets panel.

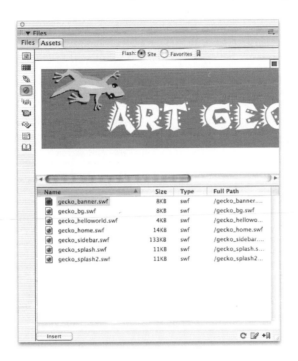

FIGURE 16.3
The Flash Property Inspector.

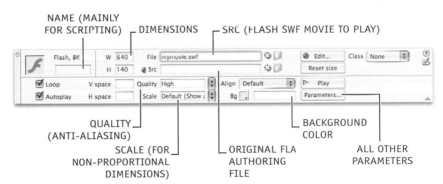

Working Smart with Flash Parameters

Flash is a unique medium, offering its own special challenges and opportunities for web authors. As noted earlier, Flash movies accept a variety of parameters, some common to all media types and some unique to Flash. Most can be added using the Property Inspector; some are set automatically by Dreamweaver and don't appear anywhere in the inspector. Some must be added using the generic Parameters dialog box. Table 16.1 lists parameters for the Flash plug-in and ActiveX player, noting which parameters must be added manually.

TABLE 16.1 **Specifications of the Parameters Accepted by the Flash Player Plug-In and ActiveX Control**

Parameter Name	Value	Description
name	Any one-word name.	Required by the <embed> tag if the movie is to referred to by scripting.
ID	Any one-word name.	Required by the <object> tag if the movie is to be referred to by name.
width	Integer or percent value.	Specifies the horizontal space the movie will be allotted on the page. If the width assigned is different from the movie's width, the movie will be resized (see the entry for the scale parameter).
height	Integer or percent value.	Specifies the vertical space that the movie will be allotted on the page. If the height assigned is different from the movie's height, the movie will be resized (see the entry for the scale parameter).
align	baseline, top, middle, absbottom, left, or right.	Determines how the browser will align the movie when text or other page elements are placed next to it (in the same table cell or paragraph, for instance).

continues

TABLE 16.1 **Specifications of the Parameters Accepted by the Flash Player Plug-In and ActiveX Control** *continued*

Parameter Name	Value	Description
bgcolor	Choose from the palette or enter a six-digit hexa-decimal number.	If the width and height values assigned are larger than the movie's dimensions, the color that will fill up the rest of the allotted space.
vspace	Integer (pixels).	Adds empty whitespace above and below the movie. Specify a number of pixels.
hspace	Integer (pixels).	Adds empty whitespace to the right and left of the movie. Specify a number of pixels.
autoplay	true or false.	Specifies whether the movie will start playing as soon as it loads.
loop	true or false.	Specifies whether the movie will repeat indefinitely or play only once. This has effect only if the movie's own internal scripting doesn't have its own looping or stopping controls.
quality	low, medium, high, best, autolow, or autohigh.	Determines whether Flash Player will antialias the movie as it plays. (Quality doesn't change the file size, but it can affect playback speed for processor-intensive animations.) See Table 16.2 for details.
scale	show all, noborder, or exactfit.	Determines how the movie's contents will be resized, if the width and height parameters are used to resize the movie object nonproportionally. Defaults to show all. See Table 16.3 for details.
* salign	left, right, top, or bottom (center and middle attributes are the defaults if salign is not present).	If the movie object has been scaled nonproportionally, determines how the movie's contents align within the object shape. See Table 16.4 for details.

Parameter Name	Value	Description
* menu	true or false.	Determines whether right-clicking on the Flash movie in the browser will cause a contextual menu to appear. Defaults to true.
* devicefont (Windows only)	true or false.	Determines whether an antialiased system font replaces text when specified fonts are not available. (Note: Normal, static text is automatically embedded in Flash movies; this setting refers to dynamic text and input fields only.) Defaults to false.
* wmode (IE/Windows only)	opaque, window, or transparent.	Determines whether the background of the Flash movie is opaque or transparent, sitting in front or in back of other layered page elements. See Table 16.5 for details.
** pluginspage	http://www.macro- media.com /shock- wave/download/ index.cgi?P1_Prod_ Version= ShockwaveFlash	Used by the embed tag. Allows users without the plug-in to link directly to Macromedia's plug-in download site.
** codebase (part of object tag, not a standard param tag)	http://download. macromedia.com/ pub/shockwave/ cabs/flash/ swflash.cab#version= 5,0,0,0	Used by the object tag. Allows IE/Windows users without the ActiveX control to automatically retrieve the control from Macromedia.

* Indicates parameters that must be set using the generic Parameters dialog box
** Indicates parameters that Dreamweaver handles automatically

Because Flash is not quite like any other plug-in media, the meaning and potential uses of some of these items are not immediately obvious.

Dimensions

Scalability is one of the most liberating aspects of designing with Flash. Unlike its handling of other plug-in media, Dreamweaver is capable of determining the original dimensions of a Flash movie, and it can reset its size if the current width and height don't represent its true dimensions. Also, unlike other plug-in media, altering a Flash movie's width and height attributes actually scales the movie, not simply adjusts its cropping. Flash movies can even safely be set to percent-based dimensions, much like tables, so that they resize as the browser window resizes. To set a Flash movie to percent-based dimensions, type a number followed by the percent symbol into the Width or Height fields (see Figure 16.4).

FIGURE 16.4
Setting a Flash movie's dimensions to percent-based numbers.

Although any graphics created within Flash are vector-based and therefore scalable, Flash movies also can contain imported pixel images. Any pixel image inside a Flash movie has the same limitations as a pixel image outside Flash: Its presence dramatically increases the movie's file size, and if the movie is scaled, it loses image quality.

Scale

Because Flash graphics are scalable, and because you can set them to percent-based sizes that change with browser window sizes, you need to determine what will happen when the movie's onscreen dimensions aren't the same proportions as the movie's true dimensions. Table 16.2 shows the details of this parameter, its possible values, and the effect of those values on the movie's appearance. If you examine the samples shown there, you'll see why Default (show all) is the default setting for this parameter—it's definitely the most useful.

TABLE 16.2

Values for the *scale* Attribute and Their Effects on Movie Appearance

Value	Description	Example
show all (default)	The movie contents are scaled proportionally, based on the smaller dimension (width or height), so that no contents are cropped away. Adding background color makes up extra space in the movie object along the larger dimension.	
noborders	The movie contents are scaled proportionally, based on the larger dimension (width or height), causing contents to be cropped along the smaller dimension.	
exactfit	The movie contents are scaled nonproportionally, to match the movie object's scaling.	

In trying to create truly full-screen Flash, some designers mistakenly think that the noborders scale setting eliminates any page borders around the movie. As you can see from the samples shown in Table 16.2, this isn't the case. To make a Flash movie hug the browser window edges when setting dimensions to 100% × 100%, use Modify > Page Properties and set the page margins to 0.

Scale Align (*salign*)

Don't confuse salign with the more standard align attribute. The purpose of salign is to work with the scale attribute to determine how a proportionally scaled movie will fill a nonproportional box. Table 16.3 shows the settings for this attribute and the effect of those values on movie appearance. Note that there are no values for centering horizontally or vertically; these are the default values and needn't be specified at all.

TABLE 16.3 **Values for the *salign* Attribute and their Effects on Movie Appearance**

Value	Description	Example
L	When used with default scaling (show all), aligns the movie at the left (L) edge of any extra horizontal space. When used with scale=noborders, shows the left side of the movie if horizontal cropping must occur.	
R	When used with default scaling (show all), aligns the movie at the right (R) edge of any extra space. When used with scale="noborders", shows the right side of the movie if horizontal cropping must occur.	
T	When used with default scaling (show all), aligns the movie at the top (T) edge of any extra vertical space. When used with scale="noborders", shows the top part of the movie if vertical cropping must occur.	

Value	Description	Example
B	When used with default scaling (show all), aligns the movie at the bottom (B) edge of any extra vertical space. When used with scale="noborders", shows the bottom part of the movie if vertical cropping must occur.	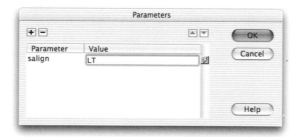
(multiple values)	To assign both horizontal and vertical salign parameters, enter both relevant letters as the parameter's value (LB, LT, RB, or RT). The resulting code will look like salign="LT", and so forth.	

The salign parameter does not appear anywhere in the Flash Property Inspector. To set this parameter, click the Parameters button in the inspector to access the generic Parameters dialog box (see Figure 16.5).

FIGURE 16.5
Setting the salign property with the Parameters dialog box.

Quality

Vector graphics such as those in Flash movies do not define pixels, but they must still be rendered by something that understands only pixels: the computer monitor. When the screen displays objects, it displays them with either aliased (jagged) or antialiased (smooth) edges. When the Flash Player plays a movie, each frame must be redrawn with either

aliased or antialiased edges. How the player handles this is determined by the quality parameter. Table 16.4 lists possible values the parameter can take.

Movies playing at low quality will have jagged edges but will play quickly. Movies set to high quality will have to be translated frame by frame into antialiased graphics, and so will have smooth edges but might not play at full speed on all computers. The other quality settings are all variations on this basic setup.

TABLE 16.4 ## Options for Setting the *quality* Attribute for Flash Movies

Option	Description
Low	No antialiasing (fastest playback).
* Medium	Some antialiasing on vector graphics; none on internal bitmaps.
High	Smooth antialiasing on vector graphics. Internal bitmaps are antialiased unless they're animated.
* Best	Anti-aliasing on vector and bitmap graphics, including animated bitmaps.
Autolow	Starts in low-quality mode and then switches to high quality if the user's computer is fast enough.
Autohigh	Starts in high-quality mode and then switches to low quality if the user's computer cannot keep up.

* Not available in the pop-up menu—must be typed into the input field

The quality setting does not affect the Flash movie itself and, therefore, has no effect on file size or download time. Its only purpose is to instruct the Flash Player how to display the movie.

The "auto" settings (Autolow and Autohigh) are the most flexible for dealing with a wide variety of computer speeds. Each tells the Flash Player to start out at a particular quality level and adjust the level as needed, depending on whether a particular user's computer can antialias and keep up with the frame rate. Of these two, Autolow always plays the first second or two of a Flash animation with jagged, aliased graphics, even on the fastest computer. Autohigh starts out with antialiasing turned on, so users with faster computers never have to see jagged graphics. If your Flash animation is at all complex, or if it includes a soundtrack, this is the best choice.

Window Mode (*wmode*)

Window mode is an attribute of the Flash ActiveX control only, so it takes effect only in IE/Windows. Within that environment, however, the wmode parameter enables you to control whether the Flash movie's background is transparent and how Flash movies interact with other page elements when DHTML layers are used. Table 16.5 details the various options for this attribute and shows the effects of each.

TABLE 16.5   **Values for the *wmode* Attribute, for Use by the Flash Player ActiveX Control**

Value	Description
opaque (default)	The background is opaque, using the Flash movie's internally specified background color. Other layers can appear in front of the Flash movie.
window	The background is opaque. All other layers appear behind the Flash movie.
transparent	The background is transparent. Other layers can appear in front of the Flash movie or show through from behind it.

If you are accessing your Flash content through the plug-in rather than the ActiveX control, Flash movies will always have opaque backgrounds, and any layer with Flash content will always show in front of all other layers.

EXERCISE 16.1   **Inserting a Flash Banner**

The exercises in this chapter give you a chance to practice working with Flash content in Dreamweaver; they also provide a chance to examine the various ways Flash can be integrated into a site. In this first exercise, you start with a page that has an animated GIF banner and replace it with a SWF banner; you examine the pros and cons of each choice. You can find all the required files for this and the other exercises in this chapter on the book's website at www.peachpit.com in the **chapter_16** folder. Before proceeding with the exercise, copy that folder to your hard drive and create a new site with that as your local root folder.

1. To start, from the exercise files on the book's website, find and open **gecko_gifbanner.html**. This sample home page includes an animated title banner made from an animated GIF. Preview the page in your browser to see how the animation works. (Figure 16.6 shows the page.) The animation is set to play only once; if you blink, you miss it!

2. Go to File > Save As, and save a copy of the file as **gecko_swfbanner.html**. (You will be comparing the animated GIF with a SWF banner, so you don't want to change the original page.) Select the GIF banner and delete it.

3. Use the Flash object to insert **gecko_banner.swf** into the banner spot. Dreamweaver will size the banner automatically and set other defaults. Do you need to change any defaults to make the new banner behave just like the old one? (*Hint*: How many times does the lizard run across the page?) Remember, you can preview the animation without previewing the entire page in a browser, by clicking the Play button in the Flash Property Inspector.

FIGURE 16.6
The gecko_gifbanner.html page as viewed in a browser.

4. Open the original file (**gecko_gifbanner.html**) and compare it to the new version. You should notice right away how much smaller the file size is for the SWF animation—GIF animations are made of pixels and, therefore, aren't suited to large graphics. One difference that you won't see unless you upload both pages to a web server and view them live is that the timing of the SWF is better than that of the GIF. This is because the first time any animated GIF plays through, the frames display as quickly as they download, regardless of their built-in timing. Only on the second and subsequent loops does the frame delay become consistent. Flash movies stream much more efficiently.

5. In **gecko_swfbanner.html**, the layout table is currently pixel-based and, therefore, nonflexible. Using the Table Property Inspector or Dreamweaver Layout view, change the table to a flexible table that is always 100% of the browser window's width. Then set the SWF banner so that it too has a width of 100%. Leave the `scale` attribute at the default so that extra space is added to make up for the excess width that could be added. Now you're taking advantage of Flash scalability. After you've done that, you might decide that the lizard animation looks silly in the middle of a big, wide page; using the generic Parameters dialog box, set the `salign` so that the image hugs the right side of the page. Figure 16.7 shows how both of these settings will look in the various parts of the Property Inspector.

6. Preview your page in the browser to see how the banner looks and how the animation resizes as you resize the window.

FIGURE 16.7
The Flash Property Inspector and Parameters dialog box, showing the gecko banner being assigned a variable width and right-side alignment.

Optional: Have you actually done anything with the SWF banner that can't also be done with the animated GIF? Because you have scaled the movie only horizontally, you haven't resized the graphics—you've only given the browser permission to add extra space on either side, if needed. The same

effect could be generated using the animated GIF by setting the table to be 100% wide and changing the bgcolor of the banner's table cell to match the brown of the banner. Then you could set the cell alignment to right to mimic the salign.

Stacking Flash Content and HTML with Layers (IE/Windows Only)

In this exercise, you'll see how much fancier your page can become if you layer HTML content over a Flash movie—although this effect will work only for visitors with Internet Explorer 4+/Windows who are using the Flash Player ActiveX control.

1. This exercise creates an alternate version of the home page you saw in Exercise 16.1. Begin by opening **gecko_layers.html**. Examine the file, and you'll see that the text and navigation bar are present, each in its own layer. This file includes an animated banner that extends under the page elements and becomes, in essence, an animated background.

2. You want to insert the background SWF movie on the page but not in a layer and therefore behind all other layered content. (You could insert the SWF in its own layer, stacked behind the other two layers, but because the movie will just be sitting in the background, this isn't necessary.) With the insertion point outside all layers, and using the Flash object, insert **gecko_bg.swf**. Leaving all the parameters at their default settings, preview the page in any browser you choose. You should get a lovely preview of the animated background, but the content layers won't show correctly, even in IE/Windows. That's because you haven't set the wmode yet.

3. Select the background SWF and assign whatever parameters you think are appropriate. In particular, use the generic Parameters dialog box to set the wmode to opaque (see Figure 16.8).

4. Change the page's bgcolor to match the background of the SWF. You want the movie to blend seamlessly with its environment so that it looks more like a background element.

To match movie color and page color, do this:

- Select the SWF and click the Property Inspector's Play button to play it (so its colors show).

- With the movie still playing, go to Modify > Page Properties. Click the Background Color button. When the eyedropper appears, use it to sample the SWF movie's color. (Figure 16.9 shows this happening.) Voilá! Seamless integration. (For more on color sampling in Dreamweaver, see "Working with the Color Picker," in Chapter 2, "The Dreamweaver Workspace.")

FIGURE 16.8
Setting the parameters for gecko_bg.swf in gecko_layers.html.

FIGURE 16.9
Playing a Flash movie in Dreamweaver, and sampling its color for the page background color.

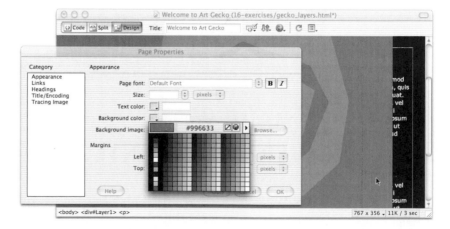

Do your colors match? If your monitor is set to display thousands of colors (16-bit color depth), you might notice that it's impossible to get the Flash movie color to match your page background. This is because the Flash Player renders colors slightly differently than the browser does. The difference won't show up on 8-bit monitors (displaying 256 colors) or in 24-bit monitors (millions of colors). However, any visitor who views your page on a 16-bit monitor will see the difference. It's not because you mismatched the colors, and there's nothing you can do about it.

5. Preview your layered page in various browsers. In IE/Windows, you should see a complete page, as shown in Figure 16.10. In other browsers and platforms, you'll just see the background movie, or the movie and partial page contents.

FIGURE 16.10

The completed gecko_layers.html page as it appears in IE/Windows, with text showing on top of animated background.

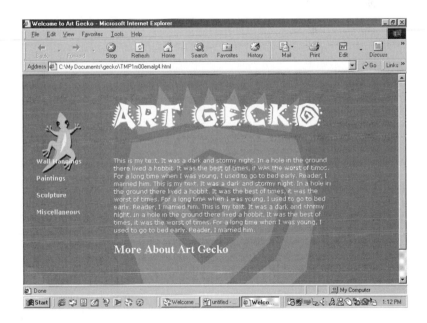

WORKING SMART WITH DREAMWEAVER/FLASH INTEGRATION

If you have current versions of both Flash and Dreamweaver on your computer, you can take advantage of some wonderful integration features to make your Flash editing easier.

Flash Launch-and-Edit

The procedure for creating a Flash movie and incorporating it into a Dreamweaver HTML page involves creating the main Flash file (FLA), exporting a SWF, and launching Dreamweaver to build an HTML document that houses the SWF. If you're working away in Dreamweaver and discover that the Flash movie needs editing, you have to launch Flash, open the FLA, make your edits, and export a new SWF before coming back to Dreamweaver and continuing work on your HTML pages.

In case you want to practice using Flash integration features on the exercise files from this chapter, the **chapter_16/FlashFiles** folder contains several of the original FLAs for the ArtGecko site.

With launch-and-edit, the procedure is somewhat simpler:

1. Create the FLA in Flash MX 2004, and export a SWF.

2. In Dreamweaver, insert the SWF into an HTML document.

3. In the Src field in the Flash Property Inspector (see Figure 16.11), browse or use Point-to-File to show Dreamweaver the FLA used to create this SWF. Dreamweaver creates a Design Note storing the information and displays a site-relative path to the source file in the Property Inspector. (This is the same mechanism used for Fireworks integration.)

FIGURE 16.11
An embedded SWF and its Property Inspector, with Flash integration features highlighted.

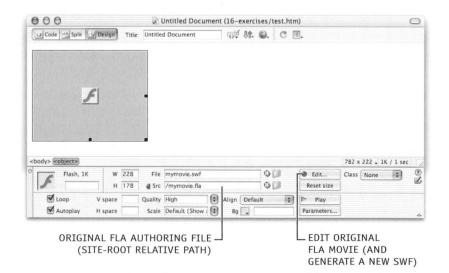

ORIGINAL FLA AUTHORING FILE (SITE-ROOT RELATIVE PATH)

EDIT ORIGINAL FLA MOVIE (AND GENERATE A NEW SWF)

4. The next time you need to edit the FLA, select the SWF in your Dreamweaver document and click the Property Inspector's Edit button (see Figure 16.11). Dreamweaver will launch Flash and open the source file you specified earlier.

5. In Flash, make your changes to the FLA. When you're done, instead of re-exporting, click the Done button (see Figure 16.12) to return to Dreamweaver. Flash exports a new SWF, and Dreamweaver now displays your document with the new movie in place.

FIGURE 16.12

The Flash authoring file (FLA) for an embedded SWF, showing in the special launch-and-edit version of the Flash application window.

In case you're curious about how all this interapplication communication works, you can open and examine the Design Note that makes it happen. Because Design Notes are invisible in the Site window, leave Dreamweaver and use Explorer (Windows) or the Finder (Macintosh) to examine your root folder. Design Notes are stored in that folder, within a **_notes** folder. Open that folder, and you'll find a text file with the name of your SWF file, followed by the .mno extension—**myFile.swf.mno**, for instance. Open that file in a text editor (or in Dreamweaver Code view), and you'll see the <infoitem> tag identifying the source FLA file, one for each original link in the SWF and one for each changed link. Dreamweaver accesses this Design Note to populate the Flash Property Inspector and to generate the Flash

items in the site map; Flash accesses it to determine whether any links need to be updated within the original FLA when you open that file for editing.

For Dreamweaver/Flash integration to work properly, Design Notes must be enabled for your site. In the Site Definition dialog box, go to the Design Notes category and make sure the Maintain Design Notes option is selected. For more on Design Notes, see the section "Using Design Notes for Improved Workflow" in Chapter 19, "Workplace Collaboration."

Cloaking Your FLAs

Here's the problem: Every Flash project involves an FLA (authoring) file and a SWF (export) file. And Flash likes to have both of these in the same folder. This means that when you're building a website involving Flash, all of your FLAs end up inside the local root folder, and Dreamweaver wants to upload the entire contents of the local root folder to the web server. But your FLA files don't need to be on the server, taking up space and upload time.

Here's the solution: Enable cloaking for your site, and tell Dreamweaver not to upload any FLA files. Do it by opening the Site Definition dialog box (choose Site > Manage Sites, select your site, and click Edit) and going to the Cloaking category. Select the Enable Cloaking option, and also select the option to cloak files ending with .png and .fla. After you've done this, all of your FLA files show up in the Site panel with a red slash through them, and Dreamweaver will ignore them whenever you select Newer Local or choose Site > Synchronize.

Updating Links in SWF Files

If your SWF file contains links (ActionScript getURL() actions), you can change these links without launching Flash at all, using the Dreamweaver site map and the Change Links command. Do it this way:

1. Configure your site map preferences to show dependent files. Choose Site > Edit Sites and, in the dialog box that appears, select your site and click Edit. In the Site Definition dialog box, choose the Site Map Layout category. If you haven't done so already, use the Home Page field to define a home page for your site. (You need to do this before you can use the Site Map feature.) Select the Show Dependent Files option (see Figure 16.13).

FIGURE 16.13
Setting site prefer-
ences so the site
map displays depend-
ent files.

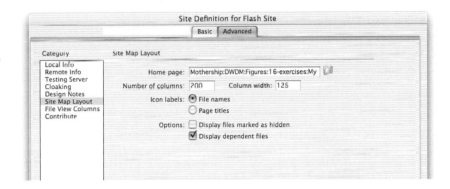

2. In the Site window, click the Site Map button to show the site map. Your embedded SWF file will show as a dependent file of its parent HTML document. All links within the SWF file will also be shown as dependents (see Figure 16.14).

FIGURE 16.14
Site map showing an
HTML document, the
SWF embedded within
it, and the link with-
in the SWF, along
with the Change
Links command.

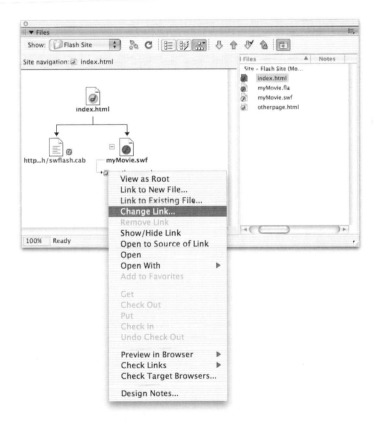

3. Right-click (Windows) or Ctrl-click (Macintosh) on the linked file you want to change to access the contextual menu (as shown in Figure 16.14), and choose Change Link. In the dialog box that appears, choose a new file that the SWF should link to.

When you do this, several things happen. Dreamweaver updates the getURL() action within the SWF. It also generates a Design Note noting that this has been done. The next time you launch the FLA in Flash, that Design Note will tell Flash that a link has been changed, and it will offer to change the link in the source file as well (see Figure 16.15). (If you don't let Flash update the link in the source file to match the link Dreamweaver altered in the SWF, the next time you export a SWF, the link will revert to whatever it was before you used Dreamweaver to change it because the SWF that Dreamweaver created will be overwritten.)

Dreamweaver has updated some URL links in the Flash Movie File (SWF). These changes will be propagated to the Flash Document (FLA).

☐ Don't warn me again.

Don't Change · OK

A more elegant solution to the link-update problem is to code your Flash movie so that its links are stored externally, either in a text file or XML file or as a URL parameter. That way, anyone with access to a text editor can update them, and the SWF doesn't have to be regenerated every time URL information changes. That's more of a Flash scripting topic than a Dreamweaver technique, however.

WORKING WITH FULL-SCREEN FLASH PAGES

In a full-screen Flash page, the Flash movie is the only content on the page, and for all viewing and interactivity purposes, it becomes the page. Full-screen Flash can be used for an entire splash screen or opening animation; for individual pages, such as the home page or main section pages; or even for an entire website.

Dreamweaver's Job: Create the HTML Framework

If the HTML document exists only as a framework to hold the Flash movie, there isn't much work to be done in Dreamweaver. Typically, your job in Dreamweaver is to do the following:

- **Set movie parameters**—The <object> and <embed> tags and their parameters govern how the browser and Flash Player will present the movie. quality, scale, loop, and autoplay must be set for the movie to play as desired. The movie can be left to its original dimensions (best if it contains photographic elements) or set to be truly full-screen by assigning width and height to 100% × 100%.

- **Set page margins**—The HTML code determines where on the page the movie sits, including how closely it's allowed to snuggle up against the top and left edges of the browser window. To make the movie completely cover the browser window space, set its dimensions to 100% × 100% and set the page margins to 0. (Do this in Modify > Page Properties, or by using CSS to redefine the body tag.)

- **Set page background color**—It's always a good idea to match the page and movie background colors so that no slivers of a different color appear at the edges of the browser window.

- **Perform plug-in and browser checks**—If the user's computer doesn't have the correct plug-in, the entire full-screen movie won't play. You can use JavaScript behaviors, which execute upon onLoad, to make sure the movie will play and to reroute visitors who can't see the movie. (See Chapter 13, "Interactivity with Behaviors," for a discussion of plug-in detection in Dreamweaver.)

Flash's Job: Create Interactivity and Links

After the page has been loaded, the Flash movie is the entire interface, so all interactivity—including links—must be built into the SWF. A Flash movie might just call another Flash movie to replace itself on the page, in

which case the document's URL doesn't change and the visitor probably won't even be aware that there has been a change. (The browser's Back button also won't work because the URL hasn't changed.) This is done internally with Flash's loadMovieNum() ActionScript command.

The Flash movie also might link to another HTML document that contains other Flash movies. In this case, the user will see the URL change, and the browser's Back and Forward buttons can be used to navigate between movies. This is done internally with Flash's getURL() ActionScript command.

EXERCISE 16.3

Creating a Flash Splash Page

In this exercise, you add an opening splash page to the Art Gecko home page created in the preceding exercise. The splash page will consist only of a full-screen Flash animation with a built-in link to the home page. All exercise are in the **chapter_16** folder on the book's website.

1. If this were a real project and you were responsible for it, you would start by creating the Flash movie and assigning a getURL() command within the movie to make it automatically load the home page. Because this isn't a real project, **gecko_splash.swf** has already been created for you, with the link in place. Figure 16.16 shows how the link has been added. (You can test-play **gecko_splash.swf** by opening it directly from your Desktop—double-clicking it should automatically launch the Flash Player.)

2. To house this movie, create a new Dreamweaver document. Save it in the **ArtGecko** folder. (It must be in the same folder as the home page because of how the relative URL has been written into the Flash movie). Call it **gecko_splash.html**.

3. Use the Flash object to insert **gecko_splash.swf**. To make the movie automatically resize with the browser window, set Width and Height to 100% × 100%. In the Property Inspector, make sure Autoplay is selected. Because you want the movie to play only once, you can deselect Looping; because of the movie's internal scripting, though, it won't loop, regardless of what setting you choose here in your HTML parameters.

FIGURE 16.16
The gecko_splash.swf
file being created in
Flash. The getURL()
action has been
assigned to the final
frame of the timeline,
so it executes auto-
matically as soon
as the animation
finishes playing.

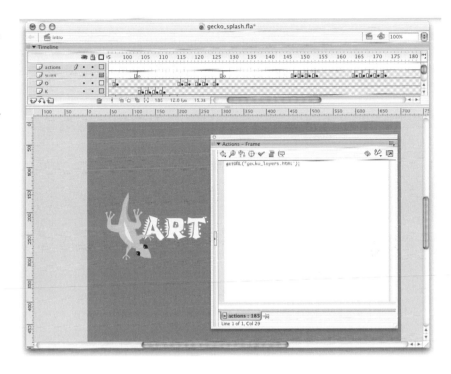

To understand how
Dreamweaver codes
page margins and
what possible
browser issues
are involved, see
Chapter 11, "Using
Cascading Style
Sheets.

4. To make the movie completely take over the page, you need to set the page's background color and margins. First, so that you can sample the color, use the Property Inspector's Play button to start the movie playing. Then go to Modify > Page Properties. Remove the page margins by setting Left Margin, Top Margin, Margin Width, and Margin Height all to 0. Using sampling, set the page background color to match the Flash movie (like you did in the preceding exercise) and click OK.

5. Save your file and try it. When the page loads, the Flash animation should take over the screen. It should play once through and then load your layered home page. (If the home page doesn't load properly, make sure the filename is still **gecko_layers.html**, and that it and the splash page are in the same folder.)

The relative pathname used in the Flash movie's internal link requires that the two HTML documents be in the same folder. The gecko_splash.swf file does not need to be stored in that same folder. Try it and see—you can move the SWF file to a subfolder (making sure to change the reference to it in gecko_splash.html). When you browse the document, it will still call gecko_layers.html.

EXERCISE 16.4

Creating a Full-Screen Flash Page

In this exercise, you create an alternate home page for the Art Gecko website, doing away with the multilayered setup from the preceding exercise by using a Flash-built version of the entire opening presentation. You'll also see how Flash's internal loadMovie() command can be used to navigate between SWF movies without creating new HTML documents or changing the URL in the browser window. All exercise files can be found in the **chapter_16** folder of the book's website.

1. For this exercise, you need two Flash movies: a revised splash movie and a movie containing the full-screen home page presentation. Again, in the real world, you would start this project by building both the **gecko_splash2.swf** and **gecko_home.swf** files in Flash. You would assign a loadMovie() action to the final frame of the splash movie, to automatically load the home page movie. You can launch both files from your desktop to see what each one contains. Figure 16.17 shows the loadMovieNum() command being added to **gecko_splash2.swf**.

FIGURE 16.17

The gecko_splash2.swf file being created in Flash, with loadMovieNum() action being added.

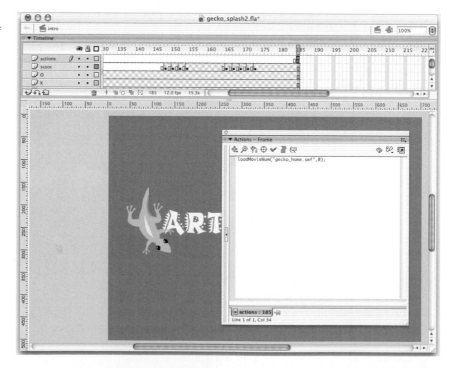

2. You now need an HTML document to hold the Flash movies. Instead of creating a new page from scratch, open **gecko_splash.html** and save it as **gecko_fullscreen.html**.

3. This page currently contains **gecko_splash.swf.** If you delete this movie and insert the new movie, you'll have to set its parameters all over again. So, instead, use the existing movie code, but just change the src parameter to point to the new movie. Select the Flash movie, and, in the Property Inspector, find the File input field and click the Browse button next to it. In the dialog box that appears, find and choose **gecko_splash2.swf.**

4. That's it! Try the movie in a browser to see it work. Can you tell at which point the new movie is being loaded? Note that the URL shown in the browser's location bar doesn't change when the new movie loads. (Unfortunately, this makes it impossible for users to bookmark the home page; they can bookmark only the splash page.)

FLASH AND JAVASCRIPT

Scripting Flash movies in the browser follows the same rules as scripting any plug-in media type (see Chapter 15, "Plug-Ins, ActiveX, and Java," for more on this). Whenever you want Flash movies to talk to the browser or the browser to give commands to the Flash Player, you use Flash ActionScript to send JavaScript instructions, or JavaScript to send ActionScript code.

Scripting In: Using JavaScript to Control Flash

A variety of JavaScript commands exist for communicating with the Flash Player, in its plug-in and its ActiveX forms. Table 16.6 lists some of the most commonly used of them. As you can see from examining the figure, it's possible to send the Flash movie to a certain frame in its timeline, to start and stop playback, and even to control embedded movie clips by setting their properties and controlling their timelines.

(The more you know about Flash authoring, the more useful this information will be to you.) Before relying on any of these commands, remember that although ActiveX media controls support extensive scripting for IE/Windows, no commands given to media objects will work within IE/Mac. Netscape 6 also has some difficulties passing commands to Flash movies.

TABLE 16.6

A Selection of JavaScript Methods Available for Controlling the Flash Player

Name	Syntax	Description
Play()	myMovie.Play()	Starts playing the specified movie.
StopPlay()	myMovie.StopPlay()	Stops playing the specified movie.
Rewind()	myMovie.Rewind()	Sends the movie to its first frame.
GotoFrame()	myMovie.GotoFrame ➡(frameNumber)	Sends the movie to a specified frame number.
Zoom()	myMovie.Zoom(percent)	Zooms the view by a factor() specified by *percent*. Numbers smaller than 100% increase the magnification.
SetZoomRect()	myMovie.SetZoomRect (left, top, right, of the movie. Values are integers bottom)	Zooms in on a rectangular area representing twips (1440 twips per inch, 17 twips per point).
SetVariable()	myMovie.SetVariable (varName, value)	Sets the value of a specified Flash variable. Both arguments are strings.
GetVariable()	var a = myMovie. ➡GetVariable ➡(varName)	Returns the value of a specified Flash variable as a string.
TCallFrame(), TCallLabel()	myMovie.TCallFrame ➡(target, frameNumber) myMovie.TCallLabel ➡(target, frameLabel)	In the target timeline, executes any frame actions in the specified frame. (Similar to the Flash call() method.)

continues

TABLE 16.6 ## A Selection of JavaScript Methods Available for Controlling the Flash Player *continued*

Name	Syntax	Description
TPlay()	myMovie.TPlay(target)	Plays the specified movie clip.
TStopPlay()	myMovie.TStopPlay ⮕(target)	Stops playing the specified movie clip.
TGotoFrame(), TGotoLabel()	myMovie.TGotoFrame ⮕(target, frameNumber) myMovie.TGotoLabel ⮕(target, frameLabel)	Sends the timeline of the specified movie clip to the specified frame.
TCurrentFrame(), TCurrentlabel()	var a = myMovie. ⮕TCurrentFrame ⮕(target), var b = myMovie. ⮕TCurrentLabel ⮕(target)	Returns the number or label of the current frame for a specified movie clip.

Not all methods work with the Flash plug-in. For a complete list of supported JavaScript methods, visit www.macromedia.com/support/flash/publishexport/scriptingwithflash/scriptingwithflash_03.html.

Scripting Within Dreamweaver: The Control Shockwave or Flash Behavior

For basic Flash control using JavaScript, the Control Shockwave or Flash behavior lets you use HTML page elements to start, stop, rewind, and send movies to specific frames without writing a lick of code. (Note that the only reason to use this behavior is if you want non-Flash page elements to control the movie. Flash movies are capable of containing their own internal buttons that will start, stop, and so on. If the movie contains its own interactivity, you don't need to add any JavaScript in Dreamweaver.)

To control a Flash movie using this behavior, follow these steps:

1. Insert a Flash movie in your document.

2. Give the movie a one-word name. You can do this in the Flash Property Inspector by filling in the name field in the upper-left corner.

3. Decide what sort of page element and event you want to trigger the action (when the user clicks a text link, when the page loads, and so forth).

4. Select the element that should trigger the action (page, text link, and so on), and use the Behaviors panel to apply the behavior. Figure 16.18 shows the behavior being chosen and the resulting dialog box with its various options.

FIGURE 16.18

Choosing and configuring the Control Shockwave and Flash behavior.

As its name implies, the Control Shockwave or Flash behavior also can be used to control a Director Shockwave movie. The same procedure outlined here would apply. (See Chapter 15 for more on working with Shockwave.)

Scripting Out: Using Flash to Send JavaScript Instructions

Just as you can (theoretically, anyway) send scripting messages from the browser to the Flash Player, you can send messages from the Flash movie to the browser. Because this is done in Flash, not in Dreamweaver, it's beyond the scope of this discussion. But it's handy knowledge to have anyway. Just as in the preceding exercise you used javascript: in a link field to send a JavaScript command in to Flash, Flash uses the same syntax in its getURL link command to send out commands.

Figure 16.19 shows the Flash file **gecko_helloworld.swf** with this link in place. To see how the link works, find that file in the **chapter_16** folder, place it in an HTML document, and preview it in a browser. Note that because this is JavaScript coming out of a Flash movie instead of going in, it should work much more reliably in the different browser/ platform combinations.

FIGURE 16.19
The gecko_ helloworld.swf file being created in Flash.

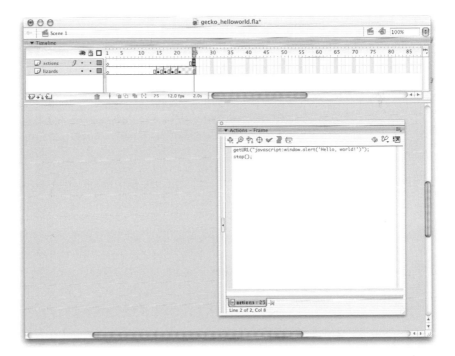

FLASH TEXT AND FLASH BUTTONS

You've seen how complex Flash content, including interactive movies, can be inserted into HTML pages within Dreamweaver. The Flash Button and Flash Text objects (available in the Media menu of the Common category of the Insert bar) enable you to create, customize, and insert simple Flash-based page elements (buttons and text) into a web page without ever leaving Dreamweaver, and without having to own or know how to use Flash (see Figure 16.20). This opens all sorts of new horizons for integrating different kinds of Flash content in your websites quickly and inexpensively.

FIGURE 16.20
The Flash Button and Flash Text objects, as they appear in the Common Insert bar.

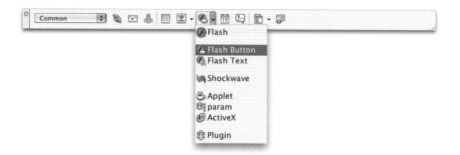

How Dreamweaver Creates SWF Files

The technology that makes Dreamweaver-created SWF files possible is Macromedia Flash Generator. *Generator* is a software system for creating Flash graphics dynamically from changing information in a database, similar to the way ASP and ColdFusion create text and page layouts dynamically. To work with Generator, the Flash author creates a special *SWT* (small web template) *file*, which is essentially a SWF file with placeholders for collecting and displaying dynamic data. When the page is uploaded to a web server, as visitors access it, the Generator application server, which sits on the server, creates SWF files to display on the page by filling in the SWT placeholders with data from a server-side database.

Using Generator technology, Dreamweaver creates Flash Text and Flash Button objects from SWT files stored in its **Configuration** folder. Whenever you choose one of the Flash objects from the Insert bar, Dreamweaver collects information from you (text to enter, typestyle, and so on), feeds that information into placeholders in one of its SWT files, and generates a SWF file. Figure 16.21 shows an overview of the whole process.

FIGURE 16.21
How Dreamweaver creates the SWF files for Flash Button and Text objects from SWT templates.

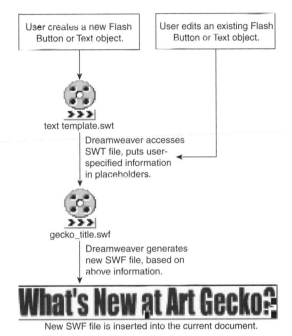

Creating and Inserting Flash Objects
===

You create Flash buttons and text at the same time as you insert them—by clicking the Flash Button or Flash Text object in the Insert bar. When you click the object, a dialog box displays, enabling you to customize the button or text that will be created. When you click OK to exit the dialog box, the SWF file is created and the object is inserted.

Figures 16.22 and 16.23 show the dialog boxes for the Flash Button and Flash Text objects. They give you similar choices for specifying type, color, and linkage. The Flash Button dialog box also enables you to choose a button style.

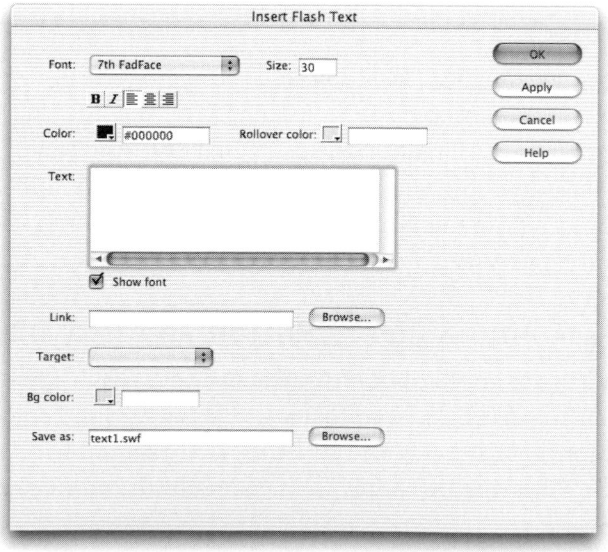

LIST OF BUTTON STYLES (THE GENERIC SAMPLE SHOWN WILL NOT REFLECT TEXT CHANGES MADE BELOW)
CLICK HERE TO YOUR BROWSER AND CONNECT TO THE MACROMEDIA EXCHANGE
Insert Flash Button
Sample:
Button Text
OK
Apply
Cancel
Get More Styles...
Help
Style:
Beveled Rect-Blue
Beveled Rect-Bronze
Beveled Rect-Green
Beveled Rect-Grey
Blip Arrow
Blue Warper
TEXT AND FONT INFORMATION (ALL FONTS WILL BE EMBEDDED IN THE SWF)
Button text:
Font:
Verdana
Size:
12
LINKS MUST BE ENTERED HERE, AND WILL BE EMBEDDED IN SWF FILE
Link:
Browse...
Target:
Bg color:
Save as:
button1.swf
Browse...
COLOR THAT WILL APPEAR BEHIND TEXT (UNLESS WMODE IS USED)
NAME AND LOCATION OF SWF TO CREATE

FIGURE 16.22
The Flash Button dialog box, which enables you to choose a button "style" or template to work from, and to customize its text and behavior.

Insert Flash Text
Font:
7th FadFace
Size:
30
OK
Apply
Cancel
Help
Color:
#000000
Rollover color:
Text:
Show font
Link:
Browse...
Target:
Bg color:
Save as:
text1.swf
Browse...

FIGURE 16.23
The Flash Text dialog box, which enables you to specify text and type style, colors, and links for the new text.

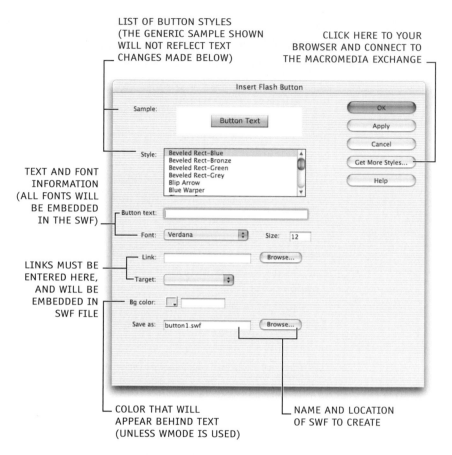

Button Style (Flash Button Object Only)

When you insert a Flash button, Dreamweaver creates a SWF file based on one of a dozen or more SWT templates. Each template contains the graphic elements for a different button. In this dialog box, each SWT template is shown as a separate button style. The graphic appearance of the button styles (color, shape, decorations, and so on) is not customizable because this information is built into the SWT. Any rollover effects also are built into the button style and can't be edited here.

To get more button styles from the Macromedia Exchange, click the Get More Styles button in the editing dialog box. This launches your browser and connects you to the Exchange (if your computer is connected to the Internet). When at the Exchange, navigate to the Flash Media category of extensions to see currently available buttons and other Flash-related extensions. Each set of button styles is saved as a Macromedia Extension Package (MXP) file, ready for use with the Extension Manager.

Text and Typestyle (Button and Text Objects)

If you're inserting Flash text, or if the Flash button style you're inserting includes a text label, you can determine what text will appear and how it will be formatted. Note that because fonts are automatically embedded in all Flash movies, you can set the typeface to any font installed in your system. This font then becomes part of the SWF movie.

Link and Target Information (Button and Text Objects)

If you want your Flash objects to contain any links, you need to assign the link information in this dialog box. The link then becomes part of a getURL() command in the generated SWF file. This is because, unlike images and text, media objects cannot just be wrapped in an <a> tag—so you can't use the Property Inspector to assign links. (For more on links and targets, see Chapter 6, "Links and Navigation.")

Background Color (Button and Text Objects)

Like pixel images, Flash content always exists inside its own rectangle. This means you'll need to assign it a background color that matches the color of whatever it will be sitting on (page, table cell, layer, and so on). The following tips apply to assigning background colors:

- Color sampling works here like it does throughout Dreamweaver. To match your web page's background color, just position the Flash object dialog box so that you can see some portion of your document behind it, and then click the color swatch; when the eyedropper cursor appears, click to sample the page or other desired background color.

- Background color is not just for Flash text! Even for rectangular Flash buttons, you want to assign a background color, unless you want your button to be surrounded by a little white halo on the page.

- Although this will have an effect only when seen in IE/Windows, you can use the `wmode` parameter to make the background invisible. After you've exited the dialog box, select the Flash object and use the generic Parameters dialog box from the Property Inspector to assign `wmode=transparent`.

Previewing Your Work (Button and Text Objects)

Note that the dialog box offers only limited preview capabilities as you're creating the SWF. You can preview in general what a button style will look like, but other than that, you have no visual feedback as you're working. This is because, as you're making your choices in the dialog box, Dreamweaver has not yet created the SWF file it will be inserting, so there's nothing to preview. If you're using the dialog box to create a new Flash object, instead of editing an existing one, you can't even use the Apply button to see your changes in the Document window because Dreamweaver can't apply changes to a SWF that it hasn't created yet. For this reason, creating Flash Button and Text objects usually involves several trips to the editing dialog box.

Working with Flash Objects

After it is inserted, the Flash button or text is coded into your HTML the same way that any SWF file would be, using `object` and `embed` tags. Just like any Flash movie, you can assign any of the parameters listed in Table 16.1. By default, Dreamweaver assigns Flash Text objects a scale value of `exactfit`, allowing nonproportional scaling. Unlike standard Flash movies, the movie contents are always visible in Dreamweaver Design view, so you don't have to use the Property Inspector's Play

button to preview them. This makes resizing more intuitive because you don't have to stop the playback before using the object's resize handles. Here are a few other things to consider when working with these Flash objects.

Editing

You edit a Flash Button or Text object by going to the Property Inspector and clicking the Edit button or by double-clicking the object itself. Either method reopens the original Flash object dialog box, ready to accept customization changes. Be aware that because SWF files can't be edited after creation, when you open the dialog box, make changes, and click OK, Dreamweaver is generating a new SWF, not editing the existing one. If you change the name in the Save As input field, you'll generate a separate SWF. If you leave the name the same, you'll overwrite the original SWF.

Undoing

Again, because Dreamweaver is creating SWF files as it goes, you can't use Edit > Undo or the History panel to undo edits made to Flash text or buttons. It makes sense when you think about it: When you perform your edits, Dreamweaver creates an uneditable SWF file and saves it to your hard drive. Because that file is not editable and is already saved, there's nothing to undo. The only way to undo changes to Flash Text and Button objects is to reopen the editing dialog box and manually change things back to the way they were.

Resizing

It's an obvious statement, but one worth repeating: Flash objects are resizable. Have a blast, with no worries about losing image quality if you scale up an object.

Duplicating

After you've created a Flash object, you can, of course, duplicate it as you would any page element (copy and paste, or Option/Ctrl-drag). Be aware, however, that each duplicate is an instance of the same SWF file. To change the text, color, link information, or other embedded properties in a Flash object, you'll need to tell Dreamweaver to generate a new SWF file instead of replacing the original. The procedure is as follows:

Every program has its own way of handling dragging to duplicate. To Ctrl-drag in Dreamweaver/Windows, click the Flash button and hold down the mouse button until the cursor changes to an arrow with a dotted square. Then press Ctrl, and a plus sign (+) will appear in the square; then drag. If you don't wait for the cursor change, the duplication might not work.

1. Duplicate the Flash Button or Text object in the Document window.

2. Double-click the new object to open its editing dialog box, and make whatever changes you like.

3. Before closing the dialog box, go to the Save As Input field at the bottom of the dialog box, and enter a new filename.

4. Click OK to exit the dialog box. Dreamweaver now generates a second SWF for you.

EXERCISE 16.5

Populating a Page with Flash Buttons and Text

It's time to create yet another Art Gecko home page! This time, you'll use **gecko_banner.swf** for the top banner, but you'll create your own navigation sidebar from Flash Button objects. Then you'll dress up the text headings by replacing them with Flash Text.

1. From the **chapter_16** folder, open **gecko_flashobjects.html**.

2. First, replace those boring headings. Select "Welcome to Art Gecko" and cut it to the Clipboard (Edit > Cut). With the insertion point still in position, go to the Media tab of the Insert bar and click the Flash Text object. Create a new "Welcome to Art Gecko" heading, pasting the Clipboard text into the Flash Text dialog box and using whatever font, size, style, and color your heart desires.

   Leave the Link field and rollover color swatch blank; you don't need your heading text to link anywhere.

   For a filename, you'll probably want to choose something more descriptive than **text1.swf**. Set the filename to **welcome.swf**.

   Finally, don't forget to set the background color to match the page color, or else your new heading will appear in its own little white box.

   When everything is set, click OK to close the dialog box.

3. Back in Design view, resize the new Flash heading until it's just the

right size and shape for you. Note that the scale parameter for this Flash object defaults to exactfit, so you can squish and stretch the type if you like. (*Warning:* Typographic purists frown on this sort of activity. Resizing type nonproportionally distorts the letter shapes and can make them ugly.)

4. To replace the "What's New at Art Gecko?" heading, start by deleting the text heading that's currently there. Then copy the Flash Text heading that you created in the previous step and paste it into position where the text heading was. Double-click the new Flash Text heading and change the wording to "What's new at Art Gecko?" Use the Save As Input field to enter a new filename; call the new file **whatsnew.swf**.

5. Next, add your own sidebar buttons. With the insertion point in the sidebar table cell, go to the Objects panel and click the Flash Button object. Choose any button style you like, as long as it includes a text label.

   For a text label, type in **Wall Hangings**. Format the type any way you please. Because you won't be able to preview the type without creating the button, you have to guess at what type size will be appropriate.

   For the link, browse to **ArtFiles/art1.html**. For the filename, enter **art1_button.swf**. And don't forget to set the background color!

   When you have finished, click OK to close the dialog box.

6. Back in Design view, you might discover that you don't like the button's size or the size of the type you put in it. You can resize the button by dragging its selection handles. (Note that the scale parameter for this Flash object has been set to show all, so the button maintains its proportions as you scale it. Of course, you can change this to exactfit if you like, although you risk making the button and its label look ugly.) To resize the text label in relation to the button, you have to double-click to re-enter the Flash Button dialog box and change the number in the Type Size field. Keep tweaking the button until you like how it looks on your page.

7. You have three more buttons to create. You can start by copying and pasting the Flash button you just created three times.

To change each Flash button's text and link information, double-click the button to open the editing dialog box, change whatever settings you need to, and then, in the Save As field, enter a new filename for the new SWF file that must be generated.

When duplicating Flash text or buttons, it's crucial to change the filename in the Save As Input field. If you don't remember this step, you'll be changing the original SWF file you duplicated from.

8. When you have finished, your page should look something like the one shown in Figure 16.24. Preview it in a browser to check it all out.

FIGURE 16.24
The gecko_ flashobjects.html home page, with Flash objects in place.

Using Flash Objects to Trigger JavaScript Commands

What if you want to use your Flash Button or Text object not as a standard link, but as a link that triggers a JavaScript action? You can't just select a Flash object and assign a behavior to it, as you would with regular text or images, because in HTML, the object and embed tags don't

accept event handlers. (See Chapter 15 for more on this.) JavaScript links, like other links, must be embedded in the Flash file itself.

If you read the earlier section on sending JavaScript out of Flash movies, however, you already know that it's possible to embed a JavaScript command in a Flash link. Therefore, just as you can add links to Flash Button and Text objects, you can add JavaScript links. You just use the `javascript:` keyword, followed by whatever command you want to execute. The Flash Button dialog box shown in Figure 16.25, for instance, creates a button that opens an alert window with the message "Hello, world!"

FIGURE 16.25

Creating a Flash Button object that will execute a Java-Script command when clicked.

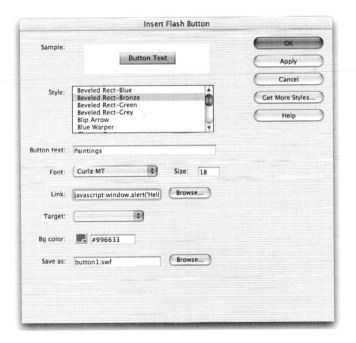

This is fine if you like writing short little JavaScript statements by hand. To execute more complex scripts, write the code as a function in the document head and use the previous technique to embed the function call in the Flash object.

By following the procedure described in Chapter 13 for "hijacking" behavior function calls, you can even use the Flash object to trigger a Dreamweaver behavior, adding complex scripting functionality to your Flash object with minimal coding on your part. The steps are as follows:

1. Create a dummy text link—a temporary page element that can be discarded later.

2. Select the text link and use the Behaviors panel to apply the desired behavior, configuring the behavior as you like.

3. Switch to Code view and find the text link, along with its function call. Copy the function call (everything between the quotation marks, after the onClick event handler).

4. Create the Flash button. In the button's dialog box, in the Link field, type **javascript:**. Then paste the function call in after the colon.

5. Back in Code view, find and delete the fake text link. Check the document <head> to make sure Dreamweaver hasn't deleted the function itself.

Figure 16.26 shows a Flash button configured to call the Open Browser Window behavior function.

FIGURE 16.26

"Hijacking" a Dreamweaver behavior's function call for use in a Flash button.

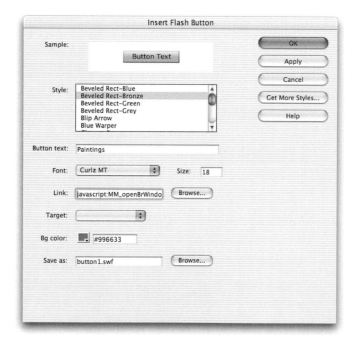

FLASH ELEMENTS

New to Dreamweaver MX 2004, Flash Elements are Flash page components (SWF files) that Dreamweaver creates for you, and that are highly customizable through the Tag Inspector. You can find Flash Elements in the Flash Elements Insert bar (see Figure 16.27).

FIGURE 16.27

The Flash Elements Insert bar, showing the Flash Image Viewer object

Currently, Dreamweaver ships with just one Flash Element: the Flash Image Viewer. This slick little item creates a display interface for a slide show of your images, complete with captions, clickable links, back and forward links, and so on. To insert and work with a Flash Image Viewer, do this:

1. Collect the series of images you'd like to show in the image viewer, and place them within your site (unless you're working without a site).

2. Open a document and place the insertion point where you want the image viewer to appear.

3. From the Flash Elements Insert bar, choose the Flash Image Viewer object. A dialog box will appear asking you to name the SWF file Dreamweaver is about to create. Choose a name and location, and click OK to close the dialog box.

   In your Document window, a new Flash movie is in place. The Property Inspector tells you it's a Flash movie with a few special parameters set (see Figure 16.28).

4. To customize the movie, use the Tag Inspector. Here, you can specify the names of the images to display, captions to display with them, and much more (see Figure 16.28). Sample entries are in place to show you the proper syntax for your entries.

FIGURE 16.28
An image viewer SWF built with the Flash Image Viewer element, along with its Property Inspector and Tag Inspector.

Flash Elements allow Flash developers to create components that can be used from within Dreamweaver. Look for additional Flash Elements to appear on the Dreamweaver Exchange before too long.

SUMMARY

In this chapter, you got a taste of the possibilities for integrating Flash into a website, and you saw how Dreamweaver makes this task easier. Each of the different Art Gecko home pages that you created represents a different approach to Flash/HTML coexistence. Each has its advantages and disadvantages. In your web design experience, you'll find that each project has its own needs and limitations, so you might use different strategies at different times. No matter what your Flash authoring strategy is, though, Dreamweaver's Flash text, Flash buttons, and Flash integration features will make publishing and maintaining your Flash website easier.

PART IV:

SITE MANAGEMENT WITH DREAMWEAVER

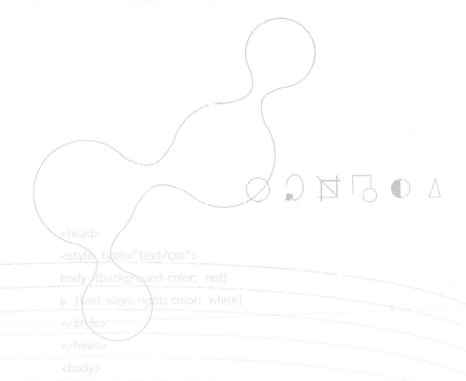

```
<head>
<style type="text/css">
body {background color: red}
p {text-align: right; color: white}
</style>
</head>
<body>
```

CHAPTER 17

LOCAL SITE MANAGEMENT

NO WEB PAGE IS AN ISLAND. IN WEB DEVELOPMENT, EACH DOCUMENT THAT you work on exists as part of a collective. In that collective might be linked pages, images, multimedia files, and other resource files. All of these parts must be tracked, uploaded, and maintained as a unit. Managing all of those files can be a daunting task. Exactly which files need to be part of the website? How should they be organized into directories and sub-directories? What colors are to be used site-wide? What about external style sheets or script documents? What if you decide halfway through building the site that you really should have been more consistent in naming your pages, or that you want your images in their own folder? You can't even think of uploading your site to a web server and sharing it with the world until you have these management concerns taken care of.

Luckily for those of us who are more creative than organized, Dreamweaver MX 2004 offers a whole set of easy-to-use, powerful tools to make local site management a breeze, from link checking to doing site-wide searches and diagnostic tools, to keeping track of files for you. Dreamweaver will even help you visualize your site's logical structure as you build it. Is it magic? No, it's just good organization.

This chapter discusses the process of defining a local site in Dreamweaver, how to work with the Site panel, and Dreamweaver tools available for file and asset management.

HOW DREAMWEAVER HANDLES LOCAL SITES

At the core of Dreamweaver site management is the concept of the local site. The *local site* is a complete version of your website that exists on your computer. It consists of all the same documents and resources that will eventually become your published website, in the same arrangement of files and folders. Your local site is your developmental testing ground. You store pages that you are currently working on, as well as any other resources, in the local site. You create an organized folder structure for your elements and manage your page content from here. Local site tools built into Dreamweaver allow you to perform spell checks, find-and-replace operations, and consistency checks.

You define a local site in Dreamweaver by pointing Dreamweaver to the folder on your computer where you plan to store all of your local site files. This folder is called the *local root folder*. After you've designated a folder as the local root folder, Dreamweaver treats any item placed within that folder as part of your site. To add a document or resource to your site, simply put it in this folder; to remove a document or resource without actually deleting it from your computer, move it out of this folder. All the while you're working on the various files in your site, Dreamweaver is watching the local root folder, keeping track of which files are being added or removed, noting whenever files or folders are renamed or rearranged, and examining the relationships between documents to make sure the site's relative links are accurate. The local root folder is integral to your Dreamweaver site-building experience.

DEFINING A LOCAL SITE

Creating and managing sites in Dreamweaver is done through the Site > Manage Sites command. Setting up each site's options is done in the Site Definition dialog box.

To create a new site or change the settings of an existing site, use the Site Definition dialog box. Choose Site > Manage Sites (or, in the Site

panel toolbar, choose Manage Sites from the site drop-down menu). This opens the Manage Sites dialog box. This dialog box is the central launching point from which you can click New to create a new site or Edit to change the settings for an existing site (see Figure 17.1).

FIGURE 17.1

Managing sites through the Manage Sites dialog box.

The Site Definition dialog box offers two modes for setting up your site information: Basic mode (also known as the Site Wizard) and Advanced mode. Unless you're very new to creating websites, Advanced mode is much more efficient to use. It allows you to set all the same basic information that the Site Wizard collects, plus many more options. The information is presented in logical categories, but without the friendly question-and-answer approach of the wizard.

To define a local site using the Advanced method, start by accessing the Site Definition dialog box (Site > New Site or Site > Manage Sites > New) and clicking the Advanced tab to make it active. The site information is divided into categories covering all aspects of static and dynamic sites. To define a local site, only the information in the Local Info category (shown in Figure 17.2) needs to be filled in, and only two items from this category are absolutely required to define a site.

Required information in the Local Info category (this information is also collected by the Site Wizard) is as follows:

- **Site Name**—This enables you to specify the name with which Dreamweaver will associate with your site.

- **Local Root Folder**—This sets the local folder on your computer that will be used as the root for your site. Click the Browse button to select this folder.

FIGURE 17.2
The Advanced tab of the Site Definition dialog box.

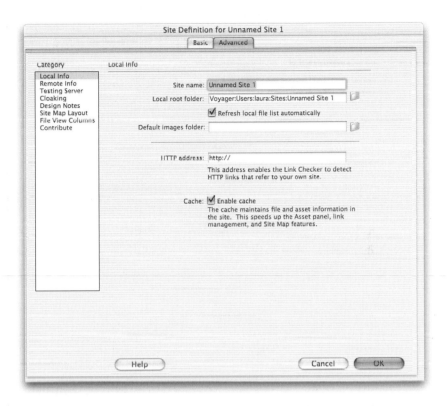

Optional information in the Local Info category (this information cannot be set in the Site Wizard) is as follows:

- **HTTP Address**—Enter the complete HTTP address that your site will eventually have as its root when it is uploaded to the web server—for example, `http://www.mydomain.com`. If your site uses absolute links between site documents, Dreamweaver can use this information to verify these links when you perform link-checking operations. If you won't be using absolute links for internal site navigation, you can leave this field alone. (See the section "Managing Links," later in this chapter, for more information on this.) If you have used the Site Wizard to define your site, this address defaults to `http://`.

- **Enable Cache**—As discussed earlier, Dreamweaver automatically keeps track of file and asset information for your local site as you work. It does this by maintaining a *site cache*, or temporary storage area, in your computer's memory. For small to medium sites, using the cache can significantly speed up site-wide operations such as Find and Replace, spell checking, and link management. For very large sites, the site cache can actually slow these operations (because there's too

much information for Dreamweaver to remember). A good general strategy is to enable the cache when you first define a site; if you later notice that site-wide operations are sluggish, try disabling it.

Dreamweaver lets you create as many sites as you need. Each site must have at least its local information specified, although it can also include remote and other information.

MANAGING SITES

Dreamweaver site management is handled through the Manage Sites dialog box (see Figure 17.1), the Site Definition dialog box (see Figure 17.2), and the Site panel, with its drop-down site menu.

The current site displays in the Site panel. Its name shows in the Site panel's drop-down site menu. To switch the current site to a different site, you can also open the Manage Sites dialog box by choosing Manage Sites from this menu. You can open the Site Definition dialog box for the current site by clicking on its name in this drop-down menu.

The Site Definition dialog box, used in creating new sites, is also used to edit settings for existing sites. Access it by choosing Site > Manage Sites, choosing a site, and clicking the Edit button; or by clicking twice on the current site's name in the Site panel's drop-down site menu.

The Manage Sites dialog box lists all currently defined sites, giving you the option to create new sites, edit existing sites, delete sites, and more (see Figure 17.1). Access this dialog box by choosing Site > Manage Sites, or by choosing Manage Sites from the Site panel's drop-down site menu. It's also accessible from a button in the Preferences > Site dialog box.

- To edit a site from this dialog box, select a site and click Edit to open that site's Site Definition dialog box.

- To delete a site, select it and click the Delete button. Note that deleting a site does not delete any of the files that are part of that site from your computer, nor does it change the local root folder in any way. It deletes only the site information that you specified when you created the site—including the site name and the designation of a specific folder as the local root folder.

- To create a new site from this dialog box, click the New button.

WORKING IN THE SITE PANEL

When you have a site defined, the Dreamweaver Site panel is your interface for performing any and all site-related tasks (see Figure 17.3). It's your window on the world of your site. It's a good idea to always leave it open while you work. Use this window to see your site's files and hierarchical structure at a glance, to perform file-management tasks, and more.

FIGURE 17.3
The Site panel
(shown in expanded
and contracted
modes).

Expanding and Contracting the Site Panel

The Site panel with all of its information showing can take up a lot of screen real estate, which can be a problem unless you have a very large monitor or a dual monitor set up at your workstation. To alleviate this problem, the panel can be shown in full or abbreviated form. Switch between these two modes by clicking the Expand/Collapse button in the Site panel toolbar (see Figure 17.3). Like other panels, it can also be docked in with the rest of the Dreamweaver panels, or undocked and used as a free-standing panel. (This feature is new for Dreamweaver/Mac users.) When docked, it's always in abbreviated form.

The details of the Site panel vary slightly on Mac and Windows.

- **Windows users**—When the Site panel is docked, expanding it causes it to temporarily undock and take over the entire Dreamweaver application window. When it is used as a free-standing window, it expands without taking over the entire application window. In its expanded form, the panel includes a special Site panel menu bar, with File, Edit, View, and Site menus. In its abbreviated form, this menu disappears, but the panel options menu (accessed by clicking the Options icon in the panel's upper-right corner) includes them as submenus. Throughout this chapter, this is referred to as the Site panel menu bar.

- **Mac users**—When the Site panel is docked, expanding it causes it to temporarily undock and become a free-standing window. It doesn't take over the entire screen like its Windows counterpart, and it doesn't provide a Site panel menu bar. But the panel options menu (accessed by clicking the icon in the upper-right corner of the panel) includes File, Edit, View, and Site submenus. Throughout this chapter, this is referred to as the Site panel menu bar.

For both Windows and Mac, the Site panel cannot be reinserted into the dock while in an expanded state.

Site Files View

In the expanded Site panel, the right column shows the Site Files list. In the abbreviated panel, the Site Files list shows by default. It can also be shown by choosing Local View from the view drop-down menu (see Figure 17.3). The Site Files list shows all of the contents of your local root folder, arranged hierarchically as if you were viewing it in Windows Explorer or the Macintosh Finder's List view. Just like the lists of files in your operating system, every folder shows with a plus/minus (+/−) sign (Windows) or triangle (Mac) to show or hide its contents. Most of the powerful file-management features in Dreamweaver center on the Site Files view.

Working with the File View Columns

When the Site panel is expanded, the Site Files list becomes more than just a list of names. It includes columns of information about each file: name, size, type, modified date, and more. If your Site panel is wide enough, you can learn a lot about your files by just looking at their column information. Just as you can with Windows Explorer or the Macintosh Finder List view, you can also choose to view your files organized by any column, by clicking on that column.

If the Site panel is not organized optimally for your work habits, you can change it. Dreamweaver allows you to customize how you view your Site panel with the File View Columns category in the Site Definition dialog box (see Figure 17.4). In addition to the methods already mentioned for accessing this dialog box, you can open the dialog box and go directly to the File View Columns category by choosing View > File View Columns from the Site panel menu bar.

In this window, you can see all the names of the columns visible in the Site panel, whether the columns are built-in by Macromedia or created by you. You can also see whether the columns are visible.

Read Chapter 19, "Workplace Collaboration," to learn how to use file view columns with Design Notes.

If you want to add your own custom column, click the plus (+) button. You can then name the new column, specify whether you want to assign a Design Note to it, specify how the information in the column is to be aligned, and specify whether the column is visible or not. When you create your own column, its type is Personal. To delete a column you have created, click the − (Delete) button.

FIGURE 17.4

The Site Definition dialog box showing the File View Columns category.

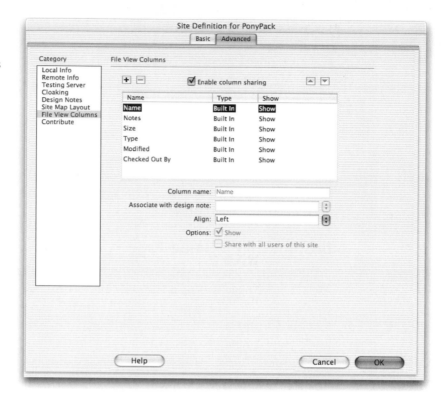

To understand where the new column you create appears in the Site panel, you need to use your imagination. Visualize the Site panel. Recall that the first column in the window contains the names of files located in your local site. The next column holds Design Notes. The third column indicates the size of the files, and the fourth column tells you the types of files. Here, you see the names of the columns (which appear horizontally in the Site panel) vertically. Dreamweaver places the new column at the bottom of the list by default, which means that the new column is placed on the far right of the Site panel. If you want to change the location of your new column, use the up and down arrows located in the upper-right portion of the Site Definition window. By clicking the up arrow, you are moving your column to the left in the Site panel. Click the down arrow if you want to move your column to the right of the Site panel. You can also move the built-in columns, except for the Name column; that always must remain at the top of this list.

You cannot delete a Dreamweaver default column. If you don't want to see it, however, you can deselect the Show option. This hides the column from your view, giving the appearance that it has been deleted.

Site Map View

So far, you have looked at the elements of your site as a list. However, this list doesn't tell you how the files relate to each other. Which file is the first one viewed when someone goes to your site? How many pages link to your first page? Dreamweaver gives you an easy way to answer all these questions: Site Map view.

Designating a Home Page

Before you can use Site Map view, you need to tell Dreamweaver what your "home" page is. This is the page that is first visible when someone goes to your site. Just because it's called the home page doesn't mean that the document itself needs to be named home.html. In fact, the home page is typically named index.htm, index.html, default.htm, or default.html. This is because web servers are usually configured to recognize one or more of these names automatically so that visitors don't need to specify the page name when entering a site's URL in the browser's address fields. (Before choosing the home page filename for your site, check with your web server administrator or your ISP's tech support staff to see which default names its servers are configured to recognize.)

Default filenames won't be recognized by Dreamweaver or a web server if too many of them exist. Don't put index.htm and index.html files in the site.

To define a home page for your site, open the Site Definition dialog box and go to the Site Map Layout category (see Figure 17.5). You can also go directly to that category by choosing View > Layout from the Site panel menu bar. In the dialog box, click the folder icon to browse for your home page, or type its name in the home page field.

If you have chosen one of the standard default filenames for your home page, you don't need to explicitly define it as a home page in Dreamweaver. Like a web server, Dreamweaver recognizes these names and assumes that a file with a default name is the home page.

FIGURE 17.5
The Site Definition
dialog box, ready to
define a home page.

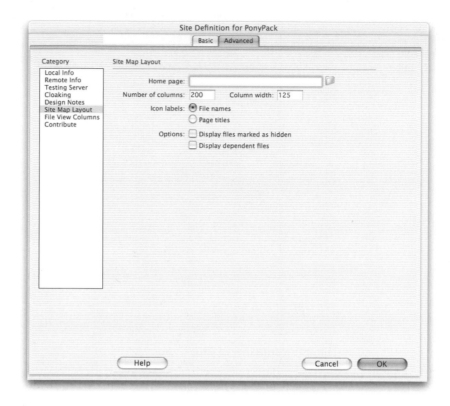

Viewing a Site with the Site Map

After you have selected your home page, you can view the site map.
With the Site panel expanded, press the Site Map button (refer to
Figure 17.3) and, from the drop-down menu, choose Map Only or Map
and Files. Figure 17.6 shows the Site panel displaying Map Only.

As Figure 17.6 shows, the Site Map view displays your site as a hierarchy
of linked files, with the topmost file being your home page. Below the
home page are files linked directly from the home page. Included as well
are email links, external links, and links to any sort of media embedded
in the page.

Options for how the site map displays are set in the Site Map Layout category of the Site Definition dialog box. Some options can also be set
using commands in the View menu in the Site panel menu bar.

FIGURE 17.6
The Site panel show-
ing the site map for a
simple site.

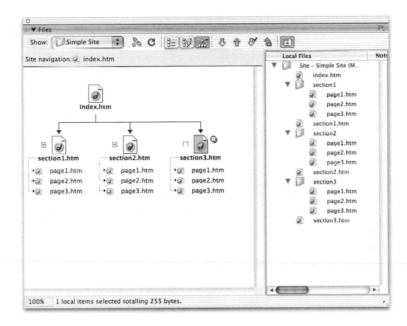

Icons, Names, and File Types

The site map uses small icons to give visual clues to a file or link's status.
When you get used to the visual language being used, a glance will tell
you a world of information about your site:

- **Icons**—Each kind of item in the site map has its own icon to represent
  it. Dreamweaver file icons with black labels represent files. A globe icon
  with a blue label represents absolute URLs and other special links.
  Broken links are represented by a broken chain icon with a red label.

- **Labels**—If you'd rather label your icons with page titles instead of
  filenames, choose Page Titles in the Site Definition dialog box, or
  choose View > Show Page Titles from the Site panel menu bar. To
  turn filenames back on, choose Filenames from the Site Definition
  dialog box, or choose View > Show Filenames from the Site panel
  menu bar.

What Shows and What Doesn't

By default, dependent files (such as linked media, and linked script and
CSS files) don't display in the site map. To see these files, choose Display
Dependent Files in the Site Definition dialog box, or choose View >
Show Dependent Files from the Site panel menu bar. To hide them
again, use the same commands.

Showing the Hierarchy

If your site is complex, the site map might be difficult to read because of all the icons and links shown. But you can simplify the view by hiding and showing links.

To hide all the links coming from a particular file, click the minus (–) button next to the file icon. To show the links again, click the plus (+) button. (The button changes state depending on whether links are shown or hidden.)

To view only a portion of the site at a time (for instance, to show only the Menswear section of a clothing catalog website), right-click the file at the top of the hierarchy that you want to view and choose View as Root from the contextual menu. The site map shifts so that the selected file appears as the new home page at the top of the hierarchy, with all of its child links showing. No other parts of the website are visible. At the top of the site map window, a special icon shows the relationship of the current view to the home page (see Figure 17.7).

To return to viewing the entire website after you've switched to this temporary view, click the home page icon at the top of the site map window (see Figure 17.7).

FIGURE 17.7
Viewing a page as the root of the hierarchy and returning to view the entire hierarchy.

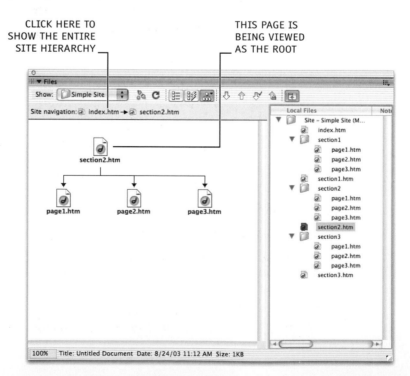

Modifying the Site Map Home Page

Dreamweaver lets you change the existing home page to either an existing page or a completely new one, including non-HTML files such as an image or a SWF file. Select Site > New Home Page from the Site panel menu bar. This brings up the New Home Page dialog box. You can enter the filename and page title of your new home page here. After creating this new page, you can re-create your links using the Link to Existing File command as well as the Point to File icon. This process was discussed in the previous sections of this chapter.

To set an existing page as the new home page in the site map, select that file from the local Site panel (you must be in Map and Files View mode to do this). Then select Site > Set as Home Page from the Site panel menu bar. This re-creates the site map with the newly defined home page and its links. You can also right-click a file in the Site panel and choose Set as Home Page from the contextual menu.

Customizing Site Map Layout

You can customize your current site's site map in the Site Definition dialog box's Site Map Layout category. From this window, you can select the number of columns and the column width for your site map display. This number specifies the number of pages to display on each row; the default is 200. You will typically not need to adjust this value because you will rarely have more than 200 pages linked to from your main page.

Next you can select whether the site map should represent documents by their filenames or their page titles. If you have been diligent in creating effective page titles, using the page titles in the Site Map view might be a good way to display your site. Displaying your site files by their page titles also gives you an idea of whether the titles are easy to understand. You might be surprised how confusing some page titles can be when you're not looking at the page itself.

Finally, you can choose options that you want to include in your site map. The first option enables you to specify whether the site map should show files marked as hidden. When this is checked, hidden files will be shown. The other option, Display Dependent Files, displays all dependent files (such as images and other files linked in the HTML) in the site map. These files are listed in the order in which they are located in the HTML code.

Creating an Image from the Site Map

How handy would it be if you could save your site map as an image that you could then email to or print out for your client? Dreamweaver makes this task incredibly easy!

To save the site map, choose File > Save Site Map. In the Save Site Map dialog box, name your image and choose the location in which to save it. For Windows users, in the File Type drop-down menu, choosing .bmp saves the file as a bitmap, and choosing .png saves it as a PNG file. For Mac users, the file automatically is saved as a JPEG.

FILE AND LINK MANAGEMENT WITHIN A SITE

The biggest ongoing chore of website development is site management—keeping track of all the files in the site and making sure the folder structure is logical, that the filenames make sense, that the links all work, and that everything is where you can find it quickly for editing and uploading. After you've defined your Dreamweaver site, all the formidable power of its local site-management tools is at your disposal. Working from your "central command window"—in other words, the Site panel—you can keep your finger on the pulse of your site and control your files like a general marshalling her troops.

Managing Files and Folders

Think of the Site panel as a substitute for Windows Explorer or the Macintosh Finder. Leave it open all the time as you work on your site. Use it to perform all basic file operations across your site. Site Files view is your key to managing the file structure of your site; Site Map view is your key to managing its links.

Opening Files

As always, there's more than one way to open files in Dreamweaver. The first and perhaps most popular method is to select File > Open from the menu. You can then use the Open dialog box to navigate to the file that

you want and click Open. A faster method is through the Site panel. You can double-click a file in the Site panel (Site Files or Site Map view), and it will open. It's as simple as that! Now that you know this snazzy new way to open a document in one step, will you ever use the old way again?

Creating Files and Folders

Always close all documents before performing any file-management operations on them. Dreamweaver can't properly update links, change filenames, and so on if the files are open.

To create a new file or folder from Site Files view, click the folder that you want to contain the new item and Choose File > New File or File > New Folder from the Site panel menu bar. Or, you can right-click on the folder that you want to contain the new item and, from the contextual menu, choose New File or New Folder.

A new, untitled file or folder will appear in the Site Files list. (For new files, Dreamweaver creates files of the default document type for this site.)

Renaming and Rearranging Files and Folders

Regular humans who aren't super-organizers rarely get the best possible organization system going until they're at least a little way into a site-development project. They might also come across the perfect naming scheme after already creating a half dozen files with useless names that must be changed. The nightmare of this scenario is that, after you've started building a website—complete with links to graphics and links between files—any little change in the location or name of a file means having to update every single relative link that points to or comes from that page.

If you use the Dreamweaver Site Files view to perform any of these naming or organizing tasks, Dreamweaver automatically updates all links as needed.

To move a file or folder from one location in the file structure to another, just drag the item to its new location in the Site Files view.

To rename a file or folder, click twice on its name in Site Files view or Site Map view, or select the file and choose File > Rename from the Site panel menu bar. Then type in a new name. Note that if you change the filename of the home page, the site map won't display properly until you refresh it by choosing Site > Re-create Site Cache from the Site panel menu bar.

If your change will require any links to be updated, Dreamweaver presents you with the Update Links dialog box showing you all the files that will need to be updated as a result of your action (see Figure 17.8). From here, simply click Update, and Dreamweaver changes all links in the listed files, so none of your links is broken.

Dreamweaver's link updates work only on relative links encoded in anchor (a) tags. Absolute links and those coded as part of JavaScript commands need to be updated manually.

FIGURE 17.8
Automatic link updating in the Site panel.

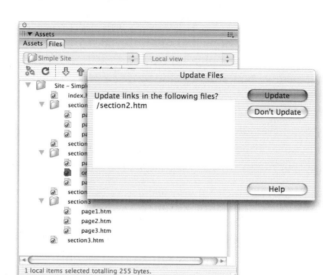

Why would you ever not want to update links? Imagine a scenario in which you have two alternate home pages—maybe one for when the company is having a sale, and one for other times—with identical links coming from them but different content. You might leave both home pages in the local root folder, one called index.html and the other called index-sale.html. The next time there's a sale going on, you can easily switch home pages by renaming them index-nosale.html and index.html. When you change the name of index.html to index-nosale.html, Dreamweaver will offer to update your links for you. Don't do it! You still want all links in the site pointing to index.html. When you change the name of index-sale.html to index.html, all links in the site will now point to the alternate home page.

Managing Links

You've already seen some pretty wonderful link management in the way Dreamweaver updates links when you update your file structure. But that's only the first step in a comprehensive link-management system. By utilizing the site map, various Site menu commands, and Site Reports, you can truly be in command of your site's link structure without moving from your command chair.

Creating Links with Point to File

Do you like dragging and dropping? Is it your dream to create a site-wide navigation system quickly and easily, possibly without even opening a single file? You're going to love point to file.

Point to File from Within a File

If you have a document open and the Site panel at least partially visible on your computer screen, you can create a link from within that file to another file in your site using point to file. Do it this way:

1. Open the file that you want to contain the link. Make sure your Site panel is open and visible.

3. Select the text or image that will become the link.

4. In the Property Inspector, find the Link field, but instead of clicking the Browse button or typing a name in the input field, find the Point to File button.

5. Press down on this button and drag over to the Site panel. (If the Site panel is free-standing, just drag so you're over some portion of it, and it will pop to the front so you can see the whole window.) Keep dragging until you're on top of the file to which you want to link. This file becomes highlighted when you're in the right position.

6. Let go of the mouse button. If your hand-eye coordination was working right, your open document now contains a link to the item you pointed to. It's point-and-shoot! (See Figure 17.9.)

FIGURE 17.9
Using point to file to create a link.

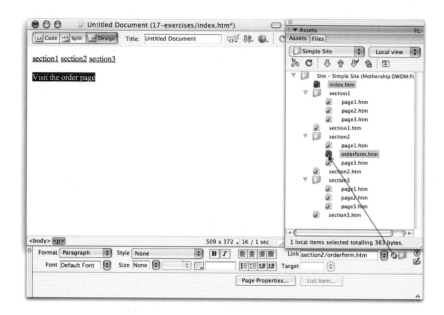

Point to File from the Site Map

If you're in a hurry to create some navigation controls in your site, and you don't even want to open the files to do it, you'll love the capability to point to file from the site map. Just do this:

1. Close all documents. (Always do this before performing file-management tasks that might require files to update their contents.)

2. Open Site Map view in the Site panel.

3. In the site map, select the file you want to link from. A little point to file icon appears beside the file.

4. Press down on that icon and drag to the file to which you want to link. You can drag to another file in the site map or to a file in the Site Files list. When you're on top of the desired file and it highlights, let go. Your link is created! (See Figure 17.10.)

The site map changes to show that a link has been added between the two files. But what kind of link is it? Open the file you linked from and scroll down to the bottom of the page. You'll see that Dreamweaver has

added a text link to the other file, with its text derived from the other file's filename. If you continue adding links from this same file, Dreamweaver eventually creates a whole text-based navigation bar along the bottom of the page. It's not fancy, but it's accessible and it works. And you didn't have to open a single file to do it. (You just opened the file to see the results.)

FIGURE 17.10
Using point to file to link two files in the site map.

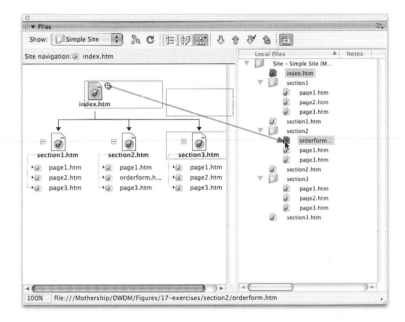

Creating Links with Menu Commands and the Site Map

If pointing-and-shooting isn't your cup of tea, you can still quickly add links from one file to another without opening either file by using menu commands. You must be in Site Map view to do this, but there's no dragging and dropping involved.

Linking to an Existing File with the Site Map View Menu

To link one file to another existing file without opening either file or using point to file, do this:

1. In Site Map view, select the file you want to link from and choose Site > Link to Existing File from the Site panel menu bar. Or, right-

informIT

www.informit.com

YOUR GUIDE TO IT REFERENCE

InformIT.com brings technical information to your desktop. Drawing from authors and reviewers to provide additional information on topics of interest to you, **InformIT.com** provides free, in-depth information you won't find anywhere else.

Articles

Keep your edge with thousands of free articles, in-depth features, interviews, and IT reference recommendations— all written by experts you know and trust.

Online Books

Answers in an instant from **InformIT Online Books'** 600+ fully searchable online books.

POWERED BY

Safari

Catalog

Review online sample chapters, author biographies, and customer rankings and choose exactly the right book from a selection of more than 5,000 titles.

real world. real training. real results.

Get more done in less time with
Macromedia Training and Certification.

Two Types of Training

Roll up your sleeves and get right to work with authorized training
from Macromedia.

1. Classroom Training

   Learn from instructors thoroughly trained and certified by
   Macromedia. Courses are fast-paced and task-oriented to get
   you up and running quickly.

2. Online Training

   Get Macromedia training when you want with affordable, interactive online
   training from Macromedia University.

Stand Out from the Pack

Show your colleagues, employer, or prospective clients that you
have what it takes to effectively develop, deploy, and maintain dynamic
applications–become a Macromedia Certified Professional.

Learn More

For more information about authorized training or to find a class near you,
visit **www.macromedia.com/go/training1**

macromedia®
**TRAINING AND
CERTIFICATION**

Macromedia® Dreamweaver® MX 2004 Demystified

Laura Gutman

Macromedia Press books are published in association with:

Peachpit Press
1249 Eighth St.
Berkeley, CA 94710
510/524-7178 • 800-283-9444
510/524-2221 (fax)

Find us on the World Wide Web at: **http://www.peachpit.com**

To report errors, please send a note to: **errata.peachpit.com**

Copyright © 2004 by Peachpit Press

Publisher: Nancy Ruenzel
Associate Publisher: Stephanie Wall
Production Manager: Gina Kanouse
Senior Acquisitions Editor: Linda Anne Bump
Executive Development Editor: Lisa Thibault
Project Editor: Jake McFarland
Copy Editors: Krista Hansing, Gayle Johnson
Indexer: Greg Pearson
Interior Design: Mimi Heft
Compositor: Molly Sharp
Cover Design: Aren Howell
Cover Illustration: Nathan Clement
Marketing: Scott Cowlin, Tammy Detrich, Hannah Onstad Latham
Publicity: Kim Lombardi, Susan Nixon

International Standard Book Number: 0-7357-1384-7

Library of Congress Number: 2003112007

07 06 05 04 03   7 6 5 4 3 2

Printed and bound in the United States of America

P9-DMF-772

MACROMEDIA®
DREAMWEAVER®
MX 2004
DEMYSTIFIED

LAURA GUTMAN

Feb. 2, 2004

macromedia®
PRESS

PART I:
WEB PAGE CONSTRUCTION WITH DREAMWEAVER

indicates that no actual hard return should be inserted here. Any code word or phrase in the text (such as the name of an HTML tag or attribute) is also set in a `monospace` font.

Keyboard shortcuts for menu commands are not generally mentioned along with their menu counterparts because they're always listed next to the menu item and because you may have customized your keyboard shortcuts, so the information would be irrelevant to you, anyway. This book is for intermediate users, and I assume that you know how to read a shortcut indicator. Your reward for not having every keyboard shortcut explicitly mentioned in the text is that it makes room in the book for lots of extra content—a great trade-off!

Mac/Windows differences for keyboard and other procedures are indicated as concisely as possible. Ctrl/Cmd refers to the Control key on Windows and the Command key on Mac. So Ctrl/Cmd+S means that Windows users press Ctrl+S and Mac users press Cmd+S. Alt/Opt similarly refers to the Alt key on Windows and the Opt key on Mac. Whenever the book refers to right-clicking anything, Mac users with a single-button mouse should Ctrl-click. If you're on a Mac, you probably already know that Ctrl-clicking is the standard alternative to right-clicking, so it's not explicitly stated in the text.

WHAT TO TAKE AWAY FROM THIS BOOK

We hope you enjoy learning about Dreamweaver as much as we enjoyed putting this book together for you. We want you to close the covers of this book with a greater understanding of how web development works, and how to use Dreamweaver to work with it, than when you started. But remember, no one ever became a better web designer just by reading books. Read the book. Then go create some websites. Then come back and read more of the book. Then go make more websites. And just about the time you think you've got everything mastered, it'll be time for a new book!

How to Use This Book

How you use this book depends on who you are and how you want to use it.

- **Reading front to back**—You could read this book from front to back; the topics are generally arranged from simpler to more challenging, and from small-scale (working with individual pages) to large-scale (working with sites and servers). Or, your could pick any section or chapter you like and start reading there. Each chapter contains enough cross-references that you should be able to pick up the story anywhere you like and still be oriented.

- **Doing the exercises or not**—The exercises are provided to give you practice with various Dreamweaver topics and examples of how to put different Dreamweaver functions to use. You'll gain a lot by doing them. You can find all the exercise files at www.peachpit.com. Sometimes, however, you just don't have time to do exercises—you need answers *now*. All topics are fully covered outside the exercises, so if you want to use the book as a reference only, you can find everything you're looking for in the text.

Book Conventions

All computer books need to establish certain conventions to simplify presentation of the material. And this book is no different!

Menu commands are separated by > indicators between menu name and command name, or between menu name and submenu name, like this: File > Save. This convention is also used to indicate particular categories or tabs within dialog boxes and windows, like this: the Preferences > General dialog box or the Results > Site FTP Log panel.

Important new terms are *italicized* the first time they appear in the text, but not after that. Filenames (for the exercises) are in **bold**.

Code samples are printed in a monospace font when separated from their surrounding text. If a line of code is too long to print on the book page, it's indicated by a ➡ arrow where it wraps to the next line. This

Part III: Interactivity, DHTML, and Multimedia

Web pages don't have to be static. An important part of the web experience is interactivity, whether it's for user engagement, efficient presentation of information, or entertainment value. The chapters in this section examine all the tools for making things hop and pop, turning the static web experience into something interactive. This includes JavaScript behaviors, DHTML (what it is and how you can use it), and how to work beyond HTML with Flash and other rich media content.

Part IV: Site Management with Dreamweaver

No web page is an island. This section covers Dreamweaver as an organizational tool for working with the dozens or hundreds of files that comprise a website. This section covers creating a local site and taking advantage of Dreamweaver file-management resources, working with remote sites, and using Dreamweaver tools for team-based or large-scale web development.

Part V: Dreamweaver and Live Data

Dynamic data (referred to as *live data* in Dreamweaver) is the future of web development. Read this section of the book to improve the way you work with ASP.NET, ColdFusion, and PHP. We cover the basics—setting up sites, using live data objects, and understanding server behaviors—and then move on to pushing the envelope with the different server technologies.

Part VI: Dreamweaver Under the Hood

Think of this section as Dreamweaver for geeks. These chapters cover using Dreamweaver as a coding tool, customizing the Dreamweaver workspace, working with extensions and the Extension Manager, and, finally, using a bit of scripting to write your own extensions.

to use them well. Each chapter includes professional tips and strategies, as well as exercises showing you how to apply the program features covered in that chapter.

New Features

Dreamweaver is always evolving. The new Dreamweaver X offers the Selection Inspector; a revised Insert bar; improved CSS handling; more powerful tools for working with PHP, ASP.NET, and ColdFusion; and more. Throughout the book, keep your eye out for the special New Features icon. Wherever we show off a new feature, you'll see that icon in the margin.

HOW THIS BOOK IS ORGANIZED

Each of the book's 29 chapters contains explanatory text, lots of pictures, and several hands-on exercises. The chapters are grouped into six sections:

Part I: Web Page Construction with Dreamweaver

These chapters cover the nuts and bolts of creating web pages with Dreamweaver, including setting up the workspace, creating documents, working with text and images, setting up links and navigation systems, and adding head content. Just because these are fundamentals doesn't mean this section is only for beginners! There's a lot to learn here about good, solid work skills for creating good foundation documents.

Part II: Designing with Dreamweaver

This section looks at Dreamweaver as a design tool. This includes creating good page layouts with tables and divs, using CSS, creating frame-based layouts, and designing forms. The focus is on creating attractive, functional, and communicative page designs, and on developing good coding skills to create well-structured pages that will display well across browsers and platforms.

WHAT (AND WHOM) THIS BOOK IS FOR

According to the blurb on the back cover, this book is for the intermediate Dreamweaver user. What does that mean? That's a good question. We assume you've opened up Dreamweaver at least a few times already. You've gone through the beginning tutorials, or you just plowed right in and started using it when you got that new assignment at work. But beyond that? Every intermediate user is a beginner at some things and is advanced at others. Consequently, for every topic, we begin with a quick trip through the basics before exploring more advanced issues and techniques.

Dreamweaver in the Larger Scheme of Things

Working with web-development software isn't like working with any other kind of program. Before you can use Dreamweaver effectively, you need to know how browsers work and how HTML, JavaScript, and other web technologies function within the browser to create web experiences. One of our goals in this book is to help you look beyond the software, to start thinking about what's possible on the web and how Dreamweaver can help you accomplish that.

To that end, this book examines every topic as it relates to browsers and W3C standards, as well as how it's implemented in Dreamweaver. Instead of just learning how to format type in Dreamweaver, you want to know what all the possibilities are for type formatting in HTML, how they work, and what their relative advantages are. Then you want to know how to use Dreamweaver to make that formatting happen. That's the emphasis throughout this book.

Dreamweaver in the Real World

We also know that no one becomes a pro by memorizing program features. To really master any software, you have to know not only what the program can do, but also how to use its capabilities to solve real problems and build real projects. This book teaches you how to use various program features. However, it also explains why to use them—and how

INTRODUCTION

WELCOME TO *MACROMEDIA DREAMWEAVER MX 2004 DEMYSTIFIED*! IT'S AN EXCITING PLACE to be. We've squeezed as much information, tips, techniques, strategies, and advice as we could fit between its covers. Each new release of Dreamweaver adds more features and improves on existing ones. And this release is no different. Grab a cup of coffee, get comfortable, and let's get started demystifying Dreamweaver.

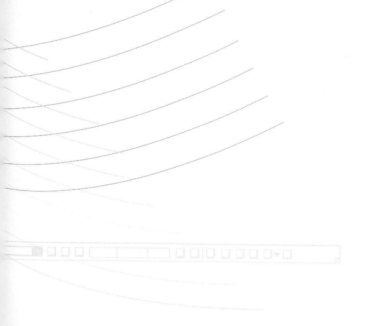

<head>

<style type="text/css">

body {background-color: red}

p {text-align: right; color: white}

</style>

</head>

<body>

PART VI: DREAMWEAVER UNDER THE HOOD

Chapter 27: Writing Code in Dreamweaver   1043

Chapter 25: Working Smart with PHP 977

Chapter 26: Working Smart with ASP.NET 991

Chapter 24: Working Smart with ColdFusion 931

Chapter 20: Site-Wide Content with Templates and Libraries   735

PART V: DREAMWEAVER AND LIVE DATA

Chapter 21: Building Dynamic Sites with Dreamweaver   795

Chapter 18: Site Publishing and Maintenance 679

Chapter 19: Workplace Collaboration 705

PART IV: SITE MANAGEMENT WITH DREAMWEAVER

Chapter 17: Local Site Management 631

Chapter 12: CSS Positioning, Dreamweaver Layers, and Page Layout   423

PART III: INTERACTIVITY, DHTML, AND MULTIMEDIA

Chapter 13: Interactivity with Behaviors   465

Chapter 7: Utilizing Head Content   201

PART II: DESIGNING WITH DREAMWEAVER

Chapter 8: Building Tables   229

Chapter 2: The Dreamweaver Workspace   23

Chapter 3: Creating and Working with Documents   49

Chapter 4: Working with Text   65

TABLE OF CONTENTS

CONTENTS AT A GLANCE

ABOUT THE TECHNICAL REVIEWERS

Bryan Ashcraft's adventure into the world of web development began by accident. Being a musician, he loved the creative outlet the web provided. But little did he know that it would lead to a career change. Having played around with HTML for about a year and hearing that some friends in a local techno group wanted their website (www.clubnation.net) redesigned, Bryan, along with the band's sound and lighting engineer, volunteered to take on the task. That was the beginning of Paragon Visuals.

As co-founder and lead developer, Bryan focuses on helping small- to mid-size businesses bring their products or services to the web, utilizing ColdFusion, ASP, and the entire Macromedia Studio suite. Paragon Visuals also designs and develops other promotional material, including interactive CDs, brochures, and logos. Bryan is a Macromedia-Certified Dreamweaver Developer and Team Macromedia Member, as well as a certified Master CIW Designer. He is also a founding partner of Community MX (www.communitymx.com) and a contributing author at Dreamweaver FAQ (www.dreamweaverfaq.com).

Laurie Casolino first discovered the Internet in 1996, and it was love at first "site." The more she surfed, the more fascinated she became with the nuts and bolts of how websites were created. She downloaded a freeware HTML editor and made her first home page. It wasn't pretty, but it was the beginning of a love affair with web design. Not happy with the lack of control she had over her page with this editor, Laurie started looking around for a good HTML editor. A friend recommended that she try Dreamweaver. She downloaded the trial version of Dreamweaver 3 and immediately knew that this was what she had been looking for.

With two young children, Laurie wanted a career that she could feel passionate about, yet still be able to work from home. In 2001, she started MJ Website Designs. Still passionate about Dreamweaver, she discovered the Macromedia newsgroups and the great bunch of volunteers who have taught her so much. A partner in Community MX (www.communitymx.com), Laurie is finding that the more she learns, the more there is to learn.

ABOUT THE CONTRIBUTORS

Donald S. Booth works as a team lead on the Dreamweaver Technical Support Team at Macromedia. He also works on the Authorware Support team as a technician and trainer. Don co-wrote *Inside Dreamweaver MX* (New Riders, 2002). He has degrees in art and philosophy from the University of Rhode Island. When not building web pages, Don likes to build other things, such as guitars, cameras, and a good library. He likes taking photographs and collecting cameras. He currently resides in San Francisco. Learn more about him at www.dbooth.net.

Matt Brown is a consultant based in the Bay Area. He has edited more than 20 Dreamweaver and Photoshop books over the years. He has taught at Foothill College and in the Multimedia Studies Program at San Francisco State University. He was on the Dreamweaver team for five years in a number of capacities, finally as community manager. Matt is married to a magnificent woman, Marcella. He keeps chickens, and he loves to cook and create all sorts of art.

ABOUT THE AUTHOR

Laura Gutman works as a multimedia web application developer and educator in the fields of multimedia, programming, and design. Her first experience in computer science was at an IBM training school in 1983, where she learned how to punch cards, dissect mainframes, and program in COBOL. In the intervening years, she earned her Ph.D. in English from the University of St. Andrews (Scotland) and has worked as a graphic designer and illustrator (for print and multimedia), technical writer, and multimedia developer. Currently Laura lives with her dog, parakeets, and hundreds of computer toys in Albuquerque, New Mexico. In addition to her development and consulting work, she teaches a range of courses in multimedia and graphic design at the University of New Mexico. You can visit her online at www.rocketlaura.com.

Acknowledgments

I would like to thank several people for their behind-the-scenes help that made this book better than it otherwise would have been. Nick Bennett, CSS guy extraordinaire, kept me honest and accurate on that topic, especially in Chapter 12, "CSS Positioning, Dreamweaver Layers, and Page Layout." Jennifer Bennett helped with Chapter 6, "Links and Navigation." And as always, my students, whom I practice on, helped make everything better throughout.

click on the file you want to link from and, from the contextual menu, choose Link to Existing File.

2. When the Select HTML File dialog box appears, browse to the file you want your file to link to. Click Choose to close the dialog box.

That's it! Your link is in place and shows up as an additional link in the site map. To see how the link was created in the originating file, open that file and scroll to the bottom of the page. You'll see that, as with the point to file links just described, Dreamweaver has added a text link to the other file, with its text derived from the other file's filename.

Linking to a New (Nonexistent) File with the Site Map View Menu

This little feature is the unsung hero of Dreamweaver site management. From the site map, you can determine what files your site will need and which should be linked to which, and essentially build the entire site without opening a single file. To create a new file and link to it all in one process, do this (see Figure 17.11):

FIGURE 17.11

Linking to a new file in the site map.

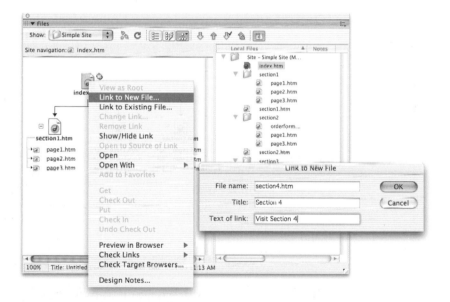

1. In Site Map view, select the file you want to link from and choose Site > Link to New File from the Site panel menu bar; or, right-click on the file you want to link from and, from the contextual menu, choose Link to New File.

2. When the Link to New File dialog box appears, fill in the following information:

- **Filename**—Dreamweaver is about to create a new file for you. What would you like it to be called?

- **Title**—What would you like the page title (contents of the `title` tag) of the new file to be?

- **Text of Link**—After the new file is created, Dreamweaver creates a text link in the original file pointing to the new file. What would you like it to say?

3. When you've got all the information entered, click OK to close the dialog box. There's your link! And there's your new file! Open the original file, and you'll see that the link has been added as a simple text link after all other page content. If you keep repeating this process, you can build an entire website starting from one lowly home page—and all without ever leaving the Site Map view.

Changing Links

You've created your site, and you've linked several pages to the gallery.html page. But then you have a brainstorm and decide that those pages should link to the slideshow.html page instead. Are you in for an afternoon of opening files and changing link field information? No! With Dreamweaver, you can modify what links point to either individually or all at once across the site—again, all without opening a single file.

The Change Link Command

To change all links in a site that point to one page, and to make them point to another page instead, follow these steps:

1. Select the linked page that you want to modify. The linked page is the page you navigate *to*, not *from*. (In the example cited previously, this would be the gallery.html page.)

2. Choose Site > Change Link from the Site panel menu bar. This brings up the Select HTML File dialog box.

3. Select the new file that you want your site's links to point to. (In the previous example, this would be the slideshow.html page.) When you're done, click Select.

4. The Update Files dialog box appears, displaying a list of all the files in the site that should be updated. To change all links and close the dialog box, click Update.

The Change Links Sitewide Command

The Change Links Sitewide command operates in much the same fashion as the Change Links command, but with a few crucial differences. As with the preceding command, its purpose is to change all links within a site that point to one file so that they point to another file instead. To use this command, do the following:

1. (Optional) Select the linked page that you want to modify. The linked page is the page you navigate *to*, not *from* (the gallery.html page, in the previous example).

2. Choose Site > Change Links Sitewide.

3. When the Change Links Sitewide dialog box appears (see Figure 17.12), enter the following information:

FIGURE 17.12

The Change Links Sitewide dialog box.

4. Click OK to close the dialog box.

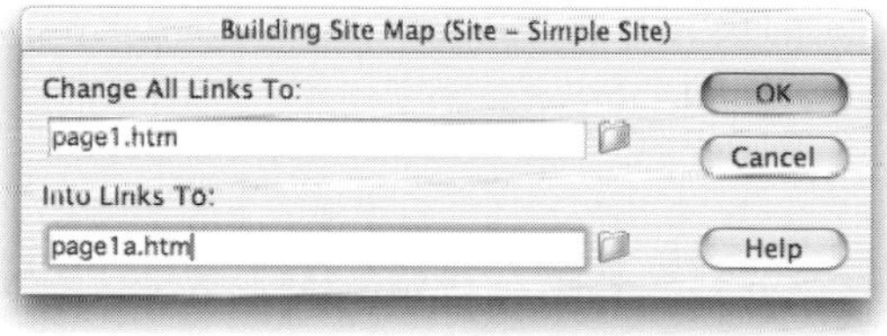

- **Change All Links To**—If you selected a file before choosing the command, this information will be filled in for you. Otherwise, enter the link here.

- **Into Links To**—Enter the new link that you want to replace the old link with (in the previous example, the slideshow.html page).

4. Click OK to close the dialog box.

5. The Update Files dialog box appears, displaying a list of all the files in the site that should be updated. To change all links and close the dialog box, click Update.

How is the Change Links Sitewide command different from the Change Links command? The purpose of Change Links is to recalculate the document-relative links between two documents in your site, and that's all the command does. Change Links Sitewide is more of a straight Find and Replace command, simply replacing the href attribute for certain links from one value to another. This has the following ramifications:

- Change Links Sitewide can be used only with absolute or root-relative links, not document-relative links. If you browse to choose a link for the Change Links Sitewide dialog box, Dreamweaver calculates that link's root-relative URL. If you type in a document-relative link, you get an error message. If you want to change all references to a document within your site and you're not using root-relative paths, use Change Links.

For more on root-relative versus document-relative links, see the section "How Links Work in the Browser" in Chapter 6, "Links and Navigation."

- Change Links can be used to change only links that point to documents. Change Links Sitewide can be used to change any href attribute into any other href attribute. For instance, you can update mailto: links when your email address changes, or change all null links from # to the safer javascript:; with Change Links Sitewide. Any time you're changing links that are not document-relative links within your site, use Change Links Sitewide.

Checking and Repairing Links

In the next few sections, you will learn how to check all of your links with Dreamweaver. Then you'll see how to fix any errors it finds.

Checking Links

You can check links one file at a time, check several files or folders at a time, or check the entire site in one massive sweep. The Dreamweaver Check Links function reports three types of possible problems:

- **Broken links**—These are files that have links located internally that don't contain the proper path for the link to work correctly. This means that Dreamweaver could not find internal links referenced on pages of your site.

- **External links**—External links are perhaps the most notorious for creating broken images and the dreaded "Error 404: File not found" message. These are files that are located outside your site (and look like http://www.somesite.com). External links are displayed so that you are aware of the possible problems associated with them. Note that a link on the external links list does not mean that the link is broken; it simply means that it's beyond the scope of Dreamweaver's link-management system to check these links.

- **Orphaned files**—These are files that have no incoming links pointing to them. In other words, these are files in which there is no navigation to get to them. Typically these files are older versions and aren't in use anymore. However, you can't just assume that all orphaned files are not used. Be careful to make sure that orphaned files aren't necessary before deleting them.

Whether you check all of your site's files simultaneously or check only one or two files as needed, the procedure is basically the same.

To check your site's links all at once, do this:

1. Save all open documents.

2. Choose Site > Check Links Sitewide, or right-click any file or folder in the Site Files list and choose Check Links > Entire Site from the contextual menu.

To check links for only a few files in the site, do this:

1. Save and close all open documents.

2. In the Site Files list or site map, select the file(s) that you want to check. Shift-click or Ctrl/Cmd-click to select multiple files.

3. Right-click any selected file and, from the contextual menu, choose Check Links > Selected Files/Folders.

To check links for only one document, do this:

1. Open the document you want to check, and save it, if needed.

2. Choose File > Check Page > Check Links.

Whichever method you choose, Dreamweaver checks your links and then shows you the results by opening the Results window with the Link Checker tab displayed (see Figure 17.13). Using the drop-down menu at the top of this window, you can view any of the three types of links reported (broken links, external links, or orphaned files). On the left side of the window, the file that has the problematic link is displayed. To the right is the specific link with which Dreamweaver is having a problem. The Orphaned Files section doesn't have a second column because no link is associated with it.

FIGURE 17.13
The Results window
showing the results
of checking links
across a site.

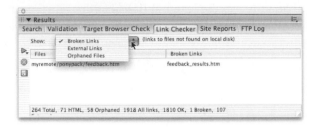

From here, you can either close the Results/Link Checker window or save the list as a tab-delimited text file. This saves all three link types as one file. You can then import the list into a page by using the Tabular Data object (from the Layout Insert bar), or import the text file into a word processor to be printed for reference.

Fixing Links

Two methods exist for fixing broken and external links (if they actually need fixing). Both are accessed via the Results/Link Checker window.

The first method is to double-click the filename of the file with the broken or external link. This opens the file in a Document window and highlights the suspect link. If your Property Inspector is open, the link also is highlighted in the Link or Src sections of this Inspector. You can then manually type the correct reference, or use the folder icon or Point-to-File icon to select the correct file that you want to link to.

The second method is probably quicker and easier, if you know your site well. From the Link Checker window, click once on the link in question in the right column. This makes the link manually editable (see Figure 17.14). If you're currently troubleshooting the broken links section, a folder icon appears that enables you to easily browse to the correct link. If there are other broken links with the same reference, Dreamweaver asks you if it should update them as well. Now, could that be any easier?

FIGURE 17.14
Fixing a broken link
with the Results
window.

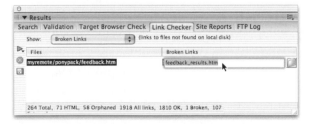

If you are using the file Check In/Check Out system on your site, Dreamweaver attempts to check out the file so that it can change the link. If it cannot do so, Dreamweaver displays a warning message and leaves the link as broken. For more on Check In/Check Out, read Chapter 19, "Workplace Collaboration."

EXERCISE 17.1

Manage Files and Links in a Dreamweaver Site

In this exercise, you'll define a local site and use the Site panel to manage its files. You'll rearrange your file structure, allowing Dreamweaver to update links for you. You'll create new files and folders. And you'll see how to use the Site panel to add links, correct links, and change links.

Before you start, download the **chapter_17** folder from the book's website at www.peachpit.com to your hard drive.

1. Start by defining a Dreamweaver site. Choose Site > Manage Sites and click the New button in the Manage Sites dialog box. When the Site Definition dialog box appears, bring the Advanced tab to the front. Make sure the Local Information category is selected. Name the site eBooks Site. (Note that the site name contains a space, which is perfectly legal for this purpose.) For the local root folder, browse to the **chapter_17** folder on your hard drive. Figure 17.15 shows the Site Definition dialog box with settings in place. Click OK to close the dialog box and create the site.

    The Site panel now shows the site files list for the eBooks site (see Figure 17.16). Have you noticed that the organization of files within the eBooks site is not too good? This is what's called a *flat structure*—all the files are loose in the main folder. That's not too easy for finding things. You want to create an images folder in the local root folder and put all of your images in there. But you don't want to break the links when you do so.

2. In the Site Files pane of the Site panel, select the folder icon that represents your local root folder (it's the one at the top of the list). Right-click on this folder to access the contextual menu, and choose New Folder.

FIGURE 17.15
The Site Definition window for setting up the eBooks site.

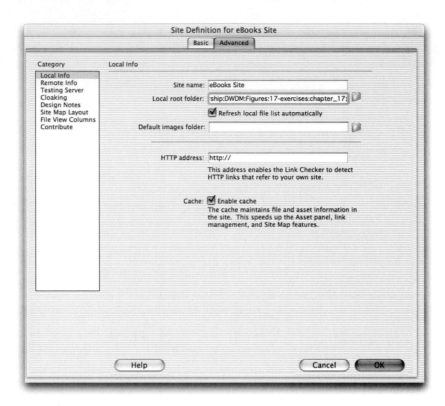

FIGURE 17.16
The Site panel for the eBooks site.

3. A new untitled folder appears in your site list, with its name selected and ready to change. Rename the folder as **images**.

4. Now it's time to move all of your image files into that folder. To make this job as easy as possible, expand the Site panel and, from the column names at the top of the panel click, the Type column. This arranges your files by type. Now all of your images (type: GIF) are displayed together in the list.

5. Select the top image in the list. Then Shift-click to select the bottom image in the list. Release the Shift key and drag the selected images into the images folder. Dreamweaver asks if you want to update your files. Click Update. After a few seconds, your images are moved. (See Figure 17.17.)

6. To test this, double-click the **index.htm** file to open it. When the home page opens, all the images still display. Select any image and examine the Src field of the Image Property Inspector. The src attribute includes the images folder as part of the relative path, indicating that the image is in an images subfolder.

FIGURE 17.17
The eBooks site with all images moved to a special images folder.

7. Now it's time for some link management. Open index.htm, if it's not already open, and choose Preview in Browser. Notice that, in the browser, you can navigate to any of the three subpages, but after you're there, you can't navigate back home. That's a definite limitation.

8. Back in Dreamweaver, close all open files. (Never perform file-management chores that will alter file contents when files are open!) Expand the Site panel so that both left and right sides are visible, and press the Site Map button to view the map in the pane that doesn't show the Site Files List (see Figure 17.18). This will probably be the left pane.

FIGURE 17.18
The expanded Site panel, showing the site map for eBooks.

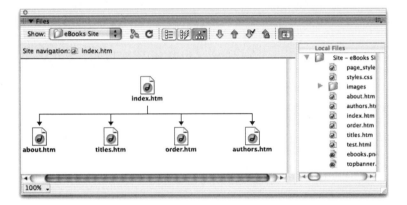

9. In the site map, select **about.htm**. Note that when the file is selected, the point to file icon appears next to it. Press down on that icon and drag back up to index.htm. When you let go of the mouse (if you were on top of index.htm when you let go), a new link appears under about.htm.

10. Repeat this same procedure to add links from **titles.htm, order.htm**, and **authors.htm** back to the home page. Then add links from each of the three subpages to each other. This creates a complete site-navigation system. When you're finished, your site map will look like the one shown in Figure 17.19.

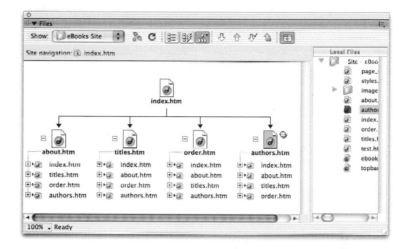

You'll also notice that it looks like you suddenly have a lot of pages in your site. If you expand all the plus (+) icons to view the entire hierarchy, your site looks immense! But you still only have four files in there. This is because the site map has no way to represent reciprocal links (such as two pages that link to each other).

11. After you've done all this, open **about.htm** and examine the new text links that have been added at the bottom of the page. There they are—serviceable, but not too pretty (see Figure 17.20). You're going to fix that.

12. Choose Edit > Find and Replace. In the dialog box that appears, set your options to match those shown in Figure 17.21. You'll be searching all the text in the current site for index and replacing it with Home.

FIGURE 17.21
Finding and replacing
the index links
with Home.

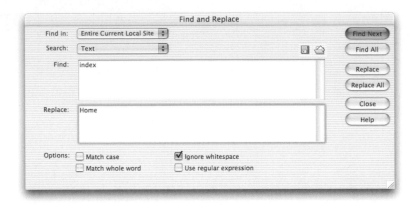

FIGURE 17.21
Finding and replacing the index links with Home.

13. Click the Replace All button. Dreamweaver warns you that this is dangerous because it's going to search all the files of the site, and you won't be able to undo its changes. For the current exercise, be brave and allow it to do so. When you're working in the real world, you might want to be more circumspect and click the Replace button instead, to change one instance at a time. Replace All is much faster but more dangerous.

14. Repeat this process four more times, changing titles to Available Titles, order to Check an Order, authors to Meet the Authors, and about to About EBooks.

15. When you've finished all this finding and replacing, open one of your pages and choose Preview in Browser (F12). How does your navigation system look and work?

ASSETS MANAGEMENT WITH THE ASSETS PANEL

The Assets panel keeps track of and enables you to easily update or insert certain elements used in the site, such as images, colors, rich media files (Flash, Shockwave, and so on), and scripts. This is particularly helpful if you plan to reuse one of these items on many pages throughout your site.

To open the Assets panel, click Window > Assets, or expand the Files panel group in your panel dock and bring the Assets tab to the front (see Figure 17.22). The panel consists of two main sections: the assets list (the lower half of the panel) and the display area (the upper half). Selecting an asset in the assets list displays it in the display area. Because assets are organized by *type* rather than by the hierarchical directory structure used in the Site panel, you'll only ever be looking at one type of asset at a time. To switch between different asset types, click the buttons along the left side of the panel. The types of assets are listed here:

- **Images**—These are image files such as GIF, JPEG, or PNG contained in your site. These are image files that are in your site folder, regardless of whether they are currently linked to a document.

- **Colors**—These are all the colors used in your site, including background colors as well as text and link colors.

- **URLs**—These are external URLs found linked to by documents in your site. These include HTTP, HTTPS, FTP, JavaScript, local file (`file://`), and email (`mailto:`) links.

- **Flash movies**—These are Flash movies found in your local root folder. Only the SWF files are listed here, not FLA source files or the SWT template files.

- **Shockwave movies**—These are Shockwave movies created with Director or Authorware found in your site.

- **QuickTime and MPEG movies**—These are movies in either Apple QuickTime (.mov or .qt files) or MPEG format.

- **Scripts**—These are JavaScript and VBScript files found in your site. Only independent script files are listed. JavaScript located in your pages is ignored.

- **Templates**—When used correctly, templates provide an easy way to build and edit similar pages quickly and easily. Before relying too heavily on template-based design, be sure to spend time learning them inside and out.

- **Library**—Libraries are similar to templates, in that you change only one instance to update many. These are typically small content elements that are used on many pages throughout a site, such as a company logo or a default navigation panel.

FIGURE 17.22
The Assets panel.

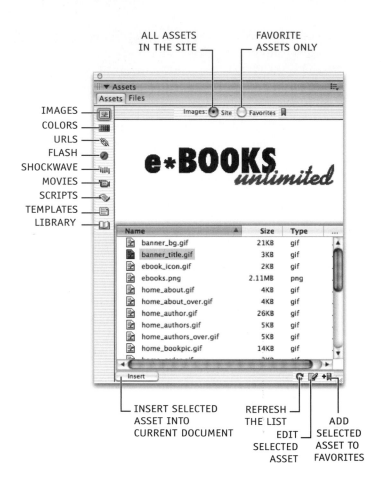

To learn more about using Flash assets, see Chapter 16, "Building Web Pages with Flash." To learn about using templates and Library items in the Assets panel, see Chapter 20, "Site-Wide Content with Templates and Libraries."

The site cache determines the contents of the Assets panel. If you have recently added a media element, color, URL, or other asset to your site, yet it doesn't show up in the Assets panel, click the Refresh button at the bottom of the panel to get an updated list of assets.

Inserting Assets

Why are assets so wonderful? For one thing, the Assets panel makes it easy to find and insert images and other assets quickly into your documents as you work.

Inserting Media Elements from the Assets Panel

Images and other media elements (Flash movies, Shockwave movies, and more) are the simplest to insert from the Assets panel. It's all a matter of dragging and dropping, or selecting and clicking. To insert a media element into a document using drag-and-drop, do this:

1. In the Document window, make sure Design view is active.

2. Open the Assets panel and click the desired icon to view the type of asset you want to insert.

3. From the assets list, grab the item you want to insert and drag it to the desired location in your document. Note that even though you can drag and drop an asset anywhere within your page, its final position within the document depends on the flow of content around it. Dragging an image into the middle of a paragraph of text causes the text to wrap around it. Dragging it to the right side of the page does not position it on the right if the page contents are aligned left.

To insert a media element using the Insert button, do this:

1. In the Document window, make sure Design view is active. Click to position the cursor where you want the asset to be inserted.

2. Open the Assets panel and click the desired icon to view the type of asset you want to insert.

3. In the Assets panel, select the asset you want to insert. Then click the Insert button.

Inserting URLs from the Assets Panel

Inserting URL assets is slightly trickier than inserting media elements because the URL must be inserted as the href for a link. To insert a URL asset, follow these steps:

1. Open a document and make sure you're in Design view.

2. In the document, select the text or image that you want to link to the URL.

3. Open the Assets panel and click the URL icon to show URL assets.

4. Either find the URL you want to apply and drag it to the selected item in the Document window, or select the URL you want to apply and click the Apply button.

Inserting Color Assets

In one way, color assets aren't quite as useful as you might think because they can't be inserted or applied to very many document elements. The only kind of page element that will accept application of a color asset is text—and when text is colored using this method, the color is added as part of a font tag (which has been deprecated in favor of CSS formatting). But used in conjunction with the Dreamweaver color picker and its sampling tool, color assets can be very handy indeed.

To use a color asset to colorize any page element in a Dreamweaver document, do this (see Figure 17.23):

FIGURE 17.23

Sampling a color from the Assets panel.

1. Open the Assets panel and click the color swatch icon to show color assets.

2. Open the document you want to work on, and either select the item that you want to colorize (layer, table, table cell, and so forth) or open the dialog box from which you'll be choosing a color (Page Properties, CSS Style Definition, or another option).

3. From whatever dialog box or Property Inspector you're in, find the color button and click it to activate the color picker.

4. Instead of choosing from the color swatches in the color picker, move the eyedropper cursor over to the Assets panel and click on the color asset swatch you want to sample. There's your color!

Your Favorite Assets

Your site's assets list contains every single asset in the site, including colors, images, and URLs that you might use only once in the entire site. Typically, as your site becomes larger, the number of assets in your site increases as well. When you begin handling a 30-page site, you can easily have 50 or 60 different images, if not more! As you can imagine, this makes the assets list rather cumbersome and slow to navigate through.

To solve this problem, Dreamweaver has favorite assets. From all the assets in your site's assets list, you can choose only those that you know you'll be using repeatedly and declare them to be Favorites. Favorite assets show in the Assets panel when you switch to Favorites view (see Figure 17.24). Not only is it easier to navigate a list of 10 favorites than a list of 100 site assets, but the Favorites view can even be organized into folders for easier and more logical access. This section shows you how to organize and use Favorites-specific features.

FIGURE 17.24
The Assets panel showing Favorite assets.

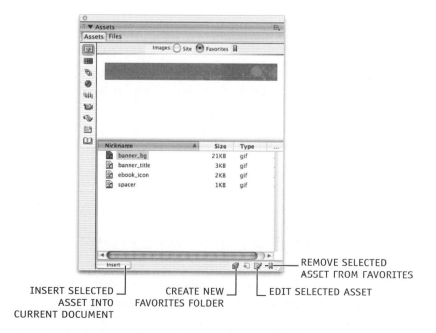

INSERT SELECTED ASSET INTO CURRENT DOCUMENT

CREATE NEW FAVORITES FOLDER

EDIT SELECTED ASSET

REMOVE SELECTED ASSET FROM FAVORITES

Viewing and Working with Your Favorite Assets

All of the functionality of the Assets panel can be applied to favorite assets just as it is to site assets. To see and work only with your favorite assets, click the Favorites radio button at the top of the Assets panel.

You can add a site asset to your favorite assets by doing one of the following:

- In the Assets window, select the asset(s) that you want to add to the Favorites list. Then click the Add to Favorites button at the bottom right of the window. This button looks like a plus (+) symbol and a purple ribbon.

- Select the asset(s) that you want to add to the Favorites list in the Assets window. Access the context menu by clicking the right arrow button on the upper-right corner of the panel. You can also bring up this menu by right-clicking on the asset(s).

Note that when adding text to your Favorites, Add to Color Favorites appears if the text does not contain a link; otherwise, Add to URL Favorites appears.

- In Design view of the Document window, select the asset(s) (or object) that you want to add. Right-click the object(s) to access the context menu. Select Add to [Asset Type] Favorites.

The Favorites list wouldn't be worth much if you couldn't change your mind and delete an item from the list. To remove an asset from your Favorites list, follow these steps:

1. Select the asset(s) that you want to remove from your Favorites list.

2. Click the Remove from Favorites button. You can also right-click the asset and select Remove from Favorites from the context menu that appears. Alternately, you can select the asset in the Favorites list and press the Delete key. You can remove the entire Favorites folder as well, which removes all the folder's contents along with it.

Assets that you remove from the Favorites list are not actually deleted from your site in any way; they're simply removed from your Favorite Assets list.

Grouping Your Favorite Assets

To reduce clutter even further, you can group your assets in folders. This enables you to keep images that are part of your main navigation in their own folder, while keeping other commonly accessed images in another.

Creating Favorites folders and placing assets inside them does not change the location of the actual file in the directory structure of your site. It simply offers an easy way to further organize your assets.

To create a Favorites folder and place assets inside it, simply do the following:

1. Access your Favorites listing.

2. Click the New Favorites Folder button located in the lower-right corner of the panel. You might also select the New Favorites folder by right-clicking the asset.

3. Name the folder and drag the desired assets into the folder (see Figure 17.25).

FIGURE 17.25
Creating a group of favorite assets.

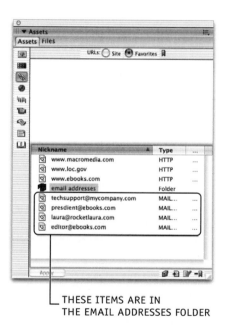

```
THESE ITEMS ARE IN
THE EMAIL ADDRESSES FOLDER
```

Customizing the Assets Panel

Like most things in Dreamweaver, you can customize the Assets panel in many ways. In addition to defining favorite assets (covered earlier), you can change the listing order of the assets. By default, the assets are listed in ascending alphabetical order (from A to Z) by name or value. You can change the order of the listing by clicking the column heading with which you want to sort. This sorts the assets ascending alphabetically by that column's attribute. Clicking a column header a second time sorts the listing alphabetically still, only in descending order (from Z to A). If you sort a column of numbers, such as file size, the ordering is sorted numerically rather than alphabetically, from smallest to largest (ascending) initially.

You can also change the width of the columns in the Assets panel. To do this, simply hold your cursor directly over the divider line that separates two columns. You will notice that the pointer changes to a double-headed arrow column. You can now click and drag the column to any width that you want. This typically holds true for most windows that use columns.

Using Assets Throughout Your Site

Dreamweaver enables you to use assets in many ways. It even enables you to copy assets and share them among various sites.

To copy an asset from one site to another, follow these steps:

1. Select the asset(s) that you want to copy to another site. You can copy entire folders of assets in your Favorites listing.

2. Click the right arrow button located in the upper-right corner of the panel.

3. Select Copy to Site from this menu. A submenu appears with a list of the possible sites to copy the asset(s) to. Choose one of these sites listed.

Selected assets are copied into the specified site and placed in folders that correspond to their locations in the current site. Any folders that don't already exist are created automatically. It's also important to note that assets copied in this fashion are automatically added to the other sites' Favorite Assets listings.

After the site on which you are working becomes rather large, you might forget where certain assets have been used. Dreamweaver will help you find them. If you would just like to find where a certain asset (or group of assets) is being used in the local site, follow these steps:

1. In the Assets panel, select the asset or assets that you want to locate.

2. Right-click to bring up the context menu. You can also access this menu by clicking the right arrow button located in the upper-right corner of the panel.

3. Choose Locate in Site from this menu. The Site panel appears, and the assets you searched for are highlighted.

The Locate in Site option is not available with colors and URLs. This is because these two asset types do not have files associated with them; they are simply strings of text inside files.

Editing Your Assets

The Assets panel provides an easy way to edit assets as well. This can come in handy when you want to edit multiple pictures but don't want to wade through the complex directory structure of the Site panel.

To edit an asset through the Assets panel, do one of the following:

- Double-click the asset name. This launches the default editor (as specified in your preferences).

- Select the asset and then click the Edit button found in the lower-right corner of the panel.

The type of asset that you want to edit dictates what happens next. With assets such as images and Flash movies, an external application is launched with the file in question open inside that program. In this case, simply edit the asset and then export it again to your local site folder, overwriting the older version.

If you are editing a color, you can get out of the color swatch box without choosing a new color by pressing the Esc key.

Colors and URLs will not launch a separate application. In fact, you can edit these types of assets only if they are in your Favorites section. Editing a color brings up a swatch box, where you can choose a new color. Editing URLs brings up an Edit URL box, where you can change the URL as well as the nickname that the Assets panel uses to describe the URL. Library items and templates are opened for editing directly in the Document window.

If nothing happens after you double-click an asset to edit it or use the Edit button, be sure to check the File Types/Editors section of your preferences to see if there's an application associated with that type of file.

Creating New Assets

Although you cannot create every type of asset from the Asset panel, you can create new color, URL, template, and library assets. (Image, Flash, and Shockwave assets are created outside of Dreamweaver.) You must be viewing your Favorites to create new colors and URLs.

To create a new color, make sure that the Favorites listing is currently being viewed, and select the Colors section. Click the New Color button in the lower-right corner of the panel. You can also use the context menu, either by right-clicking (Windows) or Ctrl-clicking (Mac) in the list, or by selecting the right arrow button in the upper-right corner of the panel and selecting New Color. This brings up a color swatch, where you can pick out your new color (see Figure 17.26). After you have selected a color, you can give it a nickname.

FIGURE 17.26
Creating a new
color asset.

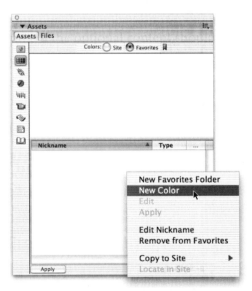

To create a new URL, make sure that the Favorites listing is currently being viewed, and select the URLs section. Click the New URL button in the lower-right corner of the panel. You can also use the context menu, either by right-clicking (Windows) or Ctrl-clicking (Mac) in the list, or by selecting the right arrow button in the upper right corner of the panel and selecting New URL. This brings up the Add URL dialog box, where you can define both the nickname and the URL path for this new asset.

Notice that any colors or URLs that you create in the Favorite Assets listing won't appear in the site listing until they've actually been used in the site.

EXERCISE 17.2

Managing Assets for a Dreamweaver Site

In this exercise, you'll do some more work with the eBooks site, this time working with image, link, and color assets.

1. With the eBooks site as your current site, open the Assets panel. Take a look at the image assets. This site has many images. Some of these images will be used only once in the site, while others you'll want to reuse. Select the ebook_icon.gif entry and press the Add to Favorites button at the bottom of the panel. Now change the panel view to Favorites. The next time you want to insert this image, it's a lot easier to find in here!

   Open **about.htm**. Wouldn't it look nice with a little ebook icon in the left margin? Drag **ebook_icon.gif** from the Assets panel to the left gutter area of the page (see Figure 17.27). That was simple! When you're done, save and close the file.

2. Now have some fun with link assets. Go to the URLs category of Assets. You don't see any entries here because the site doesn't contain any absolute URLs yet.

   You're going to add a new absolute URL. Open titles.htm. At the end of the page's text, create a new paragraph and choose Insert > Email Link. When the dialog box appears, enter the following:

   • In the Text field, enter **Contact our sales department for more information.**

   • In the E-Mail field, enter **sales@ebooksinternational.com.**

FIGURE 17.27
Adding an image
from Assets to an
eBooks page.

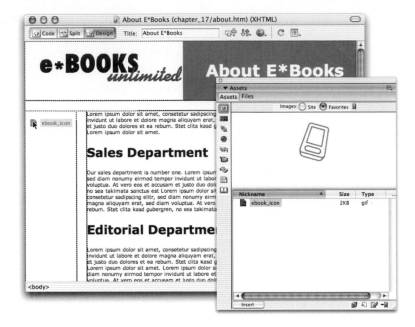

3. Click the OK button to close the dialog box and insert the link. Save and close the file.

4. In the Assets panel, your email link doesn't show up right away. Press the Refresh button at the bottom of the panel. The new email address appears (see Figure 17.28).

FIGURE 17.28
URL assets for the
eBooks site.

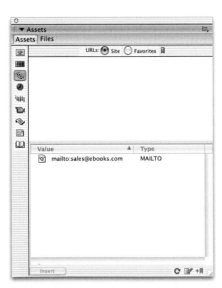

5. Now open **about.htm**. Under the Sales Department heading, the first sentence is about the sales department. Select the words `sales department`. In the Assets panel, grab the icon for the e-mail URL and drag it on top of the selected text. Then check the Property Inspector. The link has been added! Leave the file open when you're done.

6. Finally, try out the color assets. In the Assets panel, go to the Colors category. Two colors are used in the eBooks site, brown (#ce6b00) and white (#ffffff).

    You want to use that brown color for the subheadings on the About Us page. Subheading formatting is defined in a style sheet, so open the CSS Styles panel (Window > CSS Styles). Select the h2 style rule and press the Edit Style button at the bottom of the panel.

7. When the CSS Style Definition dialog box opens, find the color setting in the Type category. Click inside the color chip, and then move the eyedropper cursor over to the gold color chip in the Assets panel. Click again to sample this color. There's your color! Click OK to close the dialog box and check out your updated subheadings.

WORKING WITHOUT A SITE

New to Dreamweaver MX 2004, it's finally possible to work without a defined site of any kind. This is handy if you just have a one-off page that you need to build, and you don't want to have to stop and set up a site just for that purpose.

To work without a site, in the Site panel's site-selection drop-down menu choose Computer (see Figure 17.29). Instead of displaying a list of files in the local site folder, the Site panel now shows an expandable list view of your computer's file system. You can use this list to browse to any document that you want to open or insert. Dreamweaver won't insist that any of these files be in the local root folder, won't create absolute links for files outside any local root folder, and won't offer to copy files into a local root folder. Of course, you can't take advantage of any of the site-management features covered in this and subsequent chapters, but that's the trade-off.

FIGURE 17.29
The Site panel in siteless mode, showing the computer's file system and available servers connections.

SUMMARY

This chapter showed you the wide and wonderful world of Dreamweaver local site management. Before you ever even think of uploading your site to a web server for publication, all the behind-the-scenes work of file, link, and asset management has to take place. In this chapter, you learned how to use the Site panel—including the Site Files and Site Map views—to rearrange, rename, create, and delete files within a site. You learned how Dreamweaver can help you manage links across an entire site easily and painlessly. And you learned about managing media elements, colors, and URLs through the Assets panel. In the next chapter, you'll take your show on the road by publishing your site masterpiece to a remote web server.

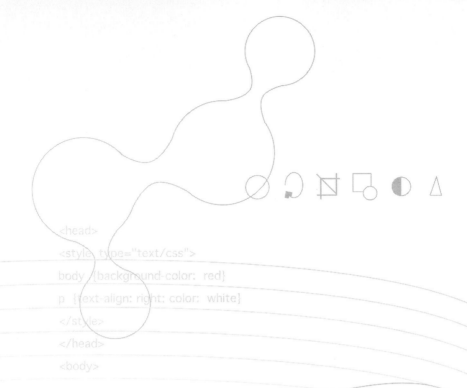

CHAPTER 18

SITE PUBLISHING AND MAINTENANCE

THE PRECEDING CHAPTER HELPED YOU SET UP A FOLDER ON YOUR COMPUTER in which to store all your files for your website. After you have the local root site folder set up, you will see that Dreamweaver MX 2004 has many tools available to help you make sure your site stays together, as well as tools that enable you to do site-wide searches and changes. However, no one but you will see the site while it lives solely on your own hard drive. You need to publish your site by putting it on a computer that anyone can access, such as a web server. This server might be for an internal intranet or for the Internet.

Where you put your site so others can see it is called the *remote site*. The remote site is generally a web server. If you are running your own server on your computer, the remote site can be as simple as another folder on your computer. In the long run, what makes your website a success (or failure) is what is in your remote site because that is what the world will see. Dreamweaver has many tools to help you keep your remote site updated and functioning properly. This chapter discusses how to define a remote site, including using various access methods, working with your remote site, uploading and downloading files, and keeping your local and remote sites synchronized.

HOW DREAMWEAVER WORKS WITH REMOTE SITES

Before delving into the remote site functions and features Dreamweaver provides, you need a basic understanding of how Dreamweaver thinks about your remote sites.

As you've undoubtedly wandered about on the Internet, you're sure to have noticed that the web page addresses typically follow a basic and, hopefully, intuitive naming scheme. For instance, many home pages, or default documents, are called index.htm. If you click to view a certain company's products page, more often than not, you'll be directed to the product's subdirectory. Not only does this allow for better organization and maintenance, but it just makes sense.

When you upload, or *put*, your website, Dreamweaver mirrors its structure as closely as possible (always with *few* exceptions) on the remote site. If you have a file called widgets.htm in the products subdirectory on your local site, after the site is published, you'll end up with a widgets.htm file in the products subdirectory on your remote site. Although this might seem rudimentary, this mirroring helps out in a few ways:

• Assists in making updating and maintaining your site easier.

• Helps prevent broken, orphaned, or otherwise incorrect links.

• Helps prevent multiple copies of a web page or image file. This conserves server space and, in some cases, the amount of bandwidth used.

• Adds to the level of professionalism your page exhibits.

• Makes it easier to understand and follow document-relative links.

In fact, to use many of the Dreamweaver remote file features, the local and remote site must mirror one another. Maintaining the file/folder structure is vital to maintaining all your links. This really isn't an issue, however, because Dreamweaver does this for you (including creating the required subdirectories) automatically with commands such as Synchronize, Get, and Put. Next, you will learn how to properly configure your remote site in the Site Definition.

DEFINING A REMOTE SITE IN DREAMWEAVER

As with defining a local site, entering remote site information in Dreamweaver can be done either in Basic (Site Wizard) or Advanced mode. The latter is more efficient—a little bit scarier for web publishing newbies—than using the Site Wizard and offers more options.

To define remote information for a Dreamweaver site using Advanced mode, open the Site Definition dialog box (choose Site > Manage Sites, or choose Manage Sites from the Site panel's site-selection drop-down menu). In the Manage Sites dialog box, select your site and click Edit. When the Site Definition dialog box appears, click the Advanced tab to bring it to the front, and go to the Remote Info category (see Figure 18.1). The only option available when you first view the Remote Info section is the Access menu. What you select here dynamically generates the remaining options. The following sections look at your choices here.

FIGURE 18.1
The Advanced Site Definition window with Remote Info selected.

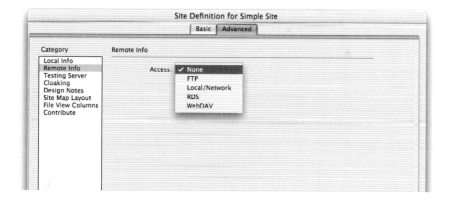

Specifying No Connection

Choosing None as your access method offers no options and restricts you from uploading your site via Dreamweaver. You also cannot utilize some of the advanced site-management features in Dreamweaver if you don't establish a remote connection.

Although having no remote access method established in the site definition prohibits you from using Dreamweaver to perform remote site functions (such as uploading your site), you can still do this with a third-party FTP client such as CuteFTP on Windows (www.cuteftp.com/) or Transmit (www.panic.com) on the Mac. If you're not familiar with such practices, however, it's recommended that you use the built-in remote site-management features of Dreamweaver.

FTP

FTP stands for *File Transfer Protocol* and is easily the most widely used method for uploading web pages to a server (see Figure 18.2). You will almost certainly use this method when creating other organizations' web pages. Similar to Hypertext Transfer Protocol (HTTP, the protocol used to transfer web pages over the Internet), FTP requires a client and server application. In this instance, Dreamweaver acts as the FTP client. Software on the remote server acts as the FTP server. If you choose FTP as your access method in Dreamweaver, the Site Definition dialog box asks you for the following information (see Figure 18.2):

FIGURE 18.2
The Site Definition dialog box ready to set up an FTP connection to the remote site.

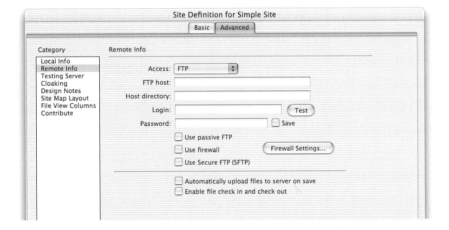

- **FTP Host**—This enables you to specify the address for the remote host of your web server. An example is ftp.remotehost.com or ftp.yourwebsite.com. If you don't know this information, contact your network administrator or host provider (ISP).

- **Host Directory**—This specifies the directory on the server where your uploaded site will be located. A directory on the server is just like a folder on your local computer. A lot of servers have the site root set as www.htdocs, or public_html/. If you are unsure about the host directory, leave it blank. This will default to the main directory of the FTP host. (Some hosts use the username/password combination to automatically direct you to the proper directory.) If there is an incorrect path in the host directory field, Dreamweaver might fail to connect even though your FTP information is correct, and you can connect with other FTP clients. If you are having trouble connecting, remove any value from the Host Directory field. After you can connect, you can verify the correct folder.

- **Login**—This is the username of your account.

- **Password**—This is the password used to authenticate your account and gain access to the FTP server.

- **Use Passive FTP**—Required by some firewalls, this enables Dreamweaver to set up the FTP session instead of having the FTP server do it. If you're unsure what this should be, leave it unchecked and ask your network administrator.

- **Use Firewall**—This dictates whether Dreamweaver should use the firewall preferences to connect to the FTP server. Ask your network administrator if you need to set these.

- **Use Secure FTP**—This enables you to encrypt your login information. It does not encrypt the files that are being transferred. To enable SSH on a Mac, Dreamweaver uses Putty, a free program that does the encrypting. You need to download Putty and install it before you can use the encryption. Go to the Dreamweaver Support Center (www.macromedia.com/support/dreamweaver/).

- **Use Check In/Check Out**—This enables Dreamweaver's versioning software and is discussed in detail in Chapter 19, "Workplace Collaboration."

You can set several more options for all of your sites' FTP connections in the Preferences > Site dialog box.

Local/Network

A local/network connection is used when the web server you will be publishing your pages on is located on the same local area network

(LAN) as you are. Often this option is used when developing a company intranet site or if you are providing the design and hosting for a site.

For this connection type, you must provide the path to the remote folder (see Figure 18.3). You can either type the information or use the Browse button to locate your remote site folder.

FIGURE 18.3
The Site Definition
dialog box ready to
set up a Local/
Network connection
to the remote site.

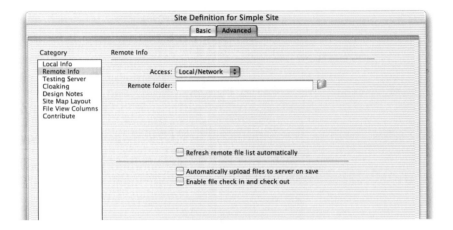

With this method of connection, you have the option of refreshing the remote file list automatically. If enabled, this causes Dreamweaver to refresh the file list for you (for example, reconnect to the remote folder and regenerate the list of remote files) every time files are added or deleted to the remote file. If you don't enable this option, you can still do this manually by clicking the Refresh button in the Site panel toolbar or choosing View > Refresh from the Site panel menu bar.

SourceSafe Database, RDS, and WebDAV

Visual SourceSafe, RDS, and WebDAV are all *versioning systems*—that is, tools that allow multiple developers to work together and keep track of files so that developers don't overwrite each others work. Visual SourceSafe (VSS) is a Microsoft program. RDS and WebDAV are *protocols* (like FTP), meaning that they are a set of rules used to communicate and track files. A protocol is a set of rules that computers agree upon to transfer files back and forth. These remote setting options are all just different ways of connecting to other computers and transferring files.

To learn more about Visual SourceSafe and WebDAV, and how they work in Dreamweaver, see Chapter 19.

What about the Site Wizard? In the Site Wizard (from the Basic tab of the Site Definition dialog box), remote site information is added in the Testing Files section. When you get to this screen of the wizard, you're asked "How do you connect to your testing server?" The answer to this wizard question gives Dreamweaver the information it needs to set up your remote site. The same basic choices are available here as in the Advanced tab of the dialog box, beginning with choosing an access method.

EXERCISE 18.1

Setting Up Remote Information for a Dreamweaver Site

In this exercise, you will set up the remote site information for the e*Books site. This is the site used in the previous chapter, built from files in the **chapter_17** folder on the boook's website at www.peachpit.com. If you haven't already done so, download the **chapter_17** folder and define a site called **e*Books**, with this as the local root folder.

1. Set up the remote folder. For this exercise, assume that your workstation will double as your web server, so your remote folder will be another folder on the same computer. For this purpose, create a new folder on your computer. Call it **webserver**.

In the real world, if you were going to use your own computer as a web server, would you bother specifying a local and remote folder? Why not just publish the local folder and not have to worry about any remote site? Even in this unlikely circumstance, you're better off defining separate local and remote folders because you can work on the local copies of your files while the general public is busy surfing your remote files.

2. Back in Dreamweaver, choose Site > Manage Sites. Select the e*Books site and click Edit.

3. This opens the Site Definition dialog box. Make sure the Advanced tab is in the front, and, from the categories at the left, choose Remote Info.

4. From the Access method pop-up menu, choose Local/Network. This adds a series of input fields to the dialog box.

5. The most important task here is to tell Dreamweaver where the remote folder is. Click the Browse button and use the dialog box that appears to navigate to your **webserver** folder.

Dreamweaver/Windows users must be inside the **webserver** folder before clicking Select. Dreamweaver/Mac users must be outside the **webserver** folder and must have it selected in the dialog box before clicking Choose.

7. You can also set your Local/Network connection options. Enable Refresh Local File List Automatically. Leave the other two options unselected.

8. That's it! Figure 18.4 shows what your settings should look like. Click OK to close the Site Definition dialog box. Then Click Done to close the Edit Site dialog box.

That's all there is to it! Now you are ready to rock and roll (and publish your site as well).

FIGURE 18.4
The Remote Info category of the Site Definition dialog box for the e*Books site.

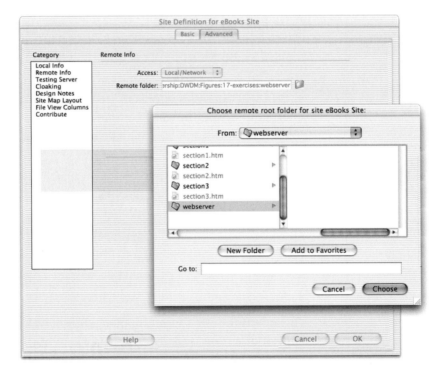

WORKING WITH A REMOTE SITE

For full information on the ins and outs of the Site panel interface, see the section "Working in the Site Panel," in the previous chapter.

When you've set up the remote site information in your Site Definition dialog box, you can interact with the remote server. This section teaches you the steps involved in basic remote site file management. More-advanced discussion, such as that on the Synchronization feature, appears later in this chapter. This section discusses two primary functions: connecting to and disconnecting from the remote server, and uploading and downloading files. Figure 18.5 shows the Site panel, with items relevant to remote site management highlighted.

FIGURE 18.5
The Site panel.

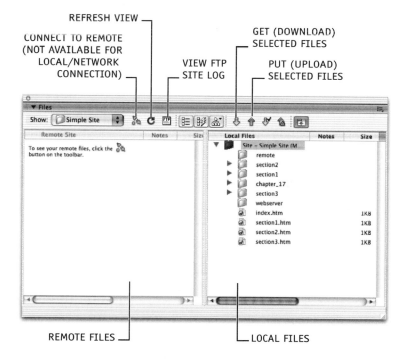

Viewing Remote Information in the Site Panel

When you expand the Site panel to show both its left and right panes, you have the option of showing the site map or the Remote File list in the left pane. To show the Remote File list, click the Files icon at the upper-left corner of the expanded window (see Figure 18.5).

In contrast to Dreamweaver, most FTP programs show local information on the left and remote information on the right. If you would prefer your Site panel to use this setup, open the Preferences > Site dialog box and reverse the order there.

Connecting and Disconnecting

The Connect/Disconnect button (see Figure 18.5) enables you to connect to and disconnect from a remote FTP server. This option also is available if you use a source control system such as SourceSafe or WebDAV. If you publish to a server located locally on your computer or your network, this button is grayed-out because you are automatically connected to the local server. This button also is grayed-out if you have not specified a remote FTP server in your site definition.

If you are using an FTP connection, you must select the Connect button to connect to the FTP server before moving your files from the local to the remote folder. When you connect, a green light appears in the lower-left portion of the Connect button icon. This lets you know that you're connected to the remote server, and it toggles the button's function to Disconnect. Pressing the button in this state disconnects you from the remote server.

If you experience problems connecting to your remote server (or perhaps if you just want to know what Dreamweaver is really doing when you press the Connect button), you can view the FTP log by choosing View > Site FTP Log from the Site panel menu bar, or by opening the Results panel (Window > Results) and bringing the FTP Log tab to the front. This provides a real-time client/server log of your FTP requests and responses. This also shows you how Dreamweaver creates directories, uploads and downloads files, and uses many other FTP commands.

 Macromedia maintains a TechNote that lists FTP commands and shows you how to interpret an FTP log. The address for this resource is www.macromedia.com/support/dreamweaver/ts/documents/ftp_errors.htm.

Getting and Putting

When you're connected to your remote site, it's time to either place your files there or download files from there to work on them. When you want to upload, or place a file on the remote server, it's called *putting* because you are putting your files on the remote site. When you want to download a file from the remote server, it's called *getting* because you are getting a file from the remote folder. In Dreamweaver, you can get and put by selecting the files you want to upload or download and doing one of the following:

• Click the Get or Put buttons in the Site panel toolbar (see Figure 18.5).

• Choose Site > Get or Site > Put from the Site panel menu bar.

• Right-click your selected files and choose Get or Put from the contextual menu.

You can also choose the fun but dangerous way: dragging and dropping your files from one site of the Site panel to the other.

When you put or get, if an older version of a file exists in the target location, it is overwritten. If a newer version exists, Dreamweaver warns you and allows you to cancel the operation.

When you select to either get or put files, the Dependent Files dialog box appears, asking whether it should include all files linked to inside the HTML documents. These files include images and other media content. Select Yes or No accordingly. You also might tell Dreamweaver whether it should ask you this in the future. If you decide to have Dreamweaver not ask you in the future, you might decide later that you would like it to. You can turn on this prompt again by going to the Site section of your Preferences and checking Prompt on Get or Put. If you decide to leave this feature hidden, you might force Dreamweaver to ask you on a one-time basis by holding Alt/Opt while selecting the Get or Put buttons.

If you press the Get or Put buttons without being connected to the remote site, Dreamweaver connects automatically, if possible.

Keeping Local and Remote Sites Synchronized

During your life as a web designer/programmer, you are sure to spend a late night or two trying to get a project done on time. It is possible that as the sun is rising and you are working away furiously, you might lose track of whether you have uploaded the most recent version of a document to the remote site. How can you keep track of the most recent files and whether they have been placed on the remote site? Dreamweaver offers two ways to do this: manually and automatically. The next section covers the old-fashioned manual method. Then the discussion turns to the powerful Synchronize command, which enables you to do this automatically.

Select Newer Local/Remote Files

You can use the Select Newer Local command or the Select Newer Remote command to manually synchronize your sites. This function compares the modified date on the local machine for each file with the modified date on the remote server for each file.

Select Newer Local

To select the newer files on the local site, right-click in the Site panel and choose Select > Newer Local, or choose Site > Select Newer Local from the Site panel menu bar. After Dreamweaver has compared the modified dates on both the local and remote sites, it highlights all the files in the local window that are more current than those on the remote site. From here, you can simply click the Put button, and all the files that are more current on your local site are uploaded to the remote site.

Select Newer Remote

If you are working as part of a team on a single site, it is possible that the remote site has a more current version of a document than you have on your local site. In this case, before you make any changes on a document, you should check to see if there is a more recent version on the remote server. You can do this by right-clicking in the Site panel and choosing Select > Newer Remote, or choosing Site > Select Newer Remote from the Site panel menu bar. In this case, the files that have a more recent modification date on the remote side, as compared to your local site, are highlighted. Then all you need to do to get the most recent versions is click the Get button, and they are downloaded to your local site.

The first time you upload your files to the server, you might notice that your local modified dates are not accurate. With the initial upload, Dreamweaver changes the local timestamp so that it matches the server time. That way, in the future, it can compare timestamps and calculate what files have been changed and should be synchronized.

If Dreamweaver cannot determine the timestamp on the server, you'll get a warning that synchronization can't occur. You can still get and put files, but you will be unable to find the newer files, on either the local or remote sites.

Because Dreamweaver highlights only files that are newer, those that are exactly the same (that is, those that have the same modification date and time) are not selected. If your site is already synchronized, no files are selected after running both of these commands. You might think that nothing happened, but it's just that the sites are already up-to-date.

Be aware that because Dreamweaver checks all the files of a site, the Select Newer Remote command could take a long time. This is the case if you have a slow connection to the remote server. Sometimes this might be mistaken as Dreamweaver "freezing." Be patient, especially if you are connecting via a modem.

The Synchronize Command

To access the Synchronize command, choose Site > Synchronize. The Synchronize command provides a much better way to synchronize your files than the method of manually selecting newer files. Part of the beauty and power of this command is that you can choose to synchronize as much or as little as you want. This means that you can synchronize just one folder, just one file, or the entire site. You also can choose to remove any file on the remote site that is not located on the local site copy, or vice versa. This is not possible with the previous (manual) method.

To synchronize your site using the Synchronize command, follow these steps:

1. Unless you want to synchronize the entire site, select the files you want to synchronize.

2. Choose Site > Synchronize. The Synchronize Files dialog box displays (see Figure 18.6).

3. From the Synchronize pull-down menu, choose whether to update the entire site or just the selected files.

4. From the Direction pull-down menu, select what you want to do from these options:

   • Put only those files that are newer locally to the remote site. (You will only send files.)

   • Get only those files that are newer remotely to the local site. (You will only receive files.)

   • Synchronize both the local site and the remote site with each other. (You will both send and receive files.)

FIGURE 18.6
The Synchronize Files dialog box.

5. If you select Get and Put Newer Files from the Direction menu, go straight to step 6. If you select one of the other two directions, you can specify one additional option. If you are putting newer files to the remote site, you can choose to delete remote files not on the local drive by checking the appropriate box. If you are getting newer files from the remote site, you have the option to delete any local files that aren't on the remote site. To select the delete option, check the box on the lower left. Remember that deleting a file is final and cannot be undone. Use this option with great care. The server often has files that need to be there, such as logs, scripts, and such, that don't have corresponding files in your local site. Similarly, you might have local files, such as PNGs, FLAs, and Template and Library folders, that haven't been uploaded to the server but that are still needed.

6. Press Preview. This processes your files for synchronization and opens the Synchronize window (see Figure 18.7). This gives you a preview of what will happen when you click OK, showing how many files are to be updated, the action that will be taken on that file (get, put, or delete), and the filename.

7. By default, all check boxes are checked in the Action column of this dialog box. Deselecting a check box removes the file from being processed. This enables you to ensure that you know exactly what is happening and lets you change what Dreamweaver does, just in case you know something that it doesn't.

8. Click OK to close the dialog box.

FIGURE 18.7
The Synchronize window showing one file needing to be uploaded.

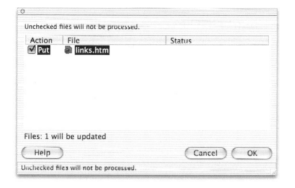

When synchronizing with the Direction option Get Newer Files from Remote, you can delete files locally that aren't found on the remote server. When synchronizing the other way, with Get Newer Files from Local, you can delete files on the remote server that aren't found locally. Be extremely careful with both of these options, however. For convenience, it is common to keep source files, such as Photoshop (.psd) files or Fireworks (.png) files, in folders within your local site that shouldn't be uploaded or deleted. Similarly, you might have necessary files on the web server (the remote site) that don't have counterparts in your local site—script files or website stats, for instance.

After you have completed the synchronization, you can see the actions that Dreamweaver performed. Dreamweaver shows the progress of the synchronization and, after it's done, enables you to save a text file of the procedure for future reference.

Cloaking

Because it is so common to keep assets in your local site folder that you never want to upload to your remote site, Dreamweaver enables you to cloak certain files and folders. *Site cloaking* enables you to exclude folders or file types in a site from certain site operations, such as a get or a put. Note that you can cloak file types, such as PNGs, but not individual files. The items that you choose to cloak are site-specific, meaning that each site on which you work can cloak different folders or file types. You can cloak folders or file types on either the local site or the remote site.

When a folder is cloaked, it is excluded from the following operations:

- Put/Get

- Check In/Check Out

- Undo Checkout

- Reports

- Select Newer Local/Select Newer Remote

- Check Links Sitewide/Change Links Sitewide

- Synchronize

- Find/Replace Sitewide

- Asset Panel Contents

- Template Updating/Library Updating

Disabling and Enabling Cloaking

The capability to use the cloaking feature is enabled by default. To turn it off, open the Site Definition dialog box (choose Site > Manage Sites, use the Site drop-down menu in the Site panel), right-click in the Site panel and choose Cloaking > Settings, or choose Site > Cloaking > Settings from the Site panel menu bar. Go to the Cloaking category (see Figure 18.8), and select or deselect the Enable Cloaking option. If you disable cloaking, all cloaked files will be uncloaked. But Dreamweaver won't forget that they were once cloaked. If you later choose to use cloaking again, previously cloaked files become cloaked.

FIGURE 18.8
Enabling cloaking
in the Preferences
dialog box.

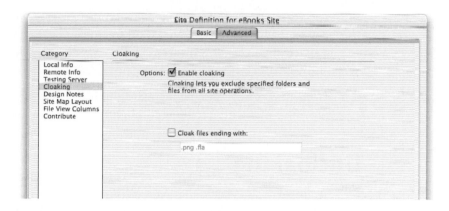

Cloaking Files and Folders

To cloak or uncloak a folder, right-click it in the Site panel and choose
Cloaking > Cloak, or select the folder and choose Site > Cloaking > Cloak
from the Site panel menu bar. A cloaked folder appears with a diagonal
red line through it (see Figure 18.9).

FIGURE 18.9
A cloaked folder in
the Site panel.

Cloaking individual files is a little different. Instead of cloaking a specific
file, you cloak a certain type of file, defined by its filename extension.
To do this, open the Site Definition dialog box (choose Site > Manage
Sites, or use the Site drop-down menu in the Site panel) and go to the
Cloaking category. Enable cloaking based on file type by clicking the
Cloak Files Ending With check box. By default, Dreamweaver offers to
cloak PNG and FLA files, the authoring files for Fireworks and Flash.

Specify the types of files to cloak by typing the three-letter extension belonging to the file type you want to cloak. Separate the entries with a space. If you don't want to cloak PNG or FLA files, just delete those entries.

From now on, all files belonging to the type you designated show up in the Site panel with a red line through them.

Uncloaking

To uncloak all cloaked files—regardless of whether they were cloaked by file type or by location—right-click in the Site panel and choose Cloaking > Uncloak All, or choose Site > Cloaking > Uncloak All from the Site panel menu bar. Dreamweaver makes sure you really want to perform this task by bringing up a dialog box that asks "Are You Sure You Want to Do This?" Click Yes. Now all files and folders are uncloaked, regardless of the technique used to cloak them.

EXERCISE 18.2

Working with the e*Books Local and Remote Sites

In this exercise, you will get some practice uploading, downloading, and synchronizing between the local and remote e*Books sites. Before going through this exercise, make sure you've defined the local and remote sites, as outlined in Exercise 18.1.

1. Make sure e*Books is the active site. Expand your Site panel so you can view both local and remote file lists at the same time.

2. To start, the remote folder for e*Books is empty. That's the way you normally start out when you create a new website. There's nothing on the server.

   To upload the entire site, select the folder at the top of your local Site Files list. This selects the entire site.

3. At the top of the Site panel, click Put. Dreamweaver will probably ask if you want to upload dependent files. Choose No. (Because you have all of your dependent files selected, it doesn't really matter what you choose in this dialog box.) Figure 18.10 shows the results of this.

FIGURE 18.10

The local and remote e*Books sites showing mirror structures.

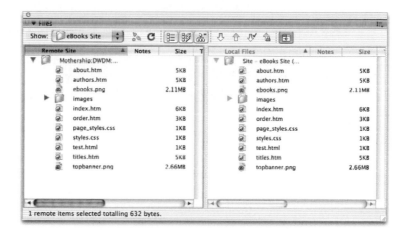

4. But wait! The site files include several PNG files that don't need to be uploaded to the server because they're Fireworks source files that are not actually used in the web pages. That's not good.

    First, select the PNG files in the list of remote files and delete them. Then open the Site Definition dialog box for e*Books (click twice on the name e*Books in the Site panel's site selection drop-down menu). Go to the Cloaking category and choose to enable cloaking and cloak files ending with the .png filename extension. When you're done, click OK to close the dialog box.

5. Now you're going to test the Dreamweaver synchronization features by altering a few of the local files and seeing if Dreamweaver notices.

    From your local Site Files list, double-click **about.htm** to open it.

6. Add a subheading for Programming Department, with a paragraph of text beneath it. When you're finished, save and close the file.

    Now open available titles and add a few book titles to the list—your favorites, whatever you like. Save and close the file.

7. Right-click in the Site panel and choose Select > Newer Local from the contextual menu. Dreamweaver thinks for a split second and then highlights **about.htm** and **titles.htm** in the local Site Files list. Remember, the goal is to make the remote site a mirror of the local site. That's what synchronizing is all about.

8. Those are your two updated files. Now that they're selected, click the Put button to put them. (There's no need to upload dependent files.)

9. That was handy! Now, though, you'll try something a bit fancier. In the local Site Files list, right-click the local root folder and, from the contextual menu, choose New Folder. When the new folder appears, name it **pages**.

   Still in the local Site Files list, move **authors.htm**, **about.htm**, **order.htm** and **titles.htm** into the **pages** folder. (You're tidying up your site organization.) When Dreamweaver asks if you want to update your links, click Update.

10. Now try synchronizing again. Right-click in the Site panel and choose Select > Newer Local from the contextual menu. When Dreamweaver makes its selection, click the Put button to upload all selected files.

    How do your remote and local sites look (see Figure 18.11)? Are they still mirroring each other? No! Dreamweaver added a new **pages** folder and filled it with pages—but it didn't remove the old HTML files. Why not? Because it doesn't realize that you haven't created any new files—you've just rearranged existing files.

FIGURE 18.11
The e*Books site after manual synchronization—not quite perfectly aligned anymore.

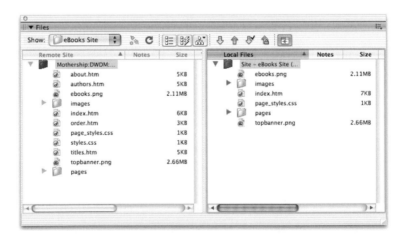

This is a good example of what happens quite frequently when dealing with local and remote sites. Slowly, over the course of editing and rearranging your files, old files start collecting on the web server; they're not doing any harm, but they're taking up vital storage space. Manual synchronization doesn't get rid of them.

11. Time to synchronize the automatic way! Choose Site > Synchronize. When the dialog box appears, choose to synchronize the entire local site, putting newer local files to remote. Enable the Delete Remote Files Not on Local Drive option.

12. When you've set your options, click the Preview button. Dreamweaver now compares the modified dates of the local site and remote site, and lists the items that are newer on the local site in the Synchronize window (see Figure 18.7). Notice that from this list you can choose whether you want to upload, or put, each item individually. This is an important safeguard, giving you every chance not to delete needed files from the server. For this exercise, don't deselect any files.

Also notice that the PNG files are not in the list of files to be uploaded. That's because they're cloaked.

13. Click Update. Now the list shows you that the extra files have been deleted and that the synchronization is complete (see Figure 18.12).

14. Click OK. Your synchronization is done!

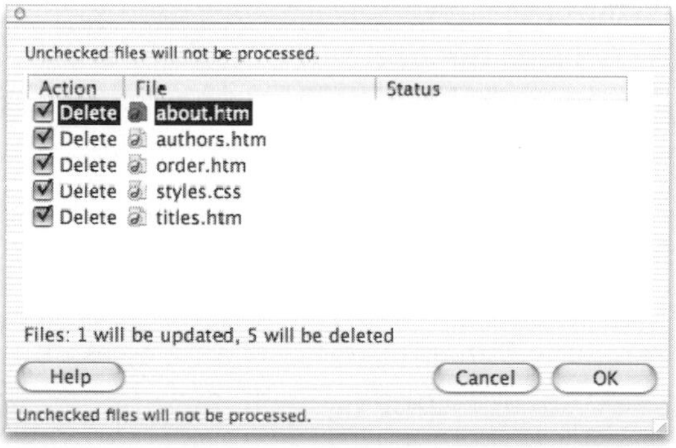

FIGURE 18.12
The Synchronize window showing the extra files that must be deleted.

WORKING WITHOUT A SITE: DEFINING REMOTE CONNECTIONS

The previous chapter introduced Dreamweaver's new siteless working mode for local development. If you don't want to work within a site, but you still want to upload your developed pages to a server, Dreamweaver lets you define remote connections without a site as well.

To create a remote connection, right-click the FTP and RDS Servers icon in the Site panel, or choose from the Servers menu in the Site panel menu bar (see Figure 18.13). The Configure Server dialog box appears. Give your connection a name that you'll recognize, and enter settings similar to those that you would add in the Site Definition dialog box's Remote Info category. When you're done, click OK to close the dialog box. The Site panel now displays a list of files and folders on the connected server (see Figure 18.14). From now on, expanding the server connection in the Site panel to show its files will connect you to the server, if you're not connected already.

To save a document to the connected server (essentially putting it), do this:

1. Open the document that you want to move to the server, and choose File > Save to Remote Server.

2. When the Save File dialog box appears, find your connection in the list on the left. This opens the server's folder structure. Select the folder where you want the document saved and click OK. This uploads the document.

To open a file from the connected server, right-click the file in the Site panel's list of server contents and click Open. This opens the copy of the file that's on the server—it doesn't get, or download, the file and open it locally. You can tell that this is happening by examining the title bar of the open document's Document window.

FIGURE 18.13
Defining a server
connection without
defining a site.

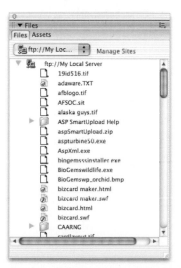

FIGURE 18.14
Accessing a con-
nected server.

SUMMARY

In this chapter, you learned how to define a remote site. You learned how to work with your remote site, including uploading and downloading files. Finally, this chapter discussed the ways that Dreamweaver enables you to keep your local and remote sites synchronized and up-to-date (manually and automatically), and how to exclude certain files from synchronization by cloaking them. The next two chapters expand your site-management horizons by looking at features aimed specifically at design teams working together on large sites.

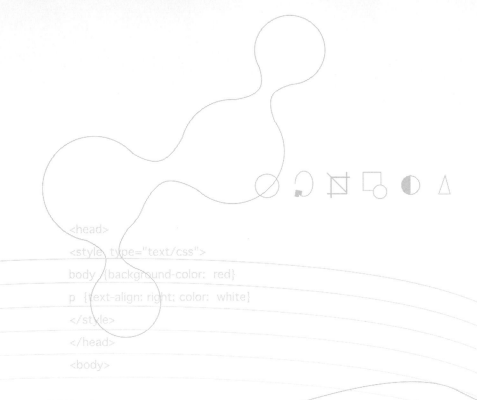

```
<head>
<style type="text/css">
body {background-color: red}
p {text-align: right; color: white}
</style>
</head>
<body>
```

CHAPTER 19

WORKPLACE COLLABORATION

SO FAR IN THIS PART OF THE BOOK, THE SITE HAS BEEN DISCUSSED MAINLY as a single-developer project. This chapter addresses difficulties that can occur when many developers are working on the same site. If you are always the sole developer of your sites, most of this information doesn't apply to you. However, some of it might prove beneficial or interesting, so you should at least skim each area. Topics discussed in this chapter include the challenges you face when working in a collaborative environment, how to use Design Notes to make managing your workflow easier, implementing and using the built-in version control system in Dreamweaver MX 2004, implementing and using other version control systems, and creating and using reports about project workflow. We will also discuss using Dreamweaver with Macromedia Contribute. Contribute is an easy-to-use website editing program for entry-level users. We will discuss how to use these two programs together on one site.

CHALLENGES OF WORKING IN A DESIGN TEAM

Often, designing, creating, and implementing a website by yourself is a daunting and challenging task. Throw in a group of people who are trying to accomplish the same tasks simultaneously, and you introduce a whole slew of potential problems and issues. Most of these issues can be categorized into one of two areas: technical or interpersonal.

Technical

Technical challenges are issues related to software (Dreamweaver or your web server software) and hardware (computers) that present themselves when you're trying to move from a single-user development arena to a multiuser situation. For web development, common technical issues include the following:

- Making sure that all developers edit the newest revisions and that their changes are immediately available for other team members to view and edit

- Making sure that some form of version control—either through the Dreamweaver Check In and Check Out or another method—prohibits developers from editing the same file simultaneously

- Providing a central repository that is accessible by the entire team where development files can be stored

Interpersonal

Interpersonal challenges are issues related to communication within the team. Functioning as part of a team involves more than just working on computers and going in and out the same door. People must work together. Communication is essential because misperceived instructions and ignorance of current information can cause disastrous delays and expense.

For web development, common interpersonal issues include the following:

- Making sure that all developers are suited to functioning in a team environment, which is different from being a "star" designer, off on one's own

- Making sure that all developers communicate regularly and understand each others' communications

SHARING SITE INFORMATION

When working on a site with many developers, it is obvious and important that you need to make sure that everyone is working on the same set of files and using the same set of options. To help ensure that everyone is on the same page, you can use a Dreamweaver feature to ensure that everyone is connected and set up properly. Dreamweaver MX lets you import and export site definitions. This feature exports a site definition file that can be saved or shared with others. It can also serve as a backup of the site definition.

When you use a site definition file to share with others, you ensure that all the sites are defined identically.

To export a site definition, follow these steps:

1. Select Site > Manage Sites to access the Manage Sites dialog box.

2. Highlight the site you want to export, and click the Export button.

3. A dialog box opens, asking whether you want to back up your site definition or share it with others. The first option saves your specific username, password, and local root folder path. The second option does not include this information. Select the Share Settings option.

4. Click OK. A dialog box asks you to save the file to your hard drive. Give the .ste (the file extension for site definitions) a filename, and save it to your desktop.

You can now send this file to other Dreamweaver users. When the other users get it, they can double click it to automatically open Dreamweaver, and the import proceeds. Or they can go to the Manage Site dialog, click the Import button, browse to the .ste file, and click OK.

When the site is imported, they are prompted to establish the path to the Local Root Folder for their machine. This is the folder where the local copy of the site is kept. Users have to open the Site Definition and enter their login and password information if any is required. They also have to establish a Check In/Check Out name and email if this feature will be used.

USING DESIGN NOTES FOR IMPROVED WORKFLOW

Design Notes as they pertain to image editing are discussed in Chapter 5, "Working with Images." Customizing your file view columns using Design Notes is covered in Chapter 17, "Local Site Management."

The idea behind Dreamweaver Design Notes is simple: A *Design Note* is a small file that contains pieces of information about a document. That file follows that document wherever it goes (from your office computer to all the other computers in the office, and even to the web server itself if necessary). It can be accessed at any time by any design team member. Therefore, Design Notes allow you to leave notes associated with specific files for yourself and your coworkers. This means that you can track changes to documents, map their progress and history, or update and change a document's completion status. Although this chapter focuses on using Design Notes to save information such as file status for HTML documents, they can potentially store any type of information you can think of and can be attached to any kind of file.

How Design Notes Work

As mentioned, Design Notes are small files that are "attached" to a document that store designer information about the document (see Figure 19.1). The Design Note is not literally attached; it is stored in a **_notes** folder next to the document. The **_notes** folder is the repository for all your site's Design Notes.

Open this folder, and you'll see a selection of files, all named after various files from your site, but with the .mno extension added. These are your Design Notes files. This folder cannot be seen within the Dreamweaver Site window. The _ before the folder name makes the folder invisible to the Dreamweaver Site window, so to see this folder, you have to go to the site folder through the operating system file explorer. Design Note files are basically small XML text files. Open one of the files, either in your favorite text editor or in Dreamweaver Code view, and you'll see a chunk of XML code that looks something like this:

```
<?xml version="1.0" encoding="iso-8859-1" ?>
<info>
    <infoitem key="status" value="draft" />
    <infoitem key="author" value="Julius Marx" />
</info>
```

FIGURE 19.1
Design Notes as they appear in the local root folder structure.

Each piece of information about the parent file is stored as an <infoitem/> tag containing a key/value pair (status/draft, for instance). The first time a document needs a piece of information about itself to be stored, Dreamweaver creates the MNO file. After that, every new piece of information that needs to be stored adds another <infoitem/> tag. Dreamweaver, Fireworks, and Flash can all access and read the same Design Notes, which is what makes the tight integration between the programs possible. And when the site files are moved from one computer to another, the Design Notes are moved as well, so various team members can all access the same pieces of information and coordinate their work.

Enabling Design Notes for a Site

Before you begin using Design Notes, you need to set up basic Design Notes capability in your site. To enable Design Notes, follow these steps:

1. Access the Site Definition dialog box by choosing Site > Manage Sites, selecting your site in the Manage Sites dialog box, and clicking

Edit. Or double-click the Site Name in the Sites drop-down menu in the File panel. This opens the Site Definition directly.

2. In the Advanced tab of the Site Definition dialog box, choose the Design Notes category, as shown in Figure 19.2.

FIGURE 19.2
The Design Notes category of the Site Definition dialog box.

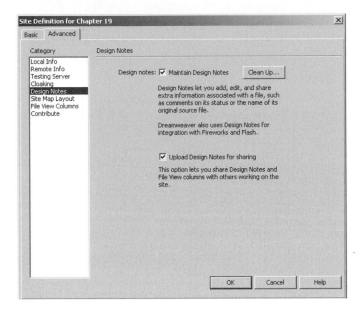

3. Check the Maintain Design Notes check box if it is not already checked. This allows Dreamweaver to start creating Design Notes. If it is checked already, you might already have some design notes.

4. If you're using Design Notes as a communication aid in a collaborative work environment, select Upload Design Notes for Sharing. With this feature enabled, every time you upload a document to the remote site, the file's associated Design Note is uploaded with it. This allows all team members who share work on a document or image to view its status quickly and easily and send notes regarding work to be done on the document.

    If you're using Design Notes only for your own benefit, in a single-user environment, leave this option deselected to speed up file transfer between local and remote sites.

Working with Design Notes

After you've enabled Design Notes, you can view, create, edit, and delete notes as needed to store any document-related information you like.

Accessing Notes

The main interface for working with Design Notes is the Design Notes dialog box. To access this dialog box, do one of the following:

- Open the file whose Design Note you want to work with, and select File > Design Notes.

- In the Site Files pane of the Site panel, right-click (Windows) or Ctrl-click (Mac) the file whose Design Note you want to work with. From the context menu that appears, select Design Notes.

The Basic Info tab, shown in Figure 19.3, contains a simple interface for assigning document status and jotting down comments to share with coworkers (or reminders to yourself). The All Info tab, shown in Figure 19.4, displays all Design Notes for the current document, including status, comments, and any other Design Notes (including those added automatically by Dreamweaver, Fireworks, or Flash for working with the document).

FIGURE 19.3

The Design Notes dialog box's Basic Info tab.

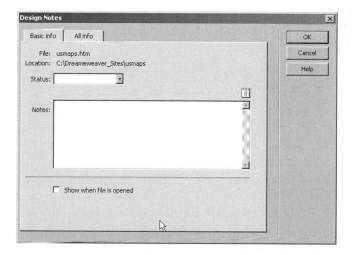

FIGURE 19.4
The Design Notes dia-
log box's All Info tab.

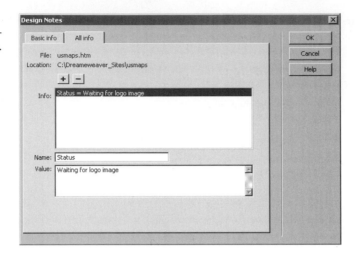

If the file Check In/Check Out system is in use, you need to check out a file before accessing its associated Design Note.

Creating, Editing, and Deleting Notes

When you are in the Design Notes interface, you can create notes, edit them, and remove them using the Basic Info and All Info tabs of the dialog box.

Setting Document Status

Labeling documents according to their current status (draft, revision1, and so on) is an important tool in a collaborative workflow.

To set the document status to one of the predefined choices, bring the Basic Info tab of the dialog box to the front, and choose from the Status pop-up menu.

To set the document status to a value not on the list of choices (such as Beta 1 or Beta 2), bring the All Info tab to the front. Click the + button to add a new note. In the Name field, enter **status**; in the Value field, enter your custom value (**beta 1**). When making custom notes such as status, make them clear to other users. It might be a good idea to have a defined set of values for everyone to reference.

Adding Comments

You can make miscellaneous notes regarding a document—instructions on what needs to be revised, peer review, whatever—by typing into the

Comment field in the Basic Info tab. To put a date stamp on the note, click the date icon above the Note field. After you've filled in a note, bringing the All Info tab to the front reveals that the note is actually saved as a name/value pair Design Note, just like status.

Adding Other Information

You can save any name/value pair as a comment by using the All Info tab of the Design Notes dialog box. For collaborative workflow, for instance, you might want to track authorship of documents, due dates, or task hours. To add any of these pieces of information, bring the All Info tab to the front, click the + button to add a new pair, and enter a name and value for that item. Check "Show when file is opened" to help ensure that the note is noticed.

Design Notes are great for job tracking because documents can be organized and searched according to the name portion of the name/value pair. If you want to use custom Design Notes for this purpose, however, make sure that you are consistent and predictable in naming your name/value pairs. For instance, it's no good trying to track authorship of documents across a site if some documents have a Design Note named author and others have a Design Note named writer.

Viewing Design Notes in the Site Panel

You can see at a glance which files in your site have Design Notes by examining the Site Files list. Any file with at least one Design Note displays an icon in the Notes column. If the Site panel doesn't display the Notes column, either because the column doesn't fit in the window pane or because the column is not enabled, you can change the File View Columns settings in the Site Definition dialog box so that this column does show in the expanded Site panel.

You can also customize the File View Columns in the Site panel to show the value of a particular Design Note. To do this, follow these steps:

1. Open the Site Definition dialog box for the site, and go to the File View Columns category.

2. Click the + button to add a column. The new column appears at the bottom of the list of columns.

3. In the Column Name input field, enter the name you want to appear the top of the column.

4. In the Associate with Design Note input field, type the name of the Design Note whose value you want to appear in the column (or choose from the pop-up menu of names).

5. Use the up/down buttons at the top of the dialog box to rearrange the columns' order if you like. Figure 19.5 shows the resulting changes to the Site panel.

FIGURE 19.5
The File View Columns category of the Site Definition dialog box showing rearranged columns and a new Design Notes column being added.

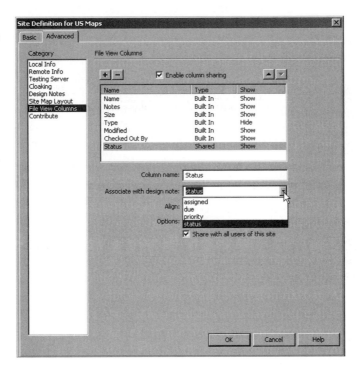

EXERCISE 19.1

Creating a Status Design Note and Viewing It in the Site Panel

In this exercise, you'll create status Design Notes for several files within a site. You'll set different status values and examine how Dreamweaver implements the Design Note.

Before you start, download the files from the **chapter_19** folder on the book's website at www.peachpit.com to your hard drive.

1. The files for this site are all in the **chapter_19/local** folder. Define a site called Chapter 19, with **chapter_19/local** as the local root folder and **chapter_19/remote** as the remote folder. (See Chapters 17 and 18, if needed, for more about defining local and remote sites.) In the Design Notes panel of the site definition, check both boxes.

2. With the Site panel expanded to view Site Files, examine the site's file structure. You see several HTML files.

3. Start by creating a note for **index.htm**. Right-click the file in the Site panel, and choose Design Notes.

   In the Design Notes dialog box that appears, make sure that you are in the Basic Info tab. From the Status pop-up menu, choose **draft**.

   To see that Dreamweaver is interpreting this note as a name/value pair, bring the All Info tab to the front. Dreamweaver has generated a name/value pair consisting of status/draft.

   When finished, click OK to close the dialog box.

   Notice in the Site panel that there is a small icon in the Notes column. This indicates that a note exists for this file.

4. To see how the Design Note has been saved as a Design Note file, use the file browser to examine the files in the local site's folders. You see a **_notes** folder, which now contains a file called **index.html.mno**. Open that file (it opens in Code view) and examine the XML code within. When you're done, close the file.

5. Repeat step 4 for **solution.htm**.

6. For the remaining file, **about_us.htm**, assign a new status called **approved**.

   Open the file, and select File > Design Notes to access the dialog box. Instead of choosing from the Status pop-up menu (which doesn't contain the word **approved**), bring the All Info tab to the front.

   Click the + button to add a new Design Note. In the Name input field, type **status**. In the Value field, type **approved**.

7. Click the top folder in the Local Site panel. Then click the Put button to upload all the files to the Remote site. If you're asked if you

want to put the entire site, click Yes. The Design Notes now show up on the other side, as shown in Figure 19.6. Other users can now download and view them.

FIGURE 19.6
The Site Files view of the website after you create and upload Design Notes.

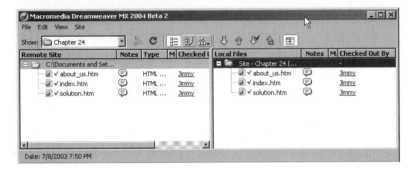

VERSION CONTROL

When you work with multiple developers, communication is important. Version control software can prevent miscommunication disasters. Version control software controls the editing of files by allowing a file to be edited by only one person at a time. It also ensures that everyone is working on the latest version of the page. There are a couple of different ways to ensure version control. One is to use Dreamweaver's built-in control system. Another is to install a full-fledged version control program on the server.

Server-Based Version Control

Dreamweaver MX 2004 continues to support source and version control systems such as Microsoft Visual SourceSafe (VSS) and WebDAV-enabled software—two large, complex pieces of administrative software that are installed on web servers to control workflow. These applications act like librarians sitting on the server. Anytime a team member wants to work on a particular file, she must "check it out" from the server, like checking a book out from the library. After a file is checked out, it still exists on the server, but no other team members are allowed to access it until the original member checks it back in. Just like a human librarian would, the server software keeps track of who checks out files and when, so team members and managers can watch the workflow progress by monitoring which files are being accessed.

If your web server uses either of these technologies, you can take advantage of its version control features while working in Dreamweaver by using special protocols to connect to the remote server, as defined in the Remote Info section of the Site Definition dialog box.

Visual SourceSafe Integration

Currently, only Windows computers can connect to a VSS server-side database. Windows users need to obtain and install the Microsoft Visual SourceSafe 6.0 client software on their computer before they can configure Dreamweaver to work with VSS.

Currently, there is no way for Macintosh users to connect to a VSS database. MetroWerks used to make a client that was used to connect Macintoshes to VSS, but it has discontinued that product. Current owners of MetroWerks VSS client should be able to connect with Dreamweaver MX 2004. To find out the latest on this, visit www.macromedia.com/support/dreamweaver/ts/documents/vss_on_mac.htm.

To set up Visual SourceSafe for your site (see Figure 19.7), follow these steps:

1. Open the Site Definition dialog box for the site, and go to the Remote Info category.

2. From the Access pop-up menu, choose SourceSafe Database. This is the method Dreamweaver uses to connect to the remote server.

3. The dialog box changes to present VSS options. Click the Settings button, which appears next to the Access menu. The Open SourceSafe Database dialog box appears. Enter the following settings:

    • For the Database Path, browse to or enter the path of the SourceSafe database you want to use. This is a **srcsafe.ini** file and is used to initialize SourceSafe.

    • For the Project, enter the SourceSafe project you want to use as the root of the remote site. Note that this field must contain $/, but anything else is optional.

    • Enter your username and password in the remaining fields. You can choose to save your password or require it to be entered each time you connect to the database.

When you're done, click OK to close the Settings dialog box.

If you're unsure of any of these settings, contact your system or network administrator for assistance, or consult the Microsoft Visual SourceSafe documentation.

4. Back in the Site Definition dialog box, choose the Check Out Files When Opening option in the check box if you want Dreamweaver to check out the files from the SourceSafe database when you double-click them in the Site panel.

5. Click OK to save these changes and close the dialog box.

FIGURE 19.7
Using the Site
Definition dialog
box to set up
Visual SourceSafe
integration.

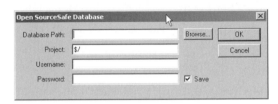

You now can connect to and disconnect from the SourceSafe database and use normal Dreamweaver file control commands such as Get, Put, Check In, Check Out, and Refresh.

WebDAV Integration

For more information
on HTTP servers—
how they work and
what they do—
see Chapter 21,
"Building Dynamic
Sites with
Dreamweaver."

Short for *World Wide Web Distributed Authoring and Versioning*, WebDAV is a protocol rather than an application. It defines additional HTTP methods and headers and is an extension to the HTTP/1.1 protocol. WebDAV can be integrated into HTTP servers such as Apache and Microsoft's Internet Information Server (IIS). Unlike VSS integration, to connect to a WebDAV server, you don't need any special client software on your computer.

To set up WebDAV integration for your site (see Figure 19.8), follow these steps:

1. Open the Site Definition dialog box for the site, and go to the Remote Info category.

2. From the Access pop-up menu, choose WebDAV. This is the method Dreamweaver will use to connect to the remote server.

3. The dialog box changes to present WebDAV options. Click the Settings button, which appears next to the Access menu. The WebDAV Connection dialog box appears. Enter the following settings:

    *   For the URL, enter the full URL of the site to which you want to connect. This includes the protocol used (`http://`) as well as the directory, if not just the domain root. *Important tip:* HTTP requests are usually routed by the server to port 80. If you want to use a port other than 80 to connect to the WebDAV server (recommended), append `:PortNumber` to the end of the URL— for example, `http://www.webdav.org:81` as opposed to `http://www.webdav.org`.

    *   Enter your username and password into their respective fields. You can choose to save your password or require it to be entered each time you connect to the database.

    *   Enter a valid email address in the Email text box. This is used on the WebDAV-enabled server to identify who is using a particular file. It offers contact information accessible via the Site panel.

    When you're done, click OK to close the Settings dialog box.

If you're unsure of any of these settings, contact your system or network administrator for assistance. You can also consult the WebDAV documentation or go to www.webdav.org for help.

4. Back in the Site Definition dialog box, choose the Check Out Files When Opening option in the check box if you want Dreamweaver to check out the files from the WebDAV site when double-clicking them in the Site panel.

5. Click OK to save these changes and close the dialog box.

FIGURE 19.8
Using the Site Definition dialog box to set up WebDAV integration.

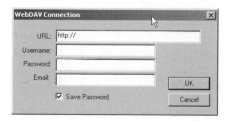

You now can connect to and disconnect from the WebDAV database and use normal Dreamweaver file control commands such as Get, Put, Check In, Check Out, and Refresh.

Version Control Using Check In/ Check Out

Unless you're working in a large corporation, you probably won't need the power of VSS or WebDAV. No matter where you're working, your design team might not have any say in the software configuration of the company web server. But you might still benefit from some sort of version control system.

The Dreamweaver Check In/Check Out feature provides a good, inexpensive alternative to server-based version control, along the same lines as that found in VSS and WebDAV, but without any server-based components. Similar to those other solutions, when using Check In/Check Out, Dreamweaver acts as a librarian, keeping track of who has accessed what files, and restricting the same file from being accessed by two different team members at the same time.

Although LCK files do not show up in the Dreamweaver interface, you can view them by accessing the remote site with another FTP program or Telnet window. Or, if the remote site is located on a Windows or Macintosh computer, and if you have local network access to that computer, you can view them by setting your system preferences to show hidden files.

Because Dreamweaver doesn't reside on the web server, like VSS and WebDAV do, it approaches this librarianship differently. When Check In/Check Out is enabled on the team members' computers, each member's Dreamweaver program treats the files on the remote server as a repository, like a library. To open files and edit them, users must "check the files out" from the server. When a user does this, Dreamweaver creates an invisible file on the server, stored in the same directory as the file being checked out and named with that file's name followed by the extension .lck. If someone checks out the file **about.htm**, for example, Dreamweaver creates a file called **about.htm.lck**. This "lock" file indicates that the file in question is currently checked out and should not be edited. When another user tries to open the same file using Dreamweaver, that user's program tries to check the file out, finds the LCK file on the server, and informs the user that the file is checked out. When the original user is done editing the file, he checks it back in, and the LCK file is deleted from the server. Other copies of Dreamweaver now recognize the file as available.

Note that because the site documents on the web server are not actually made read-only—they are just marked with LCK files that only Dreamweaver recognizes—only Dreamweaver considers the files locked. Other programs, such as other FTP programs and web editors, can open and edit the files. This means that Check In/Check Out is not a secure system. It presumes that all team members will play fair and won't try to access locked files while no one else is looking. This system is easily overcome by simply Getting or Putting the file. If Check In/Check Out is being used, everyone has to use it for it to work properly.

When a user checks a file back in, Dreamweaver makes the local version read-only. This prohibits team members from making changes to a file without "permission" to edit it.

Configuring the Check In/Check Out System

The Check In/Check Out system cannot be used until you have established remote site information in your Site Definition. This is because when you check out a file, you are doing so from the remote site (which everyone on the project has access to). Setting up your remote site is discussed in the section "Defining a Remote Site" in Chapter 18, "Site Publishing and Maintenance."

To set up your file Check In/Check Out options, follow these steps:

1. Access the Site Definition dialog box by choosing Site > Manage Sites. Select the site you want to modify, and click Edit.

2. In the Site Definition dialog box, go to the Remote Info category. Either FTP or local/network should be the access method used to enable file Check In/Check Out on your site.

3. Select Enable File Check In and Check Out. When you do this, additional entry boxes appear, as shown in Figure 19.9. Fill them out as follows:

    *   **Automatically Upload Files to Server on Save.** As it says, this option uploads the new version to the server every time you save. This might be a good choice so that you don't have to manually check in when you are done editing. But if you save the file frequently as you work, which is a good idea, this might not be a good option.

- **Check Out Files When Opening.** Selecting this option automatically checks out files whenever you open them by double-clicking them in the local Site Files list. If you open a file by choosing File > Open, you are prompted to check out the file or open it as read-only, even if this option is selected.

- **Check Out Name.** This is the name that is displayed in the Site panel next to any file you have checked out. This should be either your name, if you access files from only one computer, or perhaps a location, such as John-Home or John-Office. This helps you and others know who has checked out the file and where that person might be.

- **Email Address.** Enter your email address in this area. This causes your Check Out name to become a blue hyperlink in the Site panel. Other team members can then click this link to email you regarding the file. When they do so, their default email application opens with your email address in the To field and the file in question (as well as the site that the file is from) in the Subject line. I highly recommend that you use this feature of the Check In/Check Out system.

4. After you have selected your options, click OK.

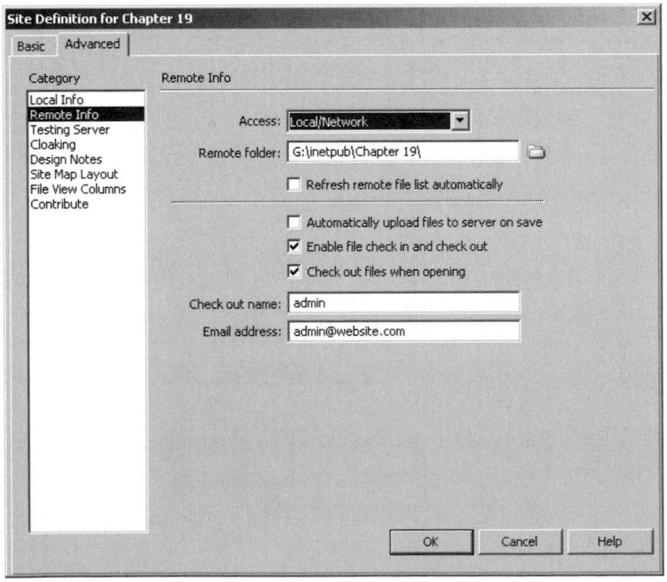

FIGURE 19.9
Configuring the Check In/Check Out feature in the Site Definition dialog box.

Check In/Check Out in the Site Panel

After you've enabled Check In/Check Out, the Check In and Check Out buttons in the Site panel become available, and the Remote and Local Site Files lists display information indicating their status, as shown in Figure 19.10.

FIGURE 19.10

The Site panel when Check In/Check Out is in use.

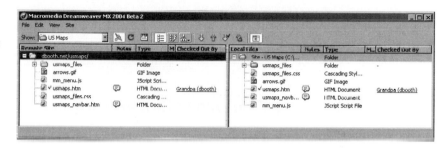

Checking Files In and Out

You can use either the Site panel or the Document window to check files in and out, as shown in Figure 19.11.

FIGURE 19.11

Site panel toolbars for working with Check In/Check Out.

To check files in and out using the Site panel, do one of the following:

- Select the file (or files) in the Local Site files pane of the window, go to the Site panel toolbar, and click the Check In or Check Out button.

- Select the file(s) in the Local Site files list, and choose Site > Check In or Site > Check Out.

- Right-click (Windows) or Ctrl-click (Mac) the file in the files list to access the context menu, and choose Check In or Check Out.

To check files in from within the Document window, do one of the following:

- With a checked-out document open, go to the Document toolbar and click the File Management icon. From the File Management menu, choose Check In.

- With a checked-out document open, select Site > Check In.

After you've checked in an open document, it remains open and editable, but the File > Save command behaves like File > Save As because the original file is now read-only.

Tips for Working with Check In/Check Out

As with any powerful organizational tool, Dreamweaver Check In/Check Out offers various handy options you can take advantage of, and a few pitfalls you can stumble into.

"Undoing" File Checkout

To "undo" a file checkout, select the file(s) you want to discard any changes to, and select Site > Undo Check Out. This differs from just checking the file back in because the original version of the file on the server is downloaded again, overwriting your local copy. You also can right-click the file(s) in the Site panel and select Undo Check Out from the context menu that appears. Choosing this action closes the files, discarding any changes made, and reverts to the version that existed before you checked out the file. It also sets your local copy to read-only and allows other teammates to check out the file.

If you check in the currently active document this way, it is saved (according to your preferences—see Chapter 28, "Customizing and Extending Dreamweaver") and then is checked in to the remote server. If you check out a currently active document this way, the copy on the remote server overwrites it, and any changes you made that don't exist in the remote version are lost.

Remembering to Check In

Many Dreamweaver users have a hard time remembering to check in files. They tend to just use the Put command instead. Although this updates the remote copy of the file, it doesn't check in the file and remove the checked-out status. If you forget to do this, you might get an email from coworkers wondering what's taking you so long with a file you were finished with two days ago. Also, if you use the regular Get and Put commands, you can overwrite files that have been checked out by others, which defeats the point of the system. Remember to use the correct command!

Unlocking Checked-In Files

After you've checked a file in, you no longer have access to it for editing because it has been set to read-only at the system level. But occasionally, you might need to edit these locked files. Your coworker might have checked the file out and gone on vacation, taking his computer with him. Or your company might have decided not to use Check In/Check Out, so you have disabled it on your computer (by deselecting it in the Site Definition dialog box).

Checked-in files can also be unlocked outside Dreamweaver. Right-click the file in Windows Explorer and choose Properties from the context menu, or select the file in the Macintosh Finder and choose File > Get Info. In Windows, turn off the read-only option. In Macintosh, deselect the Lock option.

To unlock a checked-in file, do one of the following:

- In the Site panel, right-click (Windows) or Ctrl-click (Mac) the file to access the context menu, and choose Turn Off Read Only.

- If Check In/Check Out has been disabled, select the file in the Site panel and choose File > Open, or double-click the file to open it. Dreamweaver prompts you to choose between viewing the file as read-only and making it writeable (unlocking it).

In Dreamweaver MX 2004, many of the menus have been streamlined and changed. There is no longer a Site menu on the Files panel when collapsed in the window. Right-clicking or Ctrl-clicking brings up the Site menu options. There is a Site menu at the top of the regular document view and also when the Site panel is expanded. The options in this menu change a bit depending on which view you are in.

Right-clicking usually brings up all the relevant commands for the area where you are clicking.

When to Use Check In/Check Out

So when is the Check In/Check Out feature ideally used? It is most often used in a workgroup environment where several people are working as a team on a particular site and plan to work on the same specific files or documents. It should (or could, at least) be used anytime more than one computer is accessing the files and changing them. This could even be a small office/home office environment in which you are the only person changing the site, but may do so from more than one workstation. It is also conceivable that you might take some work on the road with you via a notebook computer and you want to make sure that you or someone else doesn't inadvertently modify files from your work or home workstation.

EXERCISE 19.2

Checking Files In and Out

In this exercise, you'll work some more with the website created in the previous exercise. You'll enable Check In/Check Out and experiment with checking files in and out.

If you haven't done so already, download the **chapter_19** folder from the book's website to your hard drive. Define a site called Chapter 19, with **local** as the local root folder and **remote** as the remote folder. (See Chapters 17 and 18 for more about defining local and remote sites.)

1. To enable Check In/Check Out for the site, access the Site Definition dialog box and go to the Remote Info category.

    Select the Enable Check In/Check Out option.

    Select the Check Out When Opening option.

    For your Check Out Name, enter your name. (It's a matter of choice whether your team will want complete first and last names, or short usernames that will be easy to read in the Site panel.)

    For your Email, enter an email address.

    When you're done, click OK to close the dialog box.

2. Checking in and out involves working between the local and remote site, so expand the Site panel to show both sets of site files.

3. Files must be checked in before they can be checked out. Select all files in the Local Site Files list, and click the Check In button in the Site panel toolbar.

Note how all files in the Local site now have padlock icons next to their names. These files are now locked.

4. Check out **index.htm** by selecting it in the Remote site and clicking the Check Out button in the Site panel toolbar.

    This file appears in the Remote site and in the Local site with a green check mark by its name. You have checked out that file. (To all other design team members who access the Remote site, the file appears with a red check mark.)

    Your name also appears in the Remote site file list, in the Checked Out By column. Adjust the size of the Site panel and its panes, if necessary, until you can see this column.

    If you entered an email address when you enabled Check In/Check Out, your name appears as a link (blue and underlined). When you click it, your default email program launches, ready to send a message regarding the checked-out file.

5. From your Local site files, try opening **solution.htm** by double-clicking it. The file opens because you selected the Check Out File When Opening option when you enabled Check In/Check Out. If you look at the Site panel, the file appears with its little green check marks in place, indicating that it has been checked out.

6. Close any files that are open. Right-click the File Name tab in the Document window, and choose Close All. It's time to check in! In the Local site, select **index.htm** (it should still be checked out from earlier in the exercise) and click the Check In button on the Site panel toolbar. Its green check marks disappear, and a padlock appears in the Local site file. That file is checked in.

7. Now see what happens if you put a file without checking it in. Select **solution.htm** and click the Put button, instead of the Check In button, in the Site panel toolbar. The green check marks are still there. The file has been uploaded to the Remote site but not checked in.

8. Finally, see what happens when you disable the feature. Access the Site Definition dialog box for the site, and go to the Remote Info category. Deselect the Enable Check In/Check Out option. Click OK to close the dialog box.

9. Examine the Site panel. All the padlocks are still in place! Try to open one of the HTML files in the Local site. Dreamweaver knows that Check In/Check Out is disabled, so you aren't prompted to check the file out. But because the file is locked, you need to unlock it before you can edit it.

10. To unlock all the files in the site with one action, select all the files in the Local site, right-click, and choose Turn Off Read Only. All the padlocks disappear.

CREATING PROJECT WORKFLOW REPORTS

Workflow reports in Dreamweaver include information about file Check In/Check Out, as well as Design Notes properties. In this chapter, you will look at each workflow report in greater detail.

Before getting started, however, be aware that workflow reports require a remote connection to be set up in your Site Definition, and you must be able to connect to the remote site. If you are unsure whether you have done this, refer to the section "Defining a Remote Site" in Chapter 18.

Design Notes Reports

Running a Design Notes report lets you view Design Note names and values and search for files within a folder or site that have certain values assigned to certain Design Notes. You can run a general search to see *every* Design Notes attribute, or you can narrow the search to a particular Design Note or multiple notes. As with all the other reports, you can search a single document, an entire site, a specific folder, or the currently selected files (files selected in the local site).

To run a Design Notes report, follow these steps:

1. Choose Site > Reports to open the Reports dialog box.

2. In the dialog box, choose the scope of your search from the Report On pop-up menu (current document, entire local site, folder, selected files in site).

3. In the Select Reports section, make sure that the Workflow Reports category is expanded, and select the Design Notes option.

4. The Report Settings button becomes active. Click it to open the Design Notes dialog box.

5. In this second dialog box, enter from one to three Design Note name/value pairs to search for, along with the search criteria to use (contains, does not contain, is, is not, matches regex). The report being set up in Figure 19.12 searches for documents in a site whose status includes the word revision and whose author is Fred Smith. If your team has been using the default status choices, this search finds all documents written by Fred Smith whose status is Revision1, Revision2, or Revision3.

FIGURE 19.12
The Results window showing the results of a Design Notes workflow report.

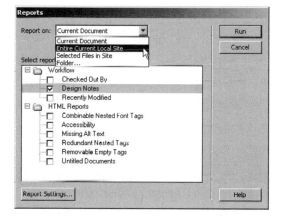

The matches regex search option allows you to perform searches based on regular expressions. For a discussion of regular expressions, see Chapter 27, "Writing Code in Dreamweaver."

6. After you've entered your settings, click OK to close the Design Notes settings dialog box, and click Run. The dialog box closes, and Dreamweaver performs the requested search and generates the report. The results appear in the Results window.

Reports on Checked-Out Files

Running a report on checked-out files lets you see who has checked out any file. You can run a general search to see *everyone* who has checked out files, or you can narrow the search to the files checked out by a particular individual. As with all the other reports, you can search a single document, an entire site, a specific folder, or the currently selected files (files selected in the local site).

To run a Checked-out Files report, follow these steps:

1. Choose Site > Reports to open the Reports dialog box.

2. In the dialog box, choose Entire Local Site from the Report On pop-up menu.

3. In the Select Reports section, make sure that the Workflow Reports category is expanded, and select the Checked Out By option.

4. The Report Settings button becomes active. Click it to open the Checked Out By dialog box.

5. What you do in this second dialog box depends on what sort of report you want to create.

   To generate a list of all checked-out files, no matter who checked them out, leave the text field blank.

   To generate a list of files checked out by a particular team member, enter the Check Out Name of the person you want to find (such as the name that person entered in the Site Definition dialog box when enabling Check In/Check Out). This search is case-sensitive, but you do not need to enter the entire string. If you are searching for files checked out by a team member named Jeffrey Stewart, for example, you can enter **Jeff**, **Jeffrey**, or **Stewart**. Remember that if you search for Jeff, multiple individuals might appear—Jeffrey Stewart as well as Jeff Daniels and Ann Jeffrey, for instance.

6. After you've entered your settings, click OK to close the Checked Out By settings dialog box, and click Run. The dialog box closes, and Dreamweaver performs the requested search and generates the report. The results appear in the Results window.

DREAMWEAVER AND CONTRIBUTE

Dreamweaver works hand in hand with Macromedia Contribute. Contribute is a program that allows website editing directly on the server. It is designed as a simple-to-use program that allows non-HTML users to add and update content on existing websites. It is limited to editing text, tables, and images. It can edit and make new pages from Dreamweaver Templates. With Dreamweaver MX 2004, you can control Contribute users, making Templates for them and controlling their editing permissions.

Contribute 2.0, which was released just before Dreamweaver MX 2004, shares many new features with Dreamweaver, including support for SFTP. Actually, they both share the completely new FTP client and Network share code. Transferring files should be faster and more stable than before!

For the Dreamweaver admin, this is the same as having other Dreamweaver editors (because you don't really care how the other files are being edited, just that they are). It's still important that everyone works with the latest files.

Between Contribute 1.0 and Contribute 2.0, a change was made in how Dreamweaver MX 2004 refers to the Contribute Administration panel. Dreamweaver MX 2004 users need to have a copy of Contribute 2.0 installed to administer Contribute sites of either version.

To enable Contribute compatibility, go to the Contribute panel of the Site Definition. Check the Enable box, and fill in the rest of the information. The Site Root URL is the path to the website's home page (or subpage, depending on the site). After you have set up the Contribute compatibility, you can enter the Contribute Admin panel and set permissions for Contribute users.

Luckily, Contribute uses the same Check In/Check Out system that Dreamweaver uses. When Contribute users make a connection to the website, they enter a username and email address that Check In/Check Out uses to track the files. Contribute also uses Design Notes to track the name of the file editor and when the file was edited. One difference is that Contribute users cannot add notes to the Design Notes, nor can they turn them off. They are always used and contain the same level of information.

When a Dreamweaver user first makes a connection to a site that has been set up for Contribute, he is asked if he wants to enable Contribute compatibility for the site definition. This means turning on Design Notes and Check In/Check Out. If you click Yes, the Site Definition panel opens. Fill in the Check In/Check Out information. Remember that your username should be unique for each machine on which you work. This goes for Contribute names, too. If you are working with both Contribute and Dreamweaver, use names such as Jim-DW and Jim-CT.

Dreamweaver users see the Design Notes icon in the Site panel from a Contribute-edited file. They also see the check marks, email links, and lock icons that indicate when another user is editing a file. Contribute users are notified if another Contribute or Dreamweaver user is editing the file.

For Dreamweaver users, this means that if Contribute users are editing the website, Dreamweaver users should enable Check In/Check Out. Again, it is important to use the Check In/Check Out system consistently.

Not only does Contribute work with Dreamweaver, but Dreamweaver can work with Contribute. This means that with Dreamweaver MX 2004 (and Dreamweaver MX with the 6.1 updater), you can serve as a Contribute administrator. This allows Dreamweaver to control and create Contribute user groups and create Connection Keys. A Contribute user group defines a set of users who have similar editing capabilities. For instance, with Dreamweaver you can control whether Contribute users can

- Create or delete new pages
- Use Dreamweaver Templates
- Add tables and images
- Create new content using CSS or HTML

Connection Keys are like automated site definitions for Contribute users. These files contain all the connection information needed to edit files with Contribute. Dreamweaver can create these Connection Keys through the Contribute admin. Because Contribute cannot create templates or CSS, using the two programs together is a perfect combination. All the administration features that are available in Contribute are available in Dreamweaver, through the exact same interface.

A full discussion of Contribute administration is beyond the scope of this chapter. More-detailed information can be found in the Dreamweaver Help Pages.

SUMMARY

This chapter discussed all the features in Dreamweaver for improving workflow in a collaborative environment. It is important to keep both technical and interpersonal requirements and considerations in mind when you're in an environment that has several developers because failing to do so will only lead to disaster. These features are used in multi-developer design environments and, for the most part, have nothing to do with problems or issues you'll run into when developing by yourself. This chapter informed you of such issues and helped you implement protocols for prevention and avoidance should you be in environments where they might occur. This chapter also introduced Macromedia Contribute and discussed issues with using the two programs together.

Hopefully, by keeping these collaborative issues in mind, your work with multiple developers can be productive and efficient.

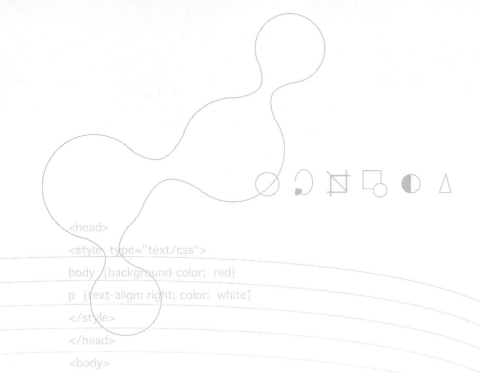

CHAPTER 20

SITE-WIDE CONTENT WITH TEMPLATES AND LIBRARIES

ALMOST EVERY WEBSITE HAS SOME REPEATED CONTENT. WHETHER IT IS A header with the company logo and tagline, a navigation bar, a footer with contact or copyright information, or other features, it's very common—and good design practice!—to use the same content on more than one page. But managing this repeated content is time-consuming and can lead to errors and inconsistencies across your site.

Working with Templates

A Dreamweaver MX 2004 template fits within the ordinary definition of the word *template* in that it is a page that serves as a pattern for others like itself. Even those who don't use Dreamweaver templates might create a template page and just resave it with a new name for each page of that type that is needed. However, Dreamweaver templates take the concept further, adding a measure of power and ease: The pages made from a template can be updated automatically, all at once, just by updating the template itself.

Therefore, a Dreamweaver template is an HTML page, but a special type of HTML page. Special code inserted by Dreamweaver makes it possible for the template and its *child pages* (the HTML pages made from the *parent* template) to be connected in such a way that an update to the template updates all child pages.

Template Basics

The basic procedure for working with templates is simple: Create a template page, including editable and noneditable regions; use the template to create one or more child pages, or apply the template to existing pages; update the template, and let Dreamweaver automatically update all child pages.

What Templates Are and Where They Live

A Dreamweaver template is an HTML document that has the .dwt filename extension and that lives in a folder called Templates in a site's Local Root folder. The file's name, minus its extension, is its template name. You can view and manage the templates for a site with the Templates category of the Assets panel, shown in Figure 20.1. Each template must belong to a particular site and can be used only from within that site.

 Don't move or rename the Templates folder! And don't move any template files out of this folder, or Dreamweaver won't recognize them as templates anymore!

FIGURE 20.1

The templates category of the Assets panel.

In addition to their HTML content, templates contain special markup embedded in HTML comments. This code is in Dreamweaver's template language and looks something like this:

```
<!-- TemplateBeginEditable name="doctitle" -->
```

Creating Templates

There are several ways to create new templates, all of them equally effective. To create a new template, do one of the following:

- In the Assets panel (select Window > Assets), choose the Templates category and click the New Template button at the bottom of the panel (see Figure 20.1). This adds a new **.dwt** file to your Templates folder and gives you the chance to rename it. To edit the template, select it in the panel and click the Edit Template button.

- Choose File > New and, in the New Document dialog box, choose Template > HTML Template from the category lists (see Figure 20.2). This creates and opens a new, empty file. The first time you save the document, instead of displaying a standard Save dialog box, Dreamweaver asks you what template name the file should have and what site it should belong to. The template is automatically stored in the Templates folder for that site with the .dwt filename extension.

• You can also turn any HTML document into a template by opening it and choosing File > Save As Template, or by going to the Common category of the Insert bar and choosing Make Template from the template objects (see Figure 20.3). Dreamweaver asks you to name the template and saves it in the Templates folder as a .dwt file.

FIGURE 20.2
Creating a new template with the New Document dialog box.

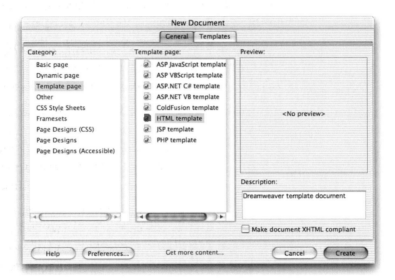

FIGURE 20.3
Turning an HTML document into a template with the Make Template object.

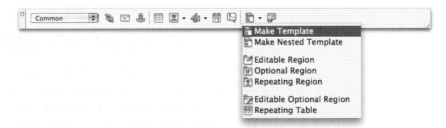

Making Regions Editable

When you build child pages from a template, all parts of the template are locked except those that you (or Dreamweaver) have specifically defined as editable. You generally want to leave things such as the title banner, navigation bar, and footer locked so that they remain the same on all child pages. You'll probably want to unlock the content area by declaring it to be an editable region so that each child page can have its own unique content. Dreamweaver automatically makes the page title an editable region.

To see how editable regions are defined, open any template page, go to Code view, and find the page title area. You'll see this:

```
<!-- TemplateBeginEditable name="doctitle" -->
   <title>Untitled Document</title>
<!-- TemplateEndEditable -->
```

The opening and closing lines surround the editable area. The name of this editable region is **doctitle**.

Any region in a template can be made editable by surrounding it with this code and assigning it a unique name. To define a region as editable, do one of the following:

- Put the cursor inside a table cell, empty paragraph, layer, or other region. From the template objects in the Insert bar, choose the Editable Region object. When Dreamweaver prompts you, give the region a unique name. You can get the same result by right-clicking inside a region and choosing New Editable Region from the context menu.

- Select the tag (such as td or table) from the Tag Selector or in Design view and choose Insert > Template Objects > Editable Region.

- If you prefer to do things manually, go to Code view, find the region you want to define as editable, and surround it with the code listed earlier. To create an editable region within a heading, for instance, you type something like this:

```
<h1><!-- TemplateBeginEditable name="main heading" -->
 
<!-- TemplateEndEditable --></h1>
```

Line breaks aren't crucial to the effect, so break lines wherever you like.

After you've created the region, it appears in Design view with a colored label. It appears in the Tag Selector as <mmtemplate:editable>. You can select the region for editing by clicking the label or the Tag Selector entry. The Property inspector then lets you change its name (the only property of editable regions).

Note that it's entirely legal to assign a block-level text element, such as a p, li, or h1 tag, to be an editable region. If you do so, every time you save the template, Dreamweaver warns you—as if you've done something stupid. You can safely ignore these warnings.

When you define the template, you can put any content you like inside the editable regions—maybe a helpful bit of text such as [title goes here]. Because this text is inside an editable region, you can overwrite it in any child page. Dummy text like this can help you visualize the design of the finished pages as you're working.

Working with Child Pages

After you've defined one or more templates, you can create new pages based on those templates or apply the templates to existing pages.

To create a new document based on a template, choose File > New. In the New Document dialog box, bring the Templates tab to the front. Choose the site you're working on, and the template you want to base your page on, and click OK to create the child page (see Figure 20.4).

FIGURE 20.4
Creating a new document based on a template.

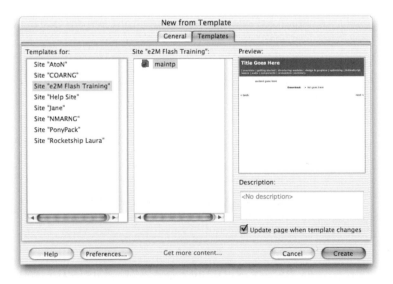

To apply a template to an existing document, open the document. From the Templates category of the Assets panel, select the template you want to apply. Either click the Apply button or drag the template to the Document window. If the page has any content, Dreamweaver needs to either put that content into editable regions in the template or throw the content away. You see a dialog box indicating what content exists in the current document body and document head (see Figure 20.5). As long as any regions are set to <Not Resolved>, you won't be allowed to continue. You must select each region and, in the Move Content to New Region drop-down, choose one of the following:

- Nowhere to delete the region's content

- Head for any existing document head content (keywords, scripts, style sheets, and so on)

- One of the named editable regions to put the content in that region

FIGURE 20.5
Applying a template to an existing document.

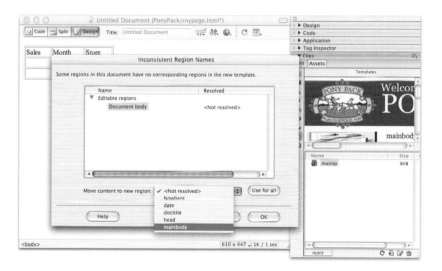

After you've created your child page, you can save it as normal (select File > Save) to any folder in your site. You can add or edit content only in the editable regions. While you're in Design view, the Tag Selector displays only tags within editable regions. Each editable region itself is marked as <mminstance:editable>. If you examine the document in Code view, you'll see that all noneditable code (code outside the editable regions) appears in gray. An HTML comment at the top of the page, and another at the bottom, indicate that this page is a *template instance*, or a child page based on a particular template:

```
<!-- InstanceBegin template="/Templates/main.dwt"
➥codeOutsideHTMLIsLocked="false" -->
  <html>
    etc
  </html>
<!-- InstanceEnd -->
```

Figure 20.6 shows a typical child page being edited.

FIGURE 20.6
A template's child
page being edited
in Code and
Design view.

Within the document's head section are two editable regions: the head region for head content such as meta tags, and the doctitle region for the page title. In Code view, they look like this (shown in bold):

```
<head>
<!-- InstanceBeginEditable name="doctitle" -->
  <title>My Web Page</title>
<!-- InstanceEndEditable -->
```

```
<meta http-equiv="Content-Type content-"text/html; charset=
➥iso-8859-1">
<!-- InstanceBeginEditable name="head" -->
  <script src="myscripts.js"></script>
<!-- InstanceEndEditable -->
</head>
```

If you're in Design view, use the View Options submenu to display head content. You see a blue box surrounding the page title, as shown in Figure 20.7. That's the doctitle region. To add other head content, such as keywords or other meta tags, you have two choices:

- Click anywhere inside the doctitle box in the Head Content bar, and use the Insert bar or menu to add head objects as normal. This puts the code for your meta tags and so forth inside the head tag in the HTML (so they'll work fine in the browser), but within the doctitle editable region. They don't belong there.

- If you want your head content inserted inside the head editable region (which is where it logically belongs!), you have to be a bit sneakier because the head editable region doesn't appear in the Head Content bar until you place some content there. Switch to Code view and place the insertion point between the opening and closing head region tags:

```
<!-- InstanceBeginEditable name="head" -->

<!-- InstanceEndEditable -->
```

Then use the Insert bar or menu to insert a head object. After you do this, the Head Content bar in the Document window shows a second blue box, representing the head region, as shown in Figure 20.7. From now on, you can place the cursor in that box and insert more head content.

FIGURE 20.7
The doctitle editable region within a child document's head section, as displayed in Design view.

A template isn't a straitjacket. You can open any child page in an editor other than Dreamweaver and change the locked code if you want to. But the next time the original template is updated, Dreamweaver overwrites your changes. If you want to divorce the child from its template parent, you can open the file in another program and manually delete the template comments, or you can open the file in Dreamweaver and choose Modify > Templates > Detach From Template. All locked regions are then editable, but the page no longer updates when the parent template updates.

Working with Template Pages

If you have more than a few child pages based on your template, updating might take a few moments. But you don't have to update every time you save. If you are in the (good!) habit of saving often, you can save time by updating only once, at the end of your editing session.

The glory of Dreamweaver templates is that they're updatable. As soon as you've created a template, you can open the template file and edit any content in the page's locked regions. Your changes are immediately applied to all child pages. To open a template for editing, you can select it in the Templates category of the Assets panel and click the Edit Template button (see Figure 20.1), or find it in the Templates folder in the Site panel and double-click to open it (as you would any file). When the template is open, you can make any changes you like to the areas that are not editable regions. You can also add, rename, or delete editable regions. Every time you save the template, Dreamweaver offers to update all child pages. If you've renamed or deleted any regions, and the template has child pages, Dreamweaver asks how content in those child pages should be disposed of. You can choose to reassign the child pages' content to a different editable region or to delete the content.

Uploading and Templates

When it's time to upload your site files to a web server, remember that you don't have to upload the template files themselves (the .dwt files in the Templates folder)—just the child pages. Two uploading habits can be helpful when working with templates:

- Use the Synchronize command (Site > Synchronize) to determine which files need uploading after editing. This guarantees that, after you've edited a template, all updated child pages get uploaded.

- Enable cloaking for your site in the Cloaking category of the Site Definition dialog box. Cloak the Templates folder by right-clicking it in the Site panel and choosing Cloaking > Cloak. Dreamweaver warns you that this doesn't work for batch site operations, but it stops the folder from being uploaded during synchronization.

Beyond the Basics with Templates

Editable regions and automatic updates are just the beginning of what you can do with Dreamweaver templates. Thanks to the template language (those special HTML comments in templates and child pages), you can use templates to generate complex websites that include optional content, editable tag attributes, repeating regions, nested templates, and more!

Optional Regions

An optional region is a piece of document content that exists in the template. You can choose to hide or show it independently in each child page. Optional regions are great if, for instance, some of the pages based on your template are long enough to require a Back to Top button and others aren't, if some pages require Next or Previous links and others don't, and so forth.

Creating Optional Regions in Templates

To define an area of your template as optional, open the template file and do the following:

1. Put the insertion point where you want the optional content to appear. If you've already created the content and just want to make it optional, select the content.

2. From the Template objects in the Insert bar, choose Optional Region.

3. When the Optional Region dialog box appears, leave the Basic tab in front and give your region a unique name. If you want the region to be invisible by default, deselect the Show by default check box. Otherwise, leave it selected. Click OK to close the dialog box and insert the region.

Check your document in Code view after doing this, and you'll see that Dreamweaver has added two sets of template instructions. In the head section, a template parameter is defined, named whatever you called your optional region, with a type of boolean and a value of true or false. Here's an example:

```
<!-- TemplateParam name="back to top" type="boolean"
value="true" -->
```

Your optional content is surrounded by more template code, like this:

```
<!-- TemplateBeginIf cond="_document['back to top']" -->
  <a href="#top">Back to top</a>
<!-- TemplateEndIf -->
```

This conditional statement determines whether the content should be included in the child page, based on the value of the parameter defined in the head.

In Design view, the optional region is marked with a colored label. In the Tag Selector, it's indicated as `<mmtemplate:if>`. If you select the region, the Property inspector lets you change its name. Or you can click the Edit button to reopen the Optional Region dialog box and change its default settings.

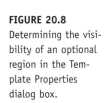
As with all template code, you are free to move these optional region delimiters if you discover they don't surround exactly the right content.

Using Optional Regions in Child Pages

As soon as your template defines an optional region, you can determine on a page-by-page basis whether the content shows. To do this, open the child page and choose Modify > Template Properties. The dialog box that appears lists any optional regions, along with a true/false value, as shown in Figure 20.8. Select the region name and select or deselect the Show [region name] check box to show or hide the region on this page. If you choose to hide the optional region, and then you check your document in Code view, you'll see that the code for this region is gone! If you choose to show it, and then check Code view, the code is back!

FIGURE 20.8
Determining the visibility of an optional region in the Template Properties dialog box.

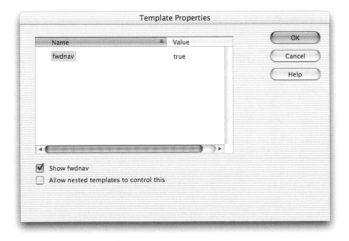

Making Optional Regions Editable

By default, optional regions aren't editable. They contain locked content (such as Back to Top or Next/Previous links). You can, however, create an optional region that contains an editable region.

To insert an optional/editable region, open your template file, go to the Template objects in the Insert bar, and choose Editable Optional Region. If you already have an optional region, and you want to make it editable, just put the insertion point inside the optional region and choose the Editable Region object from the Insert bar. No matter how you do it, Dreamweaver puts an editable region inside an optional region. In Design view, it appears as two colored labels nested one inside the other, or two tags in the Tag Selector. In Code view, it appears like this:

```
<!-- TemplateBeginIf cond="_document['myRegionName']" -->
   <!-- TemplateBeginEditable name="EditRegion4" -->
     [content goes here]
   <!-- TemplateEndEditable -->
<!-- TemplateEndIf --></td>
```

When editing your child pages, you can show or hide the specified content (indicated here by *[content goes here]*). If it's showing, you can change those contents.

Editable Attributes

Editable attributes in templates let you specify any attribute to any tag in the template's locked regions. They also allow this attribute to be controlled by the child page. Sound esoteric? It's actually amazingly useful! With editable attributes, you can insert a consistently placed and sized logo in a locked area of the page while allowing child pages to assign a different `src` attribute (so that a different logo can appear in different pages). You can include consistent Next and Previous links on every page while allowing child pages to control where the links go by making the `href` attribute editable. And you can do a lot more. Your imagination is the only limit.

Creating Editable Attributes in Templates

To specify an attribute as editable in a template, open the template and do the following:

1. Select the tag whose attribute you want to make editable.

2. Choose Modify > Templates > Make Attribute Editable.

3. In the dialog box that appears, select the desired attribute from the Attribute drop-down list. If your attribute doesn't appear in the list, click the Add button to add it. (You also might want to check that you didn't accidentally select a tag other than the one you think you should be working with.) Select the Make editable check box. For the Label, assign a unique and easily recognizable name (such as next_href or logo_src). In the Type drop-down, choose the appropriate type of value (string, URL, number, and so on) that this attribute takes. The default value is whatever value the attribute currently has; you can change this if you like. When you're done, click OK to close the dialog box.

After you've assigned the editable attribute, if you select the tag and examine the Property inspector, or go to Code view and examine the tag's HTML, you see that Dreamweaver has inserted a template parameter in place of your attribute. Here's an example:

```
<img name="logo" src="@@(logo_src)@@" width="112" height="30" />
```

If you go to Code view and look at the end of the head section of your document, where Dreamweaver defines template parameters, you'll find an additional line of code that looks something like this:

```
<!-- TemplateParam name="logo_src" type="URL"
➥value="../images/jewelry_logo.gif" -->
```

What's happening here? The code in the head section defines the logo_src parameter, with a type of URL, and assigns it a default value. The code in your tag tells Dreamweaver to insert that parameter in place of a specific attribute.

Dreamweaver doesn't interpret the parameter while you're viewing the template in Design view. So if you've used a parameter to specify an image source, for instance, you see a broken image icon as you work. When you get to the child page, however, Dreamweaver substitutes a real value for the parameter, and the page displays properly.

Using Editable Attributes in Child Pages

To edit the attribute in a child page, open the child page and choose Modify > Template Properties. The dialog box shown in Figure 20.9

appears. All editable attributes and their default values are listed. Select the attribute you want to change, enter a new value for it, and click OK to close the dialog box. Note that Dreamweaver gives more help for some parameter types than others. If your parameter type is color, the Template Parameters dialog box includes a color picker. But for URL-type parameters, you must enter the relative or absolute URL manually—there's no Browse button. (Note also that relative URLs must be relative to the template file, not the child page.)

FIGURE 20.9
Using Modify >
Template Properties
to set an editable
attribute in a
child page.

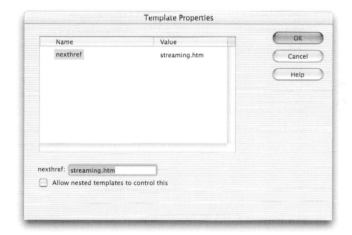

If you check a child page in Code view after setting your editable attributes, you'll see that the tag attribute now has a standard value, in place of the template parameter. In the document's head section, however, the template parameter definition is still present.

Repeating Regions

With repeating regions, you can define a chunk of page content that appears one or more times in any given child page. For instance, you can create a one-row table in the template. In one child page you could repeat that row to create a five-row table, and in another child page you could repeat the row to create a two-row table. Or your template could define one subheading and text paragraph as a repeating region so that some child pages could have several subheading/text units and others would have only one. Repeating regions are most useful when they contain editable regions so that each repeated table row or subheading can have its own unique content.

Creating Repeating Regions in Templates

To define one or more editable regions as a repeating region, open a template file and do the following:

1. Create the page element you want to repeat. This can be a table with one or more rows, text heading and/or paragraph, ordered or unordered list—you name it.

2. Assign editable regions within this element wherever you want. (See the earlier section "Making Regions Editable" if you don't know how to do this.) To create a table with a repeating row, for instance, you probably want an editable region in each table cell. For a text heading/paragraph combination, you want an editable region inside the heading and another inside the paragraph.

3. Select exactly the element(s) you want to repeat. It's a good idea to either use the Tag Selector or work in Code and Design view while doing this to make sure that you get exactly the right selection—the tr tag for a repeating table row, the li tag for a repeating list element, and so on.

4. From the Template objects in the Insert bar, choose the Repeating Region object. When the dialog box opens, give your region a unique name, and click OK.

If you examine your document in Code view at this point, you'll see that Dreamweaver has added template code to indicate the beginning and end of the repeating region, as well as code for each editable region. Your code might look something like this:

```
<ul>
  <!-- TemplateBeginRepeat name="gadget-list" -->
  <li><!-- TemplateBeginEditable name="gadget-item" -->anything
  ➥goes here
  <!-- TemplateEndEditable --></li>
  <!-- TemplateEndRepeat -->
</ul>
```

This example defines a repeating list item. You wouldn't want the repeating region code defined outside the ul tags, or you'd create multiple lists in the child pages instead of multiple list items in one list.

Using Repeating Regions in Child Pages

Using repeating regions in child pages is easy and fun. When you open a child page whose parent template contains a repeating region, and view it in Design view, you see a colored Repeat label with the name of the region, followed by a little set of control icons for adding, removing, and rearranging repeating entries (see Figure 20.10). To work with the repeating region, do the following:

1. Enter whatever content you like in the editable region(s) within the repeating region.

2. Add more repetitions by pressing the + button in the region control bar. Enter content into these editable regions as well.

3. If you end up with too many iterations, place the insertion point in the one you want to remove and press the – button in the region control bar.

4. To rearrange the iterations, place the insertion point in an item you want to move, and use the up and down icons in the control bar.

FIGURE 20.10
Working with a repeating region in a child page.

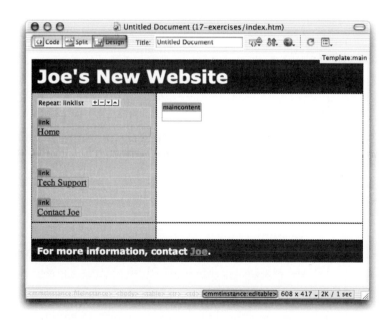

The code for the repeating region in the child page includes indications of where each iteration begins and ends:

```
<ul>
  <!-- InstanceBeginRepeat name="gadget-list" -->
  <!-- InstanceBeginRepeatEntry -->
  <li><!-- InstanceBeginEditable name="gadget-item" -->Gadget
  <!-- InstanceEndEditable --></li>
  <!-- InstanceEndRepeatEntry -->
  <!-- InstanceBeginRepeatEntry -->
  <li><!-- InstanceBeginEditable name="gadget-item" -->Doodad
  <!-- InstanceEndEditable --></li>
  <!-- InstanceEndRepeatEntry -->
  <!-- InstanceEndRepeat -->
</ul>
```

Repeating Tables

Probably the most common use of repeating regions in web pages is to build a table in which one or more rows repeats and every cell contains an editable region. Price lists, company directories, and a whole host of other layout tasks work very well with this kind of repeating table structure. And guess what? Dreamweaver provides you with a special object just for creating this structure.

To create a repeating table, open a template document and follow these steps:

1. Place the insertion point where you want the table with its repeating rows to be located.

2. From the Insert bar's category of Template objects, choose Repeating Table. The Insert Repeating Table dialog box appears, as shown in Figure 20.11, allowing you to specify the table's basic structure, as well as how many rows will repeat. To create a table that includes a header row and one repeating data row, for instance, you should create a two-row table in which the Starting Row and Ending Row of the repeating region are both set to 2.

   Give the repeating region a unique and easy-to-remember name. Then click OK to close the dialog box and insert the table.

FIGURE 20.11
Creating a simple
repeating table in a
template document.

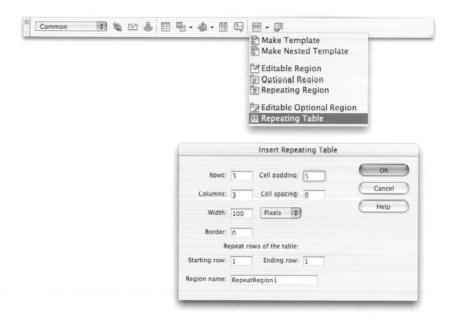

3. As soon as the table is inserted, you'll see that it contains a repeating region and, within that region, one editable region for each table cell. There's nothing magic about any of these regions. They're exactly the same as they would be if you had created them yourself using the Repeating Region and Editable Region objects. It's a good idea to rename the editable regions by selecting each and using the Property inspector. You can apply any formatting to the table—it's essentially a normal HTML table.

In the child pages based on this template, you use the repeating table exactly like you would use any repeating region.

Nested Templates

Nested templates let you define templates based on other templates, and then create child pages based on those templates. What?! It might sound daunting, but if you're willing to put a little extra thought into it, nested templates can make even extensive and complex websites easier to create and maintain. For instance, suppose you have an overall layout that you want all the pages in your site to have. That's your main template. But you also want some pages in your hierarchy—second- or third-level pages, perhaps—to have additional page elements. Or you want an over-all layout for all pages, but pages in different sections of your website should have additional requirements. You can define one main template for the entire site and then additional templates for each section, or for each level of the hierarchy, that are based on the main template.

Creating a Nested Template

To create a nested template, do the following:

1. Create the main template you want throughout your site, using any of the methods discussed earlier in this chapter. Add editable regions to this template as normal.

2. Create a new child page based on this template. It's easiest to do this by choosing File > New and selecting from the Templates tab of the New Document dialog box.

3. With the child page open, choose File > Save As Template, or, from the Insert bar's Template objects, choose the Nested Template object. Either of these actions opens the New Template dialog box. Give your template a unique name, and click OK.

You don't have to stop with one generation of nesting. It's possible to nest templates inside nested templates, as many generations deep as you like.

Congratulations! You have created a template based on a template. But the fun doesn't really begin until you learn how to handle editable regions, attributes, and other template features across your multiple generations of templates.

Editable Regions and Nested Templates

When you nest templates, editable regions always begin in the parent template. As shown in Figure 20.12, the parent template defines one or more editable regions. The nested template can then lock part of any of these regions, so the child page retains only part of it as editable. If the nested template does not specify which portion of the parent's editable region should be locked, the entire region is passed to the child page as editable.

When building the main template, you must keep in mind that you'll be defining editable regions for two purposes: some to be inherited by the nested template and locked there, and some to be passed down through the nested template to the child pages.

FIGURE 20.12
How editable regions progress from parent to nested template and ultimately to child page.

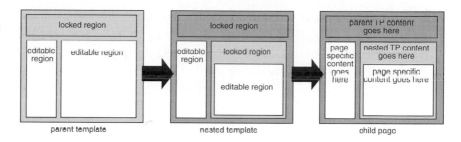

When building the nested template, keep in mind that if you do nothing to one of the parent template's editable regions, it is passed to the child page as an editable region. To lock part of one of the parent template's editable regions, define another editable region within it. For instance, a layout table in a parent template might have a row defined as an editable region; in the nested template, one of the cells in that row can be defined as an editable region, which automatically locks all other cells in the row. Figure 20.13 shows this happening in Design view. The code for the editable row looks like this:

```
<!-- InstanceBeginEditable name="edit-row" -->
  <tr>
    <td>this content will be locked in child pages</td>
    <td><!-- TemplateBeginEditable name="edit-cell" -->this
    ➡content will be editable in child pages
    ➡<!-- TemplateEndEditable --></td>
  </tr>
<!-- InstanceEndEditable -->
```

The edit-row region is defined in the parent template; the edit-cell region is defined in the nested template.

Dreamweaver uses color-coded highlights to keep track of which editable regions have been defined where. By default, the labels for all editable regions defined in a parent template are aqua (#66CCCC); labels for editable regions defined in a nested template are gold (#FFCC33). If you don't like these colors, you can change them in the Preferences/Highlighting dialog box (select Edit > Preferences).

FIGURE 20.13

A very simple nested template showing an editable region from the parent template (edit-row) containing an editable region defined in the nested template (edit-cell).

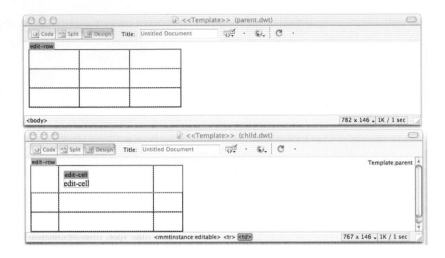

What if you want a child template to lock an entire editable region from the parent template instead of locking part of it by making another part editable? You can't do this, but you can create an empty editable region in the child template to accomplish your goal. In the nested template, place the insertion point anywhere in the parent's editable region, and create a new editable region. Then delete all contents from this editable region.

Template Parameters in Nested Templates

Optional regions, editable attributes, and any other template parameter that appears in the Template Properties dialog box can also be used with nested templates. As with editable regions, any template parameter defined in a parent template can be passed to nested templates to control, or can be passed directly to the child pages. Parameters defined in parent templates for control by child pages are called *pass-through parameters*, because they pass through the nested template.

To set up pass-through parameters in your nested template setup, do the following:

1. While creating the parent template, define an optional region, editable attribute, or other template parameter.

2. When working with the nested template, choose Modify > Template Properties to open the Template Properties dialog box. Parameters defined in the parent template appear here.

3. Select any parameter. At the bottom of the dialog box, select the option to Allow Nested Templates to Control This. The parameter's

value is replaced with the pass-through indicator, as shown in Figure 20.14. Click OK to close the dialog box.

FIGURE 20.14
Defining a pass-through parameter in a nested template.

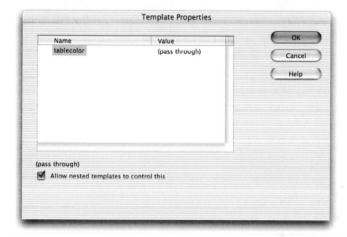

After you've defined the pass-through parameter, each child page you create based on the nested template can set the parameter independent of all other pages. Just open the child page and choose Modify > Template Properties. Select the parameter, and set its value.

EXERCISE 20.1

Creating a Template-Based Site

This exercise builds and formats a small website using basic and advanced template features. Before you start, download the **chapter_20** folder from the book's website at www.peachpit.com to your hard drive. Define a site called Chapter 20, with this folder as the local root folder.

Start by opening the **layout.html** file and examining its contents. This file holds the layout you'll use for the site, including a layout table and navigation banner, and a link to a CSS style sheet (see Figure 20.15).

1. With **layout.html** open, choose Insert > Template Objects > Make Template. When the Template dialog box appears, name the template **main**. Without closing the file, examine the Templates category of the Assets panel; the main template should be there now. Also check out the Site panel. A Templates folder has been added to the site, containing a file called **main.dwt**. (If the folder doesn't show up, click the Refresh button in the Site panel toolbar.)

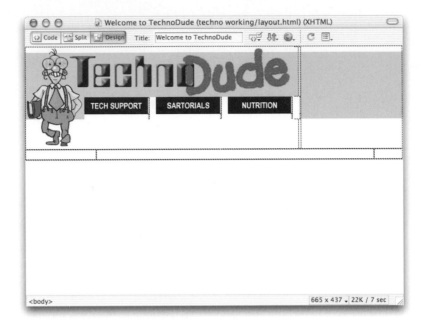

2. The template needs one editable region where the main page content will go. Place the insertion point in the central table cell, and
   choose Insert > Template Objects > New Editable Region. Name the
   region **maincontent**, as shown in Figure 20.16. Save the template file
   (select File > Save), and close it.

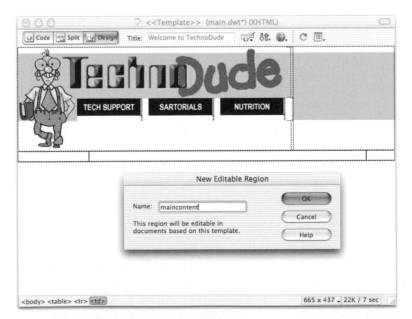

3. Create a new home page based on this template. Choose File > New. When the New Document dialog box appears, bring the Templates tab to the front, choose the Chapter 20 site and the main template, and click OK to close the dialog box. A new untitled document, which is the child page of the main template, opens. Only the main-content area is editable. Select the placeholder text there and delete it. In its place, enter a heading and a bit of text formatted with the h1 and p tags. The style sheet attached to the template changes their appearance automatically because these tags have been redefined. Save the page as **index.html**, at the site's root level, and close it.

4. The subsidiary pages of the website already exist, but they're not formatted yet. Open **nutrition/index.html** and examine it. You'll see that it contains some headings and text, but nothing more. No styles or other formatting have been applied. With this file open, find the main template in the Assets panel, and drag its file icon to the Document window. A dialog box appears, asking you how to dispose of the page's existing content. Select the body content in the dialog box, and choose maincontent from the drop-down menu to put the content in that region (see Figure 20.17). Click OK to close the dialog box. The page has been formatted, and framework elements have been added! Save and close.

FIGURE 20.17

Applying the main template to the nutrition page in the TechnoDude website.

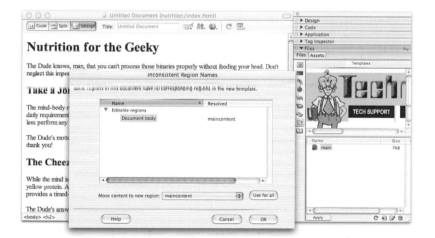

 Make sure you're dragging the main template from the Assets panel and not the Site panel. If you drag from the Site panel to the Document window, it just opens the **main.dwt** file. If you drag from the Assets panel, it applies the template to the open document.

5. Repeat step 4 to apply the main template to the **sartorials/ index.html** page. Before closing it, preview the page in a browser. The template formatting is present, and because the navigation banner and links are in the template, the three pages you just set up— **index.html**, **nutrition.html**, and **sartorials.html**—should successfully link to one another. (Don't worry about the tech support pages just yet. You're saving them for some special treatment.)

6. Navigation bars are always more user-friendly if they change to indicate which page is currently being displayed. When the nutrition page is open, the NUTRITION button at the top of the page should appear altered, along with the other buttons. The trick is, because the navigation buttons are in a locked part of the main template, they can't be changed except through template parameters and expressions. To accomplish this, you'll set up some editable attributes.

Open the main template (you can open it from the Assets panel or the Site window). Click the NUTRITION button, and choose Modify > Templates > Make Attribute Editable. The dialog box shown in Figure 20.18 appears. Choose Src as the attribute, and select the Make editable check box. Name the editable attribute **nutrition_src**. Set the attribute type to URL. Leave the default value at its current setting. When you're done, click OK to close the dialog box. In Design view, the image now shows up as a broken image. That's because, if you look at the Property Inspector, its source is set to an expression, **@@(nutrition_src)@@**—and that can't be displayed in Design view!

Repeat this procedure with the other two buttons in the navigation banner, naming the attributes **techsupport_src** and **sartorials_src**. When you're done, save and close the template, allowing it to update child pages.

To make use of these editable attributes, open the nutrition page (**nutrition/index.html**). First, note that the images show up correctly! That's because the child page has placed the default values assigned in the template in the HTML code, replacing the expressions in the template. This happened when you updated the pages.

You want the NUTRITION button to display an alternative image. Choose Modify > Template Properties. The three source parameters are present. Select nutrition_src and change its URL to

../images/nutrition_down.gif. (This image was created for you in Fireworks.) Click OK to close the dialog box. The button is now orange! (See Figure 20.19.)

FIGURE 20.18
Making an image source editable to customize the TechnoDude navigation bar.

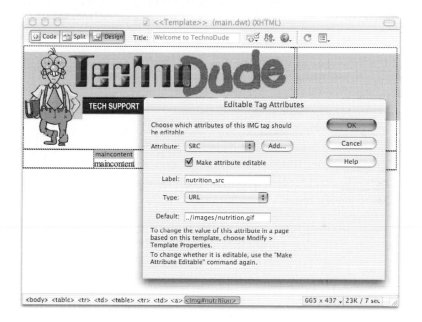

FIGURE 20.19
The TechnoDude navigation bar with a customized image source.

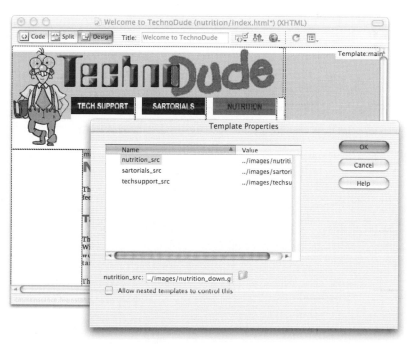

Open the sartorials page (**sartorials/index.html**) and repeat this procedure, setting the sartorials_src parameter to **../images/sartorials_down.gif**. When you're done, preview in a browser to see the newly improved navigation bar in action. Again, don't worry about the tech support pages just yet.

7. Because there are several pages in the tech support section, it merits its own template—one that's based on the main template but that has some tech support-specific features as well. This will be a nested template!

Create a new file based on the main template (choose File > New, and use the New Document dialog box, as you did previously). With this new document open, choose Insert > Template Objects > Make Nested Template. Name the template **techsupport**. This template is now a child template of the main template.

Select Modify > Template Properties to set the **techsupport_src** parameter to **../images/techsupport_down.gif**. All pages in this section should have the TECH SUPPORT button displayed in orange. When you're done, save and close.

8. The techsupport template needs a navigation bar in its left column, specifically for navigation among the tech support pages. But you can't put one there because there's no editable region for it in the main template. Remember, all editable regions must start in the parent template. Open the main template, and, in the left column, insert an editable region. Call this region **navbar**. After it's made, delete the placeholder text Dreamweaver put there. You don't want that text to appear in the nutrition and sartorials pages! For those pages, this side region will remain empty. When you're done, save and update, and close.

Open the techsupport template again. Place the insertion point inside the navbar region, and choose Insert > Images > Fireworks HTML. In the dialog box that appears, browse to the **techsupport_menu.html** page. This page contains a sliced image table made in Fireworks. It doesn't matter whether you delete the file after insertion. Click OK to close the dialog box and insert the small navigation bar (see Figure 20.20). You might get an error message, as Dreamweaver tells you the inserted code would require changing a locked region. Click OK to close the error message. The Fireworks HTML and JavaScript are inserted in the document, despite the message.

In order to make sure the navigation bar is locked in pages based on this template, you'll need to add another editable region within the navbar region. Place the insertion point immediately following the table containing your navigation bar and insert an Editable Region object from the Insert bar. Call the region **tech_navbar**. Delete the placeholder contents Dreamweaver puts in the editable region, so it will automatically be empty in child pages.

Save (choosing to update any child pages) and close the template.

FIGURE 20.20
Inserting the tech support navigation bar into an editable region in the techsupport nested template.

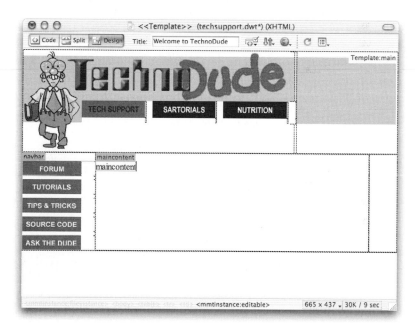

9. Apply the techsupport template to all pages within the techsupport folder, using the same method you used previously in this exercise. (If you're not a glutton for punishment, it's okay to focus on just a few of the pages. It's not really necessary for the exercise to set them all up.) While you're working, note that you can't select the new navigation bar. This area was made noneditable for all child pages when you inserted content into it in the techsupport template.

Working Smart: Using the Template Language

The code in templates might look like HTML comments, but that's just to fool browsers into ignoring it. This code is actually a scripting language (a small subset of JavaScript, in fact) that Dreamweaver uses to construct child pages from templates. If you want to become a true template power user, you should learn how to speak template.

Opening and Closing Tags

Templates and regions are defined with opening and closing tags that look like this (as defined in the template):

```
<!-- TemplateBeginEditable name="doctitle" -->
<!-- TemplateEndEditable -->
```

or this (as used in a child page):

```
<!-- InstanceBeginEditable name="doctitle" -->
<!-- InstanceEndEditable -->
```

These tags take a little more typing than your average HTML tag, but they follow the basic HTML syntax of *<tag attribute="value">*, and they can contain simple scripting constructs such as conditionals and parameters. Table 20.1 lists the main tags used in defining template-based pages and their editable regions.

TABLE 20.1 **Tag Pairs for Defining Templates and Regions**

Tag Pair	Usage	Attributes

`<!--InstanceBegin`
`➡template="/Templates/`
`techsupport.dwt"`
`➡codeOutsideHTMLIsLocked=`
`➡"false" -->`
`<!-- InstanceEnd -->`
	Surrounds the html element for a child page based on a template.	template: The root-relative URL of the DWT file this page is based on codeOutsideHTMLIsLocked: True or false, determining whether server-side code added outside the html tag is controlled by the template (true) or the child page (false)

Tag Pair	Usage	Attributes

`<!-- TemplateBeginEditable`
➡`name="myStuff" -->`
`<!-- TemplateEndEditable -->`
	Surrounds an editable region (in the template).	name: The name assigned to the region. Should be unique and easily identifiable.

`<!-- InstanceBeginEditable`
➡`name="myStuff" -->`
`<!-- InstanceEndEditable -->`
	Surrounds an editable region (in the child page).	

Parameters and Expressions

Template parameters work like variables in a scripting language. They're declared in the document head and can be used anywhere in the document. Dreamweaver uses them to set optional regions, editable attributes, and other template constructs, but you can use them for much more than this if you know the rules.

Defining Template Parameters

Parameters are defined by a statement in the template head, like this:

```
<!-- TemplateParam name="myParameter" type="color" value="red" -->
```

In the template's child page, the definition statement changes to look like this:

```
<!-- InstanceParam name="myParameter" type="color" value="red" -->
```

Like variables in a scripting language, template parameters can be of various data types, for storing different kinds of information. These types are Boolean (true/false), text, number, color, and URL. The parameter's name is how it can be referred to throughout the template; its value is the information stored in it. The general idea is to define a parameter in the template document and allow each child page to assign its own unique value.

Using Parameters in Expressions

After a parameter has been defined, it can be called on anywhere in the document by using an expression, like this:

```
@@(myParameter)@@
```

It works like this: Anywhere in the template document that the expression is present, the child page substitutes the parameter's value. So if the template page includes the following expression in its code:

```
<td bgcolor="@@(myParameter)@@">
```

a child page has code like this in its place:

```
<td bgcolor="red">
```

For this expression syntax to work properly, your parameter names must not include spaces or other special characters.

Whatever color is specified in the child page's parameter definition is used here.

Dreamweaver automatically creates parameters and expressions every time you define an editable attribute in your template. But you can also create your own parameters, for use any way you like, using this same syntax. Imagine, for instance, that you have one template governing product display pages for several categories of products. You could define a category parameter by entering the following code in the template head:

```
<!-- TemplateParam name="category" type="text" value="default"
➡--->
```

You could cause that category name to appear at the top of each page by entering an expression like this:

```
<h1>@@(category)@@</h1>
```

You have to enter the parameter definition by hand using Code view. But you can create the expression in Design view by just typing in @@(category)@@ and formatting it. When Dreamweaver notices that you've entered an expression here, it displays an expression placeholder where you typed your text, as shown in Figure 20.21.

When you open a child page based on this template, you can change the parameter's value by manually changing the definition statement in Code view or by choosing Modify > Template Properties. The category parameter appears in the dialog box, ready to accept a new value.

FIGURE 20.21

A template parameter as seen in Design view and the Property Inspector

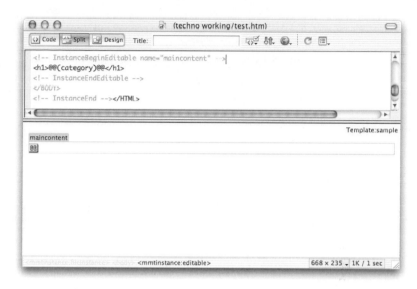

Passthrough Parameters

When you're working with nested templates, and you want to define a parameter in the main template that will be controllable by child pages (and not by the nested template), do so by opening the child template and adding a passthrough attribute to the parameter definition with a value of true:

```
<!-- TemplateParam name="myParameter" type="text"
➥value="default" passthrough="true" -->
```

When using a passthrough parameter in an expression in the child template, use this syntax:

```
@@@(myParameter)@@@
```

Any time you tinker with code, there's the possibility that things will go wrong (typos, syntax goofs, and so on). To make sure that your code is error-free after manual editing, choose Modify > Templates > Check Template Syntax. You'll get either an error message or a clean bill of coding health.

Conditional Statements and Optional Regions

In scripting, a conditional statement indicates that something should happen only if a certain condition is met. Conditional statements generally involve testing the value of variables or parameters. Every time you work with optional regions in your Dreamweaver templates, you're working with conditional statements. As soon as you know your way around conditional syntax in template language, you can start creating advanced optional regions.

Conditional Syntax

The syntax for a conditional statement in template language looks like this:

```
<!-- TemplateBeginIf cond="[true or false code]" -->
```

The cond attribute must have as its value an expression that evaluates to true or false. For instance, if the head section of the template defines a parameter like this:

```
<!-- TemplateParam name="myParameter" type="boolean" value=
➥"true" -->
```

the conditional statement can test this parameter:

```
<!-- TemplateBeginIf cond="myParameter" -->
```

If the head section defines a parameter that isn't itself a Boolean, the conditional statement can use various comparison operators to determine if the optional content should display:

```
<!-- TemplateParam name="myParameter" type="text" value="HATS" -->
<!-- TemplateBeginIf cond="myParameter=='HATS'" -->
```

Table 20.2 lists common comparison operators that can be used in conditional statements.

TABLE 20.2 ## Comparison Operators for Use in Conditional Statements

Operator	Description	Examples
==	Equality	myText == 'HATS' myNumber == 3
!=	Inequality	myText != 'HATS'
>	Greater than	myNumber > 3
>=	Greater than or equal to	myNumber >= 3

Operator	Description	Examples
<	Less than	myNumber < 10
<=	Less than or equal to	myNumber <= 10
&&	Two expressions, both of which are true	myNumber > 3 && myNumber ↪< 10
||	Two expressions, at least one of which is true	myText == 'HATS' || ↪myText == 'SHOES'

The Code Behind Optional Regions

As discussed earlier in the chapter, when you create a basic optional region using the Optional Region object, Dreamweaver defines a template parameter of the Boolean type and then uses a conditional statement that tests this parameter to determine whether the optional region should show:

```
<!-- TemplateParam name="myBoolean" type="boolean" value=
↪"true" -->
<!-- TemplateBeginIf cond="myBoolean" -->
```

But you can create more advanced optional regions using other kinds of parameters and conditionals:

```
<!-- TemplateParam name="category" type="text" value="HATS" -->
<!-- TemplateBeginIf cond="category=='HATS'" -->
```

You'd have to work in Code view to define the parameter shown here. But you can create the optional region without working in Code view by using the advanced settings for the Optional Region object. Do it this way:

1. In Design view, select whatever page content should be part of the optional region.

2. From the Insert bar, choose the Optional Region object.

3. When the dialog box opens, bring the Advanced tab to the front, and choose Enter expression. For the expression, type the conditional statement you want to use (see Figure 20.22):

    ```
    category=='JEWELRY'
    ```

    Click OK to close the dialog box.

FIGURE 20.22
Entering an expression to determine if an optional region should display.

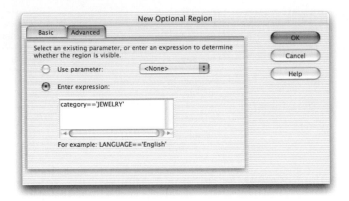

MultipleIf Statements

Standard conditionals lend themselves to things that either are or aren't true (is the category equal to JEWELRY?). But sometimes, you might have a parameter that can have any of several values, and you want to display different page content for each value (if the category is JEWELRY, do this; if the category is HATS, do this; and so on). For such occasions, the template language has a special kind of conditional called a `MultipleIf` statement. The syntax looks like this:

```
<!-- TemplateBeginMultipleIf -->
  <!-- TemplateBeginIfClause cond="[test 1]" -->
    optional content 1
  <!-- TemplateEndIfClause -->
  <!-- TemplateBeginIfClause cond="[test 2]" -->
    optional content 2
  <!-- TemplateEndIfClause -->
<!-- TemplateEndMultipleIf -->
```

For the first conditional, you might enter `category=='HATS'` and display a statement about hats or a picture of a hat as your optional content. For the second, you might enter `category=='SHOES'` and display some comparable shoe-related content. You can add as many conditional clauses as you like, each with its own set of optional content. The only downside is that the entire code must be entered in Code view because Dreamweaver doesn't provide an object for it.

Shorthand Conditional Code

You can also use conditional statements within editable attributes by using abbreviated one-line syntax (just like that found in JavaScript):

condition ? true : false

For instance, if a sale is going on, you might want the prices to appear highlighted in yellow. You could create a template parameter like this:

```
<!-- TemplateParam name="sale" type="boolean" value="true" -->
```

You could create the table cell that holds each price like this:

```
<td bgcolor="@@(sale ? 'red' : 'white')@@">
```

You can enter the expression in Code view by typing the code shown here, or in Design view by entering the expression only (starting and ending with @@) in the appropriate input field of the Property Inspector.

Advanced Coding for Repeating Regions

When you're working with repeating regions, your expressions can take advantage of the template language's _repeat object and its properties to create some sophisticated results. Table 20.3 lists _repeat properties and the syntax for accessing them.

TABLE 20.3 ## Properties of the _repeat Object for Working with Repeating Regions in Templates

Property	Value Type	Description
_index	Integer	The numerical index of the current iteration, starting at 0
_numRows	Integer	The total number of iterations in this child page
_isFirst	Boolean	Specifies whether the current iteration is the first
_isLast	Boolean	Specifies whether the current iteration is the last
_prevRecord	Object	The _repeat object for the previous iteration (or an error if there is none)
_nextRecord	Object	The _repeat object for the next iteration (or an error if there is none)
_parent	Object	The _repeat object for the enclosing repeating region (use this only when one repeating region is nested inside another)

What can you do with the _repeat object properties? By using them in expressions, you can construct conditional statements to hide or show optional content. For instance, what if you have a repeating region that consists of a subheading and paragraph, and you want to insert a horizontal rule between each subheading-paragraph combination, but no rule after the last one? To accomplish this, you put an hr tag after each repetition except the last one. You need a conditional statement that tests each time the region repeats, to see if this is the last iteration—and if it is, that inserts an hr tag. The code for your repeating region would look like this:

```
<!-- TemplateBeginRepeat name="product_list" -->
  <h2>
<!-- TemplateBeginEditable name="product_name" -->
Product name goes here
<!-- TemplateEndEditable -->
  </h2>
  <p>
<!-- TemplateBeginEditable name="product_desc" -->
Product description goes here
<!-- TemplateEndEditable -->
  </p>
  <!-- TemplateBeginIf cond="!(_repeat._isLast)" -->
    <hr>
  <!-- TemplateEndIf -->
<!-- TemplateEndRepeat -->
```

To create this effect in Design view, you can insert a Repeating Region object, and then, within the repeating area, insert an Optional Region object. In the Optional Region dialog box, bring the Advanced tab to the front, choose Enter expression, and type **!(_repeat._isLast)** in the input field. This expression uses the not operator (!) to ask if the current iteration is not the last one.

If you want your repeating entries to display numbers (like a numbered list), you can create an expression that displays the _index property:

```
@@(_repeat._index + 1)@@
```

(You add 1 to the _index each time because computer index values start from 0, and it looks a bit strange to have your numbering begin with 0.)

Finally, if you're using a table with repeating rows, you might want every other row in the table to be a different color. Enter the following code for the tr tag:

```
<tr bgcolor="@@(_repeat._index%2 ? 'orange' : 'white')@@">
```

This uses the *modulo* operator to test whether dividing the _index property by 2 will leave a remainder. If there is a remainder, the row is an odd-numbered row, and it is given an orange background. If not, the row is even-numbered and is given a white background.

If you've worked with data-driven web pages, using the Dreamweaver template language probably feels a lot like constructing pages in ColdFusion or one of the other application server languages. Dreamweaver template language lets you accomplish many of the same tasks as a server-side language—using page-specific editable regions, repeating regions, optional regions for conditional content, and parameters to construct individual pages on-the-fly from a scripted original—but without any server involvement. As you'll see in Chapter 23, "Further Dynamic Techniques," templates can also be used in conjunction with data-driven pages.

Snippetizing Your Template Code

Is all this typing and memorizing syntax getting you down? If you hand-code templates frequently, it's a good idea to create snippets for the items you type most often. You can create a snippet folder specifically for template snippets and store block and wrap snippets in it. Figure 20.23 shows a few template snippets being created.

See the section "Code Snippets" in Chapter 27, "Writing Code in Dreamweaver," for more on this.

FIGURE 20.23
Creating a block
snippet and a
wrap snippet for
different pieces of
template code.

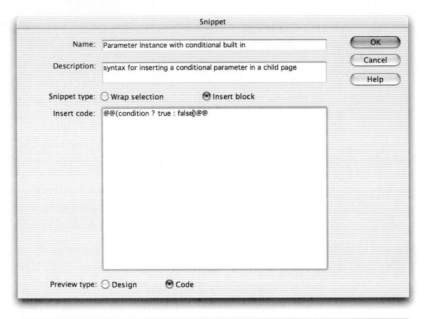

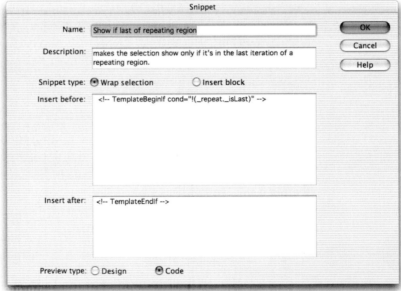

Refining the Template-Based Site

This exercise builds on the template site you started in Exercise 20.1, using optional regions and manually entered template parameters and expressions to construct a breadcrumb navigation system.

1. Start by opening the main template. Insert a new row in the layout table, directly above the row containing the maincontent and nav-bar editable regions. Using the Tag Selector or the CSS Styles panel, assign the breadcrumbs custom class to the td tag for this table cell (see Figure 20.24). Enter the following text in this row:

   TechnoDude > Section > Page

   Select the word TechnoDude, and use the Property Inspector to link it to the main **index.html** page, at the site's root level. This bread-crumb leads home.

FIGURE 20.24

Creating a bread-crumb navigation row in the TechnoDude main template.

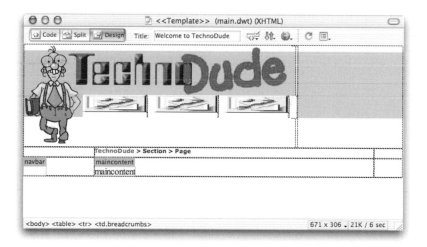

   Select the word Section, and use the Property Inspector to link it to #. You'll let child pages change this property later.

2. You want each child page of this template to be able to specify its own section and page. To do this, you need to define template parameters. Go to Code view and find the end of the head section,

where several template parameters have already been defined (the src parameters for the editable attributes in the navigation banner). After the last of these parameters, create a new line and enter the following:

```
<!-- TemplateParam name="section" type="text" value=
➥"sectiondefault" -->
<!-- TemplateParam name="section_url" type="URL" value="#" -->
<!-- TemplateParam name="page" type="text" value=
➥"pagedefault" -->
```

You can type this from scratch or copy and paste one of the other definitions and change the details as needed.

3. Now you want to display these parameters in the breadcrumbs bar. Go back to Design view, and select the word Section in the breadcrumbs. In its place, type the following:

   @@(section)@@

   Select the word Page in the breadcrumbs. In its place, type the following:

   @@(page)@@

   Select the a tag that surrounds the Section breadcrumb. (It's easiest to use the Tag Selector for this.) In the Property Inspector, in the Link field, enter the following:

   @@(section_url)@@

   Guess what you just did? You manually made the href attribute of the a tag editable. You could have accomplished the same thing using the Make Attribute Editable command.

   Before proceeding, choose Modify > Templates > Check Template Syntax, just to make sure you haven't got any typos in there. If Dreamweaver gives you an error message, troubleshoot your parameter and expression code and repeat the syntax check until your code is error-free.

   When Dreamweaver notices that these are template expressions, it displays an expression icon in Design view, as shown in Figure 20.25. If this doesn't happen right away, save the template, close it, and reopen it.

FIGURE 20.25

The breadcrumb bar with parameter expressions in place.

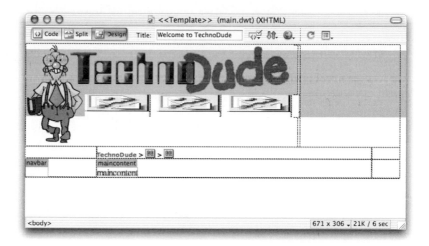

4. Open the techsupport template. The breadcrumbs are in place, but with their default parameter values:

   TechnoDude > sectiondefault > pagedefault

   That's because these parameters haven't been set for this child yet! Choose Modify > Template Properties, and in the dialog box that appears, select the section parameter. (See how it appears here, even though you entered the parameter by hand? All correctly formatted parameters show up here.) Set the value for this parameter to Tech Support.

   Select the `section_url` parameter, and set its value to `./techsupport/index.html`.

   What's the meaning of this URL? It's the relative path from within the Templates folder to the tech support main page. Remember, all URLs must start out relative to the template document itself. Dreamweaver takes care of updating the URL when the template is applied to a child page. Don't close the dialog box yet!

5. You don't want to set the page parameter here; you want the children of this template to set the parameter, so it needs to pass through this child template to its child pages. To accomplish this, select the `page` parameter and select Allow nested templates to control this. Note that the value of the parameter changes to `passthrough`, as shown in Figure 20.26.

FIGURE 20.26
Turning the page
parameter into a
passthrough
parameter.

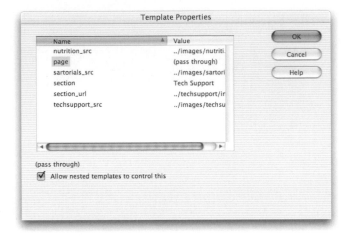

Click OK to close the dialog box. Check your document in Code view, and you'll see that a passthrough attribute has been added to the parameter definition (in the head). The page breadcrumb now sports an expression of **@@@(page)@@@**. The triple at symbol on either side marks it as a parameter that has been passed down from the parent template.

When you're done, save the template and close it.

6. Open one of the child pages based on this template. Start with **techsupport/forum.html**. When this page opens, the section breadcrumb says Tech Support (this was set in the template). The page breadcrumb is still an expression. Use the Template Properties dialog box to set the page parameter to Forum. Save the document and close it.

Repeat this procedure for all other pages in the **techsupport** folder, except the index file. You'll deal with that next.

7. So far, the breadcrumb system isn't perfect, because it always displays some sort of page breadcrumb, even if that's not appropriate. For the nutrition, sartorials, and techsupport index pages, there shouldn't be a page indicator, just a section. It's time for an optional region!

Open the main template and select the page breadcrumb, including the > symbol that precedes it. You don't want any of this content to show if there is no need for a page breadcrumb. Choose Insert > Template Objects > Optional Region. Name the region **pagecrumb**, and set it to hide by default (see Figure 20.27). Most of the sections in the current site don't need this item. Save the template and close it.

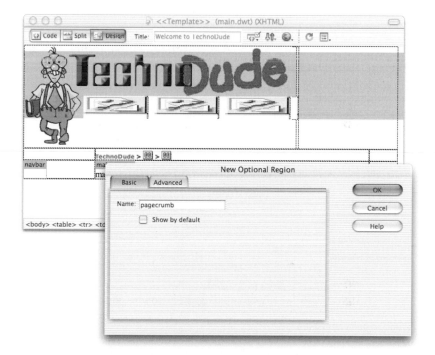

8. Open the nutrition page. The page breadcrumb doesn't show here! That's because it's hidden by default. This page doesn't need any updating, so you can close it.

9. Open the techsupport template. You need to pass the parameter for hiding and showing the pagecrumb region down to the child pages. Open the Template Properties dialog box, select pagecrumb, and select Allow Nested Templates to Control. The parameter value changes to passthrough. Click OK to close the dialog box. Then save and close the dialog box.

10. Open the **techsupport/forum.html** page. Open the Template Properties dialog box, select the `pagecrumb` parameter, and set it to show. Repeat this procedure for all pages in the **techsupport** folder except the index page.

11. Try previewing the site in a browser, and see how the breadcrumbs behave from page to page. They're almost perfect! One little niggle is that, if there is no page breadcrumb, the section breadcrumb doesn't really need to be a link because the main section page must appear. This is an opportunity for a more advanced optional region—one that hides and shows the opening and closing a tag surrounding the section crumb based on the `pagecrumb` parameter.

12. Open the main template again. Select the section breadcrumb and go to Code view. Edit the code for the breadcrumb bar so that it looks like this (new code is shown in bold, and line breaks have been added to make the code more readable):

```
<a href="../index.html">TechnoDude</a> &gt;
<!-- TemplateBeginIf cond="pagecrumb" -->
<a href="@@(section_url)@@">
<!-- TemplateEndIf -->
@@(section)@@
<!-- TemplateBeginIf cond="pagecrumb" --></a><!--
TemplateEndIf -->
<!-- TemplateBeginIf cond="_document['pagecrumb']" -->&gt;
@@(page)@@
<!-- TemplateEndIf -->
```

What's happening here? You're adding two optional regions—one around the opening a tag and one around its closing partner. Both are based on the `pagecrumb` parameter.

13. Before finishing up, check your syntax (select Modify > Templates > Check Template Syntax) and troubleshoot until you receive no error messages. Then preview the entire site in a browser. Congratulations! Some fancy template work is happening here.

Working with Library Items

Dreamweaver library items use the same basic mechanism that templates use, but on a much smaller scale.

Library Basics

A *library item* is a piece of code, usually representing a page element, that needs to appear repeatedly throughout a website. A library item exists in a document that has an .lbi filename extension, stored in a folder called **Library**, in the site's Local Root folder, as shown in Figure 20.28. Library items can be inserted into any Dreamweaver document in the site. Like templates, when the original library item (the one in the Library) is updated, all instances of it throughout the site are updated as well. Library items are managed through the Library category of the Assets panel, shown in Figure 20.29.

FIGURE 20.28
The Library folder of a Dreamweaver website and its contents.

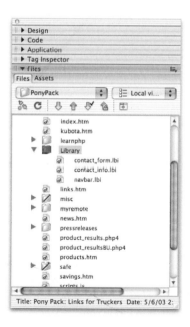

FIGURE 20.29

The Library category
of the Assets panel,
the central manage-
ment location for
library items.

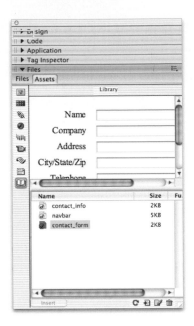

Creating Library Items

The most common way to create a library item is by grabbing some existing content in a site document. Just select the content you want to add
to the library, open the Library category of the Assets panel, and click the
New Library Item button (see Figure 20.29), or choose Modify > Library >
Add Object to Library. A new, untitled item is added to the Library (obviously, you'll want to rename it!), and the selected content in your document is turned into an instance of that item. If you check the Site panel,
you'll see that a new LBI file named after your library item now appears
in a Library folder. If you open this file, you'll see that it contains only the
code fragment that was selected when you created the item. Dreamweaver
displays it in Design view, as though it were a complete HTML document,
but it doesn't include the HTML framework.

You can also create an empty library item by clicking the New Library
Item button in the Assets panel when you have no document open or
nothing is selected in the current document.

Library Items in Documents

After you've created a library item, you can insert as many instances of it
as you like into any document in your website. Just open the document
you want to insert into and drag the item from the Assets panel to the

spot where you want it inserted, or place the insertion point where you want the item inserted and click the Insert button in the Assets panel, or choose Insert >.

When the library item is inserted, all its code is copied into the document. Any relative URLs (linked pages, images, and so on) are updated so that they will work from the document's location. The code for the library item appears surrounded by special HTML comments (similar to the comments in templates) that tell Dreamweaver this is a library item:

```
<!-- #BeginLibraryItem "/Library/contact.lbi" -->
  <a href="mailto:laura@rocketlaura.com">Contact the author</a>
<!-- #EndLibraryItem -->
```

Within the document, the item is noneditable. When you select it, the Library Item Property Inspector appears, as shown in Figure 20.30, giving you three options:

- **Open**—Opens the LBI file for editing.

- **Detach from original**—Removes the surrounding comments from the item's code, making it editable but no longer connected to the library.

- **Recreate**—If the original LBI file has been lost or damaged, clicking this button creates a new LBI file containing the code from this instance.

FIGURE 20.30
A library item in a Dreamweaver document.

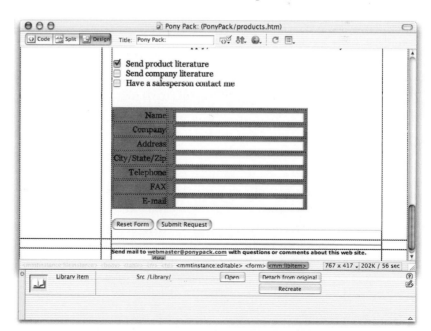

Updating Library Items

Like templates, library items are dynamically updateable. Editing the original library item automatically updates all instances of the item throughout the site. To open a library item for editing, select an instance in a document and click the Open button in the Property Inspector, or select the original in the Assets panel and click the Edit Library Item button, or double-click the LBI file in the Site panel. Make whatever changes you like. When you save the file, Dreamweaver offers to update all occurrences, as shown in Figure 20.31. Clicking the Update button copies the code to all documents containing instances of the item.

FIGURE 20.31
Updating all
occurrences of
a library item.

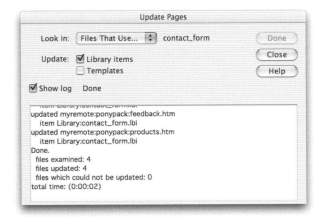

Uploading Library Items

For more on cloaking, see the section "Cloaking" in Chapter 18, "Site Publishing and Maintenance."

Every time you update a library item, you have to upload all files containing instances of the item. The easiest way to make sure this happens is to synchronize the entire site (select Site > Synchronize). There's no need to upload the original LBI file to the web server (because the code has been copied into the document files). You can even cloak the Library folder so that Dreamweaver doesn't try to upload it every time you synchronize your site. Do this in the Site panel by right-clicking the LBI file and choosing Cloaking > Cloak from the context menu. Or you can open the Site Definition dialog box, go to the Cloaking category, and add **.lbi** to the list of filename extensions that are automatically cloaked.

Working Smart with Library Items

After all the complexity and sophistication of templates, library items are refreshingly easy to understand and use. They don't have editable regions, or optional regions, or parameters. But as with everything, they have their own tricks.

Library Items and Templates Together

Library items don't have anything to do with templates, and they don't require templates to work, but you can use library items and templates together. You can put a library item into the locked region of a template, or into an editable region of a template's child page. The procedure is the same as for inserting library items into nontemplate pages. Why would you want to put library items and templates together? Maybe you have a site with three templates, each of which has a logo/contact/copyright bar at the bottom. Make that bar into a library item, and place it in the locked bottom area of each template file, and you don't have to update it separately in each of your three templates.

Or maybe you have a catalog site where periodically certain items are on sale and need a special sale notice. The notice will appear at different places within the editable region of each child page, so it doesn't belong in the template itself. But you still want to be able to update it quickly across the entire site. So you create a library item and insert it into editable regions within your template's child pages.

The Joys of Incompleteness: JavaScript, CSS, Image Maps, and Other Tricky Library Item Content

A library item is a fragment of code. Sometimes it's an incomplete fragment. That can be a problem—or an opportunity for creative sneakiness. It all depends on how you look at it.

CSS and Library Items

When you insert a library item into a document governed by CSS, the library item becomes governed by that same CSS. If you've redefined the h1 tag for your document, and you insert a library item that contains an h1 tag, the instance won't look the same as the original in the library. If you insert the same library item into another document that has h1 defined differently, that instance of the item won't look the same as the first instance. Similarly, if the library item calls on a custom class, that class might be defined differently in different documents, creating different-looking instances of the item across the site.

If you plan your styles right, you can use this CSS dependence to create multipurpose library items that blend nicely into the pages they're put into. The formalwear section of your site has blue subheadings; the beachwear section has orange subheadings. The sale notice you drop into both sections gets automatically color-coded to match its surroundings. Nice!

If you want to guarantee that all pieces of the library item are styled the same throughout the site, your best choice is to put that styling into an external style sheet that all pages in the site are linked to. But if this solution isn't feasible, you can always use an inline style within the library item itself:

```
<input type="text" name="username" style="width:150px" />
```

This overrides any other styling present in any documents the item ends up in. Of course, you can't use the CSS Styles panel to apply this styling because Dreamweaver doesn't support inline styles. You have to either code it yourself in Code view or use the Tag Editor dialog box or the Selection Inspector.

JavaScript Behaviors and Library Items

Dreamweaver behaviors are always coded with a function placed in the document head and a function call in the code for the page element the behavior is attached to. When you create a library item from a page element, only the function call goes in the library; the function itself remains behind.

This might seem like a terrible problem, but it's not. Dreamweaver is pretty smart about behaviors. After you insert the library item into a document, Dreamweaver sees the function call and automatically inserts the required function along with it. Pretty neat trick!

Image Maps and Library Items

When you create an image map in Dreamweaver, the program inserts code in two places, not always together. The map tag containing the hotspot coordinates and links is inserted toward the bottom of the body tag. The `img` tag that uses the map is placed wherever the image appears. If you select the image and turn it into a library item, only the `img` tag goes to the library; the map stays behind.

To make sure that this doesn't happen, you need to do a bit of code tweaking before creating the library item. Go to Code view in the document containing the image map. Find the `map` tag and move it so that it's right next to the `img` tag. The code should look something like this:

```
<img src="usmap.gif" width="473" height="181" border="0"
usemap="#Map">
<map name="Map">
  <area shape="rect" coords="103,88,216,119" href=
  "district1.html">
  <area shape="rect" coords="226,89,340,119" href=
  "district2.html">
  <area shape="rect" coords="349,89,464,120" href=
  "district3.html">
</map>
```

Back in Design view, the map appears as a gold icon next to the image, as shown in Figure 20.32. Make sure that both are selected before creating the library item.

FIGURE 20.32

The two parts of an image map, sitting together in Code and Design view.

If you've already created your library item, and the map didn't make it into the code, just cut and paste it from the original document into the LBI file.

When a Library Item Should Be a Server-Side Include

Library items are good and efficient at what they do, but they have one drawback: Every time you update a library item, you have to upload all the files that contain instances of that item to the web server. What if you use the item on two dozen pages or more, and the information in the item changes frequently? You'll get pretty tired of uploading and reuploading, especially if the uploading takes a while. This is a case for a server-side include.

How Server-Side Includes Work in HTML

Server-side includes can serve some of the same purposes as library items, but they're very different. They're part of the HTML specification, not just Dreamweaver tools. A *server-side include*, or *SSI*, is a placeholder that sits in an HTML document, containing instructions to the web server to replace it with some dynamically generated data. The data inserted can be anything from a chunk of predefined code to the current date or time to information collected from processing a script or querying a database. Or the data inserted can simply be another fragment of code, stored in another HTML file, to be tucked as-is into the current document. That's just like a Dreamweaver library item! The difference is, the web server (not Dreamweaver) does the inserting, and it happens at the last minute, when the page has been requested by a browser. This means that if you change the included file, you need to upload only that one file to the server, not any of the files that might call on it. For frequently updated pages, that's a big time-saver. Figure 20.33 compares the processes for library items and server-side includes.

Be aware that because SSIs require extra processing duties from the server, not all servers are configured to handle them. Before using them on any site, check with your server administrator or tech support staff to find out if they're supported.

FIGURE 20.33

The processes for Dreamweaver library items and server-side includes.

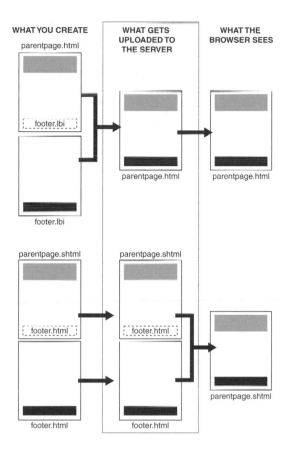

Using Server-Side Includes in Dreamweaver

A server-side include consists of a code fragment file, with an .htm or .html filename extension, and one or more documents that call on it. Each of these files has the .shtm or .shtml filename extension. (The "s" alerts the server that it needs to perform extra processing before delivering the page to a browser.) In Dreamweaver, the job of putting the include into the parent file is done with the Server-Side Include object. The whole process works this way:

1. Create both files—the parent file and the fragment file. Be sure to save the parent file with the proper filename extension. Dreamweaver doesn't add this for you.

2. Open the parent file, and put the insertion point where you want the include to appear.

3. From the Insert bar, choose the Common category, and from the Script objects, choose Server-Side Include. Or choose Insert > Script Objects > Server-Side Include. When the dialog box appears, click Browse to select the fragment file, and then click OK to close the dialog box.

In Design view, Dreamweaver displays the page with the inserted file in place, as shown in Figure 20.34. If you look in Code view, however, the code looks like this:

```
<!--#include file="myfile.html" -->
```

When you select the include, the SSI Property Inspector appears, showing the name of the included file and the type, which defaults to **file**.

FIGURE 20.34
A server-side include
in Design view and
in the Property
Inspector.

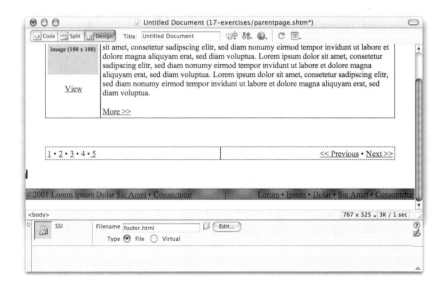

Previewing Server-Side Includes

Because a server puts the include in its parent file, it can't be previewed locally. If you have Dreamweaver configured to preview using a temporary file (do this in the Preferences/Preview in Browser dialog box), when you preview, Dreamweaver inserts the SSI code into the temporary file, along with some proprietary code indicating that this is an SSI. If you are not configured to use a temporary file, when you preview, the SSI won't show up at all.

SUMMARY

This chapter looked at Dreamweaver templates and libraries, two different (but not mutually exclusive!) ways of automating the development of site-wide content. You saw many different aspects of templates, including the template language, and you got some experience building a template-based site in the exercises. You also learned about library items and some of their idiosyncracies, and how library items compare with server-side includes, an HTML tool for creating updateable site content.

PART V:
DREAMWEAVER AND LIVE DATA

CHAPTER 21

BUILDING DYNAMIC SITES WITH DREAMWEAVER

MORE AND MORE AS THE WEB DEVELOPS, INCREASINGLY COMPLEX DATA processing needs require more than just static, or hard-coded, pages. You want your visitors to be able to ask questions, place orders, and get results immediately. You need current information posted at all times, without having behind-the-scenes humans constantly updating and uploading pages. In other words, you need web pages that can be generated and updated automatically, calling information as needed from a central source such as a database, and updating that source as visitors buy things, add their names to lists, and sign in and out. You need data-driven—dynamic—websites.

This section of the book is for you if you work in the world of dynamic data—or if you want to expand into that world. This chapter goes over what makes a site dynamic, the players and the options in dynamic development, and how Dreamweaver MX 2004 fits into that picture.

BASICS OF DYNAMIC SITES

A *static web page* is one that's completely created in advance, with all text and images in place, and housed on a web server to await a visitor coming to look at it. A *dynamic web page*, in contrast, contains placeholders for content that the server inserts at the moment a visitor requests the page—at runtime—along with instructions to the server on how to construct the completed page. A look at how web pages are processed between the server and the browser will show you how this works.

How Static Web Pages Work

Figure 21.1 shows the typical set of events in the life of a static web page. The page exists on the server. When a visitor clicks a link or types a URL in the address field, the browser sends a request in the form of the desired URL to the web server. The server software then finds the page and responds by sending it back to the browser. This is called the *request-and-response model*. The request is an HTTP request, using the `http://` protocol to begin the URL; the web server software is also called the *HTTP server*.

FIGURE 21.1
The standard request-and-response process for static web pages.

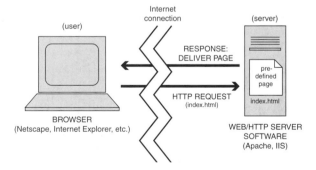

How Dynamic Web Pages Work

Dynamic data can enter into this equation in three main ways:

- Server-side includes (SSIs)
- CGI scripts
- Database connectivity using application servers

Although the purpose of this section is to show you the third method, all three are covered here so that you can see how they relate.

Server-Side Includes (SSIs)

The simplest kind of dynamic content—and the easiest to understand—is the *server-side include,* or SSI. An SSI is a placeholder that sits in an HTML document, containing instructions to the server to replace it with some dynamically generated data. The data inserted can be anything from a chunk of predefined code to the current date or time to information collected from processing a script or querying a database. The code for an SSI might look like any of the following:

```
<!--#include virtual="mydata.html" -->

<!--#echo var="DATE_LOCAL" -->

<!--#exec cgi="/cgi-bin/sample_script.pl" -->
```

The HTML document containing an SSI is saved with a special filename extension—typically .shtm or .shtml—to alert the server that SSIs are present.

For more on using SSIs in Dreamweaver, see the section "When a Library Item Should Be a Server-Side Include" in Chapter 20, "Site-Wide Content with Templates and Libraries."

Figure 21.2 shows the web page request-and-response process for an HTML page using SSIs. When the server receives a request for an SHTML document, it responds by finding any embedded SSIs in the page, executing their instructions, and inserting the resulting data into the document, which it then passes to the browser. Usually this involves substituting some real data (such as the date or time, or even the contents of another file stored on the server) in place of the SSI placeholder code.

FIGURE 21.2
The request-and-response process for web pages that use SSIs.

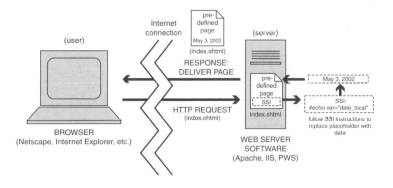

CGI-Scripted Documents

A more truly dynamic web page can be created using CGI scripting to process browser requests and respond by saving user input, delivering web pages with filled-in placeholder content, and even building pages at runtime from collections of code snippets. For this discussion, you need to know only that CGI scripts (usually written in Perl) are stored in a special folder on the web server, generally called **cgi-bin**. When a user fills out a form, the form action might contain the URL of a CGI script, like this (the URL is in bold):

```
<form name="theForm" action="http://www.domain.com/cgi-bin/
➥myscript.cgi" method="post">
```

Clicking the form's Submit button causes the browser to request the specified script, passing it the form variables as part of the URL or as an attached posting. Figure 21.3 diagrams the ensuing request-and-response process. The web server knows, because of the extension of the file that is called (.cgi or .pl, depending on how the server software is set up), that the requested page should not just be downloaded back to the browser. Instead, it finds the script and executes it. The script might perform a simple task such as emailing user input to a designated address, or it might execute much more complex operations such as performing calculations on user data, talking to a database, and so forth.

FIGURE 21.3
The request-and-response process for web pages that access CGI scripts.

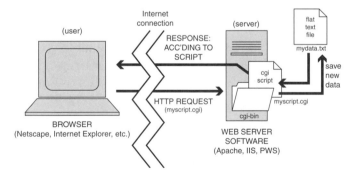

Application Servers and Database Connectivity

The third and most powerful way to create dynamic web pages—what this section of the book is all about—is using databases to provide content and special software modules called *application servers* to construct pages at runtime. Figure 21.4 diagrams the basic response-and-request process for this kind of dynamic content.

FIGURE 21.4
The request-and-
response process
for web pages built
using an application
server and database
connectivity.

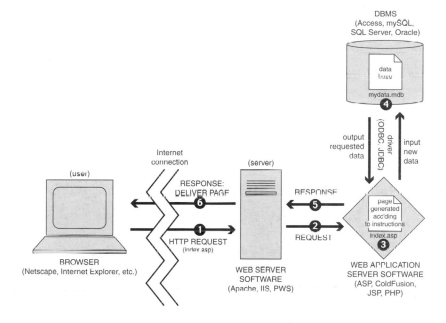

The general procedure is as follows:

1. The browser sends an HTTP request consisting of the URL for a document with a filename extension such as .asp, .aspx, .cfm, .php, or .jsp.

2. The web server software recognizes the extension, finds the requested page, and activates the application server. This might be the Active Server controls built into Microsoft web servers, ColdFusion Server, Tomcat Java server, or the PHP module.

3. The application server reads the document and either executes any scripts or interprets any custom tags it finds. These scripts and tags usually contain requests for some database information (such as "Place the contents of the Product Name database field from the Widget International database here") or instructions to change the database information (such as "Add John Smith to the User-name database field in the Books Online database").

4. The application server sends these requests and instructions—collectively called *queries*—to a database management system such as Access or MySQL, which finds the appropriate database and performs the requested actions. If any information was requested, it's sent back to the application server.

5. The application server constructs an HTML-formatted page containing the requested information formatted according to the instructions in the originally requested document, and sends the whole lot back to the web server.

6. The web server returns this page to the browser.

That's how the process works. Now it's time to take a look at who all the players are and how they all fit together.

Who's Who and What's What in the World of Dynamic Data

Obviously, setting up a database-driven website involves a lot of variables and requires learning all sorts of new names and technologies. The following sections examine the pieces of the puzzle one at a time.

The Server OS and HTTP Server Software

The web server itself is a computer, using some version of Windows or Unix/Linux (including Mac OS X) as its operating system, running special web software for processing HTTP requests. The term *web server* in a discussion of dynamic sites usually refers not to the computer itself but to the server software. This software is also called the *HTTP server* to distinguish it from the application server (discussed later in this chapter). The most common server software is described in the following sections.

Apache

Created and maintained by the Apache Software Foundation, Apache is the most popular server software today, installed on more than 50 percent of web servers worldwide. Apache is open-source software and therefore is either free or very cheap to obtain. It's stable and powerful, and it runs on just about any operating system.

Internet Information Server

Microsoft's Internet Information Server (IIS) software is second only to Apache in popularity. It's powerful and flexible, although as a Microsoft product it runs only on servers using the Windows operating system (NT, 2000, or XP).

The Database

The heart of the data-driven website is, of course, the database. For the system to work, it must have a database, and the database must reside on the web server (or on a computer accessible to the web server). To create the database and work with it offline, you must have access to a piece of software called a *database management system* (DBMS). To make the database part of an online system, a DBMS must reside on the server.

To keep things simple, this discussion focuses on all the components of server-side data processing as if they were stored on one server computer. In fact, multiple networked computers might be involved. This won't change how the system works, however.

To author database-driven web pages online, you don't need to be a database expert. However, you do need to know at least how databases store data, how to ask them questions and give them commands, and how to use drivers to communicate with them.

Hierarchical Data Storage

Databases store information in tables, as a series of fields (columns) and records (rows). Figure 21.5 shows a simple table structure at work. Adding a new customer to the database adds a new record, or row. Adding a new field, or column, means storing one more piece of information about each customer. This table structure is called *hierarchical data storage*.

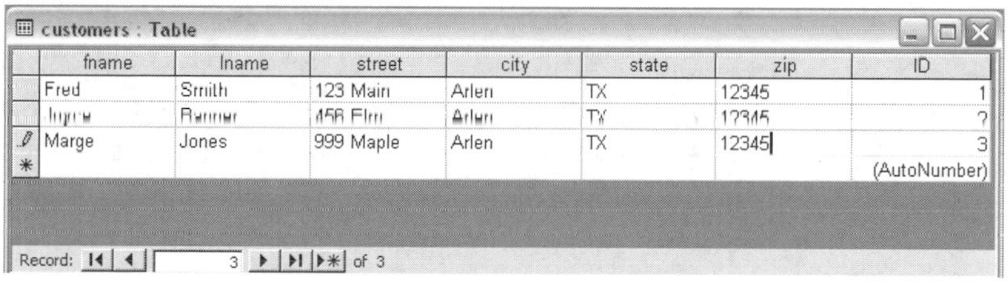

FIGURE 21.5
Data stored in a hierarchical, or table, structure.

fname	lname	street	city	state	zip	ID
Fred	Smith	123 Main	Arlen	TX	12345	1
Iryi v	Runner	456 Flm	Arlen	TX	12345	2
Marge	Jones	999 Maple	Arlen	TX	12345	3
						(AutoNumber)

customers : Table

Record: 3 of 3

Relational Databases

Hierarchical information storage is fine as far as it goes, but it doesn't go far enough to handle complex information. The more-sophisticated databases—the ones generally used with data-driven websites—are *relational databases,* run by relational database management systems (RDBMSs). Relational databases offer the following features:

- **Multiple tables**—A relational database stores information in a series of tables, related by common key fields. Figure 21.6 shows the same information table shown in Figure 21.5, but with a second and third table added to store different kinds of data.

- **Primary and foreign keys**—Keys create the relationships between the tables. Each table must contain one field designated as the *primary key field,* which contains a unique entry for each record. This lets you call up a specific record by searching for the value in this field. Each table relates to the other tables by having its primary key present in the other table as a foreign key. As the dotted lines in Figure 21.6 show, the Customer ID and Product No. primary keys become foreign keys in the Order table, establishing the relationships between the tables.

FIGURE 21.6
Three related tables
storing customer,
order, and
product data.

Queries and SQL Statements

A database is useful only if you can find, update, and analyze information in it. You do this by using the database management system to query the database. How many people have ordered product J-9995 since January of last year? Did more or fewer people order the item the year before? What is the most expensive item ordered since March? When was the last time Moe Howard ordered anything? Sort the customer database by name, zip code, or state. Raise all prices in the product database by 5 percent. The standard language used for querying databases is Structured Query Language (SQL). Hence, database queries also are called *SQL statements.*

Drivers (ODBC and JDBC)

Application servers communicate with database management systems through *drivers*—pieces of software that define how to move information into and out of databases. The most common driver formats are

Microsoft's Open Database Connectivity (ODBC) and Sun Microsystems' Java Database Connectivity (JDBC). A database management system that can connect using one of these formats is said to be ODBC-compliant or JDBC-compliant.

Standard DBMS Programs

To function as part of an online system, a database management system must be a relational database, must be able to run in whatever operating system is required by the server, must understand SQL statements, and must be compliant with ODBC, JDBC, or some other standard driver format. This section describes some common database management systems for online use.

Microsoft Access, the most popular database program for general business use, is often used for small to mid-size online databases. Access isn't the most powerful DBMS. Its main limitation for online use is that it cannot accept large numbers of users trying to access it simultaneously. It is reasonably priced, however, and easily available as part of Microsoft Office. As a Microsoft product, it runs only on Windows servers.

SQL Server is the big brother of Access, intended for large-scale sites with huge amounts of data and a significant number of simultaneous hits. This powerful program is expensive, and learning it is not for the faint of heart. Like Access, it runs on Windows only.

MySQL, a DBMS that has its roots in Unix, is a good alternative to Access if you are on a tight budget or are not working on Windows. It doesn't have the same multiple-access limitations as Access, and it's famous for its speed and stability and for being able to handle large amounts of data. But it is missing some of Access' advanced features, such as stored procedures. In its basic form, MySQL uses a command-line interface, so it might seem intimidating at first. However, several free GUI MySQL interfaces are available. Its learning curve is surprisingly gentle compared with Access. Depending on how you use it, it's either free or cheap. It runs on Windows, Unix, Linux, or Mac OS X.

PostgreSQL, sort of a big brother of MySQL, is the most advanced open-source DBMS available. It runs in Unix-based environments, including Linux and now Mac OS X. For the non-Microsoft crowd, it's a good alternative to SQL Server.

For more information on Access and SQL Server, visit www.microsoft.com. To learn about (and download) MySQL and PostgreSQL, visit www.mysql.com and www.postgresql.org. To learn about Oracle, visit www.oracle.com.

Oracle, from Oracle Enterprises, is the most powerful database management system available. It's also not a program for small businesses or anyone on a tight budget. It's very expensive, and it comes with a steep learning curve and very expensive authorized training. Oracle runs on Linux, Unix, and Windows operating systems.

The Application Server (Middleware)

Databases, and database management systems, are a big topic—but they're only half of the story. The application server software functions as *middleware*, allowing communication between the browser and the DBMS. Choosing an application server is like getting married. You (and your client, and your company) will be up close and personal with this software on a daily basis for a long time. You'll use the application server language to write your pages. You'll be limited by its limitations and empowered by its strengths.

Which web server, database, and/or application server should you choose? Unless you're in charge of your web server's configuration, these decisions probably aren't entirely up to you. Whoever hosts your site will have certain technologies available. If you're shopping for a host, it's a good idea to learn what technologies each host offers, and how those options fit your needs, before choosing one.

ColdFusion

Macromedia's ColdFusion has become a very popular alternative to ASP, largely because it uses a tag-based, rather than script-based, means of communicating with the DBMS. The core of ColdFusion functionality is ColdFusion Markup Language (CFML). Page elements can also be built using the CFScript scripting language.

The application server portion of ColdFusion is called *ColdFusion Server*. It operates on servers running Windows, Linux, HP-UX, or Solaris, and it must be purchased separately from any web server software. Because it is available only through commercial licenses, ColdFusion might not be the most immediately attractive choice for small businesses, but the speed of page construction possible using CFML makes the long-term development costs very reasonable. To learn more about ColdFusion, visit http://www.macromedia.com/software/coldfusion.

PHP

PHP (the recursive acronym for PHP: Hypertext Preprocessor) is a popular open-source alternative to commercial systems. Its commands are script-based, written in PHP scripting language.

PHP is available freely or cheaply, depending on its intended use. It has a large and friendly user community supporting it, but no commercial guarantees behind it. PHP works with Apache and Microsoft IIS web servers and on Unix, Windows, and Mac OS X operating systems. Unlike the other server technologies, PHP is database-specific. Not all installations of PHP work with all DBMSs. Dreamweaver MX 2004 supports PHP for use with MySQL. To learn more about PHP, visit `http://php.net/`.

ASP/ASP.NET

ASP (Active Server Pages) is Microsoft's basic application server. ASP is not an independent program or software module, like other application servers are. Rather, it's a functionality built into the Microsoft web server software (IIS). The language is script-based, using VBScript or JavaScript to formulate database queries and construct pages based on the results. Many developers still use ASP for less-complex websites, but it is being supplanted by the much more powerful ASP.NET.

According to Microsoft, the .NET framework, which includes ASP.NET, is the new face of dynamic web development. Programs and scripts can be written in several languages, including Managed C++, C#, JScript, and Visual Basic, and they can be executed server-side or client-side. Live data pages can also be programmed to tie in with Microsoft's COM technology. ASP.NET offers many of the advantages of using Java/JSP (see the next section), but strictly within the Microsoft fold. ASP.NET runs only on IIS web servers, and of course only on servers running the Windows OS. To learn more about ASP.NET, visit `http://www.microsoft.com/net/`.

JSP

JSP, or JavaServer Pages, is (as its name implies) a Java-based alternative to both ASP and ColdFusion. The application server is in the form of an applet—called a *container*—that resides on the server. Popular JSP containers include several commercial entities, such as Macromedia's JRun and IBM's WebSphere, as well as the popular open-source Tomcat. Generally, JSP is favored by Java programmers. It's definitely not for novices. To learn more about Java development, including JSP, visit `http://java.sun.com`.

ASP is an old technology, being replaced by ASP.NET. JSP generally is not used except by Java developers. This book focuses on ColdFusion, PHP, and ASP.NET.

SETTING UP YOUR WORKSTATION FOR DYNAMIC DEVELOPMENT

If you want to use Dreamweaver to build data-driven websites using PHP, ColdFusion, or one of the other server technologies, you can set up your development environment in one of two ways.

In a "live" or "online" setup, all the specialized software—web server, application server, DBMS, driver—is housed on a remote computer that you have FTP access to. This remote computer might even be the web server hosting your site. Developing live is easier to set up because it means you don't have to install any new software on your computer. But you can work only when you're connected to the remote server, and you're limited by the speed of your connection.

In an "offline" setup, you put all software elements on your computer—including HTTP server software, DBMS, everything—and temporarily act as hosting server and developer. When your site is fully developed, you move the relevant database files, drivers, and pages to the actual web server. This is how most developers work when they can. An extra benefit of developing offline is that you get a free education about how server software works.

It's entirely acceptable to install web server software on a computer that won't be used solely as a web server. You probably don't want to do development work on a computer while that computer is open to the public for web browsing. But simply putting server software on the computer doesn't make that computer a dedicated server.

Setting Up for Online Development

To set up for remote development, you need the following information and configuration.

The Remote Computer's HTTP Address (URL)

Even if you're connected to the remote computer over a local network, you must know its URL to send HTTP requests to it so that you can preview your data. If your remote computer is your web host, use your site's domain name. If the remote computer is simply another computer you're networked to, you have to get its IP address from the server administrator.

To learn the IP address of a Windows server, launch the command prompt or DOS prompt. At the prompt, type **ipconfig** and press Enter. A set of numbers appears, including the IP address.

To learn the IP address of a Mac server, launch the System Preferences and view the Sharing preferences. The IP address is at the bottom of the window.

Read/Write Access to the Shared Web Folder

If the remote computer you're using for development is your web host, you already have FTP access to your published files. If you have local network access to the remote computer, you don't need FTP access. But regardless of your connection method, you need to make sure you have read/write access to the folder where your files will be stored.

Correct Setup on the Remote Computer

The remote computer might be your web hosting company's web server, or it might be a computer under the administration of someone else in your office, or it might be all yours. Someone—maybe you—needs to create the setup spelled out in the previous sections: the HTTP server, the application server, the DBMS, and the driver must all be present on that computer. You also have to know any special instructions required to access these items. You can get this information from your server administrator or tech support staff.

SETTING UP FOR OFFLINE DEVELOPMENT

To develop offline, using your own computer as the development web server, you need to make sure that the HTTP server, application server, database software, and any necessary drivers are installed and correctly configured.

Setting Up the HTTP Server

Your main choices for the HTTP server are IIS and Apache. If you're setting up for ColdFusion development, you can also run the ColdFusion server as a stand-alone server (performing HTTP server and application server duties), so you'll install that instead of Apache or IIS. You should still read the upcoming section "Serving Pages Locally," however, to understand how local HTTP servers work.

Installing IIS

If you're running Windows NT, 2000, or XP Pro, the simplest HTTP server to install for development is IIS. For NT users, the IIS software is part of the Windows NT 4.0 Option Pack, which you can download from the Microsoft website. For other users, the IIS software is on your Windows Install CD.

To get help using IIS, launch your browser and type **http://localhost/iis help** in the URL field.

IIS installs as a service, meaning that it starts automatically when the computer boots. To access and configure IIS, select Start > Control Panel > (Administrative Tools) > Internet Services Manager.

Installing Apache

IIS is the most common choice as a Windows server, but it isn't the only choice. Especially if you're working with PHP, before uploading to a Unix server, you might want to more closely duplicate your eventual online environment by using Apache as your HTTP server. Apache is free and easily available.

If you have IIS on your computer, it's best not to run IIS and Apache at the same time.

Windows users can download Apache from the Apache Group (http://httpd.apache.org/). Apache is always developing, but it's usually available as a self-installing EXE file with complete instructions for configuration. You can choose to install it as a service (which starts up every time your computer starts up) or as an application, which you can start and stop from the desktop.

For Mac users, the Apache HTTP server comes preinstalled with OS X. All you have to do to turn it on is launch System Preferences, go to the Sharing pane, and enable Web Sharing. With Web Sharing enabled, Apache automatically starts and runs in the background every time you start your computer.

Serving Pages Locally

To browse locally served pages, your browser must pass an HTTP request to the server software by specifying the HTTP protocol followed by your computer's IP address or computer name, or the generic IP address (127.0.0.1) or name (localhost) that computers use to refer to themselves.

Entering any of the following into the address field of the browser acts as a request telling the server to display (or *serve*) its default page:

http://localhost/

http://127.0.0.1/

http://192.123.128.128/ (substitute your computer's IP address)

Figures 21.7 and 21.8 show this happening.

FIGURE 21.7
The IIS HTTP Server default home page served from your local computer.

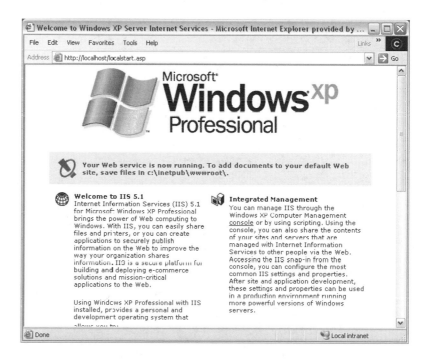

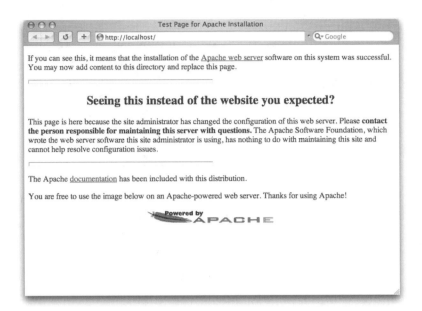

Each server has a root directory, or folder, from which it serves its pages. You can request any web document placed in the root directory, or in a subfolder within the root directory. For instance, you can request a file called **myfile.html**, stored in a folder called **myFiles**, which is stored inside the server's root directory, by entering the following into the browser's address field:

> **http://127.0.0.1/myFiles/index.html**

> **http://localhost/myFiles/index.html**

> **http://192.123.128.128/myFiles/index.html (substitute your IP address)**

For IIS, the root folder from which all pages are served is **c:\Inetpub\wwwroot**.

For Apache/Windows, the root folder is the **htdocs** folder in your **Apache** program folder. The exact path to this folder varies, depending on your installation.

For Apache/Mac, the root folder is **/Library/WebServer/Documents**.

(If you'll be using ColdFusion as your HTTP server, see the later section "Using ColdFusion as Your HTTP Server" for specific instructions on browsing served ColdFusion pages.)

The quickest way to test whether you have correctly identified your root folder is to create a simple HTML file called **mytest.html** or some other generic name and store it in what you think is the root folder. Then open your browser and type **http://localhost/mytest.html**. Your page should appear.

Setting Up the Application Server

You also need to make sure that the correct application server software is installed and correctly configured on your computer. The application servers covered in this book are ASP.NET, PHP, and ColdFusion.

Setting Up PHP

To develop and test PHP pages locally, you need the PHP server module or CGI application. Windows users can download it from the PHP website (`http://www.php.net/downloads.php`). Make sure you download a Windows binary version and not source code. This is a self-installing version with complete documentation.

For Mac users, the Apache server in OS X includes a disabled PHP module. You enable it by typing a few lines of code in the Terminal window. For full instructions, visit the Apple website at `http://developer.apple.com/internet/macosx/php.html`.

Setting Up ColdFusion

To develop and test ColdFusion pages locally, you must install the ColdFusion Server software. This is a commercial program, but a free developer's edition is available for users who want to develop and test on one computer. For Windows users, ColdFusion Server development edition is included on the Macromedia Studio MX 2004 CD, or you can download it from the Macromedia website (`http://www.macromedia.com/software/coldfusion/`). For Mac users, currently the only option available is to download the ColdFusion Java edition, also available on the Macromedia website. Be aware, though, that this is a Java installation, and installing it is not for novices.

During installation, you'll be asked to provide an administrative password to access the server for setup purposes. Be sure to remember or jot down what you enter here! You'll need it later.

Using ColdFusion as Your HTTP Server

ColdFusion can run as a stand-alone server, which means it functions as HTTP server and application server. By default, it operates through port 8500, which means it can run at the same time as IIS or Apache without getting in their way. It also means that you must access all served pages using the following URL formula:

http://localhost:8500/ ...

http://127.0.0.1:8500/ ...

The root folder from which ColdFusion Server serves its documents is CFusionMX\wwwroot\. With the default Windows installation, you'll find this on your C drive. Any files or folders placed within this folder can be accessed using these URLs.

Administering ColdFusion Server

The ColdFusion Server administrative interface, shown in Figure 21.9, is a set of web pages that you can access through your browser at http://localhost:8500/CFIDE/administrator/. You need to enter your administrative password to gain access to these pages.

FIGURE 21.9
The ColdFusion Server administrative pages.

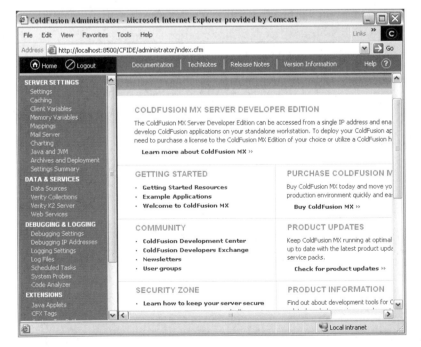

Setting Up ASP.NET

ASP itself is part of IIS, so it needs no installation. To develop and test ASP.NET locally, you must download and install the .NET framework from Microsoft (http://www.microsoft.com/net). Extensive installation and configuration help is available through the website and documentation. Be warned that this is a big download!

Databases

You can't serve pages built from databases unless you have the proper database management software (DBMS) on your computer. The most popular choices for small business and individual websites are Access and MySQL.

Setting Up Microsoft Access

For Windows users, Microsoft Access is easy to obtain. You might already have it on your computer. For local development, your database file can be stored anywhere on your computer.

Setting Up MySQL

MySQL is freely available for both Mac and Windows. It's fairly easy to use, but not that easy to set up. For full information on MySQL, visit the official website at http://www.mysql.com.

Windows users can download a self-installing EXE for MySQL from the MySQL website. (Be sure to download the Windows binary.) After it's installed, start the server portion of the program by launching WinMySQLAdmin. This program runs in the background and appears as a traffic light icon in the taskbar. You'll also probably want to obtain a GUI. MySQL Control Center, available from the MySQL website, is free and easy to use.

Mac users can also download a MySQL version from the official website, but you'll have a much easier time if you download a graphic installer such as the one from Marc Liyanage (http://www.entropy.ch). Full installation and configuration instructions are included. You'll also want a GUI, like the free CocoaMySQL, available from Source Forge (http://cocoamysql.sourceforge.net/).

Database files must be stored where the MySQL server can find them. Each database consists of several files stored in a folder named after the database, in the **mysql/data** folder. The exact location of this folder on your hard drive depends on which MySQL installation you use. Figure 21.10 shows the MySQL folder structure and database files.

FIGURE 21.10
MySQL databases stored in the mysql/data folder.

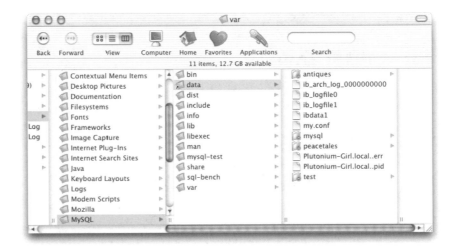

Setting Up Drivers

Each database you'll communicate with requires some sort of driver to connect to. The driver setup you need depends on which server technology you're using.

ColdFusion

If you're using Windows and you're connecting to an Access database, ColdFusion Server automatically creates a DSN for you. Read the section "ASP.NET and DSNs" for more on DSNs.

To work with ColdFusion, databases must be registered with the ColdFusion server. To do this, launch the ColdFusion administrator pages (see the earlier section "Setting Up ColdFusion" for more on this). From the main page, choose Data & Services > Data Sources to access the controls.

In the Add New Data Source section, give your data source a one-word name, and select the driver type (Access, MySQL, and so on). Then click the Add button. In the Data Source page that appears, fill in the required information (this varies, depending on the driver type you have chosen) and click Submit. If all is well, after a few moments the screen changes, and your database is listed in the Connected Data Sources section.

PHP and Drivers

When used with MySQL (as it is in Dreamweaver), PHP requires no drivers. Instead, it communicates with the MySQL server application and can access any database on the system

ASP.NET and DSNs

ASP.NET requires a Data Source Name (DSN) to communicate with databases. DSNs are ODBC drivers and are created and managed through the Data Sources (ODBC) control panel. To create a DSN, open the control panel, bring the System DSN tab to the front, and click the Add button. When the new DSN window appears, choose the appropriate driver from the list of drivers (depending on what kind of database you're using), and enter whatever additional information is required. For Access databases, it's as simple as browsing to select the database. When you're done, close all dialog boxes. You now have a method of accessing this database file from any web application on your computer. Figure 21.11 shows the interface for defining DSNs.

FIGURE 21.11
Defining a DSN for an Access database.

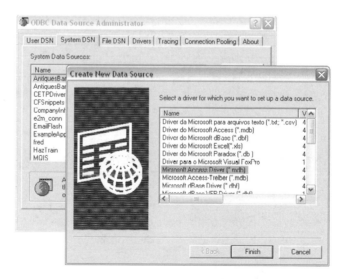

ASP.NET can also use a DSN-less connection string to establish communication with the database, in which case a DSN is unnecessary. This requires more skill to code, and you don't need to do it before you set up Dreamweaver.

How Dynamic Sites Work in Dreamweaver

Just as Dreamweaver helps you write static HTML pages, it also has plenty of tools to help you develop dynamic sites using ASP, ASP.NET, ColdFusion, PHP, or JSP. Dreamweaver can help you manage database connections, compose database queries, and display dynamic information, all within its familiar visual design environment. The basic procedure is as follows:

1. Define a site, including testing server information.

2. Define at least one database connection for the site.

3. Open individual documents and use application objects and server behaviors to query the database, collect recordsets, display dynamic data, and so on.

Dreamweaver uses the same procedure, and much of the same toolset, regardless of which server technology you're using. Therefore, as soon as you get the hang of things, switching technologies is fairly painless. The code itself, however, is not language-independent. This means that as soon as you've created a site using one server technology (such as ASP or Cold-Fusion), you can't just push a few buttons and change existing pages.

Live Data Preview and the Testing Server

The main difference between using Dreamweaver for static sites and using it for dynamic sites is how it previews your pages.

Previewing in the Browser

In a static site, when you choose Preview in Browser (F12), Dreamweaver launches the browser and passes it the local address of the current page:

```
C:\Client Files\Web\My Local Site\index.html
```

or for Mac users:

```
file:///Client Files/Web/My Local Site/index.html
```

This engages your browser through your computer's file system.

In a dynamic site, however, it's not enough just to view the pages in a browser. Dreamweaver has to activate the web server, passing it an HTTP request so that it processes the files. This requires an address like one of these:

```
http://localhost/mysite/index.php
```

```
http://127.0.0.1:8500/mysite/index.cfm
```

```
http://www.mydomain.com/index.aspx
```

This engages the web server and the browser so that pages are "served" rather than simply being called up through the file system. To develop dynamic sites, therefore, you must have access to a web server as you work.

Previewing in the Document Window

You can also engage the dynamic preview from within the Document window itself by clicking the Live Data button in the Document toolbar, as shown in Figure 21.12. When you do this, the Document window changes to show you the URL it's previewing from (it's the same as those used by the browser), and your page appears with real data replacing data or scripting placeholders, as shown in Figure 21.13. Although you can do a certain amount of work with Live Data view engaged, this slows you down and is not recommended. Instead, use this as a quick peek at the final result without having to leave Dreamweaver. To disengage Live Data view, click one of the other view icons (Design, Code, Code and Design) in the Document toolbar.

FIGURE 21.12
The Live Data view icon in the Document toolbar.

FIGURE 21.13
The Document window in Live Data viewing mode.

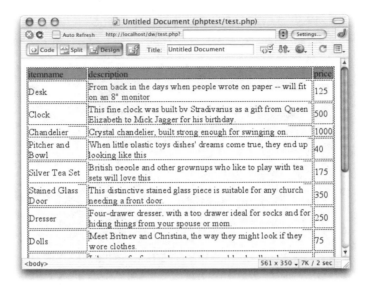

Setting Up a Dynamic Site

The first step in setting up a dynamic site in Dreamweaver is to define a site, complete with local, testing server, and (optionally) remote information. Dreamweaver needs to know where your local, testing server, and remote folders are. It also needs to know what server technology you'll be using and, if necessary, what specific scripting language you'll be using for that technology. (For instance, ASP can be coded using one of several scripting languages.) Finally, as with any remote site, it needs to know how to communicate with your web server and your testing server.

Set up a dynamic Dreamweaver site this way:

1. Choose Site > Manage Sites, and click the New button (as you normally would to define a site).

2. In the Site Definition dialog box (Advanced mode), set up the Local Info category as normal. If desired, you can also set up your Remote Info at this time, but it's not required at this point.

3. Still in the Site Definition dialog box, go to the Testing Server category, as shown in Figure 21.14. Specify the server technology/language setup you want to use, and set up communication information for your web server. If you're planning to develop online, using the remote server as your development server, the settings here should match those in the Remote Info category. If you want to develop

offline with a local testing server (a safer method), set up the connection information to your computer's server here.

FIGURE 21.14
Setting up the testing server for a Dreamweaver site (offline development).

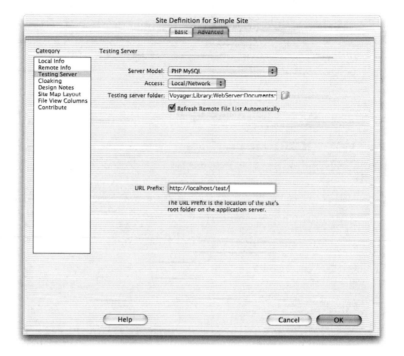

It's especially important to make sure that the URL Prefix for communicating with the testing server is correct! Dreamweaver relies on this information to create live previews of your pages. For offline development, begin with **http://localhost/** or **http://127.0.0.1/**. For online development, enter the base URL you would normally use to browse to your website—**http://mydomain.com/**, for instance.

When you're done, click OK to close the Site Definition dialog box. The dynamic development features in Dreamweaver are now enabled for this site.

The testing server is essentially a temporary remote site. It works much like the remote site in the Dreamweaver interface. To see the contents of the testing server, as shown in Figure 21.15, do one of the following:

- If the Site panel is not expanded, choose Testing Server from the site view drop-down menu (instead of Local View).

- If the Site panel is expanded, click the Testing Server button to display it in the panel's left pane.

FIGURE 21.15
Viewing the testing
server in the Site
panel (expanded and
unexpanded).

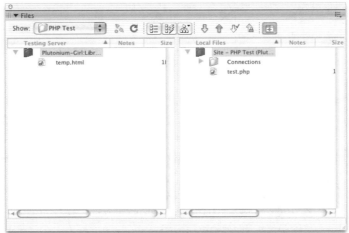

With the Site panel in expanded mode, and the testing server showing,
all Dreamweaver's file synchronizing commands—such as Get, Put, and
Synchronize—work between local and testing server sites, just as they
normally work between local and remote sites.

Connecting to a Database

The database connection is a script that either calls on the driver to talk
to the database or tells the application server how to talk to the database
without a driver. Every time you use Dreamweaver to establish a database connection, the program creates a Connections folder in your local
root folder and puts a special script file in that folder. Every time you use

that connection in one of your site documents, Dreamweaver links that document to the relevant script file. This externalization is a great thing, because it allows you to develop on a testing server and then move the site to a live remote server simply by updating the connection script.

All connections are managed by the Databases panel (select Window > Connections), located in the Application panel group. To create a connection, open the Databases panel and check out its messages. Whichever server model you're using, this panel walks you through the steps of creating a connection script within that technology.

Keep an eye on how the panels are laid out in the Application panel group. As you're defining your dynamic site and its pages, you generally start from the Databases panel (on the left) and work your way through the panels from left to right. Each panel starts with a checklist of tasks that need to be done before that panel can be used.

ColdFusion

For ColdFusion MX sites, as soon as the testing server has been defined, the Databases panel displays a list of all databases currently registered with the ColdFusion MX server, as shown in Figure 21.16. No connection script is necessary.

FIGURE 21.16
The Databases panel for a ColdFusion MX site.

PHP MySQL

If your server technology is PHP MySQL, you don't need to define a driver; the MySQL server program keeps track of databases and connections. As the Databases panel indicates, you need to define a site (which includes a testing server), open or create a PHP document, and make sure you can connect to your testing server. Then you can click the + button to create a connection.

When you click the + button, the only choice available is MySQL Connection. When you choose this, a dialog box asks you the following (see Figure 21.17):

- **Connection name**—Any one-word name will do, although many developers like their connection names to end in **conn**.

- **MySQL Server**—Enter the IP address of your testing server here. If your server is on your working computer, enter **localhost** or **127.0.0.1**.

- **User name and password**—MySQL allows only known users to connect to and access its databases. Get this information from the administrator of your MySQL server. (If you set up MySQL on your own computer, you can check the user table of the mysql database to see what usernames and passwords are available.)

- **Database**—The name of the database to connect to. Click the Select button to get a list of available databases.

FIGURE 21.17
Setting up a database connection using PHP MySQL.

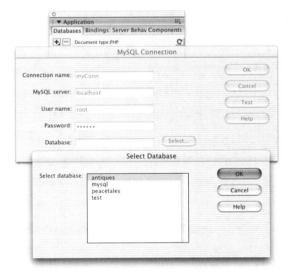

ASP.NET

For ASP and ASP.NET sites, the Databases panel gives you the choice of choosing a DSN on the server or constructing a DSN-less connection string. Choosing the former calls up a dialog box listing all DSNs currently defined for the specified server. If no DSN is defined, clicking the

Define button connects you to the server's ODBC control panel so that you can define one without leaving Dreamweaver. Choosing the latter opens a dialog box where you can type in your connection string. (To learn more about constructing connection strings, check a good ASP.NET reference.)

After you've made the connection, the Databases panel shows a database icon with your connection name. Expanding this icon lets you see the structure of the database you're connected to, as shown in Figure 21.18. If you check out the Site panel, you'll see a new Connections folder containing one file named after your connection, as shown in Figure 21.19.

FIGURE 21.18
The Databases panel showing a connected database.

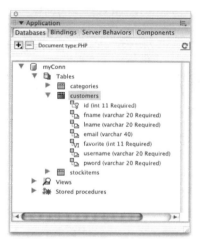

FIGURE 21.19
The Connections script as it appears in the Site panel.

EXERCISE 21.1   **Creating a Dreamweaver Site**

In this exercise, you define the Antiques Barn ColdFusion, PHP, or ASP.NET site in Dreamweaver. Make sure you've set up your workstation for online or offline development before going through the exercise.

The pages and images necessary for the exercise can be found in the **chapter_21** folder of the book's website at `www.peachpit.com`, in folders specific to each application server and language. Download the appropriate folder to your hard drive. The antiques database files are in the **chapter_21/databases** folder, in Access and MySQL format. For Access development, copy the **antiques.mdb** file anywhere on your hard drive. For MySQL development, copy the **antiques** folder to the mysql/data directory on your computer or your remote server.

1. Start by defining the site. In Dreamweaver, select Site > Manage Sites, and click the New button. In the Site Definition dialog box that appears, click the Advanced tab to bring it to the front.

2. Go to the Local Info category. Local site information for a dynamic site is no different from any other site information. Name your site **Antiques Barn**. From the local root folder, browse to the folder you copied from the website (**antiques_php**, **antiques_cf**, and so on).

3. Now go to the Testing Server category. From the Server Model drop-down menu, choose whatever server technology and language you want to use. If you choose ColdFusion, make sure the following drop-down menu is set to Dreamweaver MX 2004 Pages Only. (Dreamweaver must write different code to communicate with different versions of the ColdFusion Server.)

4. For the testing server connection, you enter different information here depending on how you set up your workstation (as discussed earlier in this chapter):

   • If you're set up for offline development, choose Local/Network as the access method, and browse to your HTTP server's root directory. (See the section "Serving Pages Locally" or "Using ColdFusion as Your HTTP Server" if you've forgotten where your root directory is.) Create a new folder in this root directory called **antiquesbarn**, and select it as the folder for your testing server files (see Figure 21.20).

FIGURE 21.20
The testing server setup for the Antiques Barn site, set up for offline development.

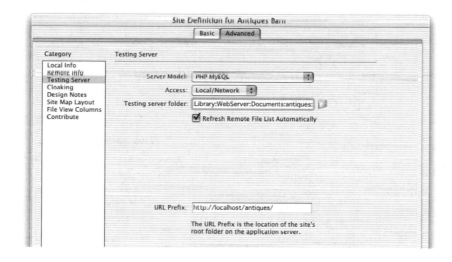

• If you're set up for online development, choose whatever access method and details you normally use to connect to the remote server. Create a folder on your remote server called **antiquesbarn,** and use it as the folder for your testing server files (see Figure 21.21).

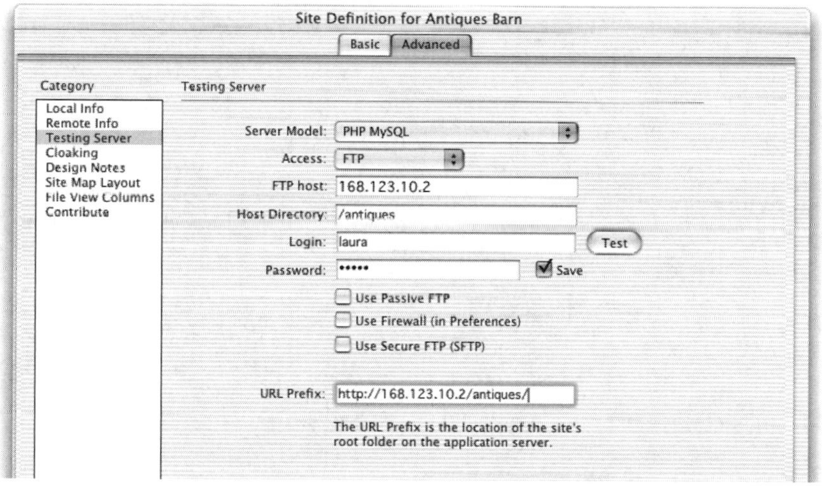

FIGURE 21.21
The testing server setup for the Antiques Barn site, set up for online development.

5. Still in the Testing Server category, examine the URL Prefix field. Dreamweaver should have filled in this information based on your previous entries, but it might be incorrect. If you're working offline, the address should be `http://localhost/antiquesbarn` or (for ColdFusion development) `http://localhost:8500/antiquesbarn`. If

you're working online, the address includes the host computer's actual IP address. This is the URL information Dreamweaver will use every time you preview your pages in the browser. It must be correct!

6. When you think all the site information is correct, click OK to close the dialog box. It's time to test things.

7. From your local root folder, open **index.html** and Preview in Browser (F12). You're probably in for a nasty surprise. Either the page displays with broken images, or you get a File Not Found error. Why is this happening?

   When you're working on a dynamic site, Dreamweaver uses the remote folder to generate its previews. (As explained earlier, this has to happen so that the page can be served rather than merely viewed.) Currently, your remote folder contains nothing! You must get in the habit of uploading files to the remote folder before previewing.

8. In the Site panel, select all the files in your site, and click the Put button to upload them all. Then try previewing again. If you entered the correct information in the Site Definition dialog box, you will be able to preview the page (see Figure 21.22). The browser's Address field shows the `http://` address of the home page, not its file location on your computer. (If you can't preview, keep double-checking those site settings until you can preview. You cannot keep working in Dreamweaver until you get this part right.)

FIGURE 21.22
Previewing in the browser in a dynamic Dreamweaver site.

EXERCISE 21.2

Defining a Database Connection

Building on the previous exercise, in this exercise you'll create the connection script that will allow your pages to communicate with the **antiques** database.

1. Because Dreamweaver has to know what kind of connection to create, you must have a dynamic document open before you can create the connection. From your local site, open **catalog.cfm**, **catalog.php**, or **catalog.aspx**.

2. From the Application panel group, open the Databases panel. What happens next depends on what server technology you're using:

    If you're working with ColdFusion, you don't have to explicitly make a connection. The Databases panel lists all the databases that the ColdFusion Server is aware of. You just need to make sure that the antiques database is here. You can also expand the antiques entry to explore the database structure, as shown in Figure 21.23.

FIGURE 21.23
The Databases panel for a ColdFusion site, showing the antiques database and its structure.

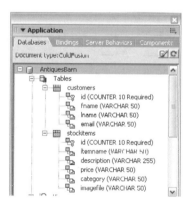

If you're working with PHP, click the + button at the top of the panel, and choose MySQL Connection. The connection dialog box opens. Set the following:

- **Name**—antiquesConn

- **Host (offline)**—localhost
  Host (online)—The IP address of the remote server

- **Username and password**—This information must belong to a registered user in the MySQL server's administrative database. It's the same username you need when you connect to MySQL using one of the GUIs, such as MySQL Control Center or CocoaMySQL. (For Windows users, if you're developing offline, you can sometimes leave these fields blank.)

- **Database**—If the host, username, and password are correct, you should be able to choose from a list of available MySQL databases. Choose antiques. If Dreamweaver can't connect to the MySQL server, you won't be able to continue. Double-check your information, and make sure that you are connected to a remote server (online development) or that the MySQL server is running on your computer (offline development). Figure 21.24 shows this happening.

As soon as you can choose your database, click OK to close the dialog box. The Databases panel now shows the antiquesConn connection. Expanding it lets you explore the structure of the antiques database.

FIGURE 21.24
Defining a database
connection for the
Antiques Barn (PHP).

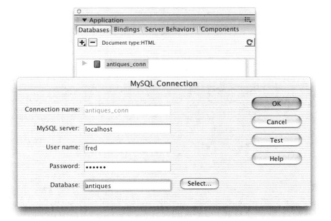

If you're working with ASP.NET, click the + button at the top of the panel and choose DSN. The DSN Connection dialog box opens. Set the following:

- **Name**—antiquesConn

- **DSN**—If your server is on your working computer, the radio buttons at the bottom of the dialog box should be set to Using

Local DSN, and there will be a pop-up list of drivers. Choose AntiquesBarn from the list. (Clicking the Define button opens the ODBC control panel.) If your server is on another computer, the radio buttons should be set to Using DSN on Testing Server, and the dialog box includes a DSN button. Click that button to get a list of DSNs, and choose AntiquesBarn from that list.

As soon as you can choose your database, click OK to close the dialog box. The Databases panel now shows the antiquesConn connection. Expanding it lets you explore the structure of the antiques database.

3. If you're using ColdFusion, you can skip this step. If you're using PHP or ASP.NET, go to the Site panel and examine your local root folder. You'll see a new **connections** folder. Inside that folder is the **antiquesConn.php** or **antiquesConn.aspx** file. That file contains your connection script.

Check out your open catalog document in Code view. At the very top of the code is a line of code connecting this page to the connection script. From now on, every time you create a dynamic page within this site that requires connecting to the database, Dreamweaver automatically inserts this code into the page to link it to the connection script. If you ever need to change your connection information, only the connection script file needs updating.

Summary

In this chapter, you learned the basics of how dynamic sites work, how to set up your workstation for online or offline development, and how to set up a dynamic site in Dreamweaver. The next two chapters look at working with dynamic content in Dreamweaver pages, as well as how to stretch your wings a little with Dreamweaver's interface for dynamic development. Most of what's covered works equally well in any of the server technologies that Dreamweaver supports. If you're curious about the possibilities of the specific languages, check out Chapters 24, 25, and 26, which cover ColdFusion, PHP, and ASP.NET.

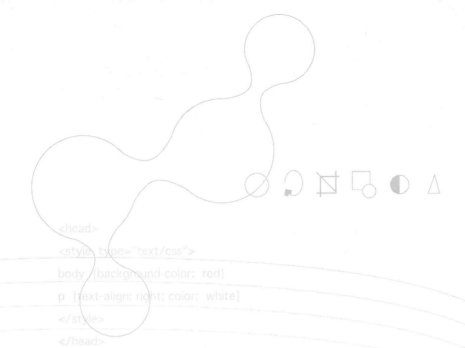

CHAPTER 22

CREATING DYNAMIC PAGES

DYNAMIC WEB PAGES DISPLAY DYNAMICALLY DETERMINED DATA, UPDATE databases with user input, and allow for just about any other data-related functionality you can imagine. Dreamweaver's application objects, server behaviors, and other tools help make these tasks easier, even if you're not a database development wizard. This chapter covers the ins and outs of creating recordsets and working with dynamic page content. It goes on to demonstrate how to create catalog pages, search-and-result pages, and simple catalog update pages.

COLLECTING DYNAMIC DATA

As soon as one or more connection scripts have been written, individual pages throughout the site can query the database. The most common kind of query is to create a recordset (a group of records that meet certain selection criteria).

The Basics of Recordsets

To create the recordset, open a dynamic document and follow these steps:

1. Open the Bindings panel, click the + button, and choose Recordset (Query); or go to the Insert bar, choose Application objects, and choose the Recordset object, as shown in Figure 22.1; or open the Server Behaviors panel, click the + button, and choose Recordset (Query).

FIGURE 22.1
Creating a database recordset.

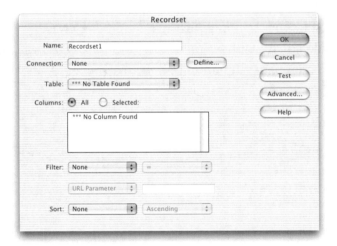

2. In the Recordset dialog box that opens, choose whichever connection, database, and specific database elements (usually table columns, which translate into record fields) you want to collect.

3. (Optional) To test the information you'll collect, click the Test button (see Figure 22.1).

4. When you're done, click OK to close the dialog box.

After you've created the recordset, the collected columns appear in the Bindings panel, as shown in Figure 22.2. Expand it to see all database fields that have been collected. Also, because Dreamweaver has to write a script to create the recordset, technically speaking, the collection action is a server-side behavior, and the recordset appears in the Server Behaviors panel (see Figure 22.3).

FIGURE 22.2
A created recordset in the Bindings panel.

FIGURE 22.3
A recordset query as it appears in the Server Behaviors panel.

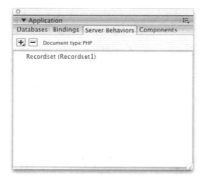

It's best not to make any drastic changes to the recordset after you start putting dynamic elements in your document because you might end up not collecting a field that is required for part of your page to display.

To edit a recordset you've already created so that it collects different data or organizes it differently, open the Server Behaviors panel and double-click the Recordset behavior there. The Recordset dialog box opens again, and you can change any of your settings. If you change the recordset's name after you've created it, Dreamweaver warns you that it's about to use Find and Replace to replace all occurrences of the recordset name throughout the document. Click OK to close this warning. The Find and Replace dialog box appears. To cancel the recordset name change, click Cancel in the Find and Replace dialog box. To change all occurrences at once, click Replace All. To change occurrences one at a time so that you can check that each one is correct, click Replace as many times as needed to fix the entire document.

What does the code for a recordset look like? Obviously, its appearance depends on what server technology and language you're working with. But at the heart of every recordset is a SQL query that looks something like one of these:

```
SELECT * FROM userTable
```

```
SELECT username,password FROM userTable
```

The first example collects all fields from all records in the userTable of your database; the second collects only the username and password fields from that table. Although it's not crucial for you to know what your recordset's SQL query looks like, in database development, as in all HTML, knowledge is power, and the more you know about what's happening behind the scenes, the better off you'll be.

Getting More Sophisticated with Your Recordsets

If all you want to do is collect all records from a database table, creating the recordset is just a matter of the steps outlined here. But all too often, your needs are more complex than that. The more you know about collecting more-complex recordsets, the easier it will be for you to collect exactly the information you need from the database.

Sorting

Unless you specify otherwise, the server collects the records from your database in whatever order they happen to be in. To put the records in any other order, you must include a sorting clause in your query. In the Recordset (Query) dialog box, use the Sort by options to do this. You can sort by any field in the table you're collecting from. Sorting is always done in alphanumeric order (0 to 9, A to Z). Choose Ascending or Descending to sort forward or backward (Z to A, 9 to 0). Figure 22.4 shows a sorted recordset being collected and viewed. The SQL query behind a sorted query uses the SORT BY clause and looks something like this:

```
SELECT * FROM userTable
ORDER BY username
```

FIGURE 22.4
Creating a sorted
recordset.

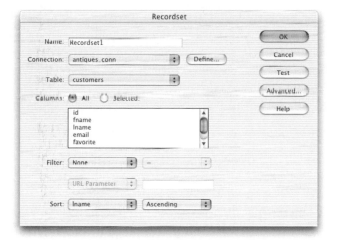

Filtering

Use filtering when you don't want to collect all the records in the database—only those that meet certain criteria. You might want only users whose last names begin with A, for instance, or only people who live in the state of Maine.

To create a filtered recordset, open the Recordset (Query) dialog box and set the Filter options. This involves three drop-down menus:

- **Filter by**—Choose any field in your recordset.

- **Comparison**—Choose any comparison operator (=, >, <, >=, <>, begins with, ends with, contains).

- **Required value**—Choose from one of the options here, or enter a value.

To find people who live in Maine, for example, your database table must have a field for state of residence. You can then choose the state field from the Filter by list, choose the equal sign for the second list, choose Entered Value for the type of filter, and type **Maine** in the input area.

Use the URL Parameter option if your page will be called from a form passing its variables using the GET method, or if the page will be called from a regular anchor tag that includes a URL parameter, like this:

```
<a href="dynamicpage.cfm?state=Maine">
```

For more on GET and POST form methods, see the section "How Forms Work in the Browser" in Chapter 9, "Working with Forms."

Use the Form Variable choice if the page will be called from a form that passes its variables using the POST method. Passing form variables and URL parameters is discussed later in this chapter in the section "Creating a Search Page." Cookies, session variables, and application variables are covered in the next chapter.

The SQL behind a filtered query uses the WHERE clause. It looks something like this:

```
SELECT * FROM users
WHERE state = "Maine"
```

Creating Advanced Recordsets with SQL

There are many more ways you might want to refine your data collection. The SQL language can accommodate just about all of them if you know how to structure your queries. Creating recordsets based on complex queries that involve joins, grouping, or other refinements requires that you work in Advanced mode and that you construct the SQL statement yourself.

To create an advanced recordset, open the Recordset (Query) dialog box and click the Advanced button. The resulting window, shown in Figure 22.5, includes a text area for typing SQL queries, a parameter definition area, and a database explorer area from which you can construct SQL queries without hand-coding.

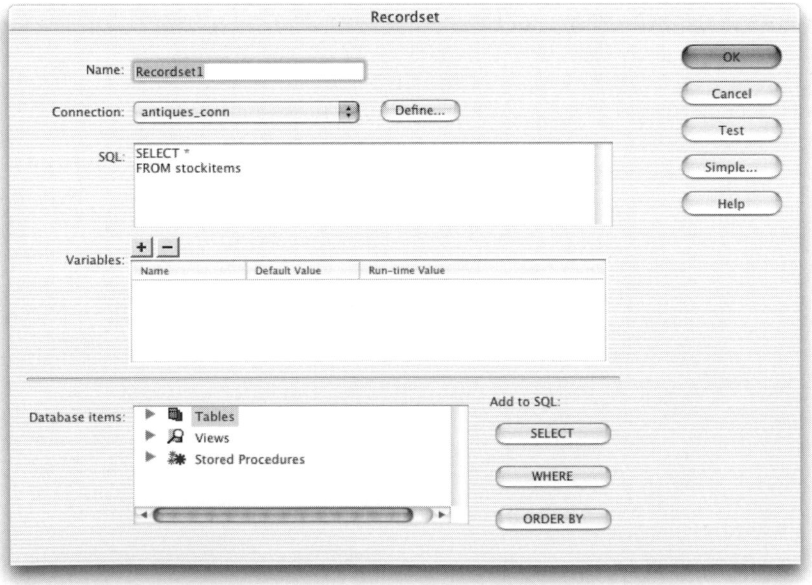

FIGURE 22.5
The Recordset (Query) dialog box in Advanced mode.

Collecting Distinct Records

Suppose you have a list of 200 people in your database, of which 25 are from Maine, 25 are from California, and 50 are from New York. You want to create a recordset that indicates which states are represented, so you collect the state field from the userTable. But you don't want to collect 25 instances of Maine, 25 instances of California, and so on. You want to collect one instance of Maine, one of California, and so forth. The DISTINCT keyword in SQL queries lets you do this:

```
SELECT DISTINCT state FROM userTable
ORDER BY state
```

To create a statement like this in Dreamweaver, do the following:

1. Open the Recordset (Query) dialog box. In Simple mode, create a query that selects only the field you want to group by. (For example, select only the state column from the userTable.) If you like, set the Sort by order here as well.

2. Click the Advanced button. In the SQL text area, add the word DISTINCT immediately before name of the field you want one instance of (see Figure 22.6). Before closing the dialog box, click the Test button to make sure you don't have any syntax errors in your SQL query.

FIGURE 22.6

Creating a recordset of distinct instances in the Recordset (Query) dialog box

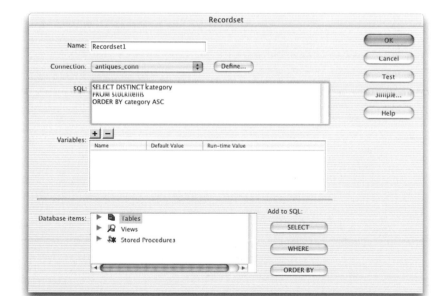

PUTTING DYNAMIC ELEMENTS IN YOUR PAGES

Dreamweaver dynamic elements allow you to display database data in your web pages and to preview them with placeholders in Design view. Building dynamic pages in Dreamweaver is largely about working with dynamic text, images, tables, and so on.

Dynamic Text Elements

Dynamic text elements are the contents of database fields, placed in your page as text. Prices, names of things, and descriptions are all good candidates to be inserted as text elements. Depending on how much text the database field contains, the dynamic element can be as short as a few letters or words, or as long as several paragraphs. Dynamic text elements all appear as placeholders in Design view:

```
(Recordset1.category)
```

or as server-side scripting in Code view:

```
<?php echo $row_Recordset1[category]; ?>
```

Remember, the placeholder does not indicate how much room the actual text will take up.

Inserting Dynamic Text

You can insert text by opening the Server Behaviors panel, pressing the + button, and choosing the Dynamic Text server behavior. Or you can choose the Dynamic Text object from the Application category of the Insert bar. Both these methods bring up a dialog box that lets you specify which database field to display as text, and whether to apply any automatic formatting to it, such as dollar signs or other currency indicators, as shown in Figure 22.7.

FIGURE 22.7
Using the Dynamic
Text object to insert
dynamic text into a
document.

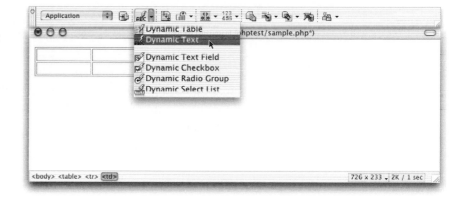

You can also insert dynamic text from the Bindings panel, either by dragging a field into the Document window or by selecting a field and clicking the Insert button (see Figure 22.8). After the text is in place, the Server Behaviors panel shows that a new Dynamic Element behavior has been added to the document. Double-click the server behavior to open the Dynamic Text dialog box and add any automatic formatting.

FIGURE 22.8
Inserting dynamic
text from the
Bindings panel.

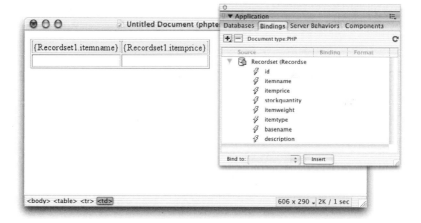

The options available for auto-formatting dynamic text vary depending on the server technology you're using.

Dynamic Text in the Document

You can use dynamic text placeholders in exactly the same way, and for the same purposes, as regular text. The dynamic text can appear in its own p, h1, or other tag, or it can appear in the middle of a block of static text. Any formatting you would normally apply to text, such as CSS custom classes, you can apply to the placeholder for dynamic text. Just select the text placeholder and use the Property inspector or CSS panel as you normally would. Figure 22.9 shows dynamic text elements in Code and Design views.

FIGURE 22.9
Dynamic text elements in a PHP document, treated as normal text.

Setting Dynamic Properties

Just as dynamic information can be substituted for text in a web page, it can also be substituted for any piece of HTML, including tag attributes.

If the database stores a user's favorite color in a field called favcolor, for instance, the following code in a PHP document dynamically sets the background of a table cell to this color:

```
<td bgcolor="<?php echo $row_Recordset1[favcolor]; ?>">
```

Dynamic Properties and the Selection Inspector

The Tag inspector provides a handy interface for entering dynamic properties. Just select the page element that should have a dynamic property, open the Tag inspector, and bring the Attributes tab to the front. Then select the attribute in question from the list of attributes and look for the little lightning-bolt icon at the right edge of the panel. Click that icon. A dialog box appears, asking which database field should have its value substituted for the attribute's value. Choose a field, click OK twice (to close all dialog boxes), and there you are (see Figure 22.10)!

FIGURE 22.10

Using the Tag inspector to assign a dynamic bgcolor property to a table cell.

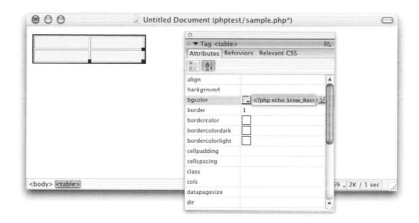

Dynamic Images

Generally, images and other media files are not stored in databases. Rather, a database field stores a filename or URL that points to the image. The dynamically generated web page can then contain an img tag that references this field in its src attribute:

```
<img src="<?php echo $row_Recordset1[filename]; ?>">
```

Assuming that the database contains a record with the filename field set to "necklace.gif", these references would generate code like this:

```
<img src="necklace.gif">
```

Inserting Dynamic Images

Inserting a dynamic image is similar to inserting a regular image. Use the Image object or Insert > Image command as normal. But when the Insert Image dialog box appears, find the Select File Name From option and click the Data Sources button. A list of available fields in the current document's recordset(s) appears. Choose one of these fields, and click OK. The image is inserted in the document with a placeholder (lightning bolt) icon, as shown in Figure 22.11.

After doing this, look in the Server Behaviors panel. You'll see that a new Dynamic Attribute behavior has been added to the page. The dynamic attribute is your image's src. Select your dynamic image, and check the Property inspector or Selection inspector. You'll see that the src attribute is defined with server-side code.

FIGURE 22.11

Inserting a dynamic image.

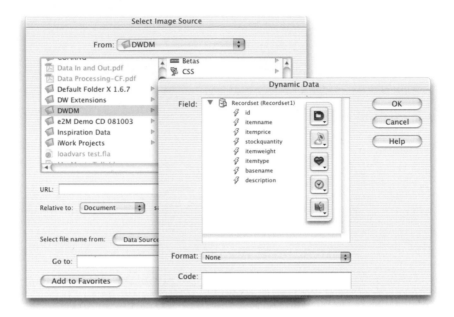

When you insert a dynamic image, Dreamweaver doesn't give it a width or height. Because the image `src` information has not yet been determined, Dreamweaver doesn't know its dimensions. If you know for certain that all images referred to in your database will have the same dimensions, and you know what those dimensions are, you can add the width and height yourself by entering them in the image Property inspector. If you're not sure of the dimensions, or if your images' dimensions might vary, leave these attributes unassigned.

Working Smart: Partial URLs

The database field used to generate the `src` does not have to contain the entire absolute or relative path to the image. For instance, if your images will be in an **images** subfolder, and the database field called on includes only the filename, you can create the rest of the path as you're placing the dynamic image. In the Insert Image dialog box, after you've chosen the database field to use as the `src`, type the rest of the path information into the URL field, like this (added code is in bold):

images/`<?php echo $row_Recordset1[filename]; ?>`

If you name your images carefully, you can do away with the `filename` database field. Suppose your database has a field called `itemname`. You can tweak the code that appears in the URL field when you insert the dynamic image (added code in bold):

images/<%=(Recordset1.Fields.Item("itemname").Value)%>.gif

Assuming that the itemname field for one of your collected records contains necklace, the generated HTML looks like this:

```
<img src="images/necklace.gif">
```

Working Smart: Dynamic Alt Labels

Dynamic images need dynamically determined alt labels. If your recordset contains any field that describes the item portrayed in the image, you can use that field to create your alt text. Use the Selection inspector for this, as outlined in the previous section.

Dynamic Data and Forms

Forms are used heavily in dynamic sites to collect information. Search pages, login pages, and information update pages all use forms to collect user input and either query or edit the data source.

If you need the form only to collect information, you don't need your form elements to be dynamic. But if you also want the form to present information from the data source—a pop-up menu of choices based on database contents, for instance, or a personal data page that users can check and update—you need to use dynamic data to determine the contents and status of the form elements.

Dynamic List/Menu

A dynamic drop-down list or form menu is created from a select form element with dynamically generated entries. To create one, open a dynamic document and create a recordset for the dynamic entries. Then do the following:

1. Create the form as normal, and use the List/Menu object (in the Form category of the Insert bar) to insert a standard list/menu.

2. In the Property inspector, click the Dynamic button. This opens a dialog box. Choose which field of the current recordset should be displayed in the list/menu, and click OK to close the dialog box. You can use this same dialog box to add static elements (those that

appear the same every time the list is generated, regardless of what's in the database). When you're done, click OK to close the dialog box.

Working Smart: Grouping Records for List Display

The preceding instructions create a dandy list/menu element, as long as your recordset contains only one value for each field to be displayed. If you have 10 necklaces to choose from, and the name of the necklace appears in the drop-down menu, all is well. But what if you have 10 necklaces, 10 bracelets, and 10 brooches, and you want the list to display the category names (necklaces, bracelets, brooches)?

The trick to creating a concise pop-up menu or list with dynamic entries is to eliminate all duplicates from the data source. To accomplish this, you need to define the recordset so that it collects only one of each entry. When creating the recordset for the document, after you have chosen which fields to collect, go to the Advanced tab of the dialog box. Edit the SQL query to add a GROUP BY clause, grouping by the field you plan to use in the dynamic list/menu. Note that if there is an ORDER BY clause, it must remain at the end of the query. To create a pop-up list of jewelry categories, for instance, your code might look like this:

```
SELECT category FROM jewelry
GROUP BY category
ORDER BY category ASC
```

After you've entered this into the SQL field, you can't return to Simple view for this recordset.

Dynamic Check Box

A dynamic check box appears checked or unchecked, depending on a field value in the recordset. To create a dynamic check box, follow these steps:

1. Insert a regular check box into your form (select Insert > Form Objects > Checkbox). Using the Property inspector, give the check box a name you'll remember.

2. Still in the Property inspector, click the Dynamic button. In the dialog box that appears, choose your check box's name. Specify which recordset field should be examined, and enter a value that the field must be equal to for the check box to appear checked. The dialog

box allows only for comparisons based on equality (no less than, more than, and so on).

Dynamic Radio Button

A dynamic group of radio buttons has one of its members selected, depending on a field value in the recordset. To create a dynamic radio group, do the following:

1. Insert a group of radio buttons as you normally would (select Insert > Form Objects > Radio Button or Insert > Form Objects > Radio Group). Use the Property inspector to give the group a name and to give each button a unique value.

2. In the Server Behaviors panel, click the + button and choose Dynamic Form Elements > Dynamic Radio Group.

3. In the dialog box that appears, choose your radio group's name. Then specify a recordset field that each button in the group should be compared to, to determine if it will be selected in the form.

Dynamic Text Field

Dynamic text fields appear in the form filled with text from a specified recordset field. To create a dynamic text field, follow these steps:

1. Insert a text field as you normally would (select Insert > Form Objects > Text Field). Use the Property inspector to give the text field a name you'll remember.

2. In the Server Behaviors panel, click the + button and choose Dynamic Form Elements > Dynamic Text Field.

3. In the dialog box that appears, choose your text field's name. Then specify the recordset field whose value should appear in the text field.

Repeating Content

By default, most dynamic elements display information from the first record found in a recordset. Repeating regions and dynamic tables let you display multiple records on one page.

Repeating Regions

A repeating region can be any page element you like—subheading and paragraph, list item, table—but the most common element to repeat is a table row. You create repeating regions with the Repeated Region application object or Repeat Region server behavior, as shown in Figure 22.12.

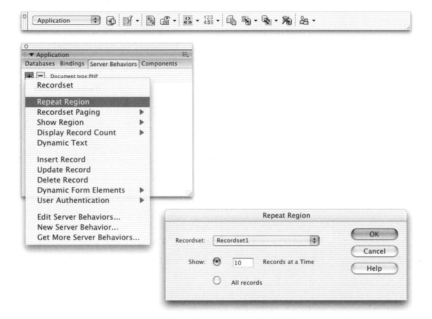

To create a repeating region, open a dynamic document, create a recordset, and do the following:

1. Determine what page area you want to repeat, and select it. The area should contain some dynamic content (such as text or images).

2. From the Application objects in the Insert bar, choose Repeated Region, or, from the Server Behaviors panel, choose Repeat Region. When the dialog box appears, choose the recordset to display and the number of records to show, and click OK.

   Your repeating region appears in Design view surrounded by a labeled box, as shown in Figure 22.13. To edit it, double-click the label.

FIGURE 22.13
A repeating region as it appears in Design view.

Dynamic Tables

The ASP.NET server model offers no Dynamic Table object. The Data Grid serves the same purpose. See Chapter 26, "Working Smart with ASP.NET," for instructions specific to ASP.NET.

A dynamic table is a table that displays information from the current recordset using repeating regions for rows. It's really just a shortcut method for creating the most common kind of repeating region setup.

To create a dynamic table, open a dynamic document, create a recordset, and do the following:

1. Place the insertion point where you want the table to appear.

2. From the Application Insert bar, in the Dynamic Data objects group, choose Dynamic Table. When the dialog box appears, choose the recordset, the number of records to show, and the table formatting options you want. Click OK to close the dialog box.

Dreamweaver inserts a table with a repeating row, exactly as if you had created the table and assigned the row to repeat. Note that the table includes all fields in the current recordset, in order. If you don't want all fields to show, you can delete columns of the table. The dynamic text in the table cells can be treated just like any other dynamic text.

Testing and Troubleshooting

Repeating regions are coded as loops containing content that should be repeated, along with instructions to the server to move through the recordset items one at a time. This code looks different depending on the language you're using. Here's how it looks in PHP:

```php
<?php do { ?>
  [repeated content goes here]
<?php } while ($row_Recordset1 =
➥mysql_fetch_assoc($Recordset1)); ?>
```

Here's how it looks in ColdFusion:

```
<cfoutput query="Recordset1" startRow="#StartRow_Recordset1#"
➥maxRows=
➥"#MaxRows_Recordset#">
   [repeated content goes here]
</cfoutput>
```

Is it important to know this? Maybe not, if everything goes according to plan and you never want to push the envelope. But as with all HTML work, the more you know about the code behind what you're doing, the easier it is to troubleshoot and tweak things.

You can make almost any page area selectable. It's important to make sure you have exactly the right things selected before you insert the repeating region. If you're making a list with repeated list items, make sure you have the li tag but not the surrounding ol or ul tag selected. If you're making a table row repeat, make sure the tr tag is chosen. The best way to keep on top of this is to use the Tag Selector, or to work in Code and Design view while keeping one eye on the code. Make sure you've selected exactly what you want to repeat.

Extra care is also important if you want to insert page content immediately beneath the repeating region, to make sure Dreamweaver doesn't put the new content inside the region. One especially tricky situation is when you have a repeating table row and you want to insert a new, non-repeating row beneath it. Normally, to add a row to a table, you place the insertion point in the last cell of the table and press Tab, or select Modify > Table > Insert Rows or Columns, or add to the number of rows in the Table Property inspector. But all these methods add the new row inside the repeating region. That's not good if it isn't what you want! What should you do?

If Dreamweaver adds the new content (the new table row, paragraph, and so on) inside the repeating region, take a quick trip into Code view. Find the code for the table row or other element that shouldn't be in the repeating region, and move it beneath the line of code that closes the region.

Paging Through Repeated Regions

Recordset paging, or navigation, comes into play when you use a repeated region but you want only a certain number of records to display at a time. These include links to Next, Previous, First, and Last, and messages indicating which records are currently being viewed (such as 2 to 14 of 500). Dreamweaver offers several methods for adding paging controls, involving various application objects and server behaviors, as shown in Figure 22.14.

FIGURE 22.14
The Recordset Paging and Recordset Count objects and server behaviors.

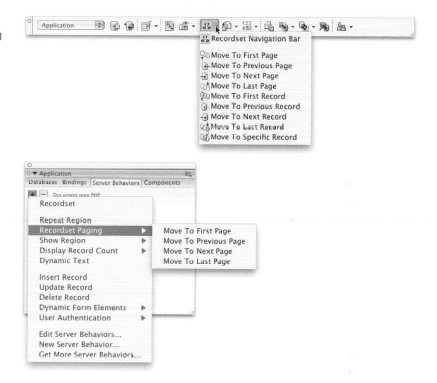

Recordset Paging Objects

To insert a Next, Previous, First, or Last link into a page containing a repeated region, you can do one of the following:

- Type the text or select the image that should function as the link. From the Insert bar, choose one of the Recordset Paging objects: Move to First, Move to Last, and so on.

- Position the cursor where you want the link inserted. From the Insert bar, choose one of the Recordset Paging objects. Dreamweaver adds default text for the link.

To automatically insert a complete set of paging controls, place the insertion point where you want the controls to appear. From the Insert bar, choose Recordset Navigation Bar. You can choose to create the bar with text or images (Dreamweaver supplies the images). The bar is built as a centered table with a cell for each link, as shown in Figure 22.15.

FIGURE 22.15
A recordset naviga-
tion bar in action.

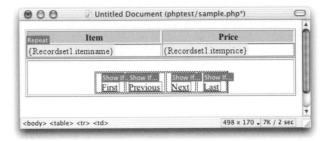

Recordset navigation links are page elements in an a tag that has a dynamic href attribute. You can safely change anything about the page element except its dynamic href attribute without disturbing the navigation. So feel free to format or change the text, add rollovers to the images, and so forth.

Recordset Count Objects

When your visitors are paging through records, they like to know where they are in the recordset—how many records there are in total, where they are in the set, and so forth. Dreamweaver includes objects for these indicators. As soon as you have a repeated region and recordset paging controls, to add the count indicators, position the insertion point where you want the indicators to appear. From the Application category of the Insert bar, choose any of the Display Record Count objects. If you choose to insert the entire Recordset Navigation bar, Dreamweaver creates a text display for you. You can also choose to insert dynamic text placeholders only, without any connecting text, by choosing the Starting Record, Ending Record, or Total Records object.

These objects insert a mixture of dynamic and static text elements into your page. As with all dynamic text, you can safely format it as you like or change any of the static text.

Conditional Content

Conditional content appears on a page only if certain requirements are met. This involves some sort of if-then statement in your server-side scripting language. With conditional content, you can fine-tune exactly what appears on a page based on various conditions. It's all done with the Show If application objects or server behaviors, as shown in Figure 22.16.

FIGURE 22.16

The Show If objects and server behaviors.

Displaying or Hiding Content If a Recordset Is Empty

If your recordset doesn't find any records in the database, you probably want to display a "Sorry, no items found" message. If records are found, you want to display the relevant dynamic elements. To create this effect, you need to put both sets of content in your page and define each as conditional based on record contents. This means using the Show If Recordset Empty and Show If Recordset Not Empty objects or server behaviors (refer to Figure 22.16).

Do it this way:

1. In your document, create the content that should display if records are found. Immediately before or after this content, create whatever content should display if there are no records. So your page first displays placeholders to display recordset data and then displays a "Sorry" message or other default content.

2. Select the set of content that should show only if records are found. Make sure you select everything, including repeating regions, HTML tags, and so on.

3. From the Insert bar (Application category, Show Region objects), choose the Show If Recordset Not Empty object. Or, in the Server Behaviors panel, click the + button and choose Show Region > Show If Recordset Not Empty. In the dialog box that appears, make sure the relevant recordset is chosen, and click OK to insert the region.

   In Design view, the selected content now appears in a box with a label, as shown in Figure 22.17. Exactly what the label says varies, depending on which server technology you're using.

FIGURE 22.17
A document with
conditional content,
set to display only if
the current recordset
contains records.

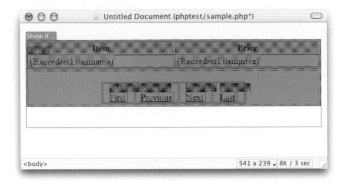

4. Select the content that should appear only if no records are found. Again, be sure to include all HTML tags and other invisible elements. (Use the Tag selector, or take a peek at Code view, to check.)

5. From the Insert bar or the Server Behaviors panel, choose the Show If Recordset Empty object. When the dialog box appears, select the recordset you're testing for (the one that must be empty before this content appears), and click OK to close the dialog box.

   In Design view, this content also appears surrounded by a labeled box. Figure 22.18 shows how the page should look at this point.

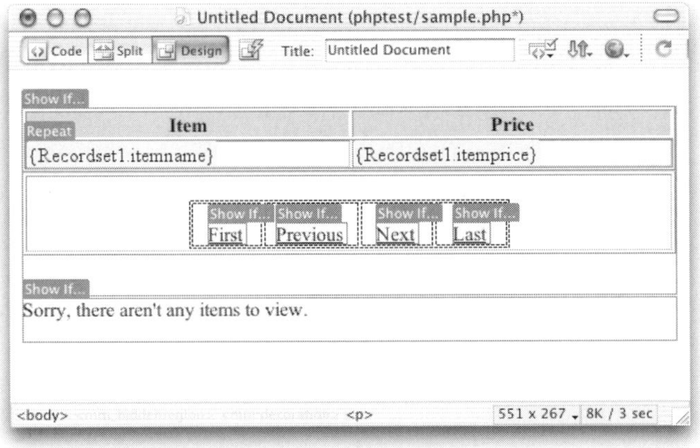

FIGURE 22.18
A document with
regions defined to
hide or show if the
recordset is empty.

Preview your page in a browser to see how it works. You can experiment by changing the definition of your recordset so that it collects no data, to see if the "Sorry" message displays as it should.

Displaying or Hiding Content Based on Recordset Paging

If you've ever inserted a Recordset Navigation Status object, you've already used this kind of conditional content. If your page includes a repeating region, with recordset paging to display only a set number of records at a time, you might want things such as the Move to Next Page object to display only if there is a next page to display. This involves using the Show If First Page, Show If Not First Page, Show If Last Page, and Show If Not Last Page objects (refer to Figure 22.16). Do the following:

1. Open a document that contains dynamic data in a repeating region that is set to display only a certain number of records at a time.

2. Select any content that should appear only if this is the first page of records. This includes any decorative elements you want, as well as dynamic elements such as the Move to First Page and Move to Previous Page objects. (See the earlier section "Paging Through Repeated Regions" for more on this.)

3. From the Insert bar (Application category, Show If objects), choose the Show If First Page object. Or choose the Show If > Show If First Page behavior from the Server Behaviors panel.

   In Design view, your new conditional content appears with a labeled box surrounding it.

4. Repeat this procedure to identify and isolate any elements that should appear only when it is or isn't the first and last page of the recordset. Figure 22.19 shows a page with this kind of conditional content in place.

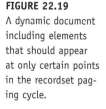

FIGURE 22.19
A dynamic document including elements that should appear at only certain points in the recordset paging cycle.

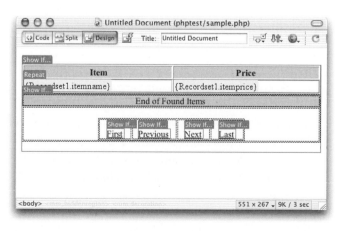

Testing and Troubleshooting Conditional Content

Like repeating regions, conditional regions are coded with beginning and ending server code surrounding the conditional content, like this (for PHP):

```
<?php if ($totalRows_Recordset_1 > 0) { ?>
  [conditional content goes here]
<?php } ?>
```

or this (for ColdFusion):

```
<cfif Recordset4.RecordCount GT 0>
  [conditional content goes here]
</cfif>
```

It's important to know this so that you can fix things that go wrong. If your conditional content isn't hiding and showing the correct content, for instance, take a trip to Code view. Any conditional content must be inside the opening and closing lines of server code. So if you didn't quite get the right selection when you inserted the conditional region, just select the stray code and move it in or out from between the opening and closing lines.

Common Dynamic Tasks

Each of the following sections briefly outlines a common type of dynamic page or task and includes an exercise demonstrating the procedure. Before performing any of the exercises, be sure you're set up for online or offline dynamic development. The **antiques** database used in the exercises is available on the book's website at www.peachpit.com in the **chapter_22** folder, in both Microsoft Access and MySQL format. You need to install the database on your server. Depending on your setup, you also might need to create a DSN and configure the ColdFusion MX server. The **chapter_22** folder on the book's website contains exercise files for ASP/VBScript, ASP.NET/C#, ColdFusion, PHP, and JSP. Use the appropriate folder for the technology you're employing. Before beginning, you also need to define a Dreamweaver site, with local and testing server information filled in. You also need to define a connection to the **antiques** database.

Creating a Catalog Page

A catalog page displays multiple records from the database. Usually, it displays multiple records at a time, using recordset paging and navigation indicators to link between displays. Catalog pages make heavy use of dynamic text and images, along with repeating regions.

EXERCISE 22.1

Creating a Catalog Page for the Antiques Barn Site

In this exercise, you'll build the Antiques Barn catalog page. This page should display all stock items from the **antiques** database, including each item's name, description, price, and picture. The finished page should look like Figure 22.20.

FIGURE 22.20
The Antiques Barn catalog page as it should look when completed.

Create a Recordset

Before you can display information from the database, you must collect it. This is called creating a recordset. It involves determining what information you need and how it should be ordered and querying the database.

1. Open **catalog.cfm**, **catalog.php**, or **catalog.aspx** and examine it. The layout framework is the same as that shown in Figure 22.20, but the central content area is currently empty.

2. Open the Bindings panel (select Window > Bindings, or expand the Application panel group).

3. Click the + button and choose Recordset (Query) from the menu.

4. In the dialog box that appears, set the following options (see Figure 22.21):

   • **Connection, or Database**—antiquesConn

   • **Table**—stockitems

   • **Columns**—all

   • **Filters**—none

   • **Sort**—itemname, ascending

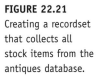

FIGURE 22.21
Creating a recordset that collects all stock items from the antiques database.

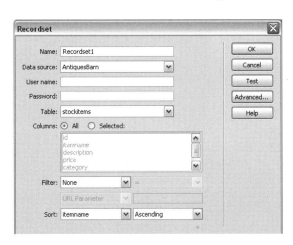

5. Click OK to close the dialog box.

The recordset now appears in the Bindings panel, as shown in Figure 22.22. Click the triangle by its name to expand it so that you can see its fields (itemname, description, price, and so on). You now have access to these pieces of information for every record in the stock items table of the **antiques** database.

FIGURE 22.22
The recordset for the Antiques Barn catalog page.

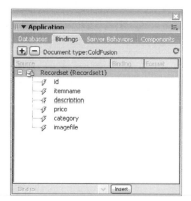

Create and Format Dynamic Text

Dynamic text elements in this page are the item's name, description, and price, which appear in the right-side column of the layout.

1. In the Bindings panel, select the itemname field and drag it to the right-side empty cell in the page's layout table.

2. Place the cursor after this item and press Enter to create a new paragraph.

3. From the Bindings panel, drag the description recordset item to the space below the item name.

4. Place the cursor after this item and press Enter to create a new paragraph.

5. From the Bindings panel, drag the price recordset item to the space below the description text.

Now that the text is in place, it appears in Design view as placeholder text. The placeholders can be formatted and treated like any other text.

1. In the document, select the paragraph containing the itemname placeholder.

2. In the Property Inspector, use the Style drop-down menu to apply the itemname style to your paragraph.

3. Repeat this process to add the price style to the price placeholder.

4. Type $ immediately preceding the price placeholder. Figure 22.23 shows what the page should look like at this point.

FIGURE 22.23
The Antiques Barn catalog page with dynamic text elements in place and formatted.

Preview the Page

It's time to see what kind of code you've created and how it will behave in the browser.

1. To see your page's code, switch to Code view. Note that server code appears above the opening `<html>` tag and below the closing `</html>` tag. This is the code for linking to the connection script (PHP and ASP.NEXT only) and creating the recordset. It also appears within the document, where your dynamic text elements are placed.

   PHP—Any code within the `<?php ... ?>` tag is PHP script.

   ASP.NET—Any code within the `<% ... %>` tag is ASP.NET scripting, written in either C# or Visual Basic.

ColdFusion—Any tag that begins with cf (such as cfoutput) is a ColdFusion markup tag, which includes scripting information that the server executes.

When the application server processes this page, it leaves the regular HTML elements alone and processes all script within the specified server tags.

2. In the document toolbar, click the Live Data View button. The formatted text placeholders for the first item in the database (the bookcase) should appear. Note also how the information at the top of the Document window changes to indicate that you're viewing your Dreamweaver document through the Apache server (see Figure 22.24).

FIGURE 22.24
Previewing the catalog page in Live Data view in Dreamweaver.

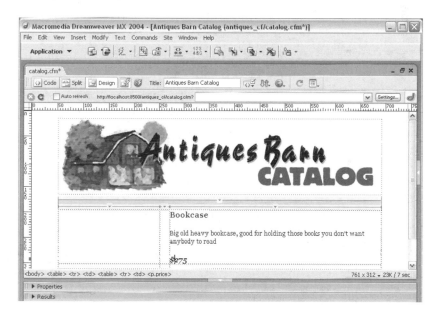

3. When you're done examining the live preview, turn off Live Preview by clicking the Live Data View button in the toolbar again.

4. Preview in the browser (select File > Preview in Browser). Note that the browser's URL field says something like http://localhost/ antiquesbarn/TMP*xxxxx*.php. This tells you that the page is being served, rather than just viewed through your computer's file system.

5. Still in the browser, view source to see the code for the file (select View > Source or View > Page Source, depending on your browser).

    Note that the page is now just plain old HTML. The text placeholders have been replaced by actual text, and the scripting before and after the <html> tags is gone. The web server executes the server-side scripting and creates regular HTML before passing the page to the browser. That's why server-side scripting is not browser-dependent, like JavaScript.

Add a Dynamic Image

The Antiques Barn catalog page also needs to display a picture of each antique in its database. For this, you use a dynamic image:

1. In the catalog page, place the cursor in the table cell where the dynamic image should appear. Choose the Image object from the Insert bar or select Insert > Image.

2. When the Insert Image dialog box opens, click the Data Sources button to choose the image source from the database rather than from an existing file (see Figure 22.25).

FIGURE 22.25
Inserting a dynamic image for the Antiques Barn catalog page.

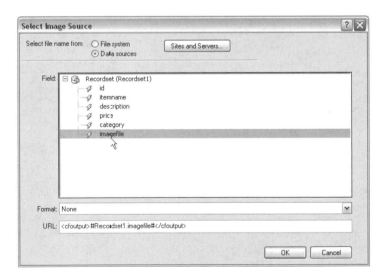

3. When the Data Sources dialog box opens, select imagefile from the list of available recordset items (see Figure 22.25).

4. Click OK to close both dialog boxes.

5. Examine the dynamic image. In Design view, it appears as a special lightning-bolt placeholder. In Code view, it's a standard img tag, but with server-side scripting in the middle. It looks like this in ColdFusion:

```
<img src="<cfoutput>#Recordset1.imagefile#</cfoutput>">
```

and like this in PHP:

```
<img src="<?php echo $row_Recordset1['imagefile']; ?>">
```

In the processed page that the browser sees, the contents of the imagefile database field are substituted for everything within the server tag.

6. Preview in a browser to see the results. The image doesn't display correctly. Why not? While still in the browser, view source code. The code for the image looks like this:

```
<img src="bookcase.jpg">
```

Using the Dreamweaver Site panel, check the files in your site. The images are in a folder called **images**. The correct link to this image should reflect this:

```
<img src="images/bookcase.jpg">
```

You need to edit the img tag in your document to include the correct path.

7. In Dreamweaver, select the dynamic image. In the Property Inspector, place the cursor at the beginning of all the text in the Src field, and type **images**/. The PHP code for the image should now look like this for ColdFusion:

```
<img src="images/<cfoutput>#Recordset1.imagefile#</cfoutput>">
```

or like this for PHP:

```
<img src="images/<cfoutput>#Recordset1.imagefile#</cfoutput>">
```

8. Preview in the browser. You'll see that the image displays properly. View the source code to see why this is so.

Add a Dynamic Alt Label

Finally, the Antiques Barn images should have alt labels to make them accessible. You can do this by using the Tag Inspector to add a dynamic property to the img tag.

1. Select the dynamic image.

2. Open the Tag Inspector panel (select Window > Selection Inspector). Bring the Attributes tab to the front if it's not already in front.

3. In the General category of attributes, find the alt attribute and select it.

4. In the right-side (value) field for the alt attribute, click the lightning-bolt icon. When the dialog box opens, choose itemname as the field you want the alt label to display, as shown in Figure 22.26.

FIGURE 22.26
Assigning the item-name database field as the dynamic alt text for an Antiques Barn image.

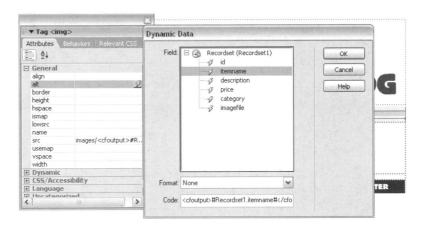

5. Click OK to close this dialog box.

6. Preview in the browser, and view source code to test your alt label. Using the lightning-bolt icons that occur in the Tag Inspector and Property Inspector, you can substitute database field information for most object attributes.

Add a Repeating Region to Display Multiple Records

So far, your dynamic page displays only the first database record it finds. That's not a very complete catalog! To display multiple records, you need to define the table row containing your dynamic elements as a repeating region.

1. Select the table row containing the dynamic image and text. (The safest way to do this is by clicking inside the row and using the Tag selector to select the tr tag.)

2. In the Application Insert bar, choose the Repeated Region object.

3. In the dialog box that opens, set the following:

   • **Recordset**—Recordset1 (the only option!)

   • **Show**—5 records at a time

4. Click OK to close the dialog box. In Design view, your repeating region is marked by a labeled box, as shown in Figure 22.27.

5. Preview in a browser to test your multiple records. Your page now contains five antiques!

Add a Recordset Navigation Bar

Unless your database is very small, it's not wise to display all records on the same page. That's why the current page displays only five records. Now you'll add a set of Recordset Paging objects.

1. You want to add a special row of the layout table to hold the navigation bar. To do this, select the row after the repeating row, and choose Modify > Table > Add Row.

2. Select all the cells of the new row, and merge them (select Modify > Table > Merge Cells).

3. Place the insertion point inside the new row.

4. From the Insert bar, choose the Recordset Navigation Bar object. In the dialog box that appears, set the following:

    *   **Recordset**—Recordset1

    *   **Display**—Text

5. Click OK to close the dialog box. There's your navigation bar! It appears in its own table, nested inside the main table, as shown in Figure 22.28.

FIGURE 22.28

Inserting a recordset navigation bar for the Antiques Barn catalog page.

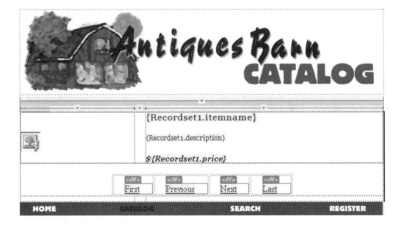

6. Select the navigation bar table, and use the CSS Styles panel to apply the nav style. This formats the text.

7. Set the table's width to 100% so that it stretches to fill the entire width of the layout.

8. Preview in the browser to test your navigation. You can use the links to navigate between pages, each of which contains five records (see Figure 22.29).

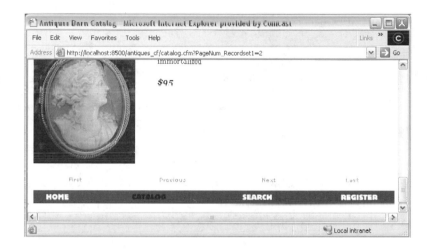

Add a Recordset Navigation Status Indicator

Now that the user can navigate between pages, it would be nice to give him an indication of which records he's looking at (the first five, the last five, and so on). This means adding a Recordset Navigation Status object. You'll add a new row at the beginning of the nested navigation bar table to contain this text:

1. Place the insertion point in the one and only row in the navigation bar table, and choose Modify > Table > Insert Row to add a new top row. (Or choose the Insert Row Above object from the Layout Insert bar.)

2. Select all cells in this row, and choose Modify > Table > Merge Cells.

3. Place the insertion point inside the newly merged cell. In the Insert bar, choose the Recordset Navigation Status object.

4. When the dialog box appears, set it to display RecordSet1. Click OK to close the dialog box.

5. Examine your document. A combination of static and dynamic text has been added, as shown in Figure 22.30. You can format this text, or change any of its static elements, without disturbing its functionality. Change the word Records to **Show Items** to be more user-friendly.

FIGURE 22.30

Inserting a recordset navigation status bar on the Antiques Barn catalog page.

6. Preview in a browser to see your navigation object in action.

Congratulations! You've created your first display page using Dreamweaver and server-side scripting.

Creating a Search Page

One of the best things about databases is that they're searchable. By adding a search function to your site, you pass that power along to your site visitors. Searches involve two pages: the search form, where the user specifies what search criteria to use, and the results page, which uses dynamic elements to display only data matching the search criteria.

EXERCISE 22.2

Creating a Search Page for the Antiques Barn Site

In this exercise, you'll add scripting to a search page, learning how to create dynamic form elements along the way and seeing how to search the database and create a results page. If you've never worked with form processing, you'll also get to see how information is passed from one HTML page to another as parameters.

You'll start by developing the search page itself, which collects user input to determine what to search for. Then you'll develop the results page, which uses this input to determine which database records to display.

Set Up a Dynamic List/Menu

The search page for the Antiques Barn lets the user choose a category of antiques to search for. It does this by presenting a form that lists the available categories as a drop-down menu (a <select> form element). Therefore, this page needs to access the database, collect a list of categories from the stockitems table, and display them.

1. Open **search.cfm**, **search.php**, or **search.aspx** from your local site files.

2. To create the recordset, open the Bindings panel, click the + button, and choose Recordset (Query). In the dialog box, set the following (see Figure 22.31):

    *   **Connection/Database**—antiquesConn

    *   **Table**—stockitems

    *   **Columns**—selected, category

    *   **Sort**—category, ascending

FIGURE 22.31
Creating a recordset
for the Antiques Barn
search page.

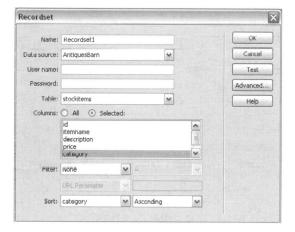

3. Before closing the dialog box, click the Test button to see what kind of data you're collecting. You get a list of categories, but there are multiple instances of each category, because the stockitems table contains multiple items in each category (see Figure 22.32).

FIGURE 22.32
Testing the search
page recordset.

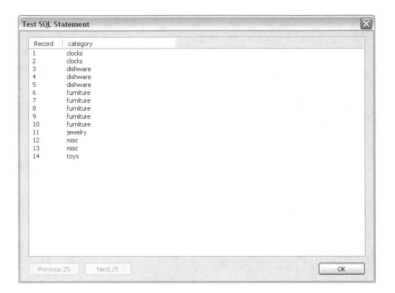

4. That's not too good! You need to collect only one instance of each
    category.

    Close the Test window and click the Advanced button in the Recordset
    (Query) dialog box. In Advanced mode, change the SQL query so that
    it reads like this (the new code is in bold):

    ```
    SELECT DISTINCT category FROM stockitems
    ORDER BY category ASC
    ```

    Click the Test button again. That's more like it! Only one of each
    category appears.

5. Click OK to close the dialog box. In the Bindings panel, you now see
    a recordset consisting of one item (category).

6. You need to use this dynamic data to populate the list/menu form
    element. Select the list in the Document window. In the Property
    Inspector, note that its name is **category**. You'll need to remember
    that for later.

7. With the list/menu still selected, in the Property Inspector click the
    Dynamic button. This opens a dialog box that lets you display
    record data in the pop-up list. In the dialog box, click the + button
    in the Static items area to add one static item. Give it a label of
    (select one) and no value. In the bottom half of the dialog box, set
    the following (see Figure 22.33):

- **Options from Recordset**—Recordset1

- **Values**—category

- **Labels**—category

- **Set select value equal to**—leave blank

FIGURE 22.33
Setting the search page's drop-down menu to display dynamic data.

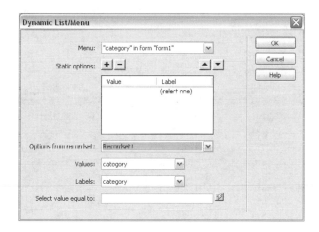

8. Click OK to close the dialog box.

9. Preview in the browser, and try out the pop-up list. It should look like the one shown in Figure 22.34.

FIGURE 22.34
The search page's dynamically populated drop-down menu in action.

Call the Results Page

The search page looks great. Now you need to make it functional. Clicking the Submit button in any form calls the page that's indicated in the form's action attribute, sending the form field values as parameters. When you're working with server-side scripting, the form action calls a dynamic page. The server sends the form values to that other page, processes any script in the page, and returns the processed page to the browser.

1. In the search document, select the form element. (Use the Tag selector if necessary.)

2. In the Property Inspector, set the Action to **results.cfm**, **results.php**, or **results.aspx**, depending on your server technology. (Just type in the name. The file doesn't exist yet, so you can't browse to it!)

3. Set the method to GET. (You'll see what this means in a later step.)

4. Save and close the search page.

Create the Results Page

The results page should display database records, so it's essentially the same as the catalog page you created in the previous exercise. The only difference is, the results page doesn't display all the records—only those requested by the search page. To create the results page, you'll start from the catalog page to save yourself some work.

1. In the Site panel, select the catalog page. Ctrl-click the file to access the context menu, and choose Edit > Duplicate. Call the duplicated file **results.cfm**, **results.php**, or **results.aspx**, as appropriate.

2. The search engine isn't fully functional yet, but it's time for a quick preview. First, upload both files (the search page and the results page) to the Testing Server.

3. Open the search page and preview it in a browser. Choose a category from the drop-down menu, and click the Search button.

   The results page should appear. (The contents won't reflect your search yet.) Examine the URL and see how the form input has been passed as a URL parameter:

   ```
   http://localhost/antiquesbarn/results.php?category=
   ➡clocks&submit=search
   ```

This shows how the search works. The parameter category and its value are both passed from the search page to the results page. All that's left is to revise the results page to make use of this parameter. (If you had specified POST as the form's method, the information would be passed invisibly instead of attached to the URL.)

Refine the Results Page

In a search-and-results page set, the results page does all the work, translating the passed parameters or form variables into useful information. You must now change the recordset in **results.php** so that it collects only records whose category matches the category in the parameters.

1. Open the results page in Dreamweaver.

2. In the Server Behaviors panel, double-click the Recordset1 behavior to open its editing window. (If the window opens in Advanced view, click the Simple button to return to Simple view.)

3. Add the following settings (see Figure 22.35):

    - **Filter by**—category

    - **Operator**—=

    - **Value**—Choose URL Parameter from the drop-down menu, and type **category** in the text field next to it. (If you had chosen POST as your search form's method, you would choose Form Variable from this drop-down menu instead of URL Parameter.)

FIGURE 22.35
The Recordset (Query)/DataSet dialog box, ready to filter the antiques recordset based on a passed form value.

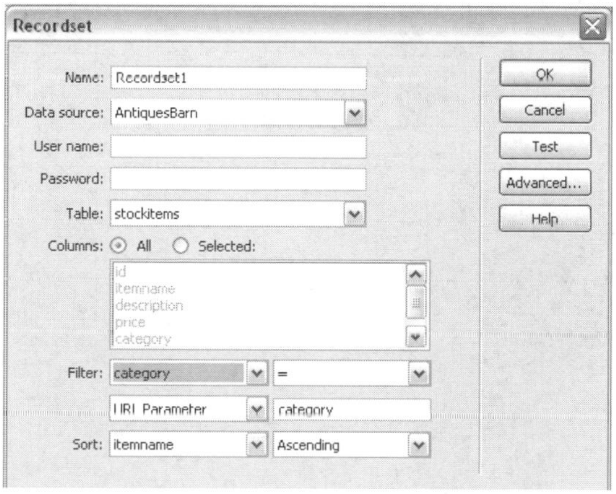

4. Click OK to close the dialog box.

5. Upload the results page, and then open the search page and preview it in the browser. Choose a category, click Search, and see your lovely results! Figure 22.36 shows the search happening.

Creating a Catalog Update Page

Another commonly used task in dynamic sites is allowing users to add information to the database. Every time a user registers as a member, or adds an item to a store's inventory, or even places an order, it involves adding or updating database records.

EXERCISE 22.3

Creating a Visitor Sign-In Page for the Antiques Barn Site

In this last exercise, you'll create a sign-up page where a user can add his or her name to a mailing list:

1. Open **register.cfm**, **register.php**, or **register.aspx**.

2. Examine the form. It has fields for fname, lname, and email. (These match the names of the fields in the database. It's not required that they do, but as you'll soon see, it makes life much easier.) The Sign Me Up button is actually a submit button (see the Property Inspector). The form element has no action specified.

Create a Recordset of Customers

Even though you won't be displaying any existing customer data on this page, you still need to create a recordset of customers so that you'll have access to this part of the database.

1. In the Bindings panel, click the + button and choose Recordset (Query)/DataSet.

2. In the dialog box that appears, set the following (see Figure 22.37):

   - **Connection**—antiquesConn

   - **Table**—customers

   - **Columns**—selected (and select all except ID)

FIGURE 22.37
Creating a recordset to allow new users to be added to the antiques database.

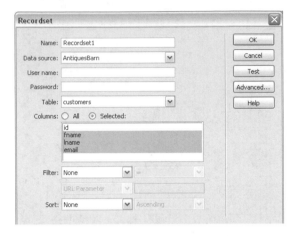

Insert a Record into the Recordset

1. Click OK to close the dialog box.

    When the user clicks the Submit button, you want to add his data to the created recordset and then send the browser to a Thank You page so that the user knows his submission has been accepted. You do this by attaching a server behavior to the Submit button.

2. Click the Submit button.

3. In the Server Behaviors panel, click the + button to show the list of available behaviors, and choose Insert Record. In the dialog box that appears, set the following (see Figure 22.38):

    *   **After Inserting, Go To**—thankyou.html (you can browse to this file or enter its name manually)

    All form fields should be matched up with the corresponding database fields. Because the form fields are named the same as the database fields, Dreamweaver should already have matched these up.

Test the Registration Process

1. Click OK to close the dialog box.

2. To make sure your registration works, you have to preview it in the browser and then examine the database to see if a new record has been added.

FIGURE 22.38
Configuring the Insert
Record server behav-
ior for use with the
Antiques Barn user
sign-up.

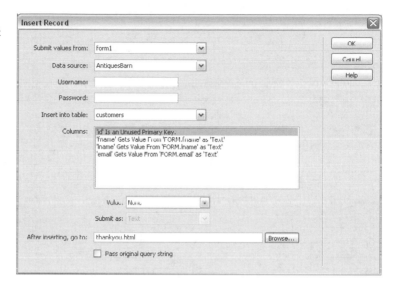

3. Preview in the browser. Fill in the form with any values you choose.

4. Click the Sign Me Up button. You should be directed to the Thank You page.

5. To check the database, leave Dreamweaver and open the **antiques** database in Access or MySQL. View the users table. Your new user is there! You've just updated the database through your web page.

SUMMARY

This chapter covered the basic Dreamweaver tools and techniques available for creating dynamic pages. This includes creating recordsets, displaying dynamic elements, and building some of the most common kinds of dynamic pages. If you completed the exercises, you now have a fully functional Antiques Barn website. The next chapter covers more advanced tasks and techniques, including more-complex pages, Dreamweaver templates, and dynamic sites.

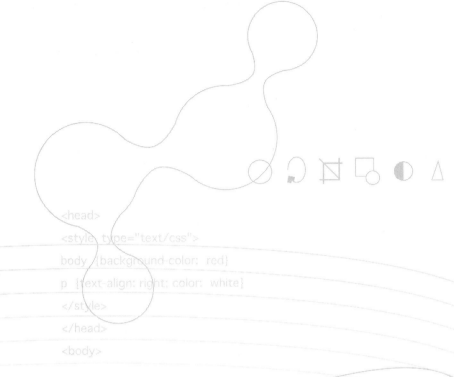

CHAPTER 23

FURTHER DYNAMIC TECHNIQUES

CREATING BASIC PAGES IS ONLY THE BEGINNING OF WHAT YOU CAN DO WITH Dreamweaver MX 2004 and dynamic sites. This chapter covers more-complex techniques, including master-detail page sets, user authentication systems, creating complex recordsets, and displaying conditional content. This chapter also looks at dynamic templates and shows how they function in a data-driven site. In the exercises, you build a more-complex version of the Antiques Barn website you worked with in the previous chapters.

DYNAMIC TEMPLATES

Dreamweaver templates can also be used with dynamic pages. This lets you create an overall look for the site using templates and still dynamically generate individual pages.

This discussion assumes that you're familiar with template basics. If you're not, check out Chapter 20, "Site-Wide Content with Templates and Libraries."

Creating Dynamic Templates

To create a dynamic template, choose File > New. In the New Document dialog box, shown in Figure 23.1, choose Template page and any of the dynamic document types listed. What's the difference between a dynamic and a normal HTML template? If you're using a server model that requires any directives to be added to the top of the page (such as the language declaration in ASP or ASP.NET), the code is added for you. Dreamweaver also saves dynamic template files with two file extensions—such as **main.cfm.dwt**—to indicate their status.

FIGURE 23.1
Creating a new dynamic template from the New Document dialog box.

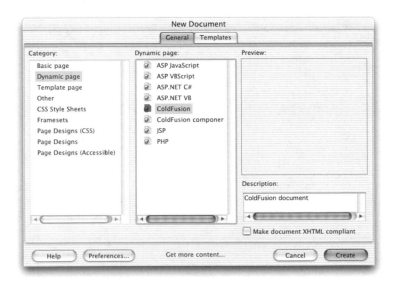

You can also create a dynamic template by opening an existing dynamic page and choosing File > Save as Template.

How Dynamic Templates Work

When a page is generated from a template, all areas are locked except for editable regions that have been specifically defined. Dynamic pages usually include server-side content that's defined outside the html tags. To accommodate this code, Dreamweaver templates consider the area outside the html tags to be editable by child pages. You can tell that this is happening by looking at the head area of any template child page, where you'll find this statement immediately following the html tag:

```
<!-- InstanceBegin template="/Templates/main.dwt"
  codeOutsideHTMLIsLocked="false" -->
```

This means that you can add recordsets and other server-side instructions to documents based on templates.

You can still add server-side instructions to the template page itself, but if any code is placed outside the HTML tag, it is treated just like content in any editable region: It isn't copied to existing child pages, and although it will be added to any new child pages created from now on, those pages can overwrite it. Dreamweaver warns you that this will happen, as shown in Figure 23.2.

If you want to keep the area outside the HTML tag locked—which means you want all child pages to use the same recordsets that the template uses—you can do so. By default, template files don't include a code-locking statement (this statement is added to the child pages only as they're created). But you can add one. In the template file, switch to Code view, and type the following code into the head section:

```
<!-- TemplateInfo codeOutsideHTMLIsLocked="true" -->
```

Creating a Dynamic Site Based on Templates

In this chapter's exercises, you'll work on an alternative version of the Antiques Barn site you worked with in the previous chapter. You don't need to have done any of those exercises to do these. But you do need to set up your workstation for dynamic development, using ColdFusion, PHP, or ASP.NET. You need to install the **more_antiques** database, in MySQL or Access format (it's in the **chapter_23** folder on the book's website at www.peachpit.com), and, depending on your technology choice, you might need to define a driver. Read the instructions in Chapter 21, "Building Dynamic Sites with Dreamweaver," if you need refreshing on this.

See Chapter 21 for a full discussion of setting up the testing server and defining a database connection.

Before beginning the exercise, from within the **chapter_23** folder on the book's website, find the folder that matches your server model and language. Copy that folder to your hard drive, and define a site called Chapter 23, using it as the local root folder. Also set up a testing server for the site. You also must define a connection to the **more_antiques** database.

1. Start by opening the layout file (**layout.cfm**, **layout.php**, **layout.aspx**). This file contains the framework elements that will be the same throughout the site. Choose File > Save as Template, or, from the Insert bar (Common), choose the Make Template object. When the dialog box appears, name your template **main**, and click Save. When asked to update links, click Yes.

    When you've done that, examine the title bar of the Document window. Note that the template's name includes both the file extension for your server model and the .dwt extension.

2. Select the text in the central area of the page. Delete it and insert an editable region there called **maincontent**. (Use the Editable Region object from the Template objects in the Common Insert bar, or choose Insert > Template Objects > Editable Region).

3. Save and close the template.

4. Open the catalog page (**catalog.cfm** and so on), and apply the main template to the page (drag the main template from the Assets panel to the Document window, and put all body contents in the maincontent region, or whatever method you prefer for applying templates).

This is your master page. The design framework is now in place, including placeholders for the dynamic elements.

5. Using the Bindings panel, create a recordset for this page. From the stockitems table, collect **id**, **itemname**, **description**, **price**, and **base-name**, as shown in Figure 23.3.

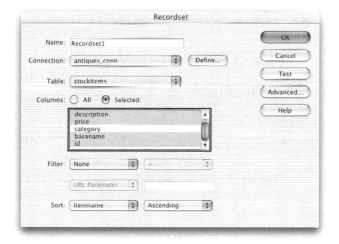

6. Substitute dynamic text for the itemname, description, and price placeholders.

7. Delete the image, and replace it by inserting a dynamic image. Do this by using the Image object and, when the dialog box opens, clicking the Data Sources button.

When the Data Source dialog box opens, you'll notice that it has no field specifying the image file. You'll use basename instead. The basename system works like this: Each antique has two images, one large and one small. The bookcase, for example, has **bookcase.jpg** and **bookcase_sm.jpg**. The basename for the bookcase is **bookcase**. You can construct the image paths for both images from this base-name. (See the following sidebar for more information on the **more_antiques** database.)

In the Data Source dialog box, choose basename. When the code appears at the bottom of the dialog box, place the insertion point before the code, and type **images**/. Then place the insertion point after the code and type **_sm.jpg**. You're creating a file path like this:

images/**bookcase**_sm.jpg

but substituting the basename for the central portion of the address.

When you're done constructing the file path, click OK as many times as you need to to close all the dialog boxes.

This method of working—using a basename to generate image paths—works only if the image files and database fields are set up this way. Otherwise, thumbnail and full-size images are specified in separate database fields. For creating catalog pages, either method works.

8. Select the table containing your dynamic elements, and turn it into a repeating region by choosing the Repeated Region object from the Insert bar. Choose to display all records so that you don't have to bother with recordset paging for this exercise. Figure 23.4 shows what the finished page should look like.

FIGURE 23.4
The finished Antiques Barn catalog page as it appears in the browser.

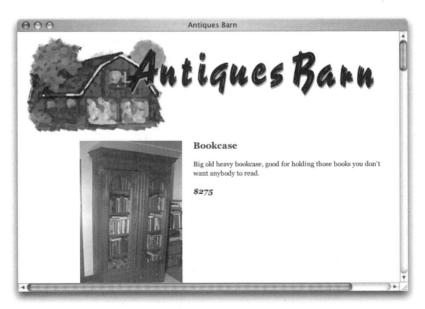

Save this file! You'll need it for another exercise later in this chapter.

What's in the more_antiques Database?

The database used for the exercises in this chapter is a more sophisticated version of the antiques database used in the previous chapters. It contains more interrelated tables to create more of a real-world experience working with fully functional databases. Figure 23.5 shows the table structure as it appears in the Microsoft Access interface, with primary keys and table relationships diagrammed.

FIGURE 23.5
The table structure of the more_antiques database.

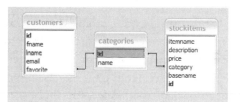

MASTER-DETAIL PAGE SETS

Building a set of master-detail pages is a fairly common dynamic task. Think of a catalog page on which all products are listed and each product entry contains a link to a page of detailed information about that product. Dreamweaver gives you two ways to build master-detail sets: manual and automatic. The manual method isn't all that manual (it doesn't involve any hand-coding), and it gives you greater control over your layout and setup. But the automatic method is (as its name suggests!) much quicker. We'll look at both methods here.

Master-Detail Sets the Manual Way

In the manual method of building master-detail pages, you create the master and detail page, create recordsets, and link the two pages using dynamic hyperlinks. The details of this procedure are described next.

Creating the Master Page

Create a page to be your main display page. As you should with any dynamic page, plan what information you want to display and how it should be laid out ahead of time. Also consider what you want the link to the detail set to look like. Do you want visitors to click an item's name, its picture, or some other generic link that says something like **Click here for more...**? Whether it's a dynamic element or not, the link must be inside the repeating region so that it appears once for every record that gets displayed.

When you've got a plan, build the design framework for the page.

Collect a recordset of information to display, as you normally would for a catalog page, with one extra consideration: Be sure to include the column that functions as the primary key or unique identifier for each item. You'll need it to tell the detail page exactly which record to display. You don't need to display the identifier field anywhere, but it must be collected.

Creating the Detail Page

Repeat the same procedure for the detail page. Start by planning what needs to be displayed and how, and build your design framework. Don't forget to include a link back to the master page. Remember, this page will display only one record at a time, so there's no need for repeating regions or recordset paging controls.

Create a recordset of information to display, again being sure to include the unique identifier or primary key. It's what will connect the two pages.

Linking the Master Page to the Detail Page

Back in the master page, select the item(s) you want to link to the detail page. You need this item to link to the detail page but with a URL parameter that specifies the record to display. Because the parameter will be different for every record, it must be dynamically determined. Create the link this way:

1. In the Property Inspector, click the Browse button next to the Link field. When the Select File dialog box opens, browse to the detail page, but don't close the dialog box yet!

2. In the dialog box, click the Parameters button. When the Parameters

dialog box opens, enter the name of the unique identifier field as the parameter name.

3. The parameter value must be dynamically assigned. Click inside the value area of the dialog box and, when the lightning-bolt icon appears, click it. When the Data Source window opens, choose the unique identifier field from the recordset. Click OK as many times as you need to to close all the dialog boxes.

If you examine the Link field at this point, you'll see that dynamic code is tucked in there. If you check out your link in Code view, it will look something like this:

PHP:

```
<a href="closeup.php?id=<?php echo $row_Recordset1['id']; ?>">
➥click for close-up</a>
```

ColdFusion:

```
<a href="closeup.cfm?id=<cfoutput>#Recordset1.id#</cfoutput>">
➥ click for close-up</a>
```

ASP.NET:

```
<a href="closeup.aspx?id=<%# DataSet1.FieldValue("id", Container)
➥ %>">click for close up</a>
```

This is the standard code for a link with a URL parameter:

```
<a href="closeup.php?id=3">
```

But server-side code has been inserted in place of the parameter value.

Filtering the Detail Page Recordset Based on the URL Parameter

Now that the master page is passing a parameter, the detail page needs to make use of it. In the detail page, open the recordset for editing (find it in the Server Behaviors panel's list of behaviors, and double-click it). In the Recordset dialog box, set the Filter options to filter the unique identifier field based on the URL parameter (see Figure 23.6). Because you're filtering based on a unique identifier, this recordset will collect only one record.

FIGURE 23.6

Filtering a detail page's recordset based on the unique identifier (ID) being passed as a URL parameter.

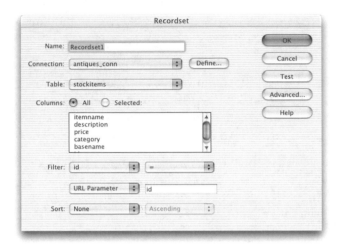

That's it! One page passes a parameter, the other receives it, and the parameter is dynamically generated.

EXERCISE 23.2

Building a Master-Detail Page Set

In this exercise, you'll work with an alternative version of the Antiques Barn catalog page, which is template-based and that uses master and detail pages. Before doing this exercise, you should have completed Exercise 23.1, which defines a template for the Antiques Barn site and creates the catalog page.

1. In the **chapter_23** folder, open the catalog page (**catalog.cfm** and so on). It displays a list of antiques with small pictures of each.

   This is your master page. The design framework is in place, and the recordset has been created. All it needs is a link to the detail page, which you'll set up later.

2. Now for the detail page. Open **catalogdetail.php**, and apply the **main** template. That's the framework for the detail page, without dynamic elements.

3. Create a recordset for the document, collecting the **basename** and **id** from the **stockitems** table. These are the only records you need for this page.

4. Delete the bookcase image and insert a dynamic image, using the

same basename technique you used in Exercise 23.1 to construct the following file path from dynamic information:

images/bookcase.jpg

You need to insert a dynamic image, starting with the **basename** field as its value and adding **images/** to the front of the dynamic URL and **.jpg** to the end.

5. Your detail page is now ready for action.

6. Link the two pages. Open the catalog page, and select the dynamic image placeholder. This is what will link to the detail page.

7. In the Property Inspector, click the Link field's Browse button. When the dialog box opens, browse to the detail page. Then click the Parameters button. When the parameters dialog box opens, enter **id** as the parameter name. For the value, click in the value field, click the lightning bolt, and choose id from the Data Source dialog box (see Figure 23.7). When you're done, click OK as many times as you need to to close all the dialog boxes.

The master page now passes a record ID to the detail page. The final step is to alter the detail page recordset so that it uses that record.

FIGURE 23.7
Assigning a dynamic URL parameter for the Antiques Barn master catalog page.

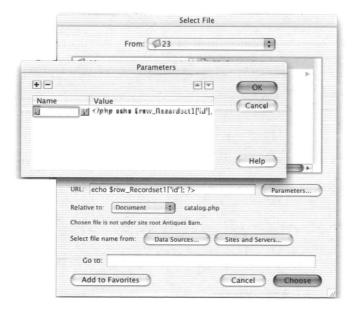

8. Open the catalogdetail page. In the Server Behaviors panel, double-click its recordset to open it for editing. Set the Filter options to filter by the ID passed in the URL parameter, as shown in Figure 23.8.

To make sure you're collecting only one record at a time, click the Test button in the Recordset dialog box. Dreamweaver asks for a value to use as a default URL parameter. Enter **3**, which is the ID of the chandelier. You should see a recordset consisting of only that one record, as shown in Figure 23.9.

FIGURE 23.8
Filtering the record-set for the Antiques Barn detail catalog page.

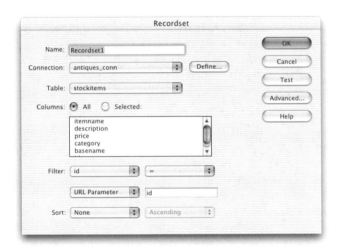

FIGURE 23.9
Testing the filtered recordset from within the Record-set dialog box.

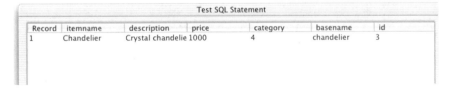

Record	itemname	description	price	category	basename	id
1	Chandelier	Crystal chandelie 1000		4	chandelier	3

9. That's it! Save both pages, and upload them to the testing server. Then preview the set.

Working with the Master-Detail Page Set Object (ColdFusion and PHP)

The advantage of manually building master-detail page sets is that you can determine your layout options ahead of time and then fill in the dynamic blanks. The Master-Detail Page Set object, on the other hand, builds the layout for you—although you can change that layout after the fact. But all the dynamic linking and even recordset paging are built for you with a few mouse clicks, so it's a very quick way to work.

The Master-Detail Page Set Object is not available for ASP.NET. ASP.NET uses a separate application object called a DataGrid that presents data and provides links to detail pages you create. For an explanation of the DataGrid, see Chapter 26, "Working Smart with ASP.NET."

To use the Master-Detail object, do this:

1. Create a blank detail page and then close it.

2. Create a blank master page. You don't need any page content in place.

3. With the master page open, create a recordset that includes all the fields you want to display in both the master and detail pages. Be sure to include the unique identifier field for each record.

4. From the Application Insert bar, choose the Master-Detail Page Set object (or choose Insert > Application Objects > Master-Detail Page Set). The dialog box shown in Figure 23.10 opens. Its options are as follows:

   • **Master page fields**—The top portion of the dialog box determines what will be displayed in the master page. The master page will be built with a dynamic table displaying all fields listed here, in the order they're listed. Generally, you won't want to display all information in the master page. Remove from the top list any fields you don't want to display there. Also rearrange the list to suit your display needs.

   • **Link to detail from**—You can also determine which item in the master page should function as a link to the detail page. Do you want the user to click the item's name to access the detail page? If so, choose that field from the Link to detail from menu.

   • **Pass unique key**—You need to specify which field is the unique identifier key that will be passed from master to detail to determine what is displayed in that page. Choose the unique identifier field from the Pass unique key menu.

Also choose how many records at a time to display on the master page. Dreamweaver will insert recordset paging controls as needed.

- **Detail page name and fields**—In the bottom portion of the dialog box, you set the detail page options. Browse to select the blank detail page you created earlier. Adjust the list of fields to include only those that the detail page should show, in the order you want them shown. The detail page, like the master page, will be built with a dynamic table.

FIGURE 23.10

The Master-Detail page Set dialog box.

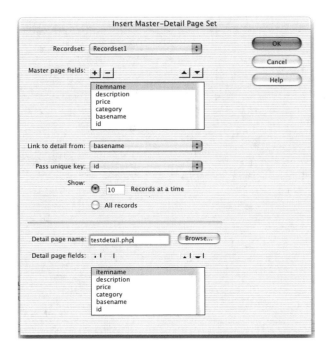

5. When you're done, click OK to create the page set. Dreamweaver puts dynamic tables in both pages, adds recordset paging where needed, and assigns dynamic URL parameters to link between the two pages, as shown in Figure 23.11. Of course, the result isn't formatted very prettily, but you can dress it up and rearrange it all you like at this point.

You can't use template child pages as the blank master and detail pages, but you can apply templates after the fact. Create your master-detail set using blank pages that aren't child pages of any template when Dreamweaver has finished. Then apply the template to the pages.

FIGURE 23.11
Master and detail pages as built by the Master-Detail Page Set object.

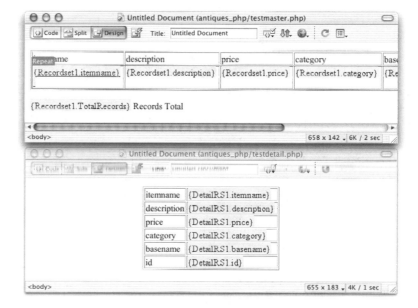

WORKING WITH COMPLEX RECORDSETS

SQL is a powerful language that can collect data in all sorts of ways. To help you with this, the Recordset dialog box can operate in simple or advanced mode. Simple mode is quick and easy for collecting, filtering, and sorting basic recordsets. But for table joins, grouping, using calculated fields, and other more sophisticated tasks, only advanced mode will do (see Figure 23.12). In this mode, you can write your own SQL, use the Data Tree to help create complex statements, and incorporate variables (parameters) into your SQL.

FIGURE 23.12
The Recordset
dialog box in
Advanced mode.

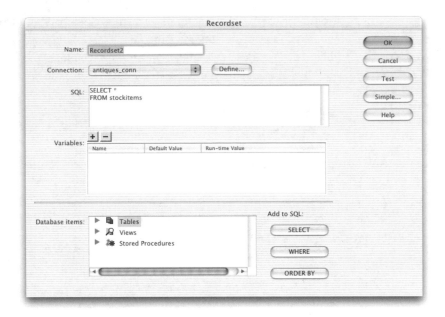

Writing SQL Queries

For online SQL help,
check out the
Dreamweaver
Reference panel.
From the Book drop-
down menu, choose
O'Reilly SQL
Reference.

Welcome to the wonderful world of SQL! SQL is a straightforward language on the surface, with an amazing amount of complexity hidden
in its depths. It's not hard to get into, though. A good way to get used
to the syntax for simple statements is to create a recordset in Simple
mode and then peek into Advanced mode to see what code created the
recordset. SQL is not case-sensitive, but it's customary to use all caps
for SQL keywords. SQL statements can also be written on multiple
lines for easier reading.

The Basics

The kinds of recordsets created in Simple mode use selecting, filtering,
and ordering to collect their data:

- **Selecting**—Data is collected with SELECT statements. The statement
  must specify which fields are being collected. An asterisk indicates
  that all fields should be collected. There must also be a FROM
  clause, specifying which table to use:

```
SELECT * FROM stockitems
```

```
SELECT itemname, price FROM stockitems
```

Other data-collection refinements all build on the SELECT statement by adding clauses to it.

- **Filtering**—Data is filtered by adding a WHERE clause to the SELECT statement:

```
SELECT * FROM stockitems WHERE price < 300
```

```
SELECT * FROM stockitems WHERE category = 'clocks'
```

Note that string values (text) are placed in single quotes within a SQL statement, but numeric values are not. WHERE clauses can also specify multiple search criteria using logical operators such as AND and OR:

```
SELECT * FROM stockitems WHERE price < 300 AND category =
➡'clocks'
```

- **Sorting**—Records are sorted by adding an ORDER BY clause. Records can be ordered by any field and can be ordered in ascending (ASC) or descending (DESC) order:

```
SELECT * FROM stockitems ORDER BY itemname ASC
```

The ORDER BY clause must be the last item in the SELECT statement. If you omit the ASC/DESC keyword, the records are sorted in ascending order by default.

Getting Fancier

Beyond these basics, a whole world of complexity awaits. Data can be collected from multiple tables at once, have calculations performed on it during collection, and more.

Collecting One Instance Only

You can collect only one instance of every different value in a particular field by adding the DISTINCT keyword to the statement's SELECT clause:

```
SELECT DISTINCT category FROM stockitems
```

Calculations

You can perform calculations on the data as it's being retrieved from the database by using various calculation keywords and operators, creating calculated fields. Calculations can be used to summarize information across multiple records or to process record information as it's being retrieved. Calculations can be used with the AS keyword to assign the calculated value a descriptive name, which then shows up in the recordset. Tables 23.1 and 23.2 show the SQL syntax for some common calculations.

TABLE 23.1 ## Calculations for Summarizing Data

Calculation	Description	Example
SUM()	Adds the values of all records for that column	SELECT SUM(price) AS total ⟿price FROM stockitems
COUNT()	Counts the number of records	SELECT COUNT(*) AS totalitems ⟿FROM stockitems
AVG()	Returns the average value of all record values for the specified field	SELECT AVG(price) AS ⟿avgprice FROM stockitems
MAX()	Returns the highest value for all records in the specified field	SELECT MAX(price) AS ⟿highprice FROM stockitems
MIN()	Returns the lowest value for all records in the specified field	SELECT MIN(price) AS ⟿lowprice FROM stockitems

TABLE 23.2 ## Calculations That Process Data from Each Record Before Collecting It

Calculation	Description	Example
Concatenation	Collects text values in multiple fields as one value	SELECT fname + ' ' + lname ⟿AS fullname FROM customers
Mathematical calculation	Performs mathematical calculations on numeric field values before returning them	SELECT price/2 AS saleprice SELECT price - discount AS ⟿saleprice

Joining

Databases are made up of multiple tables, and sometimes you need to collect pieces of data from several tables. You do this by temporarily joining the tables with a join statement. There are different kinds of joins and different requirements for different database systems. A simple join just collects fields from multiple tables, specifying the table name as well as the field name where needed:

```
SELECT stockitems.itemname, stockitems.price, customers.* FROM
➥stockitems, customers
```

This statement collects the itemname and price fields from the stock-items table, as well as all fields from the customers table.

The more complex your database (the more it relies on interrelated tables) the more important joins are. For instance, look again at the table structure of the **more_antiques** database (see Figure 23.5), used in this chapter's exercises. Each customer's favorite category of antiques is identified by an ID, which matches an item in the categories table. Finding out the name of a particular customer's favorite category requires accessing both tables:

```
SELECT categories.id, categories.name, customers.favorite
FROM categories, customers
WHERE customers.id = 2 and customers.favorite = categories.id
```

Using the Database Items Tree to Write SQL

At the bottom of the Advanced Recordset window, the database items tree area lets you choose items from the database structure, along with SQL keywords, to construct SQL statements without actually writing them yourself. This is a handy way to avoid all that typing and get a little help with the syntax. But you still need to know basically what the syntax should be to make this method work.

To create a SELECT statement using the data tree, do the following:

1. Look through the data tree and select the first field you want. Click the SELECT button to the right of the tree. A SELECT statement gets added to the SQL window, as shown in Figure 23.13. Note that this method always identifies each field along with the table it belongs to, which is correct although not necessary when you don't use joins.

FIGURE 23.13
Using the data tree
to select the id field
from the customers
table of a database.

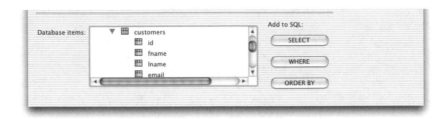

2. To select additional fields from the same table or a different table, repeat step 1. Dreamweaver doesn't add a new SELECT statement; instead, it adds the new field to the existing statement.

To add a WHERE clause, do the following:

1. From the data tree, select the field you want to filter by, and click the WHERE button. This inserts the first part of the WHERE statement but not the rest of the comparison statement.

2. It's up to you to enter a comparison operator into the SQL area where the statement is being constructed. Table 23.3 lists common comparison operators.

3. If the clause is filtering according to a hard value (such as less than 3, or equals "Fred"), you have to type that in as well. If the clause is comparing two fields, type the comparison operator yourself, select the field to compare to, and click the WHERE button again.

To add an ORDER BY clause, do the same thing: Select a field, and click the ORDER BY button to add it to the code. Dreamweaver always adds the clauses in the proper order, so the ORDER BY clause is at the end of the query.

TABLE 23.3 ## Common Comparison Operators in SQL

Operator	Meaning	Example
=	Equal to	username = "Fred"
<>	Not equal to	username <> "Fred"
!=	Not equal to	username != "Fred"
>	Greater than	price > 50
>=	Greater than or equal to	price >= 50
!>	Not greater than	price !> 50
<	Less than	price < 200

Operator	Meaning	Example
<=	Less than or equal to	price <= 200
!<	Not less than	price !< 200
BETWEEN	Between two values	price BETWEEN 50 AND 200

Using Parameters in SQL Statements

To see how a valid parameter should be entered into the parameters area, examine a recordset that uses Filter options, and take a look at it in Advanced mode.

Parameters, or variables, are pieces of the SQL query that are determined at runtime. For instance, a URL parameter, passed form variable, cookie, or session variable may determine filtering, sorting, or other elements that go into the SQL query. When you filter a recordset using the Filter options in the Simple Recordset dialog box, parameters are added to your SQL query behind the scenes. Other uses of parameters require using the parameters area of the Advanced Recordset dialog box.

The parameters area of the Advanced Recordset dialog box looks different, and behaves differently, depending on which server model you're using. They're best discussed separately.

Parameters for PHP

Figure 23.14 shows the parameters area of the dialog box for PHP.

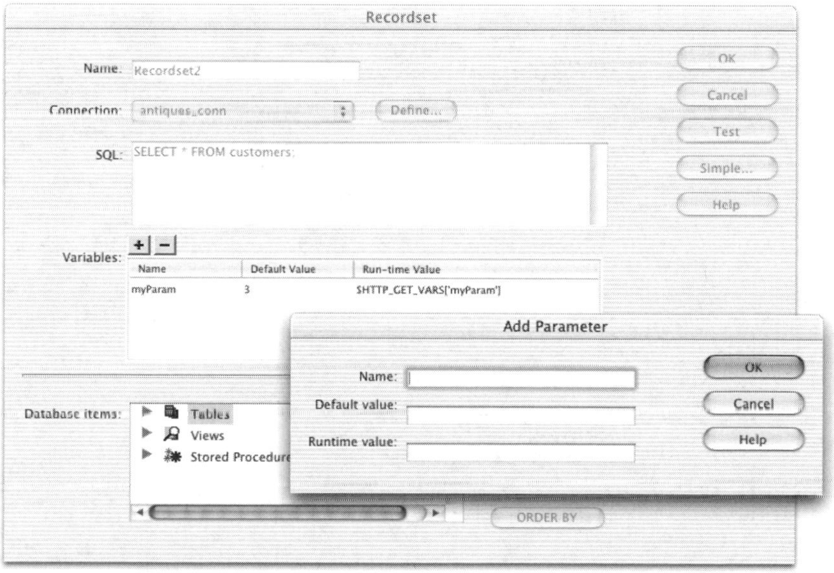

FIGURE 23.14

The parameters area of the Advanced Recordset dialog box for PHP pages.

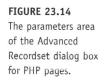

To create and use a parameter in a PHP page, follow these steps:

1. With the Advanced Recordset dialog box open, click the + button in the parameters area to create a new parameter.

2. Give the parameter a one-word name that you'll use in the SQL query to reference it. You can pick any name except reserved SQL keywords. Descriptive names make it easier to keep track of what you're doing. (Table 23.4 lists common reserved keywords.) For instance, if the parameter will determine sort order, **sortOrder** or **sortby** would be descriptive.

TABLE 23.4 ## Reserved SQL Keywords You Might Be Tempted to Use

Keyword	Keyword
ABSOLUTE	ACTION
AUTHORIZATION	AUTO
BACKUP	BULK
CATALOG	CHARACTER
CHECK	CHECKPOINT
COMMENT	COMPUTED
CONFIRM	CONNECTION
COUNT	CUBE
CURRENT	DATABASE
DATE	DATETIME
DAY	DESCRIBE
DOMAIN	DOUBLE
DUMMY	DUMP
ESCAPE	EXIT
EXTERNAL	FILE
FLOAT	FLOPPY
IDENTITY	INDEX
LANGUAGE	MONTH
MINUTE	MODULE

Keyword	Keyword
NATIONAL	NATURAL
OPTION	ORDER
OUTPUT	OVERFLOW
PAD	PAGE
PAGES	PASSWORD
PERCENT	PERMANENT
POSITION	PROCEDURE
REFERENCES	RELATIVE
SEGMENT	SEQUENCE
SHADOW	SHARED
SIZE	SNAPSHOT
SPACE	STATISTICS
TEMPORARY	TIME
TRANSACTION	TRANSLATE
TRIGGER	TRIM
UPDATE	USER
VOLUME	WHEN
WHERE	WORK
YEAR	ZONE

3. Supply a default value for the parameter. This makes it possible to test your query before runtime, but more importantly, it keeps the page from generating an error if for some reason the parameter doesn't get supplied at runtime. (For instance, if the parameter will come from a URL parameter, what if the page gets called with no URL parameter?) If the parameter is supposed to determine sort order, a default value would be the name of a field to sort by.

4. Supply a runtime value. This is the dynamic value that is actually used when the page is run. It must be a valid PHP expression calling up a URL parameter, session variable, and so on. Table 23.5 lists the required syntax for different kinds of runtime values.

The Syntax column of Table 23.5 lists two syntax examples for each parameter. Either syntax is correct. Dreamweaver uses the first.

5. Finally, incorporate the parameter's name into the SQL query. You have to do this by typing, so you have to know enough SQL syntax to know how to do that. Just substitute the name where the value should go. For example, if the parameter determines sort order, and its name is sortby, you would want the following in the SQL area:

SELECT * FROM stockitems ORDER BY **sortby**

TABLE 23.5 ## Syntax for the Runtime Values of PHP Parameters

Type of Parameter	Syntax
URL parameter (or form value passed using GET)	$_GET['myParam'] $HTTP_GET_VARS['myParam']
Form variable passed using POST	$_POST['myParam'] $HTTP_POST_VARS['myParam']
Cookie collected from the user's computer	$_COOKIE['id'] $HTTP_COOKIE_VARS['myParam']
Session variable set for this user's browsing session	$_SESSION['myParam'] $HTTP_SESSION_VARS['myParam']
Environment variables	$_ENV['myParam'] $HTTP_ENV_VARS['myParam']
Server variables, storing information about settings on the server	$_SERVER['myParam'] $HTTP_SERVER['myParam']

Parameters for ColdFusion

Figure 23.15 shows the parameters area of the Advanced Recordset dialog box for ColdFusion.

To create and use a parameter in a ColdFusion page, do the following:

1. With the Advanced Recordset dialog box open, click the + button in the Page Parameters area to create a new parameter.

FIGURE 23.15
The Parameters area
of the Advanced
Recordset dialog box
for ColdFusion pages.

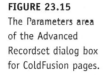

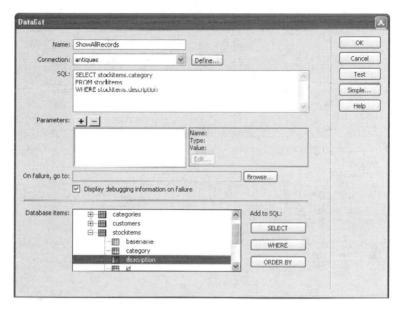

2. When the Edit Parameter dialog box opens, enter a name indicating what kind of parameter it is (URL, form variable, and so on) and its name. Table 23.6 lists the kinds of parameters available in ColdFusion and their syntax; your entry in the Edit Parameter dialog box should match the Name column in this table. If the parameter will be a URL parameter called sortby, for instance, your entry should be **URL.sortby**, or just **sortby**. (Either is correct.)

3. Still in the Edit Parameter dialog box, enter a default value. This value makes it possible to test your query before runtime, but more importantly, it keeps the page from generating an error if for some reason the parameter doesn't get supplied at runtime. (For instance, if the parameter will come from a URL parameter, what if the page gets called with no URL parameter?) If the parameter is supposed to determine sort order, a default value would be the name of a field to sort by.

4. Click OK to close the Edit Parameter dialog box.

5. Finally, incorporate the parameter's name into the SQL query. You have to do this by typing, so you have to know enough SQL syntax to know how to do that. Substitute the name, surrounded by pound signs (#), where the value should go. If the parameter is a URL parameter that determines sort order, and its name is sortby, you

would want one of the following in the SQL area:

```
SELECT * FROM stockitems ORDER BY #URL.sortby#
SELECT * FROM stockitems ORDER BY #sortby#
```

(This corresponds to the information in the Usage column in Table 23.6.)

The Syntax column of Table 23.6 lists two syntax examples for each parameter. Either syntax is correct. Dreamweaver uses the first.

TABLE 23.6 ## Syntax for Defining and Using ColdFusion Parameters

Type of Parameter	Name	Usage in SQL Query
URL parameter (or form value passed using GET)	URL.myParam	#URL.myParam# #myParam#
Form variable passed using POST	FORM.myParam	#FORM.myParam# #myParam#
Cookie collected from the user's computer	COOKIE.myParam	#COOKIE.myParam# #myParam#
Session variable set for this user's browsing session	SESSION.myParam	#SESSION.myParam# #myParam#
Application variable	APPLICATION.myParam	#APPLICATION.myParam# #myParam#

Parameters for ASP.NET

Figure 23.16 shows the parameters area of the Advanced Recordset dialog box for ASP.NET.

FIGURE 23.16
The parameters area of the Advanced Recordset dialog box for ASP.NET pages.

To create and use a parameter in a .NET page, follow these steps:

1. With the Advanced DataSet dialog box open, click the + button in the parameters area to create a new parameter.

2. When the Edit Parameter dialog box opens, click the + button to add a new parameter.

3. When the Add Parameter dialog box opens, name your parameter. The name is what you will refer to in the SQL query, so make it descriptive. In ASP.NET, you want to name the variable with an @ symbol. If you want to filter the query on the id field, name the Parameter @id.

4. In the Type drop-down menu, pick the variable's type. This can be complicated if you don't know what the type of the field is in the database. For numbers, it usually is Integer. For text, it usually is WChar. For a complete description of each type, check an ASP.NET reference.

You can add the ASP.NET code to the value field by hand, but it is easier to click the Build button.

1. In the Build Value dialog box, shown in Figure 23.17, the name defaults to the name in the Add Parameter dialog. In this case, it is @id. Leave the name unchanged.

    In the Source drop-down, you can specify where the variable is coming from: a URL Parameter, Session Variable, Application Variable, Cookie, or Form Variable. Select URL Parameter.

    In the Default Value field, you can set a default value if you want a result to be returned even if no value is passed in. You can leave this blank.

    Click OK to exit the Build Value dialog box.

FIGURE 23.17
The Build Value dialog box set for a variable named @id.

2. In the Add Parameter dialog box, shown in Figure 23.18, the Value field is now filled with the ASP.NET code to test for the existence of a form.

3.   Click OK to return to the DataSet dialog box.

4.   Now that the parameter is defined, you need to add it to your query.
     If your parameter is designed to be used as a filter in a WHERE
     clause to limit the query to finding only records that have a specific
     ID, you would put the following in the SQL area:

```
SELECT basename, id
FROM stockitems
WHERE id = ?
```

5.   Click the Test button to make sure your syntax is correct. Then click
     OK to close the dialog box.

Table 23.7 lists the syntax for defining and using ASP.NET parameters.

TABLE 23.7 ## Syntax for the Runtime Values of ASP.NET Parameters

Type of Parameter	Name	Value
URL parameter (or form value passed using GET)	@id	IIf((Request.QueryString("id") <> ➡Nothing), Request.QueryString("id"), ➡"")
Form variable passed using POST	@id	IIf((Request.Form("id") <> Nothing), ➡Request.Form("id"), "")
Cookie collected from the user's computer	@id	IIf((Not Request.Cookies("id") Is ➡Nothing), Request.Cookies(IIf((Not ➡Request.Cookies("id") Is Nothing), ➡"id", 0)).Value, "")
Session variable set for this user's browsing session	@id	IIf((Not Session("id") Is Nothing), ➡Session("id"), "")
Application variable for long-term storage of information	@id	IIf((Not Application("id") Is Nothing), ➡Application("id"), "")

EXERCISE 23.3

Collecting a Complex Recordset to Create a Dynamically Sortable Display (ColdFusion, PHP, and ASP.NET)

A dynamic page presents recordsets that have been sorted based on one of the recordset fields. But what if the page visitor needs the information sorted some other way? A popular interface feature is to let visitors click the different headers of a dynamic table to re-sort the contents according to that header. Click the Date column to sort by date, click the Author column to sort by author, and so on (see Figure 23.19).

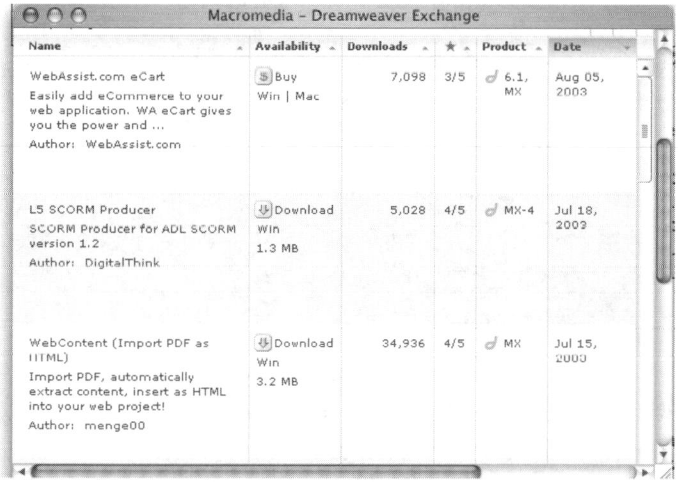

FIGURE 23.19

The Macromedia Exchange displays information in tables that can be dynamically sorted by Date, Software, and so on.

The mechanism works like this: Each column header links back to the current page, passing it a URL parameter that must be used to determine the recordset's sort order. This is similar to how a search-and-results page works, but it has to be created differently in Dreamweaver.

In this exercise, you'll add dynamic sorting links to the column headers in the Antiques Barn pricelist table.

1. Working within the Chapter 23 site, create a new file based on the main template. (Choose File > New to bring the Templates tab to the front, and choose Main.) Save it as **pricelist** (plus your filename extension).

2. You need to create a recordset that includes each item's name and price and the name of its category. These records reside in fields

across two tables. The stockitems table includes itemname and price. It contains a category field as well, but the field contains only a category ID number, not the category's name. For each record, you need to collect the name field from the categories table, and you need to compare the stockitems table's category field to the categories table's ID field to determine which category name goes with which stock item. Whew! You need to use a join (joining fields from the category and stockitems tables) with a WHERE clause to construct this set of data.

Create a recordset by using either the Bindings panel or the Recordset object in the Insert bar. When the Recordset dialog box opens, go to Advanced mode.

Using the Database Tree, expand the Tables hierarchy until you see the fields in the stockitems table. Select itemname, and click the SELECT button. Select price from the stockitems table, and click the SELECT button. Then expand the categories table and use the same method to add the name to your SQL query. In the SQL area, place the insertion point immediately following categories.name and type the following:

```
AS category
```

Next, you need a WHERE clause to specify which category names should be collected. In the data tree, expand the stockitems table, and select the category field. Click the WHERE button to begin the clause. Go to the SQL area, make sure the insertion point is at the end of the text that's there, and type in the rest of the WHERE clause:

```
= categories.id
```

From the data tree, select the itemname field of the stockitems table. Click the ORDER BY button to sort the records. At this point, your query should look like the one shown in Figure 23.20. Click the Test button to make sure your SQL query has no errors. Then click OK as many times as you need to to close all the dialog boxes.

3. For ColdFusion and PHP, insert a dynamic table into the **maincontent** editable region. Set the table to display all records, with border and cellspacing of 0 and cellpadding of 10 (see Figure 23.21). For the purposes of this exercise, you know there aren't very many entries in the database, so there's no need to deal with recordset paging.

FIGURE 23.20
The recordset for
the Antiques Barn
pricelist page.

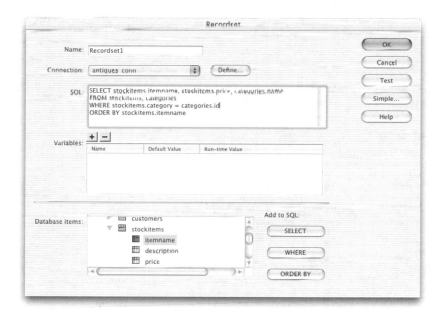

FIGURE 23.21
Inserting a dynamic
table into the
pricelist page.

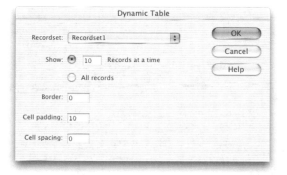

For ASP.NET, insert a table into the **maincontent** editable region
with two rows and three columns. Set the table border and cellspacing to 0 and the cellpadding to 10. In the first row of the table, add
the headers for each column: itemname, price, and name. From the
Bindings panel, expand the DataSet you just created, and drag the
itemname binding to the table cell below the itemname label you
just entered. Drag the price and name bindings from the DataSet
to the corresponding cells in the table. Select only the row containing the bound data, and apply a Repeat Region server behavior. In
the Repeat Region Server Behavior dialog box, select the DataSet you
created, and set it to show all records.

4. When the table is in place, assign it the CSS class **.pricetable**. Also select the top row of cells and convert the cells to header cells (for accessibility and styling).

5. Before previewing, remember to upload your entire site to the testing server. Figure 23.22 shows the price table as it should look now.

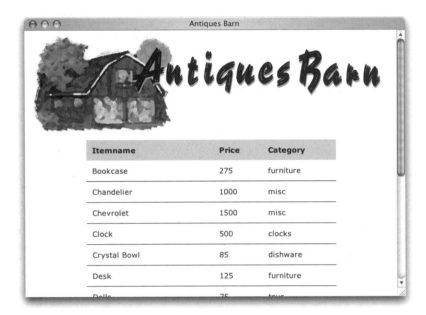

6. Now it's time to add dynamic sorting. Each of the headers must link back to the current page, but with a URL parameter indicating which field of the recordset to sort by.

   Select the itemname column header. In the Property Inspector's Link field, click the Browse button to open the Select File dialog box. Browse to the pricelist page, and select it. Click the Parameters button to open the Parameters dialog box. For the parameter name, enter **sortby**. For its value, enter **itemname**, as shown in Figure 23.23. Close all the dialog boxes by clicking OK.

7. Repeat step 6 for each of the other column headers, each time assigning a URL parameter with the name sortby and the value matching the column header's name (price, category).

FIGURE 23.23
Linking the itemname column header back to the current page, but with a URL parameter to indicate sorting order.

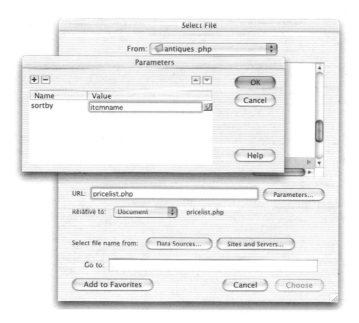

8. You need to change the recordset so that it uses the sortby parameter. In the Server Behaviors panel, open the recordset by double-clicking it. The Recordset dialog box should open in Advanced mode.

9. What you do next depends on which server model you're using:

   In PHP, in the Parameters area, click the + button to add a new parameter. Name it **sortby**, give it a default value of itemname, and enter the following for its runtime value:

   ```
   $_GET['sortby']
   ```

   This collects the value of a URL parameter whose name is sortby.

   In the SQL area, find the ORDER BY clause, and change it to look like this:

   ```
   ORDER BY sortby
   ```

   Click Test to make sure that you have no errors. Then close all the dialog boxes by clicking OK.

   In ColdFusion, in the Page Parameters area, click the + button to add a new parameter. In the Edit Parameters dialog box, name it **URL.sortby**, and give it a default value of **itemname**.

In the SQL area, find the ORDER BY clause, and change it to look like this:

```
ORDER BY #URL.sortby#
```

Click Test to make sure you have no errors. Then close all the dialog boxes by clicking OK.

In ASP.NET, in the Parameters area, click the + button to add a new parameter. Name it **sortby**, set the type to Wchar, and click the Build button.

In the Build Value dialog box, set the Source to URL Parameter, and set the Default value to itemname. Click OK to go back to the Add Parameter dialog box. At this point, you need to do a little more work. Dreamweaver's ASP.NET DataSet accepts parameters in the WHERE clause, but not in the ORDER BY clause. To make this parameter work, you have to hand-code a little bit in the Advanced DataSet dialog using the values created here in the Add Parameter dialog box. In the Value area of the Add Parameter dialog box, select the entire contents and copy them by pressing Ctrl+C. Click Cancel to close the dialog box. You don't want the parameter to actually be added; you just want the code it would have added.

At the beginning of the SQL statement in the SQL area, add a double quote (").

Find the ORDER BY clause, delete the itemname, and replace it with another double quote ("). After the double quote you just added, add a space, an ampersand (&), and another space. Then paste the code you copied from the Add Parameter dialog box.

Your code should look like this:

```
"SELECT stockitems.category, stockitems.itemname,
➥stockitems.price,
➥ categories.name
FROM stockitems, categories
WHERE stockitems.category = categories.id
ORDER BY " & IIf((Request.QueryString("sortby") <> Nothing),
➥ Request.QueryString("sortby"), "itemname")
```

You can check most queries by clicking the Test button to make sure you have no errors. In this case, because the query you have built is not what Dreamweaver expects to see, the test function doesn't work properly. Close the DataSet dialog box by clicking OK.

10. Finally! Preview the result in the browser. Clicking each of the column headers reloads the page, with the contents sorted by that header.

CREATING A USER AUTHENTICATION (LOGIN) SYSTEM

Many websites employ user authentication to control access to all or some of their pages. For the ColdFusion and PHP server models, Dreamweaver has an easy-to-use set of User Authentication server behaviors. These include signing users up, logging them in and out, and restricting access to those who haven't logged in.

The User Authentication tools are available for ColdFusion, PHP, ASP, and JSP server models, but not for ASP.NET. Rather than using scripts on each page to check users' access to a particular page, like the other server models, ASP.NET uses application-wide and directory-wide configuration files to secure access to different parts of your site. This topic is beyond the scope of this book. For complete coverage of user authentication, check out *ASP.NET Development with Macromedia Dreamweaver MX* from Peachpit Press or *Macromedia Dreamweaver MX 2004 and Databases* from New Riders.

Enabling Sessions for ColdFusion

User authentication systems rely on session management—keeping track of the sessions of each user visiting your site. If you're using ColdFusion, you need to explicitly enable sessions for your web application (your site) before your user authentication will work. To enable sessions, create an empty file called **Application.cfm** (be sure to start it with a capital A) and upload it to your web server as part of your site. Put the following code in the file:

```
<cfapplication name="myApp"
sessionmanagement="yes"
sessiontimeout="#CreateTimeSpan(0,0,20,0)#">
```

continues

continued

The first line of this code assigns your web application a name. You can substitute your own one-word name for *myApp*. The last line specifies that the session will end after 20 minutes of user inactivity. You can change that time by entering a different value in place of the *20*.

This is only the bare beginnings of what you can do with the **Application.cfm file.** For more information, check out Bryan Ashcraft's tutorial "Enabling Session Variables in ColdFusion," available at http://www.communitymx.com.

User Registration

Signing up a user, or adding him or her to the login system, is just a matter of creating a form and using it to insert a new record into the database. This was covered in Chapter 22, "Creating Dynamic Pages." To prevent duplicate usernames, the Check for Duplicate Username behavior is also available.

To set up a user sign-up page, do the following:

1. Plan your setup. Determine where the user should be redirected if the sign-up is successful or if it's not. Create those pages in advance.

2. In your database, create a table to hold user information, including username and password, as well as a unique ID.

3. ColdFusion users should enable sessions on the server by creating the **Application.cfm** file. See the preceding sidebar, "Enabling Sessions for ColdFusion," for details.

4. Create a dynamic page and build a form for collecting this information from visitors. If your page requires database recordsets for any of its display, add them now. (No recordset is required to add a user.)

5. Select the form. From the Server Behaviors panel or the Application Insert bar, choose Insert Record. You see the dialog box shown in Figure 23.24. Align each form field with a database field. Also assign the page that users will be sent to on successful signup.

FIGURE 23.24

The Insert Record dialog box for entering a new user into the system.

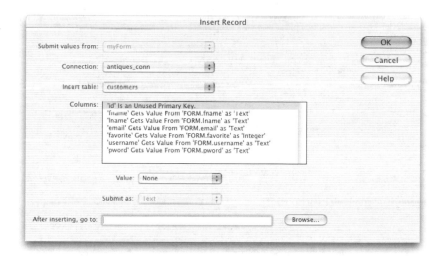

6. From the Server Behaviors panel, choose User Authentication > Check New Username. When the dialog box opens, specify which field must be unique and what page to redirect the user to if a duplication is found.

EXERCISE 23.4

Creating a User Registration Page for the Antiques Barn Site (ColdFusion and PHP)

The Antiques Barn has turned into a members-only site, so now users need to sign in to browse the catalog. The first step in setting this up is presenting users with a sign-up page. In this exercise, you'll build the Antiques Barn membership sign-up page. Before starting this exercise, you need to have completed at least Exercise 23.1, which defines the site and builds the main template.

1. Three pages are involved in the sign-up: the sign-up page itself, a thank-you page for successful submission, and a sorry page for errors. All three are in your site folder (with the relevant filename extensions). Start by opening the sign-up page (**signup.cfm** and so on). Apply the main template to it, putting all body content in the **maincontent** region.

   While you're here, take a moment to examine the form fields in the file. Select each field. You see that the text fields have names such as fname, lname, email, and pword. The drop-down menu is called favorite. These names match the field names in the database's customers table. Although it's not necessary to match form field names and database field names, it's a good convention to use, and it will come in handy when you fill out the Insert Record dialog box.

2. The form needs a dynamic drop-down menu that displays the antique categories in the database. This means collecting a recordset. In the Bindings panel, click the + button, and choose Recordset (Query). Collect all fields from the categories table, ordered by name, as shown in Figure 23.25.

FIGURE 23.25
Collecting the record-
set for displaying
antique categories.

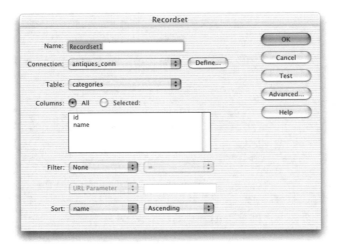

(Recalling a similar exercise task from Chapter 22, can you tell why you don't have to worry about collecting only a single instance of each different category? In the revised database structure, categories have their own table, which lists each category once. So no use of the DISTINCT keyword is necessary.)

Select the Favorites menu. In the Property Inspector, click the Dynamic button to open the Dynamic List/Menu dialog box, shown in Figure 23.26. Leave the static option at (select one). For the dynamic values, choose the category name as the label and the category ID as the value. The name is what the user needs to see, but the ID is what the database needs to store as this user's favorite kind of antique.

3. The form is now set up. The next step is to submit the form and add a new user to the database. In the Server Behaviors panel, click the + button and choose Insert Record. When the dialog box shown in Figure 23.27 opens, choose to insert this record into the customers

table of the **more_antiques** database. The field names should automatically match up to database fields because they've been named to match database field names. The id database field doesn't have a matching record, but it is automatically assigned by the database.

Before closing this dialog box, choose the thankyou page (**thankyou.cfm** and so on) in the After inserting, go to field. Then click OK.

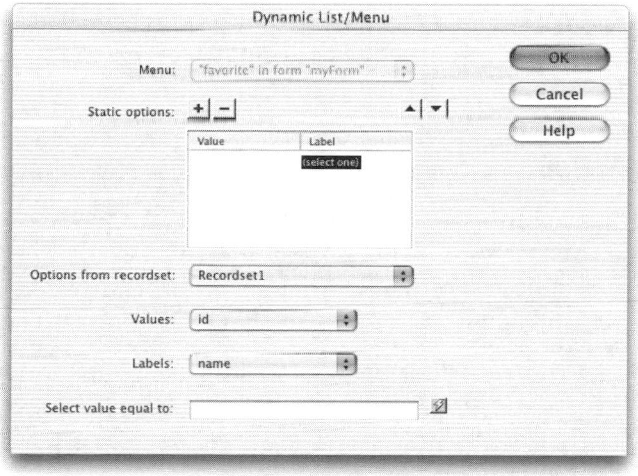

FIGURE 23.26
Setting up the dynamic list of favorite categories for the Antiques Barn sign-up page.

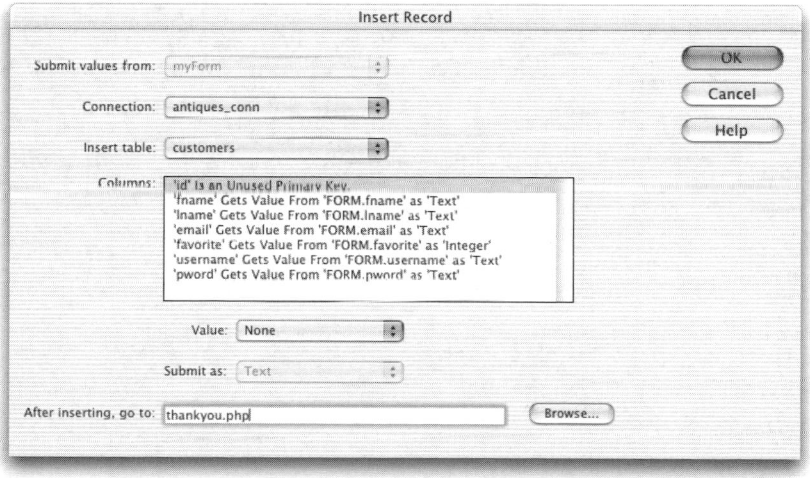

FIGURE 23.27
Settings for inserting a new user into the customers table.

4. You don't want two matching usernames, so you also need to check for duplicates before processing the record. From the Server Behaviors panel, click the + button and choose User Authentication > Check New Username. When the dialog box opens, choose username as the field

that must be unique, and enter the sorry page (**sorry.cfm** and so on) to redirect to if the name isn't unique. Click OK to close the dialog box.

5. One more refinement: The database requires values for all fields except email, so you don't want users submitting forms without these fields filled in. This is done with good old JavaScript. Select the form and, from the regular Behaviors panel, choose the Validate Form behavior. The fname, lname, username, and password fields are required to have a value (they must be filled in), although it doesn't matter what their values are. When you're done, click OK to close the behavior's dialog box.

6. Try it out! Preview it in a browser. Try creating a new user, and also try submitting the form without any data and being redirected to the sorry page by entering a username that's already in use (fred is being used, so try giving yourself that username). When the sorry page appears, notice the URL for the page—a URL parameter containing the problematic username has been appended.

This means that you can easily dress up the sorry page with some personalized information. Open the sorry page. In the Bindings panel, click the + button and choose URL Parameter. For the parameter name, enter the same name that appeared in the sorry page URL: **requsername**. When you close the dialog box, the parameter appears as one of your page's data bindings. (Note that you can also apply the main template to this page to dress it up further. You can do the same to the thankyou page if you're so inclined.)

In the Document window, select the word USERNAME. Then select the requsername parameter from the Bindings panel, and click Insert (at the bottom of the panel). Your sorry document should now look like the one shown in Figure 23.28.

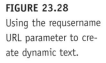

FIGURE 23.28
Using the requsername URL parameter to create dynamic text.

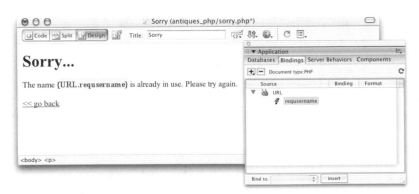

User Login

After a user has signed up and is in the database, he or she needs to be able to log in, which requires a login page. This involves creating another form and applying the Log In User behavior.

To create a login page, do the following:

1. Plan your setup. Determine where the user will be redirected if he logs in successfully and where he will be sent if his login is unsuccessful. Create these pages in advance.

2. Create a new dynamic page, and build a form containing fields for username and password and a Submit button. If any recordsets are required for other parts of this page, collect them now.

3. Select the form and, from the Server Behaviors panel, choose User Authentication > Log In User. In the dialog box that appears, shown in Figure 23.29, choose the form fields to validate from and the database fields to validate against. (This is easiest if you've named things carefully!) Then assign the redirection destinations for successful and unsuccessful login.

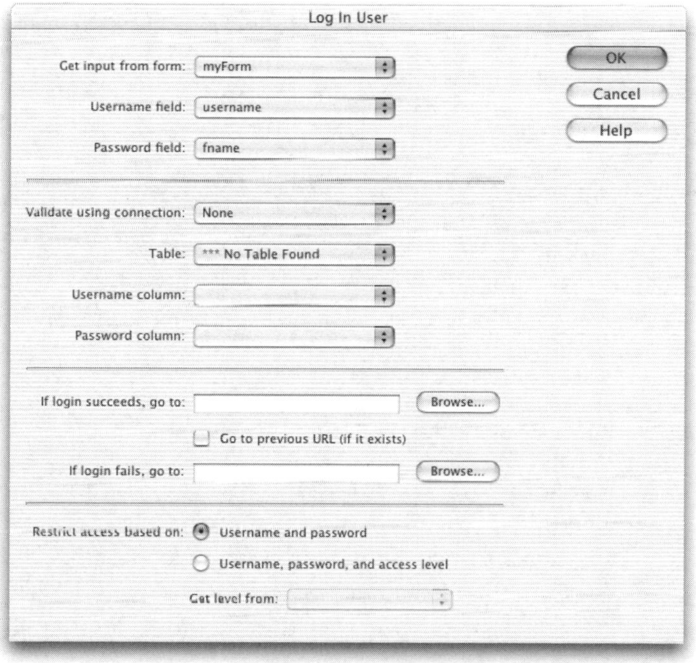

FIGURE 23.29
The dialog box for the Log In User behavior.

Creating a User Login Page (ColdFusion and PHP)

In this exercise, you continue building the user sign-up system by adding a login page. You must have completed Exercise 23.4 before attempting this one.

1. Start by opening the login page (**login.cfm** and so on). This file contains a form with a username and password field and an image being used as a Submit button. To make it look its best, apply the main template, putting all body content in the maincontent area.

2. Add the login script. From the Server Behaviors panel, choose User Authentication > Log In User. In the dialog box that appears, match your settings to those shown in Figure 23.30. Note that if login is successful, the user is merrily sent along to the catalog page. If it fails, the user stays on the current page.

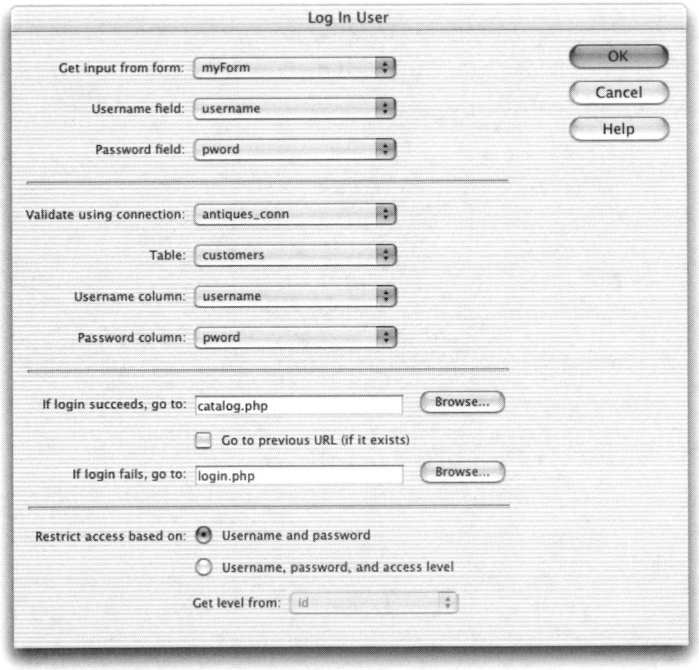

FIGURE 23.30

Log In User settings for the Antiques Barn login page.

3. Check things out in a browser. If you've already signed yourself up (and therefore added your name to the database), use the username and password you signed in with. If not, use fred and fred. If you enter everything correctly, you'll be sent to the catalog page.

Restricting Access

There's not much point in requiring users to log in if it doesn't affect their ability to see things on your site. As soon as the login system is in place, restricting access to certain pages makes use of it. In Dreamweaver, the Restrict Access to Page behavior accomplishes this. You should apply this behavior to any page in the site that should be seen only by authenticated users.

To restrict access to a page, follow these steps:

1. Plan your setup. What should happen if an unauthorized user tries to access the page? Where should he or she be redirected? Create this page if necessary.

2. Open a dynamic page. The behavior is added to the page as a whole, so you don't need to select anything.

3. From the Server Behaviors panel, choose User Authentication > Restrict Access to Page. In the dialog box that appears, restrict access based on username and password, and assign the page that the user is redirected to if he doesn't have access.

Remember to repeat this process for all restricted pages, not just the main entrance page. In the normal course of browsing, of course, users can't get to any internal pages except through the main page. But that won't stop someone from typing the detail page's URL directly into the browser address field and viewing the page that way. If you really want your site to be restricted, you have to restrict more than just the main entry page.

Logging Out

For security purposes, it's good to give users a chance to explicitly log themselves out. That's as simple as attaching a Log User Out server behavior to a logout text link or button. Because only logged-in users can log out, these logout actions should be placed on restricted pages.

To create a logout system, do the following on every restricted page:

1. Plan the setup. Determine where the user should be redirected when he logs out. (He can't stay here on the restricted page!) This might be a page that says, "You have been logged out," it might be the

login page, or it might just be the site's main unrestricted page. Create the page if it doesn't already exist.

2. Determine where in your page layout you want the logout link to appear, and add it.

3. Select the link (text link or linked image). From the Server Behaviors panel, choose User Authentication > Log User Out. In the dialog box that appears, choose to log the user out when he clicks the selected link (this option should be set by default if you had a link selected when you chose the behavior). Assign a page to redirect the user to on successful logout.

Remember, users also automatically log out if they don't interact with any of your site's pages within a certain amount of time or if they quit their browsers.

EXERCISE 23.6

Creating Restricted Access Pages (ColdFusion and PHP)

Only Antiques Barn subscribers are allowed to browse the antiques catalog. This means that the catalog and catalogdetail pages must be restricted to logged-in users. In this exercise, you'll add restricted-access scripts to both of those pages.

1. Start by opening the catalog page. In the Server Behaviors panel, click the + button, and choose User Authentication > Restrict Access to Page. When the dialog box opens, choose to restrict based on username and password. If access is denied, go to the login page. Click OK to close the dialog box.

2. Users also like the opportunity to log out. To add this, you need to edit the main template. Open the main file (from the Templates folder in the Files list, or from the Assets panel), and insert a new editable region in the left margin cell. Call this region **sidebar**, as shown in Figure 23.31. Save the template and close it, letting it update all pages.

3. Back in the catalog page, place the cursor in the new sidebar region, and insert the **logout.gif** image (in the **images** folder).

With this image selected, go to the Server Behaviors panel, and choose User Authentication > Log Out User. On logout, redirect the user back to the login page.

FIGURE 23.31
Adding a new editable region to the main template.

4. Check things out in a browser. If you've been practicing logging yourself in, quit your browser and relaunch it to start a new session. Then try visiting the catalog page without logging in. You should go directly to the login page.

5. For full security, you should also restrict access to the catalogdetail page. For this exercise, you can skip this extra step if you like. But if you want to protect the detail page, open it and repeat what you did in steps 1 and 2.

CONDITIONAL CONTENT

Conditional content is page content that displays only if certain conditions are met. It can be dynamic or static content, but it must be in a dynamic page. In the various server-side scripting languages, it's usually created with some sort of `if` statement (if x is true, display this) or `if-else` statement (if x is true, display this; else display that). The Dreamweaver Show Region objects let you show or hide contents based on recordset conditions. Any other kind of conditional content (based on URL parameters, session variables, and so on) you can create yourself if you know the proper syntax for your server model.

The Show Region Objects

The Show Region objects, shown in Figure 23.32, let you show or hide selected page content based on various recordset conditions: if the recordset is empty or not, or if recordset paging controls are displaying the first or last records of the set. This is very handy for creating special messages, such as "We're sorry; no records matched your search criteria." Show Region objects are also used in the Recordset Navigation Status object to hide or show the paging links for navigating through records.

FIGURE 23.32
The Show Region objects in the Insert bar.

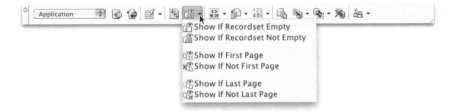

To use a Show Region object, do the following:

1. Create the content you want to hide or show based on the recordset.

2. Select that content (make sure you get all of it, including opening and closing tags!), and choose one of the Show Region objects. The display in Design view shows your conditional content surrounded by a labeled box.

Other Kinds of Conditional Content

There are all sorts of conditions besides these few recordset conditions that you might want to use to hide or show page content. How about hiding or showing a dynamic image depending on whether the current record has any data for a dynamic image? Hiding or showing top-secret information depending on whether a user is logged in? Hiding or showing titles or messages depending on the presence of URL parameters?

Conditional content makes it possible to use one page for multiple purposes instead of having to create separate pages.

Turning Dreamweaver page elements into conditional content isn't difficult if you don't mind a little bit of typing in Code view and if you know the syntax required by your server language. To create any conditional content, first create the content in Design view. Then surround it with the if statement required by your server language.

Displaying Content Only If a Record Field Is Not Empty

Some records in a database might contain empty fields. If so, you don't want to try displaying their data. You can create conditional content to be displayed only if the current record has data in that field, or only if the record has no data. You can also choose to display alternative sets of content—one if there's content and one if there's not. Tables 23.8 and 23.9 list the syntax requirements for the different server models covered here. For all examples, substitute the name of your recordset for **Recordset1** and the name of your field for **myField**.

TABLE 23.8 **PHP Syntax for Displaying Content Based on Whether a Field Has Content**

	Syntax

Show if field is not empty	`<?php  if ($row_Recordset1['myField'] != "") {   ?>`
	`[display this content if the field is empty]`
	`<?php } ?>`

Show if field is empty	`<?php  if ($row_Recordset1['myField'] == "") {   ?>`
	`[display this content if the field is empty]`
	`<?php } ?>`

Show alternate content	`<?php  if ($row_Recordset1['myField'] != "") {   ?>`
	`[display this content if the field is not empty]`
	`<?php }else{   ?>`
	`[display this content if the field is empty]`
	`<?php } ?>`

TABLE 23.9 ## ColdFusion Syntax for Displaying Content Based on Whether a Field Has Content

	Syntax

Show if field is not empty	`<cfif #Recordset.myField# NEQ "">`
	`[display this content if myField is not empty]`
	`</cfif>`

Show if field is empty	`<cfif #Recordset.myField# EQ "">`
	`[display this content if myField is empty]`
	`</cfif>`

Show alternate content	`<cfif #Recordset.myField# NEQ "">`
	`[display this content if the field is not empty]`
	`<cfelse>`
	`[display this content if the field is empty]`
	`</cfif>`

Displaying Content Based on a URL Parameter

You can repurpose and tweak pages to suit different visitors by passing different URL parameters in their addresses. For instance, the first time a user visits the login page, no extra content is displayed; if the login fails, the page includes an error message; if the user was redirected here after trying to visit a restricted page, a redirect message appears; and so forth. The conditional statement you write must test for the existence of a URL parameter and then must test for its value. Tables 23.10 and 23.11 show the required syntax for this kind of conditional content in the different server languages. For each example, substitute the name of your parameter for `myParam` and the value to test for for `myValue`. (Note that no recordset needs to be collected for this to work.)

TABLE 23.10 ## PHP Syntax for Displaying Content Based on a URL Parameter

	Syntax

Show if parameter exists and has a certain value	`<?php if isset($_GET['myParam']) &&`
	`➥$_GET['myParam'] == 'myValue') { ?>`
	`[content to display]`
	`<?php } ?>`

	Syntax

Show alternate content	`<?php  if isset($_GET['myParam']) &&`
	`⮞$_GET['myParam'] == 'myValue') {  ?>`
	`[content to display]`
	`<?php }else{  ?>`
	`[alternate content to display]`
	`<?php }  ?>`

TABLE 23.11 ## ColdFusion Syntax for Displaying Content Based on a URL Parameter

	Syntax

Show if parameter exists and has a certain value	`<cfif isdefined("URL.myParam") AND`
	`⮞#URL.myParam# EQ "myValue">`
	`[content to display]`
	`</cfif>`

Show alternate content	`<cfif isdefined("URL.myParam") AND`
	`⮞#URL.myParam# EQ "myValue">`
	`[content to display]`
	`<cfelse>`
	`[alternate content to display]`
	`</cfif>`

EXERCISE 23.7 ## Adding Conditional Content to the Antiques Barn Login Page (ColdFusion and PHP)

If you've completed all the exercises in this chapter, you've sent your visitors to the login page from a variety of other pages. You can make your user interface more understandable by adding custom messages to the login page depending on why the user got sent here. Before doing this exercise, you need to have completed the login exercises earlier in this chapter.

1. Start by opening the login page. This page redirects the user back to itself if the user's login is unsuccessful. You want it to pass a parameter as it's doing this.

   In the Server Behaviors panel, double-click the Log User In behavior to open it for editing. In the field that specifies where to redirect the user if the login fails, change the entry by adding an msg parameter set to sorry. You can type this parameter in by hand or use the Browse and Parameter buttons. The code in the input field should look like this:

```
login.php?msg=sorry
```

(The filename extension, of course, depends on your server model.) When you're done, click OK to close the dialog box.

2. Add a paragraph of text immediately preceding the form that says something like **Sorry, username or password is incorrect; try again**, as shown in Figure 23.33. Using the Property Inspector or Tag selector, apply the sorry class to the paragraph.

FIGURE 23.33
Adding a Sorry! message to the login page for unsuccessful logins.

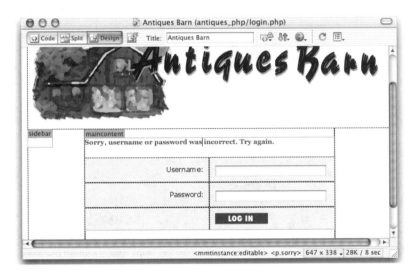

3. Switch to Code view, and find your sorry paragraph. You need to surround it with conditional statements, to display only if the msg parameter is present and is set to sorry. The exact code you'll enter depends on the server language you're using:

In PHP:

```
<?php if isset($_GET[msg]) && $_GET[msg] == 'sorry') { ?>
 <p class="sorry">Sorry, login was unsuccessful...</p>
<?php } ?>
```

In ColdFusion:

```
<cfif isdefined("URL.myParam") AND #URL.msg# EQ "sorry">
<p class="sorry">Sorry, login was unsuccessful...</p>
</cfif>
```

4. Switch back to Design view. Your conditional content appears. If you're using PHP (and if invisible elements are showing), it is surrounded by gold server-side script icons, as shown in Figure 23.34. If you're using ColdFusion, a labeled box surrounds your content, as if you had applied the Show If server behavior.

FIGURE 23.34
Conditional content in the Antiques Barn login page, as seen in Design view.

5. Try things out in a browser. If you preview the login page, the conditional content doesn't show. If you manually add the ?msg=sorry parameter to the URL field, the sorry message shows. If you try to log in, and you fail, the URL parameter and the sorry message appear.

6. Open the catalog page. This page has restricted access. Users without access are redirected to the login page.

    In the Server Behaviors panel, double-click the Restrict Access to Page behavior to open it for editing. If access is denied, send the user to the login page with the msg parameter set to a different value:

    `login.cfm?msg=noaccess`

    Click OK to close the dialog box.

    Double-click the Log Out User behavior to open it. When the logout is complete, send the user to the login page with another msg:

    `login.php?msg=logout`

Click OK to close the dialog box, and save and close the file.

7. Go back to the login page. You need two more sets of conditional content. Select your existing conditional content, including the gold server-code icons, and select Edit > Copy. Place the insertion point after the closing icon, and select Edit > Paste twice. Change the second conditional paragraph to say something like **You need to log in to view this page**. Change the third to say something like **You have been logged out**. Your page should now look like Figure 23.35.

FIGURE 23.35

The Antiques Barn login page with three sets of conditional content.

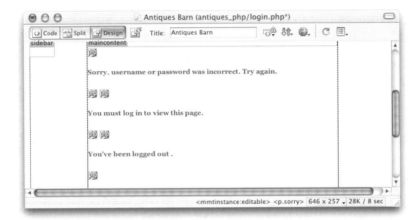

8. You need to change the conditional scripting for the new conditional regions. You could go to Code view, but you can also use the Property Inspector. Select the opening tag for the second set of content. (For PHP, click the gold icon; for ColdFusion, use the Tag selector to select the `cfif` tag.) In the Property Inspector, change the `msg` value from `sorry` to `noaccess`. Select the opening tag for the third set of content, and in the Property Inspector, change the `msg` value from `sorry` to `logout`. These values match those you entered in the other pages.

9. Try your pages in a browser. Log yourself in and out, successfully and unsuccessfully, and see how the login page customizes itself.

SUMMARY

Data-driven sites in Dreamweaver offer a world of possibilities, and this chapter investigated some that go beyond the basics. All exercises in this chapter were built using dynamic templates. This chapter looked at more-complex catalog pages with master-detail pages, more-complex database updates with user authentication, and working with complex recordsets and other data sources. It also peeked into the world of conditional content using Dreamweaver tools and hand coding. Almost everything covered here works with all server models supported by Dreamweaver. The next three chapters take you further into the specifics of the three most popular server models: ColdFusion, PHP, and ASP.NET.

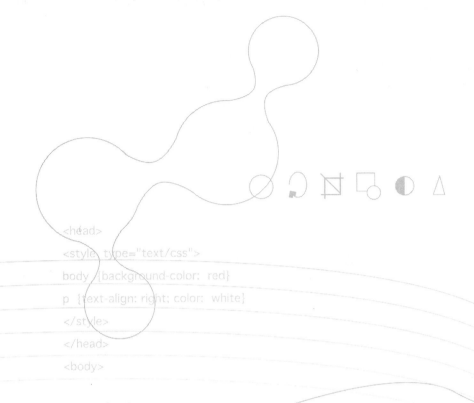

CHAPTER 24

WORKING SMART WITH COLDFUSION

DREAMWEAVER MX 2004 IS DESIGNED TO BE A COMPLETE SOLUTION FOR developing ColdFusion applications. Unlike other server models supported in Dreamweaver, ColdFusion is a "tag-based" language for developing dynamic applications. Rather than using a scripting language, like PHP, ColdFusion reads embedded custom tags in the page's regular HTML for the server to execute commands and return data to the browser. From within Dreamweaver, developers can access all the tags available in ColdFusion from the insertion bar.

Dreamweaver has several ways to access ColdFusion tags. The most basic way to work with ColdFusion is to use the built-in server behaviors and application objects that were covered in Chapter 22, "Creating Dynamic Pages." The server behaviors and application objects insert one or more ColdFusion tags into your code with one dialog box that makes it easy to create complete blocks of code to accomplish particular tasks, such as inserting a record into a database or protecting a page with user authentication. Dreamweaver also allows you to insert individual ColdFusion tags into the code so that you can include more-complex or customized commands for the ColdFusion server. Individual tasks also allow you to modify blocks of code that Dreamweaver inserts if you need to add additional commands or simply hand-code your own ColdFusion applications tag by tag.

Some of the tags available in this chapter have many attributes. This chapter details the most common attributes. If you want complete information on each tag, try using the Allaire CFML Reference, available from the Reference Panel.

Another ColdFusion feature available in Dreamweaver MX 2004 is the ability to create and consume (use) ColdFusion Components (CFCs). These are pieces of ColdFusion functionality that are broken out from your main application and that are available to multiple applications. CFCs make your applications more robust and reusable and are the preferred way to design applications professionally.

COLDFUSION OBJECTS IN THE INSERTION BAR

Developers can access all tags that ship with ColdFusion from the insert bar in a ColdFusion page in a ColdFusion site. Most of the common ColdFusion tags have their own icons. Some ColdFusion tags are available to insert from the More Tags dialog box.

Server Variables

Server variables are tremendously useful constructions that return information about the environment of the browser, the server, and the page that is requesting information. You can use server variables to return information to the screen when the server variable is wrapped in a CFOUTPUT tag. You also can use the variable in a query to insert data into a database. When you click the server variable icon in the CFML insert bar, you can select one of several variables from a drop-down list, as shown in Figure 24.1. You can insert as many server variables as you like, but you have to insert them one at a time.

FIGURE 24.1

The Server Variable dialog box.

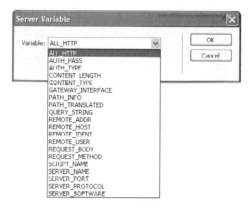

The server variables are as follows:

- **ALL_HTTP**—Returns all the HTTP information for the request from the browser.

- **AUTH_PASS**—Returns the password that the user logged in as if the server supports user authentication.

- **AUTH_TYPE**—Returns the authentication method used to validate the user if the server supports user authentication.

- **CONTENT_LENGTH**—Returns the length of the content.

- **CONTENT_TYPE**—Lists whether the query is using GET or PUT to interact with the server.

- **GATEWAY_INTERFACE**—Lists the revision of the CGI on the server.

- **PATH_INFO**—The return path to the requested page from the root of the application.

- **PATH_TRANSLATED**   Returns the physical address of the page on the server.

- **QUERY_STRING**—Displays the query information following the ? when a form is submitted.

- **REMOTE_ADDR**—The IP address of the remote browser that is hitting the page.

- **REMOTE_HOST**—The hostname of the server that is hitting the page. If the server does not have this feature enabled, it returns the REMOTE_ADDR.

- **REMOTE_IDENT**—If the HTTP server is configured to support RFC 931 identification, this returns the remote username from the server.

- **REMOTE_USER**—If the server supports user authentication, the username that the user used to log in is returned.

- **SCRIPT_NAME**—The path to the script that is executing.

- **SERVER_NAME**—The name of the server, IP address, or DNS alias from the server.

- **SERVER_PORT**—The port number that the request was sent to.

- **SERVER_PROTOCOL**—Shows the server's protocol and the version number. (Usually this is HTTP.)

- **SERVER_SOFTWARE**—Returns the server software and version of the remote server.

Inserting the HTTP_ALL server variable inside a CFOUTPUT tag looks like this:

```
<cfoutput>#CGI.HTTP_ALL#</cfoutput>
```

and returns this:

```
HTTP_ACCEPT:*/* HTTP_ACCEPT_LANGUAGE:en-us
➡ HTTP_CONNECTION:Keep-Alive HTTP_HOST:www.3981.com
➡ HTTP_REFERER:http://localhost/test/TMPwtvOnhbkmb.cfm
➡ HTTP_USER_AGENT:Mozilla/4.0 (compatible; MSIE 6.0; Windows
➡ NT 5.1; .NET CLR 1.1.4322) HTTP_CONTENT_LENGTH:13
➡ HTTP_CONTENT_TYPE:application/x-www-form-urlencoded
➡ HTTP_ACCEPT_ENCODING:gzip, deflate HTTP_CACHE_CONTROL:no-
➡ cache
```

Note that you get the host, the URL of the page that called the page with the server variable, the user agent or browser type, and the version all in one server variable.

CFQUERY

The CFQUERY tag is inserted when you create a Recordset (Query) from the Application panel. When you insert the CFQUERY from the Insert menu, many more attributes are available to set, but you don't have the query builder or the ability to test the connection.

The general attributes for CFQUERY are as follows:

- **Query Name** (required)—The query's name. This is how you reference the query in the code to display data. The query's name should not have spaces.

- **Data Source** (required)—The name of the ODBC datasource that you have set up in the ColdFusion Administrator.

- **User Name** (optional)—The database's username (if one is set).

- **Password** (optional)—The password for the database (if there is one).

- **SQL** (required)—The SQL that goes between the opening and closing CFQUERY tag.

Inserting the CFQUERY tag produces code like this:

```
<cfquery name="getemployees" datasource="employeedatabase">
SELECT *
FROM employeetable
</cfquery>
```

This code returns a set of data of all the records in the employee table in the employee database.

out CFOUTPUT

CFOUTPUT, as shown in Figure 24.2, is the tag used to display information from a query or other operation to the browser.

FIGURE 24.2
The CFOUTPUT dialog box.

The attributes for CFOUTPUT are as follows:

- **Query Name** (optional)—The name of the query that contains the data you want to display. When you add the name attribute, you create a loop in which each returned record is output in the order in which it was received from the query.

- **Group Field** (optional)—The name of the field you want to use to group your results. For example, a query that gets the information for all the employees in a database lets you group the results by department or last name or some other field you specify.

- **Start Row** (optional)—The row of data from which to begin showing data. If your result set of data from the query has 30 records, setting the Start Row to 100 displays only records 100 through 130. This attribute requires that the name attribute be set.

- **Max Rows** (optional)—Sets the maximum number of records shown from the result set of data from the query. If your query has 30 records with Start Row set to 10 and Max Rows set to 10, the output shows only records 10 through 20. This attribute requires that the name attribute be set.

- **Group Case Sensitive** (optional)—SQL query results are generally case-insensitive. Use this attribute if you want to group your results and respect their case.

Inserting the CFOUTPUT tag produces code like this:

```
<cfoutput query="getemployees" group="department"
➥startrow="100" maxrows="100"></cfoutput>
```

To display the results in the browser, you would reference each field name you want to display, wrapped in # signs between the beginning and end of the CFOUTPUT tag:

```
<cfoutput query="getemployees" group="department" startrow="10"
➥ maxrows="10"> #LastName#, #FirstName#, #Department#<br>
</cfoutput>
```

The result in the browser looks like this:

Smith, Bill, Accounting

Wilson, James, Accounting

Washington, Martha, Accounting

Russell, Dave, Engineering

Mugler, Sarah, Engineering

Louis, Ben, Engineering

Brown, Matt, Executive Staff

Davis, Karen, Human Resources

Davis, Andy, Human Resources

Lyons, Aaron, Human Resources

CFINSERT

CFINSERT inserts data from a form into a database table. This is shorthand for a SQL insert query.

The attributes for CFINSERT are slightly more confusing than other tags. There are more attributes available than you should use. Dreamweaver MX 2004 allows the development of ColdFusion documents for ColdFusion MX and earlier versions. The dialog includes attributes for connectString, dbName, dbServer, dbtype, provider, and providerDSN. These are all deprecated and should not be used if you are working with ColdFusion MX.

For the CFINSERT tag to work properly, you need to have the form elements named the same as the fields in your database for ColdFusion to map the data from the form to the database.

CFINSERT works only with forms using the post method. It fails silently if the form uses the get method.

Why would you use CFINSERT rather than a regular SQL update query? Because it is easier to type the CFINSERT tag, and it allows less room for errors than an insert query, which can get messy. However, it has the limitation of not being able to insert into multiple tables, and it cannot accept any input that doesn't come through a form.

If the table you are inserting data into has a primary key that is not auto-generated, CFINSERT must have a field from the form passed that is inserted into that key, or it generates an error. If you have a key that is auto-generated, it works fine.

The CFINSERT attributes that are valid for ColdFusion MX are as follows:

- **Data Source** (required)—The datasource into which you want to insert the record.

- **User Name** (optional)—The username (if one is needed) to access the database being inserted into.

- **Password** (optional)—The password (if one is needed) to access the database being inserted into.

- **Table Name** (required)—The name of the table you need to insert data into.

- **Table Owner** (optional)—An optional attribute for databases that support table ownership, such as SQL Server and Oracle.

- **Table Qualifier** (optional)—An optional attribute for databases that support table ownership, such as SQL Server and Oracle.

- **Form Fields** (optional)—A comma-delimited list of fields you want to insert into the datasource. This attribute is optional. If you don't specify the form fields attribute, CFINSERT processes all the form fields. In effect, you use the Form Fields option to limit the fields you want to process to only the fields you list.

Here's an example:

```
<cfinsert datasource="employeedata" tablename="employees"
➡ formfields="FirstName, LastName, Department">
```

This code takes the data entered in a form that has fields named FirstName, LastName, and Department and inserts those values into the employees table of the employeedata datasource.

CFUPDATE

CFUPDATE updates data from the form into a database table. This is shorthand for a SQL update query.

CFUPDATE works only with forms using the post method. It fails silently if the form uses the get method.

The attributes for CFUPDATE, like CFINSERT, are slightly more confusing than other tags. There are more attributes available than you should use. Dreamweaver MX 2004 allows the development of ColdFusion documents for ColdFusion MX and earlier versions. The dialog box includes attributes for connectString, dbName, dbServer, dbtype, provider, and providerDSN. These are all deprecated and should not be used if you are working with ColdFusion MX.

Like CFINSERT, the names of the fields in the form must match the field names in the database for the CFUPDATE tag to be able to map the data correctly.

The CFUPDATE attributes that are valid for ColdFusion MX are as follows:

- **Data Source** (required)—The datasource into which you want to insert the record.

- **User Name** (optional)—The username (if one is needed) to access the database being inserted into.

- **Password** (optional)—The password (if one is needed) to access the database being inserted into.

- **Table Name** (required)—The name of the table you need to insert data into.

- **Table Owner** (optional)—An optional attribute for databases that support table ownership, such as SQL Server and Oracle.

- **Table Qualifier** (optional)—An optional attribute for databases that support table ownership, such as SQL Server and Oracle.

- **Form Fields** (optional)—A comma-delimited list of fields you want to insert into the datasource. This attribute is optional. If you don't specify the form fields attribute, CFINSERT processes all the form fields. In effect, you use the Form Fields option to limit the fields you want to process to only the fields you list.

Here's an example:

```
<cfupdate datasource="employeedata" tablename="employees"
  formfields="FirstName, LastName, Department">
```

This code takes the data entered in a form that has fields named FirstName, LastName, and Department and updates those values in the employees table of the employeedata datasource.

▣ CFINCLUDE

CFINCLUDE includes a ColdFusion file at the location of the tag in the document. This allows the developer to encapsulate functionality into separate files and then reuse them in multiple locations. It is also a great way to include footers and headers in documents that can be updated separately from the main file.

CFINCLUDE has only one required attribute—`template`—which points to the location of the file you want to include.

Here's an example:

```
include file footer.cfm
<address>123 Elm Street </address>
```

Here's a sample file with CFINCLUDE calling the **footer.cfm** file:

```
<html>
<head>
<title>My page</title>
</head>
<body>
<h1>lots of things to say</h1>
<p>Maybe not so much</p>
<cfinclude template="footer.cfm">
</body>
</html>
```

Here's the resulting code in the browser:

```
<html>
<head>
<title>My page</title>
</head>
<body>
<h1>lots of things to say</h1>
<p>Maybe not so much</p>
<address>123 Elm Street </address>
</body>
</html>
```

CFLOCATION

CFLOCATION redirects the browser to the specified URL. If you check the Append Client Variables to the URL check box, the parameters after the ? in the URL that calls the CFLOCATION are sent to the new URL that the CFLOCATION redirects to.

CFLOCATION has two attributes:

- **URL** (required)—The URL of the HTML or CFML file you want your user to be redirected to.

- **Addtoken** (optional) Appends the parameters after the ? from the calling URL to the URL to the new page that the user is being redirected to. If the addtoken is not specified, it defaults to yes.

Here's an example:

```
<html>
<head>
<title>My page</title>
</head>
<body>
<p>You are being redirected to a new address.</p>
<cflocation url="newresults.cfm">
</body>
</html>
```

When the user gets to this page, he or she is redirected to the **newresults.cfm** page.

When you use the CFLOCATION tag, it is processed in the order of tags on the page. If you include a CFLOCATION tag in a page after a CFUPDATE or CFINSERT, that CFUPDATE or CFINSERT is executed before the CFLOCATION is executed. This is very handy to use in different cases of CFIF clauses to route users to failure pages or login pages.

set **CFSET**

CFSET sets a ColdFusion variable in your code.

Here's an example:

```
<html>
<head>
<title>My page</title>
</head>
<body>
<cfset foo = "bar">
My cat is named <cfoutput> #foo# </cfoutput>!
</body>
</html>
```

This code displays the following:

> My cat is named bar!

! **CFPARAM**

CFPARAM tests for the existence of a variable and sets its type. It also can set a default value for the variable. This tag is used to test whether a variable exists and if it is a specified type. It also allows you to set the value of the variable if it does not exist.

CFPARAM has three attributes:

- **Name** (required)—The name of the variable you're testing.

- **Default** (optional)—Sets the value of the variable if it is not already set.

- **Type** (optional)—Sets the variable's data type. The choices are any, array, binary, boolean, date, numeric, query, string, struct, UUID, and variableName.

Here's an example:

```
<html>
<head>
<title>My page</title>
</head>
```

```
<body>
<cfset foo="cat">
<cfparam name="foo">
My cat is named <cfoutput> #foo# </cfoutput>!<br>
<cfparam name="pooh" default="bear">
My dog is named <cfoutput> #pooh# </cfoutput>!
</body>
</html>
```

When this code is executed, it sets a variable named foo with a value of cat. The value is checked to exist with the first CFPARAM and is output in the next line. The second CFPARAM checks for a variable called pooh, which has not been defined. Then, with the `default` attribute, it assigns a value of bear, which is output in the next line.

This produces the following in the browser:

My cat is named cat!

My dog is named bear!

ColdFusion Comments

ColdFusion uses a special comment syntax for comments it should not process or render. ColdFusion comments use `<!---...--->` instead of `<!--...-->`. The ColdFusion Comments object takes your selection and wraps it in ColdFusion comments. Normal HTML comments are sent to the browser, but ColdFusion comments are not passed to the browser.

Surrounding Variables with #...#

ColdFusion treats everything between # signs as a server variable. When you are hand-coding, you can type your variable names, highlight them, and wrap them in # signs. This is a very handy hand-coding feature.

CFSCRIPT

ColdFusion has a less-used syntax of CFSCRIPT that allows you to code ColdFusion in a script syntax more like PHP or ASP. This is seldom used, but it is available to you in Dreamweaver MX 2004. When you insert a CFSCRIPT object into your document, Dreamweaver simply inserts a beginning and end CFSCRIPT tag and centers the insertion point in the middle so that you can begin scripting.

Here's an example:

```
<cfscript></cfscript>
```

CFTRY and CFCATCH

CFTRY and CFCATCH are debugging and error-handling tags that work together to process exceptions in ColdFusion pages. An exception is any event that disrupts the flow of the instructions on the page, such as missing include files, failed database operations, or events specified by the developer.

Developers need to build error-catching into industrial-strength applications.

Each CFTRY must have at least one CFCATCH. It may have more CFCATCHes to test for more than one problem. ColdFusion processes the CFCATCH tags in the order they appear in the code. See Figure 24.3.

FIGURE 24.3
CFCATCH options.

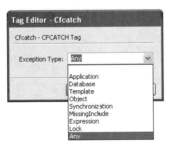

CFCATCH has the following attribute:

- **Exception Type** (optional)—The type of exception the CFCATCH is looking for. The choices are `application`, `database`, `template`, `security`, `object`, `missinginclude`, `expression`, `lock`, `custom_type` (catches developer-defined exceptions defined in a CFTHROW tag), `searchengine` (catches Verity search engine exceptions), and `any` (catches all exceptions). If you do not specify one of the exception types, the tag defaults to `all`.

Here's an example:

```
<cftry>
<!--- Note the misspelled tablename "employees" as "eemployees"
➡--->

  <cfquery name - "getemployees" datasource = "employeedatabase">
    SELECT *
    FROM eemployees
  </cfquery>

  <cfcatch type = "Database">
    <p>You've encountered a database Error</p>
    <cfoutput>
      <!--- and the diagnostic message from the ColdFusion
      ➡server --->
      <p>#cfcatch.message#</p>
      <p>Caught an exception, type = #CFCATCH.TYPE# </p>
    </cfoutput>
  </cfcatch>

</cftry>
```

In this code, instead of just adding a query, the query is inside the CFTRY and has a CFCATCH to check for a database error. Because the name of the employees table is misspelled, the code inside the CFCATCH is executed. If there were no error, the page would process normally. If the CFCATCH were not there, ColdFusion would either throw an error or fail silently.

⊗ CFTHROW

CFTHROW is used in a CFTRY block. It can be caught by a CFCATCH tag with the custom_type, application, or any type.

The CFTHROW tag has the following attributes:

- **Type** (optional)—An application or a custom type. If application is specified, you don't need to specify a type for CFCATCH.

- **Message** (optional)—A message that describes the exception event.

- **Detail** (optional)—A description of the event.

- **ErrorCode** (optional)—A custom error code that you supply.

- **ExtendedInfo** (optional)—A custom error code that you supply.

- **Object** (optional)—Throws a Java exception when using CFOBJECT. Requires the value of the name of the CFOBJECT. If you use this attribute, you cannot use any other attribute for the CFTHROW tag.

Here's an example:

```
<cftry>
<cfif NOT IsDefined("URL.employeeid")>
    <cfthrow message = "employeeid is not defined">
</cfif>

<cfcatch type = "application">
<cfoutput>
    <p>You have thrown an exception</p>
    <p>#cfcatch.message#</p>
</cfoutput>
</cfcatch>
</cftry>
```

In this code, a CFTRY block is opened, and a condition is tested. If the test is true, the CFTHROW is executed, and a custom message is written. In the CFCATCH tag, if there is an error from the CFTHROW, the code in the CFCATCH block is executed.

🔒 CFLOCK

CFLOCK locks processes on a page temporarily so that multiple requests don't execute at the same time. CFLOCK has two kinds of locks. Exclusive locks allow only one request to be processed at a time. No other requests can begin processing until the first request is finished. Read-only locks allow multiple requests, but only to read data, not to write or modify data. If a request has an exclusive lock on shared data, the read-only lock waits for the exclusive lock to terminate.

In production, CFLOCK is used to ensure that modifications to shared data are made sequentially so that no two requests try to write to the same data at the same time. Also, if you are using any file manipulation, CFLOCK ensures that only one request writes to a file at one time. If two requests try to write to the same file, one request fails.

The CFLOCK tag has the following attributes:

- **Name** (optional)—Only one request can execute within this tag with a given name. This lets different parts of your application have access to data but provides more-specific control than the scope attribute. You can use either the name attribute or the scope attribute, but not both.

- **Timeout** (required)—The maximum length of time in seconds for the lock to remain in place.

- **Type** (optional)—Read-only locks allow more than one thread to read data, but not write. Exclusive locks allow one request to read or write shared data.

- **Scope** (optional)—application sets the lock to cover the application so that only the one application defined in the **Application.cfm** file can access the data. server sets the lock to all the applications on the server. session locks the data to only the active session. You can use either the scope or the name attribute, but not both.

- **Throw On Timeout** (optional)—Tells the timeout attribute to behave when the timeout is reached. yes generates an exception (that you can catch with CFCATCH). no allows the request's execution to continue without an error.

Here's an example:

```
<cflock scope = "Session"  timeout = "30" type = "Exclusive">
    <cfif NOT IsDefined("session.username")>
      <cfset session.username = "guest">
    </cfif>
    <cfif NOT IsDefined("session.password")>
      <cfset session.password = "guest">
    </cfif>
  </cflock>
```

This code locks the session for 30 seconds. The code takes a lot less time, but in 30 seconds, if it cannot execute for some reason, it throws an error. If it does execute, it checks to see whether a username and password are assigned in the session. If they are not, it sets both the username and password to "guest."

case def CFSWITCH, CFCASE, and CFDEFAULTCASE

CFSWITCH, CFCASE, and CFDEFAULTCASE are related flow control tags that allow you to branch your function to achieve different results based on results that occur while processing a page. CFSWITCH evaluates a passed expression and then passes control to a CFCASE that corresponds to the result. The CFDEFAULTCASE provides the default behavior if the CFSWITCH does not evaluate to any of the CFCASEs available in the CFSWITCH code block.

Here's an example:

```
<cfquery name = "GetEmployees" dataSource = "employees">
  SELECT  *
  FROM    Employees
</cfquery>

<cfoutput query="GetEmployees">
<cfswitch expression="#Trim(Department)#">
  <cfcase value="Sales">
    #FirstName# #LastName# is in sales<br>
  </cfcase>
  <cfcase value="Accounting, Administration" delimiters=",">
    #FirstName# #LastName# is in accounting or administration<br>
  </cfcase>
  <cfdefaultcase>
    #FirstName# #LastName# is not in sales or accounting or
    ➥administration.<br>
  </cfdefaultcase>
</cfswitch>
</cfoutput>
```

This code queries a database to get a returned data set of all the employees. A CFOUTPUT is started that loops through and prints all the names in the database; however, the CFSWITCH catches each record and evaluates what department each employee is in. If the department is Sales, it prints the first name and last name, with a note that the person is in sales. If the department is Accounting or Administration, then it prints the first name and last name with a note that the person is in accounting or administration. If the employee is in any other department, the CFDEFAULTCASE kicks in, and the first name and last name are printed with a note that the employee is not in sales, accounting, or administration.

The CFSWITCH tag has one attribute, expression (required), which sets the expression to evaluate to determine which case to pass the request to.

The CFCASE tag has two attributes: value (required) and delimiters (optional). The value is the possible result of the expression that the CFSWITCH evaluates. delimiters is the character that separates the values in the list if you want a CFCASE to execute for more than one value. The default delimiter is a comma.

CFDEFAULTCASE has no attributes.

if else elsif CFIF, CFELSE, and CFELSEIF

CFIF, CFELSE, and CFELSEIF are flow-control tags like CFSWITCH, CFCASE, and CFDEFAULTCASE. The difference between CFIF and CFSWITCH is that CFSWITCH executes faster than CFIF, although CFSWITCH can check against only one expression. CFIF can check against multiple expressions, one in each CFIF or CFELSE tag.

Here's an example:

```
<cfquery name = "GetEmployees" dataSource = "employees">
  SELECT  *
  FROM    Employees
</cfquery>

<cfoutput query="GetEmployees">
<cfif Trim(Department) is "Sales" OR Trim(Department) is
➥"Accounting" >
    #FirstName# #LastName# is in #Department#<br>
<cfelseif Trim(Department) is "Administration" >
    #FirstName# #LastName# is in Administration and available
    ➥to answer questions.<br>
<cfelseif Trim(Department is "Engineering")>
    <b>Engineers rule and #FirstName# is one of them</b>
<cfelse>
    #FirstName# is not in any of the departments we're looking
    ➥for.
</cfif>
</cfoutput>
```

This code queries a database to get a returned data set of all the employees. A CFOUTPUT is started that loops through and prints all the names in the database. However, the CFIF/CFELSEIF/CFELSE catches each record, evaluates what department each employee is in, and prints different results based on the department. This example could easily be done with a CFSWITCH.

Here's an example:

```
<cfquery name = "GetEmployees" dataSource = "employees">
  SELECT  *
  FROM    Employees
</cfquery>

<cfoutput query="GetEmployees">
<cfif Trim(Department) is "Sales" AND Trim(Region) is "West
➥Coast" >
    #FirstName# #LastName# is in #Department# for the West
    ➥Coast<br>
<cfelse>
    #FiretName# #LastName# is in #Department# for non-West
    ➥Coast regions.<br>
</cfif>
</cfoutput>
```

This code could not be done with a CFSWITCH because in the CFIF, two expressions are evaluated—the department and the region.

The CFIF and CFELSEIF tags have no attributes other than the expression they are evaluating. CFLESE has no attributes.

CFLOOP and CFBREAK

CFLOOP allows you to loop through a set of commands in a number of different ways:

* An index loop repeats for a set number of times, as defined by a numeric value. Traditionally, this is known as a for loop.

* A conditional loop repeats a set of instructions as long as the condition is true. Traditionally, this is known as a while loop.

- Looping over a query is very much like a CFOUTPUT, in which the instruction is repeated for each member of the returned dataset from a CFQUERY.

- Looping over a list or file steps through lists contained in variables, values returned from an expression, or a file.

- Looping over a COM collection or structure loops over a COM collection or object.

CFBREAK is used in CFLOOP constructions to terminate the loop in a given set of circumstances. Usually it is found in a CFIF inside the loop that is checked for every iteration of the loop.

The CFLOOP index loop has the following attributes:

- **Index** (required)—This counter is incremented or decremented by the CFLOOP as it iterates. When it equals the to value, the loop stops.

- **From** (required)—The index's beginning value.

- **To** (required)—The index's ending value.

- **Step** (optional)—The increment by which the index is changed with each iteration. If the step attribute is not set, this defaults to 1.

Here's an example of an index loop:

```
<cfloop  index = "counter" from = "1" to = "5" step = "1">
  <cfoutput>The index of the loop is #counter#</cfoutput>.<br>
</cfloop>
```

This block of code produces the following in the browser:

The index of the loop is 1.

The index of the loop is 2.

The index of the loop is 3.

The index of the loop is 4.

The index of the loop is 5.

The CFLOOP conditional loop has only one attribute—the condition that is required for the tag. The condition is tested with every iteration; while it is true, the loop continues.

Here's an example:

```
<cfset CountVar = 0>
<cfloop condition = "CountVar LESS THAN OR EQUAL TO 5">
  <cfset CountVar = CountVar + 1>
  The loop index is <cfoutput>#CountVar#</cfoutput>.<br>
</cfloop>
```

This code block sets a variable called CountVar to 0. The loop checks to see if the value of CountVar is less than or equal to 5. If it is, CountVar is increased by 1 in a CFSET tag, and the loop index is printed. The loop is repeated, and now CountVar equals 1. This continues until CountVar equals 5. At that point, the condition is false and the loop stops.

CFCOOKIE

The CFCOOKIE tag defines browser cookies, including cookies with security and expiration options.

The CFCOOKIE tag has the following attributes:

- **Name** (required)—The name of the cookie variable.

- **Value** (optional)—The value to assign to the cookie variable.

- **Expires** (optional)—Specifies when the cookie expires. This can be a date, a number of days, now, or never.

- **Path** (optional)—A subset of a domain to which the cookie applies. You might want the cookie to apply to only a portion of your site.

- **Domain** (required if the path attribute is specified)—The domain in which the cookie is valid. You have to start the domain with a period, such as .newriders.com. For domains that end in a country code, you need to include the last three components of the domain, as in .tepapa.gov.nz. You cannot use an IP address as a domain.

- **Transmit cookie securely** (SSL) (optional)—Requires that the browser support Secure Sockets Layer (SSL), or the cookie is not sent.

Here's an example:

```
<cfif IsDefined(#Form.username#)>
    <cfcookie name="username"
```

```
        value-"Form.username"
        expires="5">
    <cfcookie name="Cookie.userIPaddress"
        value="#CGI.REMOTE_ADDR#"
        expires="5">
</cfif>

<cfoutput>
The username is #Cookie.username# and their IP address is
➡#userIPaddress#
</cfoutput>
```

This code checks to see if data is passed from a form with a field called username. If there is, it writes a cookie with the username from the form and the IP address of the visitor from a server variable.

CFCONTENT (Advanced)

CFCONTENT downloads a file from the server to the client.

For more information on the CFCONTENT tag, consult the ColdFusion documentation that was installed with your ColdFusion server.

CFHEADER (Advanced)

CFHEADER generates custom HTTP responses to send to the client.

For more information on the CFHEADER tag, consult the ColdFusion documentation that was installed with your ColdFusion server.

ColdFusion Page Encoding (Advanced)

The ColdFusion Page Encoding object inserts a set of tags in the head of the document. You can modify them to set the page encoding for other character sets for foreign languages.

For more information on the Page Encoding tag, consult the Function Reference in the ColdFusion documentation that was installed with your ColdFusion server.

▤ CFAPPLICATION

CFAPPLICATION defines the scope of a ColdFusion application, controls the storage of client variables, enables session variables, and sets various timeouts. This tag is typically used in the **Application.cfm** file that sets all the defaults for a ColdFusion application. (Case is important in the filename. The filename must be initial cap.)

The attributes of the CFAPPLICATION tag are as follows:

- **Application Name** (required)—The application's name, such as Employee_Stock_Benefit_Application

- **Session Timeout** (optional)—Sets the lifespan of session variables using the CreateTimeSpan function. For this option, Client Management must be enabled in the ColdFusion Administrator.

- **Application Timeout** (optional)—Sets the lifespan of application variables using the CreateTimeSpan function.

- **Client Storage** (optional)—Sets where client variables are stored. The choices are datasource_name, which sets the storage in an ODBC datasource, registry, which uses the system registry, and cookie, which stores client variables on the client computer. For this option, Client Management must be enabled in the ColdFusion Administrator.

- **Enable client variables** (optional)—yes enables client variables. no (the default) blocks client variables.

- **Enable session variables** (optional)—yes enables session variables. no (the default) blocks session variables.

- **Set client cookies** (optional)—yes enables client cookies. no means that CFID and CFToken must be passed to each page that requires them manually via the URL or some other method.

- **Set domain cookies** (optional)—yes sets the CFTOKEN and CFID cookies for a domain. no means that CFID and CFToken must be passed to each page that requires them manually via the URL or some other method. This is primarily for use in clustered server environments.

You need to have this turned on to use the default login and authentication server behaviors.

Here's an example.

```
<cfapplication name="GetUsers"
clientmanagement="no"
sessionmanagement-"yes"
setclientcookies="no"
setdomaincookies="no">
```

This code sets an application name of GetUsers and sets session management to yes. This would be the entire contents of an **Application.cfm** file needed to use the login and authentication behaviors in Dreamweaver MX 2004.

CFERROR (Advanced)

CFERROR displays a custom HTML page when an error occurs, letting you set up custom error pages to match your site's look and feel.

For a full explanation of the CFERROR tag and all the available error variables, consult the ColdFusion documentation that was installed with your ColdFusion server.

The CFERROR tag has the following attributes:

- **Error Type** (required)—The type of error handled. The choices include application, database, template, security, object, missinginclude, expression, lock, custom_type, and any.

- **Message Template** (required)—The path to a custom error page.

- **Administrator Email** (optional) An email address for the site's administrator.

- **Exception**—The type of the exception thrown—either an exception of the CFTRY tag or a custom exception in a CFTHROW tag.

Here's an example:

```
<cferror type = "database"
    template = "customerror.cfm"
    mailTo = "admin@mywebsite.com">
```

This code returns an error and calls a custom error page that can list error variables for the user.

CFDIRECTORY (Advanced)

The CFDIRECTORY tag allows ColdFusion to interact with directories on the server to create, delete, and rename folders and to list the files in a given directory. To use the tag, it must be enabled in the ColdFusion Administrator.

Enabling CFDIRECTORY allows people to delete or rename directories. Be sure that you want this available on your server and that you have adequate protections enabled.

CFDIRECTORY has the following attributes:

- **List:**

- **Directory** (required)—The absolute pathname to the directory you are listing.

- **Query Name** (required)—The name of the output recordset of listed files.

- **File Filter** (optional)—The file extension filter to return only files of a certain type.

- **Sort Specification** (optional)—Sets the sort order of the list of the files returned.

- **Create:**

- **Directory** (required)—The absolute pathname to the directory you are creating.

- **Mode** (optional)—Octal values for permissions uploaded. Solaris and HP-UX only.

- **Delete:**

- **Directory** (optional)—The absolute pathname to the directory you are deleting.

- **Rename:**

- **Directory** (optional)—The absolute pathname to the directory you are renaming.

- **New Directory** (optional)—The directory's new name.

💾 CFFILE (Advanced)

The CFFILE tag allows ColdFusion to transfer files from the client browser to the server, move files on the server, rename files on the server, copy files on the server, delete files on the server, read files on the server, read files as binary on the server, write files on the server, and append files on the server. The syntax and attributes for each function are different. For a full explanation of the CFFILE tag, consult the ColdFusion documentation that was installed with your ColdFusion server.

This tag needs to be enabled in the ColdFusion Administrator.

The CFFILE tag to upload files to the server from the browser has the following attributes:

Using the CFFILE tag to upload files can create a security problem for your server by introducing files that have not been checked for viruses.

- **Action** (required)—upload in this case. Other options are copy, move, rename, delete, append, write, read, and read binary.

- **File Field** (required)—The name of the form field used to select the file. You do not need to use # signs around the name of the field for this tag.

- **Destination Path** (required)—The absolute pathname of the directory or file on the server. The trailing slash in the directory name is optional in ColdFusion MX.

- **Accept Files** (optional)—Limits the MIME type of files to accept. A comma-delimited list of file types.

- **Attributes** (optional)—You can set the file to be hidden, read-only, or normal on the server after uploads.

- **Mode** (optional)—Octal values for permissions uploaded. Solaris and HP-UX only.

- **Filename Resolution** (optional)—Specifies what the server should do when the file is uploaded if the filename is not unique. error does not save the file and returns an error to the user. skip does not save the file and skips. overwrite overwrites the file on the server if the filename is the same as the uploaded file. MakeUnique makes a unique filename for the uploaded file if there is a file of the same name on the server in the directory specified.

Here's an example:

```
<cffile action = "upload"
  fileField = "contents"
  destination = "c:\inetpub\wwwroot\uploads\"
  accept = "text/html"
  nameConflict = "MakeUnique">
```

This code uploads a file specified in a form with a field called contents. The file is saved to the server to the c:\inetpub\wwwroot\uploads\ directory. (This presents a security problem, because the file is sent to a directory on the server within the web root, where it can be accessed by any user who figures out the path. If this were a virus, you would be in big trouble. For a more secure location, upload the files to a folder outside the web root.) The server accepts HTML files and makes the filename unique so as not to overwrite existing files.

The CFFILE tag to write a file to the server has the following attributes (see Figure 24.4):

- **Action** (required)—write in this case. Other options are copy, move, rename, delete, append, read, and read binary.

- **Write to File** (required)—The absolute pathname to the file on the web server. Remember to use backslashes in Windows.

- **Attributes** (optional)—You can set the file to be hidden, read-only, or normal on the server after uploads.

- **Mode** (optional)—Octal values for permissions uploaded. Solaris and HP-UX only.

- **Output String** (required)—The content of the file being written. Most of the time, this contains dynamic data that you will want to create by hand in the code after the object has been inserted in the document.

- **Add New Line** (optional)—Appends the newline character to the ends of lines written to the file.

FIGURE 24.4

The CFFILE dialog box.

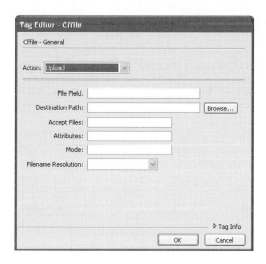

Here's an example:

```
<cffile action = "write"
  file = "c:\files\updates\#Form.FileName#.txt"
  output =  "#Form.Content#">
```

This code creates a file in the location specified, the title of which is specified in a form with a field called file. The contents of the file come from the Content field in the `output` attribute. The output could also have come from a CFQUERY.

CFMAIL (Advanced)

The CFMAIL tag allows ColdFusion to send mail from your application if your server administrator has enabled the mail features in the ColdFusion server. For a full explanation of the CFMAIL tag, consult the ColdFusion documentation that was installed with your ColdFusion server.

The CFMAIL tag has the following attributes (see Figure 24.5):

- **General:**

- **To** (required)—The address or addresses of the mail's recipients. This can be generated dynamically from a query.

- **From** (required)—The sender of the email—either a static string or dynamic data.

- **Subject** (required)—The message subject. It can be static or dynamically generated.

- **CC** (optional)—The address or addresses to copy the mail to.

- **BCC** (optional)—The address or addresses to blind-copy the mail to.

- **Dynamic Content:**

- **Query Name** (optional)—The name of a CFQUERY to draw data from for the mail.

- **Group Field** (optional)—Sets the field on which to group your mail if you are getting the data dynamically. For instance, you can group on CustomerID to send out a set of records in one mail that relate to that CustomerID.

- **Group Case Sensitive** (optional)—Specifies whether to consider case in the grouping.

- **Start Row** (optional)—The row in the query to start from.

- **Max Rows** (optional)—The maximum number of rows to return from the query.

- **Message Body:**

- **Message Type** (optional)—Informs the receiving mail client that there is HTML in the message if the mail client previews HTML content in emails.

- **Message**—A quick way to insert the content that goes out in the body of the mail. You'll probably want to hand-edit this portion of the mail after inserting the object.

- **MIME Attachments:**

- **MIME Attachment** (optional)—The path to a MIME-encoded file attached to the mail.

- **Server Settings:**

- **Server** (optional)—The SMTP server address to send messages. A server has to be specified here or in the ColdFusion Administrator. Any setting here overrides the setting in the ColdFusion Administrator.

- **Port** (optional)—The TCP/IP port for the SMTP server.

- **Timeout** (optional)—The number of seconds to wait for an SMTP server to respond.

FIGURE 24.5
The General section of the CFMAIL dialog box.

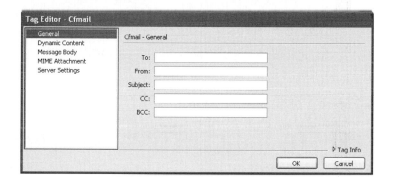

Here's an example:

```
<cfif IsDefined("form.mailto")>
  <cfif form.mailto is not ""
        AND form.mailfrom is not ""
        AND form.Subject is not "">
    <cfmail to = "#form.mailto#"
        from = "#form.mailfrom#"
        subject = "#form.subject#">
        #form.body#
    </cfmail>
    <p>Thank you, <cfoutput>#mailfrom#: your message,
    ➥#subject#, has been sent to #mailto#</cfoutput>.
  </cfif>
</cfif>
```

This code sends mail to a recipient defined in the mailto field of the form that calls this .cfm page. The first line checks to see if the mailto field exists in the URL that calls the page. If there is a variable in the URL called mailto, the code checks to see whether the values mailto, mailfrom, and subject are not empty. If there is data in each field of the form, the page adds the contents of the body field inserted into the mail and sends the mail. Note that the form does not check to see if the body is empty.

✉ CFPOP (Advanced)

The CFPOP tag allows ColdFusion to receive and manipulate mail in POP3 mailboxes. You can use this tag to create your own mail client in the browser if your administrator has enabled the mail features of the ColdFusion server.

The CFPOP tag has many attributes and features. For a full explanation of the CFPOP tag, consult the ColdFusion documentation that was installed with your ColdFusion server.

CFHTTP and CFHTTPPARAM (Advanced)

CFHTTPPARAM is a required tag for a CFHTTP to set the name and type of parameter passed with a POST operation.

For more information on the CFHTTP and CFHTTPPARAM tags consult the ColdFusion documentation that was installed with your ColdFusion server.

CFLDAP (Advanced)

CFLDAP provides an interface to a Lightweight Directory Access Protocol (LDAP) server. The tag also allows you to search, add, edit, and delete data.

For more information on the CFLDAP tag, consult the ColdFusion documentation that was installed with your ColdFusion server.

CFFTP (Advanced)

CFFTP controls FTP operations between the ColdFusion server and FTP sites. The CFFTP tag does not move files from the browser to the ColdFusion server. To move files from a browser to the server, use the CFFILE tag.

For more information on the CFFTP tag, consult the ColdFusion documentation that was installed with your ColdFusion server.

CFSEARCH (Advanced)

CFSEARCH searches Verity collections using either the ColdFusion or K2Server, depending on which search engine the collection is registered by.

For more information on the CFSEARCH tag, consult the ColdFusion documentation that was installed with your ColdFusion server.

CFINDEX (Advanced)

CFINDEX populates a Verity search engine collection with a list of documents from the file system or from the results of a CFQUERY.

For more information on the CFINDEX tag, consult the ColdFusion documentation that was installed with your ColdFusion server.

CFMODULE (Advanced)

CFMODULE invokes a custom tag that is installed on your server.

For more information on the CFMODULE tag, consult the ColdFusion documentation that was installed with your ColdFusion server.

CFOBJECT (Advanced)

CFOBJECT creates a ColdFusion object of a specific type, component, COM object, CORBA object, Java object, or web service object.

For more information on the CFOBJECT tag, consult the ColdFusion documentation that was installed with your ColdFusion server.

CFCHART (Advanced)

The CFCHART tag generates and displays a chart from a specific set of data. It is used with the CFCHARTDATA and CFCHARTSERIES tags to provide data to chart and the format of the chart. For more information on the CFCHART tag, consult the ColdFusion documentation that was installed with your ColdFusion server.

More Tags (Advanced)

There are more ColdFusion tags available than are displayed in the insert bar for CFML. When you access the More Tags object a dialog box opens that lets you pick any ColdFusion tag to insert and to add whatever attributes are available for that tag. You would use this object if you know ColdFusion well and you want to insert a tag for which there is no specific object.

COLDFUSION COMPONENTS

Designing your ColdFusion application generally starts when you have a particular problem to solve. For example, maybe you need to build a shopping cart or build a system to take care of your Human Resources information. You have one problem and a solution designed specifically for that problem. However, as your site grows and the functionality becomes more complex, having applications in multiple places that need access to the same data or that need to perform many of the same functions becomes a liability. You end up with more and more processing pages in different locations that all do the same thing. If you need to make a change, you end up having to change multiple locations.

One solution that ColdFusion provides is ColdFusion Components (CFCs). CFCs are files that encapsulate your application's information or functionality into separate files that can be maintained and accessed separately by multiple pages and applications.

For a detailed look at ColdFusion Components, check out *Macromedia ColdFusion MX Web Application Construction Kit* by Ben Forta et al.

Dreamweaver allows you to build CFCs quite easily by adding them as a document type that you can select from the New File dialog box. When you select Dynamic Page and ColdFusion Component, Dreamweaver opens a new page and inserts the necessary code framework:

```
<cfcomponent>
    <cffunction name="myFunction" access="public"
    ➥returntype="string">
```

```
        <cfargument name="myArgument" type="string"
        ➥required="true">
        <cfset myResult="foo">
        <cfreturn myResult>
    </cffunction>
</cfcomponent>
```

The CFCOMPONENT tag starts the file just like <html> starts an HTML file and indicates that the file is a CFC. Each CFC can contain multiple CFFUNCTION tags, each of which is a method of the component. Each CFFUNCTION can accept one or more arguments that are data passed to the function. It also returns some information that is handed back to the page that called the CFC.

A simple CFC would be one that gets a list of employees from a database and lists them with their departments. To make this interesting, though, the CFC also allows you to pass a variable from a form to limit the search to look for employees in a particular department. This is the CFC you will create in the exercise for this chapter.

EXERCISE 24.1

Make Sure Your Workstation Is Properly Set Up

You need to have ColdFusion MX installed on your machine, and the service needs to be running. You also need to have a web browser installed and running. You can test this by starting the ColdFusion administrator. In the Administrator, check the Data Sources. You should see that a data source named cfsnippets is installed. It comes with ColdFusion MX when you install it. If you see all that, you are set up correctly.

Set Up Your Site

If you don't have a site set up for ColdFusion, set up one now. If you have a ColdFusion site defined already, you can skip to the next section.

You don't need any supporting files for this exercise. You will create the entire project from scratch, so you don't need to move any files around for this exercise.

1. Expand the Site Files panel, and choose Site > New Site to open the Site Definition dialog box. In this dialog box, bring the Advanced tab to the front.

2. For Local Info, set the following:

    • **Name**—SearchEmployeeExercise

    • **Local Root Folder**—Create a new folder. Call it SearchEmployeeExercise. Set it as your local folder.

3. For Testing Server, set the following:

    • **Server Type**—ColdFusion

    • **Access**—Local/Network

    • **Testing Server Folder**—Browse to the SearchEmployeeExercise folder.

    • **URL Prefix**—`http://localhost/SearchEmployeeExercise/`.

4. Click OK to close the Site Definition dialog box. The Site panel now shows your site. Note that the left portion of the panel shows the testing server, not the remote site, which appears when you're working with static sites (unless you have changed your preferences to change the locations of the panels).

5. When you're working with a dynamic site, Dreamweaver uses the files on the testing server for previewing in the browser. Because you will create everything from scratch, you don't need to move anything around.

Create the ColdFusion Component

1. Select File > New.

2. In the Category column, select Dynamic Page, and in the Dynamic Page column, select ColdFusion Component, and click Create.

    Your page should look like this:

```
<cfcomponent>
    <cffunction name="myFunction" access="public"
    ➥returntype="string">
        <cfargument name="myArgument" type="string"
        ➥required="true">
        <cfset myResult="foo">
        <cfreturn myResult>
    </cffunction>
</cfcomponent>
```

Save the file as **EmployeeDataCFC.cfc** in the SearchEmployeeExercise folder.

You now have the basis of the CFC created and ready to modify in Code view. To edit CFCs, you need to stay in Code view.

3. In the CFFUNCTION tag, change the name of the function to `GetEmployeeFunction`. You can have multiple functions in one CFC, so naming them with as much information as you can is helpful.

4. In the CFFUNCTION tag, change the returntype to `query` from `string`. This function returns a query that the calling page can use to display.

5. In the CFARGUMENT tag, change the name to `SearchString`, and delete the type attribute.

6. In the CFARGUMENT tag, set the required attribute to No. You want to be able to call the function whether or not an argument is passed from the calling page.

7. Delete the CFSET tag following the CFARGUMENT.

8. Change the value of the CFRETURN from the placeholder `myResult` to `SearchEmployees`.

You are ready to add the code to actually do something in the CFC now that you have the framework for the tag ready.

9. Place the insertion point between the CFARGUMENT and the CF-RETURN tag. Click the CFQUERY object in the CFML insertion bar.

10. In the General tab of the Tag Editor for CFQUERY, enter the following:

Query Name—SearchEmployees

Data Source—cfsnippets

User Name—Leave blank

Password—Leave blank

```
SQL—SELECT *
FROM employees
ORDER BY LastName
```

Click OK to close the dialog box.

Your code should look something like this:

```
<cfcomponent>
    <cffunction name="GetEmployeeFunction" access="public"
    ➡returntype="query">
        <cfargument name="SearchString" required="No">
<cfquery name="SearchEmployees" datasource="cfsnippets">
SELECT *
FROM employees
ORDER BY LastName
</cfquery>
        <cfreturn SearchEmployees>
    </cffunction>
</cfcomponent>
```

You now have a query that selects everything in the employees table and then returns it to the calling page. This works fine for cases when your user wants to return all the records, but with the CFARGUMENT, the component is set to accept some input to limit that search. You need to add that condition to the query.

11. Place the cursor after the `FROM employees` line, and press Enter to create a new line.

12. Click the CFIF object in the CFML insertion bar.

    You need to enter the condition to check for. In this case, you have an argument in CFARGUMENT called `arguments.SearchString`, and you need to see if it has a value. Enter the following:

    arguments.SearchString NEQ ""

    You are asking if `arguments.SearchString` is not equal (NEQ) to nothing. This is the same as asking if it is equal to anything. If it is equal to anything, the CFIF is true, and the code in the CFIF is executed.

13. Move the cursor to the end of the CFIF and before the /CFIF. Press Enter to create a new line.

14. On the new line, type

    WHERE Department LIKE '%#arguments.SearchString#%'

    Save the file.

    You have added a WHERE clause to the SQL that limits the search to records in which the Department is like the variable arguments.SearchString, which contains whatever value is passed to the component from the calling page.

Your code should look like this:

```
<cfcomponent>
    <cffunction name="GetEmployeeFunction" access="public"
    ➡returntype="query">
        <cfargument name="SearchString" required="No">
<cfquery name="SearchEmployees" datasource="cfsnippets">
SELECT *
FROM employees
<cfif arguments.SearchString NEQ "">
WHERE Department LIKE '%#arguments.SearchString#%'</cfif>
ORDER BY LastName
</cfquery>
        <cfreturn SearchEmployees>
    </cffunction>
</cfcomponent>
```

If you want to, you can reformat it a little to make it easier to read.

Create the Search Employees Page

Now that you have created the CFC that executes the query and returns the result, you need to make the page that calls the CFC.

1. Create a new ColdFusion page from the New File dialog box. You don't need a CFC, just a regular ColdFusion page. You should be in Design view.

2. Save the page as **searchemployees.cfm**.

3. From the Forms insert bar, insert a form in the form type:

    Enter Department:

4. On the same line, insert a text field from the Forms insert bar. Name the text field **department** in the Property Inspector. Press Enter to create a new line.

5. Insert a Submit button on the new line.

6. Save the file. Your page should look like Figure 24.6.

FIGURE 24.6

Searchemployees.cfm.

7. Change the title of the page to Search Employees.

8. You have the form for the user to enter the department to search. Now you need to invoke the component you built and set up the page so that if it is called without any form input, the component is not called. This is the case when the page is called the first time or from any link directly to the page. However, when the page is called from itself with or without any input, the component is invoked.

9. Switch to Code view.

10. Place the cursor at the end of the form tag. Press Enter a few times to give yourself some space to work.

11. On one of the blank lines, insert a CFIF.

12. In the CFIF tag, you need to test to see if a form variable is being passed to the page using the `IsDefined()` function. Type

    IsDefined("Form.department")

13. Place the cursor between the CFIF and the /CFIF tags. Press Enter to give yourself more space.

14. Open the Application panel group, and bring the Components panel to the front. Select CF Component from the drop-down list at the top left of the panel if it is not showing.

15. You should see an entry in the panel for SearchEmployeeExercise, as shown in Figure 24.7. Expand the entry to see the CFCs available.

16. Select the query called GetEmployeeFunction(SearchString) in the EmployeeDataCFC in the Components panel. Click the Insert button (the second from the right at the top of the panel) to insert the CFINVOKE into the document.

Your code should look something like this:

```html
<html>
<head>
<title>Search Employees</title>
<meta http-equiv="Content-Type" content="text/html;
➥charset=iso-8859-1">
</head>

<body>
<form name="form1" method="post" action="">
<p>Enter Department:
    <input name="department" type="text" id="department">
</p>
<p>
  <input type="submit" name="Submit" value="Submit">
</p>
</form>

<cfif IsDefined("Form.department")>
<cfinvoke
 component="SearchEmployeeExercise.EmployeeDataCFC"
 method="GetEmployeeFunction"
 returnvariable-"GetEmployeeFunctionRet">
</cfinvoke>

</cfif>

</body>
</html>
```

You need to add the CFARGUMENT to the CFINVOKE tag to specify the name of the variable that is passed to the CFC.

FIGURE 24.7

The SearchEmployee-Exercise CFC in the Components panel.

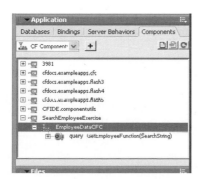

17. Place the cursor at the end of the CFINVOKE tag, before the /CFINVOKE tag, and type

    <cfinvokeargument name="SearchString" value= "#Form.department#">

    This sets a value of the contents of the form's department field to the variable SearchString, which is passed to the CFC.

18. Save the file.

    The page is mostly done. Now that you are calling the CFC and passing it the variable SearchString, you need to add a place to display the information that gets returned from the CFC.

19. Place the cursor after the end of the /CFINVOKE and before the /CFIF tag. Press Enter a few times to give yourself space to work.

20. Click the CFOUTPUT from the CFML insert bar, and enter **GetEmployeeFunctionRet** for the query. Remember that this is the name of the return variable from the CFINVOKE tag.

21. Press Enter to create a new line, and type

    `<b>#FirstName# #LastName#</b> works in #Department#<br>`

    This takes the results of the query in the CFC and iterates through the records, printing the first name, last name, and department that are returned.

22. Save the file.

Test the Application

Now you can test your application. When you preview the **searchemployees.cfm** file in the browser, you see the page with just the search box and the Submit button. When you call the page for the first time, no form value is defined. The CFIF condition tests and finds nothing, so the CFINVOKE is not called.

Enter nothing in the search box, and click Submit. The CFIF tests to see if a Form.department variable is defined. There is, even though it has no value. Because the variable is present, the CFINVOKE is called in the CFIF.

In the CFC, the CFARGUMENT is checked. The CFC finds that it is unnecessary to have an argument passed in, so the CFQUERY is executed. The CFQUERY has another CFIF that checks to see if the variable SearchString from the CFARGUMENT tag is empty. Because SearchString is empty, the CFIF does not evaluate as true. Therefore, the WHERE clause, which would limit the search to one department, is not executed. The CFQUERY finishes executing and passes that back as a query to the calling page, **searchemployees.cfm**.

On the calling page, the CFOUTPUT tag iterates through the returned data and prints the names of all the employees.

Now test the page and enter **Sales** for the department.

The CFIF tests to see if a Form.department variable is defined. Because the variable is present, the CFINVOKE is called in the CFIF.

In the CFC, the CFARGUMENT is checked. The CFC finds that it is unnecessary to have an argument passed in, so the CFQUERY is executed. The CFQUERY has another CFIF that checks to see if the variable SearchString from the CFARGUMENT tag is empty. Because SearchString has the value of Sales, the CFIF evaluates as true. Therefore, the WHERE clause, which limits the search to the one department specified, is executed. The CFQUERY finishes executing and passes that back as a query to the calling page, **searchemployees.cfm**.

On the calling page, the CFOUTPUT tag iterates through the returned data and prints the names of only the employees in the Sales department.

COLDFUSION RESOURCES

There are many good resources for ColdFusion. The following lists a few that are of great value. You might find that these lead you to other resources that make your ColdFusion coding easier and more powerful.

- *SAMS Teach Yourself SQL in 10 Minutes*. Ben Forta. SAMS Publishing. The very best resource for SQL. Small, simple, and complete. No coder should be without this.

- *Macromedia ColdFusion MX Web Application Construction Kit*. Ben Forta et al. Macromedia Press. The definitive work on ColdFusion.

- *ColdFusion MX from Static to Dynamic in 10 Steps*. Barry Moore. New Riders. An excellent introduction to ColdFusion. Mostly deals with hand-coding, but gives a good basis to work from with more-complicated books.

- *ColdFusion MX Documentation*. This is installed with your ColdFusion server and should be available from the Start menu.

SUMMARY

Dreamweaver MX 2004 has superb support for ColdFusion. All the tags are available. The most important and useful tags are very easy to access from the user interface. With the full complement of tags, code completion when you're hand-coding, and a connection to the testing server, there is no better way to code ColdFusion.

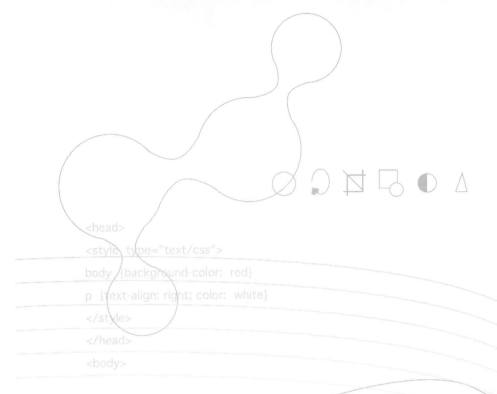

CHAPTER 25

WORKING SMART WITH PHP

THE PHP HYPERTEXT PREPROCESSOR (PHP) IS A POWERFUL, WIDELY USED, and easy-to-learn scripting language and application server. PHP has been around for years, but Dreamweaver began supporting PHP only minimally in Dreamweaver MX. Dreamweaver MX 2004 has great support for PHP, placing it for the most part on par with ASP.NET and ColdFusion MX.

To work with the PHP/MySQL Server model, you need to have both PHP and MySQL loaded and working. For information on where to find the downloads, see the resources section at the end of this chapter.

PHP Objects in the Insertion Bar

Developers can access several objects in the PHP insertion bar. Most of these objects are designed to be used alone. For instance, each object inserts a beginning and ending PHP tag that you need only once in your code block. If you want to hand-code PHP and not use the server behaviors that are detailed in Chapter 23, "Further Dynamic Techniques," you are better off using the tag-completion features of Code view.

For instance, if you start a PHP code block in Code view by typing `<?php $HTTP_`, a drop-down list pops up listing all eight HTTP variables: COOKIE_VARS, ENV_VARS, FILES_VARS, GET_VARS, POST_VARS, REQUEST_VARS, SESSION_VARS, and SERVER_VARS, where the objects in the Insertion bar give you only four of the possible options.

The bottom line is that, with PHP, you are better off hand-coding or using the existing server behaviors and whatever server behaviors are available from the community and the Macromedia Exchange.

Form Variables

Whenever a page with a form with a post action calls a PHP page, the variables from the form are put in an array to make them accessible to PHP. The HTTP_POST_VARS array holds each value passed in from the calling form.

The object inserts the following code:

```
<?php $HTTP_POST_VARS[];?>
```

When you insert the object, you need to enter the name of the post variable that you want to use in quotes. For example, the following code would get the post variable named "department":

```
<?php $HTTP_POST_VARS["department"];?>
```

Example:

```
<?php echo $HTTP_POST_VARS["department"];?>
```

This code echoes the value of department to the screen.

URL Variables

Whenever a page with a form with a get action calls a PHP page, the variables from the form are put in an array to make them accessible to PHP. The HTTP_GET_VARS array holds each value passed in from the calling form.

The URL Variables object inserts the following code:

```
<?php $HTTP_GET_VARS[];?>
```

When you insert the object, you need to enter the name of the get variable that you want to use in quotes. For example, the following code gets the get variable named department:

```
<?php $HTTP_GET_VARS["department"];?>
```

Example:

```
<?php echo $HTTP_GET_VARS["department"];?>
```

This code echoes the URL variable value of department to the screen.

Session Variables

Session information keeps information on a visit to a PHP site in an array that can be accessed from page to page or that can be preserved from visit to visit in a database.

```
<?php $HTTP_SESSION_VARS[];?>
```

When you insert the object, you need to enter the name of the session variable that you want to use in quotes. For example, the following code gets the get variable named visitdate:

```
<?php $HTTP_ SESSION_VARS["visitdate"];?>
```

Example:

```
<?php echo $HTTP_ SESSION_VARS["visitdate "];?>
```

This code echoes the session variable value of department to the screen.

Cookie Variables

The Cookie Variables object keeps information that you have saved to or read from the cookie in an array that can be accessed from anywhere in the application.

```php
<?php $HTTP_COOKIE_VARS[];?>
```

When you insert the object, you need to enter the name of the cookie variable that you want to use in quotes. For example, the following code gets the get variable named username:

```php
<?php $HTTP_ COOKIE_VARS["username"];?>
```

Example:

```php
<?php echo $HTTP_ COOKIE_VARS["username"];?>
```

This code echoes the cookie variable value of username to the screen.

Include

The Include object enables you to insert a link to a separate file, the contents of which can be referenced in the page with the include statement. Parts of your logic can be separated into distinct files for many reasons. If you have a piece of functionality such as a shipping calculator or ZIP code locator that you want to access from multiple applications or from multiple locations in one application, this is the tag you want to use. Any variable or function defined in the included file can be referenced in the file that has the include placed in it.

The Include object inserts the following code:

```php
<?php include(); ?>
```

If you were going to include a file called shippingfunction.php, your code would look like this:

```php
<?php include("shippingfunction.php"); ?>
```

Require

The Require Object enables you to insert a link to a separate file, the contents of which can be referenced in the page with the require statement. Unlike the related Include object, if a file that is required is not present, PHP produces a fatal error and stops processing. Parts of your logic can be separated into distinct files for many reasons. Any variable or function defined in the required file can be referenced in the file that has the require placed in it.

The Require object inserts the following code:

```php
<?php require(); ?>
```

If you were going to require a file called shippingfunction.php, your code would look like this:

```php
<?php require("shippingfunction.php"); ?>
```

If the application could not find the shippingfunction.php file, it would throw an error and processing would stop.

PHP Page Encoding

The PHP Page Encoding object adds the mb_http_input and mb_http_output functions to the page. Both functions are used with multibyte input.

The mb_http_input() function detects the HTTP input character encoding. If there is no string specified, it returns the last input type processed.

The mb_http_output() function sets the HTTP output character encoding if the encoding is set in the function. If it is omitted, the function returns the current HTTP output character encoding.

Example:

```php
mb_http_input("iso-8859-1");
mb_http_output("iso-8859-1");
```

Code Block

The Code Block object inserts a beginning and end delimiter for PHP if you want to hand-code. If you make a selection before inserting, the selection is wrapped in the PHP tag.

```php
<?php ?>
```

echo Echo

The Echo object inserts an echo language construct (technically, it is not a function) into the page that outputs a string to the browser. You can output multiple strings in a single Echo.

Example:

```
$username = "mbrown";
$userpassword = "passmatt";

echo "Username is $username and password is $passmatt"
```

This code outputs:

```
Username is mbrown and password is passmatt
```

/* */ Comment

The Comment object inserts comments in the form /*...*/, which you need to do in PHP code blocks. If you have a selection highlighted in Code view, inserting the object wraps the selected text in the comment delimiters.

if else If and Else

The If object inserts the If control structure to control the flow of the program through the check of some condition. If the condition is true, the enclosed code can be executed. The Else object controls flow by checking for a second condition.

```
<?php
$a = 14;
$b = 12;

if( $a > $b ){
    print "a is bigger than b";
} else {
    print "b is bigger than a";
}
?>
```

In this code, there are two variables, a and b, set to different values. In the If statement, the values are checked to see if a is larger than b. If it is, the print statement a is bigger than b is executed. If b is larger than a, the else statement is true and "b is bigger than a" is printed.

More Tags (Advanced)

More PHP tags are available than are displayed in the Insert bar for PHP. When you access the More Tags object, a dialog box opens that lets you pick the other available tags and functions.

EXERCISE 25.1

Mailing PHP Data

In this exercise, you will use PHP to take data from a form and mail it to you instead of putting it into a database. You might use this functionality to send notification of orders from a shopping cart, or you might set up a form to allow constituents to mail their representatives over a given issue. Because email has become such a ubiquitous form of communication, being able to access it from your applications is a very powerful tool.

Make sure your workstation is properly set up.

You need to have PHP installed and running. MySQL must be installed and running a database; however, for this exercise, you will not actually need the database. You do need to have a PHP site set up in Dreamweaver. You will also need a working local mail server set up and available to use.

SMTP mail is included with Microsoft IIS, and there are versions for other servers. If you have access to an SMTP mail server that allows mail relays, you can use that address. Unfortunately, the capability to relay mail has become less available because it leaves the server open to use by spammers and creates a liability for the ISPs that offer the service.

PHP uses the mail server set up in the PHP.ini file, in the Windows directory of your machine. If you don't find it there, do a search for it: Some versions of Windows place it in other locations.

About halfway through the PHP.ini file, you should find the following lines:

```
[mail function]
; For Win32 only.
SMTP = localhost ; for Win32 only
; For Win32 only.
sendmail_from = me@localhost.com ; for Win32 only
; For Unix only.  You may supply arguments as well (default:
➥"sendmail -t -i").
;sendmail_path =
```

You can leave the `SMTP = localhost` set as is if you are using your own machine for the mail. If you are using an SMTP mail server that allows you to relay to it, enter that IP address. You should set `sendmail from` to be your address or an address where the person being mailed can respond.

Creating the Mail Form

You will create a form to capture the information, name, and address for the user to enter to mail to you.

1. Select File > New to create a new PHP page in your site.

2. Add a form to the page.

3. In the form, type **Name:** and then a space.

4. Insert a text field into the form on the same line, and name the field name in the Property Inspector.

5. Press Return to get a new paragraph. Type **email address:** and a space.

6. Insert a text field into the form on the same line. Name the field email in the Property Inspector.

7. Press Return to get a new paragraph. Type **Comment:** and a space.

8. Insert a text field into the form on the same line. Name the field comment in the Property Inspector, and set Type to Multiline.

9. Press Return and enter a Submit button. Your code should look like this:

```
<html>
<head>
<title>Untitled Document</title>
<meta http-equiv="Content-Type" content="text/html;
 charset-iso-8859-1">
</head>

<body>
<form name="form1" method="post" action="mailform.php">
<p>Name:
    <input name="name" type="text" id="name">
</p>
<p>email address:
   <input name="email" type="text" id="email">
</p>
<p>Comment:
   <textarea name="comment" id="comment"></textarea>
</p>
<p>
   <input type="submit" name="Submit" value="Submit">
</p>
</form>
</body>
</html>
```

10. Save your file as **mailform.php**.

Creating the Mail Processor

You next will create the page that accepts the information from the form, formats that to an email, and then sends that to you.

1. Select File > New to create a new PHP page in your site.

2. Save the page as **mailform.php**.

3. Go to Code view of the page and put your cursor in the body.

4. From the PHP Insert bar, insert a PHP Code Block object. Your cursor will be in the code block, so press Return a couple times to give yourself some space to work.

5. Type in the following:

```
$mail_to = you@youraddress.com;
$mail_subject = "Comment from web form";
$mail_name = "Comment from web form";
$mail_body = "Name: ";
$mail_body .=
```

In PHP, the = sign assigns a value to a variable. .= appends a value to a variable. You will construct one long variable, piece by piece, that you will enter into the mail.

6. Insert a Form Variable from the PHP Insert bar. Notice that Dreamweaver has inserted not only the code for the Form Variable, but also a set of begin and end PHP tags. You want to remove those so that your code looks like this:

```
$mail_to = you@youraddress.com;
$mail_subject = "Comment from web form";
$mail_name = "Comment from web form";
$mail_body = "Name: ";
$mail_body .= $_POST[];
```

7. You need to enter the name of the variable from the form so that the code looks like this:

```
<?php
$mail_to = you@youraddress.com;
$mail_subject = "Comment from web form";
$mail_name = "Comment from web form";
$mail_body = "Name: ";
$mail_body .= $_POST['name'];
?>
```

8. For the next line, will add a line break after each variable. Add /n to indicate a new line before each form variable. Type the following code:

```
$mail_body .= "\nE-Mail: ";
```

This adds a new line and E-Mail: to the mail_body variable.

9. Add the following lines to complete the `mail_body` variable with the values passed in from the form.

```
$mail_body .= $_POST['email'];
$mail_body .= "\nComment: ";
$mail_body .= $_POST['comment'];
```

Your code should now look like this:

```
<?php
$mail_to ="you@youraddress.com";
$mail_subject = "Comment from web form";
$mail_body -  "Name: ";
$mail_body .= $_POST['name'] ;
$mail_body .= "\nE-Mail: ";
$mail_body .= $_POST['email'];
$mail_body .= "\nComment: ";
$mail_body .= $_POST['comment'];


?>
```

Finally, you want to create the function to mail the variables that you have built here in the mailform.php. You are going to do that, but you will wrap that in an `if` statement. In PHP, if the mail is sent successfully, the `mail()` function returns a yes to the flow of the program. If it fails, it sends nothing back. This is important because you want to have some way to know whether the mail was sent or failed. For a production site, you can generate a value in a database or log file, but here you simply show a message onscreen.

1. On a new line, type the following:

```
if(mail($mail_to, $mail_subject, $mail_body))
    echo "Mail Sent";
else echo "Mail Failed"
```

This tells PHP to test whether the mail has been sent or and to respond accordingly. The actual function takes three arguments: `$mail_to`, which is the address for which the mail is intended; `$mail_subject`, which is the subject of the mail; and `$mail_body`, which is the body of the mail.

The entire file should look like this:

```
<html>
<head>
<title>Untitled Document</title>
<meta http-equiv="Content-Type" content="text/html;
charset=iso-8859-1">
</head>

<body>
<?php
$mail_to ="you@yourdomain.com";
$mail_subject = "Comment from web form";
$mail_body =  "Name: ";
$mail_body .= $_POST['name'] ;
$mail_body .= "\nE-Mail: ";
$mail_body .= $_POST['email'];
$mail_body .= "\nComment: ";
$mail_body .= $_POST['comment'];

if(mail($mail_to, $mail_subject, $mail_body))
    echo "Mail Sent";
else echo "Mail Failed"
?>
</body>
</html>
```

2. Save your file.

You are now ready to test your file. Open the form and fill out some information and press the Submit button. You should be taken to a page that gives you a message telling whether the mail was sent. If you run into an error that says you don't have the right to relay mail, you need to set the relay options on your server to allow the localhost machine to send mail. In IIS, that is found in the IIS Administrator, where you need to set that option for the default SMTP server in the SMTP Properties.

PHP RESOURCES

Many good resources for PHP are available. Here are a few that are of great value. You might find that these lead you to other resources that will make your PHP coding easier and more powerful.

- **php.net (www.php.net)**—The official PHP website. Here you can access the latest downloads, look up information on add-on products, and get technical help in setup and usage. You'll find lists of PHP-related events around the world and the latest news on the various projects.

  If you are looking for the latest version of PHP, you can find it here under the Downloads link. Sometimes beta versions are available. You want to always download the latest production version of PHP, for production and stability.

- **MySQL (www.mysql.com)**—The source for MySQL database. Here you'll find the latest versions, support, and purchase options for different licenses.

- **Macromedia Exchange (www.macromedia.com/cfusion/exchange/ index.cfm?view=sn120)**—The place to check for the latest extensions from around the community. Many extensions exist for adding functionality to Dreamweaver, and many are for the PHP server model.

SUMMARY

The PHP Server Model in Dreamweaver is specifically designed to allow connections to MySQL and to provide a set of built-in functions in the form of the server behaviors described in earlier chapters. The PHP objects that are included in Dreamweaver are very specific and are most useful to hand-coders who are familiar with PHP already. If you are learning PHP, Dreamweaver is a great environment to do that. You can use the built-in server behaviors for many features, and you can hand-code with the help of the objects, but remember that a lot more power is open to you if you hand-code your PHP in Dreamweaver.

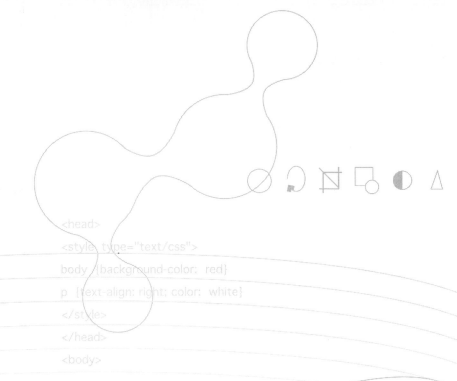

```
<head>
<style type="text/css">
body {background-color: red}
p {text-align: right; color: white}
</style>
</head>
<body>
```

CHAPTER 26

WORKING SMART WITH ASP.NET

DREAMWEAVER MX 2004 IS DESIGNED TO BE A COMPLETE SOLUTION FOR developing ASP.NET applications. ASP.NET is a little different from the other server models in Dreamweaver because it is not really an application server language. It is a more comprehensive way to build web applications in a couple of different languages. ASP.NET is a framework for developers that allows you to develop web applications in a more object-oriented way, accessing classes and controls that allow you to build larger, more robust applications without having to code everything from scratch each time.

ASP.NET has a number of great features. A chapter in a Dreamweaver book, even a great book like this one, has to pick and choose what to detail. This chapter includes the following:

- Installation notes. Although you can go many places for information on installing the ASP.NET Framework, I've run into several "gotchas" that you might benefit from.

- A reference for all the ASP.NET objects Dreamweaver provides.

- An exercise that shows you how to use a DataGrid.

The examples here are for VBScript. Dreamweaver MX 2004 also includes support for C# (C-sharp), so the code you generate might be slightly different, but the concepts are the same and, in most cases, the details are as well.

ASP.NET INSTALLATION NOTES

Installing ASP.NET is generally straightforward. However, a few "gotchas" are worth noting if you are installing ASP.NET for the first time. For general installation instructions, follow the instructions in the download from Microsoft because they might change. The steps are well-documented in whatever their current configuration is.

Where Is the Current ASP.NET Download?

The current ASP.NET download is available free from the Microsoft site at http://msdn.microsoft.com/netframework/. Look for the Redistributable download, not the SDK version.

What Versions of Windows Does ASP.NET Work On?

You need to be using Windows 98, Windows 2000, Windows Me, Windows NT, Windows Server 2003, or Windows XP Pro. Note that Windows XP Home Edition is not a supported configuration. You also need to have Microsoft Internet Information Server installed.

Turn Off Simple File Sharing

The default for Windows XP is to have Simple File Sharing enabled. This does not give you a security tab that you need to set permissions. To turn off Simple File Sharing, open My Computer (or your computer name if you have changed it) and choose Tools > Folder Options. On the View tab, in the Advanced Settings panel, uncheck the Use Simple File Sharing box. Click OK to apply the change.

Setting Permissions for the Folders

Do *not* change the format of your drive without checking with your system administrator or help desk. If you change a FAT32 partition to NTFS, you cannot change back without reformatting the drive.

You might not have the permissions set correctly to access the folder that contains your application. To set the security for the folder, you need to right-click the folder that contains your application and select Preferences. You should see a tab for Security. If you don't, your disk might be formatted in FAT32. You might need to format it as NTFS to be able to give the correct security permissions. The Windows Help system has instructions on converting a FAT32 volume to NTFS without losing your files.

In the Security tab, you need to add two users to have access to the folder.

1. Click the Add button.

2. In the Select Users or Groups dialog box, click the Advanced button.

3. Click the Find Now button.

4. In the Name (RDN) column, select the ASP.NET user. Click OK to go back to the Select Users or Groups dialog box.

5. Click the Advanced button again.

6. In the Name (RDN) column, select the IUSR user. Click OK to go back to the Select Users or Groups dialog box.

7. In the Security tab of the Properties, you should now see the two new users added in the Group or user names box.

8. Select the ASP.NET Machine Account (the ASP.NET user account) and grant it full control.

9. Select the Internet Guest Account (the IUSR user account) and grant it full control.

10. Click OK to save the changes.

This creates two new accounts that need to be able to write and execute to the folders where the application is.

Setting the Permissions in the IIS Administrator

You also have to explicitly make the folder you will use for your application in your web root into an application.

1. Open the IIS (Internet Information Services) server Administrator by selecting Start > Programs > Administrative Tools > Internet Information Services.

2. In the IIS tree control, open the machine, open the Web Sites folder, open the Default Web Site, and find the folder that will contain your web application.

3. Select the folder, and right-click to open the Properties for the folder.

4. In the Directory tab, set the Execute Permissions drop-down to Scripts and Executables. Click Create, and then click OK.

This sets the folder in your web root to be recognized by ASP.NET as an application that can be executed.

ASP.NET HAND-CODING OBJECTS IN THE INSERTION BAR

ASP.NET is based on a scripting paradigm that is significantly different from ColdFusion MX. Scripting gives developers tremendous power, but the trade-off is that the code beyond the provided server scripts mostly has to be hand-coded. Many of the objects in the insertion bar are just shortcuts for hand-coding.

Register Custom Tag (Advanced)

The Register Custom Tag object inserts code into the page to lay out and access custom server controls on the page.

Several Macromedia custom tags are inserted with the ASP.NET server behaviors. Inserting them and looking at the resulting code is a good place to start with Custom Tags.

For detailed explanations of ASP.NET tags, see the "ASP.NET Resources" section at the end of this chapter.

The server variables are as follows:

- **TagPrefix**—Sets the tag's prefix, which associates it with a namespace.

- **TagName** Sets the tag's name, which associates it with a class in the namespace.

- **Src**—Sets the namespace to associate with the TagPrefix.

```
<%@ Register
TagPrefix="MM"
Namespace="DreamweaverCtrls"
Assembly="DreamweaverCtrls,version=1.0.0.0,
➥publicKeyToken=836f606ede05d46a,culture=neutral" %>
```

This code is inserted by the DataSet server behavior. It sets a namespace of DreamweaverCtrls that contains the custom controls used by Dreamweaver. Inserting any ASP.NET server object also inserts the @Register tag to the same namespace. The TagPrefix is the first part of the custom tag name.

Import Namespace (Advanced)

The Import Namespace tag inserts a reference to a custom namespace or a part of the .NET Framework. ASP.NET allows you to use custom controls and abstracted snippets of code. Importing a namespace explicitly declares the path to any of those controls you are using in the application.

The Import Namespace object inserts the following code:

```
<%@ Import Namespace="" %>
```

Trimmed Form Element (Advanced)

The Trimmed Form Element inserts the Trim( ) method into an expression that removes any spaces from the beginning and/or end of the value of the form element you are trimming.

The Trimmed Form Element object inserts the following code:

```
Trim(Request.Form(""))
```

Trimmed QueryString Element

The Trimmed QueryString element inserts the `Trim()` method into an expression that removes any spaces from the beginning and/or end of the URL parameter you are trimming.

```
Trim(Request.QueryString(""))
```

Runat Server

The Runat Server object simply inserts `'runat="server"'` into the code. The Runat Server attribute is necessary in a number of tags. The tag is simply a shortcut for hand-coding.

```
'runat="server"
```

Bound Data

As soon as you have a DataSet defined in a page, you can bind the data from each field of the table to objects on the page. The notation for this is `<%#  %>`.

Here's an example:

```
<%# FindDepartment.FieldValue("departmentname", Container) %>
```

In this code, the departmentname field from the FindDepartment DataSet will be placed on the page.

```
<ASP:Repeater runat="server" DataSource='<%#
FindDepartment.DefaultView %>'>

<ItemTemplate>
<%# FindDepartment.FieldValue("departmentname", Container) %>
</ItemTemplate>

</ASP:Repeater>
```

In this code, the same data is bound to the page, but in this case it is wrapped in a Repeater that loops through the set of data found in the Data Set and prints each record.

📄 Page_Load (Advanced)

Page_Load is an event that is executed every time a page is loaded. Dreamweaver inserts more than just the Page_Load event; it inserts a code block that checks to see whether a page is posting back to itself. If it is, code gets executed. If the page is not posting back, the code does not get executed. Dreamweaver inserts the code block, but you still need to hand code the functions that get executed.

The Page_Load object is especially useful when you have to process a form that posts back to itself. In this case, you might have a large control like the DataGrid that works with data from the form only if the form is filled out. If the page is called for the first time without the form information being filled out, the code to populate the DataGrid should not be executed.

Dreamweaver inserts the following code:

```
<script runat="server">
Sub Page_Load(Src As Object, E As EventArgs)
If Not IsPostBack Then DataBind();
End If
End Sub
</script>
```

ASP.NET WEB SERVER CONTROL OBJECTS IN THE INSERTION BAR

ASP.NET has a tremendous set of controls to use as objects in forms that provide a lot more control than regular form elements. When you use the Dreamweaver server behaviors to create forms in insertion pages or update pages, Dreamweaver uses these web server controls. Having access to the controls separately allows you to customize forms or create your own without having to use the built-in behaviors.

▰ asp:Button

The asp:Button object displays a clickable pushbutton on the form, like the regular HTML button object, but with much more interaction with the application server.

asp:Button has the following attributes:

- **General:**

    - **ID**—Sets the object's ID so that it can be referred to by name in scripts. This has to be an alphanumeric value. If you use a number alone, you get an error from the server.

    - **Text**—Sets the control's label.

    - **Command Name**—Specifies the command associated with the control. A regular HTML button object can have only one submit. The asp:Button object can have multiple buttons that have different functions when clicked.

    - **Command Argument**—Sets a parameter to pass to the command specified in the Command Name.

- **Layout:**

    - **Height**—Sets the height of the control on the page.

    - **Width**—Sets the width of the control on the page.

    - **Border Width**—Sets the width of the control's border.

    - **Background Color**—Sets the control's background color.

    - **Border Color**—Sets the control's border color, creating a beveled look around the control. Borders are always beveled.

    - **Foreground Color**—Sets the control's foreground color.

- **Style Information:**

    - **CSS Class**—Allows you to assign a CSS class to the control's appearance. Like HTML and CSS inheritance, the properties directly defined in the control override properties set in the definition for the class.

- **Border Style**—The style of the border set with the Border Width and Border Color attributes in the Layout section. The choices are notset, none, dotted, dashed, solid, double, groove, ridge, inset, and outset.

- **Font Name**—Sets the font name for the display of the text.

- **Font Names**—Sets a font list that the browser iterates through until it finds a corresponding font it can display.

- **Font Size**—Sets the size of the text label.

- **Bold**—Sets the font to bold.

- **Italic**—Sets the font to italic.

- **Overline**—Produces an overline over the text.

- **Strkeout**—Sets the font to strikeout.

- **Underline**—Produces an underline under the text.

- **Enabled**—Sets the control's view status to enabled. Disabled controls are visible but not selectable. You can change this in ASP.NET by scripting the control to make it enabled or disabled based on other choices made in the form.

- **Enable Viewstate**—View state is maintained automatically in ASP.NET. This attribute allows you to explicitly disable automatic view maintenance.

- **Visible**—Sets the control to view or be invisible. Normally, you would use this attribute only in combination with scripting to make a control visible or invisible based on some other choice made dynamically.

- **Accessibility:**

  - **Tool Tip**—Sets a ToolTip for accessibility. This ToolTip should be short, descriptive, and unique for each control.

  - **Tab Index**—Sets the control's order so that you can control the order in which the controls are selected when the user tabs through the page.

  - **Access Key**—Sets a single key to access the control so that the user can access the control from the keyboard. For example, specifying k makes the control accessible by pressing Alt+K.

- **Events:**

    - **OnClick**—Presents an event when the control is clicked.

    - **OnDataBinding**—Presents an event when the control binds data to a data source.

    - **OnDisposed**—Presents an event when the control is released from memory.

    - **OnInit**—Presents an event when the control is initialized.

    - **OnLoad**—Presents an event when the control is loaded.

    - **OnPreRender**—Presents an event that allows you to script any updates before the output is rendered.

    - **OnUnload**—Presents an event when the control is unloaded from memory.

The asp:Button object inserts the following code (with only the general attributes set):

```
<asp:Button
CommandName="GetEmployees"
ID="submitid"
runat="server"
Text="Submit" />
```

☑ asp:CheckBox

The asp:CheckBox object inserts an asp:CheckBox element into a form. Check boxes represent choices that are either true or false. The asp:CheckBox has attributes that allow for much more control than the standard check box in HTML.

asp:CheckBox has the following attributes:

- **General:**

    - **ID**—Sets the object's ID so that it can be referred to by name in scripts. This has to be an alphanumeric value. If you use a number alone, you get an error from the server.

    - **Text**—Sets the control's label.

- **Text Alignment**—Specifies whether the text is displayed to the right or left of the check box.

- **Auto Postback**—Specifies whether the control posts the form back to the server.

- **Checked**—Indicates whether the control is selected.

- **Group Name**—Sets the name of the group of check boxes that the check box is assigned to.

- **Layout:**

  - **Height**—Sets the height of the control on the page.

  - **Width**—Sets the width of the control on the page.

  - **Border Width**—Sets the width of the control's border.

  - **Background Color**—Sets the control's background color.

  - **Border Color**—Sets the control's border color, creating a beveled look around the control. Borders are always beveled.

  - **Foreground Color**—Sets the control's foreground color.

- **Style Information:**

  - **CSS Class**—Allows you to assign a CSS class to the control's appearance. Like HTML and CSS inheritance, the properties defined in the control directly override properties set in the definition for the class.

  - **Border Style**—The style of the border set with the Border Width and Border Color attributes in the Layout section. The choices are notset, none, dotted, dashed, solid, double, groove, ridge, inset, and outset.

  - **Font Name**—Sets the font name for the display of the text.

  - **Font Names**—Sets a font list that the browser iterates through until it finds a corresponding font it can display.

  - **Font Size**—Sets the size of the text label.

  - **Bold**—Sets the font to bold.

  - **Italic**—Sets the font to italic.

  - **Overline**—Produces an overline over the text.

- **Strkeout**—Sets the font to strikeout.

- **Underline**—Produces an underline under the text.

- **Enabled**—Sets the control's view status to enabled. Disabled controls are visible but not selectable. You can change this in ASP.NET by scripting the control to make it enabled or disabled based on other choices made in the form.

- **Enable Viewstate**—View state is maintained automatically in ASP.NET. This attribute allows you to explicitly disable automatic view maintenance.

- **Visible**—Sets the control to view or be invisible. Normally you would use this attribute only in combination with scripting to make a control visible or invisible based on some other choice made dynamically.

- **Accessibility:**

  - **Tool Tip**—Sets a ToolTip for accessibility. This ToolTip should be short, descriptive, and unique for each control.

  - **Tab Index**—Sets the control's order so that you can control the order in which the controls are selected when the user tabs through the page.

  - **Access Key**—Sets a single key to access the control so that the user can access the control from the keyboard. For example, specifying k makes the control accessible by pressing Alt+K.

- **Events:**

  - **OnCheckedChanged**—Presents an event when the control is changed. If you want the function to fire on the event as the event happens, you need to set AutoPostBack to true in the General tab of the dialog box.

  - **OnDataBinding**—Presents an event when the control binds data to a data source.

  - **OnDisposed**—Presents an event when the control is released from memory.

  - **OnInit**—Presents an event when the control is initialized.

  - **OnLoad**—Presents an event when the control is loaded.

- **OnPreRender**—Presents an event that allows you to script any updates before the output is rendered.

- **OnUnload**—Presents an event when the control is unloaded from memory.

The asp:CheckBox object inserts the following code (with most of the attributes set):

```
<asp:CheckBox
BackColor="#999999"
BorderColor="#CCCCCC"
BorderWidth="6"
ForeColor="#000000"
Height="40"
ID="checkbox1"
runat="server"
Text="Male"
TextAlign="left"
Width="40" />
```

This code produces the control in the browser shown in Figure 26.1.

FIGURE 26.1
The asp:CheckBox with the TextAlign, Width, Height, BackColor, BorderColor, Border-Width, and ForeColor attributes set.

asp:CheckBoxList

The asp:CheckBoxList object inserts a set of check boxes from which the user can select multiple items. The list can contain any number of items that are pulled from a data source.

Note that if you have a form that allows users to pick multiple items from the same database field, your processor needs to loop through the results, or it will take only the first choice that has that name. For instance, if your form allows people to pick several toppings for pizza via check boxes, you need to loop through the result for as many times as there are toppings chosen, or only the first topping chosen will be processed.

asp:CheckBoxList has the following attributes:

- **General:**

    - **ID**—Sets the object's ID so that it can be referred to by name in scripts. This has to be an alphanumeric value. If you use a number alone, you get an error from the server.

    - **Text Alignment**—Sets the text's alignment in the check box list.

    - **Auto Postback**—Specifies whether the control posts the form back to the server.

- **Layout:**

    - **Height**—Sets the control's height on the page.

    - **Width**—Sets the control's width on the page.

    - **Border Width**—Sets the width of the control's border.

    - **Cell Padding**—Sets the HTML Cell Padding attribute to the <FORM> tag that is generated by the server.

    - **Cell Spacing**—Sets the HTML Cell Spacing attribute to the <FORM> tag that is generated by the server.

    - **Background Color**—Sets the control's background color.

    - **Border Color**—Sets the control's border color, creating a beveled look around the control. Borders are always beveled.

    - **Foreground Color**—Sets the control's foreground color.

- **Data:**

    - **Data Member**—Retrieves the specified table in the data source.

    - **Data Source**—Retrieves the data source to use to populate the drop-down list. The data source has to be an object that uses the IEnumerable interface, such as the DataView, ArrayList, Hashtable, or DataSet defined on the page from the Server Behavior panel.

    - **Data Text Field**—Sets the field in the data source to use as the text label for each item—that is, the text that appears on the menu.

- **Data Text Format String**—Sets the formatting string used to set the format of the data displayed in the list control.

- **Data Value Field**—Sets the field in the data source to use as the value for each item that appears on the menu.

- **Repeat Columns**—Sets the number of columns to display in the control.

- **Repeat Direction**—Sets the control to display the check boxes either vertically or horizontally.

- **Repeat Layout**—Sets the output to be in a table or in regular HTML flow.

- **Style Information:**

  - **CSS Class**—Allows you to assign a CSS class to the control's appearance. Like HTML and CSS inheritance, the properties defined in the control directly override properties set in the definition for the class.

  - **Font Name**—Sets the font name for the display of the text.

  - **Font Names**—Sets a font list that the browser iterates through until it finds a corresponding font it can display.

  - **Font Size**—Sets the size of the text label.

  - **Bold**—Sets the font to bold.

  - **Italic**—Sets the font to italic.

  - **Overline**—Produces an overline over the text.

  - **Strkeout**—Sets the font to strikeout.

  - **Underline**—Produces an underline under the text.

  - **Enabled**—Sets the control's view status to enabled. Disabled controls are visible but not selectable. You can change this in ASP.NET by scripting the control to make it enabled or disabled based on other choices made in the form.

  - **Enable Viewstate**—View state is maintained automatically in ASP.NET. This attribute allows you to explicitly disable automatic view maintenance.

- **Visible**—Sets the control to view or be invisible. Normally you would use this attribute only in combination with scripting to make a control visible or invisible based on some other choice made dynamically.

- **Accessibility:**

  - **Tab Index**—Sets the control's order so that you can control the order in which the controls are selected when the user tabs through the page.

  - **Access Key**—Sets a single key to access the control so that the user can access the control from the keyboard. For example, specifying k makes the control accessible by pressing Alt+K.

- **Events:**

  - **OnSelectedIndexChange**—Presents an event when the list changes and is posted back to the server. This is usually used with Auto Postback turned on, which posts the form back to the server when an item on the list is selected.

  - **OnDataBinding**—Presents an event when the control binds data to a data source.

  - **OnDisposed**—Presents an event when the control is released from memory.

  - **OnInit**—Presents an event when the control is initialized.

  - **OnLoad**—Presents an event when the control is loaded.

  - **OnPreRender**—Presents an event that allows you to script any updates before the output is rendered.

  - **OnUnload**—Presents an event when the control is unloaded from memory.

The asp:CheckBoxList object inserts the following code (with some of the attributes set and a data set previously defined as GetProducts):

```
<asp:CheckBoxList ID="SelectProducts"
runat="server"
TextAlign="left"
DataSource="<%# GetProducts.DefaultView %>"
DataTextField="productname"
DataValueField="productsid">
</asp:CheckBoxList>
```

This code sets the data source to the data set called SelectProducts that I created with the DataSet server behavior. It then binds the productname field in the database to the DataTextField and the productsid to the DataValueField. The result looks like Figure 26.2.

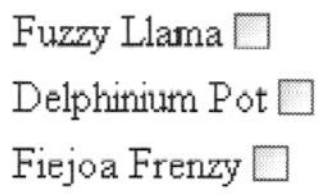

FIGURE 26.2

The asp:CheckBoxList with the TextAlign attribute set.

Fuzzy Llama ☐
Delphinium Pot ☐
Fiejoa Frenzy ☐

```
<asp:CheckBoxList BorderColor="#000000"
BorderWidth="1"
CellPadding="2"
DataSource="<%# GetProducts.DefaultView %>"
DataTextField="productname"
DataValueField="productsid"
ID="SelectProducts"
RepeatDirection="horizontal"
RepeatLayout="table"
runat="server"
TextAlign="left">
</asp:CheckBoxList>
```

This code sets the data source to the data set called GetProducts that I created with the DataSet server behavior. It then binds the productname field in the database to the DataTextField and the productsid to the DataValueField. The RepeatDirection is set to horizontal, and the RepeatLayout is set to put the check boxes in a table. The table is set to have a BorderWidth of 1 and a CellPadding of 2. Note that the border is set as a CSS style in the <TABLE> tag and not with the HTML attribute of BORDER. The result looks like Figure 26.3.

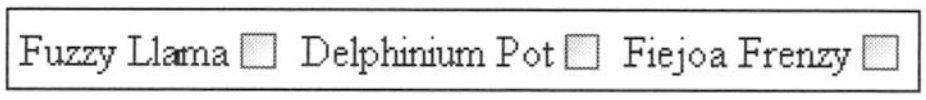

FIGURE 26.3

The asp:CheckBox-List with the Text-Align,BorderWidth, CellPadding, Repeat-Direction, Repeat-Layout, and TextAlign attributes set.

Fuzzy Llama ☐ Delphinium Pot ☐ Fiejoa Frenzy ☐

▦ asp:DropDownList

The asp:DropDownList object inserts drop-down menu from which the user can select a single item. The list can contain any number of items that are pulled from a data source.

asp:DropDownList has the following attributes:

- **General:**

  - **ID**—Sets the object's ID so that it can be referred to by name in scripts. This has to be an alphanumeric value. If you use a number alone, you get an error from the server.

  - **Auto Postback**—Specifies whether the control posts the form back to the server.

- **Layout:**

  - **Height**—Sets the control's height on the page.

  - **Width**—Sets the control's width on the page.

  - **Background Color**—Sets the control's background color.

  - **Foreground Color**—Sets the control's foreground color.

- **Data:**

  - **Data Member**—Retrieves the specified table in the data source.

  - **Data Source**—Retrieves the data source to use to populate the drop-down list. The data source has to be an object that uses the IEnumerable interface, like the DataView, ArrayList, Hashtable, or DataSet defined on the page from the Server Behavior panel.

  - **Data Text Field**—Sets the field in the data source to use as the text label for each item—that is, the text that appears on the menu.

  - **Data Text Format String**—Sets the formatting string used to set the format of the data displayed in the list control.

  - **Data Value Field**—Sets the field in the data source to use as the value for each item that appears on the menu.

- **Style Information:**

  - **CSS Class**—Allows you to assign a CSS class to the control's appearance. Like HTML and CSS inheritance, the properties defined in the control directly override properties set in the definition for the class.

  - **Font Name**—Sets the font name for the display of the text.

  - **Font Names**—Sets a font list that the browser iterates through until it finds a corresponding font it can display.

  - **Font Size**—Sets the size of the text label.

  - **Bold**—Sets the font to bold.

  - **Italic**—Sets the font to italic.

  - **Overline**—Produces an overline over the text.

  - **Strkeout**—Sets the font to strikeout.

  - **Underline**—Produces an underline under the text.

  - **Enabled**—Sets the control's view status to enabled. Disabled controls are visible but not selectable. You can change this in ASP.NET by scripting the control to make it enabled or disabled based on other choices made in the form.

  - **Enable Viewstate**—View state is maintained automatically in ASP.NET. This attribute allows you to explicitly disable automatic view maintenance.

  - **Visible**—Sets the control to view or be invisible. Normally, you would use this attribute only in combination with scripting to make a control visible or invisible based on some other choice made dynamically.

- **Accessibility:**

  - **Tab Index**—Sets the control's order so that you can control the order in which the controls are selected when the user tabs through the page.

  - **Access Key**—Sets a single key to access the control so that the user can access the control from the keyboard. For example, specifying k makes the control accessible by pressing Alt+K.

- **Events:**

  - **OnSelectedIndexChange**—Presents an event when the list changes and is posted back to the server. This is usually used with Auto Postback turned on, which posts the form back to the server when an item on the list is selected.

  - **OnDataBinding**—Presents an event when the control binds data to a data source.

  - **OnDisposed**—Presents an event when the control is released from memory.

  - **OnInit**—Presents an event when the control is initialized.

  - **OnLoad**—Presents an event when the control is loaded.

  - **OnPreRender**—Presents an event that allows you to script any updates before the output is rendered.

  - **OnUnload**—Presents an event when the control is unloaded from memory.

The asp:DropDownList object inserts the following code (with some of the attributes set and a data set previously defined as GetProducts):

```
<asp:DropDownList
ID="SelectProductID"
runat="server"
DataSource="<%# GetProducts.DefaultView %>"
DataTextField="productname"
DataValueField="productsid">
</asp:DropDownList>
```

This code sets the data source to the data set called GetProducts that I created with the DataSet server behavior. It then binds the productname field in the database to the DataTextField and the productsid to the DataValueField. The result looks like Figure 26.4.

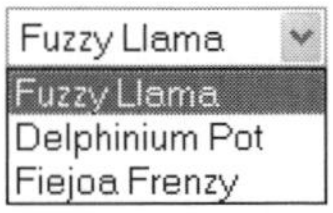

FIGURE 26.4

The asp:DropDownList control in the browser.

▣ asp:ImageButton

The asp:ImageButton object displays an image as a clickable pushbutton on the form, like the regular HTML button object but with much more interaction with the application server.

asp:ImageButton has the following attributes:

- **General:**

  - **ID**—Sets the object's ID so that it can be referred to by name in scripts. This has to be an alphanumeric value. If you use a number alone, you get an error from the server.

  - **Image URL**—Sets the image's URL to be displayed as the button. The path should be relative to the page being created or root-relative, just as any static image on the page would be. Absolute paths are supported as well.

  - **Alternate Text**—Sets the alt attribute of the image that will be the control.

  - **Command Name**—Specifies the command associated with the control. Each asp:ImageButton object can have different functions when clicked.

  - **Command Argument**—Sets a parameter to pass to the command specified in the Command Name.

- **Layout:**

  - **Height**—Sets the control's height on the page.

  - **Width**—Sets the control's width on the page.

  - **Image Alignment**—Sets the HTML `align` attribute on the image when the page is rendered in the browser. It does not use a CSS style.

  - **Border Width**—Sets the width of the control's border.

  - **Background Color**—Sets the control's background color.

  - **Border Color**—Sets the control's border color, creating a beveled look around the control. Borders are always beveled.

  - **Foreground Color**—Sets the control's foreground color.

- **Style Information:**

  - **CSS Class**—Allows you to assign a CSS class to the control's appearance. Like HTML and CSS inheritance, the properties defined in the control directly override properties set in the definition for the class.

  - **Border Style**—The style of the border set with the Border Width and Border Color attributes in the Layout section. The choices are `notset`, `none`, `dotted`, `dashed`, `solid`, `double`, `groove`, `ridge`, `inset`, and `outset`.

  - **Font Name**—Sets the font name for the display of the text.

  - **Font Names**—Sets a font list that the browser iterates through until it finds a corresponding font it can display.

  - **Font Size**—Sets the size of the text label.

  - **Bold**—Sets the font to bold.

  - **Italic**—Sets the font to italic.

  - **Overline**—Produces an overline over the text.

  - **Strkeout**—Sets the font to strikeout.

  - **Underline**—Produces an underline under the text.

  - **Enabled**—Sets the control's view status to enabled. Disabled controls are visible but not selectable. You can change this in ASP.NET by scripting the control to make it enabled or disabled based on other choices made in the form.

  - **Enable Viewstate**—View state is maintained automatically in ASP.NET. This attribute allows you to explicitly disable automatic view maintenance.

  - **Visible**—Sets the control to view or be invisible. Normally you would use this attribute only in combination with scripting to make a control visible or invisible based on some other choice made dynamically.

- **Accessibility:**

  - **Tool Tip**—Sets a ToolTip for accessibility. This ToolTip should be short, descriptive, and unique for each control.

- **Tab Index**—Sets the control's order so that you can control the order in which the controls are selected when the user tabs through the page.

- **Access Key**—Sets a single key to access the control so that the user can access the control from the keyboard. For example, specifying k makes the control accessible by pressing Alt+K.

- **Events:**

  - **OnCommand**—Presents an event when the user clicks the ImageButton.

  - **OnClick**—Presents an event when the user clicks the ImageButton.

  - **OnDataBinding**—Presents an event when the control binds data to a data source.

  - **OnDisposed**—Presents an event when the control is released from memory.

  - **OnInit**—Presents an event when the control is initialized.

  - **OnLoad**—Presents an event when the control is loaded.

  - **OnPreRender**—Presents an event that allows you to script any updates before the output is rendered.

  - **OnUnload**—Presents an event when the control is unloaded from memory.

The asp:ImageButton object inserts the following code (with only the general attributes set):

```
<asp:ImageButton
AlternateText="Order Button"
CommandName="orderitems"
ID="ImageButtonID"
ImageAlign="Middle"
ImageUrl="images/button.gif"
runat="server" />
```

abc asp:Label

The asp:Label object inserts an asp:Label element into a form. The asp:Label displays dynamically generated static text in a form that can be manipulated by the server.

asp:Label has the following attributes:

- **General:**

    - **ID**—Sets the object's ID so that it can be referred to by name in scripts. This has to be an alphanumeric value. If you use a number alone, you get an error from the server.

    - **Text**—Sets the control's label.

- **Layout:**

    - **Height**—Sets the control's height on the page.

    - **Width**—Sets the control's width on the page.

    - **Border Width**—Sets the width of the control's border.

    - **Background Color**—Sets the control's background color.

    - **Border Color**—Sets the control's border color, creating a beveled look around the control. Borders are always beveled.

    - **Foreground Color**—Sets the control's foreground color.

- **Style Information:**

    - **CSS Class**—Allows you to assign a CSS class to the control's appearance. Like HTML and CSS inheritance, the properties defined in the control directly override properties set in the definition for the class.

    - **Border Style**—The style of the border set with the Border Width and Border Color attributes in the Layout section. The choices are notset, none, dotted, dashed, solid, double, groove, ridge, inset, and outset.

    - **Font Name**—Sets the font name for the display of the text.

    - **Font Names**—Sets a font list that the browser iterates through until it finds a corresponding font it can display.

- **Font Size**—Sets the size of the text label.

- **Bold**—Sets the font to bold.

- **Italic**—Sets the font to italic.

- **Overline**—Produces an overline over the text.

- **Strkeout**—Sets the font to strikeout.

- **Underline**—Produces an underline under the text.

- **Enabled**—Sets the control's view status to enabled. Disabled controls are visible but not selectable. You can change this in ASP.NET by scripting the control to make it enabled or disabled based on other choices made in the form.

- **Enable Viewstate**—View state is maintained automatically in ASP.NET. This attribute allows you to explicitly disable automatic view maintenance.

- **Visible**—Sets the control to view or be invisible. Normally you would use this attribute only in combination with scripting to make a control visible or invisible based on some other choice made dynamically.

- **Accessibility:**

    - **Tool Tip**—Sets a ToolTip for accessibility. This ToolTip should be short, descriptive, and unique for each control.

    - **Tab Index**—Sets the control's order so that you can control the order in which the controls are selected when the user tabs through the page.

    - **Access Key**—Sets a single key to access the control so that the user can access the control from the keyboard. For example, specifying k makes the control accessible by pressing Alt+K.

- **Events:**

    - **OnDataBinding**—Presents an event when the control binds data to a data source.

    - **OnDisposed**—Presents an event when the control is released from memory.

    - **OnInit**—Presents an event when the control is initialized.

- **OnLoad**—Presents an event when the control is loaded.

- **OnPreRender**—Presents an event that allows you to script any updates before the output is rendered.

- **OnUnload**—Presents an event when the control is unloaded from memory.

The asp:Label object inserts the following code (with only the general attributes set):

```
<asp:Label ID="ColorChoiceID"
runat="server"
Text="The item is available in multiple colors, select one
➥here:">
</asp:Label>
```

asp:ListBox

The asp:ListBox object inserts a list from which a user can select a single item or multiple items. The list can contain any number of items that are pulled from a data source.

Note that if you have a form that allows users to pick multiple items from the same database field in the list box, your processor needs to loop through the results, or it will take only the first choice that has that name. For instance, if your form allows people to pick several toppings for pizza via check boxes, you need to loop through the result for as many times as there are toppings chosen, or only the first topping chosen will be processed.

asp:ListBox has the following attributes:

- **General:**

  - **ID**—Sets the object's ID so that it can be referred to by name in scripts. This has to be an alphanumeric value. If you use a number alone, you get an error from the server.

  - **Rows**—Sets how many rows are shown in the list. If there are more choices than there is space, scrolling arrows appear in the list.

- **Selection Mode**—Sets the selection mode to single or multiple items in the list.

- **Auto Postback**—Specifies whether the control posts the form back to the server.

- **Layout:**

  - **Height**—Sets the control's height on the page.

  - **Width**—Sets the control's width on the page.

  - **Background Color**—Sets the control's background color.

  - **Foreground Color**—Sets the control's foreground color.

- **Data:**

  - **Data Member**—Retrieves the specified table in the data source.

  - **Data Source**—Retrieves the data source to use to populate the drop-down list. The data source has to be an object that uses the IEnumerable interface, like the DataView, ArrayList, Hashtable, or DataSet defined on the page from the Server Behavior panel.

  - **Data Text Field**—Sets the field in the data source to use as the text label for each item—that is, the text that appears on the menu.

  - **Data Text Format String**—Sets the formatting string used to set the format of the data displayed in the list control.

  - **Data Value Field**—Sets the field in the data source to use as the value for each item that appears on the menu.

- **Style Information:**

  - **CSS Class**—Allows you to assign a CSS class to the control's appearance. Like HTML and CSS inheritance, the properties defined in the control directly override properties set in the definition for the class.

  - **Font Name**—Sets the font name for the display of the text.

  - **Font Names**—Sets a font list that the browser iterates through until it finds a corresponding font it can display.

  - **Font Size**—Sets the size of the text label.

- **Bold**—Sets the font to bold.

- **Italic**—Sets the font to italic.

- **Overline**—Produces an overline over the text.

- **Strkeout**—Sets the font to strikeout.

- **Underline**—Produces an underline under the text.

- **Enabled**—Sets the control's view status to enabled. Disabled controls are visible but not selectable. You can change this in ASP.NET by scripting the control to make it enabled or disabled based on other choices made in the form.

- **Enable Viewstate**—View state is maintained automatically in ASP.NET. This attribute allows you to explicitly disable automatic view maintenance.

- **Visible**—Sets the control to view or be invisible. Normally you would use this attribute only in combination with scripting to make a control visible or invisible based on some other choice made dynamically.

- **Accessibility:**

  - **Tab Index**—Sets the control's order so that you can control the order in which the controls are selected when the user tabs through the page.

  - **Access Key**—Sets a single key to access the control so that the user can access the control from the keyboard. For example, specifying k makes the control accessible by pressing Alt+K.

- **Events:**

  - **OnSelectedIndexChange**—Presents an event when the list changes and is posted back to the server. This is usually used with Auto Postback turned on, which posts the form back to the server when an item on the list is selected.

  - **OnDataBinding**—Presents an event when the control binds data to a data source.

  - **OnDisposed**—Presents an event when the control is released from memory.

  - **OnInit**—Presents an event when the control is initialized.

- **OnLoad**—Presents an event when the control is loaded.

- **OnPreRender**—Presents an event that allows you to script any updates before the output is rendered.

- **OnUnload**—Presents an event when the control is unloaded from memory.

Here's an example:

```
<asp:ListBox
BackColor="#CCCCCC"
DataSource="<%# GetProducts.DefaultView %>"
DataTextField="productname"
DataValueField="productsid"
ID="SelectListID"
Rows="2"
runat="server"
SelectionMode="multiple">
</asp:ListBox>
```

This code sets the data source to the data set called GetProducts that I created with the DataSet server behavior. It then binds the productname field in the database to the DataTextField and the productsid to the DataValueField. The number of rows visible is set to 2 so that there will be scroll arrows if there are three or more results in the list. The selection mode is set to multiple so that people can select more than one item at a time in the control. The BackColor sets the list's background color to light gray. The result looks like Figure 26.5.

FIGURE 26.5
The asp:ListBox control with three results and rows set to 2, showing scrollers.

◉ asp:RadioButton

The asp:RadioButton object inserts an asp:RadioButton element into a form. Radio buttons represent related choices, where only one option can be selected. The asp:RadioButton has attributes that allow for much more control than the standard radio button in HTML.

asp:RadioButton has the following attributes:

- **General:**

  - **ID**—Sets the object's ID so that it can be referred to by name in scripts. This has to be an alphanumeric value. If you use a number alone, you get an error from the server.

  - **Text**—Sets the radio button's label.

  - **Text Alignment**—Specifies whether the text is displayed to the right or left of the check box.

  - **Auto Postback**—Specifies whether the radio box posts the form back to the server.

  - **Checked**—Indicates whether the radio button is selected.

- **Layout:**

  - **Height**—Sets the control's height on the page.

  - **Width**—Sets the control's width on the page.

  - **Border Width**—Sets the width of the control's border.

  - **Background Color**—Sets the control's background color.

  - **Border Color**—Sets the control's border color, creating a beveled look around the control. Borders are always beveled.

  - **Foreground Color**—Sets the control's foreground color.

- **Style Information:**

  - **CSS Class**—Allows you to assign a CSS class to the control's appearance. Like HTML and CSS inheritance, the properties defined in the control directly override properties set in the definition for the class.

  - **Border Style**—The style of the border set with the Border Width and Border Color attributes in the Layout section. The choices are notset, none, dotted, dashed, solid, double, groove, ridge, inset, and outset.

  - **Font Name**—Sets the font name for the display of the text.

  - **Font Names**—Sets a font list that the browser iterates through until it finds a corresponding font it can display.

- **Font Size**—Sets the size of the text label.

- **Bold**—Sets the font to bold.

- **Italic**—Sets the font to italic.

- **Overline**—Produces an overline over the text.

- **Strikeout**—Sets the font to strikeout.

- **Underline**—Produces an underline under the text.

- **Enabled**—Sets the control's view status to enabled. Disabled controls are visible but not selectable. You can change this in ASP.NET by scripting the control to make it enabled or disabled based on other choices made in the form.

- **Enable Viewstate**—View state is maintained automatically in ASP.NET. This attribute allows you to explicitly disable automatic view maintenance.

- **Visible**—Sets the control to view or be invisible. Normally you would use this attribute only in combination with scripting to make a control visible or invisible based on some other choice made dynamically.

- **Accessibility:**

  - **Tool Tip**—Sets a ToolTip for accessibility. This ToolTip should be short, descriptive, and unique for each control.

  - **Tab Index**—Sets the control's order so that you can control the order in which the controls are selected when the user tabs through the page.

  - **Access Key**—Sets a single key to access the control so that the user can access the control from the keyboard. For example, specifying k makes the control accessible by pressing Alt+K.

- **Events:**

  - **OnCheckedChanged**—Presents an event when the control is changed. This stores the function to be executed to be submitted when the form is submitted. If you want the function to fire on the event as the event happens, you need to set the AutoPostBack to true in the dialog box's General tab.

- **OnDataBinding**—Presents an event when the control binds data to a data source.

- **OnDisposed**—Presents an event when the control is released from memory.

- **OnInit**—Presents an event when the control is initialized.

- **OnLoad**—Presents an event when the control is loaded.

- **OnPreRender**—Presents an event that allows you to script any updates before the output is rendered.

- **OnUnload**—Presents an event when the control is unloaded from memory.

The asp:RadioButton object inserts the following code (with most of the attributes set):

```
<asp:RadioButton AccessKey="c"
AutoPostBack="false"
BackColor="#CCCCCC"
BorderColor="#333333"
BorderStyle="groove"
BorderWidth="5"
Checked="true"
CssClass="textstyleforcontrol"
Enabled="true"
EnableViewState="true"
Font-Bold="true"
Font-Italic="false"
Font-Name="Arial"
Font-Names="Times"
Font-Overline="false"
Font-Size="12"
Font-Strikeout="false"
Font-Underline="true"
ForeColor="#FFFFFF"
Height="30"
ID="radio12"
runat="server"
TabIndex="5"
```

```
Text="Blue"
TextAlign="left"
ToolTip="color choice - blue"
Visible="true"
Width="30" />
```

This code produces the control in the browser shown in Figure 26.6.

▤ asp:RadioButtonList

The asp:RadioButtonList object inserts a set of radio buttons from which a user can select a single item. The list can contain any number of items that are pulled from a data source.

asp:RadioButtonList has the following attributes:

- **General:**

  - **ID**—Sets the object's ID so that it can be referred to by name in scripts. This has to be an alphanumeric value. If you use a number alone, you get an error from the server.

  - **Text Alignment**—Sets the text's alignment in the check box list.

  - **Auto Postback**—Specifies whether the control posts the form back to the server.

- **Layout:**

  - **Height**—Sets the control's height on the page.

  - **Width**—Sets the control's width on the page.

  - **Border Width**—Sets the width of the control's border.

  - **Cell Padding**—Sets the HTML Cell Padding attribute to the <FORM> tag that is generated by the server.

  - **Cell Spacing**—Sets the HTML Cell Spacing attribute to the <FORM> tag that is generated by the server.

- **Background Color**—Sets the control's background color.

- **Border Color**—Sets the control's border color, creating a beveled look around the control. Borders are always beveled.

- **Foreground Color**—Sets the control's foreground color.

- **Data:**

  - **Data Member**—Retrieves the specified table in the data source.

  - **Data Source**—Retrieves the data source to use to populate the drop-down list. The data source has to be an object that uses the IEnumerable interface, like the DataView, ArrayList, Hashtable, or DataSet defined on the page from the Server Behavior panel.

  - **Data Text Field**—Sets the field in the data source to use as the text label for each item—that is, the text that appears on the menu.

  - **Data Text Format String**—Sets the formatting string used to set the format of the data displayed in the list control.

  - **Data Value Field**—Sets the field in the data source to use as the value for each item that appears on the menu.

  - **Repeat Columns**—Sets the number of columns to display in the control.

  - **Repeat Direction**—Sets the control to display the RadioButtons either vertically or horizontally.

  - **Repeat Layout**—Sets the output to be in a table or in regular HTML flow.

- **Style Information:**

  - **CSS Class**—Allows you to assign a CSS class to the control's appearance. Like HTML and CSS inheritance, the properties defined in the control directly override properties set in the definition for the class.

  - **Font Name**—Sets the font name for the display of the text.

  - **Font Names**—Sets a font list that the browser iterates through until it finds a corresponding font it can display.

- **Font Size**—Sets the size of the text label.

- **Bold**—Sets the font to bold.

- **Italic**—Sets the font to italic.

- **Overline**—Produces an overline over the text.

- **Strkeout**—Sets the font to strikeout.

- **Underline**—Produces an underline under the text.

- **Enabled**—Sets the control's view status to enabled. Disabled controls are visible but not selectable. You can change this in ASP.NET by scripting the control to make it enabled or disabled based on other choices made in the form.

- **Enable Viewstate**—View state is maintained automatically in ASP.NET. This attribute allows you to explicitly disable automatic view maintenance.

- **Visible**—Sets the control to view or be invisible. Normally you would use this attribute only in combination with scripting to make a control visible or invisible based on some other choice made dynamically.

- **Accessibility:**

  - **Tab Index**—Sets the control's order so that you can control the order in which the controls are selected when the user tabs through the page.

  - **Access Key**—Sets a single key to access the control so that the user can access the control from the keyboard. For example, specifying k makes the control accessible by pressing Alt+K.

- **Events:**

  - **OnSelectedIndexChange**—Presents an event when the list changes and is posted back to the server. This is usually used with Auto Postback turned on, which posts the form back to the server when an item on the list is selected.

  - **OnDataBinding**—Presents an event when the control binds data to a data source.

- **OnDisposed**—Presents an event when the control is released from memory.

- **OnInit**—Presents an event when the control is initialized.

- **OnLoad**—Presents an event when the control is loaded.

- **OnPreRender**—Presents an event that allows you to script any updates before the output is rendered.

- **OnUnload**—Presents an event when the control is unloaded from memory.

Here's an example:

```
<asp:RadioButtonList BorderColor="#000000"
BorderWidth="1"
CellPadding="2"
DataSource="<%# GetProducts.DefaultView %>"
DataTextField="productname"
DataValueField="productsid"
ID="SelectRadioList"
runat="server"
RepeatColumns="2"
RepeatDirection="Horizontal"
RepeatLayout="table"
TextAlign="left">
</asp:RadioButtonList>
```

This code sets the data source to the data set called GetProducts that I created with the DataSet server behavior. It then binds the productname field in the database to the DataTextField and the productsid to the DataValueField. The RepeatDirection is set to horizontal, and the Repeat-Layout is set to put the radio buttons in a table. The table is set to have a BorderWidth of 1 and a CellPadding of 2 and to have two columns. Note that the border is set as a CSS style in the `<TABLE>` tag and not with the HTML attribute of BORDER. The result looks like Figure 26.7.

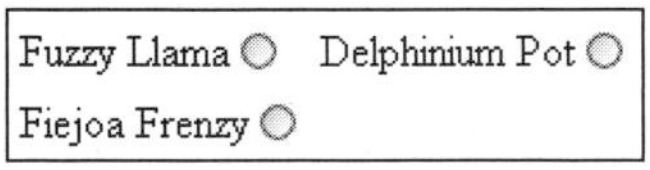

FIGURE 26.7
The asp:Radio-ButtonList control in the browser with RepeatDirection set to horizontal and RepeatLayout set to table.

ab asp:TextBox

The asp:TextBox object inserts an asp:TextBox element into a form. Text boxes can be single line, multiline, or password.

asp:TextBox has the following attributes:

- **General:**

  - **ID**—Sets the object's ID so that it can be referred to by name in scripts. This has to be an alphanumeric value. If you use a number alone, you get an error from the server.

  - **Text**—Sets the control's label.

  - **Text Mode**—Allows you to set the text box to have the text be either single line, multiline, or password.

  - **Rows**—Specifies how many rows to show in the control if the Text Mode is set to multiline.

  - **Columns**—Sets the control's width in characters, as opposed to Width, which sets the control's visual width in the browser.

  - **Max Length**—The maximum number of characters allowed in the text box.

  - **Auto Postback**—Specifies whether the control posts the form back to the server.

  - **Read-only**—Specifies whether the contents of the textfield can be modified.

  - **Wrap**—Sets the element to wrap entered text. This has no effect unless the Text Mode is set to multiline.

- **Layout:**

  - **Height**—Sets the control's height on the page.

  - **Width**—Sets the control's width on the page.

  - **Border Width**—Sets the width of the control's border.

  - **Background Color**—Sets the control's background color.

- **Border Color**—Sets the control's border color, creating a beveled look around the control. Borders are always beveled.

- **Foreground Color**—Sets the control's foreground color.

- **Style Information:**

  - **CSS Class**—Allows you to assign a CSS class to the control's appearance. Like HTML and CSS inheritance, the properties defined in the control directly override properties set in the definition for the class.

  - **Border Style**—The style of the border set with the Border Width and Border Color attributes in the Layout section. The choices are notset, none, dotted, dashed, solid, double, groove, ridge, inset, and outset.

  - **Font Name**—Sets the font name for the display of the text.

  - **Font Names**—Sets a font list that the browser iterates through until it finds a corresponding font it can display.

  - **Font Size**—Sets the size of the text label.

  - **Bold**—Sets the font to bold.

  - **Italic**—Sets the font to italic.

  - **Overline**—Produces an overline over the text.

  - **Strkeout**—Sets the font to strikeout.

  - **Underline**—Produces an underline under the text.

  - **Enabled**—Sets the control's view status to enabled. Disabled controls are visible but not selectable. You can change this in ASP.NET by scripting the control to make it enabled or disabled based on other choices made in the form.

  - **Enable Viewstate**—View state is maintained automatically in ASP.NET. This attribute allows you to explicitly disable automatic view maintenance.

- **Visible**—Sets the control to view or be invisible. Normally you would use this attribute only in combination with scripting to make a control visible or invisible based on some other choice made dynamically.

- **Accessibility:**

  - **Tool Tip**—Sets a ToolTip for accessibility. This ToolTip should be short, descriptive, and unique for each control.

  - **Tab Index**—Sets the control's order so that you can control the order in which the controls are selected when the user tabs through the page.

  - **Access Key**—Sets a single key to access the control so that the user can access the control from the keyboard. For example, specifying k makes the control accessible by pressing Alt+K.

- **Events:**

  - **OnCheckedChanged**—Presents an event when the control is changed. This stores the function to be executed to be submitted when the form is submitted. If you want the function to fire on the event as the event happens, you need to set the AutoPostBack to true in the dialog box's General tab.

  - **OnDataBinding**—Presents an event when the control binds data to a data source.

  - **OnDisposed**—Presents an event when the control is released from memory.

  - **OnInit**—Presents an event when the control is initialized.

  - **OnLoad**—Presents an event when the control is loaded.

  - **OnPreRender**—Presents an event that allows you to script any updates before the output is rendered.

  - **OnUnload**—Presents an event when the control is unloaded from memory.

The asp:TextBox object inserts the following code (with most of the attributes set):

```
<asp:TextBox Columns="50"
ID="textarea2"
MaxLength="100"
Rows="5"
runat="server"
Text="Enter your comments here."
TextMode="MultiLine" />
```

This code produces the control in the browser shown in Figure 26.8.

FIGURE 26.8
The asp:TextBox control in the browser.

⌨ More Tags

The More Tags object opens the Tag Chooser dialog box, shown in Figure 26.9. Here you have access to many more ASP.NET objects to insert into the page. For complete details on these objects, check out the "Resources" section at the end of this chapter, where a number of ASP.NET resources are listed.

FIGURE 26.9
The Tag Chooser dialog box.

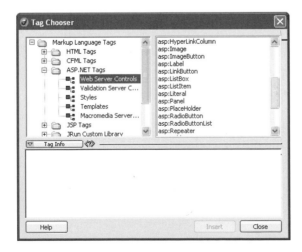

EXERCISE 26.1	## Using the DataGrid

You need to have Microsoft IIS up and running on the machine. You need to have the ASP.NET Framework installed, and the service needs to be running. You also need to have a web browser installed and running.

Create a new folder in your web root called **gardenshop**, where you will build your application. Unzip the support files for this chapter (available from this book's website at www.peachpit.com) into the gardenshop folder. Browse to **test.aspx** in the browser. You can't use the File > Open functionality to access the page; the server wouldn't know how to serve the file. Therefore, you have to browse to it. For instance, your address line might look like this:

http://127.0.0.1/gardenshop/test.aspx

Here are the contents of **test.aspx**:

```
<script runat="server" language="vb">
Sub Page_Load(Src As Object, E As EventArgs)
    labelText.Text = "Your ASP.NET server is up and running"
End Sub
</script>

<html>
<head>
<title>test</title>
</head>
<body>
<asp:Label ID="labelText" runat="server"></asp:Label>
</body>
</html>
```

When you browse to the file, you should see this:

Your ASP.NET server is up and running

If you get an error saying that the server application is unavailable, you need to go into the IIS Administrator and set the gardenshop folder's Directory Properties to match Figure 26.10.

FIGURE 26.10
IIS Administrator showing the properties for the gardenshop website.

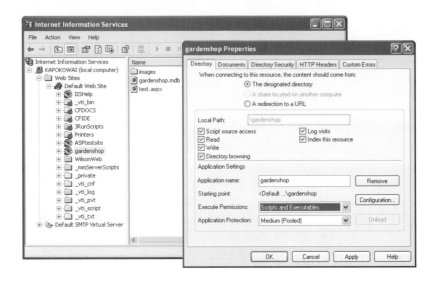

Setting up the Site in Dreamweaver

Now that you have the server set up and working, and the gardenshop folder set up, you are ready to set up the site in Dreamweaver and get going with the DataGrid. We assume that you know how to set up a site in Dreamweaver. In this case, you want to set up a site called "The Garden Shop." Set the Local Info to have your local site as the gardenshop folder in your web root that you set up in the last step. As shown in Figure 26.11, set the testing server to have a server model of ASP.NET VB. Set the access to Local/Network and then point that to the gardenshop folder.

After you set up the site, there is one more thing you need to do with an ASP.NET site. You need to deploy the Macromedia custom controls that let you use all the server behaviors that are included with Dreamweaver.

1. Select Site > Advanced > Deploy Supporting Files.

2. In the Deploy Supporting Files To Testing Server dialog box, select the bin directory that will be in the root of your web server, and click Deploy. If you don't have a bin directory in your site root, you need to create that folder first.

   In my case, that path is C:\Inetpub\wwwroot\gardenshop\bin\.

If you don't put the files in the right place, you get an error when the page is served that says that the server cannot find all the components. The error kindly lists all the locations the server is looking in to find the controls. You can simply take one of these paths (it looks in several places), enter it in the Deploy dialog box, and redeploy the support files.

FIGURE 26.11
The Site Definition dialog box for The Garden Shop with the testing server information filled in.

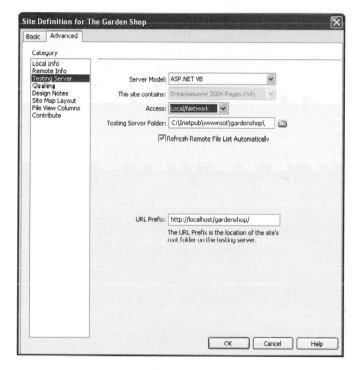

Inserting a DataGrid

The DataGrid is an amazing server control that is available in Dreamweaver. It is the be-all-and-end-all of displaying data to the page. What would take quite a while and thought to set up in ColdFusion or ASP takes only seconds to lay out in a DataGrid in ASP.NET.

You will create a new page in the Garden Shop site, create a connection to the sample **gardenshop.mdb** database, and insert a DataSet to get values for the DataGrid to display.

1. Select File > New, and select a new ASP.NET VB page.

2. Change the title of the file to View Products, and save the file as **viewproducts.aspx** in the gardenshop folder.

3. Make sure that the Server Behavior panel is showing.

4. Click the + button to add a server behavior, and select DataSet.

5. You need to have a connection to the database defined, so click the Define button.

6. In the Connections for Site 'The Garden Shop' dialog box, click the New button, and select OLE DB from the drop-down.

7. In the OLE DB Connection dialog box, name the connection GardenShopConn, and click the Build button.

8. Click the Provider tab of the Data Link Properties, and select Microsoft Jet 4.0 OLE DB Provider from the list of available connectors.

9. Click Next to go to the Connection tab, and browse to the **garden-shop.mdb** file in the gardenshop folder. Leave the user name blank, and test the connection. If it doesn't succeed, check that you selected the Microsoft Jet 4.0 OLE DB Provider.

    Click OK to close the Data Link Properties dialog box. Your OLE DB Connection dialog box should look like Figure 26.12.

FIGURE 26.12
The OLE DB Connection dialog box showing the settings for the GardenShopConn.

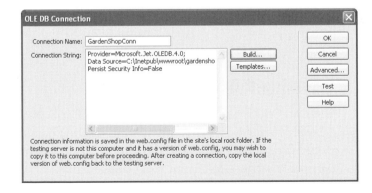

10. Click OK to close the OLE DB Connection dialog box. Click Done to close the Connections dialog box.

11. Name the DataSet Get Products. In the Connection drop-down in the DataSet dialog box, select your new GardenShopConn connection.

12. Select tableProducts from the Table drop-down, and click OK. You will select everything in the table.

You should have a DataSet on the page from which the DataGrid can get values to populate itself. You are ready to insert the DataGrid.

1. Click in the page, and make sure you are in Design view.

2. Select Insert > Application Objects > Dynamic Data > DataGrid. You can also insert a DataGrid from the Dynamic Data icon of the Application section of the Insert bar.

3. In the DataGrid dialog box, set the ID to ViewProducts.

4. Select the GetProducts DataSet you just created in the DataSet drop-down.

5. Show three records at a time.

6. Set the Navigation drop-down to Links to Previous and Next Pages. Your dialog box should look like Figure 26.13.

FIGURE 26.13
The DataGrid dialog box.

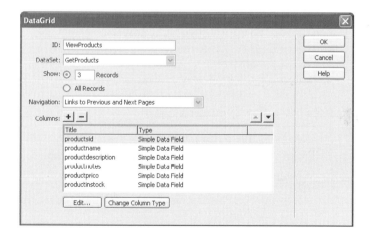

7. Click OK to close the dialog box. A placeholder for the DataGrid is inserted onto the page.

8. Save your page.

9. Preview your page in the browser. You should see something like what appears in Figure 26.14.

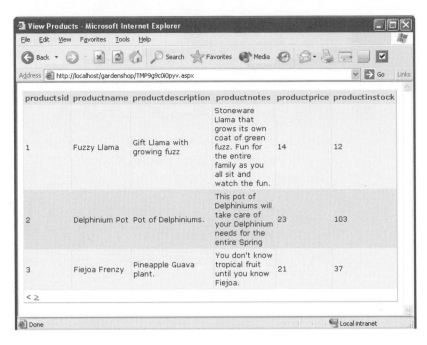

You now have a formatted table displaying data from the database in rows of alternating color with page navigation, all in one action.

This is pretty nice, but you're not done yet! You will add a way to edit data in each record without creating any more forms or pages. You can do all this directly in the DataGrid.

1. In the Server Behavior panel, double-click DataGrid (ShowProducts) to get the DataGrid dialog box back onscreen.

2. Select the productsid column in the Columns area. Click the Change Column Type button, and select Edit > Update and Cancel from the drop-down menu.

3. In the Edit, Update, Cancel Button Column dialog box, set the following values:

   Title—Edit

   Button Type—Push Button

   Update Table—tableProducts

   Primary Key—productsid

   Submit As—Integer

The dialog box should look like Figure 26.15.

FIGURE 26.15
The Edit, Update,
Cancel Button Column
dialog box.

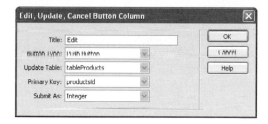

4. Click OK to close the Edit, Update, Cancel Button Column dialog box.

5. Select the productnotes column in the Columns area. Click the Change Column Type button, and click the Edit button.

6. In the Simple Data Field Column dialog box, uncheck the Read Only check box, and then click OK.

7. Repeat steps 5 and 6 for the productprice column.

8. Click OK to close the DataGrid, and save the page.

9. Preview the page in the browser. You should see something like what appears in Figure 26.16.

FIGURE 26.16
The DataGrid served
in the browser with
edit buttons added.

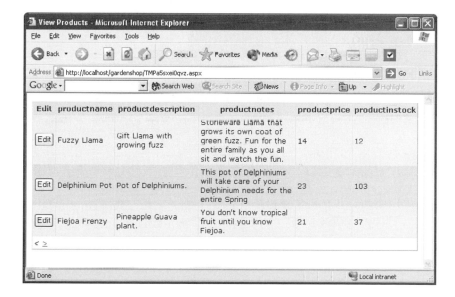

10. Test your edit button by clicking one of the edit buttons, changing the product notes or the price, and then clicking Update.

You can make right your simple edits in the DataGrid rather than having to create a separate update form. You can also insert Delete buttons to delete items from the database. If you believe, as I do, that the more pages you have in a site, the more potential you have for mistakes to occur, doing all this work in one place is easy.

You can apply many other options to the DataGrid. This information would require several chapters. Check out some of the resources listed next for more samples and exercises.

ASP.NET Resources

Many good resources for ASP.NET are available. The following lists a few that are of great value. You might find that these lead you to other resources that make your ASP.NET coding easier and more powerful.

- *SAMS Teach Yourself SQL in 10 Minutes*. Ben Forta. Sams Publishing. The very best resource for SQL. Small, simple, and complete. No coder should be without it.

- *ASP.NET for Web Designers*. Peter Ladka. New Riders. A very good and enjoyable book for people who want to understand the code. It isn't too complicated, but you will do best with this book if you are comfortable looking at code.

- *Visual Quickpro Guide: ASP.NET Development with Macromedia Dreamweaver MX*. Ryan Parnell and Joel Martinez. Peachpit Press. An excellent and concise guide to using ASP.NET in Dreamweaver.

- ASPXtreme ASP.NET Web WorkShop, `http://www.aspalliance.com/aspxtreme/index.aspx`. An excellent resource that has technical documentation, tutorials, and many other resources.

- MSDN Developer Library, `http://msdn.microsoft.com/nhp/default.asp?contentid=28000440`. The source for documentation. All levels of articles and information are available.

SUMMARY

Dreamweaver MX 2004 includes excellent support for ASP.NET. You can use the extensive set of form controls to create and format smart forms that draw their content from the database. You can use the DataGrid to display your dynamic information in a few clicks. This would take much more work in other server models. With what you have learned in this chapter, you should be able to create fairly complex applications. If you want to move to the next level of creating ASP.NET applications, you might want to check out *Macromedia Dreamweaver MX 2004 and Databases* by Sean Nicholson, published by New Riders.

PART VI:

DREAMWEAVER UNDER THE HOOD

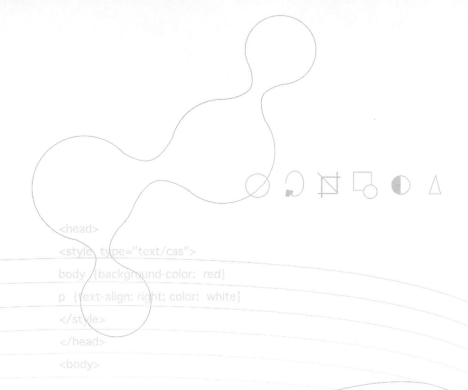

```
<head>
<style type="text/css">
body {background-color: red}
p {text-align: right; color: white}
</style>
</head>
<body>
```

CHAPTER 27

WRITING CODE IN DREAMWEAVER

DREAMWEAVER MX 2004 IS A LOT OF THINGS TO A LOT OF PEOPLE, BUT AT heart it's a code-editing tool. This chapter reviews the Dreamweaver built-in text editor and covers how to make the most of it; how to facilitate working with Dreamweaver and external text editors, such as HomeSite and BBEdit; and how you can use Dreamweaver with more than just HTML, embracing various markup and scripting languages such as XML and JavaScript.

USING DREAMWEAVER AS A TEXT EDITOR

The power of Dreamweaver has always been its close integration between visual and text-based editing. The program's built-in text editor, accessible through the Document window's Code view, or the Code portion of Code and Design view, or the separate Code Inspector panel, offers many features generally found only in dedicated text-editing programs. These include line numbers, word wrap control, syntax-based color coding, complex text searches using regular expressions, and several features adopted from HomeSite, such as code hints and tag completion. In addition, because the Dreamweaver text editor also is responsible for writing the code created when you work in Design view, it includes built-in source formatting and error-correction functions.

Accessing the Text Editor

You can access the Dreamweaver text editor from the main Document window by choosing Code view or Code and Design view. (For a full discussion of the Document window, see Chapter 2, "The Dreamweaver Workspace.") Alternatively, you can open the text editor in its own tabbed panel window by accessing the Code Inspector (choose Window > Code Inspector). All text-editing features work the same in both Code view and the Code Inspector. If you're short on screen space, you'll probably want to use Code view (or Code and Design view) in the Document window. If you have a dual monitor setup at your workstation, you might prefer to display the Document window, set to Design view, on one monitor and the Code Inspector, along with any other open panels, on the other monitor. Figure 27.1 shows Code view and the Code Inspector, side-by-side for comparison.

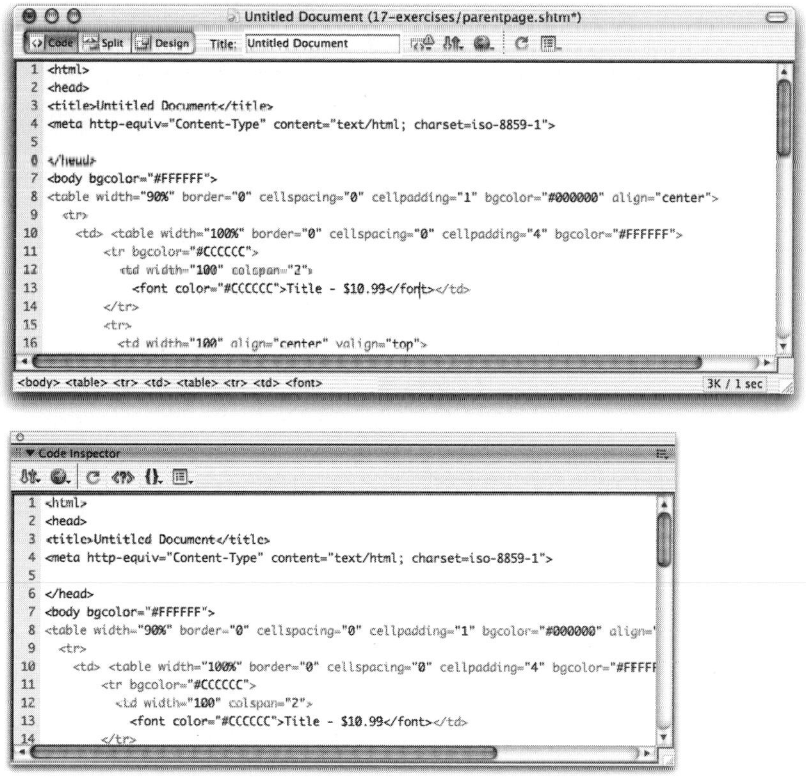

FIGURE 27.1
The Dreamweaver
built-in text editor as
it appears in Code
view in the main
Document window
(top) and in the sep-
arate Code Inspector
panel (bottom).

Code View Options and Preferences

Options for setting up the text editor's workspace can be found on the
Code View Options menu, which is accessible from the View menu, the
Document toolbar, or the Code Inspector toolbar (see Figure 27.2). Note
that only choices made in the Code Inspector toolbar affect the display
in that panel. Choosing from the Document toolbar or from the View
menu affects only the Document window's Code view display.

Preferences for other aspects of code display can be found in various categories of the Preferences dialog box (select Edit > Preferences). Choices
made here affect both Code view and the Code Inspector.

FIGURE 27.2

Accessing the Code
View Options menu
from the Document
toolbar and from the
View menu.

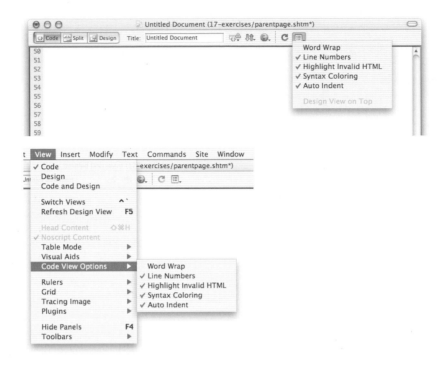

Setting Text Size and Font

By default, all text in the code editor is displayed in 10-point Courier
New (Windows) or 10-point Monaco (Macintosh). Because this text is
used only to display code in Dreamweaver, you can change the size/font
to anything that suits you without affecting your files.

You might prefer to put your code in "large-print" format for easy
onscreen reading without squinting. Or you might prefer to look at
fonts other than Courier or Monaco. One bit of advice, however:
Certain text-editing tasks, such as counting characters, are much easier
to perform on monospaced fonts (such as Courier and Monaco) than
on proportionally spaced fonts.

To change the text size or font of the code display, open the Preferences
dialog box (select Edit > Preferences) and select the Fonts category, as
shown in Figure 27.3.

FIGURE 27.3
Setting the text size and font in the Fonts dialog box.

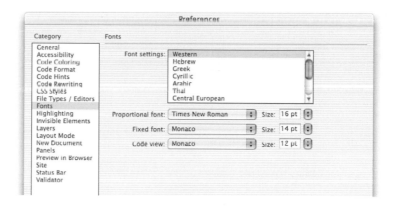

Syntax Coloring

One of the most useful visual aids in text processing is syntax-based color coding. By setting certain code elements to certain colors, you can tell at a glance how a document is structured. Dreamweaver goes a step further, allowing you to set other styling attributes, such as bold, italic, and underlining, to differentiate different syntax elements. You also can specify different formatting options for different document types (HTML, PHP, JS, and so forth).

To turn syntax coloring (and styling) on or off, choose Code View Options > Syntax Coloring.

The Reference panel's context-based lookup works only if syntax coloring is on.

To customize which elements are assigned which color and styling, open the Preferences dialog box, and select the Code Coloring category (see Figure 27.4). Choose the document type whose styling you want to change, and click the Edit Coloring Scheme button. In the new dialog box that opens, choose any element from the list in the upper left; choose color and styling options from the options in the upper right. You can see how your changes will look in the preview area at the bottom of the panel, as shown in Figure 27.4.

FIGURE 27.4
Customizing the code coloring and styling in the Code Coloring dialog box and Edit Coloring Scheme dialog box.

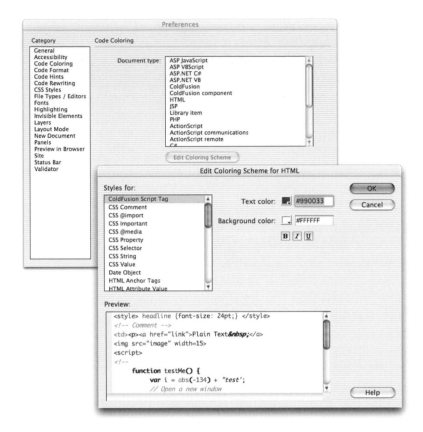

Line Numbers

Line numbers are handy for finding exactly where something happens in the code. They're mostly useful for web pages that involve scripting, as an aid to debugging (see "Writing JavaScript in Dreamweaver," later in this chapter, for more on this). Dreamweaver reports and invalid-code warnings also use line numbers for identification.

To show or hide line numbers, choose Code View Options > Line Numbers.

Word Wrap (Soft Wrapping)

Wrapping means sending text to a new line. In text-processing terms, *soft wrapping* is something the text editor does on-the-fly to make the text fit in the window. The Dreamweaver code editor lets you view your code with or without soft wrapping. Viewing code that has no wrapping often involves a lot of sideways scrolling to read long lines. Not being able to see an entire line at a time can make it more difficult to understand what's happening in the code. On the other hand, code displayed without wrapping more accurately conveys a document's overall structure. Figure 27.5 shows the differences between code with and without soft wrapping.

FIGURE 27.5

An HTML code fragment shown with (top) and without (bottom) soft wrapping.

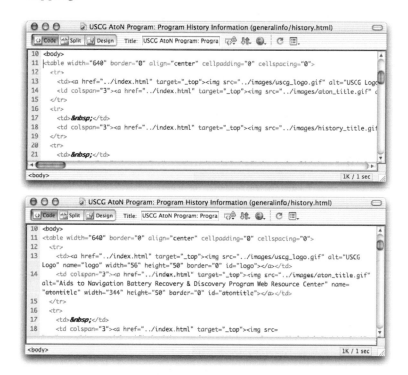

To turn soft wrapping on or off, choose Code View Options > Word Wrap. Note that if you work with line numbers showing, soft wrap doesn't affect line numbering because wrapping is a temporary visual convenience only. If you save a file created with soft wrapping on and then you open it in another editor, no soft wraps will have been saved as part of the file.

Auto-Indenting

Indenting lines of code to indicate nested elements is another way to make code more easily readable. Lines are indented by adding tabs or spaces. When you manually enter code into the Dreamweaver text editor, you indent your lines as you see fit. As you're typing, the Dreamweaver Auto-Indent feature automatically indents each new line to match the indent of the previous line. This is a handy timesaver if you're coding nested tags, where each tag's indent is based on the indent of the preceding tag.

To automatically indent each new line based on current indents, choose Code View Options > Auto-Indent.

Code Formatting Options

Although the Dreamweaver built-in code editor is in many ways comparable to other text-editing software, in one way it is unique. When you author in Design view, Dreamweaver writes—and formats—the source code for you. When you author in Code view, you are in charge of formatting your own source code. When you move freely between Code and Design view, you might write code that Dreamweaver will later edit and reformat. This is called *applying source formatting*. It's rather like having Mom looking over your shoulder as you work, tidying up after you, making sure you've indented properly, wrapped your text nicely, and so forth.

Dreamweaver (almost) never rewrites your code, but it will reformat it if you let it. Dreamweaver automatically applies source formatting to a page element whenever that item is edited from within Design view. You can force the program to apply source formatting to an entire document or to a selection within a document by choosing Commands > Apply Source Formatting or Commands > Apply Source Formatting to Selection.

Like Mom, this source formatting can be intrusive or helpful, depending on your point of view. You can turn the different aspects of source formatting on and off, and you can customize what kind of formatting is applied. Most of this customizing can be done in the Preferences dialog box, under the Code Format category, as shown in Figure 27.6. Some customizing requires tinkering with tag libraries (discussed later in this chapter).

FIGURE 27.6
The Preferences dialog box showing the Code Format category.

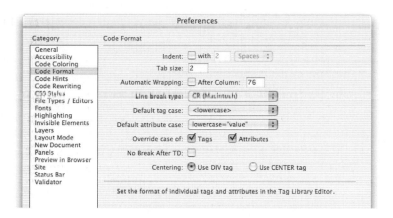

Automatic Text Wrap (Hard Wrapping)

Hard wraps are returns coded into the text using a carriage return (CR), line feed (LF), or both. As you're coding, every time you press Enter you're hard wrapping. Just as you might use soft wrapping to make your code more readable, some web authors like to insert manual (hard) returns into the code to force line breaks for easier readability. When Dreamweaver writes code for you (that is, when you're working in Design view), by default it adds hard wraps to avoid long lines of code. When you type your own code, you control the hard wraps by deciding when to press Enter. Even when you enter the code yourself, however, as soon as you edit it in Design view or choose one of the Apply Source Formatting commands, Dreamweaver takes over and adds its own hard wraps wherever it finds excessively long lines.

Hard wrap or soft wrap? If you rely on soft wrapping to display more-readable code, switching between wrapped and unwrapped views is as simple as turning Word Wrap on and off. If you rely on hard wrapping, your code's line breaks are fixed unless you manually remove them. In addition, although hard wraps do not affect how a document appears on the web, CRs and LFs are characters and take up file space. Long documents can take slightly longer to download if their coding contains many hard wraps.

To control automatic hard wrapping, select Preferences > Code Format. You see the dialog box shown in Figure 27.7. If the Automatic Wrapping option is disabled, no hard wraps will be added within a tag or text element, no matter how long the line becomes. If this option is enabled, you can specify how many characters Dreamweaver should allow in a line before it adds a hard wrap. Note that if you work with line numbers showing, hard wrapping affects the line numbers because it adds lines to the code. If you save a file created with hard wrapping on, and you open it in another editor, the hard wraps will still be there. They are part of the file.

FIGURE 27.7
The Code Rewriting dialog box.

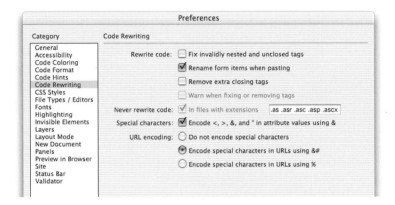

To determine how hard wraps are encoded, select Preferences > Code Format and choose one of the Line Break options from the pop-up menu. This is important because different operating systems expect hard returns to be coded differently. Obviously, you want the web server where your pages will reside to recognize your hard wraps for what they are. If you will be uploading your pages using FTP set to ASCII Transfer mode, Dreamweaver takes care of this for you, coding each return character as needed based on the server's OS. If you will be uploading your HTML documents using FTP set to Binary mode, you must set the correct return character yourself before uploading.

Indenting

Do you like your code indented? How large an indent do you prefer? Do you want your indents to consist of tab or space characters? The controls in the Code Format dialog box determine how and when Dreamweaver indents your code during source formatting:

- **Indent or don't indent**—To turn indenting off completely, so that all new lines are flush left, deselect the Use option. Selecting the Use option enables all the other choices controlling indentation.

- **Tabs/spaces**—You can specify whether indents should be created from tab characters or multiple spaces. Generally, spaces are preferable unless you plan to import your text to a word processing program for eventual printing.

- **Indent size**—Determines how many spaces or tabs each indent will have.

- **Tab size**—Determines, in characters, how big each tab will be. (If you tell Dreamweaver to calculate your indents in tabs, and you set the indent size to 2 and the tab size to 3, each indent will be 6 characters wide.)

Case Control

Standard HTML browsers aren't case-sensitive when interpreting HTML. But any browser or other device that uses XML or XHTML validation is case-sensitive. In addition, many web authors prefer their code to be written consistently in one case (upper or lower).

To specify a case for code that Dreamweaver writes, in the Code Format dialog box set the Default Tag Case and Default Attribute Case (refer back to Figure 27.6).

To have Dreamweaver change the case of existing code during source formatting, choose one or both of the Override Case Of options.

Code Rewriting

Dreamweaver promises to never rewrite your code. Well, almost never. There are a few special circumstances when you might want a tiny bit of rewriting. They're all governed by the Code Rewriting dialog box (refer to Figure 27.7).

Fixing Invalid Code

Dreamweaver warns you about, and optionally tries to fix, any invalid code it sees. Invalid code consists mainly of incorrectly nested or closed tags, such as the following:

```
<b><i>This is bad nesting! </b></i>

<h1>I have too many tags!</h1></h1>

<h6>I'm missing something...
```

To display or hide warnings for invalid code, choose Code View Options > Highlight Invalid HTML. (Note that this option governs only the various Code views. Dreamweaver always highlights invalid HTML in Design view.) To allow Dreamweaver to fix the invalid code, select Preferences > Code Rewriting and set the options as desired there (refer to Figure 27.7).

To exclude file types from error checking, go to the Code Rewriting dialog box and add the file extension to the Never Rewrite Code options list. Each new file extension must be separated from the others in the list by spaces on either side.

Dreamweaver performs its error checking, and optional error fixing, whenever a document is opened. If you have set your preferences to Warn When Fixing or Removing Tags, at this point Dreamweaver opens an alert window specifying any invalid code found and how it has been fixed. If you haven't turned the warning feature on, you won't even be aware that code is being rewritten.

Why would you want to turn warnings on? Although fixing invalid code is, in theory, a good thing, Dreamweaver isn't always perfect in determining what the desired valid code should look like. For instance, here's a segment of code with a missing `</h1>` tag:

```
<html>
<head>
<title>My Page</title>
</head>
<body bgcolor="#FFFFFF" text="#000000">
<h1>My Home Page
<p>Welcome to my wonderful website.</p>
</body>
</html>
```

Where should the closing tag be inserted? Directly in front of the `<p>` tag, probably. Here's where Dreamweaver inserts it:

```
<html>
<head>
<title>My Page</title>
</head>
```

```
<body bgcolor="#FFFFFF" text="#000000">
<h1>My Home Page
<p>Welcome to my wonderful website.</p>
</h1></body>
</html>
```

This is definitely an occasion when author intervention is needed to correct the Dreamweaver error correction. Figure 27.8 shows the warning message that appears when Dreamweaver opens a document containing this code.

FIGURE 27.8

The Dreamweaver alert window listing invalid code that has been fixed in a document.

Note that the Dreamweaver alert window doesn't give you the opportunity to cancel the code rewriting. If you don't like any of the changes that have been made to your code, you can isolate them (by turning on line numbering in the code editor and using the line references from the alert message) and fix them, or you can just close the document without saving, and all changes are ignored. From there, either open the document in another text editor, or select Preferences > Code Rewriting and temporarily disable the rewriting features.

URL Encoding

By default, Dreamweaver also applies URL encoding to spaces and other nonstandard characters in URLs. A link to a page such as **my page.html** is written as **my%20page.html**. Dreamweaver applies this encoding automatically to any URLs as it notices them. If you enter the URL while working in Design view (for instance, entering it into the Property Inspector's Link field), the encoding is immediately applied in Code view. If you type in the URL while working in Code view, Dreamweaver doesn't apply the encoding until you switch to Design view and edit the URL (through the Property Inspector, for instance).

To control how, and whether, Dreamweaver encodes URLs, select Preferences > Code Rewriting and choose one of the following options for URL Encoding:

- **Do not encode special characters.**

- **Encode special characters in URLs using &#**—This replaces the special character with an HTML entity if one exists—&quot for an apostrophe, for instance.

- **Encode special characters in URLs using %**—This replaces the special character with an ASCII code, such as %20 for a space or %27 for an apostrophe.

Code Writing and Editing

In addition to helping you format your code for readability and display, the Dreamweaver text editor offers a variety of tools to make working with the code easier.

Editing Commands and Shortcuts

If you like working with code, presumably you like typing. A few commands on the Edit menu, each with its own keyboard shortcut, can keep you typing instead of reaching for the mouse while you work. Table 27.1 lists these commands.

TABLE 27.1 ## Code-Editing Commands

Command	Keystroke		Description
	Windows	**Macintosh**	
Select parent tag	Ctrl+Shift+<	Cmd+Shift+<	Selects any tag completely nesting the current selection.

Command	Keystroke		Description
	Windows	**Macintosh**	
Select child	Ctrl+Shift+>	Cmd+Shift+>	Selects the first tag nested within the currently selected tag.
Indent code	Ctrl+]	Cmd+]	Increases the indent level of a selected line by one.
Outdent code	Ctrl+[	Cmd+[	Reduces the indent level of a selected line by one.

Code Hints

Code hints engages every time you type the opening characters of a tag, offering drop-down menus of possible tags, attributes, and even attribute values (see Figure 27.9). These hints aren't just for reference. You can navigate through and choose from any menu without moving your hands from the keyboard, for maximum efficiency. The main techniques for navigating the hint menus are as follows:

- By default, the first item in the hint menu is selected. To move down or up in the list, use the arrow keys on the keyboard.

- Menus containing lists of text items are arranged alphabetically. To jump to a particular place in the list, type the first letter of the item you want to select. Keep typing more letters to get closer to your desired selection.

- Depending on the values expected for an attribute, different hint menus appear. If the expected value is a color, the color picker appears (use the arrow keys to navigate through the swatches). If the expected value is a relative file path, a menu containing only a browse option appears (press Enter to open a browse dialog box). If the expected value is unspecified text or a number, no code hint appears. Figure 27.10 shows the color palette code hint menu.

- To choose a selected item and have Dreamweaver enter it in your code for you, press Enter. The item is inserted, and the insertion point is positioned so that you can continue typing.

FIGURE 27.9
Code hints at work,
presenting a menu of
possible attributes
for the table tag.

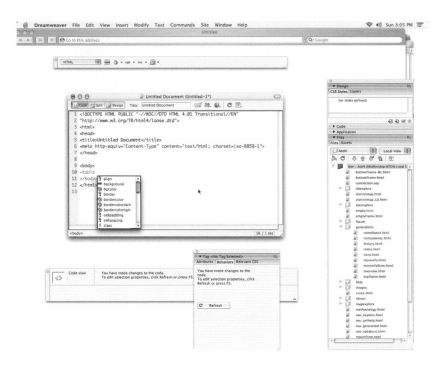

FIGURE 27.9
Code hints at work,
presenting a menu of
possible attributes
for the table tag.

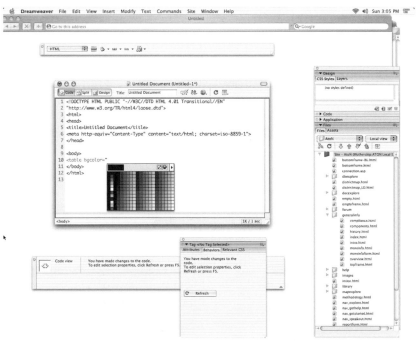

FIGURE 27.10
Using code hints to
choose a color value
for the bgcolor
attribute.

To configure code hints, select Preferences > Code Hints (see Figure 27.11). From here, you can enable or disable code hints. You also can configure the following aspects:

- The Delay slider determines how quickly after you type the menus of code hints appear. With a delay of 0, each hint menu appears immediately. With a longer delay, the menus don't appear unless you stop typing for the specified number of seconds. If you don't like hint menus popping up all over the place, but you still want to take advantage of them the next time you get stuck or feel lazy, set the delay to a few seconds, and see how you like it.

- The list of Menus determines which code hint menus appear. Do you want Dreamweaver to finish typing tag names for you, or just suggest attributes? Do you want suggestions for each attribute's value, where appropriate? To edit the contents of the hint menus, you can click the link to the Tag Library Editor. (For more on this, see the section "Tag Libraries and the Tag Library Editor" later in this chapter.)

FIGURE 27.11
The Preferences dialog box showing the Code Hints category, which governs code hints and auto tag completion.

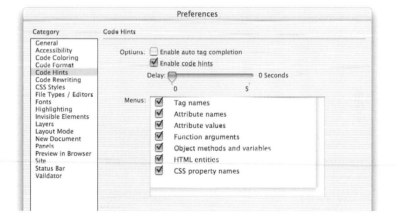

Auto Tag Completion

Auto tag completion engages every time you type the opening tag of a pair, causing Dreamweaver to automatically type the closing tag, leaving the insertion point between the two tags. If you type <p>, you get </p>, and the cursor is correctly positioned to type the text you want between the two tags, as shown in Figure 27.12. If you've ever forgotten to type that closing tag, and then wondered why your page wouldn't preview properly, this is the feature for you!

FIGURE 27.12
Auto tag completion
at work, creating an
italic section of a
page heading.

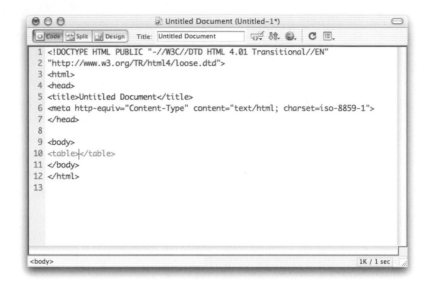

To turn auto tag completion on or off, select Preferences > Code Hints, as shown in Figure 27.13.

FIGURE 27.13
The Snippets panel,
part of the Code
panel group.

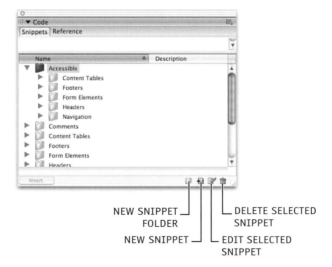

NEW SNIPPET — FOLDER

NEW SNIPPET —

DELETE SELECTED SNIPPET

EDIT SELECTED SNIPPET

Code Snippets

Snippets allow you to save frequently needed chunks of code and insert them into a document with a few mouse clicks. Snippets can be used to store anything from comments to formatting wrapped around a selection to entire tables and page layouts.

Using the Snippets Panel

Snippets are created, organized, and inserted using the Snippets panel, which is part of the Code panel group. Access this panel by choosing Window > Snippets, or by expanding the docked panel interface to view the Code panels and bringing the Snippets tab to the front. Figure 27.13 shows the Snippets panel in all its glory. Dreamweaver ships with a wide selection of snippets ready for you to use.

Inserting Snippets

You can insert a snippet into a document by dragging and dropping or by selecting the snippet and clicking the Insert button at the bottom of the panel. You will, however, want to investigate what code the snippet contains and how it will be inserted before trying to use it.

Inserting in Code View vs. Design View

Because a snippet can contain any portion of code, including incomplete tags and tags that must be nested inside other tags, not all snippets can be inserted everywhere. Some snippets can be inserted into Design view; others might require that you be in Code view before inserting. Some can be inserted as nested content inside tables or other tags; others may not. The Meta > No-Cache snippet, for instance, can be inserted only while Code view is active. If Code view is active, the snippet is inserted at the current insertion point, wherever that is—regardless of whether the insertion point is in the head or the body section, or even in the middle of another tag. Obviously, you need to know where meta tags can and cannot go before using this snippet.

Inserting Block vs. Wrapped Snippets

Most snippets insert a single block of code—a table, a set of form elements, a <meta> tag. Some snippets insert two blocks of code, wrapped around whatever you currently have selected when you insert them. You can use the various comment snippets, for instance, to "comment out" any selected page element by wrapping it in <!-- --> comment tags. If nothing is selected when you insert a comment snippet, Dreamweaver inserts an empty pair of comment tags into your document.

Editing Snippets

Snippets are easy to edit. In the Snippets panel, either select a snippet and click the Edit button, or double-click the snippet itself, to open the Snippet dialog box, shown in Figure 27.14. You can change any snippet's name, description, or type (block or wrapped), as well as edit the code the snippet will insert. You can also determine how the snippet will be previewed within the Snippets panel.

FIGURE 27.14
The Snippet dialog box, for creating and editing snippets.

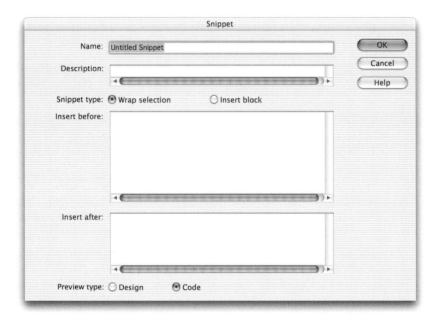

Nothing stops you from entering invalid code into a snippet. If you break one of the Dreamweaver default snippets by fiddling with its code, the only way to restore the undamaged snippet is by reinstalling Dreamweaver or tinkering around inside the Dreamweaver **Configuration** folder (another inherently dangerous activity).

Snippet Housekeeping

Snippets are organized in folders, some of which are nested inside other folders. You can rearrange this hierarchy as you like by dragging and dropping snippets and folders. You can rename snippets by editing them. You can rename folders by double-clicking them. You can even delete snippets or folders by selecting them and clicking the trash can icon at the bottom of the panel (refer to Figure 27.13)

Creating Your Own Snippets

The best feature of snippets is that you can easily create your own snippets, and even your own folders to store them in.

To create a new snippet folder, do the following:

1. If you want your folder to appear at the root level of the Snippets panel, start by deselecting any other folders in the Snippets panel. If you want your folder to be nested inside an existing folder, select that folder.

2. Click the Folder icon at the bottom of the panel (refer to Figure 27.13). Your new folder appears.

3. Name your folder! It's ready for action.

To create a new snippet, do the following:

1. (Optional) If you already have the chunk of code that the snippet should contain, open the document containing that code, and select it in Code view.

2. In the Snippets panel, select the folder you want to contain the new snippet, and click the New Snippet icon at the bottom of the panel (refer to Figure 27.13). Or right-click the folder and choose New Snippet from the context menu. This creates a new, untitled snippet and automatically opens the Snippet dialog box. If you had code selected, it appears in the Content field. Otherwise, type it in now. (You can't create an empty snippet!)

3. If you're creating a *wrapped snippet* (a snippet that inserts code before and after any selection), make sure the proper portions of code are in the Before and After fields.

4. Fill in all the other options of the dialog box, and click OK. Your snippet now appears in the Snippets panel and behaves just like any other snippet. You can insert it, edit it, delete it, move it around— whatever you like.

Creating and Inserting Snippets

In this exercise, you'll create various block and wrapped snippets to make building generic forms easier. Start by downloading the **chapter_27** folder from the book's website at www.peachpit.com to your hard drive, if you haven't done so already. Because this exercise works with invisible elements, choose View Options > Visual Aids, and make sure Invisible Elements are turned on before doing the exercise.

1. In the **chapter_27** folder, open the **generic_form.html** file, and examine it in Code and Design view. You'll see that it contains a simple form with various personal information fields, as shown in Figure 27.15. Each form element is named and includes an accessible label. If you ever find yourself repeatedly creating forms that request miscellaneous personal information from users, turning this form into a series of snippets will streamline your workflow.

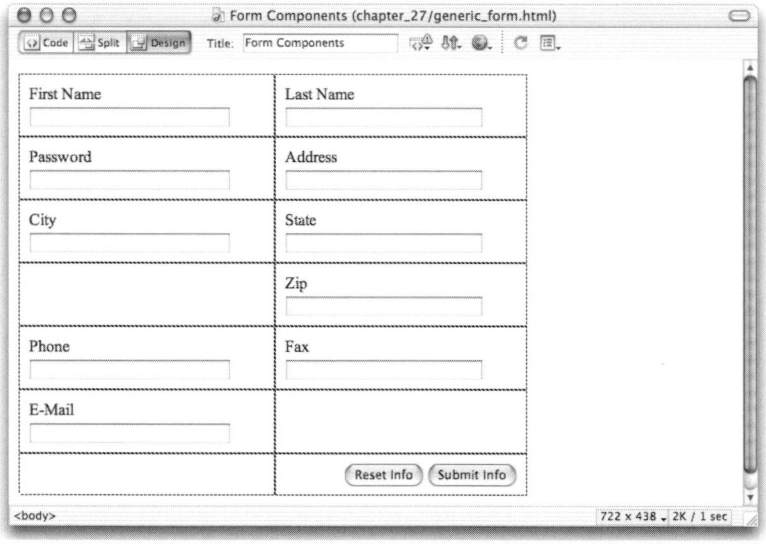

FIGURE 27.15

The generic_ form.html document, in Code and Design view.

2. Open the Snippets panel (expand the Code panel group, or select Window > Snippets). You want to create a new folder to hold the snippets you'll create for this exercise. Make sure that no existing snippet folders are selected, and click the New Folder icon at the bottom of the panel. Name your new folder **Personal Info Form**, as shown in Figure 27.16.

FIGURE 27.16

Creating a Personal
Info Form snippets
folder in the Snippets
panel.

3. To create a snippet for the First Name field, select the First Name label and its text field. You can make your selection in the Code or Design portion of the Document window, but make sure you select the complete label tag and the input tag!form field/label unit in the current document.

   After you've made your selection, in the Snippets panel, select your Personal Info Form folder, and click the New Snippet button (or right-click the Personal Info Form folder and choose New Snippet). When the Snippet dialog box opens, your selected code appears in the Code section. Name the snippet **First Name**, enter a description, and set its type to Block. Figure 27.17 shows what your settings should look like.

4. Repeat this process to make snippets for the remaining form elements, including one snippet for the Reset Info and Submit Info buttons.

5. The final snippet you'll make contains the <form> tag that should enclose the other tags. Because this is a simple snippet, you can create it entirely in the Edit Snippets dialog box.

   With no code selected, create a new snippet. Set the options to match those shown in Figure 27.18. This creates a wrapped snippet called Wrap Form, which contains any selected page contents in a <form> tag.

FIGURE 27.17
Creating the First
Name snippet from
selected code.

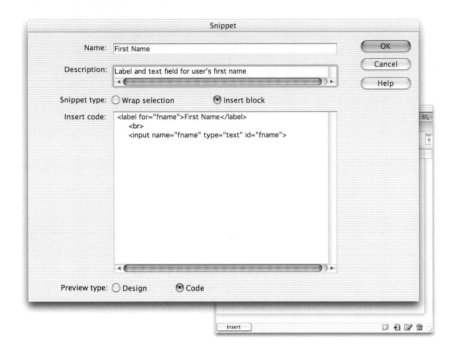

FIGURE 27.18
The Edit Snippet dia-
log box for the Wrap
Form snippet.

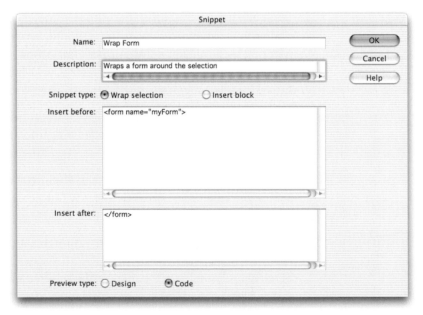

6. It's time to try out those snippets to build a quick login page. In the **chapter_27** folder, open the **login_form.html** file, and examine it. You'll see that it contains a simple table, ready to have some form elements inserted.

   Place the insertion point in the first table cell, and insert the First Name snippet. Repeat this procedure to add the Last Name, Password, and Submit Buttons snippets to the other table cells. (Do you notice that the form elements look a bit different in this document than they did before? That's a bit of CSS at work. By redefining the label and input tags in any page where you use these form elements, you can customize how they look without having to alter each snippet individually.)

7. You need to wrap the entire login form in a form tag. Select the table, and insert the Wrap Form snippet. Figure 27.19 shows the completed login page.

FIGURE 27.19

The login_form.html page, with form elements in place.

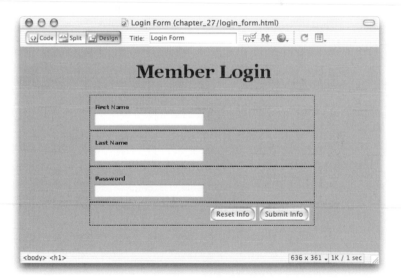

LINKING TO EXTERNAL TEXT EDITORS

So, you like working with code, and you like Dreamweaver, but you prefer your favorite text editor to the Dreamweaver Code view. You can set up a link between Dreamweaver and your external text editor and have the best of both worlds. For both Windows and Macintosh, you have the choice of standard integration with any text editor you choose, or the special options of an integrated HTML editor (HomeSite+ for Windows, or BBEdit for Mac).

Setting Up an External Text Editor (Nonintegrated)

The procedure for linking to and working with an external text editor other than HomeSite or BBEdit is simple and is basically the same across platforms.

To set up integration with an external editor, follow these steps:

1. In the Preferences dialog box, access the File Types/Editors category, as shown in Figure 27.20.

FIGURE 27.20
The File Types/Editors dialog box, showing options for enabling an external text editor.

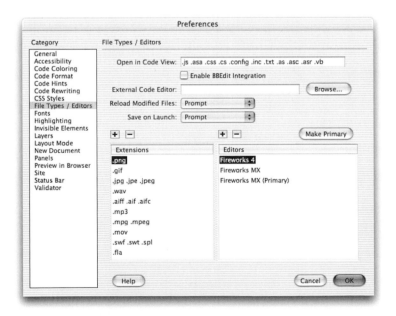

2. (Mac only) Find and deselect the Enable BBEdit Integration option.

3. Find the External Code Editor input field. Browse to select the text editor of your choice.

   The Reload Modified Files option determines what happens when you have edited a document in an external editor and then return to Dreamweaver. For more seamless integration, choose Always Reload; the changes are incorporated automatically. For more control over possible discrepancies that might occur between programs, choose Prompt; Dreamweaver warns you that changes have been made.

   The Save on Launch option determines whether Dreamweaver saves a document before launching an external text editor. Again, for more seamless integration, choose Always. If you want to be given the chance to review document changes before saving, choose Prompt.

Your chosen editor appears on the Edit menu as part of the Edit with *application* menu command (see Figure 27.21). Choose this option to open your current document in the new editor.

FIGURE 27.21

The Edit menu ready for integration with the TextPad text editor.

Text Editors Beyond HomeSite and BBEdit

Many people already have a favorite text editor. No matter what your platform, if you're in the market for a newer, better, more intuitive editor, you have all sorts of choices, from freeware to commercial.

For Windows, popular shareware/freeware text editors include UltraText, TextPad, CuteHTML, and good old NotePad.

For Macintosh, BBEdit's little brother, TextWrangler, is still commercial but less expensive. And TextEdit comes free with OS X.

Integrating HomeSite+ and Dreamweaver (Windows)

Macromedia's popular HomeSite+ text editor, which ships with Dreamweaver MX 2004/Windows, integrates easily and tightly with Dreamweaver.

To set up HomeSite integration in Dreamweaver, follow the steps outlined earlier for linking to an external editor.

You also can set up Dreamweaver integration in HomeSite. By default, HomeSite should have integration enabled. In HomeSite, go to Options > Settings, and choose the Dreamweaver category to check this and to configure how HomeSite treats modified files' other options.

To edit a Dreamweaver document in HomeSite, open a document in Dreamweaver, and go to Edit > Edit with HomeSite. That program launches, if it's not already running, and your document opens for editing.

To edit a HomeSite document in Dreamweaver, open a document in HomeSite. On the Editing toolbar, click the Dreamweaver icon.

If you have enabled both programs to automatically reload modified files and save before launching, and if you have a large monitor or dual-monitor setup at your workstation, you can leave the same document open in both programs and work back and forth fairly seamlessly, almost like working with the Code Inspector.

Integrating BBEdit and Dreamweaver (Macintosh)

Dreamweaver/Mac includes tight integration with BBEdit, unlike anything available for any other editor on either platform. If both of these applications are present on your system, integration between the two is automatically enabled; no setup is necessary.

To edit a Dreamweaver document in BBEdit, open a document in Dreamweaver, and select Edit > Edit with BBEdit. That program launches, if it's not already running, and comes to the front. Your document opens for editing.

To edit a BBEdit document in Dreamweaver, open a document in BBEdit, and select Markup > Misc > Dreamweaver.

Any code you have selected in Dreamweaver is selected in BBEdit, and vice versa. Any changes made on a document in one program are immediately visible in the other, as soon as that program is activated. If you have a large monitor or dual-monitor setup at your workstation, you can leave the same document open in both programs and work back and forth seamlessly, almost like working with the Code Inspector.

TAG LIBRARIES AND THE TAG LIBRARY EDITOR

Tag libraries are at the heart of Dreamweaver functionality. A *tag library* is a database of information about a set of tags—HTML tags, ASP tags, ColdFusion tags, and so on. In that database is the information that Dreamweaver uses to perform most of its tag-related tasks, from populating code hint menus, to applying source formatting, to generating the information presented in the Tag Chooser and Edit tag editor boxes.

The Tag Library Editor is your window to the tag libraries, and your tool for editing and adding to the information stored there. Has the latest version of Internet Explorer started supporting a tag or attribute that Dreamweaver doesn't know about? Add it to the library! Do you hate how Dreamweaver indents table code, or where it inserts line breaks between tabs? Change the library! It's all done with the Tag Library Editor.

Using the Tag Library Editor Dialog Box

Before you can start tinkering with tag libraries, you need to know what information and options are available to you through the Tag Library Editor dialog box. To open the Tag Library Editor, choose Edit > Tag Libraries. You can also access it from the Preferences/Code Format and Code Hints windows. As Figures 27.22 and 27.23 show, the interface contains a wealth of nested information.

FIGURE 27.22
The Tag Library Editor dialog box showing all the tag libraries in the Dreamweaver database.

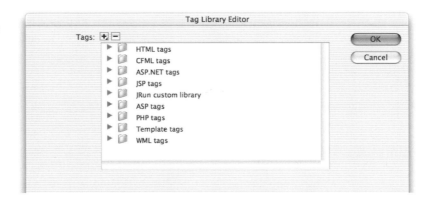

FIGURE 27.23
The Tag Library Editor dialog box showing settings for individual tags within a library.

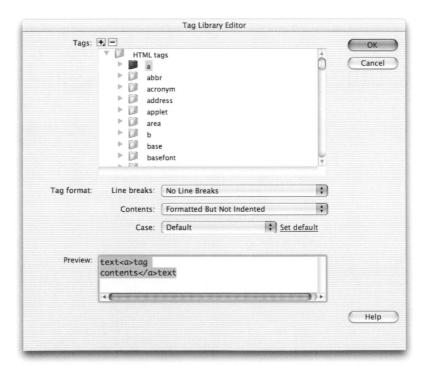

The Tags List

If you use Dreamweaver templates, note the library of template tags available here. These tags are written in Dreamweaver's template language. See Chapter 20, "Site-Wide Content with Templates and Libraries," for more on template language.

The upper half of the dialog box is taken up by the *tags list*, an expandable tree structure showing all tag libraries, the tags they contain, and the tags' attributes. The tag libraries are shown in the order in which Dreamweaver searches them for tag information (refer to Figure 27.22). In other words, when Dreamweaver is determining how to handle a certain tag, only if that tag does not exist in the HTML library does Dreamweaver search for it in the ColdFusion and other libraries. Within each library, the individual tags and attributes are listed in alphabetical order (refer to Figure 27.23).

Tag Library Options

If you have a tag library selected in the tags list, the bottom half of the dialog box displays a list of document types that might contain tags in that library (refer to Figure 27.22). This doesn't mean that Dreamweaver allows only certain tags in certain document types, but it does mean that tags in a certain library are meaningful to Dreamweaver only within those document types. For instance, within a JavaScript document, HTML tags such as a and table are meaningless. Dreamweaver doesn't provide code hints or other code editing help for those tags in that context.

Tag Options

When a tag is selected in the tags list, the bottom half of the dialog box displays Tag Format options for that tag (refer to Figure 27.23):

- **Line breaks**—Should Dreamweaver insert a hard return in the code before and/or after the tag, or between a tag pair and its nested contents? The options in this pop-up menu determine that.

- **Contents**—Should any contents nested within a tag pair be indented beyond the tag's indentation, and should the contents be formatted? Choose from this menu to determine that.

- **Case**—Should the tag be uppercase, lowercase, or mixed case? Or should it follow an application-wide default? (Click the Default link to establish the default case for all tags.)

The Preview area at the bottom of the dialog box shows the results of whatever formatting options have been chosen for the current tag.

Attribute Options

When a tag attribute is selected in the tags list, the bottom half of the dialog box displays formatting options for that attribute, as shown in Figure 27.24:

- **Attribute Case**—As with tags, case can be set to uppercase, lower-case, or mixed case for each attribute, or the attribute can use an application-wide default for all attributes. (Click the Default link to establish the default case.)

- **Attribute Type**—The option selected from this pop-up menu deter-mines what kind of help will be available to users—in the form of code hints and Tag Inspector options, for instance—when working with this attribute. If Dreamweaver is expecting a text value, for instance, no code hint will be given; if a color value is expected, the color picker will appear; if an enumerated value is expected, a list of possible choices will appear in the Code Hint menu. Table 27.2 lists the attrib-ute types and how they are treated in the Dreamweaver interface.

- **Attribute Value**—If the attribute type is set to Enumerated, this input area should hold a comma-delimited list of possible values. These will become the entries in the Code Hint menu.

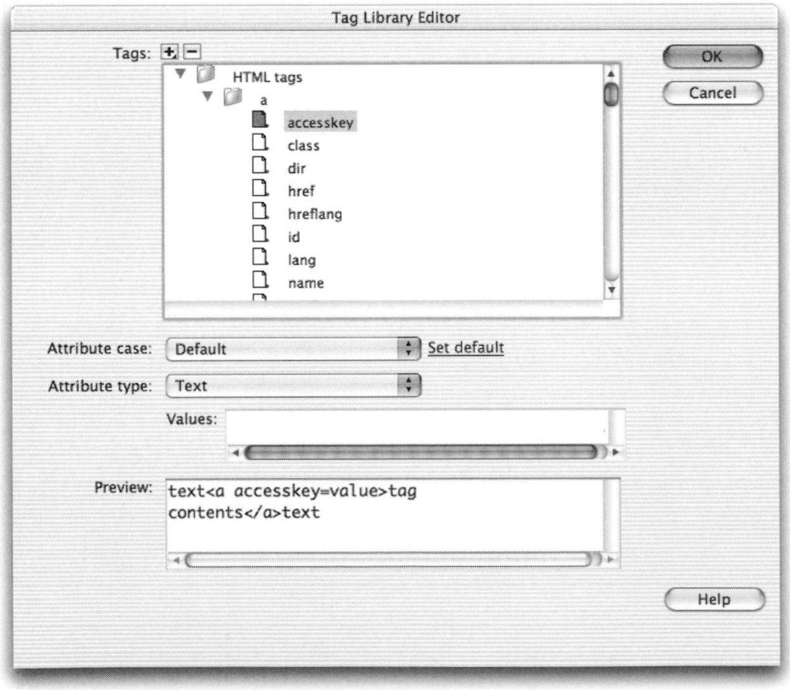

FIGURE 27.24
The Tag Library Editor dialog box showing settings for an indi-vidual tag attribute.

TABLE 27.2 **Possible Attribute Types for Entries in a Tag Library**

Attribute Type	Description	Code Hints
Text	Any text can be entered	None
Enumerated	Only select values are acceptable	Menu populated with comma-separated list entered in the Attribute Value field
Color	Color name or hexa-decimal color value	Color palette
Directory	Absolute URL for a directory	Menu of protocols: ftp://, http://, and so on
File Name	Absolute URL for a file	Menu of protocols: ftp://, http://, and so on
File Path	Absolute URL for a file	Menu of protocols: ftp://, http://, and so on
Flag	No value at all; the mere presence of the attribute is the flag (for example, the nowrap attribute for table cells)	None
Font	One or more fonts	Menu of defined font lists
Relative Path	Relative URL	Browse option
Style	CSS or other style name	List of available classes

Editing Tag Library Entries

As you have probably figured out by now, you can change any setting for any library, tag, or attribute simply by selecting the desired item in the tags list and changing the settings that appear. Here are a few tips on making changes:

- You can't do much serious damage to Dreamweaver just by changing the line break or capitalization settings for tags, but you can make features such as code hints unusable for certain attributes if you aren't careful with your settings. Proceed with caution.

- Don't override the default case of tags and attributes unless you have good reason to. The application-wide default becomes meaningless when most of the elements involved override it.

- Try your changes to see how you like them! After you've changed a formatting option, try creating and editing some samples of the changed tags in Code view. How do the code hints work? What happens when you apply source formatting? If you don't like it, go back to the Tag Library Editor and change things back.

If you're interested in extending Dreamweaver, the Tag Library information is stored in the Dreamweaver **Configuration/Tag Libraries** folder. Each tag library is represented by a folder within this main folder. Within a library, each tag exists as an XML file with the .vtm filename extension. For more information on working with the **Configuration** folder, see Chapters 28 and 29.

Adding (and Removing) Entries

Adding and removing attributes, tags, and even entire libraries is a little more complex (and can be a lot more dangerous!) than editing existing entries. But it's also where the true customizable power of Dreamweaver tag libraries comes to your aid. All adding and removing can be done with the + and – buttons at the top of the Tag Library Editor dialog box.

Adding a Tag Library

To create a new, empty tag library, do the following:

1. Click the + button at the top of the tags list, and choose New Tag Library from the pop-up menu.

2. In the dialog box that appears, give your new library a name. (This name is for your benefit only, so be descriptive and concise.)

3. Click OK to close the dialog box. You'll see your new library at the bottom of the tags list. (New libraries are like the new kids at school—they have to go to the end of the line.)

4. With your new library selected in the tags list, select what document types should support the tags in this library.

Your new library is ready to rock and roll! The next step is to add tags to the library so that it will have some functionality.

Adding a Tag

To add a new tag to a library, follow these steps:

1. Click the + button at the top of the tags list, and choose New Tags from the pop-up menu.

2. The New Tags dialog box appears, as shown in Figure 27.25. Specify what library the tag should be added to, and enter the tag's name. (The name is what appears between the opening and closing < > symbols. Don't include the symbols themselves.)

FIGURE 27.25

The New Tags dialog box, part of the Tag Library Editor.

3. If the tag will consist of an opening and closing pair, select the Have Matching End Tags option. If the tag will be a single tag only (such as <img> or <hr>), deselect this option.

4. When you're finished, click OK. Check out the tags list. Your tag appears as an entry in the library you specified. Select the tag in the list, and edit its formatting options as desired.

After you've done this, you can try it out! Open a document of a type that supports the library containing your tag, go to Code view, and type the first few characters of your new tag. If you have code hints enabled, a hint menu should appear, with your tag as one of the entries.

Adding an Attribute

To add a new attribute to a tag, do the following:

1. Click the + button at the top of the tags list, and choose New Attributes from the pop-up menu.

2. The New Attributes dialog box appears, as shown in Figure 27.26. Specify the library and tag the new attribute will belong to, and enter the attribute's name.

3. When you're finished, click OK. Check out the tags list. Your attribute appears as an entry for the tag you specified. Select the attribute in the list, and edit its formatting options as desired.

EXERCISE 27.2

Adding a Custom Tag Library and Elements

You want to get some practice working with tag library elements, but you probably don't want to risk upsetting the program's built-in functionality. So, in this exercise, you'll create a new tag library, populate it with a new tag, and assign various attributes to that tag. When you're finished, you'll remove the whole lot.

1. Choose Edit > Tag Libraries to open the Tag Library Editor.

2. In the tags list, contract all categories so that you see a list of libraries like the one shown in Figure 27.22.

3. Create a new library by clicking the + button and choosing New Library from the pop-up menu. Call the library **Practice Tags**.

4. In the tags list, select the Practice Tags library and make sure that HTML documents are selected as one of the document types where these tags may be found, as shown in Figure 27.27.

5. The Practice Tags library needs a tag of its very own. With Practice Tags selected in the tags list, click the + button, and choose New Tags from the pop-up menu. In the dialog box that appears, make sure that the tag will be added to the Practice Tags library, as shown in Figure 27.28. Call the tag **grin**. This imaginary tag has no closing tag, so deselect the Have Matching End Tags option. Click OK to close the New Tags dialog box.

FIGURE 27.27
The Practice Tags library set up so that its tags will be recognized when found in HTML documents.

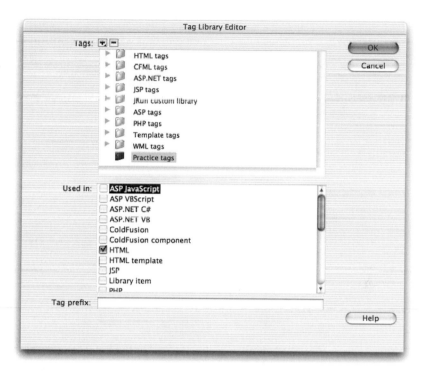

FIGURE 27.28
Adding the grin tag to the Practice Tags library.

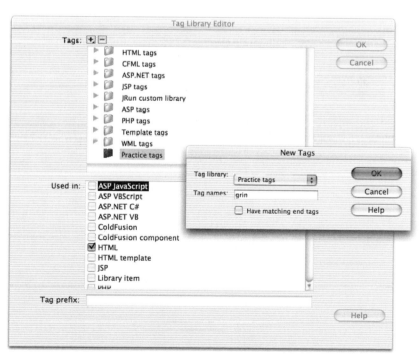

6. Back in the Tag Library Editor, select grin in the tags list, and set its options. Choose whatever formatting options you like. Use the Preview area to see how your choices will affect the code structure.

7. Try out your new tag! Click OK to close the Tag Library Editor, and open a new HTML document. Make sure code hints are enabled (select Edit > Preferences > Code Hints).

    Go to Code view, and between the <body> </body> tags, type <g. Unless your code hint delay is set to 0, pause a moment before continuing. The Code Hint menu appears, taking you right to your new tag! Press Enter to insert the rest of the tag: **<grin>**. Congratulations!

8. Add a few attributes to your tag. Select Edit > Tag Libraries to open the Tag Library Editor. From the tags list, find and select your grin tag. Click the + button, and choose New Attributes from the pop-up menu.

9. In the New Attributes dialog box, make sure your Practice Tags library and grin tag are selected. Call your attribute **kind**. Click OK, and go back to the Tag Library Editor.

10. In the editor, select the new kind attribute. Set its Attribute Type to Enumerated, and enter a comma-separated list of possible grins in the Attribute Value field (**sly**, **sneaky**, **crooked**). Figure 27.29 shows this happening.

 When defining an enumerated list in the Tag Library Editor, be sure not to put any spaces between your commas, or the list won't work.

11. Set whatever other attribute formatting you like, and click OK to close the Tag Library Editor. Try your attribute! In your open document, still in Code view, try entering a new grin tag. This time, type this much: **<grin**.

    A Code Hint menu showing your grin types appears! Choose one, and let Dreamweaver finish coding your grin tag for you. Figure 27.30 shows this happening.

FIGURE 27.29
Adding the kind
attribute to the
grin tag.

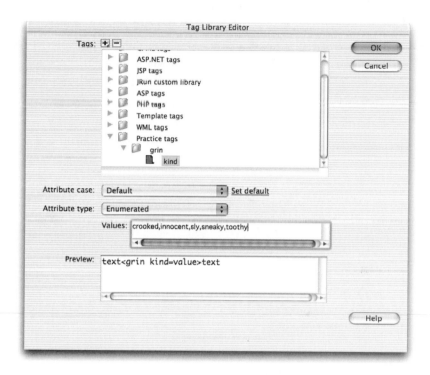

FIGURE 27.30
The grin tag in
action in Code view.

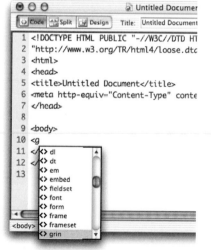

12. See how the new tag behaves in the Tag selector and Tag Inspector. Open the Tag Inspector (select Window > Tag Inspector), and bring the Attributes tab to the front. Switch to Design view, and refresh if necessary (click the Refresh button in the Tag Inspector).

In the Document window, switch to Code and Design view. In the Code portion of the window, make sure the cursor is within the `grin` tag. At the bottom of the window, `grin` shows up in the Tag selector. Select it and look in the Tag Inspector.

There's your `kind` attribute and its value! Select the value. Note that the Inspector shows a triangle icon, indicating that there's a drop-down list of values for that attribute. If you click the icon, you're presented with your list of attributes.

Advanced Find and Replace

Although the Dreamweaver Find and Replace command doesn't necessarily have to be used in Code view, sophisticated searching is a feature usually associated with code editing. The Dreamweaver Find and Replace command is a powerful tool that supports regular expressions for searching source code (for the true geeks among us), as well as the ability to construct complex searches using a simple drop-down menu interface (for the rest of us).

Advanced Text Searches

With a basic text search, Dreamweaver lets you search the text elements in an HTML document (that is, the text that is actually visible on the page, as opposed to HTML tags). With advanced text searching, you can limit the search to text elements within, or outside, specific tags. You can specify that the text element be within one tag or multiple tags; you can even require that the enclosing tags have certain attributes. The Advanced Text search option is available through the Search and Replace window. With the window open, from the Search For pop-up menu, select Text (Advanced).

Advanced text searches are useful any time you're working with complex documents and you want to refine your searches as much as possible. Maybe you want to change all instances of Minnesota to MN, except not in titles, for instance. You would search for the state name, but only when it's not in an <h1> or other title tag. Especially if you're doing sitewide changes, this sort of refinement can make it possible to complete a Replace All search in 5 minutes, rather than an item-by-item Replace search that might take an hour.

Figure 27.31 shows the Find and Replace dialog box set up to perform a complex advanced text search. Table 27.3 explains the various search criteria available in the pop-up menus. Use the + and – buttons to add or remove search criteria.

FIGURE 27.31
The Find and Replace dialog box set up to perform an advanced text search.

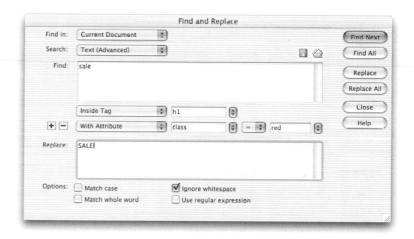

TABLE 27.3 ## Criteria for Advanced Text and Specific Tag Searches

Criterion	Description
Inside tag Not inside tag	Limit the search to text elements contained (or not contained) within a certain pair of tags. Note that only tags that occur in pairs, such as <p>...</p>, produce valid search results.
With attribute Without attribute	Limit the search to tags that have (or don't have) a certain attribute set to a certain value. To search based only on the presence or absence of the attribute, regardless of value, leave the Value field blank.
Containing Not containing	Limit the search to tags that contain (or don't contain) a specified nested tag or text element.

Specific Tag Searches

This type of search lets you find and modify the attributes of different HTML tags, as well as add, change, and even remove specific tags. This is powerful code-editing functionality, although it isn't something you normally associate with searching and replacing.

After you've tried it a few times, you'll be amazed at how handy this kind of search is. What if you use the company logo throughout your site and then discover you forgot to give it an `alt` label? A sitewide search for every `<img>` tag with the attribute `src="logo.gif"`, setting the `alt` attribute to `"Your Logo"`, will fix the problem in no time flat. Or maybe you need to find all 100-percent-width tables across an entire site and change them to 90-percent width; one easy search will do it.

Figure 27.32 shows the Find and Replace dialog box set up to perform a specific tag search with several criteria. Note that instead of replacing, you can choose an action to perform on any found tags. The (slightly-less-than-intuitive) procedure for this type of search is to click the Find button to search for instances of the specified tag and then click the Replace button to perform the specified action on any found tags. Table 27.4 explains the choices available in the Action pop-up menu.

FIGURE 27.32
The Find and Replace dialog box set up to perform a specific tag search.

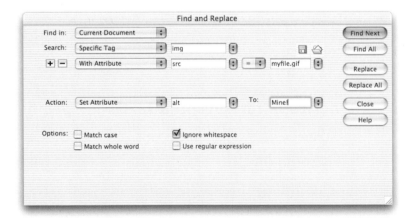

TABLE 27.4 **Actions for Specific Tag Searches**

Action	Description
Replace tag and contents	Completely replaces opening and closing tags and any nested tags or other contents with specified text. To remove the tag and its contents entirely, leave the specified text field blank.
Replace contents only	Replaces everything within the opening and closing tags with specified text, but leaves the tags in place. To remove the contents, leave the specified text field blank.
Strip tag	Removes opening and closing tags, but leaves any contents in place. Note that this action is not executed if it would result in invalid code (such as stripping a single `<td>` from within a table while leaving the table contents in place).
Change tag	Replaces the opening and closing tags with another specified pair of opening and closing tags, leaving any contents intact. Note that if an unclosed or self-closing tag (such as `<img>` or `<img/>`) is specified as the replacement for a tag pair (such as `<p></p>`), all contents of the original tag pair are lost.
Set attribute	Sets a specified attribute of the tag to a specified value.
Remove attribute	Removes a specified attribute of the tag.
Add before start tag	Adds specified text immediately before the opening tag.
Add after end tag	Adds specified text immediately following the closing tag.
Add after start tag	Adds specified text immediately following the opening tag. This can be used to add a new row to the top of certain tables, for instance.
Add before end tag	Adds specified text immediately preceding the closing tag. This can be used to add a new row to the end of certain tables, for instance.

Using Regular Expressions

Regular expressions aren't a kind of search, and they aren't unique to Dreamweaver. Regular expressions offer a powerful way to search code for patterns rather than specific character-by-character matches. For instance, if you're searching for all the phone numbers in a group of web pages, but you don't want to search for each phone number individually, you can use a regular expression to search for a pattern of numbers, dashes, and parentheses that all the phone numbers follow. Regular expressions are a part of Perl, JavaScript, and other scripting and programming languages. They can be remarkably simple or very sophisticated and complex, depending on what you're trying to accomplish.

If you are technically minded, be aware that Dreamweaver's searching capabilities are built from JavaScript. Therefore, all the features of regular expressions supported by JavaScript work in defining criteria for the Find and Replace command.

Writing Regular Expressions

A *regular expression* is a description of a text string that contains certain characters in certain positions or patterns. The simplest regular expressions just consist of the letters or numbers you want to search for, and they find only instances of those specific characters. For instance, the following three search strings are all regular expressions that find exactly the text strings specified, wherever they occur in a document:

```
Fred Flintstone
```

```
87125
```

```
laura@rocketlaura.com
```

However, regular expressions also can include various *metacharacters,* which are used to describe and count characters in a document. Tables 27.5 and 27.6 list the most commonly used metacharacters. Built from metacharacters shown there, a search for phone numbers might be encoded into a regular expression like one of these:

```
(\d\d\d) \d\d\d-\d\d\d\d
```

```
(*\d{3})*[\s-]\d{3}-\d{4}
```

The second option is fancier but more flexible, finding any of these phone numbers:

(800) 123-4567

(800)123-4567

800 123-4567

800-123-4567

TABLE 27.5 ## Character-Matching Regular-Expression Metacharacters

Expression	Kind of Character to Match	Example
\d	Numeral (0 to 9)	\d matches the 2s in R2D2, but nothing in Skywalker.
\D	Not a numeral	\D matches any character in Skywalker and the R and D in R2D2.
\w	Any alphanumeric character, including underscore	\w matches every character except the spaces and period in "R2D2 ran down the road."
\W	Not any alphanumeric character or underscore	\W matches only the spaces and the period in "R2D2 ran down the road."
.	Any character except newline	r.n matches ran and run, but not rain or region.
[xyz]	Any character in the brackets (specify a range of characters with a hyphen)	[a-f] is equivalent to [abcdef]. It matches the f and a in favor and the e, a, and f in leaf.
[^xyz]	Any character not in the brackets (specify a range of characters with a hyphen)	[l-p] is equivalent to [lmnop]. It matches any character in Chewbacca but none in moon or pool.
\b	Word boundary	\bh matches hello but not bother.
\B	Not a word boundary	\h matches bother but not hello.
\s	A single whitespace character (space, tab, form feed, line feed)	\sone matches one in "Is he the one?" but nothing in "Someone's there!"
\S	A single nonwhite space	\Sone matches one in "Someone's there!" but nothing in "Is he the one?"
^	The beginning of a string or line	^ a matches the a in "all for one" but nothing in "one for all."
$	The end of a string or other selection	s$ matches the second s in biscuits but not the first.
\t	Tab	

continues

TABLE 27.5 **Character-Matching Regular-Expression Metacharacters** *continued*

Expression	Kind of Character to Match	Example
\f	Form feed	
\r	Carriage return	
\n	Line feed	
\x	The literal value of x (used to search for occurrences of special characters that would otherwise be interpreted as metacharacters)	hi. matches hit, hid, and so forth; hi\. matches hi.

TABLE 27.6 **Character-Counting Regular-Expression Metacharacters**

Expression	How Many Characters	Example
*	The preceding character, zero or more times	om* matches om in mom, omm in mommy, and o in son.
+	The preceding character, one or more times	om+ matches om in mom, omm in mommy, but nothing in son.
?	The preceding character, zero or one time	so?e?n matches son in Anderson, sn in snack, but nothing in soon.
{n}	The preceding character, exactly *n* times	c{2} matches cc in Chewbacca but nothing in charcoal.
{n.}	The preceding character, *n* or more times	6{1.} matches the 6s in 976 and 97662, but not in 666.
{n,m}	The preceding character, at least *n* times and at most *m* times	F{1,3} matches the Fs in #F204CA and #FFCCCC, but nothing in #FFFFFF.

To learn more about regular expressions, check out *Mastering Regular Expressions* (published by O'Reilly). Many JavaScript and Perl books also have in-depth discussions of this topic.

Finding and Replacing with Regular Expressions

To use regular expressions in Dreamweaver, just enable the Use Regular Expressions option in the Find and Replace dialog box, and enter characters and metacharacters in any of the dialog box's Find text fields. (It makes no sense to use regular expressions as replacement strings.)

Figure 27.34 shows examples of three search types using regular expressions. The top example shows a basic Text search that finds variant spellings of *labeled* and makes them consistent. The center example shows an Advanced Text search that finds all occurrences of the word *and* in headers only (h? returns h1, h2, h3, and so on) and replaces them with &. The bottom example shows a Specific Tag search that finds all tables with percent-based widths (\d*% finds numbers with any number of digits that end in a percent sign) and removes the width attribute.

The Use Regular Expressions and Ignore White Space options can't both be enabled at the same time because white space cannot be ignored within regular expressions.

The most powerful feature of the Dreamweaver Find and Replace command is its capability to save search criteria for later reuse. Any setup you create in the Find and Replace dialog box can be saved. This feature really makes it worthwhile to spend time and thought to create flexible, complex searches. A good set of search criteria is like your very own utility program, ready to run on any document with a few mouse clicks.

After you've filled in all the Find and Replace options as desired, you can save any set of criteria by clicking the Save button (the one with the disk icon). You're presented with a standard Save dialog box. Choose a location and name. After you have finished, your criteria are saved to a file with a .dwr extension. Figure 27.34 shows this happening.

To load a saved criteria file, open the Find and Replace dialog box, and click the Load Query button (the one with the file icon). A dialog box appears, asking you what file to load. Browse to where you stored your DWR file, and open it. The Find and Replace interface is set to your saved settings.

FIGURE 27.33

Find and Replace dialog boxes showing different search types using regular expressions: basic Text search (top), Advanced Text search (middle), and Specific Tag search (bottom).

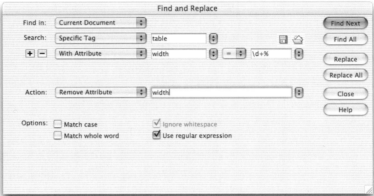

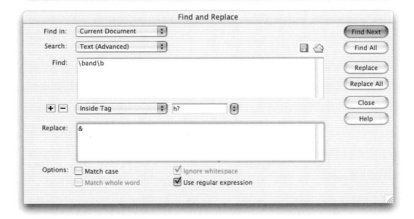

FIGURE 27.34
Saving the settings
from a Find and
Replace dialog box.

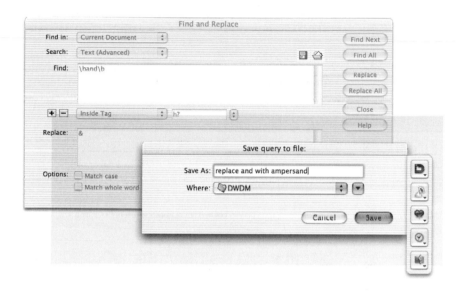

You also can modify the saved criteria file. After all, DWR files are just
XML files storing the various search parameters as attributes of custom
tags. If you love working with code, you can always open the DWR file in
a text editor (Dreamweaver, even!) and modify the criteria there. The
code for the search shown in Figure 27.33, for instance, looks like this:

```
<?xml version="1.0"?>
    <dwquery>
        <queryparams matchcase="false" ignorewhitespace="false"
        ➥ useregexp="true"/>
        <find>
        <qtag qname="table">
            <qattribute qname="width" qcompare="="
            ➥qvalue="\d*%"></qattribute>
        </qtag>
        </find>
    <replace action="removeAttribute" param1="width"
➥param2=""/>
</dwquery>
```

Finding and Replacing for Maximum Efficiency

In this exercise, you use various kinds of searches to efficiently edit a document that would otherwise be a nightmare of boring, repetitive tasks.

1. From the **chapter_27** folder on the book's website, find and open **states.html**, and examine its contents (see Figure 27.35). You can see that it consists of two types of tables: a layout table for the overall page structure, and lots of colored data tables. Your job is to make sweeping changes to those data tables.

FIGURE 27.35

The states.html file with multicolored data tables.

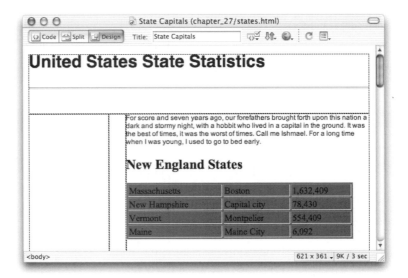

2. First, you want to add a row of header cells to each data table (with the headings State, Capital, and Pop.). You can do this with a Specific Tag search, but what tag do you search for? You can't search for all `table` tags, or the layout table will be included. You can't search by background color because each table's color is different. If you look at the code for this document, however, you'll see that each data table has a class of `state` assigned to it. You can search by class. For each data table, you want to add a `tr` with specific contents. Therefore, when you find each appropriate `table` tag, you add the following code after the `start` tag:

```
<tr><th>State</th><th>Capital</th><th>Pop.</th></tr>
```

To do this, perform a search with the setting shown in Figure 27.36.

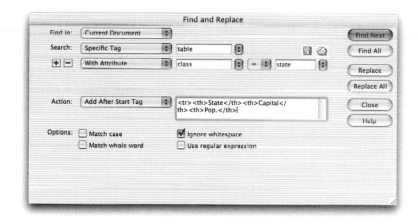

3. You've seen how a class assignment can help identify items for mass changes. You can use custom classes along with CSS to more easily format your table cells. Open the CSS Inspector, and you'll see that two custom classes have been defined for this document: `statetitle` and `statedata`. You want to apply these to the cells of your data tables. Can you see how a Specific Tag search can help with this? The `statetitle` class is easy; it should be assigned to all th tags. The `statedata` class is harder; you need to find some combination of characteristics that is unique for all data cells. For this document, examining the code shows that the data cells have no attributes at all, whereas the layout cells have height, width, or both. Figure 27.37 shows the Find and Replace dialog boxes to perform the searches required here. Perform these searches, and examine your code to make sure you get the results you want.

    Here's an extra: Now that you have a class providing color for the th tags, you don't need the `bgcolor` attribute in those tags. Can you use a Specific Tag search to remove that attribute?

4. One of the header cells has the text `Pop.`, but you've changed your mind and want it to say Population. This might be a simple Text search, but what if some text somewhere else in the document says Pop.? You want an Advanced Text search that finds only this text when it's in a `statetitle` th tag. Can you perform this search? Its setup isn't shown here.

5. The boss says he wants the cells with population numbers in them to have a white background so that they stand out. You need to do a tag search for all `td` tags with a class of `statedata`, but only those that contain numbers. It's time for a regular expression! Can you think this one through? Figure 27.38 shows a setup that works.

FIGURE 27.37
Find and Replace dialog boxes for the searches that add statetitle and statedata classes to the data tables.

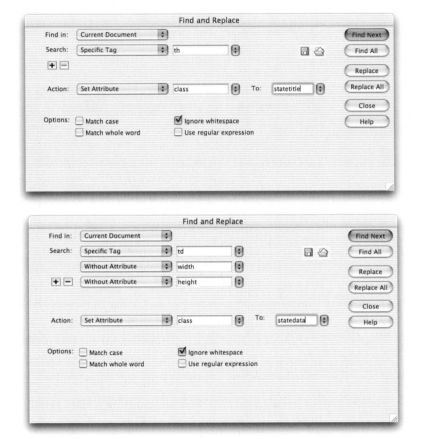

6. Here's your last big challenge: If you examine the code for the style sheet in this document's `head`, you'll see that all styles refer to a group of sans-serif fonts, but each font list differs slightly. You want all font lists for sans-serif fonts to be identical. You want them to read like this: Verdana, Arial, Helvetica, Geneva, Swiss, sans-serif. This requires a Source search with a regular expression; you want to

replace every font list that contains the word *sans-serif* with your font list. In regular-expression terms, you want to find the following:

```
font-family:[^;}]*sans-serif;
```

and replace it with the following:

```
font-family: Verdana, Arial, Helvetica, Geneva, Swiss,
➡sans-serif
```

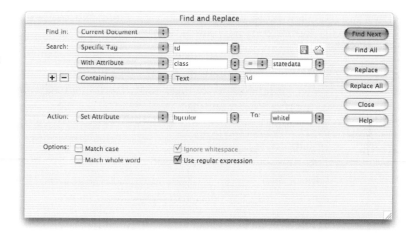

Can you see how the regular expression works? Try it. Perform the search and then examine your document code to make sure the changes were made successfully. If they weren't, select Edit > Undo as many times as necessary, and try again.

That is a pretty handy search. It might not have been too difficult to make a manual code change for just this one document, but what if you want to change internal style sheets across an entire site? More than that, you might find yourself needing a similar search again in the future. Do you want to have to figure out that regular expression every time? Of course not! This is a good set of search criteria to save. Open the Find and Replace dialog box again. Your preceding settings should still be in place. Save the search criteria as **Set Sans-Serif Font List**, in whatever centralized location you like. You now have a handy tool for future use.

EDITING NON-HTML MARKUP WITH DREAMWEAVER

For more on .mxi installer files for Dreamweaver extensions, see the section "Packaging Your Extensions" in Chapter 29, "Creating Your Own Extensions."

The Dreamweaver code editor can be used to edit kinds of code other than the default markup languages (HTML, XML, XHTML, ASP, CFM, and so on), although you can't display those files in Design view or use the Preview in Browser feature to view them. What other languages might you want? If you're into authoring for multimedia, you might want to try your hand at SMIL (Synchronized Media Integration Language), used to build audiovisual presentations, or SVG (Scalable Vector Graphics), for creating vector graphics. Both of these XML-based languages are growing in popularity. If you work with Windows Media, you might want to edit the text metafiles it uses (.wvx and .wax files). If you're authoring RealMedia presentations, you might want to edit RealText (.rt) or RealPix (.rp) files. Dreamweaver's own XML-based configuration files also can be edited here (.mno, .dwr, and so on). Dreamweaver extension authors might want to edit their installer files (.mxi) here.

If Dreamweaver doesn't know the filename extension of your non-HTML document, it won't be able to open the file. To add new filename extensions to Dreamweaver's list, select Edit > Preferences, and choose the File Types/Editors category. Find the Open in Code View option, and add the new file extension to the text field, as shown in Figure 27.39. Note that each extension must be separated from others in the list by spaces on either side. Don't forget to include the period (.). If your file type might have alternate extensions (such as .smi, .smil, or .sml for SMIL), be sure to add each one you might need.

Mac users should be aware that unlike many other Mac programs, Dreamweaver/Mac uses filename extensions to determine file types. Even if a file created in Dreamweaver appears on your desktop with the Dreamweaver icon, the program won't be able to open or preview it unless it includes the proper extension.

To make sure that Dreamweaver doesn't rewrite the code for this file type, select Edit > Preferences, and choose the Code Rewriting category. Find the Never Rewrite Code options list, and add the new extension. Each new file extension must be separated from others in the list by spaces on either side. (See the earlier section, "Code Rewriting," for more on this.)

FIGURE 27.39

Configuring Dreamweaver to open additional file types in the Preferences File Types/Editors category.

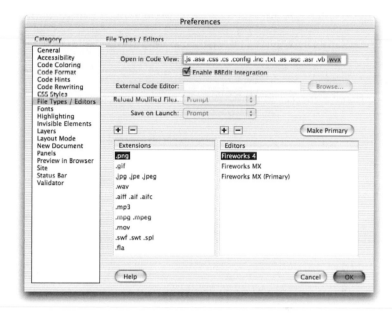

To get code hints and tag completion help for specialized markup languages, you can also create a custom tag library. (For full instructions, see the earlier section "Tag Libraries and the Tag Library Editor.") If you plan to work with a particular specialized document type frequently, the time you invest in setting up a tag library can really pay off.

WRITING JAVASCRIPT IN DREAMWEAVER

In addition to other code-writing chores, Dreamweaver has several features specifically to help you hand-code JavaScript.

The Reference Panel

In previous chapters, you have seen how the Reference panel can give you context-sensitive help for HTML and CSS. For scripting help, the Reference panel also provides JavaScript help. To access the JavaScript help in the Reference panel, click the <?> button on the Document toolbar, and choose O'Reilly JavaScript Reference from the panel's Book drop-down menu. Figure 27.40 shows the JavaScript section of the

Reference panel with all its parts labeled for easy browsing. It's organized by object, as most JavaScript dictionaries are, so you need to know your object structure to take full advantage of it.

FIGURE 27.40
The JavaScript section of the Reference Panel, a handy source of information for scripters.

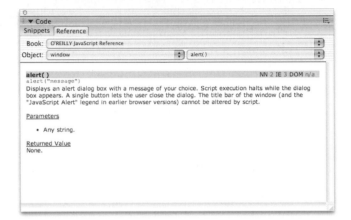

Scripting Without Using Code View

If you want to be able to add your own scripts to your page without having to navigate through one of the code editor views, you have two choices: the Call JavaScript behavior or the Script object. The Script Property Inspector also lets you edit existing script tags.

Call JavaScript Behavior

You apply and edit this behavior the same way you would any other item in the Behaviors panel. Instead of inserting some prewritten JavaScript action, however, the behavior adds whatever JavaScript statement(s) you specifically tell it to add.

Follow these steps:

1. Open a document, and select whichever page element you want to attach the behavior to.

2. Open the Behaviors panel, and from the + menu, choose Call JavaScript.

3. In the dialog box that appears, type in whatever JavaScript statement(s) you want to execute. (Separate multiple statements with semicolons.) After you have finished, click OK.

How useful is Call JavaScript? It's great if you're not really into writing scripts, or if you're in a hurry. But because of how Dreamweaver codes its behaviors, Call JavaScript can lead to some cumbersome coding. Dreamweaver behaviors must always insert their JavaScript as a noncustomizable function (in the head) and a function call with parameters. Say you wanted to insert a line of code that sends the browser back to the previous page when the user clicks a particular item. You'd insert a Call JavaScript behavior and type **history.back()** into its dialog box. Dreamweaver would add the following function to your document's head:

```
function MM_callJS(jsStr) { //v2.0
  return eval(jsStr)
}
```

And the following event handler and function call to the selected page element:

```
<a href="javascript:;" onClick="MM_callJS('history.back()')">
```

If you're familiar with how JavaScript works within the HTML framework, you'll recognize that it's much more efficient to just tuck the JavaScript statement inside the href, like this:

```
<a href="javascript:window.back()">
```

In fact, in this particular instance, you can still avoid going to Code view if you really want to. Just select the page element that will trigger the link, and type **javascript:window.back()** in the Link field of the Property Inspector.

For more on how Dreamweaver behaviors are coded, see the section "Behaviors in Dreamweaver" in Chapter 13, "Interactivity with Behaviors." For more on using Call JavaScript, see the section "Tiny Bits of Hand-Coding: The Call JavaScript Behavior," also in Chapter 13.

The Script Object

The Dreamweaver Script object is a quick way to insert a complete script tag into a document without going to Code view. Scripts entered this way aren't limited to JavaScript. They can include anything a script tag normally contains, including links to separate JS files.

To insert a script block into a document using the Script object, follow these steps (see Figure 27.41):

1. Open a document.

2. To insert the script into the body section, position the insertion point where the tag should be added. To insert the script to the head section, use the View Options menu to turn Head Content on, and click in the head content bar (along the top of the Document window) to activate it.

3. In the Insert bar, go to the HTML category. From the Script group of objects, choose the Script object. Or choose Insert > HTML > Script Objects > Script.

4. In the dialog box that appears, choose a scripting language. JavaScript (various versions) and VBScript appear in the drop-down menu. To choose any other language, enter the information directly into the text field.

5. Enter the complete script contents you want to enter, minus the opening and closing `<script>` tags (and the script-hiding comment tags).

FIGURE 27.41
Using the Script object to insert a script tag into the document.

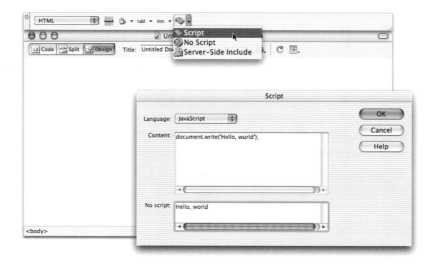

Dreamweaver inserts your script inside `script` tags and with the proper language specified. It also includes comment tags to hide the script from noncompliant browsers.

To edit a script block using the Script Inspector, follow these steps (see Figure 27.42):

1. Open a document containing script tags.

2. If the script is in the document head, show the head content bar (select View Options > Head Content). If the script is in the document body, turn on invisible elements (select View Options > Visual Aids > Invisible Elements). Each script tag in the document should now show in the head content bar or in Design view as a script icon.

3. Select the script icon representing the code you want to edit.

4. Use the Property Inspector to change any script parameters. Click the Edit button to access and edit the code.

FIGURE 27.42
The Property Inspector for Script objects.

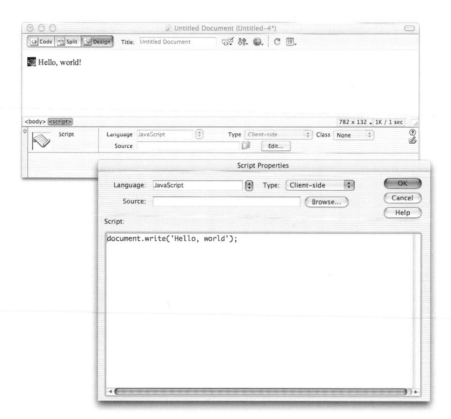

When you insert a Script object, you're not given the choice to add a script link. The dialog box assumes you'll type in your own script. However, you can subvert the process (although it's easier just to use the Assets panel, as discussed in the next section).

To insert a link to a client-side or server-side JS file, using the Script object, follow these steps:

1. Open a document and insert a Script object, as described earlier.

2. In the Script object dialog box, leave the code field blank, and click OK. This inserts an empty `script` tag into your document.

3. Turn on either the head content bar or invisible elements, find the script icon, and select it.

4. In the Script Object Property Inspector, choose the file to which you want to attach.

Scripts in the Assets Panel

If you're working within a defined site and you want to add links to JS files to your documents, the easiest way is to use the Assets panel. Every JS file within your local site folder appears in the Scripts section of the Assets panel, as shown in Figure 27.43. To add a script link to a document this way, follow these steps:

1. Open the document to which you want to add the link.

2. Make sure the head content bar is showing (select View Options > Head Content).

3. Open the Assets panel, and click the script icon to show the site's script files.

4. Find the file you want to link to, and drag its icon from the Assets panel to the head content bar of your document. Figure 27.44 shows this happening.

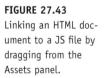

FIGURE 27.43
Linking an HTML document to a JS file by dragging from the Assets panel.

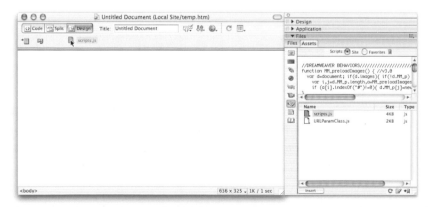

JavaScript Tools in Code View

If you're editing your scripts in Code view or the Code Inspector, you can take advantage of colored syntax, function navigation, auto-balancing, and various debugging tools.

Syntax Coloring for Scripts

You have already seen how syntax coloring works in Dreamweaver—how to enable it and customize text colors and styling. The Preferences > Code Coloring dialog box includes special settings for coloring text within scripts, including reserved keywords, other keywords, and strings (refer to Figure 27.4). This coloring applies to any code between a pair of script tags. It doesn't affect any code that is part of an event handler in the HTML because that code is not within a script tag.

JavaScript Snippets

Snippets, discussed earlier in this chapter, can also be used to store frequently used JavaScript code fragments. In fact, Dreamweaver ships with a variety of handy JavaScript snippets that you might want to explore.

Code Navigation Menu

Whether you're working in the Code Inspector, Dreamweaver lets you easily jump to different JavaScript functions with the Code Navigation menu. You can access this menu from the Code Inspector toolbar by clicking the double curly braces icon, as shown in Figure 27.44. The menu lists any JavaScript functions. Choosing a function moves the cursor to the first line of that function and scrolls the display if necessary to show it. (This feature is not available in the Document window's Code view.)

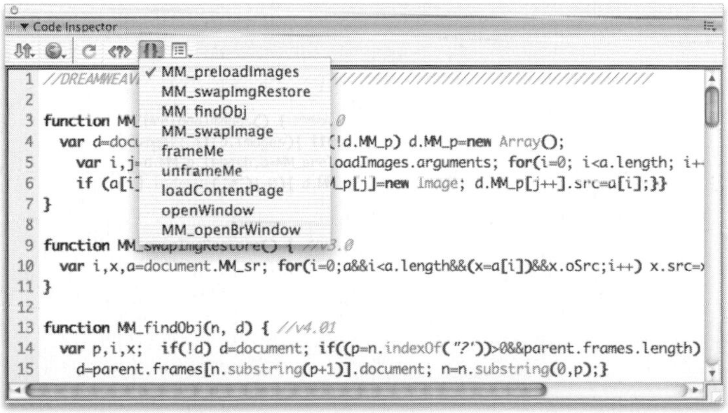

FIGURE 27.44
Accessing the Code Navigation menu (available only in Code view).

Auto-Balancing Braces

Losing track of opening and closing curly braces, parentheses, and quotation marks is a common problem in scripting. In Dreamweaver, you're on your own with determining whether all your open quotes close properly, but the program helps you with your braces (curly braces, square brackets, parentheses). To test whether your punctuation marks are correctly paired, follow these steps:

1. In Code view or the Code Inspector, select an opening brace (curly brace, square bracket, or parenthesis).

2. Select Edit > Balance Braces. Dreamweaver selects all code between that brace and the corresponding closing brace.

If you're used to how auto-balancing is implemented in some text editors (such as BBEdit), the Dreamweaver Balance Braces command might take some getting used to. You can't use it to balance anything but braces. Also, it works only when you select an opening brace, not a closing brace. It responds with an error beep if you have incorrectly balanced braces (for instance, more openers than closers, or vice versa). For example, selecting the first opening brace in the following code would generate an error sound, because the braces don't balance:

```
function helloWorld() {
    if (a==0) {
    window.alert("Hello, world");
}
```

Selecting the second opening brace, however, would not result in an error; Dreamweaver would just select the code inside the if statement braces.

SUMMARY

In this chapter, you have seen how the Dreamweaver coding environment works, and how to make the most of integrating it into your authoring workflow. You can use Dreamweaver for coding tasks from markup to scripting, and you can configure it to handle whatever file types you need to edit. And you have a great deal of control over how the code editor formats, rewrites, and displays your code. Finally, if you don't want to use the internal code editor, you can configure Dreamweaver to link to an external text editor. If you use HomeSite (Windows) or BBEdit (Mac) for this task, special integration features are available, but you can use any text editor you choose. From a coder's point of view, who needs Design view?

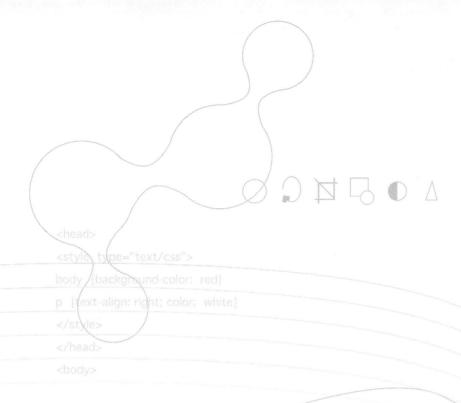

```
<head>
<style type="text/css">
body {background-color: red}
p {text-align: right; color: white}
</style>
</head>
<body>
```

CHAPTER 28

CUSTOMIZING AND EXTENDING DREAMWEAVER

DREAMWEAVER MX 2004 IS UNIQUE IN THE WORLD OF COMMERCIAL SOFTWARE because of the degree to which it can be tweaked, customized, and extended. Not only can you change defaults, tweak preferences, and rearrange panel groups, but you can actually change the program's functionality by creating new panels, commands, menu entries, and more. And it's all because of extensions.

This chapter examines how extensions work within the Dreamweaver architecture and how you can start customizing your Dreamweaver program—without needing any programming knowledge—by changing settings in Dreamweaver configuration files. This chapter also introduces the Extension Manager and the Macromedia Exchange for Dreamweaver, which you can use to download and install some of the hundreds of free and commercial extensions that have been created by other developers for your use.

HOW DREAMWEAVER IS CONFIGURED

Dreamweaver is unlike other commercial software. Most programs are created in a programming language like C++ and then are compiled into executable programs, meaning that you cannot delve into their structure to see how they were built or to adjust their functionality. It's become increasingly popular, over the last several years, for programs to offer plugin architecture, which allows third-party developers to create independent program modules—called plugins, or Xtras, or Xtensions, or even filters, depending on the software involved. But these modules generally must also be constructed as compiled programs built in C++ or comparable languages.

See Chapter 29, "Creating Your Own Extensions," for a discussion of how to create your own extensions.

Dreamweaver, on the other hand, was built with the express idea of allowing users to modify or add to the basic core of the program. To do this, the engineers built Dreamweaver as a combination of a compiled C core, with most of the interface and many of its functions coded into external JavaScript, XML, and HTML files. These external files are called *extensions*. By editing these extensions, you can customize how Dreamweaver looks and works. By adding to them, you can add to Dreamweaver functionality. Although you have to know your way around JavaScript to create your own extensions, it takes only a fundamental knowledge of HTML and XML to customize an extension's interface. And the Macromedia Exchange for Dreamweaver has hundreds of extensions written by other developers, available free or commercially for download and installation.

Working with the Configuration Folder

The key to all these menus, commands, and functions is the *Configuration folder*. This folder, located in the Dreamweaver **Application** folder, contains all the extension files for the program. Examine the **Configuration** folder, shown in Figure 28.1, and you'll recognize many of the folders inside it as matching Dreamweaver elements: Objects, Behaviors, Commands, Menus, Inspectors, and so on. Within those folders are the individual files that control the appearance and functionality of the different Dreamweaver interface elements. The general breakdown of file types within the folder is as follows:

- HTML files provide the layout and interface elements for individual dialog boxes, panels, and inspectors.

- The JavaScript files—and any JavaScript code embedded within the HTML files—provide the functionality for the different extensions.

- The XML files (with various filename extensions) provide the instructions Dreamweaver follows on how the different extensions should be integrated into the main program interface.

FIGURE 28.1

The Dreamweaver Configuration folder and its contents.

If you feel adventurous enough to tinker with these files, you can customize and even extend your Dreamweaver program. In this chapter, you'll get a chance to explore the HTML and XML files in the **Configuration** folder and changes you can make within them. The next chapter covers extending program functionality using JavaScript.

Before making *any* changes to the **Configuration** folder, it is vital that you make a backup copy so that you can return Dreamweaver to its original state in case anything gets corrupted. You can store your backup wherever you want; just make sure that you copy the whole folder!

Multiuser Support: The User Configuration Folder

Like all recent operating systems, Dreamweaver assumes that you might be working in a multiuser environment. This means that more than one person might be logging on to your computer, launching programs and customizing preferences. Dreamweaver creates multiuser configuration by having multiple **Configuration** folders. While the program's default configuration tasks are carried out by the main **Configuration** folder stored within the Dreamweaver application folder, each user also has his or her own **Configuration** folder.

For Dreamweaver/Windows, each user's personal configuration files are stored in

```
c:\documents and settings\username\application data\macromedia\
➥dreamweaver mx\configuration\
```

For *username*, substitute your name, or perhaps Owner or Default User (depending on how your system is set up). Note that, unless you've been tinkering with your system settings, the Application Data folder is probably invisible. You need to make it visible (in Explorer, select Tools > Folder Options > View) before you can see, access, and possibly tweak any configuration files.

None of this applies to Windows 98, which is the only operating system still supported by Dreamweaver that doesn't use a multiuser setup. Windows 98 Dreamweaver users have only one **Configuration** folder—the main folder in the **Programs** folder.

For Dreamweaver/Mac, each user's personal configuration files are stored in

```
/users/username/library/application support/dreamweaver mx/
configuration
```

Substitute your login name for *username*. The folder is visible and not locked.

Examine one of these extra folders, and you'll see that it isn't a complete duplicate of the main **Configuration** folder. It contains only certain files, representing interface elements that need to be customized differently for each user. (In fact, if you've never launched Dreamweaver, the folder doesn't exist yet. It's only created as needed.) Preferences such as code coloring, menus that can be customized with keyboard shortcuts, commands that can be recorded using the History panel, and even objects that save their dialog box settings from one work session to another are all represented in the individual user's **Configuration** folder.

How important is this to you? If you're interested in being just a general Dreamweaver user, all you need to know about multiuser configuration is that it's happening. If you're a tinkerer, however, working with configuration files to customize your program, you need to know which **Configuration** folder contains the files you want to work with for any given task. The general rule is this: When looking for extension files, Dreamweaver always looks in the user's **Configuration** folder first. This means that if a file exists in that folder, Dreamweaver uses it (and doesn't use the duplicate file that exists in the main folder). Only if a particular extension file has no counterpart in the user's folder does Dreamweaver use the file in the main **Configuration** folder.

RECONFIGURATIONS, FROM SIMPLE TO FANCY

Everything you do to customize Dreamweaver affects the **Configuration** folder. But not everything requires that you climb into the **Configuration** folder and tinker with it. The following sections look at different reconfiguring tasks you might want to perform, starting from simple changes with a friendly interface and working toward the more geeky (and potentially scary) changes that can be done only in the guts of the machine. Have fun in there!

Modifying Keyboard Shortcuts

Keyboard shortcuts are a great way to quickly access Dreamweaver functions and commands. The default Dreamweaver setup includes keyboard shortcuts for most menu commands, as well as various shortcuts for selecting, scrolling, and editing in Design or Code view. And in case your favorite command or operation doesn't have a shortcut, or if you just don't like the shortcuts Macromedia has chosen for you, the shortcuts are completely customizable. You can add, subtract, and reassign shortcuts as you like. You can even create different sets of shortcuts for different purposes and switch between them at will.

Working with the Keyboard Shortcuts Editor

The main interface for working with keyboard shortcuts is the Keyboard Shortcuts editor, shown in Figure 28.2. You access it by choosing Edit >

Keyboard Shortcuts (Windows) or Dreamweaver > Keyboard Shortcuts (Mac). In this window, you can choose from one of the predefined sets of shortcuts supplied with Dreamweaver, or create and customize your own set.

FIGURE 28.2
The Keyboard Shortcuts editor.

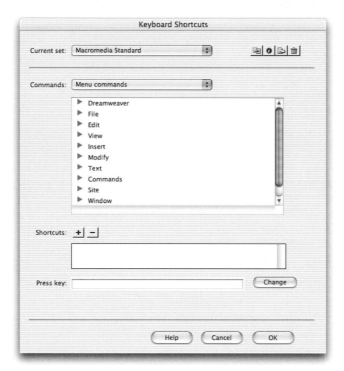

Dreamweaver ships with four sets of keyboard shortcuts:

- **Macromedia Standard shortcuts**—The default set, for best integration with the rest of the Macromedia MX 2004 programs (Fireworks MX 2004, Flash MX 2004).

- **Dreamweaver 3 shortcuts**—For upgrading users who don't want to memorize a whole new set of commands every time there's an upgrade.

- **HomeSite shortcuts**—Very helpful for Windows users who switch frequently between Dreamweaver and the HomeSite+ text editor.

- **BBEdit shortcuts**—Equally helpful for Mac users who switch between Dreamweaver and the BBEdit or BBEdit Lite text editors.

TIP

To get a nice, handy reference sheet listing all the shortcuts in a particular set, click the Export Set as HTML button in the Keyboard Shortcuts dialog box. In the Save File dialog box, give your export file a name and save it anywhere you like. After the export file has been created, open it in a browser to see a nicely formatted table listing all commands and shortcuts.

To switch between one of these default sets, just choose its name from the Shortcut Set drop-down menu. The new shortcut set goes into effect as soon as you click OK to close the dialog box. (There's no need to restart Dreamweaver!)

Although you can't modify these sets, you can duplicate any of them to create your own set, and modify that set to your heart's content. Just activate the set you want to duplicate, and click the Duplicate Set button. Name your set anything you like, and click OK to close the dialog box and create it.

To create a new shortcut in your custom set or to change an existing shortcut, search through the menu list in the editor window, and select the command you want to change. Any shortcuts assigned to it appear in the Shortcuts field. To change the existing shortcut, select it in the Shortcuts field. To add a new shortcut, click the + button above the Shortcuts field. Then click inside the Press Key field, type your desired key combination, and click Change.

Here are a few tips on working with the Shortcuts editor:

- As soon as you activate the Press Key field, Dreamweaver interprets every keystroke you make as a keyboard shortcut you're trying to assign. If you press the wrong key combination, you can't press Delete to remove it or Ctrl/Cmd+Z to undo your typing. Just remember, as long as you don't click the Change button, nothing you've entered in the Press Key field will become a shortcut.

- Only certain key combinations are considered valid for shortcuts. Function key combinations are allowed, with or without modifiers. But number and letter combinations must begin with Ctrl (Windows) or Cmd (Mac). If you enter an invalid key combination in the Press Key field, Dreamweaver warns you and won't let you assign it.

- If you enter a key combination in the Press Key field that has already been assigned to some other menu item, Dreamweaver warns you. If you click the Change button, Dreamweaver asks if you want the key combination reassigned. Of course, there's nothing wrong with that.

Any changes you make to a shortcut set are not saved until you switch to another shortcut set (at which time you're given a prompt to save changes to the previous set) or you click OK to close the Keyboard

Shortcuts editor. For instance, if Dreamweaver freezes or quits before you can do either of these things, your shortcut changes won't be saved.

How Shortcuts Are Configured

Thanks to the Keyboard Shortcuts editor, you don't have to know about the nuts and bolts of configuration to modify shortcuts. But in case you want to tinker around under the hood, keyboard shortcuts are controlled by several XML files located in the **Configuration/Menus/Custom Sets** folder (see Figure 28.3). Each file in this folder—**Macromedia.xml**, **HomeSite.xml**, and so on—represents a set of keyboard shortcuts. The file contents look something like this:

```
<SHORTCUTSET name="Macromedia Standard" type="factory">
  <SHORTCUT ID="DWMenu_File_Save"  keys="Cmd+S"/>
  <SHORTCUT ID="DWMenu_File_SaveAs"  keys="Cmd+Shift+S"/>
  <SHORTCUT ID="DWMenu_File_SaveAsTemplate"  keys=""/>
  etc
</SHORTCUTSET>
```

FIGURE 28.3
The files of the Custom Sets folder in the Configuration folder govern keyboard shortcuts in Dreamweaver.

If you've created any custom shortcut sets, they appear in your user **Configuration** folder, each as another XML file named whatever you called your shortcut set, with the .xml filename extension. In the same folder, the **Active.txt** file tells Dreamweaver which set of shortcuts is currently active. If for some reason you just don't like working with the Keyboard Shortcuts editor (it's too slow, for instance, or you just can't get the hang of the Shortcut and Press Key fields, or, dang it, you just prefer typing things), you can edit the files in your user **Configuration** folder to make any shortcut changes you like. Just remember that your XML syntax must be correct, and it is possible to goof up Dreamweaver's functioning by doing this. If you accidentally hose your shortcut set by manually editing it, quit Dreamweaver, throw away your set's XML file, and change the **Active.txt** file so that it lists some other set as active. That's the price of being a code monkey.

Customizing the Favorites Category of the Insert Bar

You're working hard, creating pages, inserting content, trying to be as efficient as possible. Do you ever get tired of bouncing around from category to category in the Insert bar, skipping past all those objects you hardly ever use to get to the ones you use all the time? New to Dreamweaver MX 2004, you can easily add your favorite objects to the Favorites category of the Insert bar—without a lick of code monkeying.

Using the Customize Favorite Objects Window

The first time you visit the Favorites Insert bar, it's empty except for a message encouraging you to click to customize the category. When you click this message, Dreamweaver opens the Customize Favorite Objects dialog box, as shown in Figure 28.4.

To add a favorite, in the left portion of the window, choose a favorite object from the list. Then click the >> button to move the object to the Favorites list on the right.

Your favorite objects appear in the Favorites Insert bar in the order they appear in the Favorites list. To organize your favorites (when you have several of them), select an item in the list, and press the up or down arrow to move it up or down.

To add a vertical separator bar to the Insert bar (so that you can clump objects in logical groups), select the object that should be followed by a separator bar, and click the Add separator button.

FIGURE 28.4
The empty Favorites Insert bar and Customize Favorite Objects dialog box.

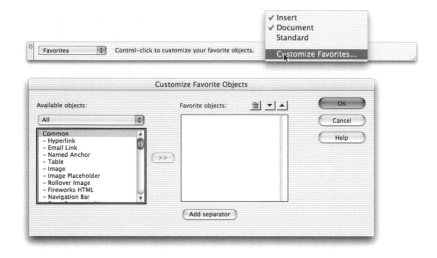

To remove an object from the Favorites list, select it and click the trash can icon. (This doesn't delete the object from the rest of the Dreamweaver interfaces—just from your Favorites category.)

When you're done creating favorites, click OK to close the dialog box, and there are your favorites (see Figure 28.5)!

FIGURE 28.5
The populated Favorites category, ready for more customizing.

You can come back to this window at any time to update your Favorites category. Just right-click an empty part of the Favorites Insert bar, and choose Customize Favorites.

How the Insert Bar Is Configured

You don't need to know how Dreamweaver configures the Favorites category, or any of the categories in the Insert bar. But in case you're curious—or you just love to tinker—here's how it works: In the **Configuration/Objects** folder, the **Insertbar.xml** file contains instructions for configuring the Insert bar, including categories, object buttons, object groups, and so on. The code framework looks like this:

```
<category>
   <button />
   <separator />
   <menubutton>
      <button />
      <button />
   </menubutton>
</category>
```

Each pair of category tags creates an Insertbar category. Within each category, button tags create object buttons, and menubutton tags containing other button tags create object drop-down menus populated by object buttons. Vertical separator bars are created from separator tags.

The actual code includes various attributes for each tag, which ends up looking like this:

```
<category id="DW_Insertbar_Common"
➥ MMString:name="insertbar/category/common" folder="Common">
   <button id="DW_Anchor" image="Common\Anchor.gif"MMString:
   ➥name="insertbar/anchor" file="Common\Anchor.htm"/>
   <separator />
   <menubutton id="DW_LayoutTools" MMString:name=
   ➥"insertbar/layoutTools"
   ➥ image="Common\Table.gif" folder="Tables">
      <button id="DW_Table" image="Common\Table.gif" enabled="!
      ➥_VIEW_LAYOUT" MMString:name="insertbar/table"
      ➥file="Common\Table.htm"/>
      <button id="DW_Div" image="Common\Div.gif" enabled="!
      ➥_VIEW_LAYOUT" MMString:name="insertbar/div" file=
      ➥"Common\Div.htm"/>
</menubutton>
<category>
```

Customizing Insertbar.xml: Creating Object Menus in the Favorites Category

What if you want to add a drop-down menu of objects to your Favorites category, like those found in the other categories? The Customize Favorite Objects dialog box doesn't give you that choice in its friendly interface. To add a custom object group or drop-down object menu to your Favorites, do the following:

1. First, of course, you have to have some objects in your Favorites category. If you don't, use the Customize Object Favorites dialog box to add them. Examine your Favorites Insert bar category, and determine which objects you'd like to group in a drop-down menu (maybe table-creating objects, or form elements, or any other grouping that makes sense to you). Make sure these objects appear together in the Insert bar so that they'll be easier to find and modify in the **Insertbar.xml** file.

2. Open **Insertbar.xml** in your favorite text editor. Remember, because you have customized the content of your Insert bar, you need to find the user-specific copy of this file in your user-specific **Configuration/Objects** folder.

3. Look in the code for a `menubutton` tag pair (it doesn't matter which one). Select the opening tag and choose Edit > Copy. You should end up copying something like this:

    ```
    <menubutton id="DW_Images" name="Images" image=
    ➥"Common\Image.png">
    ```

4. Scroll almost to the bottom of the code, where you find the code for the Favorites category (it's the last category). Look for this tag, which marks the beginning of the category:

    ```
    <category id="DW_Insertbar_Favorites" name="Favorites"
    ➥folder="Favorites">
    ```

5. Examine the `button` tags in this category, looking for the tags representing the objects you want to group. When you find them, insert a blank line immediately preceding them and another immediately following them so that they're isolated and easy to spot. Place the insertion point in the blank line preceding your buttons, and select Edit > Paste to paste the `menubutton` tag you copied in step 3. Place the insertion point in the blank line following your buttons, and type a closing `menubutton` tag:

    ```
    </menubutton>
    ```

6. Now you need to configure the `menubutton` tag.

    The `id` attribute is used by Dreamweaver, and it must be unique.

Select the existing value and replace it with something unique to yourself, such as Fred_TableObjects. If you put your own name in there, you can use your text editor's Find command to find this group easily the next time you want to edit it.

The name appears in the ToolTip that appears when you hover the mouse over the object menu. Change it to something that describes your group, such as Table Stuff or Form Elements.

The image represents the object menu in the Insert bar, along with the tiny triangle indicating that it's a menu. Choose one of the image attributes specified in your button tags, and copy it here.

That's it! Save and close the file. The next time you launch Dreamweaver, check out your custom object menu in the Favorites Insert bar (see Figure 28.6).

FIGURE 28.6
The Favorites category with a drop-down object menu in place.

Automating Tasks with Custom Commands

If you're one of those ultra-efficient workers who likes saving steps whenever possible, you've probably already used *macros* in other programs. Macros let you record all the steps involved in performing a certain task and save them to be played back later, usually triggered by a keyboard shortcut or menu command. In Dreamweaver, instead of macros, you create and deploy *custom commands*. Custom commands include temporary recorded commands, permanent commands saved using the History panel, and more-complex commands that must be programmed (written as scripts). The following sections look at the first two kinds of custom commands; the more-complex scripted commands are discussed in the section "Creating Command Extensions" in Chapter 29.

Recording Commands

A *recorded command* is a series of steps that you tell Dreamweaver to record and then tell it to play back as many times as you need those steps performed.

To record a command, follow these steps:

1. Plan out the steps you'll record, and, if necessary, set up the conditions for the recording. (For instance, if you want to record formatting a table in a certain way, you need to open a document and create a table before you can start recording the formatting steps.)

2. Choose Commands > Start Recording.

3. Perform whatever steps you want to record. To format a table, for instance, you use the Property Inspector to apply background color, cell padding or spacing, border width and color, and any other table properties. Dreamweaver can't record steps such as changing the selection or changing the active document; if you perform any of those steps while recording, they're ignored. But you can choose from the Property Inspector, type, and choose menu commands as part of your recorded steps.

4. When you're done recording, choose Commands > Stop Recording.

The command you've recorded stays in memory, ready to be played back, until you record over it or until you quit Dreamweaver.

To play back a recorded command, follow these steps:

1. Set up whatever conditions need to be in place before the command can be executed. (To replay a recorded command that formats a table, for instance, you must first select a table.)

2. Choose Commands > Play Recorded Command. The individual steps you recorded are executed.

3. Repeat this procedure as many times as you want, to execute the command as many times as needed.

As you can see, recorded commands are pretty wonderful. But they do have their limitations. They're meant to be quick, temporary aids in performing certain repetitive tasks. They can't do anything more complex or long-term than that. For example:

- Dreamweaver can store only one recorded command at a time in memory. As soon as you record a new command, whatever command was previously being remembered is overwritten.

- Recorded commands don't include dialog boxes and therefore can't be customized according to user input. Each command always performs exactly the same set of steps, with exactly the same parameters.

- Not all actions can be recorded. If you try to record a set of steps that includes changing a selection, for instance, that step won't be recorded. When the command is played back, this might lead to undesired results.

- There is no error checking. For instance, if you don't make the appropriate selection before replaying a recorded command, the command simply won't work. You won't get a nice, friendly alert message telling you what went wrong.

Saving Commands with the History Panel

If you like the idea of recording and replaying your actions, but you want more control and flexibility, the History panel offers two alternatives to recorded commands. Its Replay Steps and Save As Commands features let you save and reproduce sets of consecutive or nonconsecutive steps temporarily or permanently. Repeated steps are intended for use when you want to perform a set of actions and then immediately repeat those actions one or more times. Saved commands are for when you want to save your set of actions as a permanent item in the Dreamweaver interface, ready for replaying at any time in the future.

The procedure for repeating steps and saving steps as commands is basically the same. Just do the following:

1. Plan out the steps you want to save. If necessary, set up the conditions for them (create a table to format, for instance).

2. Open the History panel (select Window > History) so that you'll be ready to work with it. To make sure you're starting with a clean History panel and can capture as many steps as possible, choose Options > Clear History.

3. Perform whatever set of actions you want to repeat. Each action shows up as a step in the History panel, as shown in Figure 28.7). As with recorded commands, repeated or saved History steps cannot include certain kinds of actions (such as changing the selection or moving the mouse). If your actions include any of these, they appear in the History panel as a horizontal red line or black mouse-movement indicator line.

FIGURE 28.7

Repeating steps from the History panel.

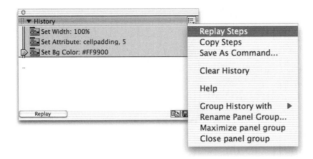

4. When you're finished performing your procedure and are ready to repeat it, select all the steps in the History panel that you want to repeat:

- To select contiguous steps, Shift-click each.

- To select noncontiguous steps (for instance, to skip over a mouse movement), Ctrl-click (Windows) or Cmd-click (Mac) each.

5. If you want to repeat these steps without saving them permanently, from the History panel choose Options > Replay Steps. Each selected step is performed again (unless it's a mouse movement or other unrepeatable action), and the History panel shows a new step called Replay Steps. Choose Replay Steps as many times as you need to. Each replay generates a new Replay Steps step in the panel.

6. If you want to save these steps as a permanent part of the Dreamweaver interface, from the History panel choose Options > Save As Command. (If your steps include any that can't be captured, Dreamweaver warns you of this and gives you the opportunity to cancel the operation.) You're prompted to give your new command a name. After you've done this and clicked OK to close the dialog

box, your new saved command appears in the bottom portion of the Commands menu.

After you've saved a set of History steps as a command, you can replay those steps any time by choosing your command from the Commands menu. Unlike the recorded commands described earlier, your saved command stays saved until you get rid of it. So if you like saving commands, you'll likely end up with a variety of them. To rename or delete a saved command, choose Commands > Edit Command List (see Figure 28.8).

FIGURE 28.8
The Edit Command List dialog box for working with saved commands.

How Saved Commands Are Configured

Just like other pieces of the Dreamweaver interface, saved commands live in the **Configuration** folder. Specifically, they live in your user **Configuration** folder, in the **Configuration/Commands** folder. Each saved command exists as an HTML file with the command's name and the .htm filename extension, as shown in Figure 28.9. If you want to climb under the hood and mess with those commands, you can open the files in any text editor and tinker with them. (You'll learn more about this in the next chapter.) Of course, doing so could destabilize Dreamweaver if you don't do it right. If that happens, open the **Configuration/Commands** folder and delete the saved command file that's causing the trouble.

FIGURE 28.9
The user Configuration/Commands folder, showing a saved command file (and a few other items).

EXERCISE 28.1

Saving History Steps As a Custom Command

Are you already dreaming of all the commands you'd like to create? Before you get too excited, remember that mouse actions (such as selecting and drawing) can't be captured, so your commands can't include them. This limits the kinds of procedures you can turn into saved commands. In this exercise, you'll go through some procedures for working with tables, saving a few as custom commands.

1. Start by creating a new HTML document.

2. Open the History panel (select Window > History). Because you've just created this document, the panel should be empty, but if it's not, choose Options > Clear History.

3. Using the Table object in the Insert bar, create a new table. Give it three rows and three columns and whatever other properties you like. (The table is just for practicing, so what it looks like doesn't matter.)

   Look at the History panel. You should have one step called Insert Table. This is a recordable step, so there's no red x in the step icon.

4. Without deselecting the table, use the Property Inspector to change any of its properties. Then look at the History panel. For each property changed, you should have another step, without any red x's in the step icons and without any black lines between the steps (see Figure 28.10). Everything you've done so far could be recorded as one big command (macro) if you like.

FIGURE 28.10

The History steps for creating a table and changing some of its properties.

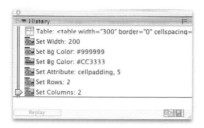

5. Put the insertion point inside one of the table's cells, and change a property or two. The History panel has a black horizontal line between the changes you made to the table and those you made to the cell. That's because you changed the selection (you clicked inside a cell), and Dreamweaver can't record that. So you can't make one big command out of your steps so far. But you can make a command out of any one or more steps not separated by a black line.

6. Now for something potentially useful that you will save into a command. With the insertion point still inside a cell, choose Modify > Table > Split Cell (or click the Split Cells button in the Property Inspector). When the dialog box appears, choose to split the cell into two columns. Click OK to close the dialog box and split the cell.

7. Look in the History panel, and you'll see that this is a recordable step. Select that step and choose Options > Save as Command. When prompted, name your command **Split 2 Columns** and click OK. Take a peek at the Commands menu, and you'll see your new command, as shown in Figure 28.11.

8. Now create another cell-splitting command. Put the insertion point in another table cell, and split the cell into three columns. Then select that step in the History panel and save it as **Split 3 Columns**.

9. How about one or two more cell-splitting commands? Split a few more cells to create the Split 2 Rows and Split 3 Rows commands.

10. Try out your saved commands. Delete the table you created, and insert another table. Experiment with putting the insertion point in a cell and choosing one of your commands. (After doing this, check out the History panel. You'll see that executing your command counts as a History step.) Sure, it's just a macro built from one

History step, but by saving it as a command, you've just saved your-self the trouble of having to use the dialog box to determine what gets split and how every time. That's a tiny little time-saver.

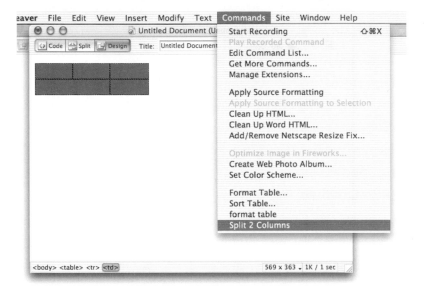

12. If you want to see how your custom commands are configured, go to Windows Explorer or the Macintosh Finder and open your user **Configuration** folder. Within it, open the **Commands** folder. (See the discussion earlier in this chapter on how to find this folder.) You'll see files such as **Split 2 Columns.htm** and **Split 3 Columns.htm**. Those are your commands!

Customizing Dialog Boxes Using HTML

Most objects, commands, and behaviors that provide dialog boxes store the layout information for those dialog boxes in HTML files with-in the **Configuration** folder. Input fields, check boxes, pop-up menus, and so on are created from standard HTML form elements and are for-matted using tables or layers. Although you can't add or remove input fields without compromising functionality, you can change the dialog box layout by changing the HTML layout. Strange as it might seem, you can use Dreamweaver to do this editing—although you have to quit Dreamweaver and relaunch before your changes take effect.

Dreamweaver loads HTML and JavaScript files into memory at startup and generally doesn't access them again as it's running. This is why it's safe to work on these files while the program is running.

To customize a particular dialog box, you first need to locate its configuration file. Table 28.1 lists locations for the elements you'll be most likely to customize. Within these locations, look for an HTML file named after the object, command, or other extension you want to customize.

TABLE 28.1 ## Locations of Common Extension Types Within the Configuration Folder*

Extension Type	Location
Objects (items in Insert bar and Configuration/Objects (within subfolders according Insert menu) to category	Configuration/Objects
Behaviors	Configuration/Behaviors/Actions
Commands	Configuration/Commands_Configuration/ Menus/MM
Inspectors**	Configuration/Inspectors
Panels**	Configuration/Floaters

*All these elements can be found in the main Configuration folder. Each piece is added to the user-specific Configuration folder only as needed (for example, as user-specific customizations occur).
**Most panels, and many Inspectors, are hard-coded into the main Dreamweaver application file, so you can't customize them.

For instance, say you wanted to customize the Call JavaScript dialog box. Because Call JavaScript is a behavior, you look in **Configuration/ Behaviors/Actions**. In that folder, you find **Call JavaScript.js** and **Call JavaScript.htm**. The JS file contains the functionality for the behavior; the HTML file contains the dialog box layout. If you open the HTML file in Dreamweaver, you see the dialog box layout as a form and table, as shown in Figure 28.12. Any changes you make to the layout here are reflected in the dialog box. Just don't rename the form or its elements, or add or subtract any form elements, or you might break the behavior.

For multiuser environments: Because the Call JavaScript dialog box does not hold any settings from session to session, it does not exist as a user-specific file in the user's **Configuration** folder. It exists only in the main **Configuration** folder.

FIGURE 28.12

The Call Java-Script.htm file as it appears in Dreamweaver Design view and in the Call JavaScript dialog box.

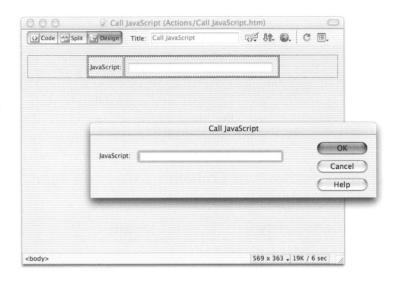

Customizing Dreamweaver Menus with menus.xml

Every command that appears in the Dreamweaver menu system—including application menus, context menus, and others—is determined by the menu configuration file, **menus.xml**. This file governs what menus appear in the menu bars, what commands appear on each menu, and what action Dreamweaver should take when that command is chosen. (The action is usually to open and execute a configuration file, such as **Objects/Common/Table.htm**.)

Menus.xml is located in the **Configuration/Menus** folder. Like **Insertbar.xml**, it is a well-formed XML document. It contains a <menubar> tag pair as its root element, with various other elements (tags and tag pairs) nested within it. The main element structure is as follows:

```
<menubar>
    <menu>
        <menuitem/>
        <menuitem/>
    </menu>
    etc.; more menus
</menubar>
```

The **Configuration/Menus** folder also contains **menus.bak**, a backup file for **menus.xml**. If you accidentally trash your only copy of **menus.xml**, you can duplicate **menus.bak**, change its extension to .xml, and resurrect your Dreamweaver menu system. (This doesn't mean you shouldn't back up your **Configuration** folder! If you rely on the BAK file for your backup, and it becomes corrupted, you'll need to reinstall Dreamweaver to get your menus back in working order.)

Each tag has a set of attributes that govern how each menu and command appears and what happens when it is launched. Figure 28.13 shows a section of **menus.xml** and how it translates into a menu in Dreamweaver.

FIGURE 28.13
A section of menus.xml and the Dreamweaver menu it creates.

```
<MENU name="_Text" id="DWMenu_Text">
    <MENUITEM name="_Indent"              key="Cmd+Opt+]" domreqi
    <MENUITEM name="_Outdent"             key="Cmd+Opt+[" domreqi
    <MENU name="Paragraph _Format" id="DWMenu_Text_Format">
        <MENUITEM name="_None"            key="Cmd+0" file="Menus
        <MENUITEM name="_Paragraph"       key="Cmd+Shift+P" file=
        <MENUITEM name="Heading _1"       key="Cmd+1" file="Menus
        <MENUITEM name="Heading _2"       key="Cmd+2" file="Menus
        <MENUITEM name="Heading _3"       key="Cmd+3" file="Menus
        <MENUITEM name="Heading _4"       key="Cmd+4" file="Menus
        <MENUITEM name="Heading _5"       key="Cmd+5" file="Menus
        <MENUITEM name="Heading _6"       key="Cmd+6" file="Menus
        <MENUITEM name="P_reformatted Text" file="Menus/MM/Text
    </MENU>
    <MENU name="_Align" id="DWMenu_Text_Alignment">
        <MENUITEM name="_Left"            key="Cmd+Opt+Shift+L"
        <MENUITEM name="_Center"          key="Cmd+Opt+Shift+C"
        <MENUITEM name="_Right"           key="Cmd+Opt+Shift+R"
        <MENUITEM name="_Justify"         key="Cmd+Opt+Shift+J"
    </MENU>
```

Although you can't add an entirely new menu item and give it functionality without scripting, you can still customize your menu system by tweaking the XML. You can move menu items, add separators between them, and even copy them so that they appear in multiple places—once in a regular menu and once in a context menu, for instance. One caveat related to duplicating menu items is that each item in **menus.xml** has an id attribute that must be unique. If you duplicate an item, you must change the duplicate's id so that it differs from the original item.

EXERCISE 28.2

Adding a Command to a Context Menu

In this exercise, you'll climb around inside **menus.xml** and copy the Check Spelling command from its location at the bottom of the application menu bar's Text menu to another location at the bottom of the context menu for text items.

Before you begin this or any other exercise in this chapter, make sure that you have a backup copy of the **Configuration** folder so that you can restore the default Dreamweaver configuration at any time.

1. Quit Dreamweaver (if it's running), and open **menus.xml** in your text editor. Note that this is a big file, and it's easy to get lost! To help you out, if your text editor supports line numbers and word wrap control, turn on line numbering and turn off word wrap (called *soft wrap* in some programs). This makes navigating and seeing the structure of the XML tags easier.

2. The hardest part of this whole procedure is finding your way around **menus.xml**. You're looking for the Check Spelling menu item, which is at the bottom of the Text menu. This menu item has the unique ID DWMenu_Text_CheckSpelling, so the easiest thing to do is to search for this. (If you're doing this for any other command, you probably won't know the ID, so you'll probably have to do more-creative searching, such as looking for spelling.)

3. Select the entire Check Spelling menu item, and choose Edit > Copy. Your selected code should look like this:

```
<menuitem name="Check Spelling" key="Shift+F7" enabled=
➥"dw.getDocumentDOM() != null &&
➥dw.getDocumentDOM().getParseMode()
➥ == 'html' && (dw.getFocus() == 'textView' ||
```

```
⇒dw.getFocus(true)
⇒ == 'html' || dw.getFocus() == 'document' &&
⇒ dw.getDocumentDOM().getFocus() == 'body')" command="
⇒if (dw.getDocumentDOM().getView() == 'code')
⇒{dw.getDocumentDOM().setView('split')}dw.setFocus
⇒('document');
⇒ dw.getDocumentDOM().checkSpelling()" id=
⇒"DWMenu_Text_CheckSpelling" />
```

What's all this code for? The Check Spelling command doesn't call on an extension file; instead, all the code for the spell check is contained in the menu entry itself.

4. Now you have to find the Text context menu. Search for **DWTextContext**, which is the unique ID for this menu. After you've found that, you can search for </menubar> because the next occurrence of that tag will be the end of this menubar. The last menuitem entry should be Page Properties.

5. You want to create a new line after the Page Properties entry, and before the </menu> entry. To create a separator line so that your new entry sits by itself at the bottom of the menu, type the following into the new line:

```
<separator/>
```

Create another new line, and select Edit > Paste to insert the Check Spelling menu item.

6. You need to find the new menu item's id attribute and change it slightly so that it's unique. Find the end of that very long <menuitem/> tag, and change the id to the following (the new code is in bold):

```
DWMenu_Text_CheckSpelling_Context
```

Just to make sure your new id is unique, search **menus.xml** for this name. You should find just one occurrence of it—the one you just added.

7. Launch Dreamweaver and try out your new menu! Type some text into a document, select the text, and right-click (Windows) or Ctrl-click (Mac). The context menu that appears looks like the one shown in Figure 28.14.

FIGURE 28.14
The Text context
menu with a sepa-
rator and Check
Spelling command
added.

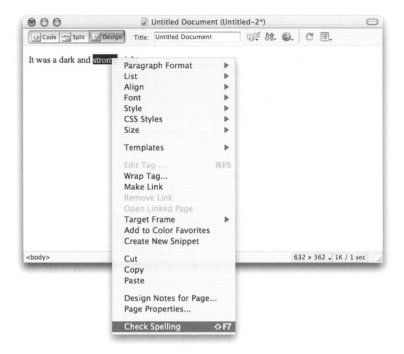

THE WORLD OF THIRD-PARTY EXTENSIONS

If you want to move beyond customizing Dreamweaver into extending
its functionality, you're ready for some new extensions. If you want to
take advantage of the programming prowess of others without having to
write extensions yourself, you're ready for the Macromedia Exchange for
Dreamweaver and the Extension Manager.

Finding Extensions: The Macromedia Exchange

The Macromedia Exchange for Dreamweaver is a huge storehouse of
extensions that Macromedia has collected and put on the Web for all
to use. Although Macromedia wrote some of these extensions, the major-
ity were written by independent developers who created the extensions
to help themselves and who have agreed to share them with the
Dreamweaver community. These extensions have been packaged in a

common format (MXP) and put on the Exchange for everyone to use. Most are free, but a few are commercially produced and might have a small cost.

The Exchange is not the only place to find extensions. Many extension-writing Dreamweaver developers have extensions and have placed them and others on various websites.

You access the Macromedia Exchange for Dreamweaver, shown in Figure 28.15, by pointing your browser to www.macromedia.com/exchange/dreamweaver. Hundreds of different extensions are available for adding all sorts of functionality to Dreamweaver—everything from enabling site searches to installing lists of country codes to adding new Flash button styles. All extensions have been tested by Macromedia to ensure that they'll install and function correctly. Those with Macromedia approval have been tested more rigorously and meet Macromedia UI guidelines, so they blend in smoothly with the Dreamweaver interface. You can browse extensions by category or search by title or author. To download extensions, you need to sign up for a free Macromedia Exchange account.

FIGURE 28.15
The Macromedia Exchange for Dreamweaver, home to hundreds of (mostly) free extensions.

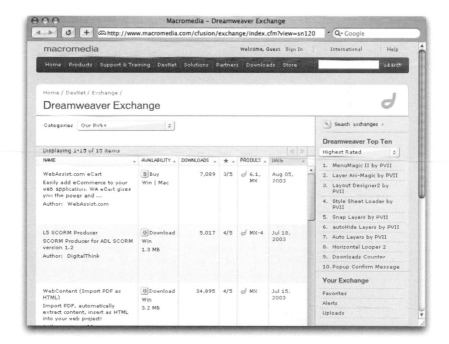

You can also access the Exchange from within Dreamweaver by choosing Help > Dreamweaver Exchange or any of the Get More commands, such as Insert > Get More Objects, Commands > Get More Commands, or the Get More Behaviors command at the bottom of the Behaviors panel's Actions pop-up menu. Choosing any of these commands launches your browser and takes you to the Exchange home page.

To download an extension from the Exchange, find the extension you want and follow the links to its download page. Choose the Windows or Mac version, and download. Extensions are usually very small files (most are less than 100KB) and therefore download quickly, even on slow connections. The downloaded file is a special installer file with the .mxp extension (Macromedia eXtension Package), which can be installed into Dreamweaver using the Extension Manager utility.

Installing and Managing Extensions: The Extension Manager

The Extension Manager (EM), shown in Figure 28.16, is a utility program used to install and manage your downloaded extensions. You can launch the Extension Manager from within Dreamweaver by choosing Commands > Manage Extensions or Help > Manage Extensions. You can also launch it from the desktop by selecting Start > Programs > Macromedia > Macromedia Extensions Manager (Windows) or by finding and launching it from within the **/Applications/Macromedia Extension Manager** folder (Mac). From the desktop, you can also double-click any MXP file to automatically launch the Extension Manager.

The Extension Manager isn't just for Dreamweaver. It also installs and manages Flash and Fireworks extensions.

To install an extension using the Extension Manager, double-click the MXP file on your hard drive, which launches the EM and starts the installation process. You also can launch the EM separately and then choose File > Install Extension or click the Install icon in the Extension Manager window. During the installation process, extension files are added to the appropriate places in the user's **Configuration** folder, and the user copies of any relevant XML files (such as **Insertbar.xml** or menus.xml) are updated. Some extensions require that Dreamweaver be restarted before they appear in the interface; the EM alerts you if this is the case.

FIGURE 28.16
The Extension Manager interface showing several Dreamweaver extensions already installed.

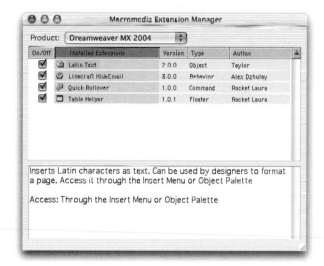

After the extension is installed, you can read all about it in the EM interface (refer to Figure 28.16). You can temporarily deactivate the extension by deselecting it in the extensions list. Or you can permanently delete it by selecting it and choosing File > Remove Extension or by clicking the Uninstall icon in the Extension Manager window.

In addition to installing extensions, the Extension Manager can be used to package files that make up an extension into MXP files, and even to submit them to the Macromedia Exchange for Dreamweaver. See the section "Packaging Your Extensions" in Chapter 29 for more on this.

EXERCISE 28.3

Downloading and Installing the Line Remover Extension

In this exercise, you will download and install Sascha Frinken's Line Remover extension, a simple but handy command that stops Internet Explorer from leaving those ugly highlight boxes around links after you've clicked them. The boxes are meant to show that the link has focus and are intended to enhance usability, but they are very unpopular with many web designers. They are especially distracting when used with irregular-shaped hotspots in image maps.

 The Line Remover extension is available on this book's website at www.peachpit.com, in case it's not available on the Exchange by the time you read this.

1. From within Dreamweaver, choose Commands > Get More Commands. This launches your browser and takes you to the Macromedia Exchange for Dreamweaver.

2. If you haven't already created a Macromedia user account, take a moment to do so now. It's as simple as entering a user ID and password.

3. Because you know the extension you want, you can search for it. In the Exchange's search field, type **Frinken**, and click Search.

4. After a moment, a list of Sascha Frinken's extensions appears. Find Line Remover and download it.

5. Find the line remover file on your hard drive—it's an MXP file called **MX15575_line_remover.mxp**—and double-click it to launch the Extension Manager. You're prompted to agree to the Macromedia license for extensions (click Agree to continue). After a second or two, you get a message telling you that the extension was successfully installed. Congratulations!

6. Examine the EM interface to learn more about this extension (see Figure 28.17). You'll see that it's a command, accessed through the Commands menu, and that it removes the lines from selected links. What could be simpler?

7. If Dreamweaver was running when you installed this extension, you didn't get prompted to quit and relaunch. That means that the extension should work right away. If Dreamweaver isn't running, launch it now.

8. In Dreamweaver, create a new document, unless one is already open. Type **click me**. Select the words and use the Property Inspector to assign a null link (type # in the Link input field). Save the page.

FIGURE 28.17

The Line Remover extension as it appears in the Extension Manager.

9. Preview the page in Internet Explorer, and see what happens when you click the link. The browser puts a line around the linked text.

10. Back in Dreamweaver, choose Commands > line_remover. A dialog box opens, explaining what the extension will do, as shown in Figure 28.18. Click Do it! If you take a look at the Behaviors panel, or the code for your page, you'll see that some JavaScript has been added to cause the link to lose focus as soon as it's clicked. This makes the outline disappear.

FIGURE 28.18

The Line Remover command in action.

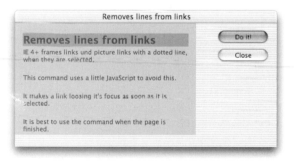

11. Preview the page in Internet Explorer again, and click the link. The blue box appears and then almost immediately disappears. That's your extension in action!

Summary

Customizing Dreamweaver is a great way to maximize your working efficiency and enjoyment. Thanks to the **Configuration** folder, with its HTML, XML, and JS files, almost all aspects of the program's interface and functionality can be customized and added to relatively easily. If you enjoy tinkering with HTML and XML, the nonscripted files of the **Configuration** folder allow you to customize menus, dialogs, and even some panels. If you love souping up your program with extra functionality, but you don't want to become a programming geek, the Macromedia Exchange for Dreamweaver and Extension Manager open up a world of extensions that are easily installed and immediately useful. If you want to dip your toes a little deeper into the pool, keep reading. The next chapter introduces you to the wonderful world of scripting, packaging, and sharing your own extensions with the Dreamweaver community.

CHAPTER 29

CREATING YOUR OWN EXTENSIONS

YOU LEARNED IN THE PRECEDING CHAPTER HOW TO TAKE ADVANTAGE OF Dreamweaver extensions written by other people. For ultimate power in Dreamweaver, you also can write your own extensions. This chapter discusses how Dreamweaver uses JavaScript, HTML, and XML to create extensions, and how you can create two of the most popular and accessible types of extensions—objects and commands.

BEFORE YOU GET STARTED

If you're a JavaScript newbie, or if your skills are rusty, you might want to have a JavaScript reference available as you work. The handiest reference is the JavaScript section in the Dreamweaver Reference panel. If you want more in-depth information, the O'Reilly series on JavaScript (*JavaScript in a Nutshell*, *JavaScript Pocket Reference*) is a valuable resource.

Although writing Dreamweaver extensions isn't just for propeller-heads, it isn't for sissies, either. To work with object and command files, you need to be fairly comfortable with reading and writing HTML code, and you need some understanding of JavaScript. In particular, you should be familiar with the basic language structure, syntax requirements, and concepts of JavaScript (expressions, variables, functions, and so on), and how to use JavaScript to process data collected by HTML forms.

Writing extensions is also an inherently dangerous occupation. Because you are messing around in the guts of Dreamweaver, you can very easily break the program. In the previous chapter you learned about the **Configuration** folder and its role in Dreamweaver functionality. Writing extensions involves altering the **Configuration** folder. Always make a backup of this folder before you begin exploring and tinkering. If disaster strikes and Dreamweaver stops functioning properly, just quit Dreamweaver, trash the corrupted **Configuration** folder, and replace it with your backup. The next time you launch the program, all should be well.

You'll also need a text editor to create all the code involved in extending Dreamweaver. Odd as it might sound, many extending tasks can be done using Dreamweaver itself as the text editor. This isn't recommended, though. Editing some configuration files, such as **menus.xml** or **insert-bar.xml**, while Dreamweaver is running can cause problems. You can also get very confused while trying to create code in Dreamweaver. However, you might want to use Dreamweaver Design view to help you design the interfaces for your extensions.

THE DREAMWEAVER API

Dreamweaver extensions are constructed following the Dreamweaver application programming interface (API), which consists of all the procedures, file construction specifications, custom functions, and formatting instructions that determine how and when commands will be processed and dialog boxes will appear, and so on. Learning how to write your own extensions means becoming familiar with the API. The official "dictionary" that explains and documents the API is Macromedia's *Extending Dreamweaver* manual. This manual comes in PDF format on the Dreamweaver application CD-ROM; you also can download the PDF from the Macromedia website (www.macromedia.com/support/dreamweaver/).

How Extensions Are Constructed

Each extension (object, behavior, command, inspector, floating panel, report, translator, and so on) consists of one or more files in the **Configuration** folder. The file types are as follows:

Every rule has an exception. Although most extensions exist in HTML and JS files, it is possible to create simple extensions that exist solely as command lines built into **menus.xml**. How that works is beyond the scope of this chapter.

- **HTML file**—Each extension begins with an HTML file. Every command, object, and behavior has one HTML file that *is* the extension. Form elements, placed in the body, become the extension's user interface.

- **JS file**—Each extension gains its functionality through JavaScript. The script functions can be placed in the head of the main HTML file. More frequently, they are found in JS files linked to the HTML file. Complex extensions might link to several JS files.

- **GIF files**—Icons, buttons, and any other graphic elements that appear in the user interface are created from GIF images, which are also stored in the **Configuration** folder.

In addition to these files, each extension might have an entry in one of the XML files, such as **menus.xml** or **insertbar.xml**, that Dreamweaver uses to populate many of its interface elements.

How Extensions Are Processed

For each extension type, the Dreamweaver API has a procedure that determines how the extension's JavaScript instructions will be processed. This procedure often involves custom JavaScript functions that Dreamweaver executes automatically at certain times (on startup, when the user clicks something, and so on).

How Extensions Talk to Dreamweaver

How does an extension tell Dreamweaver to open a new document, insert or edit document contents, or whatever else you want it to do? The API includes a variety of predefined JavaScript objects, each of which contains various methods (functions) that you use to communicate with different parts of the program:

- **The Dreamweaver (dw) object**—This object contains dozens of methods to control application-wide behavior. Some sample methods are dw.openDocument(), dw.browseForFileURL(), dw.openWithExternalEditor(), and dw.undo(). This object also contains child objects representing different parts of the application, each of which has its own set of methods, such as dw.cssStylePalette.editSelectedStyle() and dw.historyPalette.startRecording().

- **The Document (dom) object**—This object contains hundreds of methods, controlling all aspects of document editing. Document object methods and properties can be used to manipulate the selection (dom.getSelectedNode(), dom.setSelection()), can change any document property (dom.body.bgcolor="000000"), and can access and edit any item in a document (dom.deleteTableRow()).

- **The Site object**—This object contains methods for working with sites and the Site panel. Site methods let you get and put files (site.get(), site.put()), perform sitewide file-management chores (site.findLinkSource(), site.locateInSite()), and work with the Site panel itself (site.editColumns(), site.setFocus()).

In addition to these main objects, other custom JavaScript objects give you access to specific areas of Dreamweaver, such as working with web servers (the MMHttp object), working with Flash and Fireworks (SWFFile, FWLaunch), working with Design Notes (MMNotes), and so on. All these objects, methods, and properties are detailed in the *Extending Dreamweaver* manual, mentioned earlier.

CREATING OBJECT EXTENSIONS

The simplest kind of Dreamweaver extension to understand and create is the object. An *object*, in terms of the Dreamweaver API, is an HTML file that contains, or uses JavaScript to construct, a string of HTML code to insert into the user's document. The user clicks an icon in the Insert bar or selects an item from the Insert menu, and the specified code is inserted into the current document, usually at the insertion point.

Objects in the Configuration Folder

As you learned in the preceding chapter, object files are stored in sub-folders of the **Configuration/Objects** folder that correspond to object categories in the Insert bar. Most objects consist of from one to three files, all with the same name but different extensions:

- **An HTML file (such as table.htm)**—This is the object file itself—the file that contains or returns the code to be inserted. This is the only file that *must* be present to constitute an object.

- **A JavaScript file (such as table.js)**—This file contains JavaScript instructions for constructing the code to be inserted, in the form of one or more JavaScript functions, and is called on from the HTML file. This file is optional. It is entirely legal to contain the JavaScript functions in the head section of the object file instead of saving it to an external file. As experienced scripters know, it can be easier to keep track of and update JavaScripts if the code is in a separate file—but this isn't necessary.

- **An image file (such as table.png)**—This file contains an 18×18-pixel image that Dreamweaver uses to represent the object in the Insert bar. This file is also optional: If there is no image file, Dreamweaver supplies a generic image icon to represent the object in the panel.

Figure 29.1 shows some typical sets of object files.

FIGURE 29.1

Files for the Date object (two files only) and the Image object (three files), both found in the Configuration/Objects /Common folder.

 Date.htm

 Date.png

 Image.htm

 Image.js

 Image.png

Objects in the Insert Bar: insertbar.xml

Dreamweaver MX 2004 relies heavily on XML files to help construct a unified interface from its many files and extensions. The **insertbar.xml** file, stored in the **Configuration/Objects** folder, contains a series of nested XML tags that govern what objects appear where in the Insert bar. Examine this file in a text editor, and you'll see that each object category is created from a pair of category tags. Within a category, subcategories are created by a pair of menubutton tags. Each object's presence in the panel is determined by a button tag. The button tag includes attributes specifying what files the object will call on, when it will appear in the panel, and what its unique identifier is. The Table object, which appears inside the Layout objects subcategory of the Common objects category, looks like this:

```
<category id="DW_Insertbar_Common" MMString:name=
➥"insertbar/category/common" folder="Common">
[etc]
    <menubutton id="DW_LayoutTools" MMString:name=
    ➥"insertbar/layoutTools"
    ➥ image="Common\Table.png" folder="Tables">
[etc]
        <button id="DW_Table" image="Common\Table.png" enabled=
        ➥"!_VIEW_LAYOUT" MMString:name="insertbar/table"
        ➥ file="Common\Table.htm"/>
[etc]
    </menubutton>
[etc]
</category>
```

The API for Objects

Some objects, such as the Email Link object, use dialog boxes to collect user information; others, such as the Horizontal Rule object, don't. The overall structure and procedure for both is the same.

Object File Structure

Figure 29.2 shows the HTML file for a simple object that doesn't call a dialog box. Note that the body section is empty. Also note that the objectTag() function is not called anywhere in the file. Dreamweaver calls the function automatically. Figure 29.3 shows the file for the same object, with a dialog box. The body contains a form, which will become the contents of the dialog box. Note that the form does not include a Submit button. Dreamweaver supplies this.

Both files contain the following key elements:

- **Filename**—This becomes the Insert menu entry for the object.

- **Page title**—This becomes the ToolTip that pops up to identify the object in the Insert bar.

- **objectTag() function**—This JavaScript function is the most important element of the object file. This function returns the exact code you want the object to insert into your document, enclosed in quotes. The objectTag() function is part of the Dreamweaver API, so it doesn't need to be defined. It also doesn't need to be called; Dreamweaver calls it automatically when the object is chosen.

- **HTML form (optional)**—This becomes the dialog box for collecting user input and customizing the code. Dreamweaver supplies the OK and Cancel buttons automatically.

- **displayHelp() function (optional)**—If there is a dialog box, and this function is defined, Dreamweaver adds a Help button to the dialog box. When the user clicks that button, the function is executed.

In the example shown in Figure 29.2, the code returned by the objectTag() function is a simple level 1 heading. Everything between the quotation marks, in the return statement, becomes part of the user's document. In the example shown in Figure 29.3, form input is collected and used to construct the return statement.

FIGURE 29.2
The HTML file for a simple object that does not call a dialog box.

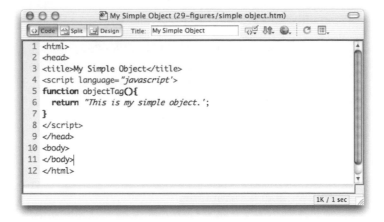

```
1  <html>
2  <head>
3  <title>My Simple Object</title>
4  <script language="javascript">
5  function objectTag(){
6    return "This is my simple object.';
7  }
8  </script>
9  </head>
10 <body>
11 </body>
12 </html>
```

FIGURE 29.3
The HTML file for an object that does call a dialog box.

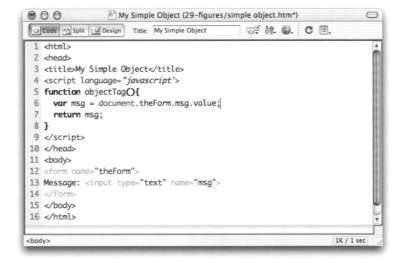

```
1  <html>
2  <head>
3  <title>My Simple Object</title>
4  <script language="javascript">
5  function objectTag(){
6    var msg = document.theForm.msg.value;
7    return msg;
8  }
9  </script>
10 </head>
11 <body>
12 <form name="theForm">
13 Message: <input type="text" name="msg">
14 </form>
15 </body>
16 </html>
```

The Procedure for Objects

The API procedure for processing objects determines how and when Dreamweaver uses the file elements previously discussed. The procedure is as follows:

1. At startup, Dreamweaver reads the **insertbar.xml** file and populates the Insert bar using its entries. It also populates the Insert menu using the filename as the menu entry.

2. When the user mouses over the object in the panel, Dreamweaver uses the `<title>` from the object file to create the ToolTip that will appear.

3. When the user clicks an object, Dreamweaver reads the object file. If the file includes body content, Dreamweaver displays a dialog box containing the content, supplying OK and Cancel buttons automatically. If the file contains a `displayHelp()` function, a Help button also appears.

4. The final step in the API process is calling the `objectTag()` function. If there is a dialog box, the function is called when the user clicks OK. If there is no dialog box, the function is called as soon as the user clicks the object icon in the Insert bar. Whatever string of text is returned by the `objectTag()` function is inserted into the user's document, usually at the insertion point. (An exception to this is when the `return` string contains head content, such as a `<meta>`, `<base>`, or `<link>` tag. In this situation, even if the insertion point is in the body, Dreamweaver inserts the code into the head.)

Pretty simple, eh? To create an object extension, all you have to do is decide what code you want inserted and create a file that matches the structure shown in Figures 29.2 and 29.3. Then create an entry for the object in **insertbar.xml** to make it part of the Dreamweaver interface.

Not all objects are created equal! Some items lurking in the Insert bar—especially those representing server-side code for live data pages—are very complex commands in object disguise. They're way beyond the scope of this chapter.

EXERCISE 29.1

Setting Up Shop

In this exercise, you'll get your workspace in order and learn about some of the basic extension-developing features available in Dreamweaver. You will create a custom folder within the **Objects** folder to store your exercise objects and add data to **insertbar.xml** so that your custom folder becomes a custom Insert bar category.

1. Make sure that Dreamweaver isn't running. You are doing this exercise to experiment with how and when Dreamweaver loads extensions.

2. Find your user-specific **Configuration** folder. (Check the section "Multiuser Support: The User Configuration Folder" in Chapter 28, "Customizing and Extending Dreamweaver," for more on user-specific Configuration items.) If there's an **Objects** folder here,

open it. If there isn't, create a folder and call it **Objects**; then open it. Create a new folder inside this folder, and name it **Development**. When you're developing new objects, it's a good strategy to put them in a special folder called **Custom** or **Development**, at least until you're sure they're running properly.

Never store your object files loose in the **Configuration/Objects** folder, or Dreamweaver won't recognize them. Objects must be placed in an existing or new subdirectory within that folder.

3. If your user-specific **Configuration/Objects** folder contains an **insertbar.xml** file, open it in a text editor. If it doesn't, find the **insertbar.xml** file in the main Dreamweaver Configuration folder, and make a copy of it in your user-specific folder. Then open the copy in a text editor. Scroll to the end of the entries. Immediately above the closing `</insertbar>` tag, add the following code:

```
<category id="DW_Insertbar_Development" folder="Development">
</category>
```

This creates a Development object category in the Insert bar, matching your **Development** folder.

4. Save and close **insertbar.xml**.

5. Launch Dreamweaver. At startup, the program checks the **Configuration** folder and loads all extensions that are inside it.

6. Check the Insert bar for a new category called Development. Because you added the code at the end of **insertbar.xml**, it should appear as the last item in the category drop-down menu, as shown in Figure 29.4. Of course, if you choose that category, it will be empty. You'll address that next.

FIGURE 29.4

The new Development objects category in the Insert bar.

EXERCISE 29.2 ## Making a Simple Object

The simplest objects are those that don't call up a dialog box for user input, and therefore always return the same code. The simple object you will create in this exercise is a copyright statement—just the sort of thing you might want to put at the bottom of all your web pages.

To create this object, use the text editor of your choice. Save all the exercise files in the **Development** folder you created in the preceding exercise.

1. The first step when creating any object is to decide exactly what code you want the object to insert. In this case, you want a one-line piece of text, formatted however you like, utilizing the special HTML entity for ©. Figure 29.5 shows the copyright statement with formatting applied.

FIGURE 29.5
Formatting the Tom Thumb copyright statement for inclusion in an object file.

 Use Design view to create and format the copyright statement, and then go to Code view. The code will be there, written for you.

2. Create the basic object file, with all structural elements in place. Open your text editor and enter the basic required code for an object without a dialog box. You can leave out the details specific to this object for now. Your code framework should look like this

(elements that you will replace later with custom text appear in italic):

```
<html>
<head>
<title>Title Goes Here</title>
<script language="JavaScript">
function objectTag() {
return 'inserted code goes here';
}
</script>
</head>
<body>
</body>
</html>
```

3. Enter a page title into the code. This will become the ToolTip that shows in the Insert bar. A logical title for the current file might be "Tom Thumb Copyright Info." The top portion of your code should now look like this (the new code is in bold):

```
<html>
<head>
<title>Tom Thumb Copyright Info</title>
```

4. Insert the desired line of code as the return statement of the objectTag() function. If you've already typed this line of code, you can just copy and paste it in; otherwise, type it in manually now.

Note that the entire return statement has to be in quotation marks. They can be single or double quotes; just make sure that they're in balanced pairs.

Your code should now look like this (the new code is in bold):

```
<html>
<head>
<title>Tom Thumb Copyright Info</title>
<script language="JavaScript">
function objectTag() {
return '<p>&copy; 2003, Tom Thumb</p>';
}
</script>
</head>
```

Working with Word? As with any JavaScript return statement, no hard returns can occur within the statement. Make sure your code is written in one long line, or it won't work!

```
<body>
</body>
</html>
```

You can get more control over how the object name appears in the Insert menu by editing **Configuration/ Menus/menus.xml**.

5. Save your file in the **Development** folder. Call it **Tom Thumb Copyright.htm**. The filename will become the menu command that appears in the Insert menu, so it's good practice to name it something descriptive. Capitalization and spacing also carry through to the menu entry. (The extension can be .htm or .html—Dreamweaver accepts either.)

6. To make the new object appear in the interface, you need to add a `<button/>` tag to **insertbar.xml**. Quit Dreamweaver, if it's running, and open **insertbar.xml** in your text editor. Find the Development category tag you added earlier, and add the following code (the new code is in bold):

```
<category id="DW_Insertbar_Development" folder="Development">
          <button name="Tom Thumb Copyright Info" image=
➡"Development\Copyright Statement.gif" id="DW_TomThumb-
➡Copyright" file="Development\Tom Thumb copyright.htm" />

</category>
```

You might notice that you're referring to an image (Copyright Statement.gif) that doesn't exist yet. That's okay! You must specify an image for your object to display properly in the Insert bar—even if you specify a non-existing image.

7. Test your object! Launch Dreamweaver and create a new document, if one isn't already open.

8. Check the Development category of the Insert bar; the new object should be there, represented by a generic icon. Position the cursor over the icon. The ToolTip should appear, as shown in Figure 29.6.

9. While you're at it, check the Insert menu. Your new object appears at the bottom of the menu, identified by its filename.

FIGURE 29.6
The new custom object, with ToolTip.

Don't waste your time making custom icon files for objects while they're still in the development phase. Wait until the object is all polished and perfectly functioning, and then dress it up with a custom icon. (Exercise 29.4 shows how to make an icon file.)

10. Position the insertion point where you want the object inserted, and click the object. The desired code should be inserted into the document at the current cursor position. Congratulations! You've made your very first object.

What If It Doesn't Work?

If your object doesn't show up in the Insert bar, you either saved it in the wrong place, you didn't append the .htm/.html extension to the filename, or there might be a syntax error in the **insertbar.xml** file.

If your object shows up, but something is wrong with the code, you'll probably get an error message when Dreamweaver tries to execute the objectTag() function. Dreamweaver error messages are fairly specific as far as what went wrong and what needs fixing. Examine the message, and fix your code accordingly.

| EXERCISE 29.3 | **Creating an Object with a Dialog Box** |

Your simple object is fine as far as it goes, but it's not very flexible or useful because it always returns the same code, no matter what. What if you want to assign a copyright to someone besides good old Tom Thumb? A fully functional object would bring up a dialog box that would ask for user input and would enter that information into the code. That's the object you will build in this exercise.

1. Open **Tom Thumb Copyright.htm** (from the preceding exercise) and save it as **Copyright Statement.htm** in the **Development** folder. Why reinvent the wheel? You can just build on your previous success by adding a dialog box and tweaking the objectTag() function's return statement to collect user input.

2. Change the title of the new object file to **Copyright Statement**.

3. Decide what pieces of the code you want to replace with user input. Check Figure 29.5 as a reminder of what the end product should look like. For this object, you want to ask the user for a copyright name (rather than Tom Thumb) and a copyright year. (If your JavaScript skills are up to it, you could have Dreamweaver automatically calculate the year; for this exercise, just ask the user to insert it.)

4. You need to create an HTML form that will serve as a dialog box to collect this information. To be functional, your form needs two text fields: one to collect the name and another to collect the year. Open **Copyright Statement.htm**, and build the form in the body section of that file. If you like coding forms by hand, go to it. If you would rather use a visual editor, open the file in Dreamweaver, and use Design view to build it, as shown in Figure 29.7.

If you want to improve your skills in creating user-friendly forms, pay attention to all the user interface elements in Dreamweaver. The dialog boxes, inspectors, and panels are beautiful examples of clean, transparent interface design, and they're constructed almost entirely from standard form elements.

FIGURE 29.7
The form for the
Copyright Statement
object dialog box
as it appears in
Dreamweaver Code
and Design view.

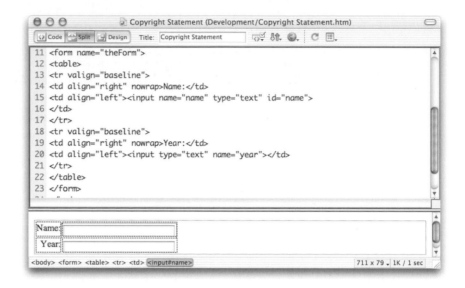

Your form code should look like this:

```
<form name="theForm">
<table>
<tr valign="baseline">
<td align="right" nowrap>Name:</td>
<td align="left"><input type="text" name="copyrightname">
➡</td>
</tr>
<tr valign="baseline">
<td align="right" nowrap>Year:</td>
<td align="left"><input type="text" name="copyrightyear">
➡</td>
</tr>
</table>
</form>
```

Note that neither the table nor the text has any formatting. Dreamweaver supplies the formatting when it processes the extension. If you enter your own formatting, your dialog box won't meet Macromedia user interface guidelines and might not look good on all computers. So don't do it!

If you're building your form in the Dreamweaver visual editor, method and action properties are automatically added to the <form> tag. Your form doesn't need either of these because it won't be processed in the standard way. You can safely remove these properties from your code.

6. Your form is now pretty. To make it functional, you need to rewrite the `return` statement of the `objectTag()` to include the collected user input. If you're an old hand at coding, this will be a piece of cake. If you're a novice at JavaScript, the trickiest bit is balancing the opening and closing quotes so that you don't end up with any unterminated string literals. Your `objectTag()` function should now look like this (the new code is in bold):

If you think the `return` statement is too unwieldy to read easily, you can collect the form input into variables and use those to construct the final statement.

```
function objectTag() {
return '<p>&copy; '+document.theForm.copyrightyear.value+',
➥ '+document.theForm.copyrightname.value+'</p>';
}
```

7. Quit Dreamweaver if it's running. To add the new object to your Insert bar, open **insertbar.xml** and add the following code to your Development category tag:

```
<button name="Copyright Statement" id="DW_CopyrightStatement"
➥ file="Development\Copyright Statement.htm" />
```

8. Launch Dreamweaver, and create a new document to try out your new object. You should get a lovely dialog box that looks like the one shown in Figure 29.8.

FIGURE 29.8
The dialog box for the Copyright Statement object.

Copyright Statement	
Name:	OK
Year:	Cancel

9. When you fill in your information and click OK, a customized copyright statement line should appear in your document.

What If It Doesn't Work?

As with the earlier exercise, if there's a problem with your code, Dreamweaver should give you a helpful error message. Read the error message, try to guess what it means, and then go back to your code and look for problems. Compare your code to the code listed in this exercise to see what might be wrong.

The most common things that go wrong in this kind of object file are incorrect references to form elements and mismatched single and double quotes in the return statement.

EXERCISE 29.4

Adding an Object Icon

Professional-looking objects have their own icons. When the development phase of your object is finished, the final touch is to make an icon file to represent it in the Objects panel.

The requirements for an icon file are as follows:

- The file must be a GIF, JPEG, or PNG image file, preferably no larger than 18×18 pixels. (Larger images work, but they're squashed into an 18×18-pixel space in the panel.)

- It's customary, though not required, to give the image the same name as the object file it goes with. For this exercise, therefore, name the image **Copyright Statement.gif**.

- It's customary, though not required, to store the image file in the same folder as the object file it goes with. For this exercise, the icon file must be stored in the **Development** folder.

- The icon must be called on in **insertbar.xml** by adding the image attribute to the <button> tag.

Icon files can have any colors you like, and the icon can look like anything you can imagine. You'll quickly discover, however, that designing icons that clearly communicate what they represent, when there are only 324 pixels to play with, is a real art.

1. Create, adapt, or borrow an 18×18-pixel GIF file containing an icon. If you have access to a good graphics program (such as Macromedia Fireworks), and you want to create your own icon, do it. Otherwise, use the **Copyright Statement.gif** file in the **chapter_29** folder on the book's website at www.peachpit.com. (The image in this file is just a big © symbol, which is not hard to create.)

2. Put the icon file in the **Development** folder. The instructions you wrote earlier in the insertbar.xml file specified that the image would be stored here.

3. Launch Dreamweaver, create a new document if needed to activate the Insert bar, and take a look at your icon! Figure 29.9 shows the **Development** folder, with a cool custom icon in place.

FIGURE 29.9
The Copyright Statement object as it appears in the Insert bar, with its new custom icon in place.

Making the Most of Objects

Congratulations! You now have the foundation skills for making Dreamweaver objects. How can you make objects work for you? As you have seen, any piece of HTML code that you repeatedly use in web pages is a candidate for an object. The best object candidates, however, are pieces of code that you need to customize and then insert — changing the name and email address, specifying a certain URL to link to, and so forth.

Any time you find yourself going through the same steps repeatedly as you add content to web pages, ask yourself the following questions:

- Is the code I'm inserting similar enough each time that I could create an object from it?

- Are there differences in the code each time, or is it exactly the same? (If the code is exactly the same each time, requiring no customization, it might be more efficient to use a recorded command or snippet.)

- How many more times do I think I'm likely to need to insert this code? Will my need continue after today? After the current assignment? Indefinitely? Creating an object is a time-consuming solution (not smart for a need that is only very temporary).

- Do I have some extra time right now to devote to making this object? (Never try a new, challenging solution when your deadline is 45 minutes away.)

Depending on your answers, you'll know whether it's time to crack open Dreamweaver and fit a new custom object inside.

CREATING COMMAND EXTENSIONS

Commands are extensions that appear as entries on the Commands menu. (Actually, if you manipulate the **menus.xml** file, as discussed in the previous chapter, you can make commands appear on any menu. But they appear on the Commands menu by default.) They are the most versatile and powerful of the extension types, allowing you to perform almost any edits on a document or site. Their API requirements are simple, but because they are so flexible, they are not easy to master. This section covers what's involved in creating simple (and also not-so-simple) Dreamweaver commands.

Commands in the Configuration Folder

Like all extensions, commands are made from HTML and JavaScript. Each command consists of an HTML file (the command file itself) and optional, associated JS files and/or graphics. Command files are stored in the **Configuration/Commands** folder. By default, all files in this folder appear on the Commands menu.

If you have ever recorded commands or saved history steps as commands, you've created simple command files! Look in your user-specific **Configuration/ Commands** folder, and you'll find an HTML file for every saved command. The filename is the name you gave the command when you saved it.

The API for Commands

Like objects, commands can exist with or without dialog boxes. They can be simple or complex. A number of API-defined functions can be part of the command file, but the file also can be very simple, with no special functions. The API procedure is simple or complex, based on the file structure. (Note also that these are flexible extensions!)

Command File Structure

There are no required API functions for commands, although a variety of optional functions exist. Figure 29.10 shows a very basic command file, with only required elements in place. Note that the body section is empty. Note also that there are no API functions, and the main function is called onLoad.

FIGURE 29.10

The HTML file for a simple command that does not call a dialog box.

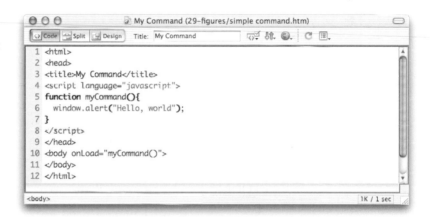

```
 1  <html>
 2  <head>
 3  <title>My Command</title>
 4  <script language="javascript">
 5  function myCommand(){
 6    window.alert("Hello, world");
 7  }
 8  </script>
 9  </head>
10  <body onLoad="myCommand()">
11  </body>
12  </html>
```

This kind of file has the following elements:

- **Filename**—The filename, minus its extension, becomes the menu entry. Command filenames can include spaces, and capitalization is respected.

- **Main function**—This is the function that makes the command do whatever you want it to do. It's a locally defined function, not part of the API, which means that it must be called explicitly. If the command has no dialog box, the function should be called in the <body> tag, using the onLoad event handler. If the command has a dialog box, the function should be called as part of the commandButtons() function (described in the following list).

Believe it or not, that's all that's absolutely required of a command file without a dialog box.

If the command includes a dialog box, a few more API elements are required. Figure 29.11 shows a sample command file with a dialog box, again containing only the necessary elements. Note that the form does not include a Submit button. The main command is now called from the commandButtons() function, not from the <body> tag.

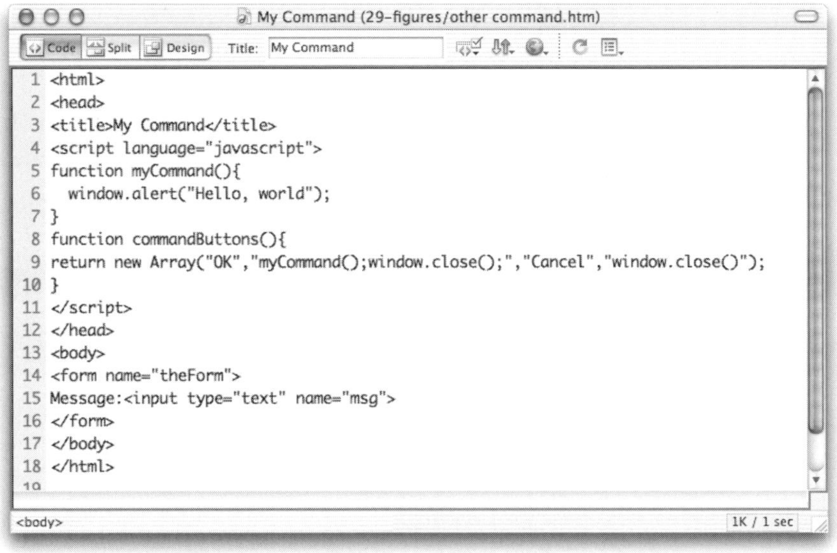

FIGURE 29.11

The HTML file for a command that calls a dialog box.

```
 1  <html>
 2  <head>
 3  <title>My Command</title>
 4  <script language="javascript">
 5  function myCommand(){
 6    window.alert("Hello, world");
 7  }
 8  function commandButtons(){
 9  return new Array("OK","myCommand();window.close();","Cancel","window.close()");
10  }
11  </script>
12  </head>
13  <body>
14  <form name="theForm">
15  Message:<input type="text" name="msg">
16  </form>
17  </body>
18  </html>
19
```

The required elements for a command that calls up a dialog box are as follows:

- **Page title**—The title is required if the command includes a dialog box. It becomes the title of the command's dialog box if there is one. If there isn't a dialog box, the title is not required.

- **HTML form**—As with all extensions, this creates the user interface (in this case, the dialog box). Note that, as with objects, the form does not include a Submit button. Unlike objects, however, command dialog boxes are not automatically supplied with buttons; instead, command buttons must be defined and given functionality using the commandButtons() function.

- **commandButtons() function**—If there is a dialog box, this function creates the buttons that appear. If this function doesn't exist, the user will have no way to activate or close the dialog box! The command-Buttons() function must return an array consisting of the name of each button, followed by the code to be executed when the button is clicked. Note that because the main command function must be called here, it should no longer be called using the <body> tag's onLoad handler.

In addition to these required elements, several optional API functions can be included. The most useful of these is canAcceptCommand(). This function determines whether the command should appear grayed-out (disabled) in the menu. A command that operates on the contents of a document, for instance, shouldn't be accessible if a document isn't open. If the function returns true, the command is accessible; if it returns false, the command is grayed-out. The API includes a whole slew of enablers (functions that determine whether something is possible) to help with this.

The Procedure for Commands

The API procedure for processing commands determines how and when Dreamweaver uses the file elements discussed in the preceding section. The procedure is as follows:

1. When the user clicks the Commands menu, Dreamweaver looks through all files that should appear on the Commands menu, checking each for the canAcceptCommand() function. If it's present, and if it returns false, that command is grayed-out in the menu. If it's not present, or if it returns true, the command is available.

2. When the user chooses a command from the menu, if there is no form, Dreamweaver executes whatever function is defined in the <body> tag's onLoad handler, and the procedure is complete.

3. If the command file includes a form, Dreamweaver calls the commandButtons() function to determine what buttons to add to the form. It calls any function called onLoad (such as an initializeUI() function). It then presents the dialog box, displaying the <title> in the dialog box's title bar.

4. When the user clicks any of the buttons in the dialog box, Dreamweaver executes the code attached to that button by the commandButtons() function. Typically, an OK button calls the main function and closes the window, an Apply button calls the main

function but doesn't close the window, and a Cancel button just closes the window. Note that the dialog box does not close until one of the buttons uses the `window.close()` statement.

So far, it all sounds pretty simple. The complex aspect of commands is that you usually want them to act on documents. And acting on documents means dealing with the Dreamweaver DOM.

The Dreamweaver DOM

If you've ever torn your hair out struggling with the conflicting DOMs of Internet Explorer and Netscape, working with Dreamweaver commands will be a welcome relief, because there's only the Dreamweaver DOM to worry about.

If you've worked in depth with JavaScript—especially if you've created DHTML effects using JavaScript—you're already familiar with the concept of the *document object model (DOM)*. The DOM is the hierarchical, or tree, structure of objects (tags, pieces of text, and so on) that makes up an HTML document. To gain access to any part of the document, you must navigate up and down the hierarchy, or climb up and down the tree.

Understanding Objects (Nodes)

An *object* is any page element that you can control by scripting. They have properties that you can access and change and methods that represent things you can do with them. Objects are also called *nodes*.

Parents, Children, and Siblings

Just as an HTML document is constructed from tags nested inside each other, and text blocks nested inside tags, so objects, or nodes, can have parents, children, and siblings. In the following example, the `<ul>` object is the parent node of the three `<li>` objects, which are siblings of each other:

```
<ul>
    <li>Moe</li>
    <li>Larry</li>
    <li>Curly</li>
</ul>
```

The text block `Moe` is the only child node of the first `<li>` object, and so on. Figure 29.12 shows a typical document diagrammed as a tree of objects.

FIGURE 29.12
A simple HTML document shown as it appears in Dreamweaver and as a diagrammed document tree.

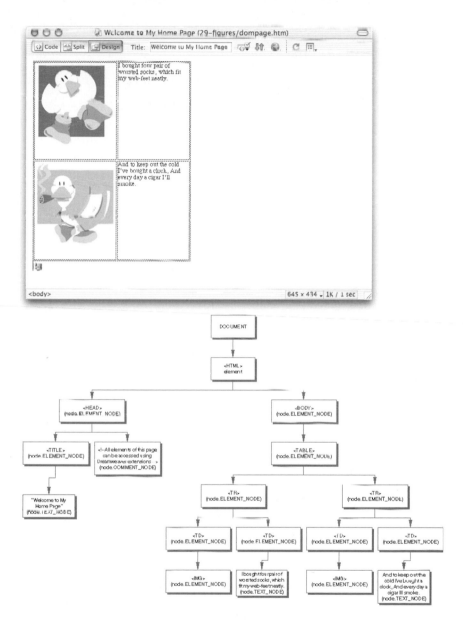

Node Types

A document has four kinds of objects, or nodes:

- **The document node type**—The document itself, as an entity.

- **The element node type**—All HTML tags belong to this type.

- **The text node type**—Each block of text is an object of this type.

- **The comment node type**—HTML comments.

In the earlier example, the Moe object is of the text node type; its parent
`<li>` object is of the element node type. Different node types have different properties and methods. Tables 29.1 through 29.4 list the properties
and methods of the different node types as they exist in the
Dreamweaver DOM.

TABLE 29.1 *DOCUMENT_NODE* **Objects**

Property/Method	Return Value	Read-Only?
nodeType	9	Yes
parentNode	Null	Yes
parentWindow	An object representing the document's parent window	Yes
childNodes	A NodeList containing all children	Yes
documentElement	The <html> tag element	Yes
body	The <body> tag element	No
URL	The document's absolute address (or an empty string if the document hasn't been saved)	No
getElementsByTagName	A NodeList containing all instances of the given tag (tagName)	No
hasChildNodes()	true	No

TABLE 29.2 *ELEMENT_NODE* **Objects**

Property/Method	Return Value	Read-Only?
nodeType	1	Yes
parentNode	The parent tag	Yes

Property/Method	Return Value	Read-Only?
childNodes	A NodeList containing all immediate children	Yes
tagName	The tag's HTML name (TABLE, A, IMG, and so on)	Yes
attrName	A string containing the value of the specified tag attribute	No
innerHTML	HTML code contained within the element's opening and closing tags	No
outerHTML	HTML code contained within the tag and the opening and closing tags	No
getAttributes (*attrName*)	The value of the *attrName* attribute	No
setAttribute	attrName, attrValue	No
removeAttribute	attrName	No
getElementsByTagName	A NodeList of children of the current element that are (*tagName*)tagName elements	No
hasChildNodes()	true/false	No

TABLE 29.3 *COMMENT_NODE* **Objects**

Property/Method	Return Value	Read-Only?
nodeType	8	Yes
parentNode	The parent tag	Yes
childNodes	An empty NodeList	Yes
data	A string of text between the opening and closing comment tags	No
hasChildNodes()	false	No

TABLE 29.4 **TEXT_NODE Objects**

Property/Method	Return Value	Read-Only?
nodeType	3	Yes
parentNode	The parent tag	Yes
childNodes	An empty NodeList	Yes
data	A string of text that comprises the current object	No
hasChildNodes()	false	No

Gaining Access to the DOM

In addition to all the standard JavaScript means of accessing and controlling DOM objects, the Dreamweaver API includes the document, or dom, object and its methods. These are the primary methods you use to edit documents using Dreamweaver extensions. Before you can use any of these methods on a document, however, you have to officially gain access to the document's structure using the dw.getDocumentDOM() function. Table 29.5 lists the specifications for this function. This function lets you gain scripting access to the contents of user documents.

TABLE 29.5 **Specifications for dw.getDocumentDOM()**

Syntax	dw.getDocumentDOM()
Description	This function creates a DOM object, giving access to the contents of a document's object structure.
Arguments	No arguments are required. If no arguments are present, the currently active document is used as the source of the DOM object. The optional arguments are as follows: document parent parent.frames[*number*] parent.frames['*framename*'] A URL. (URLs must be absolute or relative to the extension file.)
Returns	The document object at the top of the DOM hierarchy (DOCUMENT_NODE type).

You access the current user document's DOM by assigning it to a variable:

```
var theDOM=dw.getDocumentDOM();
```

After you have done this, you have access to an object of the first node type previously listed. You are officially climbing the document tree. You can now use the methods and properties of the various nodes to navigate through the document and edit it, as in these examples:

```
//change the background color to black
var theDOM=dw.getDocumentDOM();
var theBody=theDOM.body;
theBody.bgcolor="#000000";


//determine what kind of object the current selection is
var theDOM=dw.getDocumentDOM();
var theSel=theDOM.getSelectedNode();
if (theSel.nodeType=="1") {
    window.alert(theSel.tagName);
    } else if (theSel.nodeType=="3") {
    window.alert(theSel.data);
    }
```

The subject of DOM access is much bigger than this chapter covers, and it takes practice to master. But the rewards are great. After you know how to navigate a document, you can use your command or other extension to tell Dreamweaver to do almost anything to a user document. (Such power!)

For more information on working with the DOM, and scripting extensions in general, read *Dreamweaver MX Extensions,* published by New Riders, or *Building Dreamweaver 4 and UltraDev 4 Extensions,* published by Osborne.

EXERCISE 29.5

Making a Simple Command

In this exercise, you will create a command that finds all the images in an open document and assigns them a border width of 2. You won't need a dialog box, so this will be a simple file to create. You will, however, get some practice accessing the DOM.

1. In your text editor, create a new HTML file. Enter the basic code framework for a command with no dialog box. You will leave the

details blank for now (placeholder code is in italic):

```
<html>
<head>
<title>Set Image Border</title>
<script language="JavaScript">
function setImageBorder() {
//command code goes here
}
</script>
</head>
<body onLoad="setImageBorder()">
</body>
</html>
```

You set the `<title>`, although it won't be called on. You also create a local function, `setImageBorder()`, and call it `onLoad`. That's all the framework you need.

2. Custom commands, like custom objects, should be saved in your user-specific **Configuration** folder, to keep the main **Configuration** folder clean. Look in your user-specific **Configuration** folder. If it doesn't contain a **Commands** folder, create a new folder there and call it **Commands**. Save the file you just created in your user-specific **Configuration/Commands** folder as **Set Image Border.htm**.

Plotting out the main steps of a function as comments inside the function can help whittle major scripting tasks into manageable chunks. This is often called pseudocode.

3. The only remaining step is to fill in the main function code. Before accessing the DOM, plan out the required functionality for `setImageBorder()`. Using the `dw.getDocumentDOM()` function, and the node methods and properties listed in Tables 29.1 through 29.4, you can determine that your function needs to do the following (the new code is in bold):

```
function setImageBorder() {
//get document access
//get image access (collect images as an array)
//set the border property of each array item
}
```

4. You start by getting document access (the new code is in bold):

```
function setImageBorder() {
//get document access
```

```
var theDOM=dw.getDocumentDOM();
//get image access (collect images as an array)
//set the border property of each array item
}
```

5. Next, you climb the tree to get the images. Table 29.1 shows that the document node type object has a property called body, which gives you access to the body tag. Because the images are all in the body, you'll start with that. Then, because the body tag is of the element node type, you'll use its getElementsByTagName() method to collect all the body's img tags into an array:

```
function setImageBorder() {
//get document access
var theDOM=dw.getDocumentDOM();
//get image access (collect images as an array)
var theBody=theDOM.body;
var theImages=theBody.getElementsByTagName("IMG");
//set the border property of each array item
}
```

6. You have now collected the images into an array of objects of the element node type. Any tag attribute can be accessed as an object property. So you can step through the image array, setting the border property to 2 (the new code is in bold):

```
function setImageBorder() {
//get document access
var theDOM=dw.getDocumentDOM();
//get image access (collect images as an array)
var theBody=theDOM.body;
var theImages=theBody.getElementsByTagName("IMG");
//set the border property of each array item
for (var a=0;a<theImages.length;a++) {
  theImages[a].border="2";
  }
}
```

7. That's all there is to it! Save your document and close it. If Dreamweaver is running, quit. Then launch Dreamweaver and open a document that has several images.

What If It Doesn't Work?

If your command file contains a syntax error, Dreamweaver gives you a handy error message as soon as you try to choose the file. Read the error message, go back to your file, and find the error.

If your object doesn't cause any errors, but it doesn't change any images, there's a logic error. Probably you didn't accurately access the DOM. The getElementsByTagName() function requires that all parameters be specified in uppercase, so make sure your code refers to IMG, not img, or it won't work. Make sure all your variable names match as you proceed into the document tree. Match your code against the code shown here, and keep tinkering until it works.

EXERCISE 29.6

Creating a Command with a Dialog Box

The command so far is handy—if users want a two-pixel border around their images. How about letting the user specify how wide the border should be? (The ability to set the border to 0 might come in handy if you ever inherit someone else's HTML pages from a web editor that doesn't set that feature automatically.) You'll now add a dialog box to the command created in the preceding exercise, asking for a width.

1. In your text editor, open the **Set Image Border.htm** command file, and save it as **Set Image Border 2.htm**.

2. Create a simple form in the file's body section. As always, you can code the form by hand or open the file in Dreamweaver and create the form in Design view. Figure 29.13 shows how the form might look when complete.

   Wherever you create the form, remember to name it. Here, the form is named theForm, and the name of the text box is borderwidth.

3. Because there's now a form, you need to add the commandButtons() function. You will want an OK button that calls the main function and closes the window, an Apply button that calls the main function but doesn't close the window, and a Cancel button that just closes the main window. The code looks like this:

```
function commandButtons() {
return new Array("OK","setImageBorder(); window.close();",
➡"Apply",
➡  "setImageBorder()", "Cancel","window.close()");
}
```

After you've done this, be sure to remove the function call from the
<body> tag. You don't want the main function to execute as soon as
the dialog box opens!

FIGURE 29.13

The form for the Set
Image Border dialog
box, as seen in
Dreamweaver Code
and Design view.

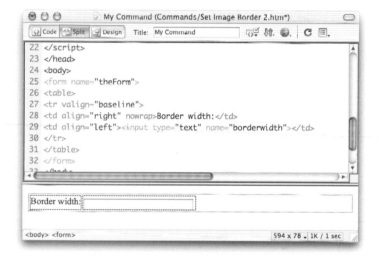

4. Finally, you need to adjust the main function so that it includes the
   form input collected in the dialog box. Rewrite the statement inside
   the for loop like this (the new code is in bold):

   ```
   for (var a=0;a<theImages.length;a++) {
   theImages[a].border=document.theForm.borderwidth.value;
   }
   ```

5. Try it out! Your dialog box should look like the one shown in
   Figure 29.14. Make sure that the commands get executed properly
   and that all three command buttons behave as they're supposed to.

FIGURE 29.14

The dialog box
for the Set Image
Borders command.

Refining Your Command

You can improve the functionality of this little command in all sorts of ways. Maybe you just want to set the border for images with or without links. Maybe you want to let the user choose which images get borders. Maybe you want to give the user the opportunity to remove the border attribute completely. With DOM access, all is possible. (To work with linked images, just determine which <img> tags have an <a> tag as their parent node.) For now, however, add the canAcceptCommand() function. If the current document doesn't have any images, it makes no sense for the command to be available. So you'll return true if there are images and false if there aren't.

1. In your text editor, open the **Set Image Borders 2.htm** command file. Add the framework for the new function, along with an indication of what you want it to do:

```
function canAcceptCommand() {
//access the document
//if there is no document, return false
//access the body
//access the images, collected as an array
//if the array is empty, return false
//otherwise, return true
}
```

2. As you might have noticed, the first several steps are the same as those in your main function. You can just copy and paste that code into this function, and then tack on a conditional:

```
function canAcceptCommand() {
//access the document
var theDOM=dw.getDocumentDOM();
//if there is no document, return false
if (!theDOM) return false;
//access the body
var theBody=theDOM.body;
//access the images, collected as an array
var theImages=theBody.getElementsByTagName("IMG");
```

```
//if the array is empty, return false
if (theImages.length--"0") return false;
//otherwise, return true
else return true;
}
```

3. Try your command now to see how it works. First, try it on a document with images, and then on one without.

Do you get tired of repeatedly quitting and relaunching Dreamweaver every time you tweak an extension? Here's a shortcut: Ctrl-click (Windows) or Opt-click (Mac) the Insert bar's categories drop-down menu. The Reload Extensions option appears. When you choose this, the program reloads its extensions without quitting.

Making the Most of Commands

Are you already full of ideas for your next command? If so, there's no stopping you. If not, you might need to broaden your horizons a little bit. Try these inspiration generators:

- Whenever you're working in Dreamweaver, keep a notebook handy. If you find yourself often repeating the same manual procedure, wasting time performing tedious tasks, try to imagine what kind of command you could write to help yourself out. Jot down that inspiration.

- Take a spin through the *Extending Dreamweaver* manual, especially the list of API methods that takes up the last half of the book. Just seeing all the different things you can tell Dreamweaver to do is likely to get your imagination moving.

- Unless you enjoy coding for its own sake, don't spend hours and hours writing a command before you check out the Exchange. You might come across a command that does exactly what you need.

The more you work with the DOM, the easier it will be. Pretty soon, you'll want to create custom Property Inspectors, floating panels, reports, translators, and more.

PACKAGING YOUR EXTENSIONS

The Extension Manager has become the standard method of installing and sharing extensions. Although you could share your extensions by just giving away the raw files, along with instructions on where to put them, it's much safer, and more user-friendly, to provide an installation package or MXP file for use with the Extension Manager.

Luckily, the Extension Manager not only installs extensions, it also neatly packages them into special installation files. The process is even relatively painless:

1. Put all the required files (help files, HTML files, JS files, GIF icons) in one folder, outside the **Configuration** folder.

2. Create an installation file. This is an XML document named **extension.mxi**. It contains all the instructions needed for installation: where the files should be stored, what versions of Dreamweaver and what platforms the extension requires, author's name, type of extension, and description. The formatting required is very exact. The best approach for beginners is to start from the Samples included with the Extension Manager. These files include a blank file (**blank.mxi**) to use as a template and a sample file (**sample.mxi**) filled in with information for a simple command.

3. Launch the Extension Manager, and select File > Package Extension.

Figure 29.15 shows a sample folder containing all the proper files to package the **Copyright Statement** file.

FIGURE 29.15
The assembled elements of the Copyright Statement object, all ready for packaging.

Copyright Statement.gif   Copyright Statement.htm   Copyright Statement.mxi

EXERCISE 29.8

Packaging an Extension

This last exercise takes you through the steps to create an MXP file from this extension.

1. Start by copying all needed files into one folder. Somewhere on your hard drive, outside the **Configuration** folder, create a new folder. Name it whatever you like and will remember—something like **Copyright Statement Files**.

   Find the files that make up the object, and copy them there. This includes **Copyright Statement.htm** and **Copyright Statement.gif**.

2. On your hard drive, find the **Extension Manager** application folder. Inside that folder, find the **Dreamweaver/Samples** folder. Inside there, you'll see **blank.mxi**. (Figure 29.16 shows where to find these items.) Duplicate that file in your **Collection** folder, and call it **C_Statement.mxi**. (Naming conventions apply here. You can't use spaces, special characters, or long names.)

   After you've made the duplicate file, open it in your text editor.

FIGURE 29.16
The Extension Manager application folder structure, showing sample.mxi and blank.mxi.

 You can download a PDF file containing detailed instructions for creating installation files from the Macromedia website. Go to the Macromedia Exchange for Dreamweaver page (www.macromedia.com/exchange/ dreamweaver), and click the Site Help topic Macromedia Approved Extensions.

3. Fill in the blanks with the information for your object.

The blank file has all the framework you need. By examining the sample file, you can get an idea how it should be formatted. For your extension, fill in the blanks until your code looks like that shown in Listing 29.1. Information that has been added to the framework from **blank.mxi** is in bold. Pay special attention to the following when filling in the code:

- **For the author name**—Enter your name. (You've already entered **Tom Thumb, Big-Time Genius**—there's no law against being fanciful.)

- **For the filenames**—Enter the relative path from the MXI file you're creating to the copies of the extension files you've saved for packaging. If all these files are in the same folder, you can just enter the filename.

- **For the destination**—Enter the complete path from the Dreamweaver application folder root, as shown. If you want your extension to create any new folders in existing folders, enter them as part of the path. (You have entered **ThumbThings** to create a new folder within the **Objects** folder.)

- **For the version number**—Your extension, like any other piece of software, gets its own version number. Start with 1.0, and increment the number if you later revise the extension.

- **For the insertbar-changes area**—The `insertbar-insert` element governs where the new category will be inserted. Set the `insertAfter` attribute to the ID of whatever category you want your category to follow. (In this case, the ThumbThings category follows the Application category, which has an ID of `DW_Insertbar_Server`.) Within the `insertbar-insert` tag, the code is the same code you entered in **insertbar.xml** when you created this object. This code tells Dreamweaver to automatically enter that code.

LISTING 29.1 **The Complete Code for C_Statement.mxi**

```
<macromedia-extension
    name="Copyright Statement"
    version="1.0.0"
    type="object">
```

```
<!   List the required/compatible products -->
<products>
      <product name="Dreamweaver" version="3" primary=
      ➡"true" />
</products>

<!-- Describe the author -->
<author name="Tom Thumb" />

<!-- Describe the extension -->
<description>
<![CDATA[
Inserts a formatted copyright statement, with user input
➡for name and year.
]]>
</description>

<!-- Describe where the extension shows in the product's
➡UI -->
<ui-access>
<![CDATA[
Access this extension via the ThumbThings category in the
➡Insert bar.
]]>
</ui-access>

<!-- Describe the files that comprise the extension -->
<files>
        <file name="Copyright Statement.gif"
destination="$dreamweaver/configuration/Objects/ThumbThings/" />
<file name="Copyright Statement.htm"
destination="$dreamweaver/configuration/Objects/Thumbthings/" />

</files>

<!-- Describe the changes to the configuration -->
<configuration-changes>
```

```
                    <insertbar-changes>
                            <insertbar-insert insertAfter="DW_Insertbar_
                            ⇒Server">
                                    <category folder="ThumbThings"
                                    ⇒ id="DW_Insertbar_ThumbThings">
                                    <button enabled=""
file="ThumbThings\Copyright Statement.htm" id="DW_ThumbThings_
⇒Copyright"
image="ThumbThings\Copyright Statement.gif" showIf="" />
                                    </category>
                            </insertbar-insert>
                    </insertbar-changes>
            </configuration-changes>

</macromedia-extension>
```

4. Finally, you package everything together with the Extension Manager. Launch the Extension Manager, and select File > Package Extension. For the name of your extension, choose something descriptive that obeys the standard naming conventions (no empty spaces, no more than 20 characters, no special characters). It's good practice to use the same name you used for the MXI file, just to keep your file organization tidy. Make sure you leave the .mxp extension in place.

    When you're asked to choose a file, choose **C_Statement.mxi**.

    If there aren't any problems, the Extension Manager generates an extension file in the same folder as the MXI file. If there are problems, you get an error report. Most often, these are problems with the MXI file. Go back to your text editor, fix the reported errors, and try again. Figure 29.17 shows how this process looks in the Extension Manager.

5. Use the Extension Manager to install the new extension. Start by quitting Dreamweaver if it's running. Open the **Configuration/ Objects** folder, and remove the development version. Then open **insertbar.xml** and delete the code that created your Development category. Finally, install the MXP file using the Extension Manager. (See Chapter 28 for a full discussion of using the Extension Manager to install MXP files.) If everything's hunky dory, you should get an alert message telling you that the extension was installed successfully.

Your custom extension also should now appear in the Extension Manager window, as shown in Figure 29.18.

FIGURE 29.17
The steps through the packaging process as they appear in the Extension Manager.

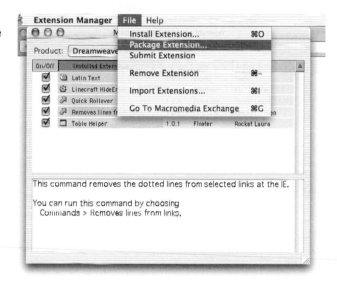

FIGURE 29.18
The Extension Manager window showing the installed Copyright Statement object.

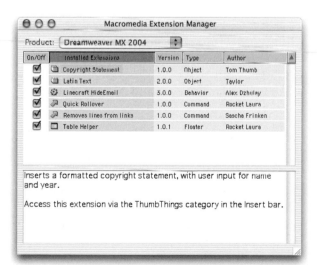

6. Finish up by launching Dreamweaver and checking that everything installed correctly.

Submitting Your Extension to the Macromedia Exchange

The ultimate in sharing is submitting your extension file to the Macromedia Exchange. After you have the MXP file, the procedure is simple: Go to the Macromedia Exchange website, and click the Uploads button (in the Your Exchange category, on the right side of the page). Then follow the instructions to submit, as shown in Figure 29.19.

FIGURE 29.19
The Macromedia Exchange Uploads page.

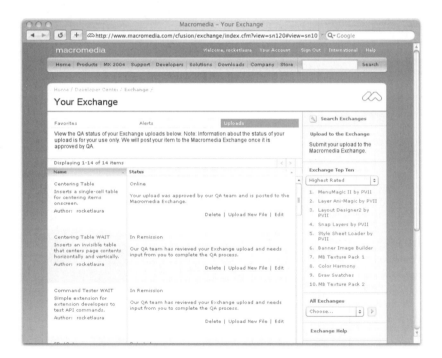

After you submit an extension, Macromedia engineers run it through a series of tests. One of three things will happen:

• If it fails, it gets returned to you with comments.

• If it passes the basic tests, it gets put on the website with Basic Approval.

- If it also passes the more comprehensive tests, it becomes a Macromedia Approved Extension.

To keep track of your submission's progress, visit the Uploads page periodically.

To learn more about the testing process and how to get your extensions accepted and approved, visit the Dreamweaver website, and click any one of the Site Help FAQ topics. This takes you to an extensive categorized list of questions and answers.

SUMMARY

You already know that Dreamweaver is a terrific web-editing environment. This chapter showed you how you can make it into a perfectly personalized web editor for your workflow needs. As much as you have seen, however, you've only touched the surface of all that is possible with extensions. Check out the *Extending Dreamweaver* manual. Visit the Exchange website and read the various support files there. If you're really serious, you can join the Extensibility Newsgroup (go to www.macromedia.com/support/forums/). Dust off your JavaScript books. And start rewriting history.

INDEX